Technological Entrepreneurship

The International Library of Entrepreneurship

Series Editor: David B. Audretsch
*Max Planck Institute of Economics, Jena, Germany
and Ameritech Chair of Economic Development
Indiana University, USA*

Wherever possible, the articles in these volumes have been reproduced as originally published using facsimile reproduction, inclusive of footnotes and pagination to facilitate ease of reference.

For a list of all Edward Elgar published titles visit our site on the World Wide Web at
www.e-elgar.com

Technological Entrepreneurship

Edited by

Donald S. Siegel

Professor, A. Gary Anderson Graduate School of Management, University of California at Riverside, USA

THE INTERNATIONAL LIBRARY OF ENTREPRENEURSHIP

An Elgar Reference Collection
Cheltenham, UK • Northampton, MA, USA

Published by
Edward Elgar Publishing Limited
Glensanda House
Montpellier Parade
Cheltenham
Glos GL50 1UA
UK

Edward Elgar Publishing, Inc.
136 West Street
Suite 202
Northampton
Massachusetts 01060
USA

A catalogue record for this book is available from the British Library

ISBN-13: 978 1 84542 251 6
ISBN-10: 1 84542 251 1

Printed and bound in Great Britain by MPG Books Ltd, Bodmin, Cornwall.

Contents

Acknowledgements

The editor and publishers wish to thank the authors and the following publishers who have kindly given permission for the use of copyright material.

Administrative Science Quarterly for article: Karen Seashore Louis, David Blumenthal, Michael E. Gluck and Michael A. Stoto (1989), 'Entrepreneurs in Academe: An Exploration of Behaviors among Life Scientists', *Administrative Science Quarterly*, **34** (1), March, 110–31.

American Economic Association for articles: David B. Audretsch and Paula E. Stephan (1996), 'Company-Scientist Locational Links: The Case of Biotechnology', *American Economic Review*, **86** (3), June, 641–52; Lynne G. Zucker, Michael R. Darby and Marilynn B. Brewer (1998), 'Intellectual Human Capital and the Birth of U.S. Biotechnology Enterprises', *American Economic Review*, **88** (1), March, 290–306; Richard Jensen and Marie Thursby (2001), 'Proofs and Prototypes for Sale: The Licensing of University Inventions', *American Economic Review*, **91** (1), March, 240–59.

Elsevier for articles: P. Westhead and D.J. Storey (1995), 'Links Between Higher Education Institutions and High Technology Firms', *Omega, International Journal of Management Science*, **23** (4), 345–60; Sarfraz A. Mian (1996), 'Assessing Value-Added Contributions of University Technology Business Incubators to Tenant Firms', *Research Policy*, **25**, 325–35; Massimo G. Colombo and Marco Delmastro (2002), 'How Effective are Technology Incubators? Evidence from Italy', *Research Policy*, **31** (7), September, 1103–22; Donald S. Siegel, David Waldman and Albert Link (2003), 'Assessing the Impact of Organizational Practices on the Relative Productivity of University Technology Transfer Offices: An Exploratory Study', *Research Policy*, **32** (1), January, 27–48; Dante Di Gregorio and Scott Shane (2003), 'Why Do Some Universities Generate More Start-ups than Others?', *Research Policy*, **32** (2), February, 209–27; Donald S. Siegel, David A. Waldman, Leanne E. Atwater and Albert N. Link (2003), 'Commercial Knowledge Transfers from Universities to Firms: Improving the Effectiveness of University–Industry Collaboration', *Journal of High Technology Management Research*, **14** (1), Spring, 111–33; Albert N. Link and John T. Scott (2003), 'U.S. Science Parks: The Diffusion of an Innovation and Its Effects on the Academic Missions of Universities', *International Journal of Industrial Organization*, **21** (9), November, 1323–56; Donald S. Siegel, Paul Westhead and Mike Wright (2003), 'Assessing the Impact of University Science Parks on Research Productivity: Exploratory Firm-Level Evidence from the United Kingdom', *International Journal of Industrial Organization*, **21** (9), November, 1357–69; Bhaven N. Sampat, David C. Mowery and Arvids A. Ziedonis (2003), 'Changes in University Patent Quality after the Bayh–Dole Act: A Re-examination', *International Journal of Industrial Organization*, **21** (9), November, 1371–90; Gideon D. Markman, Philip H. Phan,

David B. Balkin and Peter T. Gianiodis (2005), 'Entrepreneurship and University-Based Technology Transfer', *Journal of Business Venturing*, **20** (2), 241–63; Frank T. Rothaermel and Marie Thursby (2005), 'University–Incubator Firm Knowledge Flows: Assessing Their Impact on Incubator Firm Performance', *Research Policy*, **34** (3), 305–20; Wendy Chapple, Andy Lockett, Donald Siegel and Mike Wright (2005), 'Assessing the Relative Performance of U.K. University Technology Transfer Offices: Parametric and Non-Parametric Evidence', *Research Policy*, **34**, 369–84.

INFORMS (Institute for Operations Research and the Management Sciences) for articles: Jerry G. Thursby and Marie C. Thursby (2002), 'Who Is Selling the Ivory Tower? Sources of Growth in University Licensing', *Management Science*, **48** (1), January, 90–104; Maryann Feldman, Irwin Feller, Janet Bercovitz and Richard Burton (2002), 'Equity and the Technology Transfer Strategies of American Research Universities', *Management Science*, **48** (1), January, 105–21; Scott Shane and Toby Stuart (2002), 'Organizational Endowments and the Performance of University Start–ups', *Management Science*, **48** (1), January, 154–70.

MIT Press Journals and the President and Fellows of Harvard College for articles: Neil Bania, Randall W. Eberts and Michael S. Fogarty (1993), 'Universities and the Startup of New Companies: Can We Generalize from Route 128 and Silicon Valley?', *Review of Economics and Statistics*, **75** (4), November, 761–66; Edwin Mansfield (1995), 'Academic Research Underlying Industrial Innovations: Sources, Characteristics, and Financing', *Review of Economics and Statistics*, **77** (1), February, 55–65.

MIT Press Journals and the President and Fellows of Harvard College and the Massachusetts Institute of Technology for article: Rebecca Henderson, Adam B. Jaffe and Manuel Trajtenberg (1998), 'Universities as a Source of Commercial Technology: A Detailed Analysis of University Patenting, 1965–1988', *Review of Economics and Statistics*, **80** (1), February, 119–27.

Springer Science and Business Media for articles: Lynne G. Zucker and Michael R. Darby (2001), 'Capturing Technological Opportunity Via Japan's Star Scientists: Evidence from Japanese Firms' Biotech Patents and Products', *Journal of Technology Transfer*, **26** (1–2), January, 37–58; Bronwyn H. Hall, Albert N. Link and John T. Scott (2001), 'Barriers Inhibiting Industry from Partnering with Universities: Evidence from the Advanced Technology Program', *Journal of Technology Transfer*, **26** (1–2), January, 87–98; Jason Owen-Smith and Walter W. Powell (2001), 'To Patent or Not: Faculty Decisions and Institutional Success at Technology Transfer', *Journal of Technology Transfer*, **26** (1–2), January, 99–114; Magnus Henrekson and Nathan Rosenberg (2001), 'Designing Efficient Institutions for Science-Based Entrepreneurship: Lessons from the US and Sweden', *Journal of Technology Transfer*, **26** (3), June, 207–31; Albert N. Link and John T. Scott (2003), 'The Growth of Research Triangle Park', *Small Business Economics*, **20** (2), March, 167–75; Andy Lockett, Mike Wright and Stephen Franklin (2003), 'Technology Transfer and Universities' Spin-Out Strategies', *Small Business Economics*, **20** (2), March, 185–200; Peter Lindelöf and Hans Löfsten (2003), 'Science Park Location and New Technology-Based Firms in Sweden – Implications for Strategy and Performance', *Small Business Economics*, **20** (3), May, 245–58; Richard Ferguson and Christer Olofsson (2004), 'Science Parks and the Development of

NTBFs – Location, Survival and Growth', *Journal of Technology Transfer*, **29** (1), January, 5–17.

Every effort has been made to trace all the copyright holders but if any have been inadvertently overlooked the publishers will be pleased to make the necessary arrangement at the first opportunity.

In addition the publishers wish to thank the Marshall Library of Economics, University of Cambridge, UK, the Library at the University of Warwick, UK, and the Library of Indiana University at Bloomington, USA, for their assistance in obtaining these articles.

Introduction

Donald S. Siegel

In the late 1970s, there was growing concern among U.S. policymakers regarding the pervasive slowdown in productivity and the concomitant decline in the global competitiveness of American firms in several critical high technology sectors. An alleged culprit of the productivity slowdown was a diminution in the rate of technological innovation. More specifically, universities were criticized for being more adept at conducting basic research than at fostering diffusion and commercialization of university-based inventions. There was also a sense that the long lag between the discovery of new knowledge at American universities and its use by American firms had enabled Japanese companies to establish first-mover advantages in key embryonic, high-tech industries, such as memory chips.

In an effort to remove obstacles to university technology transfer, Congress passed the Bayh–Dole Act in 1980.[1] This legislation established a uniform patent policy across federal agencies, lifted numerous restrictions on licensing and, most importantly, allowed universities to own patents arising from federal research grants. The framers of this legislation asserted that university ownership and management of intellectual property would accelerate the commercialization of new technologies and promote economic development and entrepreneurial activity.

Although it is difficult to establish cause and effect, it appears that Bayh–Dole has accelerated technology transfer, by bringing research universities closer to practitioners seeking to commercialize university-based technologies. In the aftermath of this legislation, almost all research universities have established technology transfer offices (henceforth, TTOs) to manage their intellectual property portfolios. The number of patents granted to U.S. universities increased from 300 in 1980 to over 4000 in 2003, while licenses have increased almost twelve-fold since 1991. Membership of the Association of University Technology Managers (AUTM), which represents licensing officers at universities and other research institutions, increased from less than 100 in 1980 to over 3000 in 2003. Annual licensing revenue rose from about $160 million in 1991 to over $1.2 billion in 2002, now constituting about 2.6 percent of university R&D expenditures. AUTM (2004) reports that the number of startup firms at U.S. universities rose from 35 in 1980 to 374 in 2003. These U.S. trends have stimulated interest among policymakers in other OECD nations in adopting legislation similar to Bayh–Dole, which they hope will spur technology-based economic growth in their countries.

The rapid increase in university-based technological entrepreneurship has also attracted considerable attention in the academic literature, since this trend has important managerial and policy implications. As a result, there are numerous papers on university licensing, patenting and startup formation. This emerging literature is interdisciplinary, with contributions from scholars in many disciplines, such as economics, sociology, political science, public administration and several fields in management, such as strategy, entrepreneurship, and technology and innovation management. There is also considerable international evidence on this phenomenon. Finally, given the complexity of the issues raised by the rise of technological entrepreneurship at universities, many authors have employed qualitative methods to address key research questions.

Most papers have focused on institutions that facilitate commercialization and entrepreneurship, such as TTOs, science parks and incubators. Other studies focus on agents involved in technology commercialization, such as academic scientists. These authors assess the antecedents and consequences of faculty involvement in university technology transfer, such as their propensity to patent, disclose inventions, co-author with industry scientists and form university-based startups.

The purpose of this volume is to synthesize the burgeoning, heterogeneous literature on institutions and agents engaged in technological entrepreneurship at universities. These studies highlight the importance of institutional incentives and organizational practices in stimulating this activity. They also clearly demonstrate the considerable heterogeneity in stakeholder objectives, perceptions and outcomes relating to this activity. On the other hand, the evidence is much less clear on the effectiveness of property-based institutions designed to promote technological entrepreneurship, such as science parks and incubators.

The articles selected for this volume can be divided into four related topics: (1) university licensing and patenting; (2) science parks and incubators; (3) university-based startups; and (4) the role of academic science in stimulating entrepreneurial activity. In the remainder of this introduction, I place these papers in context and discuss selected studies.

Part I   University Licensing and Patenting

The process of university technology transfer begins with a discovery by a laboratory scientist working on a federal research grant. The Bayh–Dole Act stipulates that this scientist must then file an invention disclosure with the TTO, which then considers whether to patent the invention.[2] If a patent is awarded, the university can potentially license the technology to an existing firm or a startup company. The next stage involves the negotiation of a licensing agreement involving the two parties, which could include royalties or an equity stake in the startup.

Even after the agreement is signed, universities often continue their involvement with the firm. For instance, the TTO typically devotes additional resources to maintenance of the agreement. In the case of university-based startups, faculty members often serve as technical advisors to the startup or on its board of directors. Universities and individual faculty members may also have an equity stake in the startup. A seminal theoretical paper by Jensen and Thursby (2001) demonstrates that inventor involvement in university technology transfer potentially attenuates the deleterious effects of informational asymmetries that naturally arise in technological diffusion from universities to firms.

Several authors have attempted to assess the 'effectiveness' of university technology licensing in the U.S. and U.K. Siegel, Waldman and Link (2003, Chapter 6, this volume) assess and 'explain' the relative productivity of 113 U.S. university TTOs. They found that variation in relative TTO performance cannot be completely explained by environmental and institutional factors. The implication of this finding is that organizational practices are likely to be an important determinant of relative performance.

The authors supplemented their econometric analysis with qualitative evidence, derived from 55 structured, in-person interviews of 100 university technology transfer stakeholders (i.e. academic and industry scientists, university technology managers, and corporate managers and entrepreneurs) at five research universities in Arizona and North Carolina.

The field research, which was extended in Siegel, Waldman, Atwater and Link (2003, Chapter 8, this volume), identified three key impediments to effective university technology transfer. The first was informational and cultural barriers between universities and firms, especially for small firms. Another impediment was insufficient rewards for faculty involvement in university technology transfer. This includes both pecuniary and non-pecuniary rewards, such as credit towards tenure and promotion. Some respondents even suggested that involvement in technology transfer might be detrimental to their careers. Finally, there appear to be problems with staffing and compensation practices in the TTO. One such problem is a high rate of turnover among licensing officers, which is detrimental towards the establishment of long-term relationships with firms and entrepreneurs. Other concerns are insufficient business and marketing experience in the TTO and the possible need for incentive compensation.

Thursby and Thursby (2002, Chapter 5, this volume) assess whether the growth in licensing and patenting by universities can be attributed to an increase in the willingness of professors to patent, without a concomitant, fundamental change in the type of research they conduct. The alternative hypothesis is that the growth in technology commercialization at universities reflects a shift away from basic research towards more applied research. The authors find support for the former hypothesis. More specifically, they conclude that the rise in university technology transfer is the result of a greater willingness on the part of university researchers to patent their inventions, as well as an increase in outsourcing of R&D by firms via licensing.

In sum, the extant literature on TTOs suggests that the key impediments to effective university technology transfer tend to be organizational in nature (Siegel, Waldman and Link (2003); Siegel, Waldman, Atwater and Link (2003)). These include problems with differences in organizational cultures between universities and (small) firms; incentive structures, including both pecuniary and non-pecuniary rewards, such as credit towards tenure and promotion; and staffing and compensation practices of the TTO itself.

As noted earlier, in the aftermath of the Bayh–Dole Act, universities are patenting more, since they are allowed to patent publicly funded inventions and retain the royalties that these patents generate. An important policy question is whether the 'quality' of university patents has declined since the enactment of this legislation. Henderson, Jaffe and Trajtenberg (1998, Chapter 2, this volume) analyzed an early version of the NBER Patent Citation Database (Hall, Jaffe and Trajtenberg (2001)) to 'deflate' university patents (and the value of a control group of patents) and concluded that there has been a decline in the quality of university patents since Bayh–Dole.

Sampat, Mowery and Ziedonis (2003, Chapter 7, this volume) extend and refine this analysis by examining more recent citation data to test whether the Henderson, Jaffe and Trajtenberg (1998) results are sensitive to truncation bias. This could arise if there is a considerable lag in patent citations, which could be more likely for university patents, since they tend to relate to early-stage research. They also estimate negative binomial regressions of the determinants of patent citations, formally test for a 'Bayh–Dole' effect in these regressions, and use several alternative procedures to control for truncation bias. Contrary to Henderson,

Jaffe and Trajtenberg (1998), the authors conclude that there is no evidence of a decline in the relative quality of university patents in the post-Bayh–Dole era.

Part II   Science Parks and Incubators

In recent years there has been a substantial increase in global investment in science parks and incubators. This increased level of activity has stimulated an important debate concerning whether such property-based initiatives enhance the performance of corporations, universities and economic regions. Policymakers and managers are also interested in identifying best practices. Unfortunately, few academic studies address such issues.

Link and Scott (2003, Chapter 13, this volume) analyze the growth and development of U.S. science parks and their influence on academic missions of universities, employing econometric methods and a qualitative survey of university provosts. Their findings imply that the existence of a formal relationship with a science park yields three benefits for the university: (1) more academic papers; (2) better placement for Ph.D. students; and (3) easier recruitment and retention of star scientists. The authors also report that there is a direct relationship between the proximity of the science park to the university and the probability that the academic curriculum will shift from basic towards applied research.

The best available evidence on the effects of science parks is from the United Kingdom. These studies were based on longitudinal data containing performance indicators for firms located on university science parks and a carefully matched set of firms that are not located on university science parks (e.g. Westhead and Storey (1994); Westhead, Storey and Cowling (1995)). Westhead and Storey (1995) found a higher survival rate among science park firms with a university link (72 percent) than firms without such a link (53 percent). Westhead (1997), examining differences in R&D 'outputs' (i.e. counts of patents, copyrights and new products or services) and 'inputs' (i.e. percentage of scientists and engineers in total employment, the level and intensity of R&D expenditure, and information on the thrust and nature of the research undertaken by the firm), of firms located on science parks and similar firms located off science parks, found no significant differences between science park and off-park firms.

Siegel, Westhead and Wright (2003, Chapter 15, this volume) analyze the same database and estimate an R&D production function. They conclude that U.K. science park firms have higher research productivity than comparable non-science park firms, in terms of generating new products and services and patents, but not copyrights. Their results are robust to alternative specifications of the R&D production function and controls for the possibility of an endogeneity bias.

In sum, these studies underscore the importance of a university link in enhancing the performance of science park firms. Unfortunately, the precise nature of the university contribution has not been identified. Speculation has ranged from explanations of knowledge spillovers to the proximity of the requisite competencies to staff these firms.

There has also been substantial growth in technology incubators. According to the National Business Incubation Association, there are over 1000 business incubators in North America, up from 12 in 1980. Linder (2003) reports that 37 percent of these incubators are focused on developing technology businesses. Twenty-five percent have an affiliation with an academic institution.

There have been few empirical studies of the effectiveness of incubators. Mian (1996, Chapter 11, this volume) presented qualitative evidence on the 'value added' of university-based technology incubators at the University of Maryland, Georgia Tech, the University of North Carolina at Charlotte, Northwestern, Lehigh and Case Western Reserve. He concluded that the university's image, laboratory facilities and equipment, and students added significant value to firms located on these facilities.

The first 'matched pairs' analysis of the effectiveness of technology incubators was conducted by Colombo and Delmastro (2002, Chapter 12, this volume), who analyzed firm-level data from Italy. The Italian incubators were located in science parks. The authors reported that incubator firms grew faster and performed better than comparable non-incubator firms. They were also able to attract better entrepreneurs. The only systematic U.S. evidence was reported in Rothaermel and Thursby (2005, Chapter 18, this volume), who analyzed longitudinal data on 79 firms located on Georgia Tech's technology incubator. They found strong evidence of knowledge flows from universities to incubator firms, which enhance their absorptive capacity and may constitute a source of competitive advantage.

Part III   University-Based Startups

Studies using the university as the unit of analysis typically focus on the role of university policies in stimulating entrepreneurial activity. Roberts and Malone (1996) conjecture that Stanford generated fewer startups than comparable institutions because the university refused to sign exclusive licenses to inventor-founders. Degroof and Roberts (2004) examine the importance of university policies relating to startups in regions where environmental factors (e.g. technology transfer and infrastructure for entrepreneurship) are not particularly conducive to entrepreneurial activity. The authors derive a taxonomy of four types of startup policies: an absence of startup policies, minimal selectivity/support, intermediate selectivity/support and comprehensive selectivity/support. Consistent with Roberts and Malone (1996), they find that comprehensive selectivity/support is the optimal policy for generating startups that can exploit venture with high growth potential. However, such a policy is an ideal that may not be feasible, given resource constraints. The authors conclude that while spinout policies do matter in the sense that they affect the growth potential of ventures, it may be more desirable to formulate such policies at a higher level of aggregation than the university.

Di Gregorio and Shane (2003, Chapter 22, this volume) present an econometric analysis of the factors influencing the rate of startup formation at 101 U.S. universities. Based on estimates of count regressions of the number of university-based startups, they conclude that the two key determinants of startups are faculty quality and the ability of the university and inventor(s) to assume equity in a startup in lieu of licensing royalty fees. Interestingly, the availability of venture capital in the region where the university is located and the commercial orientation of the university (proxied by the percentage of the university's research budget that is derived from industry) do not have a positive effect on the rate of startup formation. The authors also find that a royalty distribution formula that is more favorable to faculty members reduces startup formation, a finding that is confirmed by Markman, Phan, Balkin and Gianiodis (2005). They attribute this result to the higher opportunity cost associated with launching a new firm, relative to licensing the technology to an existing firm.

Lockett, Wright and Franklin (2003, Chapter 23, this volume) report that U.K. universities generating the most startups have clear, well-defined strategies regarding the formation and management of spinouts. The most successful universities tend to use surrogate (external) entrepreneurs, rather than academic entrepreneurs, to manage this process. These institutions appear to have greater technical expertise and vast social networks that help them generate more startups. In the case of the more successful universities, equity ownership was found to be more widely distributed among the members of the spinout company.

The paper by Markman, Phan, Balkin and Gianiodis (2005, Chapter 30, this volume) yields an interesting result. The authors find that the most 'attractive' combinations of technology stage and licensing strategy for new venture creation, i.e. early stage technology combined with licensing for equity, are *least* likely to be favored by the university and thus not likely to be used. That is because universities and TTOs are typically focused on short-term cash maximization, and are extremely risk-averse with respect to financial and legal risks. Markman et al.'s findings are consistent with evidence presented in Siegel, Waldman, Atwater and Link (2003), who found that TTOs appear to do a better job of serving the needs of large firms than of small, entrepreneurial companies. The results of these studies imply that universities should modify their technology transfer strategies if they are serious about promoting entrepreneurial development.

Part IV   The Role of Academic Science in Stimulating Entrepreneurial Activity

There are numerous studies demonstrating that university research generates local technological spillovers. Bania, Eberts and Fogarty (1993, Chapter 19, this volume) report that there is a positive relationship between university R&D and the number of firm startups in the same standard metropolitan statistical area (SMSA). Jaffe, Trajtenberg and Henderson (1993) find that patents issued within the same state and SMSA are more likely to be cited by firms in the same state or SMSA. Audretsch and Stephan (1996) directly examine interactions between academic scientists and local firms and find that these formal and informal linkages play an important role in promoting innovation in biotechnology.

One of the first papers to study the entrepreneurial behavior of individual faculty members was Louis, Blumenthal, Gluck and Stoto (1989, Chapter 24, this volume). These authors analyzed the propensity of leading life-science faculty at 50 research universities to engage in various aspects of technology transfer, including commercialization. They found that the most important determinant of involvement in technology commercialization was local group norms. They report that university policies and structures had little effect on this activity.

The seminal papers by Lynne Zucker and Michael Darby and various collaborators explore the role of 'star' scientists in the life sciences on the creation and location of new biotechnology firms in the U.S. and Japan. In Zucker, Darby and Armstrong (2000), the authors assessed the impact of these university scientists on the research productivity of U.S. firms. Some of these scientists resigned from the university to establish a new firm or kept their faculty position but worked very closely with industry scientists. A star scientist is defined as a researcher who has discovered over 40 genetic sequences, and affiliations with firms are defined through co-authoring between the star scientist and industry scientists. Research productivity is measured using three proxies: number of patents granted, number of products in development and number of products on the market. They find that ties between star scientists and firm scientists have a positive effect on these three dimensions of research productivity, as well as other aspects of firm performance and rates of entry in the U.S. biotechnology industry (Zucker, Darby and Armstrong (1998), Zucker, Darby and Brewer (1998, Chapter 26, this volume)).

In Zucker and Darby (2001, Chapter 27, this volume), the authors examine detailed data on the outcomes of collaborations between 'star' university scientists and biotechnology firms in Japan. Similar patterns emerge in the sense that they find that such interactions substantially enhance the research productivity of Japanese firms, as measured by the rate of firm patenting, product innovation and market introductions of new products. However, they also report an absence of geographically localized knowledge spillovers resulting from university technology transfer in Japan, in contrast to the U.S., where they found that such effects were strong. The authors attribute this result to the following interesting institutional difference between Japan and the U.S. in university technology transfer. In the U.S., it is common for academic scientists to work with firm scientists at the firm's laboratories. In Japan, firm scientists typically work in the academic scientist's laboratory. Thus, according to the authors, it is not surprising that the local economic development impact of university technology transfer appears to be lower in Japan than in the U.S.

Notes

1. See Stevens (2004) for a description of the enactment of Bayh–Dole.
2. Several field studies (Siegel, Waldman and Link (2003); Siegel, Waldman, Atwater and Link (2003)) and survey research (Thursby, Jensen and Thursby (2001)) indicate that many faculty members are not disclosing inventions to the TTO.

References

Association of University Technology Managers (AUTM) (2004). *The AUTM Licensing Survey, Fiscal Year 2003*. Norwalk, CT: AUTM, Inc.

Audretsch, David B. and Paula Z. Stephan (1996). 'Company-Scientist Locational Links: The Case of Biotechnology', *American Economic Review*, **86**(3), 641–52.

Degroof, Jean-Jacques and Edward B. Roberts (2004). 'Overcoming Weak Entrepreneurial Infrastructure for Academic Spin-off Ventures', *Journal of Technology Transfer*, **29**(3–4), 327–57.

Hall, Bronwyn H., Adam B. Jaffe and Manuel Trajtenberg (2001). 'The NBER Patent Citation Data File: Lessons, Insights and Methodological Tools', NBER Working Paper 8498.

Henderson, Rebecca, Adam B. Jaffe and Manuel Trajtenberg (1998). 'Universities as a Source of Commercial Technology: A Detailed Analysis of University Patenting, 1965–1988', *Review of Economics and Statistics*, **80**(1), 119–27.

Jensen, Richard and Marie C. Thursby (2001). 'Proofs and Prototypes for Sale: The Licensing of University Inventions', *American Economic Review*, **91**(1), 240–59.

Linder, S. (2003). *2002 State of the Business Incubation Industry*. Athens, OH: National Business Incubation Association (NBIA) Publications.

Link, Albert N. and John T. Scott (2003). 'Science Parks and the Generation of University-Based Knowledge: An Exploratory Study', *International Journal of Industrial Organization*, **21**(9), 1323–56.

Louis, Karen S., David Blumenthal, Michael Gluck and Michael A. Stoto (1989). 'Entrepreneurs in Academe: An Exploration of Behaviors Among Life Scientists', *Administrative Science Quarterly*,

34(1), 110–31.

Monck, C.S.P., R.B. Porter, P. Quintas, D.J. Storey and P. Wynarczyk (1988). *Science Parks and the Growth of High Technology Firms*. London: Croom Helm.

Poyago-Theotoky, Joanna, John Beath and Donald S. Siegel (2002). 'Universities and Fundamental Research: Reflections on the Growth of University–Industry Partnerships', *Oxford Review of Economic Policy*, **18**(1), 10–21.

Roberts, Edward and D.E. Malone (1996). 'Policies and Structures for Spinning Off New Companies from Research and Development Organizations', *R&D Management*, **26**, 17–48.

Sampat, Bhaven, David C. Mowery and Arvids A. Ziedonis (2003). 'Changes in University Patent Quality After the Bayh–Dole Act: A Re-examination', *International Journal of Industrial Organization*, **21**(9), 1371–90.

Stevens, Ashley (2004). 'The Enactment of Bayh-Dole', *Journal of Technology Transfer*, **29**(1), 93–99.

Thursby, Jerry G. and Marie C. Thursby (2004). 'Are Faculty Critical? Their Role in University Licensing', *Contemporary Economic Policy*, **22**(2), 162–78.

Thursby, Jerry G., Richard Jensen and Marie C. Thursby (2001). 'Objectives, Characteristics and Outcomes of University Licensing: A Survey of Major U.S. Universities', *Journal of Technology Transfer*, **26**, 59–72.

Westhead, Paul (1997). 'R & D "Inputs" and "Outputs" of Technology-Based Firms Located On and Off Science Parks', *R&D Management*, **27**, 45–62.

Westhead, Paul and Michael Cowling (1995). 'Employment Change in Independent Owner-Managed High-Technology Firms in Great Britain', *Small Business Economics*, **7**, 111–40.

Westhead, Paul and David J. Storey (1994). *An Assessment of Firms Located On and Off Science Parks in the United Kingdom*. London: HMSO.

Westhead, Paul, David J. Storey and Michael Cowling (1995). 'An Exploratory Analysis of the Factors Associated with the Survival of Independent High-Technology Firms in Great Britain', in F. Chittenden, M. Robertson and I. Marshall (eds), *Small Firms: Partnerships for Growth*. London: Paul Chapman, pp. 63–99.

Zucker, Lynne G., Michael R. Darby and Jeff Armstrong (1998). 'Geographically Localized Knowledge: Spillovers or Markets?', *Economic Inquiry*, **36**(1), 65–86.

Zucker, Lynne G., Michael R. Darby and Jeff Armstrong (2000). 'University Science, Venture Capital, and the Performance of U.S. Biotechnology Firms', mimeo, UCLA.

Part I
University Licensing and Patenting

[1]

ACADEMIC RESEARCH UNDERLYING INDUSTRIAL INNOVATIONS: SOURCES, CHARACTERISTICS, AND FINANCING

Edwin Mansfield*

Abstract—There has been no systematic study of the characteristics of the universities and academic researchers that seem to have contributed most to industrial innovation. Nor do we know how such academic research has been funded. This paper, based on data obtained from 66 firms in seven major manufacturing industries and from over 200 academic researchers, sheds new light on the sources, characteristics, and financing of academic research underlying industrial innovation. The findings should be of interest to economists concerned with technological change and to policy makers attempting to increase the economic payoff from the nation's academic research.

ers attempting to increase the economic payoff from the nation's academic research. In this paper I report the results of a study based on data obtained from 66 firms in seven major manufacturing industries and from over 200 academic researchers. Although the findings are subject to many limitations, they shed new light on the sources, characteristics, and financing of academic research underlying industrial innovation.

I. Introduction

IN recent years there has been a great deal of interest in the process by which firms benefit from externally performed research and development (R&D), and the extent and importance of such spillovers. Research by Acs, Audretsch, and Feldman (1992), Jaffe (1989), Mansfield (1991a, 1991b, 1992), Nelson (1988), von Hippel (1988), and others indicate that technological change in important segments of the economy has been based significantly on academic research. However, there has been no systematic study of the characteristics of the universities and academic researchers that seem to have contributed most to industrial innovation. Nor do we know where such universities or academic researchers have obtained funding for the relevant R&D projects or how big or small their projects have been.

Information of this sort would be of interest to economists and other scholars concerned with the process of technology transfer and to policy mak-

II. Academic Research and Industrial Innovation

To begin with, it is worthwhile reviewing some earlier findings regarding the extent to which technological innovations in various industries have been dependent on recent academic research. Based on data obtained from 76 firms in the seven industries listed in table 1, about 11% of their new products and about 9% of their new processes could not have been developed (without substantial delay) in the absence of recent academic research (defined as academic research occurring within 15 years of the commercialization of the innovation).[1] As shown in table 1, the percentage of new products and processes based in this way on recent academic research seems to be highest in the drug industry and lowest in the petroleum industry.[2]

Received for publication March 1, 1993. Revision accepted for publication February 7, 1994.

* University of Pennsylvania.

The research on which this paper is based was supported by a grant from the National Science Foundation, which, of course, is not responsible for the findings. I am indebted to Leonard Lederman of the Foundation for his encouragement and advice. Thanks also go to the many firms (76 in section II, and 66 in subsequent sections), as well as about 220 academic researchers that provided data. This paper was presented at the January 1993 annual meetings of the American Economic Association. A preliminary version was presented at the National Science Foundation, Lehigh University, and the Maine Science and Technology Commission.

[1] By "substantial delay," we mean a delay of a year or more, according to rough estimates made by the firms.

[2] New products and processes sometimes could have been developed without the findings of recent academic research, but it would have been much more expensive and time-consuming to do so. In table 1, such cases are designated as ones where development occurred with "very substantial aid from recent academic research." Approximately 8% of these firms' new products and approximately 6% of their new processes during 1975–85 fell into this category. Often, while it was technically possible for the firm to have developed them without the findings of recent academic research, it seemed economically undesirable to have tried it. Consequently, in a practical sense, many of these innovations could not have been developed (without substantial delay) in the absence of recent academic research.

56   THE REVIEW OF ECONOMICS AND STATISTICS

TABLE 1.—PERCENTAGE OF NEW PRODUCTS AND PROCESSES
BASED ON RECENT ACADEMIC RESEARCH, SEVEN INDUSTRIES, UNITED STATES, 1975–85

Industry	Percentage that Could Not Have Been Developed (without substantial delay) in the Absence of Recent Academic Research		Percentage that Was Developed with Very Substantial Aid from Recent Academic Research[a]	
	Products	Processes	Products	Processes
Information processing	11	11	17	16
Electronics	6	3	3	4
Chemical	4	2	4	4
Instruments	16	2	5	1
Pharmaceuticals	27	29	17	8
Metals	13	12	9	9
Petroleum	1	1	1	1
Industry mean	11	9	8	6

Source: Mansfield (1991a).
[a] See footnote 2.

To prevent confusion, it is worthwhile to note that many of the innovations based on recent academic research were not invented at universities. Academic research often provides new theoretical and empirical findings and new types of instrumentation that are essential for the development of a new product or process, but does not provide the specific invention itself. Thus, to cite an old and well-known case, academic studies by Professors Kipping and Staudinger provided basic information concerning organo-silicon chemistry which laid the groundwork for industrial silicones.[3]

For each firm's new products and processes introduced in 1975–85 that, according to the firm, could not have been developed (without substantial delay) in the absence of recent academic research, information was obtained concerning the mean time interval between the relevant academic research finding and the first commercial introduction of the product or process. (If more than one such research finding was needed for the development of the innovation, this time interval was measured from the year when the last of these findings was obtained.) The mean time lag in these industries was about 7 years. In interpreting this result, note once again that these data pertain only to recent academic research.

Particularly in industries like drugs, instruments, and information processing, the contribution of academic research to industrial innovation has been considerable. In the seven industries in

[3] Jewkes, Sawers, and Stillerman (1969). Also see von Hippel (1988).

table 1, new products first commercialized in 1982–85 that could not have been developed (without substantial delay) in the absence of recent academic research accounted for about $24 billion of sales in 1985 alone. And in these industries, new processes first commercialized in 1982–85 that could not have been developed (without substantial delay) in the absence of recent academic research resulted in about $7 billion in savings in 1985 alone. While these figures are rough, they certainly indicate that industrial innovation in these industries has been based to a substantial degree on recent academic research, and crude estimates suggest that the social rate of return from academic research has been high.[4]

III. Sources of Academic Research Underlying Industrial Innovations

Although the foregoing results indicate that recent academic research has made a significant contribution to innovation in these industries, they tell us nothing about the kinds of academic research that the innovating firms believe to have been most important in this regard. To help illuminate this topic, we drew a random sample of 70 major firms from these industries. Each firm was

[4] Mansfield (1991a). The problems in allocating the social returns between academic and industrial research are obvious. However, crude estimates suggest that the social rate of return from academic research remains substantial even if seemingly generous assumptions are made concerning the social rate of return from industrial research and other industrial innovation costs. See Mansfield (1992). Of course, as I have stressed here and elsewhere, these estimates of social rates of return are only rough. See Mansfield (1977, 1980, 1991b).

asked to cite about five academic researchers whose work in the 1970s and 1980s contributed most importantly to the firm's new products and processes introduced in the 1980s.

Although our initial requests for information and cooperation were made to the firms' chairmen, the respondents generally were the top R&D executives who based their responses in considerable part on detailed data obtained from people at lower levels of their organizations. Most of the firms went to a considerable amount of trouble to provide these data. Written responses often were supplemented with interviews with relevant company personnel. Eventually, usable data were obtained from 66 of the 70 firms in the sample.[5] Since these firms account, on the average, for about a third of the R&D expenditures in these industries, the sample seems quite adequate.

Taken as a whole, these 66 firms cited 321 academic researchers.[6] Table 2 lists the universities and types of departments cited most frequently by the firms in each industry. In most industries, the most frequently-cited universities are world leaders in science and technology. For example, MIT, Berkeley, Illinois, Stanford, and CMU are most frequently cited in electronics; and Harvard, UCSF, Stanford, and Yale are most frequently cited in pharmaceuticals. But not all of the most frequently-cited universities are world leaders in the relevant fields. Thus, neither Washington University nor the University of Utah are among the top dozen departments of chemistry, according to the assessments of the National Academy of Sciences.[7]

With regard to type of department, it appears that the bulk of the cited academic research took place in departments closely related to the technology of the industry in question. In the electronics industry, over 60% of the cited academic researchers were in electrical engineering or mechanical engineering departments. In the chemical industry, almost 70% were in chemistry or chemical engineering departments. In the pharmaceutical industry, the cited academic researchers seemed to be scattered over a wider variety of fields and departments than in the electronics or chemical industries, but this may have been due to the fact that the pharmaceutical industry, as defined here, includes some medical products firms.[8]

IV. Effects of Faculty Quality, Scale of Research Effort, and Geographical Proximity on Perceived University Contribution

As pointed out in the previous section, one factor that would be expected to influence how frequently a particular university is cited in this way is the quality of the university's faculty. Another factor that is often stressed by policymakers is the scale of a university's R&D activities in the relevant area: a critical mass of researchers and equipment is often regarded as necessary to achieve high productivity in particular aspects of academic research. Still another factor is the geographical proximity of a university to the firms in the sample. Because there are obvious advantages in firms working with, and keeping abreast of developments at, local colleges and universities, one might expect that colleges and universities located near many of the firms would tend to be cited relatively often.[9]

To test whether these factors are useful in explaining the differences among universities in the number of times they were cited, we assume that

$$Y_i = \alpha_0 + \alpha_1 Q_i + \alpha_2 R_i + \alpha_3 L_i + z_i, \quad (1)$$

where Y_i is the number of citations received by

[5] The industrial distribution of the firms in the sample was as follows: electronics, 14; information processing, 16; pharmaceuticals, 8; chemicals, 13; petroleum 5; metals, 4; and instruments, 6. An attempt was made to allocate the sample optimally among industries (that is, with sample size being proportional to the total number of firms in each industry times the relevant standard deviation).
[6] The number cited by each industry was as follows: electronics, 84; information processing, 64; pharmaceuticals, 47; chemicals, 51; petroleum, 28; metals, 25; and instruments, 22. Eighteen academic researchers were cited by more than one firm, so the number of distinct researchers cited is 303, not 321. In tables 2–3, we weight each researcher by the number of firms that cited him or her.
[7] See National Academy of Sciences (1982).

[8] The frame for our sample of firms was the list of firms in *Business Week's* annual R&D Scoreboard. Included in the pharmaceutical industry were some medical products firms.
[9] For some relevant discussion, see Jaffe (1989), Jaffe, Trajtenberg, and Henderson (1993). Acs, Aubretsch, and Feldman (1992). Government–University–Industry Roundtable and Industrial Research Institute (1991), and Peters and Fusfeld (1982).

TABLE 2.—UNIVERSITIES AND DEPARTMENTS CONTAINING THE LARGEST PERCENTAGE OF ACADEMIC RESEARCHERS CITED
BY 66 MAJOR FIRMS (IN THE ELECTRONICS, INFORMATION PROCESSING, PHARMACEUTICAL, CHEMICAL, PETROLEUM,
METALS, AND INSTRUMENTS INDUSTRIES) AS CONTRIBUTING MOST IMPORTANTLY (DURING THE 1970s AND 1980s)
TO THE DEVELOPMENT OF THEIR NEW PRODUCTS AND PROCESSES INTRODUCED IN THE 1980s

Electronics				Information Processing				Pharmaceuticals			
University		Department		University		Department		University		Department	
MIT	(15%)	Elect. Eng.	(50%)	MIT	(9%)	Comp. Sci.	(38%)	Harvard	(13%)	Biology	(11%)
Berkeley	(13)	Mech. Eng.	(11)	Berkeley	(8)	Elect. Eng.	(10)	UCSF	(6)	Chemistry[a]	(22)
Illinois	(8)			Illinois	(6)	Mech. Eng.	(10)	Stanford	(6)	Pharmacology	(14)
Stanford	(7)			Minnesota	(6)			Yale	(6)		
CMU	(7)			Stanford	(6)						

Chemicals				Petroleum				Metals			
University		Department		University		Department		University		Department	
Washington	(12%)	Chemistry	(53%)	Delaware	(11%)	Chem. Eng.	(46%)	Utah	(16%)	Mat. Sci.	(32%)
MIT	(8)	Chem. Eng.	(15)	MIT	(7)	Chemistry	(8)	MIT	(12)	Civil Eng.	(20)
Utah	(6)			Notre Dame	(7)			Ohio State	(8)	Chemistry	(12)
				Princeton	(7)					Mech. Eng.	(8)
				VPI	(7)						

Instruments			
University		Department	
Yale	(9%)	Chemistry	(26%)
Indiana	(9)	Physics	(16)
		Radiology	(16)

[a] Includes biochemistry.

the ith university, R_i is the amount spent by the ith university on research and development in the relevant area[10] in 1980,[11] L_i is the percentage of firms in the sample that are located in the same state as the ith university, z_i is a random error term, and the α's are parameters. Q_i, a measure of the quality of the ith university's faculty in the relevant department, comes from the National Academy of Sciences (1982), which has published faculty ratings for departments of electrical engi-

neering, computer science, biochemistry, chemistry, and chemical engineering. These ratings range from 0 (not sufficient for doctoral education) to 5 (distinguished). For the electronics industry, we assume that the relevant department is electrical engineering; for information processing, we assume it is computer science; for pharmaceuticals, biochemistry; for chemicals, chemistry; and for petroleum, chemical engineering.

Since Y_i must be non-negative, Tobit estimates were made of the α's. Recognizing that the effects of each of the independent variables may differ from one industry to another, the statistical analysis was carried out separately in each of the five industries where the sample size is reasonably large. The results, shown in table 3, suggest that all three of the independent variables generally seem to be related directly to Y; in all but one case, the estimates of α_1, α_2, and α_3 are positive, and in about half of the cases they are statistically significant. However, there is considerable variation in Y that is unexplained by equation (1), which would be expected both because of obvious imperfections in the data and because

[10] For the electronics industry, we assume that the relevant department is electrical engineering; for information processing, we assume it is computer science; for pharmaceuticals, biochemistry; for chemicals, chemistry; and for petroleum, chemical engineering. For each industry, the relevant area of R&D is assumed to be R&D in this designated department, except for pharmaceuticals, where it is R&D in life sciences. (No data are available for pharmacology alone.) As we saw in table 2, these departments are responsible for much of the cited academic research, but by no means all of it. Thus, our analysis obviously is crude. Nonetheless, given that no information has been available heretofore on this topic, the results should be of interest. The data come from National Science Foundation (1985a).

[11] In the case of chemical engineering and electrical engineering, the R&D expenditure data pertain to 1983, not 1980. See National Science Foundation (1985a).

TABLE 3.—Tobit Estimates of Coefficients in Equation (1)

| Industry | Intercept | Independent Variables | | |
		R	Q	L
Electronics	−11.93	0.029	3.578[c]	0.030
	(2.48)	(0.093)	(0.830)	(0.035)
Information processing	−3.857[c]	0.602[b]	0.608	0.081[b]
	(1.384)	(0.264)	(0.520)	(0.037)
Drugs	−5.300[c]	0.066[c]	0.374	0.083[b]
	(1.322)	(0.022)	(0.439)	(0.035)
Chemicals	−3.987[a]	0.549	−0.171	0.096[a]
	(2.419)	(0.531)	(0.953)	(0.056)
Petroleum	−4.025[c]	0.701[b]	0.693[b]	0.014
	(1.245)	(0.300)	(0.336)	(0.024)

[a] Significant at the 0.10 level.
[b] Significant at the 0.05 level.
[c] Significant at the 0.01 level.

the independent variables are by no means the only factors influencing Y.[12]

To see the extent to which firms are willing to trade off faculty quality (as measured by Q) for geographical proximity, we chose a sample of nine major chemical, drug, and information processing firms, each of which estimated the probability that it would support research of a particular type at a university department with a specified value of Q and at various distances from the firm's R&D laboratories. The results, pertaining to 20 types of research, indicate that, holding faculty quality constant, the probability that a firm will support research at a college or university less than 100 miles away tends to be several times as great as the probability that it will support this research at a college or university 1,000 or more miles away. However, for research that (from the firm's vantage point and based on NSF's definitions[13]) is basic, geographical proximity seems to play a smaller role than for applied R&D; that is, firms seem more likely to insist on high faculty quality and pay less attention to location in choosing universities to do basic research. For applied R&D, there was about

a 1-in-5 chance that a firm in our sample would work with a university department with only a "marginal" faculty, but if so, there was an overwhelming likelihood that this college or university would be located within 100 miles of the firm's R&D laboratories.[14]

V. Size of Research Projects and Sources of Financial Support

While the foregoing findings indicate that there tends to be a direct relationship between the size of a university's R&D expenditures and its perceived contribution to industrial innovation (in the relevant area), this sheds no light on the size of the research projects carried out by the cited academic researchers. Based on data (in table 4) we obtained from about 90% of these researchers,[15] their average annual academic research expenditures during the 1970s and 1980s generally were less than $250,000 (about $425,000 in 1992 dollars).[16] Outside the pharmaceutical

---

[12] The number of colleges and universities that could be included in this analysis was electronics, 75; information processing, 48; pharmaceuticals, 84; chemicals, 93; and petroleum, 67. If ordinary least squares regressions are run, the pattern of significant regression coefficients is much like that in table 3, and R^2 is 0.30 to 0.50, except for chemicals, where it is only 0.08. If Tobit estimates are made, the normal scale parameter is about 3 in electronics and chemicals, 2 in information processing and pharmaceuticals, and 1.5 in petroleum.

[13] The National Science Foundation defines basic research in industry as research that advances scientific knowledge but does not have specific commercial objectives, although such investigations may be in fields of present or potential interest to the firm.

[14] For further discussion, see Lee and Mansfield (1994).

[15] Of the 303 distinct citations, about 70 were to academic researchers working at foreign universities or to an entire department. We corresponded with each of the remaining (roughly 235) cited academic researchers to obtain data concerning their research budgets, sources of research support, and the influence of users and funders on their choices of projects and directions taken. Eventually, after telephone and other follow-ups, these data were obtained (wholly or in part) from over 90% of them. Thus, the response rate is very high for a survey of this sort. To obtain more detailed data, we contacted a subsample of these academic researchers, and discussed these questions at length with them.

[16] The National Science Foundation and others often use the GNP (or GDP) deflator as a price index for R&D inputs. The above figures in 1992 dollars are based on this index. See Mansfield (1987).

TABLE 4.—PERCENTAGE DISTRIBUTION OF CITED ACADEMIC RESEARCHERS BY THEIR AVERAGE ANNUAL
RESEARCH EXPENDITURES, 1970–89

Average Annual Expenditure of Researcher[a]	Industry Citing the Academic Researcher						
	Electronics	Information Processing	Pharmaceuticals	Chemicals	Petroleum	Metals	Instruments
Less than $100,000	15	29	3	19	24	29	25
$100,000 to under $250,000	45	35	18	44	35	35	35
$250,000 to under $500,000	28	12	36	30	18	29	25
$500,000 to under $1 million	5	3	24	7	12	0	5
$1 million and over	8	21	21	0	12	6	10
Total	100	100	100	100	100	100	100

[a] These figures include overhead charged by the university.

industry, where the cited academic researchers tended to have comparatively large budgets, relatively few of them seemed to require total annual research budgets exceeding $500,000 (about $850,000 in 1992 dollars).[17] The median annual research budget of the cited academic researchers was about 5 times as great as the R&D expenditure per academic scientist or engineer (with a doctorate) in the relevant field, but the bulk of these projects certainly fall under the heading of "little science."[18]

Besides obtaining data from the cited academic researchers concerning the levels of their academic research budgets, we also got information from them regarding the sources of their financial support. Since our data pertain to all academic research carried out by each cited researcher during the 1970s and 1980s, they indicate the overall contours of a researcher's support, not just the support of whatever particular project the firm cited. Because various parts of a researcher's portfolio of projects often are interrelated, and because the firms often cited more than one project by a researcher, this seemed to be the best way to begin.

The first point to note is that practically all of the cited academic researchers had some government support for their research. In about two-thirds of the cases, it came, at least in part, from the National Science Foundation (NSF). The Department of Defense (DOD) was also important, particularly in electronics, and the National Institutes of Health (NIH) played a very major role in supporting academic researchers cited by the health-related industries, especially pharmaceuticals. The Department of Energy (DOE) and the National Aeronautics and Space Administration (NASA) also provided substantial, but more limited, support. In terms of dollar support, the federal government provided about two-thirds of the funding for the cited academic researchers (table 5), which was somewhat less than the percentage of R&D expenditures in colleges and universities financed by the federal government in the relevant fields (see note 10).[19]

While government support was obviously important to the vast majority of the cited academic researchers, this does not mean that industry did not support many of them as well. Over four-fifths of the cited academic researchers got research funds from industry. However, industry generally supported a substantially smaller percentage of

[17] Of course, the crudeness of these data should be emphasized. Averages over such a long period of time are very rough, and the basic data sometimes are only approximate. But the general conclusion put forth in the text seems to be quite robust; it seems unlikely to be affected much by errors of this sort.

[18] In each of the following fields in 1983, the R&D expenditures (in this field) at universities and colleges per doctoral scientist or engineer (in this field) employed by four-year colleges or universities were the following: electrical engineering, $64,991; computer science, $45,299; life sciences, $73,448; chemistry, $24,153; chemical engineering, $51,656. See National Science Foundation (1985a, c). As pointed out in footnote 10, these are regarded as the "relevant fields" for the electronics, information processing, pharmaceutical, chemical, and petroleum industries. Note that, in the pharmaceutical industry, the relevant field is not the same as the "relevant department" underlying Q_i because of the nature of the available data.

[19] For the five industries in table 5 for which a comparison can be made, the federal government provided, on the average, about 66% of the funding for the cited academic researchers, as compared with about 68% of the academic R&D in the relevant fields.

TABLE 5.—SOURCES OF FUNDING FOR CITED ACADEMIC RESEARCHERS[a]
AND FOR ALL ACADEMIC R&D IN RELEVANT FIELD

Industry Citing the Academic Researcher	Percentage of Cited Academic Researchers Where Research Was Funded (wholly or in part) by		Mean Percentage of Research Budgets of Cited Academic Researchers Funded by[b]		Percentage of Academic R&D in Relevant Field Funded by[c]	
	Federal Government	Firms	Federal Government	Firms	Federal Government	Private
Electronics	95	86	69	24	75	7
Information processing	91	65	51	22	73	9
Pharmaceuticals	91	76	85	12	61	9
Chemicals	96	78	71	21	74	8
Petroleum	100	94	56	10	58	13
Metals	89	94	44	47	—	—
Instruments	100	80	72	18	—	—
Mean	95	82	64	22	68	9

Source: See the text.

[a] For those researchers who were involved in academic research during only part of this period, the figures pertain to only this part of the period. For those who were involved in academic research during the entire period and whose pattern of support was significantly different during the 1980s than during the 1970s, we used the pattern of support during the 1970s, since this was generally the period when the work occurred for which the academic researcher was cited.

[b] For those researchers whose pattern of support was significantly different during the 1980s than during the 1970s, the figures for the federal government during the 1980s tend to be lower than those shown above, and the figures for firms for the 1980s tend to be higher than those shown above.

[c] The "relevant field" for each industry is given in footnote 10. These figures pertain to 1983, and come from National Science Foundation (1985a).

the total research budgets of the cited academic researchers than did government (22% versus 64%). Only in the metals industry, where the sample size is relatively small, did industry support exceed federal government support. Nonetheless, as might be expected, firms seemed to be more important as sources of support for the cited academic researchers than for all academic researchers in the relevant fields. The percentage of R&D expenditures in colleges and universities financed by private sources was about 10 percentage points lower, on the average, than the percentage of the cited academic researchers' budgets financed by industry.[20]

The relative importance of particular government agencies varied from industry to industry;

[20] For the five industries in table 5 for which a comparison can be made, firms provided, on the average, about 18% of the funding for the cited academic researchers; on the other hand, private sources provided, on the average, about 9% of the funding for all academic R&D in the relevant fields. Of course, the fact that the cited academic researchers received more industrial funding than the typical academic researcher in the relevant field helps to explain why, as noted in the previous paragraph of the text, the proportion of support from the federal government is somewhat less for the cited academic researchers than for all academic researchers in the relevant field.

for example, the National Institutes of Health accounted for an overwhelming percentage of the government funding of the academic researchers cited by the pharmaceutical industry, and the Defense Department supported a larger percentage of the government funding of academic researchers cited by the electronics industry than did any other agency (table 6). For a particular industry, the agencies that were the leading funders of research in the relevant field tended to provide the biggest share of support for the cited academic researchers, but they almost always were less important to the cited academic researchers than to researchers in the relevant field because a substantial proportion of the cited academic researchers were outside the relevant field. (Recall table 2.) By the same token, agencies that were not the leading funders of research in the relevant field tended to provide a bigger share of the support for the cited academic researchers than their share of research funding in the relevant field would indicate.

A substantial number of the cited academic researchers reported that their sources of financial support shifted considerably from the 1970s to the 1980s. In the later decade, more of their

TABLE 6.—MAJOR SOURCES OF FEDERAL FUNDING FOR CITED ACADEMIC RESEARCHERS[a]
AND FOR ALL ACADEMIC R&D IN THE RELEVANT FIELD

Federal Agency	Industry Citing the Academic Researcher						
	Electronics	Information Processing	Pharma-ceuticals	Chemicals	Petroleum	Metals	Instruments
	Percentage of Cited Academic Researchers with Federal Funding Whose Research Was Financed (wholly or in part) by Each Agency						
NSF	71	65	49	61	88	69	70
DOD	77	48	20	46	41	44	45
NIH	13	20	84	39	24	12	50
DOE	8	16	13	27	24	25	25
NASA	28	7	0	11	12	7	20
	Mean Percentage of Research Budgets of Cited Academic Researchers Financed by Each Agency (as percent of mean percentage financed by all federal agencies)						
NSF	32	27	6	24	57	30	36
DOD	43	31	6	14	20	36	21
NIH	7	12	65	31	11	2	18
DOE	3	6	6	17	4	9	7
NASA	7	6	0	6	2	0	6
	Percentage of Federal Obligations for Academic Research in Relevant Field by Each Agency[b]						
NSF	27	43	6	39	76	31	—
DOD	64	52	1	12	15	42	—
NIH	0	0	78	25	0	0	—
DOE	3	2	2	14	7	19	—
NASA	5	3	[c]	3	1	8	—

Source: See the text.
[a] See footnote a of table 5.
[b] The "relevant field" for each industry other than metals is given in footnote 10; for metals, it is metallurgy and materials. These figures pertain to 1981, and come from National Science Foundation (1985b).
[c] Less than 0.5%.

funding came from industry, less from government. In some cases, the shift was large; for example, for five academic researchers cited by the electronics industry, about 80% of their financial support came from the federal government (and 10% from firms) in the 1970s, as compared with about 20% from the federal government (and 80% from firms) in the 1980s.

Most of the cited academic researchers received support from multiple sources of funds. The bulk of them were supported by two or more of the following four sources: NSF, NIH, DOD, or firms. In electronics in particular, there frequently was support from three or more of them. Many of the cited academic researchers seem to have been entrepreneurial in outlook. Based on discussions with a sample of them, there was considerable interaction between them and potential sources of funding. As would be expected, a number of them complained that it was very difficult to obtain support for projects that they regarded to be of prime importance.

VI. Complementarity of Government-Funded and Industry-Funded Work of Cited Academic Researchers

Practically all of the cited academic researchers supported financially by both government and industry believe that their industry-funded work complemented their government-funded work. In the bulk of the cases, their government-funded work preceded their industry-funded work, and very often their industry-funded work was aimed at extending, deepening, or furthering the results of their previous government-funded work (table 7).[21] On the average, more than 50% felt that their government-funded work was more funda-

[21] The data underlying table 7 were collected from a subset of the academic researchers included in tables 4–6 that had obtained funding from both government and industry. In all, data were gotten from 83 of the cited academic researchers, the industry breakdown being: electronics, 35; information processing, 8; chemicals, 14; pharmaceuticals, 15; petroleum, 11. Smaller samples were collected in the metals and instruments industries.

TABLE 7.—RELATIONSHIPS BETWEEN GOVERNMENT-FUNDED AND INDUSTRY-FUNDED WORK
OF CITED ACADEMIC RESEARCHERS WITH BOTH TYPES OF FUNDING[a]

	Electronics	Information Processing	Drugs	Chemicals	Petroleum
	(percentage of cited academic researchers)				
Government-funded work preceded industry-funded work	85	62	67	86	64
Government-funded work regarded as more fundamental than industry-funded work	76	50	57	50	36
Problems worked on in academic research frequently or predominantly developed out of industrial consulting	58	62	43	57	73
Continuing consulting relationships with firms supporting academic research	65	75	100	79	82
Students took jobs with firms financing academic research	77	87	73	64	91

Source: See footnote 21.
[a] The metals and instruments industries are omitted because the sample sizes are quite small.

mental than their industry-funded work, but in the petroleum, chemical, and information processing industries, this figure did not exceed 50%.

In a large majority of the cases, the cited academic researchers had continuing consulting relationships with at least some of the firms supporting their academic research, and their students have taken jobs with at least some of these firms.[22] Moreover, in all industries other than drugs, over half of the cited academic researchers reported that the problems they worked on in their academic research frequently or predominantly developed out of their industrial consulting—and in many cases, the cited academic researchers' government-funded work stemmed

from ideas and problems they encountered in industrial consulting.[23]

Consequently, although their government-funded work tended to precede their industry-funded work, the ideas and problems they worked on (sometimes initially, and certainly later on) in both their government-funded work and industry-funded work often were influenced in an important way by their consulting and industrial

[22] One important way that these researchers became familiar with the availability of industrial funding and the needs of industrial users was through consulting. Over 90% of the cited academic researchers have been consultants to industry, the median amount of time devoted to industrial consulting being about 30 days per year. The percentage devoting 48 or more days to consulting was largest among those cited by the electronics industry, and smallest among those cited by the pharmaceutical industry.

[23] About two-thirds of the cited academic researchers in our sample felt that their own views were of primary importance in determining the nature and direction of the research they carried out. Only about one-tenth of the cited academic researchers said that potential funders or users of research had the primary influence over these matters in their case. However, this does not mean that the cited researchers did not take into account the views of potential funders and/or users of research. On the contrary, over half of them reported that their choice of problems and direction of work were influenced considerably (sometimes primarily) by potential funders and/or users. The extent of this influence seemed to be greatest for researchers cited by the electronics industry and for researchers supported heavily by DOD. Also, it seemed to be relatively great for researchers whose support was largely from industry.

experience. While much academic research is carried out with little regard for industry's needs, this does not seem to have been true of the work of most of the cited academic researchers.

VII. Summary and Conclusions

A substantial proportion of industrial innovations in high-technology industries like drugs, instruments, and information processing have been based directly on recent academic research, although in many cases the invention itself did not stem from the universities. Based on the findings of this paper, the extent to which a university is credited by firms in the electronics, information processing, drug, chemical, and petroleum industries with making major contributions to these firms' innovations tends to be related directly to the quality of the university's faculty in the relevant department (according to the NAS ratings), to the size of its R&D expenditures in relevant fields, and to the proportion of the industry's members located nearby. However, there is a considerable amount of variation unexplained by these three factors, and in all industries the effects of one or two of these factors, while they almost always have the signs indicated above, are not statistically significant.

The fact that a university's faculty rating (in the relevant department) tends to be related directly to its perceived contribution to industrial innovation seems to contradict the widely-held view that the highest-ranked university departments focus so heavily on research with a relatively long-term payoff that they would be unlikely to show up well in citations of this sort. However, the relationship between faculty rating and contribution to industrial innovation is so weak in several of these industries that it seems likely that many modestly-ranked departments play as big a role in this regard as some of the highest-ranked departments.

With regard to their research support for universities, firms tend to trade off faculty quality (as measured by the NAS ratings) for geographical proximity, particularly in the case of applied R&D. For basic research, they seem to pay less attention to location in choosing universities to work with and support, perhaps because in many kinds of applied R&D, it is very useful for academic and firm personnel to interact and work together on a face-to-face basis, whereas in basic research such ties may be weaker and more sporadic. Also, the difference between highly-rated and modestly-rated university departments in effectiveness and productivity may well be greater for basic research than for applied R&D.

With regard to government funding, the National Science Foundation, Department of Defense, and National Institutes of Health seem to play the predominant roles in financing academic research cited by the seven industries studied here. Whereas the National Institutes of Health are particularly important in supporting academic researchers cited by the health-related industries (drugs, chemicals, and instruments), the National Science Foundation and the Department of Defense are major supporters of academic researchers cited across the board. The leading role played by the National Science Foundation would probably be expected. The fact that the Department of Defense is so important in supporting academic researchers cited by such a wide swath of industries is noteworthy. The Department of Energy and the National Aeronautics and Space Administration seem to play lesser roles, at least in these industries.

Finally, the findings regarding the funding of these projects seem to reveal a complex web of financial and intellectual relationships among academic researchers, government agencies, and firms, Practically all of the cited academic researchers were supported, at least in part, by federal funds. If government agencies were trying to support work of this sort, they seemed to miss relatively few of the leading researchers, as indicated by the data presented here. Industry too supported the work of most of them, although its contribution was much smaller—and tended to come later—than that of the government. Once they achieved prominence, practically all of the cited academic researchers were involved in consulting relationships with firms, which helped to stimulate many of the ideas and topics taken up subsequently in both their government-funded and industry-funded work.

REFERENCES

Acs, Zoltan, David Audretsch, and Maryann Feldman, "Real Effects of Academic Research: Comment," *American Economic Review* 82 (1992), 363–367.
Government–University–Industry Research Roundtable and Industrial Research Institute, "Industrial Perspectives on Innovation and Interactions with Universities" (Washington, D.C.: National Academy Press, 1991).

Jaffe, Adam, "Real Effects of Academic Research," *American Economic Review* 79 (1989), 957–970.

Jaffe, Adam, Manuel Trajtenberg, and Rebecca Henderson, "Geographical Localization of Knowledge Spillovers As Evidenced by Patent Citations," *Quarterly Journal of Economics* 108 (1993), 577–598.

Jewkes, John, David Sawers, and Richard Stillerman, *The Sources of Invention*, second edition (New York: W. W. Norton, 1969).

Lee, J., and E. Mansfield, "Industrial Support of Academic Research," Center for Economics and Technology, University of Pennsylvania, 1994.

Mansfield, Edwin, "Academic Research and Industrial Innovation," *Research Policy* 20 (1991a), 1–12.

_____, "Academic Research and Industrial Innovation: A Further Note," *Research Policy* 21 (1992), 295–296.

_____, "Estimates of the Social Returns from Research and Development," in M. Meredith, S. Nelson, and A. Teich (eds.), *Science and Technology Yearbook* (Washington, D.C.: American Association for the Advancement of Science, 1991b), 313–320.

_____, "Price Indexes for R&D Inputs, 1969–83," *Management Science* 33 (1987), 124–129.

_____, "Basic Research and Productivity Increase in Manufacturing," *American Economic Review* 70 (1980), 863–873.

_____, et al., "Social and Private Rates of Return from Industrial Innovations," *Quarterly Journal of Economics* 91 (1977), 221–240.

National Academy of Sciences, *An Assessment of Research-Doctorate Programs in the United States* (Washington, D.C.: National Academy Press, 1982).

National Science Foundation, *University-Industry Research Relationships* (Washington, D.C.: Government Printing Office, 1982).

_____, *Academic Science / Engineering: R&D Funds, 1983* (Washington, D.C.: Government Printing Office, 1985a).

_____, *Federal Funds for Research and Development, 1981, 1982, and 1983* (Washington, D.C.: Government Printing Office, 1985b).

_____, *Characteristics of Doctoral Scientists and Engineers in the United States: 1983* (Washington, D.C.: Government Printing Office, 1985c).

Nelson, Richard, "Institutions Supporting Technical Advance in Industry," *American Economic Review* 76 (1986), 186–189.

Peters, Lois, and Herbert Fusfeld, "Current U.S. University-Industry Research Connections," in *University-Industry Research Relationships* (Washington, D.C.: National Science Board, 1982).

von Hippel, Eric, *The Sources of Innovation* (New York: Oxford University Press, 1988).

[2]

UNIVERSITIES AS A SOURCE OF COMMERCIAL TECHNOLOGY: A DETAILED ANALYSIS OF UNIVERSITY PATENTING, 1965–1988

Rebecca Henderson, Adam B. Jaffe, and Manuel Trajtenberg*

Abstract—This paper explores the recent explosion in university patenting as a source of insight into the changing relationship between the university and the private sector. Before the mid-1980s, university patents were more highly cited, and were cited by more diverse patents, than a random sample of all patents. More recently several significant shifts in university patenting behavior have led to the disappearance of this difference. Thus our results suggest that between 1965 and 1988 the rate of increase of important patents from universities was much less than their overall rate of increase of patenting.

I. Introduction

RECENT work in both macroeconomic theory and technology policy has focused renewed attention on the role of spillovers in general and on university research in particular in driving economic growth (Caballero and Jaffe (1993) and Romer (1986, 1990)). Since universities are in principle dedicated to the widespread dissemination of the results of their research, university spillovers are likely to be disproportionately large and may thus be disproportionately important (Dasgupta and David (1987), Jaffe (1989), Merton (1973), Zucker et al. (1997), and National Academy of Sciences (1995)).

This focus on university research comes at a time when universities have been under increasing pressure to translate the results of their work into privately appropriable knowledge. In 1980 and 1984 major changes in federal law made it significantly easier for universities to retain the property rights to inventions deriving from federally funded research. At the same time increasing competition for federal resources has forced many universities to turn to alternative sources of funding. Many universities have established technology licensing offices and are actively pursuing industrial support.

At first glance these changes appear to have had a dramatic effect on the way in which university research is transferred to the private sector. University patenting has exploded. In 1965 just 96 U.S. patents were granted to 28 U.S. universities or related institutions. In 1992 almost 1500 patents were granted to over 150 U.S. universities or related institutions. This 15-fold increase in university patenting occurred over an interval in which total U.S. patenting increased less than 50%, and patents granted to U.S. inventors remained roughly constant. However, the extent to which this explosion should be taken as evidence of a large increase in the contribution of universities to commercial technology development depends on the extent to which it represents more commercially useful inventions versus the extent to which it represents simply increased filing of patent applications on marginal inventions.

Received for publication September 5, 1995. Revision accepted for publication December 13, 1996.

* Massachusetts Institute of Technology, Brandeis University, and Tel Aviv University, respectively, and National Bureau of Economic Research.

This paper explores this issue in some detail, both as a phenomenon of interest in its own right and as a window into the changing role of universities as sources of technology for the private economy. A number of surveys and some detailed case study work have documented substantial shifts in the nature of the relationship between universities and the private sector (Blumenthal (1986), Cohen et al. (1994), David et al. (1992), and National Science Foundation (1982)). Here we focus on university patents, both because patents are a unique and highly visible method of "technology transfer" (Archibugi (1992), Basberg (1987), Boitani and Ciciotti (1990), Schwartz (1988), and Trajtenberg (1990a)), and because their accessibility allows for a more comprehensive analysis than is possible with either surveys or case study work.

We draw on a comprehensive database consisting of *all* patents assigned to universities or related institutions from 1965 until mid-1992, a 1% random sample of all U.S. patents granted over the same time period, and the complete set of all patents that cite either of these groups. We show that averaged over the whole time period, university patents are both more important and more general than the average patent, but that this difference has been declining over time, so that by the late 1980s we cannot find significant differences between the university patent universe and the random sample of all patents. We suggest that the observed increase in university patenting may reflect an increase in their "propensity to patent"—and possibly an associated increase in the rate of knowledge transfer to the private sector—rather than an increase in the output of "important" inventions.

The paper is organized into five sections. The following section describes our data, and explains some of the institutional changes that appear to be driving the growth of university patenting. Section III demonstrates the difference between university and other patents in the citation-based measures of importance, and the decline of that difference in the 1980s. Section IV explores possible explanations for that decline. Section V provides concluding observations.

II. The Growth of University Patents

A. The Basic Numbers

This paper is part of a larger research project that exploits the declining cost of access to large quantities of patent data. In prior work we have used patent data to show that spillovers are geographically localized (Jaffe et al. (1993)), that spillovers from university research are less likely to be geographically localized than privately funded research (Henderson et al. (1996)), and to explore the degree to which citation-based measures provide useful information about the scientific and economic impact of the idea captured in a patent (Trajtenberg et al. (1996)). Here we draw on these data to explore how the quantity and "quality" of university patents have changed over time, and to compare both to the overall universe of U.S. patents.[1]

We use four sets of patents: all university patents granted between 1965 and mid-1992 (12,804 patents); a 1% random sample of all U.S. patents[2] over the same period (19,535 patents); all patents after 1974 that cited the university patents (40,859 patents), and all patents after 1974 that cited the random sample patents (42,147 patents).[3] For these patents we know the year of application,[4] the identity of the institution to which it is assigned, and the "patent class," a detailed technological classification provided by the patent office.

Figure 1 illustrates the dramatic increase in patenting we have already described. Panel A compares the rate of university patenting to all U.S. patents and to domestic U.S. patents. Panel B shows university patenting relative to university research, and an analogous ratio for the U.S. industrial sector. University patenting has not only increased, it has increased more rapidly than overall patenting and much more rapidly than domestic patenting, which is essentially flat until the late 1980s. In addition, university patenting has increased more rapidly than university research spending, causing the ratio of university patents to R&D to more than triple over the period. In contrast the ratio of domestic patents to domestic R&D nearly halved over the same period. Thus universities' "propensity to patent" has been rising significantly at the same time that the overall propensity to patent has been falling. Note that the increase in university patenting has been fairly continuous since the early 1970s. There is some evidence of an acceleration in the late 1980s, but this is a period in which both university research and overall patenting accelerate as well, making it difficult to assess its significance.

This increasing propensity to patent is also evident in a significant increase in the number of universities taking out patents. Whereas in 1965 about 30 universities obtained patents, in 1991 patents were granted to about 150 universities and related institutions. Nevertheless, university patent-

[1] In our earlier paper (Henderson et al. (1996)) we documented the existence of a decline in the "quality" of university patents. However, in that paper we were not able to control for problems such as truncation bias or shifts in citation patterns over time, and we were not able to explore the causes of the decline in any detail.

[2] By "U.S. patents" we mean patents granted by the U.S. Patent Office. By the end of this period, about half of such patents were granted to non-U.S. residents. About 1% of the patents assigned to U.S. universities were taken out by individuals who gave the patent office non-U.S. addresses.

[3] A detailed description of the data set is given, Henderson et al. (1995) or is available from the authors as a technical appendix.

[4] We prefer to date patents by the year of application rather than the year of grant, because that is when the inventor identified the existence of a new invention, and there are variable lags involved between application and grant date. Because of these lags, however, totals by date of application are incomplete for years approaching the 1992 data cutoff date, since some patents applied for at the end of the period were almost certainly still under review at the time we collected our data. Thus we terminate our time-sensitive analyses in 1988.

FIGURE 1.—INCREASE IN PATENTING

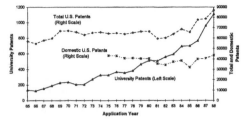

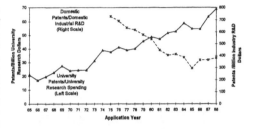

TABLE 1.—TOP 10 INSTITUTIONS FOR UNIVERSITY PATENTS, 1991

Institution	Patent Count
Massachusetts Institute of Technology	100
University of California	91
University of Texas	82
Stanford University	56
Wisconsin Alumni Research Foundation	44
University of Florida	43
Iowa State University Research Foundation Inc.	39
California Institute of Technology	32
University of Minnesota	30
Johns Hopkins University	26

ing remains highly concentrated, with the top 20 institutions receiving about 70% of the total, and MIT, the most prolifically patenting institution, alone receiving about 8%. The top 10 institutions and their total patent grants for 1991 are shown in table 1.

The increase in university patenting has not been uniform across the spectrum of technologies. Panel A of figure 2 shows the breakdown of university patents by field over time,[5] panel B shows it for all patents.[6] The differences are dramatic, if not surprising. By the end of the 1980s, drug and medical patents comprised about 35% of the university total,

[5] Full details of this classification by field are given in Jaffe (1986).

[6] This and all subsequent analyses are based on our 1/100 random sample of all patents. Given the large number of such patents (over 500 per year), the composition by field of the sample is very likely to be close to the composition by field of the universe of all patents. Note that the random sample does not exclude university patents. Even at the end of the period, however, university patents are less than 2% of the total.

FIGURE 2.—PATENTS BY BROAD FIELDS

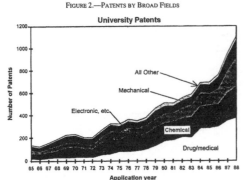

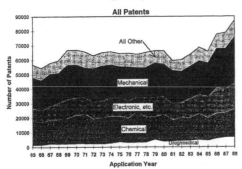

up from less than 15% in 1965; chemical patents 25–30%; electronic and related patents 20–25%; mechanical patents 10–15%; and about 5% other. In contrast, overall patenting is 30–35% mechanical; 20–25% each for chemical and electronics, 10–15% other; and less than 10% drugs and medical. Thus universities are much more interested in drugs and medical technologies, and much less interested in mechanical technologies, than other inventors, and the difference has increased over time.

B. The Broader Context of Increased University Patenting

There are several possible explanations for this dramatic increase in patenting behavior. Changes in federal law affecting university patenting in 1980 and then again in 1984 made it significantly easier for universities to patent the results of federally funded research. Industry funding of university research has notably increased and at the same time there has been a substantial increase in organized university "technology transfer" or "licensing" offices. Since all three changes occurred roughly simultaneously, their different effects cannot be easily separated, but it seems plausible that all three have played an important role in increasing the number of university patents.

Federal Law Affecting University Patenting: Before 1980 the federal government had the right to claim all royalties or other income derived from patents resulting from federally funded research. Federally funded researchers could apply for patents, and could assign those patents to universities, but the exclusive property right associated with the invention remained with the government whether or not a patent was issued. The only way that a university could profit from federally derived patents was to seek a title rights waiver from the funding agency. Since approximately 70% of university research during this period was funded by the federal government, this was a major barrier to widespread university patenting.

In 1980 Congress passed The Patent and Trademark Amendments of 1980 (Public Law 96-517), also known as the Bayh-Dole Act. The Bayh-Dole Act gave universities (and other nonprofit institutions, as well as small businesses) the right to retain the property rights to inventions derived from federally funded research. The 1984 passage of Public Law 98-620 expanded the rights of universities further by removing certain restrictions contained in the Bayh-Dole Act regarding the kinds of inventions that universities could own, and the rights of universities to assign their property rights to other parties.

Thus since 1984 universities have had very broad rights to exploit inventions derived from their research, even if it is federally funded. They can charge royalties for the use of the patent, and they can assign the patent to a third party if they so desire. As a result, major research universities now typically have explicit policies requiring faculty and other researchers to assign patents deriving from on-campus research to the university, and specifying how any income deriving therefrom is to be divided among the institution, the researcher, and research centers or departments.

Increase in Organized University "Technology" Offices:
Though it is obviously difficult to separate the chicken from the egg, since the passage of the Bayh-Dole Act there has been a dramatic increase in the scale and significance of the patenting and technology licensing function at universities. The Association of University Technology Administrators (AUTM) has recently begun conducting surveys of its members. The surveyed institutions[7] employed 767 full-time equivalent professional employees in technology transfer and licensing activities. In 1993 they received royalties totaling about $375 million on about 4016 licensing agreements; more than 4000 additional active agreements were not currently generating revenue.[8]

[7] Survey responses came from 112 U.S. institutions that were granted 1169 patents in Fiscal Year 1992, compared to our data, which indicate that about 1500 patents were granted to over 150 institutions. Thus survey totals are lower bounds on the actual numbers.
[8] *The AUTM Licensing Survey, Fiscal Years 1991, 1992, and 1993.* AUTM categories included in the quoted totals are U.S. universities, U.S. hospitals, third-party management firms, and research institutes. Excluded are government and Canadian universities. The royalty total has been adjusted to eliminate double counting, which results from shared license agreements (personal communication, Ashley Stevens, AUTM).

TABLE 2.—CORRELATION COEFFICIENTS ACROSS KEY PATENT-RELATED VARIABLES, 1993 DATA

	FTEs for Licensing Activities	Disclosures	Gross Royalties	Industry Support	Public Support
Total U.S. patents filed	0.88 (113)	0.91 (112)	0.71 (112)	0.69 (110)	0.82 (113)
FTEs		0.84 (112)	0.81 (112)	0.61 (110)	0.86 (113)
Disclosures			0.72 (112)	0.66 (109)	0.83 (112)
Royalties				0.53 (109)	0.71 (112)
Industry support					0.64 (110)

Source: *The AUTM Licensing Survey.*
Notes: Figures in parentheses are number of observations. The number of observations varies because not all universities participating in the survey provide comprehensive data.

Increased Industry Funding of University Research: Another factor that may be related to the increase in university patenting is an increase in industry funding of university research from 2.6% in 1970 to 3.9% in 1980 and 7.1% in 1994.[9]

It is clearly impossible to assign the roles of "cause" and "effect" to these different trends. The increase in university patenting predates the passage of the Bayh-Dole Act, but continued exponential growth probably could not have been sustained without removal of the cumbersome barriers to patents from federal research. The increase in universities' institutional commitment to patenting, in the form of new and expanded licensing offices, would likely not have occurred if the impetus toward more commercial research and the change in federal law had not occurred. But once created, these offices presumably facilitate the patent application process and thereby contribute to the increased patenting. Finally, increased industry funding is probably partially a response to universities' increased interest in applied research, but it, in turn, increases the resources for these activities and thereby also supports increased patenting.

Table 2 illustrates this close correlation quantitatively. For the 113 universities reporting comprehensive data to AUTM it presents correlations across patenting rates, employees in the licensing office, invention disclosures, gross royalties, and the level of industrial and publicly funded support. In these cross-sectional data patenting rates are less correlated with levels of industry funding than with levels of public funding, disclosure rates, or the size of the licensing office, suggesting that increased industry funding may be less important in driving patenting behavior than changes in the law and the expansion of technology licensing offices, but the high degree of serial correlation evident in the raw longitudinal data make it impossible to draw any firm conclusions as to the relative importance of these various factors.

III.   Characterizing University Patenting

A.   Citation-Based Measures of Importance and Generality

The flow of technology out of universities almost certainly contributes to technological innovation in the private sector (Jaffe (1989)), and there is a widespread belief that more effective transfer of technology from universities to the private sector would be beneficial to innovation and growth (U.S. GAO (1987) and National Academy of Sciences (1995)). In this light, to the extent that it signals an increase in the successful commercial application of university-derived technology, the rapid increase in university patenting would appear to be a highly desirable trend. However, patents vary tremendously in their importance, making it dangerous to draw conclusions about aggregate technology flows based on numbers of patents (Griliches (1990)). In this section we look more carefully at the university patents, to understand better what the patent data do and do not say about increases in the flow of technology out of universities.

In an earlier paper (Trajtenberg et al. (1996)) we used patent citation data to construct a variety of measures that we interpreted as capturing the importance or "basicness" of the invention covered by a patent. Implicit in this approach is a view of technology as an evolutionary process, in which the significance of any particular invention is evidenced, at least partly, by its role in stimulating and facilitating future inventions. We assume that at least some of such future inventions will reference or cite the original invention in their patents, thereby making the number and character of citations received a valid indicator of the technological importance of an invention (Trajtenberg (1990a) and Carpenter and Narin (1993)).[10]

---

[9] With federal funding at 60 to 70% of the total, the remainder is funded by state and local governments and institutions' own funds.

[10] Citations or references serve the legal function of delimiting the scope of patent protection by identifying technological predecessors of the

We use two citation-based measures: *importance* and *generality*. We define importance as

$$Importance_i = Nciting_i + \lambda \sum_{j=1}^{Nciting_i} Nciting_{i+1,j}$$

where $0 < \lambda < 1$ is defined as an arbitrary discount factor, which in the previous paper we set to 0.5. In the absence of data about "second-generation" citations in the data set on which this paper relies, we here set λ equal to zero and measure importance simply by total citations received.

The second citation-based measure that we use is *generality*. We hypothesize that patents that cover more "basic" research will be cited by work in a broader range of fields, and define generality as

$$General_i = 1 - \sum_{k=1}^{N_i} \left(\frac{Nciting_{ik}}{Nciting_i} \right)^2$$

where k is the index of patent classes and N_i is the number of different classes to which the citing patents belong. Notice that $0 \leq General \leq 1$, and that higher values represent less concentration and hence more generality. In our previous paper we were able to show that both of these measures were reassuringly high for a number of patents that are known to have had a very significant impact on their field.

Citation-based measures of importance and generality are, to some extent, influenced by variations in citation practices across time and technological areas. They are also very influenced by the fact that when we count the citations of a patent issued in, for example, 1989, we are missing many more of the citations that it will ultimately receive than we are missing in our count of the citations of a patent issued in 1975. For these reasons, when comparing importance or generality it is necessary to control for both time and technological field effects.

B.   Comparing University and Random Sample Patents

As a first step in exploring the degree to which the increase in university patenting rates reflects an increasing transfer of knowledge to the private sector, we first explore the degree to which university patents are more important or more general than the random sample of patents and the degree to which this has changed over time.

Table 3 presents the results of regressions of our measures of importance and generality on a series of dummy variables

---

patented invention. Thus if patent 2 cites patent 1, it implies that patent 1 represents a piece of previously existing knowledge upon which patent 2 builds, and over which patent 2 cannot have a claim. The applicant has a legal duty to disclose any knowledge of the prior art, but the decision as to which patents to cite ultimately rests with the patent examiner, who is supposed to be an expert in the area and hence to be able to identify relevant prior art that the applicant misses or conceals. Trajtenberg (1990a,b) showed that citation-weighted patents were a good proxy for the consumers' surplus generated by inventions. For more discussion of the value and limitations of citation data, see Trajtenberg et al. (1996).

TABLE 3.—COMPARISON OF UNIVERSITY AND RANDOM SAMPLE PATENTS

	Importance 1965–1988 n = 28,313	Generality 1975–1988 n = 14,775
Random sample mean		
Drug/medical	4.00	0.258
Chemical	3.87	0.296
Electronics, etc.	4.23	0.288
Mechanical	3.77	0.265
All other	3.47	0.203
Overall university difference, controlling for field	0.918 (0.072)	0.0452 (0.0049)
University difference by field		
Drug/medical	0.311 (0.199)	−0.0168 (0.0135)
Chemical	0.416 (0.124)	0.0480 (0.0087)
Electronics, etc.	1.718 (0.141)	0.0582 (0.0094)
Mechanical	1.290 (0.153)	0.0740 (0.0107)
All other	0.396 (0.255)	0.0148 (0.0180)

Notes: Standard errors are in parentheses. Differences are estimated controlling for application-year effects.

for application years and technological areas, and dummy variables for whether or not the original patent was a university patent. These regressions are based on application years 1965–1988 for importance and 1975–1988 for generality.[11] Over the entire period, controlling for technological field effects and time effects, university patents received almost 25% more citations on average, and this difference is highly significant statistically. They were also about 15% more general, again a statistically significant difference. These overall averages conceal a moderate amount of variation across fields. The difference between university and random sample patents is largest in electronics and mechanical patents, and smallest in the drug/medical area.

These results control for time effects, but they do not allow the university/random sample difference itself to vary over time. Results of regressions that allow each year cohort of patents to have its own university/random sample difference are shown in table 4 and again graphically in figure 3.[12] While the year-by-year differences are somewhat noisy, there is a clear overall trend: the university/random sample difference grew during the 1970s, reached a plateau during the period from about 1975 through about 1982, and fell significantly after that. The differences between the two

---

[11] The generality measure cannot be calculated for the pre-1975 patents because we lack information on the citing patents before 1975, and we terminate the analysis in 1988 because a significant fraction of 1989 applications might be granted after mid-1992, when our data end. Also, those granted in 1990 and 1991 would have very little time to receive citations.

[12] To make sure that the university/random sample difference is not due to the different technological foci of the two samples, the regressions reported in table 4 replace the five technology field dummies used in table 2 with 364 separate dummies for patent office patent classes.

TABLE 4.—COMPARISON OF UNIVERSITY AND RANDOM SAMPLE PATENTS OVER TIME

Year	University/Random Sample Mean Difference	
	Importance (1)	Generality (2)
1965	0.42 (0.29)	
1966	1.63[a] (0.52)	
1967	−0.15 (0.41)	
1968	0.10 (0.35)	
1969	0.06 (0.44)	
1970	0.82[b] (0.42)	
1971	1.35[a] (0.41)	
1972	1.48[a] (0.41)	
1973	1.84[a] (0.38)	
1974	1.08[a] (0.35)	
1975	2.54[a] (0.35)	0.053[a] (0.019)
1976	1.82[a] (0.34)	0.065[a] (0.019)
1977	1.31[a] (0.34)	0.048[a] (0.020)
1978	2.04[a] (0.34)	0.040[b] (0.019)
1979	1.13[a] (0.31)	0.052[a] (0.018)
1980	1.91[a] (0.31)	0.051[a] (0.017)
1981	1.68[a] (0.31)	0.080[a] (0.018)
1982	0.96[a] (0.31)	0.051[a] (0.018)
1983	0.97[a] (0.30)	0.028[c] (0.017)
1984	0.47[c] (0.28)	0.024 (0.017)
1985	0.40 (0.28)	0.037[b] (0.017)
1986	0.06 (0.27)	0.013 (0.017)
1987	−0.07 (0.25)	0.043[a] (0.017)
1988	−0.08 (0.24)	0.012 (0.019)
Year Dummies	Significant	Significant
Patent class controls	Significant	Significant

Notes: [a] Significant at the 1% level.
[b] Significant at the 5% level.
[c] Significant at the 10% level.

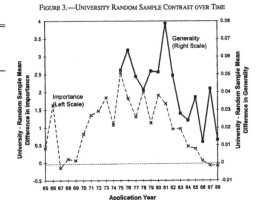

FIGURE 3.—UNIVERSITY RANDOM SAMPLE CONTRAST OVER TIME

groups are statistically significant between 1970 (1975 for generality) and about 1982 or 1983. After that the two groups are not statistically different from one another in either generality or importance.

C. Robustness of the Apparent Decline

This decline in relative importance and generality appears to be robust to a number of factors, including truncation bias or possible shifts in citation patterns over time.[13] In the first place, they are robust to time–field interaction effects. If it were the case, for example, that drug patents have become increasingly less citation intensive over time, then university patents (which are increasingly concentrated in the drug/medical area) would appear to be increasingly less important in the sense of receiving fewer citations, because the regressions reported in table 4 control only for the *average* level of citations in drug-related patent classes. However, rerunning the regressions of table 4 *separately* for each of the five major fields yields results (not reported here) that suggest that the decline in the university advantage occurs across all fields and is thus not a result of any difference in composition by field across the two groups.

A second possibility is that the decline is an artifact of the truncation of the citation information in 1992. There are a number of reasons to suspect that such bias could be present. Suppose, first, that the pattern of the distribution of citations over time is identical for both university and random sample patents, but that in every year university patents receive proportionally more citations. Thus it might take several years for the cumulative difference between university and other patents to become significant, and the apparent disappearance of the difference between the two groups at the end of the observed period could simply reflect the fact that there has been insufficient time for the difference between the two

[13] Details of the analyses summarized in this subsection are given in Henderson et al. (1995) or are available from the authors.

groups to become apparent. However, a simple test of this idea—rerunning the regression in logs, thereby capturing the *proportionate* difference between the two groups rather than the absolute difference—produces results, (not reproduced here) that are broadly consistent with those reported above.[14] Thus the results probably cannot be explained by truncation of lag distributions, if the two distributions have the same shape.

A third, more subtle possible problem is that university patents may on average come later than those for private firms, so that the truncation has a more severe effect on them than on the random sample patents. However, a regression that estimates the difference between the average university and random sample patents in a given year, controlling for the predicted levels based on the years remaining to truncation and the average citation lag structure for each sample, gives very similar results to the simpler ones reported earlier, with the university/corporate difference declining sharply around 1981 or 1982 and becoming statistically insignificant shortly thereafter.

In summary, then, university patents in all fields were more important and more general than average in the 1970s. This advantage disappeared in all fields by the mid-1980s; and this disappearance does not appear to be an artifact of truncation or of the way in which citation patterns have changed over time.

IV. The Nature of the Decline

What, then may be causing this decline? One logically plausible candidate—the increasing importance of nonuniversity patents—can probably be easily dismissed, given that, as shown in figure 1, the late 1980s were a time of increasing propensity to patent. The overall patent/R&D ratio, which had been falling for most of this century, began to rise slightly, probably in response to the creation of a special court of appeals for hearing patent cases, and the issuance of several decisions that have increased the perceived likelihood that patents will be enforced (Schwartz (1988)). We suspect that these changes have made patenting slightly more attractive, all other things equal, thus making it economic to patent ideas of lower expected quality and thereby *reducing* the overall importance of private sector patents.

Our results suggest instead that the decline in the relative importance and generality of university patents had two principal components. First the fact that an increasing fraction of university patents is coming from smaller institutions, which have always produced patents that were not as highly cited as those from the larger institutions, and second a general decline in average quality that encompasses even the best institutions triggered largely by a large increase in the number of patents that receive no citations at all.

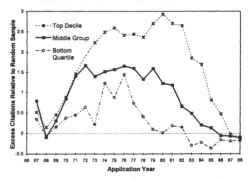

FIGURE 4.—CITATION INTENSITY OF UNIVERSITY PATENTS RELATIVE TO RANDOM SAMPLE OVER TIME BY PATENT RANKING OF INSTITUTION IN 1988

Notes: Top decile—top 10% of institutions in terms of patents in 1988; bottom quartile—bottom quartile in 1988 plus institutions that had no patents in 1988; middle group—everyone else.

Simple counts suggest that smaller institutions are indeed patenting more intensively. Since 1965 the fraction of patents going to the top four institutions has fallen from about 50% to about 25%. The Herfindahl index of concentration across institutions has also declined, from about 0.1 in 1965 to about 0.04 in 1988. These smaller institutions are indeed getting less important patents. Figure 4 shows the results of running regressions analogous to that underlying figure 3, but allowing the difference between university and random sample patents to differ not only over time but also according to the size of the institution. To control for size we grouped all institutions that got any patents over the period into three categories: (1) those institutions in the top decile in terms of the number of successful patent applications in 1988;[15] (2) those institutions that got fewer patents than the top decile but more than the bottom quartile in 1988; and (3) those institutions that were in the bottom quartile in terms of patent total in 1988 plus those that had no successful applications in 1988 but received at least one patent from some other year. The results are illustrated in figure 4. The results show that, except possibly for a few years in the second half of the 1970s, the bottom group of universities never produced patents that were statistically distinguishable from the random sample, whereas the 15 schools that comprise the top decile of institutions had patents that were even more superior to the random sample than those of other universities. Thus the fact that an increasing fraction of university patents is coming from smaller institutions does indeed seem to be partially responsible for the overall decline in the average importance of university patents. Notice that figure 4 also suggests, however, that even the

---

[14] This requires eliminating from both groups those patents with zero citations. The overall difference in importance between the two groups is about 15%. This overall difference conceals variation, with a high of about 30% in the mid to late 1970s, falling to insignificance by 1984.

[15] The distribution of patenting activities across universities is very stable over time, so that the choice of a particular year to divide the sample—in this case 1988—seems unlikely to introduce any particular bias into the results.

FIGURE 5.—TOTAL UNIVERSITY PATENTS, "WINNERS," AND "LOSERS"

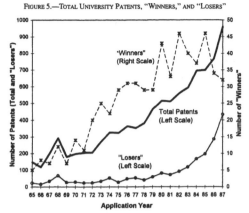

Notes: Losers—patents with no citations by end of period; winners—patents with more citations than mean of top 10% of random sample patents from same year.

very best institutions have seen a decline in the relative quality of their patents since about 1983.

The second major component of the decline in average quality appears to be the presence of an increasing number of "low quality" university patents as the institutional changes that we outlined above have substantially increased universities' propensity to patent. Figure 5 illustrates this trend dramatically. It shows the overall increase in patenting (the heavy middle line), juxtaposed with two contrasting components of that total.

The dashed line at the top is the number of high-importance patents, dubbed "winners" in the graph and plotted on the right-side axis. This is the number of patents that received more citations than the mean of the top 10% of random sample patents from the same year. This series increases *faster* than the overall total up until the early 1980s, implying that the proportion of very important patents was increasing over this period. From 1981 on, however, this series fluctuates up and down with no clear trend and despite the approximate doubling in the total number of patents after 1980, there is no increase in the number of very important patents.

The bottom line is the number of "losers"—the number of patents each year that received no citations. It is virtually flat until the early 1980s, showing that the roughly fivefold increase in overall patenting up until that time was not accompanied by much of an increase in the number of these low-importance patents. After about 1981, however, this number increases dramatically, until by 1987 nearly half of all university patents are receiving no citations. This increase appears to reflect a real change in the composition of university patents, and is quite robust to controls for both field and truncation bias.

V. Conclusion

We have shown that the relative importance and generality of university patents has fallen at the same time as the sheer number of university patents has increased. This decrease appears to be largely the result of a very rapid increase in the number of "low-quality" patents being granted to universities.

What are the policy implications of this result? From a theoretical perspective, the Bayh-Dole Act and the increase in industry funding had two distinct effects on university incentives. Both the incentive to perform research that could be expected to produce important commercial inventions, and the incentive to patent and license whatever commercial inventions were produced increased. Clearly, the Bayh-Dole Act has been a success with respect to the second of these incentive effects. Both the rate of patenting and the extent of licensing have increased dramatically. In this context it is important to emphasize that even thought the body of uncited university patents that we have observed is probably less valuable *per patent* than previous university patents, these patents are not worthless in the aggregate. Some of these uncited patents are licensed and are commercially valuable. Before the Bayh-Dole Act they would probably not have been either patented or licensed, and the invention underlying them would have been unlikely to generate commercial benefits. Thus the increase in university patenting probably reflects an increased rate of technology transfer to the private sector, and this has probably increased the social rate of return to university research.

In contrast to the impact on the *transfer* of technology, our results suggest, however, that the Bayh-Dole Act and the other related changes in federal law and institutional capability have not had a significant impact on the underlying rate of *generation* of commercially important inventions at universities. Universities either did not significantly shift their research efforts toward areas likely to produce commercial inventions, or, if they did, they did so unsuccessfully. It is unclear, of course, whether it would be socially desirable if universities shifted their research efforts toward commercial objectives. It is likely that the bulk of the economic benefits of university research come from inventions in the private sector that build upon the scientific and engineering base created by university research, rather than from commercial inventions generated directly by universities. In other words, if commercial inventions are inherently only a secondary product of university research, then it makes sense for policy to seek to ensure that those inventions that do appear are transferred to the private sector, but not to hope to increase significantly the rate at which university research directly generates commercial inventions. This appears to be what has occurred.

From a methodological perspective, our results show that it is possible to use citations to improve the usefulness of patent statistics as economic indicators. The economic usefulness of these widely available data has been limited by their perceived noisiness. Even in the time-series dimension, where cohort effects and truncation bias make citation comparisons difficult, the use of a reference group and careful controls for technology field allowed us to produce fairly clear results regarding the changing nature of university patents. We believe that this technique can be readily applied to other data, thereby greatly increasing the signal-to-noise ratio in patent data.

REFERENCES

Archibugi, D., "Patenting as an Indicator of Technological Innovation: A Review," *Science and Public Policy* 19 (1992), 357–368.

AUTM, *The AUTM Licensing Survey, Fiscal Years 1993, 1992, 1991* (Norwalk, CT: Association of University Technology Managers, 1994).

Basberg, B., "Patents and the Measurement of Technological Change: A Survey of Literature," *Research Policy* 16 (1987), 131–141.

Blumenthal, D., "Academic–Industry Relationships in the Life Sciences (Extent, Consequences, and Management)," *Journal of the American Medical Association* 268 (1986), 3344–3349.

Boitani, A., and E. Ciciotti, "Patents as Indicators of Innovative Performances at the Regional Level," in R. Cappellin and P. Nijkamp (eds.), *The Spatial Context of Technological Development* (Aldershot: Gower, 1990), 139–163.

Caballero, R., and A. Jaffe, "How High Are the Giants' Shoulders: An Empirical Assessment of Knowledge Spillovers and Creative Destruction in a Model of Economic Growth," in O. Blanchard and S. Fischer (eds.), *NBER Macroeconomics Annual*, vol. 8 (Cambridge, MA: MIT Press, 1993).

Carpenter, M., and F. Narin, "Citation Rates to Technologically Important Patents," *World Patent Information* 5 (1993), 180–185.

Cohen, Wesley, Richard Florida, and W. Richard Goe, "University–Industry Research Centers in the United States," Research Report, Center for Economic Development, Heinz School of Public Policy and Management, Carnegie-Melon University (1993).

Dasgupta, P., and P. David, "Information Disclosure and the Economics of Science and Technology," in G. Feiwel (ed.), *Arrow and the Ascent of Modern Economic Theory* (New York: NYU Press, 1987), chap. 16.

David, P. A., D. Mowery, and W. E. Steinmueller, "Analyzing the Economic Payoffs from Basic Research," *Economics of Innovation and New Technology* 2 (1992), 73–90.

Griliches, Z., "Patent Statistics as Economic Indicators: A Survey," *Journal of Economic Literature* 28 (1990), 1661–1707.

Henderson, Rebecca, Adam Jaffe, and Manuel Trajtenberg, "Universities as a Source of Commercial Technology: A Detailed Analysis of University Patenting 1965–1988," Working Paper 5068, NBER (Mar. 1995).

——— "The Bayh-Dole Act and Trends in University Patenting 1965–1988," in *Proceedings of the Conference on University Goals, Institutional Mechanisms and the "Industrial Transferability" of Research,* Stanford Center for Economic Policy Research (1996).

Jaffe, Adam, B., "Technological Opportunity and Spillovers of R&D: Evidence from Firms' Patents, Profits and Market Value," *American Economic Review* (Dec. 1986), 984–1001.

——— "Real Effects of Academic Research," *American Economic Review* 79 (1989), 957–970.

Jaffe, Adam, Manuel Trajtenberg, and Rebecca Henderson, "Geographic Localization of Knowledge Spillovers as Evidenced by Patent Citations," *Quarterly Journal of Economics* (1993).

Merton, D., in N. W. Starer (ed.), *The Sociology of Science: Theoretical and Empirical Investigation* (Chicago: University of Chicago Press, 1973).

National Academy of Sciences, *Allocating Federal Funds for Science and Technology* (Washington, DC: 1995) National Academy Press.

National Science Foundation, *University Industry Research Relationships: Myths, Realities and Potentials.* (Washington, DC: U.S. Government Printing Office, 1982).

Romer, Paul, "Increasing Returns and Long-Run Growth," *Journal of Political Economy* 94:5 (1986), 1002–1037.

——— "Endogenous Technological Change," *Journal of Political Economy* 98:5 (1990), S71–S101.

Schwartz, H. F., *Patent Law and Practice* (Washington, DC: Federal Judicial Center, 1988).

Trajtenberg, M., "A Penny for Your Quotes: Patent Citations and the Value of Innovations," *Rand Journal of Economics* 21:1 (1990a), 172–187.

——— *Economic Analysis of Product Innovation: The Case of CT Scanners* (Cambridge, MA: Harvard University Press, 1990b).

Trajtenberg, M., R. Henderson, and A. Jaffe, "University versus Corporate Patents: A Window on the Basicness of Invention," *Economics of Innovation and New Technology* 5:1 (1997), 19–50.

U.S. GAO "Patent Policy: Recent Changes in Federal Law Considered Beneficial," GAO/RCED-87-44, General Accounting Office, (1987).

Zucker, Lynn, Michael Darby, and Marilynn Brewer, "Intellectual Human Capital and the Birth of U.S. Biotechnology Enterprises," *American Economic Review* 87:3 (June 1997).

[3]

Proofs and Prototypes for Sale: The Licensing of University Inventions

By RICHARD JENSEN AND MARIE THURSBY*

Proponents of the Bayh-Dole Act argue that industrial use of federally funded research would be reduced without university patent licensing. Our survey of U.S. universities supports this view, emphasizing the embryonic state of most technologies licensed and the need for inventor cooperation in commercialization. Thus, for most university inventions, there is a moral-hazard problem with inventor effort. For such inventions, development does not occur unless the inventor's income is tied to the licensee's output by payments such as royalties or equity. Sponsored research from the licensee cannot by itself solve this problem. (JEL O31, O34, O38)

University licensing has increased dramatically since the passage of the Bayh-Dole Act in 1980, which gave universities the right to retain title to and license inventions resulting from federally sponsored research. The *Association of University Technology Managers Survey Fiscal Year 1996* (AUTM, 1997) reports that licenses executed increased 75 percent between 1991 and 1996, with 13,087 executed over the entire period. Such statistics notwithstanding, the Act has been subject to increasing congressional review and debate. At issue is whether the commercial application and diffusion of inventions from federally funded research criti-

* Jensen: Department of Economics, 245 O'Shaughnessy Hall, University of Notre Dame, Notre Dame, IN 46556; Thursby: Department of Economics, 1310 Krannert Building, Purdue University, West Lafayette, IN 47907. We gratefully acknowledge support from the Sloan Foundation and the National Bureau of Economic Research under the NBER Project on Industrial Technology and Productivity. Thursby thanks the Purdue Technology Transfer Initiative for support. Particular thanks go to Jerry Thursby, who participated in the survey and provided advice throughout, Teri Willey, and Mark Olson for advice on survey design. We thank Roko Aliprantis, Doug Curry, Neil Gandal, Adam Jaffe, Josh Lerner, Richard Nelson, Robert Plante, Scott Shane, Steve Slutsky, Gordon Wright, three referees, and seminar participants at the 25th Annual E.A.R.I.E. Conference, Hamburg Institute for Economic Research, IAW at the University of Hamburg, Mannheim Center for Economic Research, 50th Midwest Economic Theory Conference, NBER Summer Institute, Pennsylvania State University, and Purdue University, 10th Southeastern Economic Theory Conference, the Universities of Florida and Lancaster for useful comments, and Priyo Chatterjee, Barbara Newman, and Weian Zhu for research assistance.

cally depends upon allowing universities to retain title to and license them. This paper directly addresses this issue by providing survey evidence of the licensing practices of 62 U.S. universities, and analyzing several related theoretical models of licensing consistent with the types of licenses executed.

University licensing agreements, with the exception of those for software and reagent materials, invariably include both fixed fees and royalties. Many license agreements also include sponsored research clauses, and increasingly, equity. The theoretical literature on licensing has largely abstracted from institutional features of this sort and focused on inventors who maximize profit from the sale of licenses. In a university setting, profit maximization is rarely the objective. Moreover, recent legal suits suggest that there are differences in the objectives of inventors, technology managers, and university administrators.[1] Indeed, technology managers responding to our survey viewed themselves as balancing the interests of university administrators with those of inventors, who often prefer sponsored research to the objectives of administrators.

Perhaps the most striking result of the survey is that when they are licensed, most university inventions are little more than a "proof of concept." No one knows their commercial potential because

[1] In two highly publicized lawsuits, University of California System researchers sued the University, claiming the University ignored their financial interests when it negotiated license agreements (Jonathan N. Axelrod, 1996).

they are in such an early stage of development. Indeed, they are so embryonic that additional effort in development by the inventor is required for a reasonable chance of commercial success. To capture this fact, our theoretical analysis focuses on inventions for which the probability of success is zero at the time of licensing, but increases with additional inventor effort. This assumption is sufficient to show that optimal license contracts cannot rely solely on lump-sum payments, such as fixed fees or funds for sponsored research, but also must involve some sort of output-based payments, such as royalties. The intuition is simple. A lump-sum payment provides no incentive for the inventor to expend further effort in development. Because inventor effort increases the probability of commercial success, royalties solve this moral-hazard problem by linking the inventor's license income to additional effort. Other output-based payments, such as equity, solve the moral-hazard problem without the inefficiency inherent in royalties. It is important to note that assuming the probability of success is zero in the absence of inventor effort is not necessary. These results hold if this probability is positive but small enough that no firm would attempt to commercialize the invention without sufficient additional inventor effort.

Our analysis contributes to the debate over the Bayh-Dole Act, which has been the focus of a recent Government Accounting Office review (GAO, 1998) and an April 1999 U.S. Senate Hearing on Federal R&D (*Congressional Record,* 1999). The Act allows universities to retain title to federally funded inventions, in return for which they must file for patents and collaborate with businesses to promote commercial application of the inventions they elect to own. Prior to Bayh-Dole, the primary method for disseminating federally funded research was academic publication (David C. Mowery et al., 2001). Evidence based on publication citations shows that the lag between publication of scholarly research and its application by industry averages 20 years (James D. Adams, 1990).[2] Proponents of Bayh-Dole therefore argue that

university licensing accelerates the timing of commercialization and that, with the rapid growth in university technology transfer offices and patenting, businesses have better information on university inventions. The opposing view is that much of the increase in patenting involves low-quality patents and that exclusive licensing is not required for commercialization of high-quality patents. Nonetheless, there is empirical support for the view that Bayh-Dole has increased industrial application of university inventions (Rebecca Henderson et al., 1998). Our results add a new dimension to the debate by highlighting the fact that many inventions are so embryonic that they might remain in the lab without license agreements designed to induce collaboration between inventors and licensees.[3]

We also bring an institutional dimension to the theoretical literature on patent licensing by providing a new explanation for the use of royalties. With few exceptions, the main result of this literature is that inventor profit is maximized when licensees pay a fixed fee determined by an auction rather than royalties (see Morton I. Kamien [1992] for a survey).[4] The reason for this is simply that a fixed fee does not distort the licensee's output decision by increasing the marginal cost of production. However, fixed fees alone are not optimal for licensing university inventions because of the need to induce additional inventor effort.

The theoretical work closest to ours is that of Philippe Aghion and Jean Tirole (1994a, b), who examine the organization of R&D in an incomplete contract framework.[5] However,

---

[2] In a recent survey of firms that use academic research in their product and process development, Edwin Mansfield (1995) found that the average lag between research findings and commercial application was seven years. Unfortunately, it is not clear from his data whether research results were

obtained by license, consulting arrangements, or other means such as publication.

[3] In fact, commercialization by an exclusive licensee can become a problem if the inventor and licensee do not see eye to eye on how best to proceed with development. This seems to have been the case with Columbia University's invention aimed to treat glaucoma. This example was provided by Richard R. Nelson, who is developing case studies of Columbia inventions.

[4] See Nancy T. Gallini and Brian D. Wright (1990), Alan W. Beggs (1992), Jensen (1992a, b), and X. Henry Wang (1998) for exceptions.

[5] Joshua Lerner and Robert Merges (1997) test Aghion and Tirole's hypotheses for biotechnology alliances, looking at assignment of control rights and stage of the projects when alliances are signed.

their work focuses on efficiency aspects of whether an invention is owned by the research unit, final customer, or some combination. They derive conditions under which ownership is irrelevant for efficiency. One is that either the research unit or the customer can develop the invention independently. Applied to university R&D, this would mean that it does not matter whether universities or licensees own the invention. Given the dramatic response of universities to the Bayh-Dole Act, irrelevance of ownership seems unlikely. Moreover, our survey results make it clear that most university inventions could not be developed independently by either the inventor or the firm.

This paper also contributes to the empirical literature on the industrial impact of university research. With few exceptions, this literature has focused on spillovers from university research via citations to journal articles or to patents.[6] Lynne G. Zucker and Michael R. Darby (1996) point out that the commercialization of scientific breakthroughs in biotechnology depends not only on the publications of "star" scientists, but also their active involvement.[7] Our survey shows this collaboration between universities and businesses extends well beyond biotechnology.

In Section I, we focus on the survey results, and in subsequent sections, we present several closely related models of university licensing. The models in Section II highlight the role of inventor effort in commercialization. In Section III, we examine cases in which development requires both inventor effort and firm expenditure on sponsored research. We show that a contract with sponsored research does not solve the inventor's moral-hazard problem unless it also includes output-based payments. Section IV concludes the paper. We discuss survey design in Appendix A, and we sketch the proofs of all theorems in Appendix B.

I. University Technology Transfer

To understand the nature of university inventions and the types of contracts used to license them, we conducted a survey of 62 U.S. research universities.[8] Respondents were either directors or licensing officers of the technology transfer office (TTO) of each university. These offices are responsible for soliciting reports (disclosures) on faculty inventions, assessing commercial potential of inventions, filing patent applications, finding potential licensees, and executing and monitoring license agreements. Respondents were asked to complete a questionnaire concerning their licensing activities for fiscal years 1991–1995. As reported below, questions focused on the characteristics of inventions available for license, the objectives of the TTO, as well as license characteristics.[9]

A. *Invention Characteristics*

Table 1 summarizes responses on the characteristics of inventions disclosed and licensed over the sample period. Most inventions came from the schools of science, engineering, medicine, and nursing. The research leading to 63 percent of the inventions was federally funded, 17 percent was sponsored by industry, and 20 percent was unsponsored. Patentable inventions are usually considered university property rather than property of either the faculty-inventor or the sponsor. This follows from the Bayh-Dole Act in the case of federally funded inventions, and it is university policy regardless of sponsorship for all but one university in the sample.[10]

Inventions are highly variable in terms of commercial potential. Less than half of the inventions disclosed were licensed, with 31 per-

---

[6] See Nelson (1982), Adam B. Jaffe (1989), Jaffe et al. (1993), and Henderson et al. (1998).

[7] Zucker et al. (1994) and Zucker et al. (1998) use this collaboration to explain the location of biotechnology firms.

[8] These universities accounted for 67 percent of the invention disclosures, 70 percent of the licenses, and 68 percent of the revenue received by AUTM members during this period.

[9] For other issues addressed in the survey, see Jerry G. Thursby and Sukanya Kemp (2001), Thursby and Thursby (2001), and Thursby et al. (2001).

[10] Some universities grant ownership to corporate sponsors who cover all direct and indirect research costs. For copyrightable materials, 48 percent of the respondents reported inventors retain title to inventions.

TABLE 1—INVENTION CHARACTERISTICS

Invention disclosures (1991–1995)	Weighted mean[a] (Percent)
1. Filed by faculty in schools of	
Science	19
Engineering	25
Medicine and nursing	44
Agriculture	5
Other	7
2. Resulting from	
Federal-sponsored research	63
Corporate-sponsored research	17
3. Subject to	
Exclusive license	21
Exclusive license for field of use	10
Nonexclusive license	10
Not currently licensed	61
4. Revenue from top five inventions	78
5. Stage of development for inventions which were licensed[b]	
Proof of concept but no prototype	48
Prototype available but only lab scale	29
Some animal data available	25
Some clinical data available	5
Manufacturing feasibility known	8
Inventor cooperation required	71
Ready for practical or commercial use	12

[a] Weighted mean $= \Sigma\, x_i w_i / \Sigma\, w_i$, where x_i is the percentage for each university, and w_i is university i's weight. The weight is the number of invention disclosures for 1, 2, and 3, the gross revenue for 4, and the number of license agreements for 5. Data for disclosures, license agreements and revenue are from the *AUTM Survey* (1997).

[b] Stage of development at the time the license was executed. Percentages need not sum to 100.

Source: Authors' calculation.

cent either licensed exclusively or exclusively for field of use. In terms of earnings, the top five inventions licensed by each university accounted for 78 percent of gross license revenue.[11]

Our most striking result concerns the embryonic nature of the inventions that are licensed.[12]

[11] This is similar to results in Frederick M. Scherer (1996) for Harvard inventions and Dietmar Harhoff et al. (1997) for German patents.

[12] Even the most lucrative university patents tend to be quite embryonic when licensed. Neils Reimers (1987) notes the importance of the Cohen-Boyer patents was clear at the beginning, but commercial application was viewed as decades away.

Only 12 percent were ready for commercial use at the time of license, and manufacturing feasibility was known only for 8 percent.[13] Over 75 percent of the inventions licensed were no more than a proof of concept (48 percent with no prototype available) or lab scale prototype (29 percent) at the time of license! Thus, an overwhelming majority of university inventions require further development once they are licensed. Moreover, TTO managers believe efforts by licensee-firms alone to develop embryonic inventions are unlikely to succeed. For 71 percent of the inventions licensed, respondents claim that successful commercialization requires cooperation by the inventor and the licensee in further development.

B. Licensing Objectives

Respondents were asked about their own objectives and their perceptions of faculty and university administration objectives. While TTO managers execute the licenses, they report to the university administration and rely on faculty to disclose inventions with commercial potential. We were therefore not surprised to find that managers view themselves as balancing faculty and administration objectives. Managers in our pretest indicated that convincing faculty to disclose inventions is a major challenge, and a number of survey respondents stated that balancing the objectives of faculty and administrators is problematic (Thursby et al., 2001).

We asked managers about the importance of five outcomes of their work: license revenue, license agreements executed, inventions commercialized, sponsored research, and patents awarded.[14] We asked if they considered each outcome extremely important (EI), moderately important (MI), not very important (NI), or not applicable (NA), as well as how important they thought each outcome was to their administration and the faculty they work with. The stacked bar charts in Figure 1 show the proportions of EI and MI responses.

[13] The majority of inventions ready for commercial application are reagent materials or software. In many instances, these were licensed for a fixed fee.

[14] Our test group indicated that these outcomes are major criteria used by technology transfer offices to measure their success.

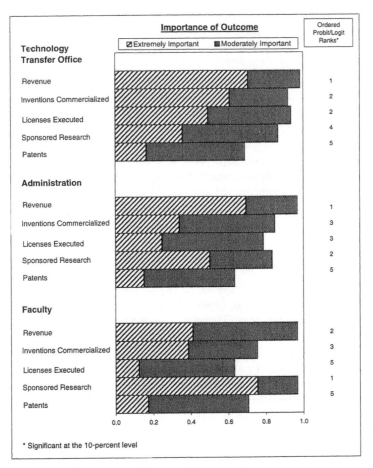

FIGURE 1. OUTCOMES OF TECHNOLOGY TRANSFER

None of the respondents view revenue as their sole motivation for licensing inventions.[15] The outcome considered least important is patents awarded. This may reflect the fact that patents are an intermediate input to licensing. Many managers said that for financial reasons their policy is to apply for a patent on an invention only after they have identified a potential licensee.[16] Finally, there are clear differences among the perceived objectives of the technology transfer office (TTO), administration (ADM), and faculty (FAC).

To examine the ranks accorded different outcomes by the TTO, ADM, and FAC, we considered both ordered logit and probit models with dependent variables equal to the manager's

---

[15] Few respondents rate any outcomes as unimportant (NI or NA). This could not have occurred had we asked for a ranking of outcomes (or allowed at most one EI choice, one MI choice, etc.), but we did not want to preclude the possibility that all of the outcomes might be elements of a manager's objective function.

[16] See Richard C. Levin et al. (1987) and Wesley Cohen et al. (1997) for similar results (for other reasons) in industry surveys. See Thursby and Thursby (2001) for a model of university patent licensing in which patents are intermediate inputs.

response for an outcome (EI, MI, or NI) and independent variables which are dummies indicating the particular question (outcome). At a 10-percent significance level, both approaches give the same rankings (which include a number of tied ranks). These ranks, along with ties, are on the right in Figure 1.[17]

Technology managers and university administrators (as perceived by TTO managers) consider license revenue more important than any other outcome. Almost as important to the TTO, however, are inventions commercialized and numbers of licenses executed. This is consistent with managers' statements identifying their job as implementing the Bayh-Dole Act. Sponsored research ranks only ahead of patents in importance to TTO managers. On the other hand, managers believe the faculty consider sponsored research more important than any other objective, and they perceive little faculty interest in patents or the execution of license agreements, per se.

Using Kendall's τ, Cohen's κ, and McNemar's Test, we tested for agreement of TTO and FAC (and of TTO and ADM) responses for each of the five outcomes. According to all three tests, TTO managers report their objectives as more closely aligned with the administration than the faculty. TTO and ADM agreement is accepted for each outcome, while TTO and FAC agreement is accepted only for inventions commercialized and sponsored research.

C. *License Characteristics*

We asked a variety of questions about license procedures. We were interested in whether the process should be modeled as an auction. Only two managers cited inventions that had been licensed in this manner. Indeed, most questioned the merits of auctioning university inventions, emphasizing that it is often difficult to find companies interested in early-stage inventions. As shown in Table 2, only 22 percent of the licenses executed had multiple bidders.

[17] We also ranked outcomes by a dual scaling procedure which allows us to estimate the scale assigned to EI, MI, NI, and NA. This procedure gives the same results as our logit and probit estimates.

TABLE 2—LICENSE CHARACTERISTICS

	Weighted mean[a] (Percent)
1. Frequency of more than one company	
Signing a confidentiality agreement	63
Bidding for a license	22
2. Percentage of revenue by payment type	
License issue or up-front fees	7
Running royalties[b]	75
Annual or minimum royalty fees	6
Progress or milestone payments	3
Patent fee reimbursement	7
Equity	3
Other	1
3. Percentage of licenses which include	
License issue or up-front fee	84
Running royalties	84
Annual or minimum royalty fees	78
Progress or milestone payments	58
Patent reimbursement	78
Equity	23
4. Percentage of licenses including equity plus	
License issue or up-front fee	67
Running royalty	79
Other	51
5. Percentage of licenses including sponsored research	33
6. Patent issued at time of license[c]	28
7. (Net revenue) distribution[d]	
Inventor[e]	40
University	35
Department, school or TTO	25

[a] Gross revenue is the weight for 2 and 8, and the number of licenses is the weight for the others.
[b] Running royalties is the common TTO term for output-based fees.
[c] Or copyright registered.
[d] Patentable inventions only. The distribution of revenue from copyrightable inventions is negotiable for 41 percent of the universities surveyed.
[e] For 15 percent of the universities surveyed, the inventors' share of net revenue is $\frac{1}{3}$; with $\frac{1}{3}$ to the university and $\frac{1}{3}$ to other university units. Also, 24 percent of the surveyed universities have sliding scales.
Source: Authors' calculations.

Table 2 also gives information on the types of payments included in licenses. Most licenses include a combination of payment types. Fixed fees (license-issue or annual) and royalties appear in roughly 80 percent of the license agreements, with fees accounting for 13 percent of revenue received and royalties accounting for

75 percent.[18] Note that milestone payments and patent reimbursement are common. While not a large fraction, equity is included in 23 percent of the license agreements. Indeed, the most recent *AUTM Survey* reported that the use of equity in licenses has increased substantially in the last five years. The managers we interviewed indicated that licenses with equity tend to be for enabling technologies to start-up companies. Agreements that include equity also tend to include fees and royalties. Finally, roughly a third of the licenses covered by the survey include sponsored research.[19]

II. University Licensing with Inventor Involvement

This section presents a theoretical analysis of university licensing. In contrast to the usual approach of characterizing optimal incentive contracts, our objective is to predict and evaluate the types of licenses executed by research universities in the United States. Key features of the analysis are the nature of the inventions to be licensed and the objectives of the managers who execute licenses. We follow the survey results in assuming that the invention is so embryonic that at the time the license is executed no one knows if it will lead to a commercially successful product or process. Although the licensee must eventually commit resources to attempt to commercialize the invention, further development by the inventor is essential early on if it is to succeed.

We assume that the invention is owned by the university and the TTO is responsible for executing the license contract. As noted, this is the case for virtually all patentable university inventions, either because of Bayh-Dole or university policy. Faculty are assumed to disclose such inventions to the TTO, at which point the TTO evaluates the invention and searches for a licensee.[20] We model the TTO's objectives as balancing those of the administration and the

inventor. This follows our survey evidence, but it is also natural since license revenue from patentable inventions is split between the university and the inventor. On average, inventors in our sample are entitled to 40 percent of revenue, with the remainder allocated to the inventor's school or department, or the TTO or some other unit within the university.

A. *Licensing by Royalties*

Given our survey results, constructing a model of university licensing involves using elements of the literatures on optimal patent licensing, principal-agent problems, and incomplete contracting. We consider a situation in which a faculty-inventor has already disclosed an invention, and the TTO has determined that a given firm is a potential licensee. The invention is either a new product or process whose profitability is uncertain; in particular, neither the inventor nor the TTO nor the firm knows whether the invention will be a commercial success.

The problem is modeled as a game that unfolds over time with the following sequence of actions. The TTO first decides either to shelve the invention, which ends the game, or offer a license contract to the firm. If a contract is offered, then the firm decides either to reject the contract, which ends the game, or accept it. If it accepts, it pays a fixed license fee, and a period of further development follows in which the inventor may expend effort to improve the probability of success. The outcome of this development is an updated probability of success, observed at the end of this period. The firm then decides either to terminate the project, which ends the game, or expend the resources necessary to attempt to commercialize the invention, after which both the TTO and the firm learn whether the invention is a success or not. If it fails, the game ends. If it succeeds, the firm produces and pays royalties.

In the development period, the inventor may expend further effort to improve the chance of success. We assume that e, the "effort cost" of the inventor I, is not contractible, but instead is chosen at the beginning of the development period (after the licensing agreement has been executed). Thus, the inventor is subject to moral hazard in that her effort cannot be effectively

---

[18] Richard E. Caves et al. (1983) and Ines Macho-Stadler et al. (1996) give similar results for business licenses.

[19] For a number of universities in the sample, the technology transfer office is not responsible for obtaining sponsored research.

[20] In the survey, 58 percent reported inventor cooperation useful in the search for potential licensees.

monitored and/or enforced. This assumption accords well with statements made by the technology managers we interviewed, who overwhelmingly viewed their own actions (and, in fact, the types of contracts they execute) as important for ensuring further development on inventions.[21] The license contract must therefore specify payoffs in a way that induces effort from the inventor. In this section, we confine our attention to licenses that specify a royalty rate (fee per unit of output) and a fixed fee paid by the firm to the university. We denote the royalty rate by r and the fixed fee by m. Given a license characterized by (r, m), the equilibrium level of effort chosen in the development stage is then written as $e^*(r, m)$.

Given any level of inventor effort e, let $p(e)$ be the probability that the invention is a commercial success. In our assumptions on $p(e)$, we are thinking of the 71 percent of university inventions that are so embryonic that commercial success requires further development by the inventor, but for which no amount of inventor effort can guarantee success. Thus, we assume $p(0) = 0$ and $p(e) \in [0, 1)$ for all $e \geq 0$. We also assume $p(e)$ is increasing and concave.

Now suppose additional development, characterized by $e > 0$, has taken place and the invention is a success. Then the firm chooses output to maximize its profit (net of any license fees). In general, as long as production occurs and marginal revenue cuts marginal cost from above, profit-maximizing output is a decreasing function of the royalty rate, but does not depend on the fixed fee.[22] The reason is that the firm's marginal cost of production depends on the royalty rate, but not the fixed fee. Thus, we denote profit-maximizing output $x(r)$. We assume this output is positive if the royalty rate is 0, and decreasing in the royalty rate when it is positive, $x(0) > 0$ and $x'(r) < 0$ for $r > 0$. We further assume that royalty revenue $rx(r)$ is

strictly concave in the royalty rate, and takes a unique maximum at some positive but finite value. These assumptions on royalty revenue hold for a broad class of new process innovations licensed to a single firm (including, but not limited to, the case of linear demand and constant marginal cost).

Next let $\Pi(x)$ be the profit (gross of any license fees) from producing x units with a successful invention, and let $E > 0$ be the lump-sum cost of attempting to commercialize the invention. Depending on whether the invention is a new product or process, E can be interpreted as a fixed cost of adoption, installation, or entry. Given a contract (r, m), the profit earned from a success is $\Pi(x(r)) - rx(r) - m - E$, while that from a failure is just $-m - E$. Hence, the firm's expected profit from the invention given a contract (r, m) and effort level e is

(1) $P_F(e, E, r, m)$

$$= p(e)[\Pi(x(r)) - rx(r)] - m - E.$$

The firm accepts this contract and attempts to commercialize the invention (after development) if and only if $P_F(e, E, r, m) \geq 0$. Note that even if the firm pays no license fees, it would not attempt to commercialize the invention if the probability of success without further inventor effort in development is "small enough," because $P_F(0, E, 0, 0) < 0$ if $p(0) < E/\Pi(x(0))$.[23] Thus, although we assume $p(0) = 0$ because it is consistent with our survey results, it is stronger than needed and could be replaced with this weaker condition.

Although effort is not contractible, it does depend on the contract (r, m). We assume that the inventor chooses effort to maximize her expected utility, and that utility takes the separable form $U_I(Y_I) - V_I(e)$, where $U_I(Y_I)$ is utility from license income Y_I and $V_I(e)$ is disutility of effort. We also assume that the marginal utility of income is positive and nonincreasing, so she is either risk averse or risk

---

[21] While we focus on inventor moral hazard, the licensee is also subject to moral hazard. Thus the Bayh-Dole Act includes a "march-in" provision allowing the government to take back inventions when a licensee shelves the invention rather than attempting commercialization.

[22] If $\Pi(x) = R(x) - C(x) - rx$, where $R(x)$ is total revenue and $C(x)$ is total cost, then profit-maximizing output $x(r)$ satisfies $x'(r) = [R''(x) - C''(x)]^{-1} < 0$ if $R''(x) < C''(x)$.

[23] It is worth noting that because the firm would not attempt to develop the invention on its own, the university does not need a patent in order to license the invention. This is also true for the analysis in Section IV.

neutral, and the marginal disutility of effort is positive and increasing. We allow the possibility of risk neutrality to emphasize that our results depend on moral hazard in development, not risk sharing. Thus, if α is her share of license revenue, then license income from a success is $\alpha[m + rx(r)]$, and that from a failure is αm, so her expected utility is

$$(2) \quad P_I(e, r, m) = p(e)U_I(\alpha m + \alpha rx(r))$$
$$+ (1 - p(e))U_I(\alpha m) - V_I(e).$$

One feature of inventor expected utility merits further discussion. It is reasonable to assume inventors also receive utility from nonpecuniary sources, such as the utility from simply solving a puzzle or from seeing an invention commercialized (see Paula E. Stephan [1996] for a survey of empirical support). In our formulation, all nonpecuniary benefits are embodied in the disutility of effort function $V_I(e)$. Thus, we have implicitly assumed that any nonpecuniary benefits associated with development are less than those associated with other basic research projects that the inventor can undertake. That is, at the time of disclosure and licensing, the inventor has already completed the most interesting research related to the invention, so additional effort in its development involves lower nonpecuniary benefits (which we formalize as the disutility of effort in development). This assumption is consistent with our survey results. As noted in Section I, in many cases TTO managers said one of their major challenges is getting productive research faculty to disclose and continue to develop inventions beyond the proof of concept stage.

When the inventor does expend effort in development, the first-order necessary condition for maximization of expected utility is:

$$(3) \quad \frac{\partial P_I}{\partial e} = p'(e)[U_I(\alpha m + \alpha rx(r))$$
$$- U_I(\alpha m)] - V'_I(e) = 0.$$

Note that if there is no royalty, then she earns the same amount, αm, whether she expends any effort or not. Because the marginal disutility of effort is positive, she does not choose to expend

effort in development unless the royalty rate is positive. However, a positive royalty rate is not sufficient to guarantee that she expends effort. This effort must result in an increase in the expected utility of income that exceeds its disutility. The firm must also accept the contract and attempt to commercialize the invention.

THEOREM 1: *Development does not occur unless the contract specifies a positive royalty rate, $e*(0, m) = 0$. Given a positive royalty rate, the necessary condition for the inventor to expend effort in development, $e*(r, m) > 0$ for $r > 0$, is*

$$(4) \qquad p'(0)[U_I(\alpha m + \alpha rx(r))$$
$$- U_I(\alpha m)] > V'_I(0),$$

which is also sufficient if the firm accepts the contract. If development occurs:

(i) Inventor effort is decreasing in the fixed fee, $\partial e*(r, m)/\partial m < 0$, if she is risk averse, but does not depend on the fixed fee, $\partial e*(r, m)/\partial m = 0$, if she is risk neutral.

(ii) Inventor effort is increasing (decreasing, constant) in the royalty rate as royalty revenue is increasing (decreasing, constant) with respect to the royalty rate; $\partial e*(r, m)/\partial r > 0(<0, =0)$ as $x + r(\partial x/\partial r) > 0(<0, =0)$.

Suppose that a contract is chosen such that the inventor undertakes development. Because the inventor receives her share of the fixed fee m before the development period, a larger fee decreases her incentive to put effort into development. That is, as long as she is risk averse, a larger m decreases the expected marginal benefit of effort, $\partial^2 P_I/\partial e \partial m < 0$, so her effort decreases. However, if she is risk neutral, then a change in the fixed fee has no effect on the expected marginal benefit of effort, and thus no effect on her effort.

The effect of a change in the royalty rate on the expected benefit of inventor effort, however, depends on its effect on royalty revenue. Suppose royalty revenue is increasing in the rate. Then an increase in the royalty rate increases the inventor's royalty income, which increases the expected marginal benefit of her effort, and so increases her effort. This is certainly the case

VOL. 91 NO. 1   *JENSEN AND THURSBY: LICENSING OF UNIVERSITY INVENTIONS*   249

for low enough royalty rates (i.e., $\partial[rx(r)]/\partial r = x(0) > 0$ at $r = 0$). Inventor effort therefore parallels royalty revenue as the royalty rate changes. That is, as the rate increases, both effort and revenue initially increase, reach a maximum, then decrease.

We emphasize that the assumption that inventor effort always has positive marginal disutility is stronger than necessary, and can be replaced with the assumption that there is some level of effort $e_o > 0$ such that $V_I'(e) > 0$ for all $e > e_o$ and $p(e_o) < E/\Pi(x(0))$. This implies that even if the inventor would expend effort in development without a royalty, she would never expend more than e_o. In this case, the firm would not attempt to commercialize this invention because $P_F(e_o, E, 0, m) < 0$ for any $m \geq 0$. The firm will not accept a contract unless it uses a positive royalty rate to induce the inventor to expend effort beyond e_o.

To complete the model, we must specify the objective of the TTO. Although its objective is not obvious, a priori, our survey indicates that technology managers view themselves as juggling the interests of faculty and administration. Moreover, the managers we interviewed clearly view their administration as risk averse, so we assume the payoff to the university administration (A) is given by the utility function $U_A(Y_A)$, where Y_A is its share of licensing revenue. We assume the marginal utility of income is positive and nondecreasing for the administration. Its expected utility is then

(5) $P_A(e, r, m)$

$\quad = p(e)U_A((1 - \alpha)[m + rx(r)])$

$\quad + (1 - p(e))U_A((1 - \alpha)m).$

Note that the administration's expected utility differs from the inventor's not only in the (possibly) different share of the license revenue, but also in the fact that it suffers no disutility from the inventor effort required to develop the invention to potential commercialization.

Based on the results of our survey, we assume the TTO's objective is to maximize a weighted average of the expected utilities of the administration and inventor. Assuming that the

weight placed on the inventor's objectives is $\beta \in (0, 1)$, the TTO's objective function is

(6) $P(e, r, m) = \beta P_I(e, r, m)$

$\quad\quad\quad + (1 - \beta)P_A(e, r, m).$

Notice we assume that the administration cannot simply treat the inventor as an agent (in the standard principal-agent paradigm) by maximizing administration utility subject to the constraint that the inventor's utility is no less that her reservation level. As justification, we note that our surveys indicate that the vast majority of university inventions require some inventor involvement in development. Moreover, the only inventions the TTO can try to license are those disclosed by inventors. It therefore seems unrealistic to give all the "bargaining power" to the administration by treating the inventor as an agent.

The TTO's problem is then to choose a contract (r, m) to maximize its objective function subject to the licensee's participation constraint,[24] or

(7) maximize $P(e^*(r, m), r, m)$

$\quad$ subject to $P_F(e^*(r, m), E, r, m) \geq 0$.

We shall consider only contracts with nonnegative royalties and fixed fees, essentially because we never observe universities subsidizing licensees. The solution to the TTO's problem thus has several possible forms. Because the royalty rate must be positive to induce effort from the inventor, the only concern is whether the

---

[24] This form of participation constraint implies that P_F is the licensee's expected increase in profit from the invention. If the licensee is an existing firm and the invention is a new product, then this constraint also implies that acceptance or rejection of the contract has no effect on profit from other products. Generalizing the analysis to inventions that may impact preinvention profit is beyond the scope of this paper. Our result that the optimal contract must include an output-based payment should be robust to any such generalization because it depends only on the behavior of the inventor and acceptance of the contract by the firm. This remark also applies to the analysis with sponsored research below.

solution has no fee, $m = 0$, or it is set so that the nonnegativity constraint on the licensee is binding, $m = p(e)[\Pi(x(r)) - rx(r)] - E$.

THEOREM 2: *The expected payoff to the TTO is strictly increasing in the fixed fee, for any positive royalty rate such that the firm accepts a license, if the inventor is risk neutral, or not too risk averse. Hence, if the invention has enough commercial potential that a contract is executed and development occurs, then that contract must involve both a positive royalty rate and a positive fixed fee.*

Ceteris paribus, an increase in m increases the income and expected utility of both the administration and the inventor. Thus, one expects the TTO to set the fee to extract all the "excess" expected payoff from the firm, in which case the participation constraint binds.[25] We assume (as do all principal-agent and patent-licensing models) that the firm accepts the contract and attempts to commercialize the invention if its expected payoff is 0. In our model, this is a particularly innocuous assumption because the fee paid is the expected profit from a success net of the fixed cost of commercialization, $m^* = p(e^*)[\Pi(x(r^*)) - r^*x(r^*)] - E$. Given a small probability of success, m^* is quite small, especially compared to the net profit actually earned if the invention succeeds, $\Pi(x(r^*)) - r^*x(r^*)$.

B. *Licensing by Equity*

In this section, we consider an alternative method of licensing. Although not as common as royalties, both our survey and the *AUTM Survey* (1997) indicate a dramatic increase in the fraction of license contracts involving equity ownership in the last few years. In 89 percent of our surveys, the university is allowed to hold equity in licensee-firms. The game analyzed now is exactly the same as that in the

preceding section except that equity replaces royalties in the contract. In particular, the contract takes the form (ρ, m), where $\rho \in [0, 1]$ is the university's equity share, the fraction of profits from the invention to which it is entitled. The optimal level of effort chosen by the inventor is now denoted $e^*(\rho, m)$.

We assume control remains with the firm, so that the university merely collects its share of the profits without influencing the decisions made by the firm. All universities in our sample either have policies that limit the extent of equity ownership or are developing them along with conflict of interest policies. All have policies that limit the type of involvement by the inventor, with many explicitly prohibiting faculty from serving in anything other than scientific advisory roles when the university holds an equity position. An overwhelming majority also explicitly limit the equity share that the university can take (most often at 10 percent).

The equity share is simply a lump-sum transfer from the firm to the university. However, unlike the fixed fee, this transfer solves the inventor's moral-hazard problem because it is made only after she expends effort in development, the invention succeeds, and production occurs. Because optimal output in this case is $x(0)$, the firm's expected profit from the invention given a contract (ρ, m) and effort level e is now

$$(8) \quad P_F(e, E, \rho, m) = p(e)(1 - \rho)\Pi(x(0))$$

$$- m - E,$$

and the inventor's expected utility is

$$(9) \quad P_I(e, \rho, m)$$

$$= p(e)U_I(\alpha m + \alpha\rho\Pi(x(0)))$$

$$+ (1 - p(e))U_I(\alpha m) - V_I(e).$$

The expected utility of the administration is $P_A(e, \rho, m) = p(e)U_A((1 - \alpha)[m + \rho\Pi(x(0))]) + (1 - p(e))U_A((1 - \alpha)m)$, and the TTO's problem is to choose a contract (ρ, m) to maximize $P(e, \rho, m) = \beta P_I(e, \rho, m) + (1 - \beta)P_A(e, \rho, m)$ subject to

---

[25] There is some possibility that, if we arbitrarily set $m = 0$, the corresponding royalty rate chosen by the TTO, r_0, is such that the firm's participation constraint binds exactly. In this case, in fact, the optimal contract is $(r_0, 0)$. Except for this razor's-edge case, we have shown that if the firm accepts the contract, it involves a positive fee.

optimal behavior by the inventor and the firm's participation constraint.[26] Again, given the positive marginal disutility of effort, the inventor does not expend effort in development unless the university's equity share is large enough.

THEOREM 3: *Development does not occur unless the contract specifies a positive equity share, $e^*(0, m) = 0$. Given a positive share, the necessary condition for the inventor to expend effort in development, $e^*(\rho, m) > 0$ for $\rho > 0$, is*

(10) $p'(0)[U_I(\alpha m + \alpha \rho \Pi(x(0)))$

$- U_I(\alpha m)] > V_I'(0),$

which is also sufficient if the firm accepts the contract. If development occurs:

(i) *Inventor effort is increasing in the equity share, $\partial e^*(\rho, m)/\partial \rho > 0$.*
(ii) *Inventor effort is decreasing in the fixed fee if she is risk averse, $\partial e^*(\rho, m)/\partial m < 0$, but does not depend on the fee if she is risk neutral, $\partial e^*(\rho, m)/\partial m = 0$.*
(iii) *The license contract also uses a positive fixed fee if the inventor is risk neutral, or not too risk averse.*

An increase in the equity share increases the inventor's income from a success and induces her to devote more effort to development. Unlike a royalty, equity has an unambiguous effect on effort because it does not distort the firm's production decision. An increase in the royalty rate reduces output and profit from a success. An increase in the equity share has no effect on output and profit from a success, but instead merely gives the university a larger share of that profit.

Given the predominant use of royalties, and

the apparent reluctance of many universities to use equity, the most interesting question is whether one method is superior.

THEOREM 4: *A contract with equity is more efficient than a contract with royalties if maximized profit from a successful invention is decreasing in the royalty rate.*

Because profit-maximizing output from a success is decreasing in the royalty rate, this result simply says that a contract with equity is Pareto superior if the output distortion introduced by royalties results in lower maximized profit (as is true for a broad class of inventions). To see this, consider the equity contract that is income equivalent to the optimal royalty rate. Let $\rho(r^*, m^*)$ be the equity share that provides the university with the same income from a success that it received under the optimal royalty rate, $\rho(r^*, m^*)\pi(x(0)) = r^*x(r^*)$. If the TTO switches from the royalty contract to this equity contract, and the inventor expends the same effort, then by construction the inventor and administration are no worse off (*ex ante*) because each anticipates the same level of expected utility. However, if maximized profit from a success is decreasing in the royalty rate, then $\pi(x(0)) > \pi(x(r^*))$, and so expected profit is greater under this income-equivalent equity contract. The optimal royalty contract is therefore Pareto inferior to this income-equivalent equity contract. The optimal equity contract is not $(\rho(r^*, m^*), m^*)$, of course, because expected profit under this contract is strictly positive. The TTO needs to adjust both the fee and equity share to attain the optimal equity contract. However, these changes simply involve reoptimization that necessarily increases the value of the TTO's objective function,[27] and cannot reduce the firm's expected profit below 0 (because it can always reject the contract). Hence, the optimal equity contract must be Pareto superior to the optimal royalty

---

[26] This form of participation constraint now also implies that, if the licensee is an existing firm, then acceptance or rejection of the contract has no effect on the value of the original owners' equity. As a referee has noted, an equity contract may not be Pareto superior for all inventions that have an impact on existing profits because the value of the original owner's equity may be diluted. However, the licensee could avoid this potential problem simply by commercializing the invention through a start-up in which it takes the equity position $1 - \rho$.

[27] Since the TTO maximizes a weighted average of inventor and administration utility, we cannot prove, in general, that the inventor and administration are both better off in the optimal equity contract. However, at least one must gain, and that gain must be large enough to offset any possible loss to the other. The same qualifier applies to Theorem 9.

contract. Finally, it is worth noting that expected consumer surplus is higher under the optimal equity contract because output with a successful invention is higher, $x(0) > x(r^*)$.

III. University Licensing with Sponsored Research

Another salient feature of our survey results is that sponsored research is the preferred form of compensation for faculty-inventors (recall Figure 1). Indeed, for the most embryonic inventions, it is not uncommon to observe research contracts funded by licensee-firms. Such license agreements typically have three important characteristics (see the *AUTM Technology Transfer Practice Manual, Volume II* [1993] for specific examples). One is that they grant exclusive rights to patents arising from the research support that the firm provides. They also very clearly specify the focus and content of the research project to be conducted. Finally, the firm typically assists the development process by providing funds to the university (to purchase equipment or hire support personnel, for example). Thus, in this section we consider a situation in which the licensee-firm is actively involved in development via sponsored research in the form of expenditures, S. The problem unfolds over time in the same way as before.

We assume e and S are chosen simultaneously at the beginning of the development period, after the licensing agreement has been executed. The outcome of this development game is again an updated probability of success. Given any (e, S), let $q(e, S)$ be this updated probability of success. We assume this is increasing at a decreasing rate in both its arguments, but that no amount of effort or sponsored research can guarantee success [i.e., $q(e, S) \in [0, 1)$ for all $e \geq 0$ and $S \geq 0$]. Moreover, inventions for which firms sponsor research tend to be so embryonic that both inventor effort and firm expenditure are necessary for any chance of commercial success. That is, $q(0, S) = 0$ for all $S \geq 0$ and $q(e, 0) = 0$ for all $e \geq 0$. Lastly, we assume $\partial^2 q/\partial e \partial S > 0$ for all $e \geq 0$ and $S \geq 0$ because additional expenditure by the firm (in the form of more or better equipment, for example) should increase the marginal impact of inventor effort on the probability of success.

A. Licensing with Royalties

We return to our benchmark case of contracts that specify a royalty rate and a fixed fee. Given a contract (r, m), the firm chooses expenditure on sponsored research to maximize expected profit

(11) $P_F(e, S, E, r, m)$

$$= q(e, S)[\Pi(x(r)) - rx(r)]$$

$$- m - S - E,$$

and the inventor chooses effort to maximize expected utility

(12) $P_I(e, S, r, m)$

$$= q(e, S)U_I(\alpha m + \alpha rx(r))$$

$$+ (1 - q(e, S))U_I(\alpha m) - V_I(e).$$

We write the Nash equilibrium outcomes of this development game as $e^n(r, m)$ and $S^n(r, m)$. In this situation the expected utility of the administration is $P_A(e, S, r, m) = q(e, S)U_A((1 - \alpha)[m + rx(r)]) + (1 - q(e, S))U_A((1 - \alpha)m)$, and the TTO's problem is to choose a contract (r, m) to maximize $P(e, S, r, m) = \beta P_I(e, S, r, m) + (1 - \beta)P_A(e, S, r, m)$ subject to optimal behavior by the inventor and firm, and the firm's participation constraint.

The first-order necessary conditions for positive choices of sponsored research by the firm and effort by the inventor are:

(13) $\dfrac{\partial P_F}{\partial S} = \left(\dfrac{\partial q}{\partial S}\right)[\Pi(x(r)) - rx(r)] - 1 = 0$

and

(14) $\dfrac{\partial P_I}{\partial e} = \left(\dfrac{\partial q}{\partial e}\right)[U_I(\alpha m + \alpha rx(r)) - U_I(\alpha m)]$

$$- V_I'(e) = 0.$$

These define best-reply (reaction) functions. That is, (13) implicitly defines the firm's best level of sponsored research for any given level of effort, $b_F(e)$, and (14) implicitly defines the inventor's best level of effort for any given level of sponsored research, $b_I(S)$. We first note that effort and sponsored research are strategic complements because they are "complements" in development. That is, they complement each other in the "production" of a positive probability of success, $\partial^2 q / \partial e \partial S > 0$.

THEOREM 5: *Inventor effort and sponsored research are strategic complements. That is, the firm's best reply $b_F(e)$ and the inventor's best reply $b_I(S)$ are both positively sloped.*

Obviously, no development is a Nash equilibrium of this game, $(e^n, S^n) = (0, 0)$. Without inventor effort, the probability of success is zero, so the firm spends nothing on development, $b_F(0) = 0$. Similarly, without firm expenditure, this probability is zero, so the inventor expends no effort, $b_I(0) = 0$. We emphasize that, again, we make these assumptions on the probability of success because they are consistent with our survey results, not because they are necessary for this "no-development" result. This equilibrium exists whenever the probability of success is too low for either the firm or the inventor to attempt to develop the invention independently.[28] Nevertheless, because the best replies are positively sloped, it is possible that there exists another equilibrium in which development does occur, $e^n(r, m) > 0$ and $S^n(r, m) > 0$. For such an equilibrium to exist and be locally stable, it is sufficient that the best replies have the properties of those graphed in Figure 2.

THEOREM 6: *No development is a Nash equilibrium, $(e^n(r, m), S^n(r, m)) = (0, 0)$. However, if*

(15) $b_F'(0) > 1/b_I'(0), \ b_I''(S) < 0,$

$$b_F''(e) < 0, \quad and$$

$b_F'(e^m) = 1/b_I'(b_F(e^m)) \ for \ some \ e^m > 0,$

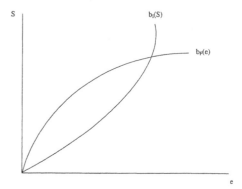

FIGURE 2. EQUILIBRIA OF THE DEVELOPMENT GAME

then there exists another Nash equilibrium with development, $e^n(r, m) > 0$ and $S^n(r, m) > 0$. Moreover, the development equilibrium is locally stable, whereas the no-development equilibrium is not.

As shown in Figure 2, the best-reply functions intersect at the origin, so that is an equilibrium. The condition $b_F'(0) > 1/b_I'(0)$ ensures that the firm's best reply is more steeply sloped than the inventor's best reply at the origin, so that this equilibrium is locally unstable. The conditions $b_I''(S) < 0$, $b_F''(e) < 0$, and $b_F'(e^m) = 1/b_I'(b_F(e^m))$ for some $e^m > 0$ guarantee that the best replies are concave enough for another intersection at $e^n(r, m) > e^m$ and $S^n(r, m) > 0$, which is a locally stable equilibrium. Naturally we are most interested in this development equilibrium, and how its existence and properties are influenced by the licensing choices of the TTO.

THEOREM 7: *Assume (15), and consider the levels of effort and expenditure in the Nash equilibrium with development, $e^n(r, m) > 0$ and $S^n(r, m) > 0$.*

(i) *Equilibrium effort and sponsored research are decreasing in the fixed fee, $\partial e^n(r, m)/ \partial m < 0$ and $\partial S^n(r, m)/\partial m < 0$, if the inventor is risk averse, but do not depend on the fixed fee, $\partial e^n(r, m)/\partial m = 0$ and $\partial S^n(r, m)/\partial m = 0$, if the inventor is risk neutral.*

(ii) *In general, changes in the royalty rate have an ambiguous effect on equilibrium effort*

---

[28] Given a contract (r, m), from (13), $b_F(0) = 0$ if $[\partial q(0, 0)/\partial S]\Pi(x(0)) < 1$, and from (14), $b_I(0) = 0$ if $[\partial q(0, 0)/\partial e][U_I(\alpha m + \alpha r x(r)) - U_I(\alpha m)] < V_I'(0)$. Note that this is where we differ from Aghion and Tirole (1994a, b), who assume a probability of success that allows independent development by the research unit or the customer.

and sponsored research. However, they are decreasing in the royalty rate, $\partial e^n(r, m)/\partial r < 0$ and $\partial S^n(r, m)/\partial r < 0$, if the inventor's best-reply effort is decreasing in the royalty rate, which occurs only for those rates such that royalty revenue is also decreasing in the royalty rate.

Suppose the inventor and firm undertake development. Comparative statics with respect to the fixed fee are similar to those in the benchmark case of Section II, subsection A. The inventor's best reply is affected by a change in the fixed fee only if she is risk averse, in which case it rotates back to the left (effort decreases for all $S > 0$). Since the firm's best reply does not depend on the fixed fee, a change in it has no effect on equilibrium effort or sponsored research when the inventor is risk neutral.

However, a change in the royalty rate affects both firm profit and inventor income. An increase in the rate decreases the firm's profit from a success, and thus its expected marginal benefit from sponsored research. Hence, an increase in r decreases sponsored research for all $e > 0$. Ceteris paribus, because they are strategic complements, inventor effort also tends to decrease. However, other things are not equal because the increase in r also changes royalty income. In a fashion similar to our benchmark case, the effect of a change in r on the marginal benefit of effort parallels royalty revenue as the royalty rate changes. As long as profit-maximizing output is inelastic with respect to the royalty rate, both royalty revenue and the expected marginal benefit of effort increase with an increase in r, so effort increases for all $S > 0$. Again, because they are strategic complements, sponsored research tends to increase. The net effect, of course, is ambiguity [consider Figure 2 when $b_F(e)$ rotates down and $b_I(S)$ rotates to the right].

These results suggest that, as in our benchmark case, the use of output-based payments such as royalties is essential in the development of embryonic inventions. The reason remains that inventor effort is required for any chance of success. As long as the inventor's effort in development is not contractible and causes disutility, there is a moral-hazard problem that cannot be solved by contracts relying only on lump-sum payments such as fixed fees or sponsored research.

THEOREM 8: *No development is the unique equilibrium if the license contract does not specify a positive royalty rate. That is, a positive royalty rate is a necessary condition for development to occur in equilibrium: $e^n(r, m) > 0$ and $S^n(r, m) > 0$ only if $r > 0$. The contract also must involve a positive fixed fee if the inventor is risk neutral or not too risk averse.*

If the inventor is risk neutral, or not too risk averse, then the TTO's objective function is strictly increasing in the fixed fee for any positive royalty rate. Hence, if the invention has enough commercial potential that a contract is executed and development occurs, then that contract must involve both a positive royalty rate and fixed fee.

B. *Licensing with Equity*

Finally, we consider equity as an alternative to royalties in the presence of sponsored research. The TTO chooses a contract (ρ, m) to maximize its expected payoff subject to optimal behavior by the inventor and the firm, and the firm's participation constraint. Compared to equity contracts without sponsored research, one important difference is that an increase in the equity share does not necessarily increase inventor effort. This is particularly interesting because, as in the case of equity without sponsored research, an increase in equity increases the inventor's marginal expected utility. This induces the inventor to provide more effort for any positive level of sponsored research. However, because the increase in equity decreases the firm's marginal expected payoff, the firm provides less sponsored research for any positive level of effort. Because effort and sponsored research are strategic complements, in equilibrium the effect on inventor effort is ambiguous. This can be easily seen from Figure 2, noting that the firm's best reply rotates down and the inventor's best reply rotates to the right.

THEOREM 9: *In the development game with an equity contract, no development is the unique equilibrium if the contract does not*

VOL. 91 NO. 1   *JENSEN AND THURSBY: LICENSING OF UNIVERSITY INVENTIONS*   *255*

specify a positive equity share. Under a condition on best replies analogous to (15), there exists a locally stable development equilibrium in which:

(i) *Changes in the equity share have an ambiguous effect on inventor effort and sponsored research.*

(ii) *Inventor effort and sponsored research are decreasing in the minimum fee if the inventor is risk averse, but do not vary with the fee if the inventor is risk neutral.*

(iii) *The contract must involve a positive minimum fee if the inventor is risk neutral or not too risk averse.*

(iv) *Even in the presence of sponsored research, an equity contract is more efficient than a royalty contract if maximized profit from a success is decreasing in the royalty rate.*

IV. Concluding Remarks

In the debate surrounding the Bayh-Dole Act, proponents argue that unless universities have the right to license faculty inventions, many results from federally funded research would remain in the research lab, finding industrial application only after a significant delay, if at all. In an effort to shed light on this debate, we surveyed technology managers from 62 universities about invention characteristics, licensing procedures, and licensing objectives in their universities. Our results show that the vast majority of inventions licensed are so embryonic that technology managers consider inventor cooperation in further development crucial for commercial success. These managers also reported challenges associated with inducing such cooperation from research faculty. Thus, for these inventions, there is a moral-hazard problem with regard to inventor effort. Our theoretical analysis shows that development would not occur unless the inventor's return is tied to the licensee's output when the invention is successful. This can be done with royalties, and in fact, our survey results show that the vast majority of agreements include royalty payments. Increasingly, however, technology managers are including equity participation by the university. In fact, we show not only that equity can induce inventor cooperation, but also that con-

tracts with equity are Pareto superior to those with royalties. We also focused on the role of sponsored research in situations where inventions could not be successful without licensee expenditure early on in the process. We find essentially the same results, which implies that sponsored research alone cannot solve the moral-hazard problem.

Opponents of Bayh-Dole, conversely, argue that no additional incentives are required to commercialize important inventions, and that it may divert faculty from more basic research and teaching. An important case we have not examined is when the inventor starts a company based on an invention developed in the course of her research, owns founder shares in the firm, and retains her job at the university. Because she holds equity in the licensee and receives a share of license revenue, there is a potential conflict of interest that we do not address. There is also a potential conflict of commitment in that the university administration may not view her allocation of time between university and firm responsibilities as appropriate. Addressing the latter issue requires extending our model to include the disutility of inventor effort in the administration's utility function. We have also not considered the case where the inventor has employment opportunities other than the university. For example, there may be a trade-off between royalties and inventor salaries that universities exploit in attracting faculty. In future work, we plan to explore these and other aspects of our survey not reported in this paper.

Appendix A: Survey Design Sample

Questionnaires were sent to the top 135 universities in terms of licensing revenue according to the 1996 *AUTM Survey*, and responses were received from 62 universities: Alabama, Birmingham; Arizona State; Baylor; California, Berkeley; California, Los Angeles; California, San Diego; California, San Francisco; California, System Office; California Institute of Technology; Carnegie Mellon; Chicago; Cincinnati; Clemson; Colorado State; Colorado; Columbia; Dartmouth College; Dayton; Duke; Emory; Florida Atlantic; Florida State; Georgia Institute of Technology; Harvard; Illinois, Urbana/Champaign; Indiana; Iowa State; Johns Hopkins; Kentucky; Lehigh; Marquette; Massachusetts Institute of Technology; Michigan

State; Michigan Technological; Michigan; Minnesota; Mississippi State; Missouri; New Jersey Institute of Technology; New Mexico State; North Carolina, Chapel Hill; Northwestern; Ohio State; Pennsylvania State; Pennsylvania; Purdue; Rhode Island; Rochester; Rutgers; Stanford; State University of New York; Tennessee; Texas A&M; Thomas Jefferson; Tulane; Utah; Virginia Tech; Wake Forest; Washington; Wisconsin; Woods Hole; and Yale.

QUESTIONNAIRE

The content of our questionnaire was influenced by: (i) the policy debate over the impact of the Bayh-Dole Act, and, in particular, the role of university licensing practices on the industrial impact of university research; (ii) potential conflicts between the objectives of inventors and technology transfer managers; and (iii) our interest in determining whether university licensing practices are consistent with results from the theoretical literatures on optimal contracts and patent licensing.

To maximize the likelihood that questions were interpreted accurately and that respondents could provide reliable information, we pretested the questionnaire on 11 experienced university technology transfer managers. These managers came from a mixture of private and public universities. The majority of managers in our test group had at least ten years of experience in university technology transfer. Each individual was asked to complete the test questionnaire for his own institution and to think about whether technology managers with less experience or from a variety of universities would be able to answer the questions. All individuals in the test group were interviewed face-to-face, and all questions in the questionnaire were discussed to minimize ambiguity. For the actual survey, follow-up telephone interviews were also used to minimize ambiguity.

There is undoubtedly noise in the survey data. In part, this is because respondents provided estimates of quantitative data which were not available from university files, but also because a number of our questions require judgment about quantitative data. Consider, for example, the question: "What percentage of the invention disclosures licensed in the last five years were in the following stages of develop-

ment at the time the license agreement was executed?" Few universities maintain files providing such information, but even so, managers' responses may be in error either because the true stage of development was misjudged or because respondents perceive questions differently. To minimize errors of this type, we used the categories listed in Table 1, part 5, all of which were identified by our test group as standard for evaluating stage of development.

For questions with a semantic scale (categorical questions), respondents may indeed perceive the same environment but use the scale differently. To minimize error of this type, we based the scale underlying Figure 1 on research results from the literature on optimal rating scales. As discussed by Jon A. Krosnick and Leandre R. Fabrigar (1997), research on the reliability of rating scales suggests people can distinguish among and have consistent interpretations of the four-point scale, "extremely important," "moderately important," "not very important," and "not applicable." One problem with this scale for our purposes is that we are interested in the importance of five outcomes that our test group suggested are the major criteria used by technology transfer offices to measure their success. Note that this necessarily implies tied responses for rankings of some outcomes.

Finally, items in Table 2 (except for part 2) are based on respondent estimates of the frequency of an event or contract term. Managers were asked to identify the frequency as "almost always," "often," "sometimes," "rarely," or "never." To quantify the responses, we assigned numerical values according to values reported by Frederick Mosteller and Cleo Youtz (1990) for the average value assigned to these terms in 20 studies on probabilities associated with categorical data. Values assigned were 0.91 for almost always, 0.65 for often, 0.28 for sometimes, 0.09 for rarely, and 0.01 for never.

APPENDIX B: SKETCHES OF PROOFS

In this Appendix, we provide brief sketches of the proofs for Theorems 1–9. Complete proofs are available from the authors.

PROOF OF THEOREM 1:
If $r = 0$, then $P_I(e, 0, m) = U_I(\alpha m) -$

$V_I(e)$ is maximized for $e \geq 0$ at $e = 0$ because $V_I'(e) > 0$ and $V_I''(e) > 0$ for $e \geq 0$. If $r > 0$, then $P_I(e, r, m)$ is maximized at some $e > 0$ because (4) implies $\partial P_I/\partial e > 0$ at $e = 0$ and $\partial^2 P_I/\partial e^2 < 0$ for $e \geq 0$. We must also assume the firm accepts the contract (otherwise the inventor expends no effort). Ordinary comparative statics on (3) gives (i) and (ii).

PROOF OF THEOREM 2:

Theorem 2 follows from observing that $\partial P(e^*(r, m), r, m)/\partial m > 0$ if the inventor is risk neutral because $\partial P_I/\partial m > 0$, $\partial P_A/\partial e > 0$, $\partial P_A/\partial m > 0$, and $\partial e^*(r, m)/\partial m = 0$ by Theorem 1. Because $\partial P(e^*(r, m), r, m)/\partial m > 0$ for $\partial e^*(r, m)/\partial m < 0$ but small enough, the same result holds if the inventor is not too risk averse.

PROOF OF THEOREM 3:

If $\rho = 0$, then $P_I(e, 0, m) = U_I(\alpha m) - V_I(e)$ is maximized for $e \geq 0$ at $e = 0$. If $\rho > 0$, then $P_I(e, \rho, m)$ is maximized at some $e > 0$ because (10) implies $\partial P_I/\partial e > 0$ at $e = 0$ and $\partial^2 P_I/\partial e^2 < 0$ for $e \geq 0$. Thus (i) and (ii) follow from comparative statics on the first-order necessary condition $\partial P_I/\partial e = p'(e)[U_I(\alpha m + \alpha \rho \Pi(x(0))) - U_I(\alpha m)] - V_I'(e) = 0$. Differentiating $P(e^*(\rho, m), \rho, m)$ with respect to m and using (ii) gives (iii) since $\partial P_I/\partial m > 0$, $\partial P_A/\partial e > 0$, and $\partial P_A/\partial m > 0$.

PROOF OF THEOREM 4:

Consider the optimal royalty contract (r^*, m^*) and the resulting inventor effort $e^*(r^*, m^*)$ defined by (3). Let $\rho(r^*, m^*)$ be the equity share that provides the same income from a success as under the optimal royalty, $\rho(r^*, m^*)\pi(x(0)) = r^*x(r^*)$. If the TTO switches from the royalty contract to this income-equivalent equity contract, and if the inventor expends the same effort $e^*(r^*, m^*)$, then by construction the inventor and university administration are no worse off (*ex ante*) because each has the same expected utility. However, if maximized profit from a success is decreasing in the royalty rate, then $\pi(x(r^*)) < \pi(x(0))$ and the firm earns more profit from a success, $[1 - \rho(r^*, m^*)]\pi(x(0)) > \pi(x(r^*)) - r^*x(r^*)$. Hence, expected profit is also greater under the income-equivalent equity contract with the same level of effort, $p(e^*(r^*, m^*))[1 - \rho(r^*, m^*)]\pi(x(0)) - m^* - E > p(e^*(r^*, m^*))[\pi(x(r^*)) - r^*x(r^*)] - m^* - E$. The optimal royalty contract is thus Pareto inferior to the income-equivalent equity

contract when the inventor expends the same effort under both. The optimal equity contract is not $(\rho(r^*, m^*), m^*)$. Because expected profit under this contract is strictly positive, the TTO must adjust both the fixed fee and equity share to attain the optimal equity contract. The resulting contract is Pareto superior to the optimal royalty contract since the reoptimization cannot reduce the firm's expected profit below 0 (the firm can always reject it) and it must increase the value of the TTO's objective function.

PROOF OF THEOREM 5:

From (13), $b_F'(e) = -(\partial^2 P_F/\partial S \partial e)/(\partial^2 P_F/\partial S^2) > 0$ because $\partial^2 P_F/\partial S \partial e > 0 > \partial^2 P_F/\partial S^2$. Similarly, from (14), $b_I'(S) = -(\partial^2 P_I/\partial e \partial S)/(\partial^2 P_I/\partial e^2) > 0$ because $\partial^2 P_I/\partial e \partial S > 0 > \partial^2 P_I/\partial e^2$.

PROOF OF THEOREM 6:

Because $q(e, 0) = 0$ for $e \geq 0$, $P_I(e, 0, r, m) = U_I(\alpha m) - V_I(e)$ is maximized for $e \geq 0$ at $e = 0$, and so $b_I(0) = 0$. Similarly, because $q(0, S) = 0$ for $S \geq 0$, $P_F(0, S, E, r, m) = -S - E - m$ is maximized for $S \geq 0$ at $S = 0$, and so $b_F(0) = 0$. Hence, $(e^n, S^n) = (0, 0)$ is an equilibrium.

Given $f(e) = b_I(b_F(e)) - e$, (e^n, S^n) is a Nash equilibrium if and only if $f(e^n) = 0$ and $S^n = b_F(e^n)$, and it is locally stable if and only if $b_I'(S^n)b_F'(e^n) < 1$. One can show that (15) implies $(0, 0)$ is not a locally stable equilibrium, and there exists another Nash equilibrium $(e^n(r, m), S^n(r, m))$ with $e^n(r, m) > e^m > 0$ and $S^n(r, m) > 0$, which is locally stable.

PROOF OF THEOREM 7:

Theorem 7 follows from comparative statics on (13) and (14) and the observation that $\partial^2 P_F/\partial S \partial m = 0$, $\partial^2 P_F/\partial S^2 < 0$, $\partial^2 P_F/\partial S \partial e > 0$, $\partial^2 P_I/\partial e \partial m < 0$ if $U_I'' < 0$ but $\partial^2 P_I/\partial e \partial m = 0$ if $U_I'' = 0$, $\partial^2 P_F/\partial S \partial r < 0$ from the envelope theorem, $\partial^2 P_I/\partial e \partial r \leq 0$ only if $x + r(\partial x/\partial r) < 0$, and $(\partial^2 P_F/\partial S^2)(\partial^2 P_I/\partial e^2) > (\partial^2 P_F/\partial S \partial e)(\partial^2 P_I/\partial e \partial S)$ by local stability.

PROOF OF THEOREM 8:

From (12), if $r = 0$, then $P_I(e, 0, m) = U_I(\alpha m) - V_I(e)$ is maximized at $e = 0$ for all S, so $b_I(S) = 0$ for all S. From (11), $P_F(0, S, E, r, m) = -m - S - E < 0$ is maximized at $S = 0$ for all e, so $b_F(0) = 0$ for all e.

Hence, $(e^n(0, m), S^n(0, m)) = (0, 0)$ is the unique Nash equilibrium for any $m \geq 0$, whence $r > 0$ is a necessary condition for an equilibrium with development. The contract involves a positive fixed fee if the inventor is risk neutral or not too risk averse because $\partial P(e^n(r, m), S^n(r, m), r, m)/\partial m > 0$ as in Theorem 2.

PROOF OF THEOREM 9:

In this development game the firm's expected profit is $P_F(e, S, E, \rho, m) = q(e, S)(1 - \rho)\Pi(x(0)) - m - S - E$, the inventor's expected utility is $P_I(e, S, \rho, m) = q(e, S)U_I(\alpha m + \alpha\rho\Pi(x(0))) + (1 - q(e, S))U_I(\alpha m) - V_I(e)$, the university's expected utility is $P_A(e, S, \rho, m) = q(e, S)U_A((1 - \alpha)(m + \rho\Pi(x(0)))) + (1 - q(e, S))U_A((1 - \alpha)m)$, and the TTO's expected payoff is $P(e, S, \rho, m) = \beta P_I(e, S, \rho, m) + (1 - \beta)P_A(e, S, \rho, m)$.

Given an equity contract, the first-order necessary conditions for positive choices of sponsored research and effort are $\partial P_F/\partial S = (\partial q/\partial S)(1 - \rho)\Pi(x(0)) - 1 = 0$ and $\partial P_I/\partial e = (\partial q/\partial e)[U_I(\alpha m + \alpha\rho\Pi(x(0))) - U_I(\alpha m)] - V'_I(e) = 0$. These implicitly define best-reply functions, which are strategic complements as in Theorem 5. The proof that no development is an equilibrium, but there also exists a locally stable development equilibrium under a condition similar to (15), is analogous to the proof of Theorem 6. Then (i) and (ii) follow from comparative statics on $\partial P_F/\partial S = 0$ and $\partial P_I/\partial e = 0$, the observation that $\partial^2 P_F/\partial S\partial m = 0$, $\partial^2 P_I/\partial e\partial m < 0$ if $U''_I < 0$ but $\partial^2 P_I/\partial e\partial m = 0$ if $U''_I = 0$, $\partial^2 P_F/\partial S\partial\rho < 0$, and $\partial^2 P_I/\partial e\partial\rho > 0$, and local stability. The proof that no development is the unique equilibrium without a positive equity share and (iii) is analogous to the proof of Theorem 8, and the proof of (iv) is analogous to that of Theorem 4.

REFERENCES

Adams, James D. "Fundamental Stocks of Knowledge and Productivity Growth." *Journal of Political Economy*, August 1990, *98*(4), pp. 673–702.

Aghion, Philippe and Tirole, Jean. "Opening the Black Box of Innovation." *European Economic Review*, April 1994a, *38*(3–4), pp. 701–10.

_____. "The Management of Innovation." *Quarterly Journal of Economics*, November 1994b, *109*(4), pp. 1185–209.

Association of University Technology Managers (AUTM). *AUTM technology transfer practice manual, volume II.* Norwalk, CT: AUTM, 1993.

_____. *Association of University Technology Managers survey: Fiscal year 1996.* Norwalk, CT: AUTM, 1997.

Axelrod, Jonathan N. "Universities Learn of Start-ups' Pitfalls." *Wall Street Journal*, August 27, 1996, p. C1.

Beggs, Alan W. "The Licensing of Patents under Asymmetric Information." *International Journal of Industrial Organization*, June 1992, *10*(2), pp. 171–91.

Caves, Richard E.; Crookell, Harold and Killing, J. Peter. "The Imperfect Market for Technology Licenses." *Oxford Bulletin of Economics and Statistics*, August 1983, *45*(3), pp. 249–67.

Cohen, Wesley; Nelson, Richard R. and Walsh, John P. "Appropriability Conditions and Why Firms Patent and Why They Do Not in the American Manufacturing Sector." Mimeo, Carnegie Mellon University, Columbia University, and University of Illinois, Chicago, 1997.

Congressional Record. Testimony of Teri Willey, Senate Committee on Federal Funding, April 15, 1999.

Gallini, Nancy T. and Wright, Brian D. "Technology Transfer under Asymmetric Information." *Rand Journal of Economics*, Spring 1990, *21*(1), pp. 147–60.

Government Accounting Office. *Technology transfer: Administration of the Bayh-Dole Act by research universities.* Washington, DC: U.S. General Accounting Office, May 7, 1998.

Harhoff, Dietmar; Scherer, Frederick M. and Vopel, Katrin. "Exploring the Tail of Patent Value Distributions." Mimeo, Harvard University, 1997.

Henderson, Rebecca; Jaffe, Adam B. and Trajtenberg, Manuel. "Universities as a Source of Commercial Technology: A Detailed Analysis of University Patenting, 1965–1988." *Review of Economics and Statistics*, February 1998, *80*(1), pp. 119–27.

Jaffe, Adam B. "Real Effects of Academic Research." *American Economic Review*, December 1989, *79*(5), pp. 957–70.

Jaffe, Adam B.; Trajtenberg, Manuel and Henderson, Rebecca. "Geographic Localization of Knowledge Spillovers as Evidenced by Patent Citations." *Quarterly Journal of Economics*, August 1993, *108*(3), pp. 577–98.

Jensen, Richard. "Reputational Spillovers, Innovation, Licensing, and Entry." *International Journal of Industrial Organization*, June 1992a, *10*(2), pp. 193–212.

_____. "Dynamic Patent Licensing." *International Journal of Industrial Organization*, September 1992b, *10*(3), pp. 349–68.

Kamien, Morton I. "Patent Licensing," in Robert J. Aumann and Sergio Hart, eds., *Handbook of game theory with economic applications*, Vol. 1. Amsterdam: North-Holland, 1992, pp. 331–54.

Krosnick, Jon A. and Fabrigar, Leandre R. "Designing Rating Scales for Effective Measurement in Surveys," in Lars Lyberg, Paul Beimer, Martin Collins, Edith de Leeuw, Catherine Dippo, Norbert Schwarz, and Dennis Trewin, eds., *Survey measurement and process quality*. New York: Wiley, 1997, pp. 141–64.

Lerner, Joshua and Merges, Robert. "The Control of Technology Alliances: An Empirical Analysis of the Biotechnology Industry." Mimeo, Harvard University and University of California, Berkeley, 1997.

Levin, Richard C.; Klevorick, Alvin K.; Nelson, Richard R. and Winter, Sidney. "Appropriating the Returns from Industrial Research and Development." *Brookings Papers on Economic Activity*, 1987, (3), pp. 783–831.

Macho-Stadler, Ines; Martinez-Giralt, Xavier and Perez-Castrillo, J. David. "The Role of Information in Licensing Contract Design." *Research Policy*, January 1996, *25*(1), pp. 43–57.

Mansfield, Edwin. "Academic Research Underlying Industrial Innovations: Sources, Characteristics, and Financing." *Review of Economics and Statistics,* February 1995, *77*(1), pp. 55–62.

Mosteller, Frederick and Youtz, Cleo. "Quantifying Probabilistic Expressions." *Statistical Science*, February 1990, *5*(1), pp. 2–34.

Mowery, David C.; Nelson, Richard R.; Sampat, Bhaven and Ziedonis, Arvids A. " The Growth of Patenting and Licensing by U.S. Universities: An Assessment of the Effects of the Bayh-Dole Act of 1980." *Research Policy*, January 2001, *30*(1), pp. 99–119.

Nelson, Richard R. "The Role of Knowledge in R&D Efficiency." *Quarterly Journal of Economics*, August 1982, *97*(3), pp. 453–70.

Reimers, Neils. "Tiger by the Tail." *CHEMTECH*, August 1987, *17*(8), pp. 464–71.

Scherer, Frederick M. "The Size Distribution of Profits from Innovation." Discussion Paper No. 96–113, Industrial Economics and International Management Series, May 1996.

Stephan, Paula E. "The Economics of Science." *Journal of Economic Literature*, September 1996, *34*(3), pp. 1199–235.

Thursby, Jerry G.; Jensen, Richard and Thursby, Marie. "Objectives, Characteristics and Outcomes of University Licensing: A Survey of Major U.S. Universities." *Journal of Technology Transfer*, January 2001, *26*(1), pp. 59–72.

Thursby, Jerry G. and Kemp, Sukanya. "An Analysis of Productive Efficiency of University Commercialization Activities." *Research Policy,* 2001 (forthcoming).

Thursby, Jerry G. and Thursby, Marie C. "Who Is Selling the Ivory Tower?: The Sources of Growth in University Licensing." *Management Science*, 2001 (forthcoming).

Wang, X. Henry. "Fee versus Royalty Licensing in a Cournot Duopoly Model." *Economics Letters*, July 1998, *60*(1), pp. 55–62.

Zucker, Lynne G. and Darby, Michael R. "Star Scientists and Institutional Transformation: Patterns of Invention and Innovation in the Formation of the Biotechnology Industry." *Proceedings of the National Academy of Sciences*, November 1996, *93*(23), pp. 12709–16.

Zucker, Lynne G.; Darby, Michael R. and Armstrong, Jeff. "Intellectual Capital and the Firm: The Technology of Geographically Localized Knowledge Spillovers." National Bureau of Economic Research (Cambridge, MA) Working Paper No. 4946, December 1994.

Zucker, Lynne G.; Darby, Michael R. and Brewer, Marilynn B. "Intellectual Human Capital and the Birth of U.S. Biotechnology Enterprises." *American Economic Review*, March 1998, *88*(1), pp. 290–306.

[4]

Barriers Inhibiting Industry from Partnering with Universities: Evidence from the Advanced Technology Program

Bronwyn H. Hall[1]
Albert N. Link[2]
John T. Scott[3]

ABSTRACT. This paper describes a small, unique set of project data that was assembled as part of a larger study on universities as research partners. Herein, we summarize, to the extent possible, our interpretation of what the project data reveal about barriers, intellectual property (IP) concerns in particular, inhibiting industry from partnering with universities.

JEL Classification: O31, O34

1. Introduction

There is a long and well-documented history of industry/university research relationships. In Europe, such relationships can be traced at least to the mid- to late-1800s and in the United States to at least the industrial revolution. Hounshell (1996) and Rosenberg and Nelson (1994) provide excellent historical overviews of the evolution of these associations. In recent decades, the nature of such relationships has become more formal through the formation of explicit research joint ventures and partnerships.

It is generally accepted, at least in the United States, that research partnerships are a critical strategic response to global competition.[1] The Council on Competitiveness (1996) in its recent policy statement, *Endless Frontiers, Limited Resources: U.S. R&D Policy for Competitiveness*, took the position that (1996, pp. 3–4), "R&D partnerships hold the key to meeting the challenge of transition that our nation now faces" and industry will increasingly rely on universities to ensure the success of the research being undertaken. Relatedly, Mowery (1998, p. 646), commenting on structural changes in the U.S. innovation system, noted that a major element of structural change is "increased reliance by U.S. firms on sources of R&D outside their organizational boundaries, through such mechanisms as ... collaboration with U.S. universities...."

In the United States, the number of new, formal research joint ventures (RJVs) formed under the National Cooperative Research Act (NCRA) of 1984 and its amendment the National Cooperative Research and Production Act (NCRPA) of 1993 has been cyclical, reaching a peak in 1995, falling for three years, and just now beginning to increase again (Brod and Link, forthcoming). However, the percentage of RJVs involving at least one university as a research partner has generally increased since 1985, as illustrated in Figure 1.[2,3]

The trend showing an increase in RJVs with university partners is not surprising given the claim by the Council on Competitiveness that university presence helps to ensure the partner-

We appreciate the comments and suggestions from William L. Baldwin, Donald Siegel, and the participants at the special issue workshop at Purdue University, June 9–11, 2000, on an earlier version of the paper.

[1] Department of Economics
University of California at Berkeley and NBER
Berkeley, CA 94720-3880
E-mail: bhhall@econ.berkeley.edu
[2] Department of Economics
University of North Carolina at Greensboro
Greensboro, NC 27412
E-mail: al_link@uncg.edu
[3] Department of Economics
Dartmouth College
Hanover, NH 03755
E-mail: john.t.scott@dartmouth.edu

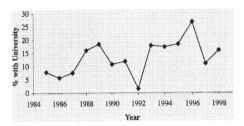

Figure 1. Percent of RJVs with at least one university.

ship's research success. Rosenberg and Nelson (1994, p. 340) make a similar claim, "What university research most often does today is to stimulate and enhance the power of R&D done in industry." Hall, Link, and Scott (2000, p. 19) conclude from their project-based study of universities as research partners that universities create research awareness among the research partners of the joint venture:

> Universities are included (e.g., invited by industry) in those research projects that involve what we have called "new" science. As such, it is the collective perception of the other research participant(s) that the university could provide a research insight that is more anticipatory of future research problems that might be encountered and could thus take on the role of an ombudsman to anticipate and translate to all concerned the complex nature of the research being undertaken. Thus, one finds universities purposively involved in projects that are characterized as problematic with regard to the use of basic knowledge.

Given the research productivity-enhancing effects of such partnerships, the trend in Figure 1 may well continue and perhaps even intensify. However, there is another issue implicit in Figure 1, and that issue serves to motivate this paper. Whereas universities are research partners in about 15 percent of all RJVs – at least all RJVs that are registered under the NCRA and NCRPA and made public in the *Federal Register* – the vast majority of research partnerships do not involve a university. Was university research participation in these projects simply not warranted because of the nature of the research? Or, was a research relationship with a university sought, but institutional barriers inhibited or even prevented the research partnership from coming about?[4]

In Section 2 we describe a small, unique set of project data that was assembled as part of a

larger study on universities as research partners in projects funded by the Advanced Technology Program (Hall, Link, and Scott, 2000). In Section 3, we summarize, to the extent possible, our interpretation of what the project data reveal about barriers, intellectual property (IP) concerns in particular, inhibiting industry from partnering with universities. Finally, in Section 4 we offer some policy observations in light of our findings.

2. The advanced technology program and the program's project data

The Omnibus Trade and Competitiveness Act of 1988 (P.L. 100–418) not only changed the name of the National Bureau of Standards to the National Institute of Standards and Technology (NIST) and broadened its scope of responsibility, but also it facilitated the ability of Congress to enact a so-called direct competitiveness program, the Advanced Technology Program (ATP). The American Technology Preeminence Act of 1991 (P.L. 102–245) later clarified the mission of the ATP.

The stated goals of the ATP are to assist U.S. business in creating and applying the generic technology and research results necessary to:

1. commercialize significant new scientific discoveries and technologies rapidly; and
2. refine manufacturing technologies.

The ATP was also designed to enhance the competitiveness of industry. The enabling legislation is explicit about that objective:

> The ATP ... will assist U.S. businesses to improve their competitive position and promote U.S. economic growth by accelerating the development of a variety of pre-competitive generic technologies by means of grants and cooperative agreements.

Towards this goal, ATP was mandated to enhance competitiveness by underwriting selected research projects. Thus by design, the ATP represents a program for direct funding of private-sector research through public-sector financial resources.[5] The first ATP awards were made in April 1991.

For this study, 38 projects funded by the ATP between 1993 and 1996 were considered.[6] This group of projects was randomly selected from the population of all completed ATP projects during that time period that were either single participant projects or one of four categories of joint venture research projects: without a university as a research partner, with a university(ies) as a research partner, with a university(ies) as a subcontractor, with a university(ies) as a research partner and a university(ies) as a subcontractor.

A complete description of the sample selection process is in Hall, Link, and Scott (2000). The sample in that paper included not only the 38 projects used here, but also 9 single-participant projects with a university(ies) as a subcontractor. Information about IP barriers was not available for those projects; hence, they could not be used in the present study.

With the assistance of the ATP, information was collected about the members of each research project and the project's funding characteristics. Also, the lead participant in each project was identified; that participant was contacted in advance about the nature of the study, asked to respond to a brief survey instrument, and assured that individual responses would remain anonymous.

We are sensitive not only about the smallness of this sample but also about the fact that the ATP-funded research projects are not necessarily representative of the population of all research undertakings, whether they be collaborative or not. Accordingly, we emphasize up front that the patterns in our project data as well as our conclusions should be interpreted (and generalized) with the utmost caution. However, to date, there is a void of research that has attempted to identify systematically barriers that inhibit industry from participating with universities in research projects, ATP-funded or otherwise.[7] Thus this research is exploratory in its nature, sample size issues aside, and should be interpreted as such.

3. Analysis of the survey data

The focus of this study is to investigate whether there are identifiable barriers – intellectual property rights related barriers in particular – that inhibit firms from partnering in research with a university(ies), and if so, to consider if such barriers are relatively more common in particular types of research projects. The issue of intellectual property vis-à-vis the relationship between firms and universities has precedence in the literature. According to Rappert, Webster and Charles (1999, p. 873), for example, drawing in part on the work of Feller (1990):[8]

> Since university research is often portrayed as a public good (e.g., characterized by free circulation), the spread of IPR [intellectual property rights] protection into university R&D activities has attracted considerable attention. Where once industry benefited from exchange systems with academia based upon transactions such as informal barter relationships, those in industry now find universities seeking contractual, exchange-value-based relationships.

Brainard (1999, p. 9), is more explicit about the differing objectives of industry and universities regarding intellectual property. And, it is these conflicting objectives that cause potential research relationships to fail, or perhaps never to begin in the first place:

> The goal of business and universities in producing and protecting intellectual property is innovation for the production of revenue. Beyond this ultimate shared goal, the interests of universities and businesses diverge. Universities value intellectual property not only as a revenue-producing resource, but also as a tool in the advancement and dissemination of knowledge. These divergent interests can result in conflicts . . . .

Hall (1999, p. 3) also discusses this issue, which she refers to as the "two worlds" of research and development:[9]

> [W]e might expect particular tensions to arise in settings where the conventions of one world (private industry) come up against the conventions of another (public R&D and university science).

Lead participants in the 38 projects studied were asked a variety of direct-response and open-ended questions from which we judged if intellectual property issues were an insurmountable barrier or a significant stumbling block with regard to a university being included as a research partner in the project.[10] Thirty-two percent of the survey respondents noted that IP issues were indeed an insurmountable barrier. Representative remarks from lead participants, in projects without university involvement, who reported that IP barriers prevented the partnership with a university are:[11]

> In general, companies such as ours believe that we own the intellectual property developed for us under sponsored

research. This view is often not shared by potential university partners.

IP is often a stumbling block for collaborations because many universities want to publish results prior to IP protection, and sometimes will not grant exclusivity of results.

In general, the difficulties that usually prevent a successful partnership [with a university] are (1) intellectual property issues and (2) the university partner's lack of understanding of our business.

Some projects, in which intellectual property issues prevented a university from being a research partner, were nevertheless able to use a university as a subcontractor.[12] Observations from lead participants in such projects are:

Universities feel that if their brainpower and equipment were used to develop a new technology then they should benefit financially as an industrial partner would. However, to do so they should be prepared to take an equity position in any commercial ventures derived from the technical work.

University licensing offices have an overinflated view of the value they bring to the project. [They have] unrealistic licensing expectations [and] an overinflated view of the value of intellectual property.

We assembled data on several characteristics of each of the 38 ATP-funded projects in the sample. In particular, we know the total budget of each project; the amount of the total budget that is funded by the ATP and hence the percentage of each project that was ATP-funded; the proposed length or duration of each project;[13] the size of the lead participant;[13] the organizational structure of the awardee (single participant, joint venture with no university involvement, joint venture with a university as a subcontractor, joint venture with a university as a research partner, joint venture with a university as a subcontractor and as a research partner); if the lead participant has previously been involved with a university as a research partner; and the technology class that characterizes the research of the project. More specifically, for the analysis that follows we define the following variables:

IPbar is a dichotomous variable equaling 1 if the lead participant in the project reported that there were intellectual property rights issues that created insurmountable barriers thus preventing a university from being a research partner in the project, and 0 otherwise;[14]

total is the total cost, including the ATP award for the research project, measured in thousands of dollars.

atppct is the percentage of total project cost funded by the ATP;[15]

length equals the length of the research project in years;[16]

small equals 1 if the lead participant is a small-sized firm, and 0 otherwise;

medium equals 1 if the lead participant is a medium-sized firm, and 0 otherwise;

large equals 1 if the lead participant is a large-sized firm, and 0 otherwise;

nonprof equals 1 if the lead participant is a nonprofit organization, and 0 otherwise;

s equals 1 if the awardee is a single participant, and 0 otherwise;

jv equals 1 if the awardee is a joint venture with no university involvement, and 0 otherwise;

jvs equals 1 if the awardee is a joint venture with a university as a subcontractor, and 0 otherwise;

jvu equals 1 if the awardee is a joint venture with a university as a research partner, and 0 otherwise;

jvus equals 1 if the awardee is a joint venture with a university as a subcontractor and as a research partner, and 0 otherwise;

prevuniv equals 1 if the lead participant has previously been involved with a university as a research partner, and 0 otherwise.[17]

All of the above information, except for *IPbar* and *prevuniv* came from the ATP; information about *IPbar* and *prevuniv* came from the surveys.

Descriptive statistics on each of these variables are in Tables I and II. The sample of 38 projects is divided into those for which the lead participant reported an insurmountable IP barrier (12 observations), and those for which IP issues were not so characterized (26 observations). Of these 26, 13 were joint ventures with university(ies) as research partners (*jvu* and *jvus*). Not surprisingly, none of these joint ventures reported an insurmountable IP barrier to partnering (see Table II).[18] Thus some of our subsequent analysis focuses only on the 25 observations for joint ventures without university partners (*jv*, *jvs*) and for single participant projects (*s*), of which 12

Table I
Sample descriptive statistics

Variable	Mean	S.D.	Median	1Q	3Q	Min	Max
	All projects ($N = 38$)						
Project size ($1000)	10,794	8,533	7,486	3,935	15,544	1,987	39,070
ATP share of funding	52.2%	8.0%	49.5%	49.0%	50.0%	43.7%	83.6%
Length (years)	3.5	1.2	3.0	3.0	5.0	1.5	5.0
	Projects excluding JVs with university partners ($N = 25$)						
Project size ($1000)	8,912	7,575	6,481	3,312	11,909	1,987	31,309
ATP share of funding	53.8%	9.5%	49.4%	49.0%	57.1%	43.7%	83.6%
Length (years)	3.2	1.1	3.0	2.0	4.0	1.5	5.0
	Projects with IP barriers ($N = 12$)						
Project size ($1000)	8,303	9,108	3,464	2,930	12,874	1,987	31,309
ATP share of funding	57.3%	10.3%	51.9%	50.0%	63.1%	49.0%	83.6%
Length (years)	2.7	1.2	2.1	2.0	3.0	1.5	5.0

reported insurmountable barriers. We show descriptive statistics for this sample of 25 observations in Table I also.

We also found that all projects with a single participant who reported prior experience with a university partner reported that IP was an insurmountable barrier in partnering with universities. Thus *s* plus *prevuniv* is a perfect predictor. However, those without prior experience also occasionally encountered IP barriers, so we included

Table II
Sample descriptive statistics (binary variables)

Variable	All projects ($N = 38$)		Projects with IP barriers ($N = 12$)		Projects with no IP barriers ($N = 26$)	
	Mean	Number = 1	Mean	Number = 1	Mean	Number = 1
IP barriers? (*IPbar*)	0.316	12	1.000	12	0.000	0
Small lead participant (*small*)	0.368	14	0.417	5	0.346	9
Medium lead participant (*medium*)	0.132	5	0.167	2	0.115	3
Large lead participant (*large*)	0.316	12	0.417	5	0.269	7
Non-profit lead participant (*nonprof*)	0.184	7	0.000	0	0.269	7
Single participant (*s*)	0.237	9	0.583	7	0.077	2
Joint venture with no university (*jv*)	0.211	8	0.167	2	0.231	6
Joint venture with university as subcontractor (*jvs*)	0.211	8	0.250	3	0.192	5
Joint venture with university as partner (*jvu*)	0.211	8	0.000	0	0.308	8
Joint venture with university as partner and subcontractor (*jvus*)	0.132	5	0.000	0	0.192	5
Prior experience with a university (*prevuniv*)	0.789	30	0.917	11	0.731	19
Info. and computer systems	0.237	9	0.250	3	0.231	6
Materials	0.211	8	0.167	2	0.231	6
Manufacturing	0.132	5	0.000	0	0.192	5
Electronics	0.079	3	0.167	2	0.038	1
Energy and environment	0.026	1	0.000	0	0.038	1
Biotechnology	0.237	9	0.250	3	0.231	6
Chemicals (*chem*)	0.079	3	0.167	2	0.038	1

all these projects in our estimating sample because they provide some information on the determinants of IP barriers.

Table I shows that the projects encountering IP problems tend to be smaller, shorter, and have a higher ATP share of the funding. Besides the fact that joint ventures with university partners and non-profit lead participants do not encounter insurmountable IP barriers, Table II shows that such barriers are enhanced, rather than diminished, by prior experience with a university. Among the three technology classes that are more highly represented – information technology, materials, and biotechnology – IP issues as an insurmountable barrier preventing universities being a research partner are not noticeably different.

In an effort to understand more systematically when intellectual property issues are an insurmountable barrier preventing university participation as a research partner (not as a subcontrac-

tor), we considered the following exploratory model:[19]

(1) *Probability (insurmountable IP barrier) = F(atppct, length, prevuniv, chem, small, large)*

where each of the variables has been previously defined, with the exception of the dummy variable that classifies projects in chemicals technology (*chem* = 1, and 0 otherwise). Equation (1) was estimated as a probit model using *IPbar* as the dependent variable and the estimates are shown in Table III. We consider 3 samples of observations, all of which give the same general conclusions. Column (1) contains estimates for the whole sample, column (2) for the sample of observations excluding those with non-profit lead participants, and columns (3) and (4) for the sample of observations excluding joint ventures with university participants (*jvu* and *jvus*).

Table III
Predicting the probability of insurmountable IP barriers

Number of observations	(1) 38		(2) 31		(3) 25		(4) 25		(4) D(prob)
ATP share	27.8	(13.2)**	25.2	(12.9)*	22.4	(12.3)*	23.7	(12.3)*	4.43
Length of project	−1.59	(0.77)**	−1.40	(0.74)*	−1.57	(0.79)**	−1.24	(0.69)*	−0.23
Prior university experience	5.35	(2.80)*	4.95	(2.72)*	4.39	(2.62)*	4.81	(2.63)*	0.90
Chemicals	4.44	(1.84)**	3.89	(1.80)**	3.77	(1.82)**	3.36	(1.70)**	0.63
Small lead participant					−1.51	(1.51)			
Large lead participant					−1.41	(1.37)			
Intercept	−15.2	(8.4)*	−13.9	(8.2)*	−10.1	(8.2)	−13.3	(8.0)*	
Log likelihood	−9.67		−9.17		−7.80		−8.49		
Pseudo r-squared	0.673		0.663		0.668		0.627		
Chi-squared for zero coefficients (p-value)	28.1	(.000)	23.0	(.000)	19.0	(.004)	17.6	(.001)	

Notes: Coefficient estimates are from the cumulative normal probability that partnering encountered insurmountable IP barriers.

Standard error estimates are shown in parentheses. *, **, *** denote significance at the 10%,5%, and 1% level respectively.

Specification (2) omits 7 observations where the lead participant is non-profit because for these observations the absence of IP barriers is predicted perfectly.

Specifications (3) and (4) omit 6 additional observations for joint ventures with university partners; these observations also predict the absence of barriers perfectly. All of the non-profit participants are also joint ventures with university partners. In specification (4), the average (over the sample) derivative of the probability with respect to the variable is shown in the last column.

Our first finding is that the size of the lead participant does not help to predict the presence of insurmountable IP barriers (column (3)) in the presence of the other variables, so our preferred specification is that in columns (1), (2), and (4), all of which have similar findings. This last fact means that the results in column (1) are not simply because of the fact that joint ventures with university participants that have not encountered IP barriers or have overcome them (the group we excluded in columns (3) and (4)) are different in other ways from the rest of the sample.

Focusing now on column (4) in Table III, we see that in spite of the small sample, the overall model is significant in predicting the probability of encountering IP barriers to partnering and that it has a pseudo R^2 of just over 60 percent. Difficulties in negotiating IP among the partners are associated positively with ATP's share in the project, the lead participant's prior experience with university partnering, and being a project in the chemicals industry, and negatively with the length of the project. We will discuss each of these factors in turn.

First, as the percentage of project costs that is funded by the ATP increases, the probability that IP issues will create insurmountable barriers inhibiting a university from joining the project as a research partner also increases. The calculated partial derivative of the probability with respect to this variable is quite large – 4.4. At the mean value of 54 percent, an increase in *atppct* of one standard deviation (10%) predicts that the probability of there being an insurmountable IP barrier increases by 0.44 or by 44 percent, albeit with a standard error of about 23 percent.[20]

Our interpretation is that the ATP share in project funding is an instrument that is highly correlated with the expected inappropriability or publicness of the research results. The larger the percentage of a project that a firm is willing to fund, the more the firm expects to be able to appropriate an adequate portion of the research results from that project and hence the less public the nature of the results. Increases in ATP's funding percentage, mirroring decreases in the firm's funding percentage, thus reflect research results that are expected by the firm to be less appropriable or relatively more public in nature.

At the same time, these firms have been unable to reach an agreement with a university partner to do the research. As a result, it logically follows that as the percentage of funding from ATP increases the "two worlds" of R&D are increasingly in conflict, with the firm trying even harder to capture all intellectual property while the university is trying to make it public. Hence, IP issues become more noticeable and act as a barrier to the industry-university research partnership as ATP's funding percentage increases.[21] Alternatively, it is possible that ATP funding is to a certain extent substituting for the university in the cases where negotiation between the potential partners broke down because of differences over IP rights.

The second finding in column (4) of Table III is that IP barriers are greater the shorter the length of the project. Again, the partial effect is large. As project length increases from the mean of 3.17 years to 3.67 years (approximately six months), the estimated probability of there being an insurmountable IP barrier decreases by 11.5 percent, with a standard error of approximately 6 percent.

Our interpretation is that the length of the project is highly correlated with the uncertainty of the research findings. The longer the expected duration of the research at the time the research is funded, the less certain the firm or the university will be as to the intellectual property characteristics of the research results. Hence, the longer the expected duration of the research project, the less likely it is that either party will face an insurmountable IP barrier because neither party is able to define meaningfully the boundaries of characteristics that the research results will have. Note that this does not rule out the possibility that unanticipated conflicts over IP rights may arise in the future, it is simply that IP barriers do not prevent the project from starting.

Our third finding is that lead participants that have been involved with universities as research partners in the past are, other factors held constant, relatively more likely to find IP issues with a university insurmountable. On average across the sample, changing *prevuniv* from 0 to 1 increases the predicted probability of insurmountable barriers by 0.9. Evidently, experience with

universities as partners does not, given the currently available IP-protection mechanisms, allow
resolution of IP issues. Instead, the experience
appears to make industry aware of the insurmountable barriers that exist given current institutional arrangements for protecting intellectual
property.[22]

Alternative specifications of equation (1) were
examined (not reported here). In all cases, the
only technology effect that was significant was
that for projects in chemicals technology, thus the
other technology class dummies were deleted.
Other researchers have shown that patent protection is especially important to firms in the chemicals industry.[23] Hence, the university would also
find it financially attractive to have ownership
rights in this technology area, and thus conflict
arises. On average across the sample, projects
involving chemicals technology have a probability
of insurmountable IP barriers that is higher than
the probability for the other technologies by 0.63.
However, we remind the reader that there are
only 3 chemical projects in our sample, so this
result for the present sample is surely a tentative
one for samples in general.

As we discussed earlier, the best predictor of
insurmountable IP barriers to partnering with a
university was to be one of those projects that
went ahead as a single participant project or as a
joint venture without a university participant.
Thus, the most important finding may be that
there are projects funded by ATP where the
participants may have desired university cooperation but found that they could not reach agreement on intellectual property issues.

4. Concluding observations

We interpret our findings from this exploratory
investigation on two levels. At one level, we have
demonstrated that IP issues between firms and
universities do exist, and in some cases those
issues represent an insurmountable barrier which
prevents the sought-after research partnership
from ever coming about. Such situations have a
greater likelihood of occurring when the research
is expected to lead to less appropriable results
that thus have a relatively greater degree of publicness and when the expected duration of the
research is relatively short term and is thus more

Table IV
Probability of insurmountable IP barriers by type of
research results

		Research results	
		Appropriable (low ATP share)	Inappropriable (high ATP share)
		No Prior University Experience	
Results of research	Certain (short projects)	0.0000	0.2173
	Uncertain (long projects)	0.0000	0.0000
		With Prior University Experience	
Results of research	Certain (short projects)	0.3160	0.9997
	Uncertain (long projects)	0.0000	0.8760

Notes: These predicted probabilities are based on the estimates in specification (4) of Table III, for projects in industries other than chemicals. The variables for ATP share and
the length of the project have been set to their mean $+/-$
one standard deviation.
Being a non-profit lead participant or a joint venture with a
university participant predicts the lack of IP barriers perfectly.
These observations have not been used for the predictions in
this table, which is based only on the 25 observations in
column (4) of Table III.

certain in terms of the characteristics of the research findings.

Table IV summarizes these findings. It shows
two panels, one for lead participants with no prior
university partnering experience and one for those
with prior experience. Across the top of the 2×2
matrix we segment the research as being either
appropriable or inappropriable (where inappropriability is an increasing function of the percentage of the research cost that is funded by the
ATP). Along the left of the matrix we segment
the results as being either certain or uncertain
(where uncertainly is an increasing function of
the length of the research project). Within each
cell of the matrix we have simulated the probability of there being insurmountable IP barriers
using the probit estimates in column (4) for projects that are not in chemicals, with inappropri-
ability/appropriability defined for purposes of
these calculations as $+/-$ one standard devia-

tion from the mean of *atppct*, and uncertainty/ certainty defined for purposes of these calculations as + / − one standard deviation from the mean of *length*.

The simulated probabilities provide an interesting descriptive conclusion. First, the probabilities are much higher when the lead participant has prior experience partnering with a university, so that they are aware of the difficulties they may encounter. Second, the probability that insurmountable IP barriers will arise between a firm and a university in terms of partnering are greatest when the intellectual property characteristics of the research are certain and the ability of the firm to appropriate such results is least. Further, the probability of barriers is least when the IP is appropriable yet uncertain. The appropriability of the IP implies less publicness, and then less tension between the "two worlds." Regarding the uncertainty, the evidence in our small sample supports the possibility that, other things being the same, when neither party can define meaningful boundaries for any resulting IP, IP is less likely to be an insurmountable issue, although we recognize that is not logically inevitable. The remaining probabilities in Table IV show the intermediate cases where the two effects of publicness and of uncertainty are to an extent offsetting, although it is clear that appropriability (as measured by the ATP share) is a more important predictor than project length.

At a second and broader level, there is some policy relevance to our findings. From other investigations, there is evidence to conclude that ATP funding is overcoming a *market* failure; in the absence of such funding the research is not likely to have occurred.[24] However, as previously noted in the introduction, Hall, Link, and Scott (2000) have found that a university participating in a research partnership can take on the important role of an ombudsman to anticipate and translate to all involved the complex nature of the research being undertaken. Thus, in such desired situations, as we have shown here, there remains an element of *government* failure. The government has not provided appropriate legal infrastructure. Firms and universities, in an effort to pursue their own research strategies in their separate worlds, are unable to partner because of limitations of the intellectual property protection mechanisms that are currently available.[25]

Notes

1. For a review of the theoretical and empirical literature on research partnerships, see Hagedoorn, Link, and Vonortas (2000).

2. Of the 741 RJVs filed by the end of 1998, 111 had at least one university involved as a research partner. In addition, the average number of university members as a share of the total number of members in an RJV has steadily increased over time.

3. The estimated slope coefficient from a linear regression on time of the percentage of RJVs with at least one university partner is positive and significant. These results and those from other specifications are available from the authors.

4. We realize that this is not a new question. The National Science Foundation hosted a one-day Workshop on Intellectual Property Rights in 1981. "The purpose of the workshop was to find out whether intellectual property issues were inhibiting cooperative research and, if so, how" (National Science Board, 1981, p. 275). The Office of the General Counsel concluded that patents are not always an effective mechanism to resolve intellectual property rights issues.

5. See Link and Scott (forthcoming) for an economic rationale for the ATP as a direct funding program. See also Link (1999) for a discussion of the ATP within the broader context of public/private partnerships in the United States.

6. Information about each project is in the Appendix at the end of the paper.

7. See Cohen, Florida, and Randazzese (forthcoming) for a discussion of intellectual property protection mechanisms that successfully facilitate industry-university collaboration.

8. These authors go on to say, as emphasis for understanding the environment associated with the imposition of IPRs, "[w]hile the university-industry interface might be a key factor in promoting innovation, the complex and varied nature of that interface needs to be understood and explored" (p. 875).

9. See also Dasgupta and David (1992).

10. The survey questionnaires are available from the authors. Each project has a designated lead participant for reporting purposes to the ATP.

11. Siegel, Waldman, and Link (1999) report that the most significant barrier to industry/university technology transfer is a lack of understanding (on the part of firms and universities) regarding corporate, university, and scientific norms and environments.

12. Our data are not rich enough for us to determine if the firm first tried to include the university as a research partner, and then when that failed it included that same university, or another, as a subcontractor.

13. Lead participants are classified by the ATP as being a small firm (less than 500 employees), a large firm (defined as a *Fortune* 500 or equivalent organization), a medium-sized firm (defined as not small or large), or a non-profit organization (such as a trade association).

Appendix:
ATP-funded projects ($n = 38$)

Project no.	Project title
91010016	Ultra-high density magnetic recording heads
91010134	Hybrid superconducting digital system
92010040	Engineering design with injection-molded thermoplastics
92010044	Genosensor technology development
93010079	Flip chip monolithic microwave integrated circuit (MMIC) manufacturing technology
94010079	Engineered surfaces for rolling and sliding contacts
94010135	Enhanced molecular dynamics simulation technology for biotechnology applications
94010178	Rapid agile metrology for manufacturing
94010228	Computer-integrated revision total hip replacement surgery
94010282	Diamond diode field emission display process technology development
94010305	Film technologies to replace paint on aircraft
94020032	Composite production risers
94020039	Low-cost advanced composite process for light transit vehicle manufacturing
94020040	Development of manufacturing methodologies for vehicle composite frames
94020043	Low cost manufacturing and design/sensor technologies for seismic upgrade of bridge columns
94020048	Manufacturing composite structures for the offshore oil industry
94040017	Automated care plans and practice guidelines
94050006	Development of rapid DNA medical diagnostics
94050027	Integrated microfabricated DNA analysis device for diagnosis of complex genetic disorders
94050030	Diagnostic laser desorption mass spectrometry detection of multiplex electrophore tagged DNA
94050033	Automated DNA amplification and fragment size analysis
95010126	Technology development for the smart display – A versatile high-performance video display integrated with electronics
95010150	Development of closed cycle air refrigeration technology for refrigeration markets
95020008	Agile precision sheet-metal stamping
95020026	Flexible low-cost laser machining for motor vehicle manufacturing
95020036	Plasma-based processing of lightweight materials for motor-vehicle components and manufacturing applications
95020062	Fast, volumetric x-ray scanner for three-dimensional characterization of critical objects
95030018	High-performance, variable-data-rate, multimedia magnetic tape recorder
95030022	Technology development for optical-tape-based rapid access affordable mass storage (TRAAMS)
95040027	Advanced distributed video ATM network for creation, editing, and distribution
95050007	Continuous biocatalytic systems for the production of chemicals from renewable resources
95050040	Breakthrough technology for oxidation of alkanes
95080006	Real-time micro-PCR analysis system
95080017	DNA diagnostics using self-detected target-cycling reaction (SD-TCR)
95100019	Healthcare information technology enabling community care
95120015	Model-driven application & integration components for MES
95120027	Advanced process control framework initiative
96010172	A portable genetic analysis system

Note: A description of each project is available at: http://jazz.nist.gov/atpcf/prjbriefs/listmaker.cfm

14. *IPbar* = 0 should be interpreted to mean that the research firm did not face any insurmountable IP barriers when including a university as a research partner, did face issues but overcame them, or did not require a university as a research partner in the project. *IPbar* = 1 should be interpreted to mean that a university was sought to be a research partner, but the relationship could not be finalized because IP issues could not be resolved.

15. By statute, ATP's maximum contribution to a single applicant project is $2 million. For joint ventures of any organizational structure, ATP cannot fund over 50 percent of direct costs.

16. There is a three-year statutory limit on single applicant projects and a five-year limit on joint venture projects.

17. Previous involvement with a university as a research partner was defined on the survey as frequent, infrequent, or never. Here, any previous involvement is captured by the variable *prevuniv*.

18. These 13 observations also included all the projects with a non-profit lead participant.

19. This specification was motivated in large part by the availability of data.

20. The exact effect of any stated change in an explanatory variable can be computed by the interested reader by calculating the effect on the probit index. For that procedure, use the estimated probit coefficients, the means of the variables as shown in Table I, and the stated settings for the explanatory variable in question. The computed index values can then be converted to the associated value of the standard normal probability function.

21. And, we expect this to be the case regardless of the funding agency.

22. As we have noted, there are institutional constraints on ATP's share of total project funding and on project duration. A careful reader might reasonably conclude that the strong effects for ATP's share and project length simply reflect those institutional constraints for single-participant projects versus joint ventures. However, that is not the case. Adding the variable *s*, the qualitative variable for single-participant projects, to the preferred specification with 25 observations, and even accounting for the perfect predictions when single-participant projects have previous experience with universities, the partial derivative for each variable can be estimated. The partial derivative for *s* is not significant, while the remaining partial derivatives tell essentially the same story as reported in Table III. The signs of the partials are the same, and their magnitude and level of significance are quite similar.

23. See, for example, Cohen, Nelson, and Walsh (2000) and particularly the references therein to Levin *et al.* and Mansfield.

24. See Link and Scott (forthcoming) and Link and Scott (1998).

25. At one level, the presence of insurmountable IP issues implies that existing IP protection mechanisms are inadequate given the culture clash between industry and the universities. At another, one might believe that the problem could be an insurmountable culture clash that mechanisms for IP protection could not ameliorate. A look at the initial ATP guidelines shows that in fact government may have failed to provide appropriate IP protection to facilitate university-industry part-

nerships for ATP projects. Technology transfer officers emphasize that a problem for universities was created by the original ATP guidelines because they required that any ATP project patents must be held by the non-university participants. The original ATP guidelines did not recognize the Bayh-Dole Act under which universities are allowed to keep the title to the inventions conceived by their employees under outside sponsorship.

References

Brainard, H.R., 1999 'Survey and Study of Technology Development and Transfer Needs in New York City', *Albany Law Journal of Science and Technology* 9, 423–470.

Brod, A. and A.N. Link, (forthcoming), 'Trends in Cooperative Research Activity: Has the National Cooperative Research Act Been Successful?' in M. Feldman and A.N. Link (eds.), *Science and Technology Policy and the Knowledge-Based Economy*, Kluwer Academic Publishers.

Cohen, W.M., R. Florida, and L. Randazzese, forthcoming, *For Knowledge and Profit: University-Industry Research Centers in the United States*, Oxford: Oxford University Press.

Cohen, W.M., R.R. Nelson, and J.P. Walsh, 2000, 'Protecting Their Intellectual Assets: Appropriability Conditions and Why U.S. Manufacturing Firms Patent (or Not)', NBER Working Paper, No. 7552.

Council on Competitiveness, 1996, *Endless Frontiers, Limited Resources: U.S. R&D Policy for Competitiveness*, Washington, DC: Council on Competitiveness.

Dasgupta, P. and P.A. David, 1992, 'Toward a New Economics of Science', Stanford University: CEPR Publication No. 320.

Feller, I., 1990, 'Universities as Engines of R&D-Based Economic Growth: They Think They Can', *Research Policy* 19, 349–355.

Hagedoorn, J., A.N. Link, and N.S. Vonortas, 2000, 'Research Partnerships', *Research Policy* 29, 567–586.

Hall, B.H., 1999, 'On Copyright and Patent Protection for Software and Databases: A Tale of Two Worlds', mimeo.

Hall, B.H., A.N. Link, and J.T. Scott, 2000, 'Universities as Research Partners', NBER Working Paper No. 7643.

Hounshell, D.A., 1996, 'The Evolution of Industrial Research in the United States', in R.S. Rosenbloom and W.J. Spenser (eds.), *Engines of Innovation: U.S. Industrial Research at the End of an Era*, Boston: Harvard Business School Press.

Link, A.N., 1999, 'Public/Private Partnerships in the United States', *Industry and Innovation* 6, 191–217.

Link, A.N. and J.T. Scott, 1998, *Public Accountability: Evaluating Technology-Based Institutions*, Norwell, MA: Kluwer Academic Publishers.

Link, A.N. and J.T. Scott, forthcoming, 'Public/Private Partnerships: Stimulating Competition in a Dynamic Market', *International Journal of Industrial Organization*.

Mowery, D.C., 1998, 'The Changing Structure of the U.S. National Innovation System: Implications for International Conflict and Cooperation in R&D Policy', *Research Policy* 27, 639–654.

National Science Board, 1981, *University-Industry Research Relationships*, Washington, DC: National Science Foundation.

Rappert, B., A. Webster, and D. Charles, 1999, 'Making Sense of Diversity and Reluctance: Academic-Industrial Relations and Intellectual Property', *Research Policy* **28**, 873–890.

Rosenberg, N. and R.R. Nelson, 1994, 'American Universities and Technical Advance in Industry', *Research Policy* **23**, 323–348.

Siegel, D., D. Waldman, and A.N. Link, 1999, 'Assessing the Impact of Organizational Practices on the Productivity of University Technology Transfer Offices: An Exploratory Study', NBER Working Paper No. 7256.

[5]

Who Is Selling the Ivory Tower? Sources of Growth in University Licensing

Jerry G. Thursby • Marie C. Thursby
Department of Economics, Emory University, Atlanta, Georgia 30322
Dupree College of Management, Georgia Tech, Atlanta, Georgia 30332,
and NBER, Cambridge, Massachusetts 02138
jthursb@emory.edu

Historically, commercial use of university research has been viewed in terms of spillovers. Recently, there has been a dramatic increase in technology transfer through licensing as universities attempt to appropriate the returns from faculty research. This change has prompted concerns regarding the source of this growth—specifically, whether it suggests a change in the nature of university research. We develop an intermediate input model to examine the extent to which the growth in licensing is due to the productivity of observable inputs or driven by a change in the propensity of faculty and administrators to engage in commercializing university research. We model licensing as a three-stage process, each involving multiple inputs. Nonparametric programming techniques are applied to survey data from 64 universities to calculate total factor productivity (TFP) growth in each stage. To examine the sources of TFP growth, the productivity analysis is augmented by survey evidence from businesses who license-in university inventions. Results suggest that increased licensing is due primarily to an increased willingness of faculty and administrators to license and increased business reliance on external R&D rather than a shift in faculty research.
(*University Licensing; Invention Disclosures; Patents; Entrepreneurial Activity*)

1. Introduction

According to the Association of University Technology Managers (AUTM) surveys, licensing activity in U.S. research universities has increased dramatically in the 1990s. For the 64 universities responding to the survey in each of the years 1994–1998, yearly invention disclosures increased 7.1% per year. Over the same period, new patent applications and licenses and options executed annually grew by 17.1% and 8.4%, respectively. In 1998 alone the 132 universities responding to the survey reported a total of 9,555 disclosures, 4,140 new patent applications, and 3,078 licenses and options executed.

This growth in the so-called "commercial outputs" of academic research has received considerable attention both from technology managers and university administrators who cite it as evidence of the increasing contribution of universities to the economy (e.g.,

AUTM press release, 1998) and policy makers who, in contrast, question the impact of commercial activity on the conduct and industrial impact of faculty research (Congressional Record 1999). Unfortunately, there is little evidence to evaluate the arguments since these growth rates alone tell nothing about the productivity of university resources devoted to technology transfer, nor do they provide evidence on the sources of increased licensing.

In this article, we explore the source(s) of this growth in university licensing. We focus on the role of inputs, including intermediate inputs, in the process, and we examine the extent to which the explosion in licensing is being driven by faculty and university administrators becoming more entrepreneurial. In particular, is the primary source of growth simply an increased propensity for university administrators to patent and attempt to license faculty inventions? To

MANAGEMENT SCIENCE © 2002 INFORMS
Vol. 48, No. 1, January 2002 pp. 90–104

0025-1909/02/4801/0090$5.00
1526-5501 electronic ISSN

THURSBY AND THURSBY
Sources of Growth in University Licensing

what extent is growth due to an increased propensity of businesses to license university inventions? Has the propensity of faculty to disclose inventions increased either because they are more willing to license as well as publish their research or because their research has shifted toward topics of more interest to industry? It is the latter element of faculty propensity that has been the focus of policy discussions.

We model technology transfer as a three-stage production process involving multiple inputs in each stage. The three stages follow the sequence of steps typically involved in licensing university inventions. First-stage outputs are invention disclosures, which are filed by faculty when they believe their research results have commercial potential. In addition to faculty, first-stage inputs include federal and industry research support as well as TTO (technology transfer office) personnel.[1] Disclosures are intermediate inputs to a second stage in which the TTO applies for patents on those disclosures they believe can be patented and licensed. Inputs for this stage also include a measure of faculty quality to capture patent potential. In turn, patent applications and disclosures are used along with other licensing inputs in a third stage to produce license and option agreements.

We provide two types of evidence on the sources of growth. The first is a productivity analysis using AUTM survey data for 64 U.S. universities for 1994–1998 that provide evidence on the extent to which growth in each stage is a direct result of increases in inputs devoted to technology transfer. The second is based on a survey of businesses that licensed university inventions over the period 1993–1997. These survey data, in conjunction with our productivity results, allow us to consider the extent to which licensing has grown because of changes in the propensity of faculty and administrators to engage in commercial activity and/or changes in business behavior toward universities.

In the productivity analysis, we use nonparametric programming techniques developed by Fare et al. (1994) to examine productivity growth. For each of

the three stages, we construct a best practice frontier that represents the maximum feasible stage output given available inputs and existing attitudes or knowledge. This approach allows us to identify both frontier performance and operation within the frontier. Thus, total factor productivity (TFP) growth can be decomposed into two components: one reflecting a frontier shift and another showing movement toward (catching up) or away from the frontier. Given the dramatic growth of licensing activity and reorganization of a number of TTOs during the early 1990s, both components of growth are likely to be important.[2]

For the 64 universities in our sample, we find TFP growth rates for disclosures and patent applications that are roughly 5% lower than the nominal growth rates noted above, and, for licenses executed, TFP growth is negative. While this implies that much of the growth in university commercial activity stems from input growth, it also suggests that changed propensities are an important element of growth. Of particular note is the negative TFP growth in licenses that, coupled with increased disclosures and patent applications, can be interpreted as evidence of universities delving more "deeply" into the available pool of commercializable inventions. To the extent that universities are trying to increase the number of inventions licensed without a concurrent shift in the underlying distribution of inventions, we would expect a decline in the commercial appeal of inventions at the margin. Thus, we would expect inventions, on average, to have less commercial potential, even though the total value of inventions licensed would increase. This result is particularly interesting in light of Henderson et al.'s (1998) evidence from an earlier period (1965–1988) that as university patenting increased, the importance (as measured by citations) of university patents declined.

To examine why propensities to engage in university/firm licensing have changed—that is, to examine the possible sources of TFP growth—we draw on the results of our business survey as well as the productivity analysis. For the first stage, our interest is in whether the growth in disclosures (net of

---

[1] TTO (technology transfer office) personnel are university employees responsible for encouraging and aiding faculty in disclosing and for executing licenses agreements with industry.

[2] Thirty-five percent of the TTOs responding to our earlier university survey were reorganized during the 1990s (Thursby et al. 2001).

inputs) is due to a reorientation of faculty research toward the needs of industry and away from basic research, or whether the growth is due to a greater willingness on the part of faculty to disclose as well as publish the results of their research. For the second stage, we focus on whether productivity growth stems from a greater receptivity of university administrations to industry contracts. In the final stage, our major interest is the extent to which growth stems from changes in industry R&D[3] or from factors leading to the growth in disclosures and patent applications.

The survey supports the view that industry reliance on university inventions increased during this period, and, in indicating the reasons, respondents weighted changes in their own R&D more heavily than a change in faculty research toward topics of greater interest to industry. Together with the productivity results, this suggests that the primary reason for increased invention disclosures may indeed be an increased propensity for faculty to disclose rather than a change in research focus. The industry survey also supports an increased receptivity of universities to industry contracts. This result, together with the fact that these businesses increased their contractual agreements with universities, reinforces our interpretation of our stage three productivity results that negative TFP growth most likely reflects university efforts to patent and license inventions with marginal commercial potential.

Finally, we find that much of the growth in TFP for the disclosure and patent stages comes from catching up by universities that were operating within the frontier. Only for the patent stage do we find both a shift in best practice and catching up. Further, we find that growth patterns differ according to public/private status and whether a university has a medical school.

These results contribute to the growing literature on the industrial impact of academic research. The bulk of this literature has focused either on the role of patents and publications in the transfer process (see Adams 1990, Henderson et al. 1998, and Jaffe et al.

1993) or on consulting, sponsored research or institutional ties (see Cohen et al. 1998; Mansfield 1995; Zucker et al. 1994, 1998). While several recent papers provide evidence on the nature of university licensing (e.g., Jensen and Thursby 2001, Mowery et al. 2001a,b, Mowery et al. 2001, Siegel et al. 1999, Thursby et al. 2001, Thursby and Kemp 2001), none of them provides a structure that allows analysis of the sources of growth.

One benefit from our structure is that we can comment on the growing policy debates on the Bayh-Dole Act of 1980, which gave universities the right to license inventions from federally funded research. Much of the concern of those who question the act's impact comes from fears that financial returns to licensing would divert faculty from basic to applied research. In their study of licensing activities at Columbia, Stanford, and the University of California system, Mowery et al. (2001a,b) point out that faculty at these universities had a long history of applied research well before the Bayh-Dole Act. Since neither their work nor ours examines the pattern of faculty research, we *cannot reject* the notion that faculty research has shifted. However, the intermediate input structure of our productivity analysis, combined with our industry survey, allows us to show that changes in the direction of faculty research appear relatively less important than other factors, such as the dramatic increase in the propensity of administrators to patent and license faculty inventions. This was, in fact, an intended effect of the Bayh-Dole Act.

2. University Technology Transfer: A Multistage Process

In this section, we provide background information on the licensing process and present our multistage model. The programming approach we adopt for the productivity analysis is described in §3, and the results are given in §4. The business survey is discussed in §5; §6 concludes.

2.1. Disclosures
The licensing process begins with a faculty member reporting a discovery that he or she believes has commercial potential. This report, or disclosure, involves

---

[3] This explanation follows from discussions with industry licensing executives.

faculty providing the TTO with information on the invention and inventors, funding sources, potential licensees, as well as barriers to patent potential (such as prior publication).

It is important to realize that invention disclosures represent a subset of university research with commercial potential. The TTO personnel we interviewed in an earlier study of university licensing in U.S. universities indicated that they believe less than half of the faculty inventions with commercial potential are disclosed to their office (Thursby et al. 2001). In some cases faculty may not realize the commercial potential of their ideas, but often they do not disclose inventions because they are unwilling to risk delaying publication in the patent and license process. Half of the firms in our industry survey noted that they include delay of publication clauses in at least 90% of their university contracts (Thursby and Thursby 1999). The average delay is nearly four months, and some firms require as much as a year's delay.

Faculty who specialize in basic research may not disclose because they are unwilling to spend time on the applied research and development that is often needed for businesses to be interested in licensing university inventions.[4] Respondents to our TTO and industry surveys noted that 88% and 84%, respectively, of licensed university inventions require further development, and that 45% and 44%, respectively, of licensed inventions are no more than a "proof of concept" at the time of license. The firms noted that for such inventions, faculty cooperate in further development more than 40% of the time. Finally, some faculty may refuse to disclose for "philosophical" reasons related to their notions of the proper role of academic scientists and engineers. Thus, for a variety of reasons, the TTO personnel we interviewed indicated that one of their major challenges is obtaining faculty disclosures.

We model invention disclosures for university u ($DISC^u$) as a function of observable and unobservable inputs. Observable inputs are faculty size, research funds, and the number of full-time equivalent personnel in the TTO ($TTOFTE^u$). Since disclosures

are generally based on research that has been ongoing for some time, we use the average over the preceding three years of the amounts of federal research support ($LAGFED^u$) and industry-sponsored research ($LAGIND^u$). For faculty size, we use the number of faculty in each of the major program areas—biological sciences, engineering, and physical sciences ($TOTFAC^u_{i=1,2,3}$). By not aggregating faculty across fields, we attempt to capture the fact that research methods and market interest in inventions can differ markedly across the sciences and engineering.[5]

The unobservable inputs are the faculty's *propensity to disclose* ($PROP^u_1$) and the probability of invention discovery (Π_1). Thus,

$$DISC^u = f_1(TTOFTE^u, LAGFED^u, LAGIND^u,$$
$$TOTFAC^u_{i=1,2,3}, PROP^u_1, \Pi_1). \quad (2.1)$$

The propensity to disclose reflects both the direction of faculty research and faculty willingness to disclose, and it can be influenced by the policies and practices of university central administrations as well as the perceived potential for monetary gain. Π_1 represents the probability of discovery, conditional on the level of research effort (e.g., research support and faculty size) and split of effort between basic or applied research. In terms of an individual invention, Π_1 represents the "black box" probability that a given amount of research effort will result in an invention, which we assume is independent of the university. Given the short time frame of our analysis (five years), it is unlikely that Π_1 has changed significantly, if at all.

2.2. Patents

Once an invention is disclosed, the TTO evaluates patent and commercial potential. From our earlier survey, it is clear that many TTOs apply for patents only when they expect to find licensees easily. Mowery et al. (2001b) note that six years after disclosure slightly more than 20% of disclosures at Stanford and the University of California system have patents.

---

[4] See Mansfield (1995) and Zucker et al. (1994) regarding faculty who are successful in both applied and basic research.

[5] As discussed in Thursby and Kemp (2001) engineering is more applied than the other fields, and it is also said that biological sciences have more of a seller's market than the other two.

Of course, many inventions, such as copyrightable software and reagent materials, are not eligible for patent protection.

We consider new patent applications ($PATENTS^u$) by university u, rather than patents awarded, as our measure of second stage output, in part because of substantial lags between application and issue, but also because patent applications are a better measure of a university's interest in commercialization than are patents awarded. Observable inputs to the patent stage are the number of disclosures, number of personnel in the TTO, and a measure of faculty quality. The latter is included to adjust for possible differences in commercial quality and novelty of disclosures across universities. Like our measure of faculty size, the quality measure is by major program field ($QUAL^u_{i=1,2,3}$). Patent applications are also a function of an unobservable *propensity to patent* ($PROP^u_2$). Since the decision to apply for a patent (which is ultimately owned by the university) is largely made by TTO personnel, the propensity to patent is indicative of the commercial aggressiveness of the university central administration.[6] Thus, university u's second-stage production is modeled as

$$PATENTS^u = f_2(DISC^u, TTOFTE^u,$$
$$QUAL^u_{i=1,2,3}, PROP^u_2). \quad (2.2)$$

Note that faculty interests in commercialization enter through the observable $DISC^u$.

2.3. License Agreements
License and option agreements executed by university u ($LCEXEC^u$) are modeled as a function of the numbers of disclosures and patent applications as well as the size of the TTO office. We include both disclosures and patent applications because some licenses are executed without patent protection and the fact that a patent application is made may well provide information about the perceived quality of patentable disclosures. As was the case with patent applications,

---

[6] It is often the decision of the TTO as to whether a patent is applied for. In our survey of TTOs we found that the TTO believes it closely reflects the interests of their central administration (see the analysis in Jensen and Thursby 2001).

we include faculty quality in an attempt to adjust for possible differences in commercial quality and novelty of disclosures and patent applications across universities, and hence likelihood of finding a licensee. Unobservable inputs are the university's *propensity to license* inventions ($PROP^u_3$) as well as the distribution of industry interest in university inventions, Π_3. Our model of licenses and options executed is

$$LCEXEC^u = f_3(DISC^u, PATENTS^u, TTOFTE^u,$$
$$QUAL^u_{i=1,2,3}, PROP^u_3, \Pi_3). \quad (2.3)$$

$PROP^u_3$ reflects the TTO's ability and knowledge as well as their aggressiveness in finding potential licensees. Π_3 represents market conditions that are independent of the other inputs. In terms of a single invention, it is the probability of finding a match in the market conditional on invention characteristics. Since both $PROP^u_3$ and Π_3 could have changed during our sample period (and our business survey indicates a change in Π_3), we are not able to identify their separate effects. Note that faculty and administration propensities enter through $DISC^u$ and $PATENTS^u$.

An alternative approach to modeling the last stage would be to include license revenue and/or sponsored research associated with licenses as outputs. This would allow us to analyze TFP in terms of the returns to licensing, and the programming techniques we employ are well suited for examining multiple outputs. There are, however, several problems with taking this approach. While AUTM collects information on royalty income and sponsored research associated with licenses, royalty income in any given year comes not only from current licenses but also from licenses executed in previous years. In many cases, the licenses executed may have been 10 or more years prior. It is also not clear how systematic the relation between royalty income and license inputs is since the distribution of royalty revenue is highly skewed. In our earlier survey, we found that on average 76% of the license revenue reported by universities is attributable to their top five inventions. Sponsored research associated with licenses is clearly a function of licenses and inputs within the same year. The problem with using this as a measure of output is that we know TTO personnel often trade off royalties and sponsored research in their negotiations.

As discussed in §4.1, we calculate TFP for sponsored research, but we believe licenses executed is a more reliable measure of output.

3. A Frontier Analysis of Total Factor Productivity

We examine productivity in each of the three stages using an approach developed by Fare et al. (1994). The approach is based on data envelopment analysis (DEA), which is a nonparametric linear programming approach to comparing inputs and outputs. For each of the three stages and for each of the universities, DEA produces a yearly efficiency rating or score by first determining the set of universities that exhibit "best practice" for the stage under consideration. These universities are said to form the production frontier that relates inputs and outputs. All other universities are then compared to the subset of best practice universities that they most resemble in terms of inputs and outputs. Thus, for each stage and for each university and year, DEA determines whether the university lies on the frontier (exhibits best practice) or, if not, how "far" from the frontier it lies. Yearly changes in the frontier and performance relative to it allow us to examine growth in each stage.

It is important to note that the programming approach is not statistically based and therefore does not allow for statistical tests of hypotheses.[7] Its advantage is that it imposes very little structure on the problem. DEA was developed to examine technical efficiency of not-for-profit institutions that provide (possibly) multiple outputs (or services) using multiple inputs where price data are either unavailable or distorted. The only data required are input and output quantities, and no assumptions are made on functional form. No restrictions are placed on institutional objectives. This is particularly important for our case since universities have multiple objectives in their technology transfer. In our earlier university survey, we found that many TTOs view themselves as

balancing a variety of objectives ranging from attracting industry-sponsored research for faculty to maximizing license income for their central administration. Others, particularly public university TTOs, view the public use of university technology within their state as one of their objectives.

The idea behind the best practice frontier is most easily seen in the case of a single input and single output. Suppose university u produces output y^u from input x^u, then any other university j with input $x^j = x^u$ should be able to produce at least y^u; otherwise, it is inefficient. If j produces more than y^u when using the same input level as u, then university u is inefficient. Similarly, if university j produces $y^j = y^u$, then it should use no more than x^u or it is inefficient. If j uses less than x^u, then u is inefficient. Best practice performance for a university in any stage and year simply means that no other university is doing better in that stage and year given their inputs and outputs.

In our case, each stage has a single output but multiple inputs so that DEA involves the maximization of the ratio of a single output to a linear combination of inputs. Essentially, in DEA each university in each stage is compared to all other universities in the same stage to determine if some combination of other universities has a larger ratio of output to a linear combination of inputs. If no combination of universities has a larger ratio, then the university under examination is said to be efficient and it lies on the best practice frontier. Otherwise, the university is said to be inefficient. An efficiency score for a university is the fraction of potential output produced by the university; for example, a score of 0.6 implies that, based on the performance of comparable universities on the frontier, the university is producing 60% of what it could be producing. A precise statement of the linear programming problem is found in Appendix A.

Once we have established the best practice frontier for each year for some stage and the position of each university vis-à-vis that frontier, we can then measure TFP changes from year to year for each university. The measure of TFP growth is the geometric mean of two Malmquist indexes, one of which is based on the best practice frontier in period t and the other based on the frontier in $t+1$.[8]

---

[7] There has been some recent work on distribution theory with regards to DEA output, but that work is nascent (see the discussion in Grosskopf 1996). A problem we face here is that the efficiency scores (and, hence, TFP growth rates) are not independent so that standard statistical tests are inappropriate.

[8] See Caves et al. (1982) for the properties of the Malmquist index.

THURSBY AND THURSBY
Sources of Growth in University Licensing

TFP growth can be decomposed into two components. One is the component of productivity change that stems from movement toward or away from frontiers in successive years; it is growth due to either catching up or lagging of universities not on the frontier in at least one period. The other is the component of productivity change that is due to frontier shifts between successive years. This effect is said to represent technical change. This notion of technical change is quite general and simply represents changes in output that cannot be attributed to a change in input usage or to a change in relative efficiency. Readers interested in a more precise statement of this measure of TFP growth and its decomposition are directed to Appendix A.

Since the DEA analysis controls for observable inputs, both technical change and changes in efficiency reflect changes in the unobservable inputs, hence they are useful in examining the sources of growth. That is, the unobservable component ($PROP_1^u$) of $DISC^u$ reflects both changes in faculty research and propensity to disclose; both of which can be influenced by university policy. In the $PATENTS^u$ stage, faculty attitudes are captured by the observable $DISC^u$, and the unobservable input ($PROP_2^u$) reflects TTO (central administration) attitudes. In the $LCEXEC^u$ stage, unobservable inputs reflect TTO and market characteristics ($PROP_3^u$ and Π_3). Thus, changes in TFP in Stage 1 reflect changes in $PROP_1^u$, while for Stage 2 TFP changes reflect changes in $PROP_2^u$, and for Stage 3 TFP changes reflect changes in $PROP_3^u$ and/or Π_3.

4. Productivity Analysis

In this section, we present both efficiency and TFP growth rates for each of the stages defined in §2 for a sample of 64 universities. The TFP growth rates are based on a constant returns to scale production frontier. Information on data is in Appendix B.

Before turning to results, we note that our sample of 64 universities represents a substantial fraction of all research conducted by and commercial activity of U.S. universities. In 1998, our sample accounts for almost 54% of federal research support and 57% of industry support to all U.S. universities. The sample

Table 1   Growth Rates, 1994–1998

	Nominal Growth Rates	Technical Change	Efficiency	Total Factor Productivity
Invention disclosures	1.071	0.983	1.045	1.027
Patent applications	1.171	1.094	1.025	1.121
Licenses	1.084	1.130	0.870	0.983

accounts for 61% of licenses executed, 59% of disclosures, and 62% of new patent applications by the 132 respondents to the 1998 AUTM survey. We are confident that our sample represents more than half of the population of research and licensing conducted at U.S. universities during the period of our observations (1994–1998).

4.1. Total Factor Productivity Growth

Table 1 gives the geometric means of our computed indexes of TFP growth, as well as the output (nominal) growth in each stage. Our measures of productivity growth give a more tempered view of growth in commercial activity than do output indexes (which are typically reported). For example, the growth rates in disclosures and patent applications are 4.4% and 5% higher, respectively, than the TFP growth rates. For licenses the difference is dramatic, with licenses executed growing at 8.4% per year and TFP falling 1.7% per year.

What immediately stands out is the large annual TFP growth rate (12.1%) in the patent stage as compared to either disclosures (2.7%) or licenses executed (−1.7%).[9] These growth rates account for growth in observed inputs, so that TFP growth can be interpreted as reflecting changes in the unobservable

---

[9] Beginning in June 1995, provisional patent applications were permitted. Some have argued that this has increased patent activity in universities since it allows faculty to more quickly publish results without compromising U.S. patent rights, although provisional patents can endanger foreign patent rights. Unfortunately, the AUTM survey counts a provisional patent application as a new patent application (although a provisional that is converted to a regular application is only counted once), thus some of the patent growth could be a result of the introduction of provisional applications. However, the TFP growth rate between 1993 and 1994 is 1.078 so that TFP growth in new patent applications was still substantial without provisional patenting.

inputs. In particular, they suggest a modest increase in the propensity of faculty to disclose ($PROP_1^u$) and a substantial increase in the propensity for university administrators to patent ($PROP_2^u$). While we cannot separate $PROP_1^u$ into effects from research focus or output, as opposed to the willingness to disclose, the industry survey results reported in §5 suggest that research focus is, at least from industry's perspective, not a major reason for growth in licensing. Further, the stark difference in TFP in the first two stages is consistent with industry responses that universities are more "receptive" to licensing.

What might account for the negative TFP growth in licenses? One possibility is a bias resulting from the fact that our growth rates do not fully account for lags between disclosure and patent application and the signing of license agreements. It is unlikely, however, that this effect is systematic. Licenses executed today may have come from disclosures and patent applications filed several years earlier, so that the measured productivity of disclosures and patent applications today may be higher than actual productivity. On the other hand, the fact that today's disclosures and patent applications may lead to licenses in later years implies that measured productivity today may be lower than the actual. Since the growth rates we report are geometric means over a four-year period, these effects may wash out.

A second explanation is that TTOs have become more demanding in their contract negotiations (i.e., conditional on commercial "quality" of a technology, asking price has increased). Several industry licensing executives with whom we spoke claimed that universities were "asking for too much." We tend to discount this explanation for several reasons. Responses to our industry survey suggest that business executives believe universities are more receptive to contracts. While this does not negate higher asking prices, it casts some doubt. We also calculated TFP growth using sponsored research as a measure of the return or valuation of licenses executed. As we noted in §2.1, sponsored research tied to licenses is flawed as a measure of current valuation since there is a trade-off between royalties and sponsored research funds. If we are willing to assume that our time frame (five years)

is sufficiently short that there have been not substantial shifts in preferences for one source of income over the other, then we can examine research funds tied to licenses as a measure of the valuation of licenses. The TFP growth in such funds is −10.7%. Valuation, therefore, is falling at a more rapid rate than are licenses executed. This leads us to our next explanation.

A third, and we believe a more plausible, explanation is that the observed growth in disclosures and patent applications reflects universities delving more "deeply" into the available pool of commercializable inventions. Increasing contracts and falling TFP together suggest declining commercial appeal for the *marginal* disclosures and patent applications. That is, since TFP growth is net of disclosures and new patent applications (which themselves have been growing), the implication is that, while many more technologies are being offered and licensed to industry, the proportion of licenses executed to those offered is falling. This productivity result reinforces Henderson et al.'s (1998) evidence of a decline in the importance of university patents (as measured by citations) from an earlier period (1965–1988).

To look further at the relation between TFP growth in licensing and growth in disclosures and patent applications, we regressed the log of the annual licensing TFP index on the logs of the growth rates in disclosures and patent applications.[10] TTO staff is the only other measured input for licenses that changes in our data, so we included the log of its growth rate. The R^2 is 0.13 and both patent applications and TTO staff are negatively related to licensing TFP and are significant (t ratios are smaller than −4.3). The disclosure TFP growth index is not significantly related to licensing TFP growth (t ratio = 0.28). The patent and TTO elasticities are −0.303 and −0.529, respectively. The negative patent elasticity is consistent with our interpretation of declining productivity of the marginal invention. While the negative TTO elasticity may seem to be an anomaly, it actually provides an additional explanation for falling

[10] The regression variances are not strictly correct as they do not account for the nonindependence of the TFP observations, which follows from DEA calculations that are based on the comparisons of a university's outcomes with that of other universities.

TFP in Stage 3. Rapidly expanding TTOs may exhibit lower TFP because there is a steep learning curve for new hires (they may be unfamiliar with faculty and industrial networks important for finding licensees, etc.) so that new staff are, on average, less productive, which implies negative effects on TFP.

4.2. Efficiency Growth and Technical Change

To what extent can we say that best practice has changed over this period, and to what extent has TFP growth reflected inefficient universities catching up to the frontier? Returning to Table 1, we again find our results differ markedly across stages. Only for the patent stage do we find both a shift in the best practice frontier and a movement, on average, of universities closer to the frontier. The latter result implies universities are becoming more similar in their patenting propensity. This increasing efficiency is modest over the four years as average efficiency rises from 0.597 in 1994 to 0.628 in 1998.

The 2.7% growth in TFP for disclosures appears to come primarily from universities moving closer to the frontier, with a slight inward shift of the frontier. As with patents, we interpret the efficiency growth as indicating universities are becoming more similar in their disclosure behavior. Average efficiency rises from 0.556 in 1994 to 0.661 in 1998. In contrast, the decomposition of licensing TFP into efficiency and technical change suggests that there is increasing diversity in the success rate of universities in turning patents and disclosures into licenses. On average, there is growth in the frontier, but there is increasing inefficiency among universities with average efficiency falling from 0.697 in 1994 to 0.517 in 1998.

4.3. Feedback Effects

In modeling the stages involved in licensing we have allowed early stage outputs to affect productivity in later stages, but we have not allowed for success in later stages to affect early-stage activity. It is natural, however, to expect faculty to disclose inventions only if they believe their TTO can successfully license them. We also know from our earlier university survey that TTOs tend to apply for patents only when the likelihood of finding a licensee is high. Thus, past success in licensing may well affect the propensity of faculty to disclose and the propensity of the TTO to patent. In this section, we consider such feedback effects.

One way to incorporate feedback effects would be to include financial rewards from licenses executed as inputs in the first two stages. The problem with this is the same problem (discussed above) with using financial returns to licenses in measuring TFP in the third stage. That is, financial returns to licenses executed can appear either as royalty income or as sponsored research money directed to the inventor's lab. In our interviews with TTO professionals we were told that some universities actively seek sponsored research at the expense of royalty income, so that information on royalty income, for many universities, is an incomplete measure of financial rewards.[11] In addition, royalty income in any given year can be attached to licenses executed in the distant past and current licenses might not result in income for a number of years.

As alternatives, we consider both the number of licenses and the ratio of licenses to disclosures in the recent past as inputs to the disclosure decision. One can think of licenses executed as a "demonstration" that the disclosure process has value, either because of potential royalty revenue and/or sponsored research or simply as an indication that companies value their work. In our earlier survey, several TTO personnel claimed that some faculty treat the very fact that a license is signed as a nonpecuniary gain, attaching value to the fact that their discoveries have commercial appeal. The ratio of licenses to disclosures is a measure of the success rate of the TTO and should also serve to encourage faculty to disclose. The measures we use are (i) the average number of licenses executed over the preceding three years and (ii) the ratio of the three-year average of licenses to the three-year average of disclosures.

Including both measures of this demonstration effect produces a marked change in the first-stage

---

[11] For more on this issue, see Thursby and Kemp (2001). It should also be noted that the tax treatments of a firm's royalty expenses and a firm's sponsored research expenses are different; the former is a deduction, while the latter can be a credit. Thus, firms are not indifferent across the two methods of payment for a license.

results. Rather than TFP growth of 2.7%, the growth rate falls to 1.5%. In decomposing this growth into technical change and efficiency change we find that there has been negative growth in technical change (−4.8% per year) and positive growth in efficiency (6.6% per year). If we drop the ratio of licenses to disclosures, the results remain virtually identical. If, however, we drop the average number of licenses and retain the ratio, the results are very similar to our results without feedback effects. The implication of this is that the growth in faculty propensity to disclose is clearly linked to licensing success as measured by the number of licenses executed in the recent past.

Finally, including these two measures of past licensing success as feedback effects in the patent stage has a smaller relative effect on the propensity of university central administrations to patent. TFP growth falls from 12.1% to 10.5%, and we continue to find TFP growth in both efficiency and technical change.

5. Industry Survey

The picture that emerges from our analysis of the AUTM data is that, while the so-called commercial outputs from university research have grown substantially, this growth reflects increased TFP only in the first two stages. We find negative TFP growth in Stage 3, which we believe is indicative of the declining commercial appeal of license disclosures and patent applications at the margin. While this highlights the role of university inputs in increased commercial activity, the productivity analysis provides limited information about the sources of TFP growth, and it does not provide any evidence on the role of business behavior in the process. That is, we cannot tell the extent to which growth in university licensing activity was due to a shift in faculty research toward topics with more commercial appeal, an increase in university attempts to market inventions, or to an increase in demand for university contracts because of changes in industry R&D.

To examine these issues we conducted a survey of businesses that transfer-in technologies via license or research agreements. The questionnaire was designed to be answered by individuals actively engaged in executing such agreements and focused on the extent to which they had executed licenses, options, and/or sponsored research agreements with universities between 1993-1997. We received responses from 112 business units that had licensed-in university inventions. As described in Appendix C, firms in our sample accounted for at least 15% of the license agreements and 17% of sponsored research agreements reported by AUTM in 1997. Seventy-nine firms in the sample responded to a question on the top five universities with whom they had contractual agreements. The 85 universities mentioned include 35 of the top 50 universities in terms of industry-sponsored research and 40 of the top 50 licensing universities in the 1997 AUTM survey. Slightly less than half the respondents are responding for business units with no more than 100 employees, and about two thirds have fewer than 500 employees. The portion of small firms in our sample is in fact representative of all university licensing; in 1998, the AUTM survey reported that 64% of all university licenses were to start-ups or existing firms with fewer than 500 employees. Sixty-three percent of those who actively license-in from universities had no more than $1,000,000 of revenues, and 20 of the respondents reported that they did not have a product in the marketplace.

We asked respondents about changes in their relationship with universities, as well as the reasons for any change. In particular, we asked whether their contractual agreements (license, option, and/or research agreements) with universities had increased, decreased, or stayed about the same over the preceding five-year period. Of the 106 answering this question, 50% indicated an increase and 16% indicated a decrease. For those with an increase or decrease in arrangements we asked, on a 5-point scale with 1 indicating *extremely important* and 5 indicating *not important* (a *don't know* response was permitted), how important a set of factors were in explaining the change. Since there are so few respondents (17) indicating a decrease, we will not consider their reasons for the decrease.

It is worth noting the magnitude of the changes reported. For those noting an increase in agreements, the number of licenses increased by 86% in 1997 compared to the average of the preceding four years, and their research funding to universities doubled. On

THURSBY AND THURSBY
Sources of Growth in University Licensing

Table 2   Relative Frequencies of Reasons Behind INCREASING Contracts

		Extremely important	2	3	4	Not important	Don't know
Q1	Cost of university research	10.4	18.8	29.2	10.4	27.1	4.2
Q2	Faculty research is more oriented toward the needs of business	10.2	20.4	26.5	18.4	20.4	4.2
Q3	A change in universities' receptivity to licensing and/or research agreements	30.6	26.5	20.4	10.2	12.2	0.0
Q4	A change in our unit's reliance on external R&D	22.4	36.7	10.2	14.3	16.3	0.0
Q5	A change in the amount of basic research conducted by our unit	18.4	22.4	20.4	14.3	24.5	0.0

average, each of these firms executed 13 licenses per year and provided $13.2 mil in sponsored research with U.S. universities.[12]

Table 2 gives the relative frequency of responses regarding the reasons for the increase in their contracts. Table 3 gives unweighted and weighted average responses where the weights are the number of licenses executed with universities over the period 1993–1997. The weighted averages are based on the 35 respondents who provided sufficient information to calculate the number of licenses—these 35 respondents represent 409 university licenses over this period. The first three questions in Tables 2 and 3 relate to changes in universities, while the last two relate to changes in corporate R&D.

Consider the two questions related to a business unit's research: "A change in our unit's reliance on external R&D"[13] and "A change in the amount of basic research conducted by our unit." Approximately 60% and 41% indicated either a 1 or a 2 for Q4 (change in reliance) and for Q5 (change in basic research), respectively, suggesting that business demand for university technologies increased as a result of changes in industry R&D. This, of course, does not rule out

the possibility (discussed below) that industry R&D changed in response to university characteristics.

The first three questions in Tables 2 and 3 relate to university characteristics: "Cost of university research," "Faculty research is more oriented toward the needs of business," and "A change in universities' receptivity to licensing and/or research agreements." What stands out is the greater importance attached to university receptivity than either costs or faculty research orientation; three times as many respondents recorded a 1 (*extremely important*) for university receptivity as recorded a 1 for costs or for faculty research.

We tested for significant differences in responses to the five questions. Our tests suggest a difference significant at the 1% level between responses to Q1 (cost) and Q3 (university receptivity) and to Q1 and Q4 (reliance on external R&D). Responses to Q2 (faculty orientation) are also significantly different from those to Q3 and Q4 at significance levels 1% and 10%, respectively. Responses to Q5 (basic research) are significantly different from Q3 (10% level) and Q4 (5% level). No other distributions of responses are significantly different.[14] These tests further support the

[12] Those who report decreased contracts indicated levels and changes in levels that are of the same order of magnitude as those who increased contracts.

[13] Note that a change in a firm's reliance on external R&D does not necessarily reflect a change in their reliance on universities as only 47% of the licenses executed in 1997 by the firms in our sample are with U.S. universities.

[14] Because the responses are not independent, the test we use is a test of difference in means where we take account of the dependence in computation of the variance of the difference in sample means. In the case of independence a more appropriate test would be to use tests for equivalence of the five-category multinomial distributions (*don't know* is excluded). The main differences in the outcomes of the two tests is the non-significance of Q5 from both Q3 and Q4.

Table 3 Average Responses of Reasons Behind INCREASING Contracts

		Unweighted	Weighted
Q1	Cost of university research	3.22	3.98
Q2	Faculty research is more oriented toward the needs of business	3.57	3.79
Q3	A change in universities' receptivity to licensing and/or research agreements	2.42	2.88
Q4	A change in our unit's reliance on external R&D	2.65	2.54
Q5	A change in the amount of basic research conducted by our unit	3.04	3.35

importance of changes in industry R&D and in university receptivity to contracts relative to costs and changes in faculty orientation.

We also calculated simple correlations of the individual responses to the five questions. Not surprisingly, the correlation between Q4 and Q5, the questions related to changes in industry R&D, is fairly high (0.6, significant at the 1% level). To examine whether changes in industrial R&D might be related to university characteristics, we consider the correlations between responses to the R&D questions and responses to the other three questions. Responses to the cost question (Q1) have correlations of 0.49 (significant at 1% level) and 0.45 (significant at 5% level) to Q4 and Q5, respectively. Neither Q2 (faculty orientation) nor Q3 (university receptivity) is significantly correlated with the R&D questions. Thus, while the cost of university research is less important to overall increases in industry/university contracts than changes in university receptivity to such contracts, university cost is an important reason behind changes in industry R&D. Finally, the correlation between Q2 and Q3 is 0.61 (significant at the 1% level), implying that, while university receptivity to contracts is more important than faculty orientation in explaining changes in industry/university contacts, changes in faculty orientation and changes in university receptivity to industry contracts go, to some extent, hand in hand.

What do these results tell us about $PROP_1^u$ and $PROP_2^u$, the propensities of faculty and central administrations to commercialize inventions? First, our

earlier finding of substantial TFP growth in patent applications indicated a substantial change in $PROP_2^u$, and the survey results corroborate this as an important source of the growth in commercial activities of universities. Second, we earlier noted that $PROP_1^u$ could change either through a reorientation of faculty research toward the needs of business or through a change in the willingness of faculty to disclose. The industry survey suggests that, while there may have been some reorientation of faculty research, a reorientation is much less important than changes in university receptivity and in industry R&D.

Finally, while we are not able through either the productivity study or the survey to disentangle the relative importance to the third stage (licenses executed) of changes in TTO ability and knowledge ($PROP_3^u$) from market conditions (Π_3), it would appear that industry demand for university technologies has increased, at least in part, due to changes in industry R&D. The latter changes are related to the cost of university research rather than a reorientation of faculty or a change in university receptivity to industry contracts.

6. Conclusion

We began this article with observations on substantial growth in disclosures, new patent applications, and licenses executed. This increased activity has prompted policy makers in government and academic circles to question the implications for faculty research, and, in particular, whether faculty research has become more applied in response to license opportunities. This has been discussed in recent Congressional hearings as an "unintended" effect of the Bayh-Dole Act of 1980. The act was intended not to redirect faculty research, but to facilitate industrial application of university research by expanding university rights to patent and license inventions from federally funded research. To the extent that increased licensing reflects a greater willingness of faculty and university administrators to facilitate technology transfer, the surge in licensing reflects the intended effect of the legislation. While our analysis is intended primarily to examine the sources of the dramatic growth in licensing activity, it also contributes to the policy debate.

In particular, we find modest TFP growth in disclosures (2.7% annual growth), which could reflect changes in faculty research or simply an increased propensity to license as well as publish their work. While our productivity analysis does not allow us to separate the two, our industry survey suggests that the modest growth in TFP of disclosures comes primarily from an increased willingness of faculty to disclose. In indicating the reasons for their increased interest in university inventions, survey respondents weighted changes in their own reliance on external R&D and increased university receptivity to industrial contracts more heavily than the orientation of faculty research toward business needs. It is worth noting that, while our evidence does not rule out some shift in faculty focus, it is consistent with statistics on the split between basic and applied research in U.S. universities as reported by universities to the National Science Foundation (*Science and Engineering Indicators*). The average proportion of basic research to total research expenditures for 1977–1980 is 0.67, while for 1994–1998 it is only 0.005 smaller. This difference represents about $119 mil of the more than $24 bil of research expenditures at all U.S. universities.

By far, the greatest growth in commercial activity is in the second stage, patent applications. Patent applications could have grown because of an increase in the propensity for university administrators to commercialize faculty inventions, but they could also have grown because of the increase in disclosures. While disclosures have increased, our productivity analysis and industry survey also support the first explanation. That is, after accounting for input growth, patent applications have grown substantially (annual TFP growth of 12.1%), and this growth is attributed to increasingly entrepreneurial university administrators. Respondents to our industry survey corroborate this result by placing a relatively high weight on a change in university receptivity to industrial contracts as being important in the growth of their university contracts. Here, again, our finding is consistent with intended effects of the Bayh-Dole Act.

Perhaps the most surprising result is the negative total TFP growth of licenses executed (−1.7% annual growth). That is, growth in disclosures and patent applications has been greater than the corresponding growth in licenses executed. We interpret this to mean that the marginal university innovation offered to the market has declined in commercial appeal; universities are apparently delving more deeply into the available pool of innovations in their efforts to increase their commercial activities. Again, delving deeply into the available pool of innovations is consistent with the intent of the Bayh-Dole Act.

Finally, we do not have evidence on the importance of learning by doing on the part of TTOs except to note our finding of a negative association between TTO growth and TFP growth in licensing, which would suggest at least the possibility of learning by doing effects.

Acknowledgments

This research has been supported by the Alan and Mildred Peterson Foundation, Purdue University, and the Sloan Foundation and the National Bureau of Economic Research under the NBER Project on Industrial Technology and Productivity. The authors would like to express their appreciation to the Licensing Executive Society, Inc. (U.S.A. and Canada) and particularly Mark Peterson and Tom Small for their support in conducting the industry survey. They are indebted to James Adams, Ashish Arora, Wesley Cohen, Shawna Grosskopf, Dan Kovenock, Richard Nelson, Barbara Newman, Jennifer Parsons, Scott Shane, Don Siegel, and John Walsh for suggestions and comments.

Appendix A: DEA and TFP Computation

Let there be $u = 1, \ldots, U$ universities using $n = 1, \ldots, N$ inputs x^{ut} in stage s to produce stage output y^{ut} in period $t = 1, \ldots, T$. The position of university u' relative to the frontier in stage s (where we suppress the stage notation) is determined by the solution to the programming problem:

$$D^{u', t}(x^{u', t}, y^{u', t})^{-1} = \text{Max } \theta^{u'} \tag{6.1}$$

$$\theta^{u'} y^{u', t} \leq \sum_{u=1}^{U} z^{u, t} y^{u, t} \tag{6.2}$$

$$\sum_{u=1}^{U} z^{u, t} x_n^{u, t} \leq x_n^{u', t} \quad n = 1, \ldots, N \tag{6.3}$$

$$z^{u, t} \geq 0 \quad u = 1, \ldots, U. \tag{6.4}$$

The inverse of $\theta^{u'}$ is a measure of the distance of u' from the frontier. If $1/\theta^{u'} = 1$, then u' lies on the frontier; otherwise, u' lies interior to the frontier, and $1/\theta^{u'}$ represents the fraction of possible output produced by u'. The best practice frontier (that is, the frontier determined by the subset of efficient universities) is given by Equations (6.2)–(6.3) for $\theta = 1$.[15]

[15] For discussions of DEA, see Seiford and Thrall (1990), Charnes et al. (1994), Ali and Seiford (1993), or Fare, Grosskopf and Lovell (1994).

THURSBY AND THURSBY
Sources of Growth in University Licensing

To examine changes in university performance over time, we compute Fare et al.'s (1994) measure of total factor productivity growth (TFP) for each stage. This measure is the geometric mean of two Malmquist indexes, one of which is based on the best practice frontier in period t and the other based on the frontier in $t+1$, and is given by

$$m(x^{u',t+1}, y^{u',t+1}, x^{u',t}, y^{u',t})$$
$$= \left[\left(\frac{D^{u',t}(x^{u',t+1}, y^{u',t+1})}{D^{u',t}(x^{u',t}, y^{u',t})} \right) \left(\frac{D^{u',t+1}(x^{u',t+1}, y^{u',t+1})}{D^{u',t+1}(x^{u',t}, y^{u',t})} \right) \right]^{1/2}, \quad (6.5)$$

where $D^{u',t}(x^{u',t}, y^{u',t})$ and $D^{u',t+1}(x^{u',t+1}, y^{u',t+1})$ are given by the solution of (6.1) for $k = t$ and $t+1$; that is, they are, respectively, DEA solutions for years t and $t+1$. $D^{u',t}(x^{u',t+1}, y^{u',t+1})$ is given by the solution to

$$D^{u',t}(x^{u',t}, y^{u',t+1})^{-1} = \text{Max } \theta^{u'}$$
$$\theta^{u'} y^{u',t+1} \leq \sum_{u=1}^{U} z^{u,t} y^{u,t}$$
$$\sum_{u=1}^{U} z^{u,t} x_n^{u,t} \leq x_n^{u',t+1} \quad n = 1, \dots, N \qquad (6.6)$$
$$z^{u,t} \geq 0 \quad u = 1, \dots, U$$

and $D^{u',t+1}(x^{u',t}, y^{u',t})$ is given by the solution to

$$D^{u',t+1}(x^{u',t}, y^{u',t})^{-1} = \text{Max } \theta^{u'}$$
$$\theta^{u'} y^{u',t} \leq \sum_{u=1}^{U} z^{u,t+1} y^{u,t+1}$$
$$\sum_{u=1}^{U} z^{u,t+1} x_n^{u,t+1} \leq x_n^{u',t} \quad n = 1, \dots, N \qquad (6.7)$$
$$z^{u,t+1} \geq 0 \quad u = 1, \dots, U.$$

Note that Equations (6.6) and (6.7) involve observations from both t and $t+1$. The solution to (6.6) involves period $t+1$ inputs and outputs in reference to the period t frontier; it gives the proportional change in output necessary to make $(x^{u',t+1}, y^{u',t+1})$ feasible given the best practice technology at t. The solution to (6.7), on the other hand, uses period t inputs and outputs in reference to the period $t+1$ frontier; it gives the proportional change in output necessary to make $(x^{u',t}, y^{u',t})$ feasible given the best-practice technology at $t+1$.

We rewrite $m(\bullet)$ by factoring the ratio of $D^{u',t+1}(x^{u',t+1}, y^{u',t+1})$ to $D^{u',t}(x^{u',t}, y^{u',t})$ from the right-hand side of (6.5) to obtain

$$m(x^{u',t+1}, y^{u',t+1}, x^{u',t}, y^{u',t})$$
$$= \left[\left(\frac{D^{u',t+1}(x^{u',t+1}, y^{u',t+1})}{D^{u',t}(x^{u',t}, y^{u',t})} \right) \right]$$
$$\times \left[\left(\frac{D^{u',t}(x^{u',t+1}, y^{u',t+1})}{D^{u',t+1}(x^{u',t+1}, y^{u',t+1})} \right) \left(\frac{D^{u',t}(x^{u',t}, y^{u',t})}{D^{u',t+1}(x^{u',t}, y^{u',t})} \right) \right]^{1/2}. \quad (6.8)$$

This ratio (the first bracketed term in (6.8)) is the ratio of the efficiency measure $\theta^{u'}$ in period t to $\theta^{u'}$ in period $t+1$, and it is the component of productivity change that stems from movement toward or away from frontiers in periods t and $t+1$; it is growth due to either catching up (the ratio is greater than 1) or lagging (the ratio is less than 1) of universities not on the frontier in at least one

period. The other term in (6.8) is the component of productivity change that is due to frontier shifts between t and $t+1$. This latter term is said to represent technical change.

Efficiency results are based on the solution to the programming problem given by Equations (6.1) through (6.4). TFP results are calculated using Equation (6.5).

Appendix B: Data
The AUTM licensing survey (AUTM, various years) has data on the technology transfer programs of many U.S. universities. In the survey is information on the output of each of the three stages (numbers of licenses executed, new patent applications, and invention disclosures) as well as the number of full-time equivalent staff employed in the TTO and federal and industry research support. These latter measures are the average level of support over the preceding three years. For universities that did not respond to all of the first three years, we use the average support values for the years in which they respond.

Data on faculty size and quality are from the National Research Council's (NRC 1995) 1993 survey of all Ph.D.-granting departments in the United States. No information is provided for departments that do not grant the Ph.D. degree. It is plausible to assume that substantial research programs have difficulty existing in the sciences and engineering—the departments from which 90% of commercial activity originate (see Thursby et al. 2001)—without the presence of Ph.D. students. We accept the reasonable proposition that science and engineering departments that do not grant the Ph.D. are not strong research departments and, hence, provide less inventive input to a university's commercial activities; the AUTM data support this proposition.

There are 64 universities with information sufficiently complete to compute frontier production functions and growth rates.

Appendix C: Survey Design
The sample was drawn from the mailing list of Licensing Executive Society, Inc. (United States and Canada). We phoned companies with multiple entries to ensure a single response from each suitable business unit and to identify the most appropriate respondent. Further calls allowed us to eliminate businesses that do not license-in technology from any source or sponsor university research, as well as firms that are no longer in business. This left us with 1,385 business units in the sample, and 300 responded (21.7% response rate); 112 indicated that they had licensed-in university technologies, and 188 indicated that their licenses were from other sources, although 61 of the latter had sponsored university research.

Many of the companies on the LES list are not publicly traded, so it is impossible to conduct the usual tests for selectivity bias. We can, however, compare the total of all licenses and industry-sponsored research reported by AUTM to the number of licenses and amount of sponsored research of our respondents. Of the 112 firms who licensed-in university technologies, 104 gave information on the number of their license agreements with universities. These 104 respondents had 417 licenses in 1997, which represents approximately 15% of the total reported by AUTM.[16] Seventy-one respondents reported $307 mil of support, which is approximately 17% of the comparable AUTM figure of $1,786 mil for 1997. If the firms with missing sponsored research expenditures had the same average research expenditure as the 71 usable responses, then our 114 respondents account for about 28% of all industry research support at U.S. universities. Seventy-nine firms listed the primary universities with whom they licensed during the preceding five years, and 64 listed the primary universities with whom they sponsored research.[17] Eighty-five universities are mentioned (many are mentioned by a number of firms), and they cover most of the major U.S. research universities; based on the 1997 AUTM survey, they represent 35 of the top 50 industry supported universities and 40 of the top 50 licensing universities. It is reasonable to conclude that our sample represents a substantial portion of all industry/university contractual agreements of the recent past.

[16]The survey is explicit in differentiating between licenses and options, whereas AUTM lumps both together, thus our estimate and the AUTM figure are not strictly comparable; however, the bulk of university contracts (aside from research agreements) are licenses. In our survey, licenses outnumbered options by about 4 to 1.

[17]Many who did not answer this question indicated confidentiality concerns. They were reluctant—in spite of assurances of confidentiality—because knowledge of the universities with whom they deal can give competitors information as to the strategic direction the firm might take in the future.

References

Adams, James D. 1990. Fundamental stocks of knowledge and productivity growth. *J. Political Econom.* **98** 673–702.

Ali, A., L. Seiford. 1993. The mathematical programming approach to efficiency analysis. H. Fried, C. Lovell, S. Schmidt, eds. *The Measurement of Productive Efficiency: Techniques and Applications.* Oxford University Press, New York.

Association of University Technology Managers, Inc. 1996–1999. *AUTM Licensing Survey,* Norwalk, CT.

Caves, Douglas W., Laurits Christensen, W. Erwin Diewert. 1982. The economic theory of index numbers and the measurement of input, output, and productivity. *Econometrica* **50** 1393–1414.

Charnes, A., W. Cooper, A. Lewin, L. Seiford. 1994. *Data Envelopment Analysis: Theory, Methodology and Applications.* Kluwer Academic Press,

Cohen, W. M., R. Florida, L. Randazzese, J. Walsh. 1998. Industry and the academy: Uneasy partners in the cause of technological advance. Roger Noll, ed. *Challenges to Research Universities.* The Brookings Institution, Washington, D.C.

Fare, R., S. Grosskopf, C. Lovell. 1994. *Production Frontiers.* Cambridge University Press, New York.

——, ——, M. Norris, Z. Zhang. 1994. Productivity growth, technical progress, and efficiency change in industrialized countries. *Amer. Econom. Rev.* **84** 66–83.

Grosskopf, S. 1996. Statistical inference and nonparametric efficiency: A selective survey. *J. Productivity Anal.* **7** 161–176.

Henderson, Rebecca, Adam Jaffe, Trajtenberg. 1998. Universities as a source of commercial technology: A detailed analysis of university patenting, 1965–1988. *Rev. Econom. Statist.* **80** 119–127.

Jaffe, Adam, Manuel Trajtenberg, Rebecca Henderson. 1993. Geographic localization of knowledge spillovers as evidenced by patent citations. *Quart. J. Econom.*

Jensen, R., M. Thursby. 2001. Proofs and prototypes for sale: The licensing of university inventions. *Amer. Econom. Rev.* **91** 240–259.

Mansfield, Edwin. 1995. Academic research underlying industrial innovations: Sources, characteristics, and financing. *Rev. Econom. Statist.* **77** 55–65.

Mowery, David C., Richard R. Nelson, Bhaven N. Sampat, Arvids A. Ziedonis. 2001a. The growth of patenting and licensing by U.S. universities: An assessment of the effects of the Bayh-Dole Act of 1980. *Res. Policy* **30** 99–119.

——, Bhaven N. Sampat, Arvids A. Ziedonis. 2001b. Learning to patent: Institutional experience, learning, and the characteristics of university patents after Bayh-Dole, 1980–1994. *Management Sci.* **48**(1).

National Research Council. 1995. *Research Doctorate Programs in the United States* (M. Goldberger, B. Maher and P. Flattau, eds.). National Academy Press, Washington, D.C.

Seiford, L., R. Thrall. 1990. Recent developments in DEA: The mathematical programming approach to frontier analysis. *J. Econometrics* **46** 7–38.

Siegel, Donald, David Waldman, Albert Link. 1999. Assessing the impact of organizational practices on the productivity of university technology transfer offices. Mimeo.

Thursby, J., S. Kemp. 2001. Growth and productivity efficiency of university intellectual property licensing. *Res. Policy* Forthcoming.

——, M. Thursby. 1999. Purdue licensing survey: A summary of results. Mimeo.

——, R. Jensen, M. Thursby. 2001. Objectives, characteristics and outcomes of university licensing: A survey of major U.S. universities. *J. Tech. Transfer* **26** 59–72.

Zucker, L., M. Darby, J. Armstrong. 1994. Intellectual capital and the firm: The technology of geographically localized knowledge spillovers. NBER working paper #4946, Boston, MA.

——, ——, M. Brewer. 1998. Intellectual capital and the birth of U.S. biotechnology enterprises. *Amer. Econom. Rev.* **88** 290–306.

Accepted by David C. Mowery and Scott Shane; received December 2000. This paper was with the authors 9 months for 1 revision.

[6]

ELSEVIER

Research Policy 32 (2003) 27–48

research
policy

www.elsevier.com/locate/econbase

Assessing the impact of organizational practices on the relative productivity of university technology transfer offices: an exploratory study ☆

Donald S. Siegel [a,*], David Waldman [b], Albert Link [c]

[a] Nottingham University Business School, Jubilee Campus-Wollaton Road, University of Nottingham, Nottingham NG8 1BB, UK
[b] School of Management, Arizona State University West, Phoenix, AZ 85069-7100, USA
[c] Department of Economics, University of North Carolina at Greensboro, Greensboro, NC 27412 USA

Received 27 April 2001; received in revised form 2 July 2001; accepted 4 December 2001

Abstract

We present quantitative and qualitative evidence on the relative productivity of university technology transfer offices (TTOs). Our empirical results suggest that TTO activity is characterized by constant returns to scale and that environmental and institutional factors explain some of the variation in performance. Productivity may also depend on organizational practices. Unfortunately, there are no quantitative measures available on such practices, so we rely on inductive, qualitative methods to identify them. Based on 55 interviews of 98 entrepreneurs, scientists, and administrators at five research universities, we conclude that the most critical organizational factors are faculty reward systems, TTO staffing/compensation practices, and cultural barriers between universities and firms.
© 2002 Elsevier Science B.V. All rights reserved.

JEL classification: D23; L31; O31; O32

Keywords: Technology transfer offices (TTOs); University/industry technology transfer (UITT); Stochastic frontier estimation (SFE)

1. Introduction

Universities in the United States have been criticized in some circles for being more adept at developing new technologies than moving them into private sector applications. This is potentially problematic

since success in university/industry technology transfer (UITT) could be a critical factor in sustaining the global competitiveness of US firms. Some federal agencies have responded to this concern by providing incentives for universities to form partnerships with firms.[1] Expectations regarding a quicker commercial "payoff" to basic research have risen accordingly. To build political support for their institutions, university leaders frequently cite the role of technology transfer

☆ A previous version of this paper was presented at the NBER Conference on Organizational Change and Performance Improvement, April 1999, Santa Rosa, CA.
* Corresponding author. Present address: Department of Economics, Rensselaer Polytechnic Institute, 110 8th St. Troy, NY 12180, USA. Tel.: +44-115-846-6629; fax: +44-115-846-6667.
E-mail addresses: don.siegel@nottingham.ac.uk (D.S. Siegel), david.a.waldman@asu.edu (D. Waldman), al_link@uncg.edu (A. Link).

[1] For instance, as noted in Cohen et al. (1998), NSF has established Science and Technology Centers and other programs that require universities to attract matching funds from industry. See David and Hall (2000), Klette et al. (2000), and Martin and Scott (2000) for more general theoretical and empirical considerations of public–private partnerships in the realm of R&D.

in stimulating local economic development. Facing tighter budgets, these administrators often promise to deliver more "bang for the buck" in technology transfer. The private sector has also chimed in, expressing frustration with obstacles that impede the process of commercialization, such as disputes that arise with the university regarding intellectual property rights.[2]

These concerns have raised the visibility of UITT in the public policy arena. In recent years, universities have attempted to formalize UITT and capture a larger share of the economic rents associated with technological innovation by establishing technology transfer offices (TTOs). TTOs facilitate technological diffusion through the licensing to industry of inventions or intellectual property resulting from university research.[3] Many institutions established a TTO in the aftermath of the University and Small Business Patent Procedures Act of 1980, otherwise known as the Bayh–Dole Act.

Bayh–Dole dramatically changed incentives for firms and universities to engage in UITT. It simplified the UITT process by instituting a uniform patent policy and removing many restrictions on licensing. Furthermore, it allowed universities to own the patents that arise from federal research grants. The framers of Bayh–Dole asserted that a streamlined federal UITT policy and university ownership and management of intellectual property would accelerate commercialization because universities would now have greater flexibility in negotiating licensing agreements and firms would be more willing to engage in them.[4]

It appears that Bayh–Dole has indeed resulted in a more rapid rate of technological diffusion.[5] Accord-ing to the Association of University Technology Managers (AUTM, 1997), the annual number of patents granted to US universities surged from about 300 in 1980 to approximately 2000 in 1996, while licensing of new technologies has increased almost two-fold since 1991. Annual streams of revenue accruing from these licenses have risen from about US$ 160 million in 1991 to US$ 611 million in 1997, now constituting about 2.5% of university R&D expenditures (GAO, 1998). Major products in a wide variety of industries have been developed through UITT, such as the Boyer–Cohen "gene-splicing" technique that launched the biotechnology industry, diagnostic tests for breast cancer and osteoporosis, internet search engines, music synthesizers, computer-aided design (CAD), and environmentally-friendly technologies.

Despite the potential importance of UITT as a mechanism for generating local technological spillovers and as a source of revenue to the university, there is little systematic empirical evidence on any dimension of the performance or productivity of UITT activity.[6] The purpose of this paper is to fill this void.

Our measures of relative productivity are constructed from benchmarking surveys conducted by AUTM for the years 1991–1996. We adjust these estimates of relative efficiency to reflect environmental and institutional factors that can influence the rate of technological diffusion at a given university. We postulate that relative performance in UITT may also depend on *organizational practices* in university management of intellectual property, which potentially attenuate palpable differences in the motives, incentives, and organizational cultures of the parties to licensing agreements (university administrators/TTO directors, managers/entrepreneurs, and academic scientists).

Unfortunately, there are no existing data on such practices, nor is it precisely clear which organizational factors are most critical to effectiveness in UITT. Therefore, we rely on inductive, qualitative methods (field research) to identify these variables, which are typically ignored in conventional productivity studies.

---

[2] Gallini and Scotchmer (2001) provides an excellent discussion of issues related to appropriate intellectual property regimes in this context.

[3] See Geroski (2000) for an excellent review article of models of technology diffusion.

[4] "We came to the realization that this failure to move from abstract research into useful commercial innovation was largely a result of the government's patent policy and we sought to draft legislation which would change this policy in a way to quickly and directly stimulate the development and commercialization of inventions" (Bayh, 1996).

[5] Mowery et al. (2001) challenge this causal interpretation of the impact of Bayh–Dole on UITT. The authors analyze pre- and post-Bayh–Dole UITT licensing and patenting at the University of California, Columbia, and Stanford, and conclude that Bayh–Dole was only one of several factors inducing a rise in UITT.

---

[6] Exceptions are papers by Thursby and Thursby (2000) and Bercovitz et al. (2001). The former is a quanitative study, based on AUTM data, which examines the productivity of university licensing. The latter is a qualitative study of the relationship between organizational structure and UITT performance at Duke, Johns Hopkins, and Penn State.

D.S. Siegel et al. / Research Policy 32 (2003) 27–48

The field research also provided a useful reality check on the specification of our econometric model. Accordingly, we conducted 55 structured, face-to-face interviews of UITT stakeholders (15 administrators, 20 managers or entrepreneurs, and 20 scientists affiliated at five universities). We solicited feedback from these individuals on the nature of the UITT "production process", barriers to effective UITT, recommendations to improve the process, and the importance of networks and relationships in UITT.

The remainder of this paper is organized as follows. Section 2 describes a set of internal and external factors that influence the extent of UITT at a given university. Differences in the actions, motives, and organizational environments of the parties to licensing agreements are also considered. We conjecture that these differences can potentially undermine efforts to commercialize university-based technologies. This discussion underscores the potential importance of organizational factors as a determinant of UITT performance. Section 3 outlines the method for assessing relative productivity in UITT. Empirical results are presented in Section 4. Section 5 describes our qualitative research design and methods. Section 6 discusses our qualitative findings. The final section consists of preliminary conclusions and suggestions for additional research.

2. Determinants of UITT

2.1. Internal inputs

To identify the appropriate "inputs", we begin with a simple description of the process of the transfer of a technology from a university to a firm or entrepreneur, through the negotiation of a licensing agreement. This description reflects the conventional wisdom among academic administrators (see AUTM, 1997) regarding how technologies are transferred. It is important to note that this linear model does not necessarily constitute an accurate representation of how *all* technologies are *actually* transferred. Indeed, a key goal of our field research is to determine whether this model understates the complexity of this process.

The first stage of the process is scientific discovery. The Bayh–Dole Act stipulates that scientists must then file an invention disclosure with the TTO. Our field research, which is described in greater detail in Sections 5 and 6, revealed that this rule is rarely enforced. Thus, TTO personnel must devote some effort to encouraging faculty members to disclose inventions. Once the invention is formally disclosed, the TTO simultaneously evaluates the commercial potential of the technology and decides whether to patent the innovation. Often, interest in the technology by an industry partner provides sufficient justification for filing a patent. In other instances, the TTO must make these judgements before industry expresses an interest in the technology. Furthermore, universities must decide whether to seek *global* or *domestic* patent protection. Domestic protection is substantially cheaper, but often much less valuable to potential licensees, particularly when foreign markets are perceived to be highly lucrative relative to the US market. As confirmed in our interviews, this decision poses a dilemma for many TTOs because they have limited resources for filing patents.

If the patent is awarded, the TTO will often attempt to market the technology. Faculty members are frequently involved in the marketing phase because they are usually in a good position to identify potential licensees and because their technical expertise often makes them a natural partner for firms that wish to commercialize the technology. It is important to note that the linear model potentially overstates the role of patents in UITT. As reported in Jensen and Thursby (2001) and confirmed in our field research, many firms will license a technology *before* it is patented.[7] This implies that a key input of UITT is invention disclosures, which constitute the pool of available technologies for licensing.

The final stages of UITT involve the negotiation of a licensing agreement with firms or individual entrepreneurs. These agreements could include such benefits to the university as royalties, "follow-on" sponsored research agreements, or an equity stake in a new venture based on the licensed technology. We discovered on our field visits that many universities, especially public institutions, are quite sensitive to the charge that they are "giving away" university-based, taxpayer-funded technologies that yield substantial

---

[7] Also, university technology managers tend to view patents as both an input and output of UITT (see AUTM, 1997, pp. 20–21).

windfall profits. As a result, many TTOs are adopting a hard line in licensing negotiations.

Interviews with university administrators revealed that TTO involvement does not end with the signing of a licensing agreement. It is quite common for TTOs to devote substantial resources to the maintenance and re-negotiation of licensing agreements. This is attributed both to the embryonic nature of the technologies and to the fledgling nature of many of the firms that license university-based technologies.

We wish to stress that our field research greatly improved our ability to model the "production process" of UITT, by helping us identify the appropriate set of outputs and inputs to include in the production function. For instance, we began this project with the view that there are multiple outputs of UITT. Discussions with university administrators, the "producers" in our model, revealed that licensing activity is by far the most critical output, so we now focus our attention on this critical dimension of UITT performance. Our qualitative work also revealed that we had greatly underestimated the importance of faculty "buy-in" to UITT. This stemmed, in part, from our literal interpretation of the language contained in the Bayh–Dole Act, which stipulates that academics working on federal research grants must disclose their inventions to the TTO. However, we discovered that this provision is rarely enforced, so that disclosure is actually not mandatory.

Thus, invention disclosures are the key intermediate input. The number of disclosures will depend, to some extent, on the efforts of the TTO to elicit them (and faculty interest in UITT). This, of course, raises the critical issue of organizational incentives for faculty and TTO personnel to engage in these activities. Consistent with recent theoretical and empirical studies summarized in Lazear (1999), we hypothesize that human resource management and other organizational practices that influence such incentives could explain some of the variation in UITT performance across universities.

Our initial field research also demonstrated the importance of intellectual property attorneys in UITT. Some universities use these lawyers to help them obtain copyrights and in various aspects of patenting and licensing, especially in support of prosecution, maintenance, litigation and interference. At some institutions, external attorneys are also involved in ne-

gotiation and re-negotiation of licensing agreements. Thus, expenditure of external lawyers should also be viewed as an input to UITT.

In sum, we conjecture that the following internal factors are inputs of UITT: invention disclosures (a proxy for the set of available technologies), labor employed by the TTO, and (external) legal fees incurred to protect the university's intellectual property.[8] That is, we have specified a TTO "production function" where the relevant inputs are assumed to be under the control of the "producer" or the TTO director.

We also seek to explain *deviations* from the production frontier, which are presumed to be a function of a set of environmental and institutional variables, which are outside of the control of the TTO director. These variables are not conventional inputs (i.e. resources under the direct control of the producer), but rather external factors that could enhance or reduce the rate at which universities transfer technologies to the private sector. We conjecture that organizational practices (as yet undefined) could also constitute determinants of inefficiency. In the following subsections, we discuss these factors.

2.2. Environmental/institutional factors

University licensing activity may also depend on a vector of environmental and institutional variables. For instance, the presence of a medical school and the public status of the university may be important institutional factors. Pressman et al. (1995) report that over 60% of university licenses result from a biomedical invention. Public universities may have less flexible UITT policies than private universities regarding startup companies and interactions with private firms. Furthermore, public universities may be less focused on UITT as a source of revenue than private universities. The age of the TTO may also be relevant, as universities with more experience in formal management of UITT may be efficient than comparable universities with less experience. An example of an environmental variable is state-level economic growth, which can be viewed as a proxy for the ability of firms in the local region to sponsor R&D at the university.

---

[8] This amount includes expenditures in support of prosecution, maintenance, litigation, and interference costs relating to patents and/or copyrights (see AUTM, 1997).

D.S. Siegel et al./Research Policy 32 (2003) 27–48   31

In explaining the relative efficiency of TTOs, it may also be important to control for the R&D activity of local firms. A plethora of recent studies provide support for the notion that university research generates local technological spillovers. Bania et al. (1993) find that there is a positive relationship between university R&D and the number of firm startups in the same SMSA. Jaffe et al. (1993) report that patents (new technologies) generated within the same state (and SMSA) are more likely to be cited by firms in the same state or SMSA. Zucker et al. (1998) and Audretsch and Stephan (1996) directly examine interactions between academic scientists and local firms and find that these formal and informal linkages play an important role in promoting innovation in biotechnology.

2.3. Organizational factors

An understanding of the potential importance of organizational practices begins with a consideration of the actions, motives, and organizational cultures of UITT stakeholders. As shown in Table 1, we conjecture that a primary motive of university scientists is recognition within the scientific community, which emanates from publications in top-tier journals, presentations at prestigious conferences, and federal research grants. This is an especially strong motive for untenured faculty members. Other possible motives include financial gain and a desire to secure additional funding for graduate assistants, post-doctoral fellows, and laboratory equipment/facilities. The norms, standards, and values of scientists reflect an organizational culture that values creativity, innovation, and especially, an individual's contribution to advances in knowledge (basic research).

The TTO must work with scientists and managers or entrepreneurs to structure a deal. We hypothesize that the primary motive of the TTO is to protect and market the university's intellectual property. Secondary motives include promoting technological diffusion and securing additional research funding for the university via royalties, licensing fees, and sponsored research agreements. Recall that a primary reason for the federal government's relinquishment of intellectual property rights, as stipulated in Bayh–Dole, was to accelerate the commercialization of university-based technologies. Many managers and scientists remarked that TTOs were especially committed to their role as guardian of the university's intellectual property. As such, technology licensing officers tend to be somewhat inflexible and conservative in structuring deals. This inflexibility is consistent with the bureaucratic organizational culture of the university.

Firms and entrepreneurs seek to commercialize university-based technologies for financial gain. They also wish to maintain proprietary control over these technologies, which can potentially be achieved via an exclusive worldwide license. The entrepreneurial organizational culture of most firms (especially startups) rewards timeliness, speed, and flexibility. Reflecting these cultural values, many managers we visited stressed the importance of "time to market" as a determinant of success in UITT, in part, because they are convinced that there are significant first mover advantages in high technology markets.

Table 1 reveals that there are palpable differences in the motives, incentives, and organizational cultures of UITT stakeholders that can potentially impede

Table 1
Characteristics of UITT stakeholders

Stakeholder	Actions	Primary motive(s)	Secondary motive(s)	Organizational culture
University scientist	Discovery of new knowledge	Recognition within the scientific community	Financial gain and a desire to secure additional research funding	Scientific
TTO	Works with faculty and firms/entrepreneurs to structure deal	Protect and market the university's intellectual property	Facilitate technological diffusion and secure additional research funding	Bureaucratic
Firm/entrepreneur	Commercializes new technology	Financial gain	Maintain control of proprietary technologies	Entrepreneurial

technological diffusion. Thus, we hypothesize that some of the variation in UITT performance across universities can be attributed to organizational behaviors that potentially serve to resolve these differences. Our inductive, qualitative analysis, described in Sections 5 and 6, will help us identify these factors.

3. Assessing relative productivity in UITT

In the previous section, we identified a set of potential determinants of UITT, which include internal inputs, environmental and institutional factors, and a set of organizational variables. To assess relative productivity in UITT, we use the *stochastic frontier estimation* (SFE) method developed by Aigner et al. (1977) and Meeusen and Van den Broeck (1977). SFE generates a production (or cost) frontier with a stochastic error term that consists of two components: a conventional random error ("white noise") and a term that represents deviations from the frontier, or relative inefficiency.

SFE can be contrasted with data envelopment analysis (DEA), a *non-parametric* estimation technique that has been used extensively to compute relative productivity in service industries (Charnes et al., 1994). Thursby and Kemp (1998) use DEA to assess the relative efficiency of TTOs. DEA and SFE each have key strengths and weaknesses. DEA is a mathematical programming approach that does not require the specification of a functional form for the production function. It can also cope more readily with multiple inputs and outputs than parametric methods. However, DEA models are deterministic and highly sensitive to outliers. SFE allows for statistical inference, but requires restrictive functional form and distributional assumptions. We believe that SFE and DEA are complements, not substitutes.

In SFE, a production function of the following form is estimated:

$$y_i = X_i \beta + \varepsilon_i \tag{1}$$

where the subscript i denotes the ith university, y the output, X the vector of inputs, β the unknown parameter vector, and ε is an error term with two components, $\varepsilon_i = V_i - U_i$, where U_i represents a non-negative error term to account for technical inefficiency, or failure to produce maximal output, given

the set of inputs used, and V_i is a symmetric error term that accounts for random effects. The standard assumption (see Aigner et al., 1977) is that the U_i and V_i have the following distributions:

$$U_i \sim \text{i.i.d.} N^+(0, \sigma_u^2), \quad U_i \geq 0$$

$$V_i \sim \text{i.i.d.} N(0, \sigma_v^2)$$

That is, the inefficiency term (U_i) is assumed to have a half-normal distribution, i.e. universities are either "on the frontier" or below it. An important parameter in this model is $\gamma = \sigma_u^2/(\sigma_v^2 + \sigma_u^2)$, the ratio of the standard error of technical inefficiency to the standard error of statistical noise, which is bounded between 0 and 1. Note that $\gamma = 0$ under the null hypothesis of an absence of inefficiency, signifying that all of the variance can be attributed to statistical noise.

In recent years, SFE models have been developed that allow the technical inefficiency term to be expressed as a function of a vector of environmental and organizational variables. This is consistent with our notion that deviations from the frontier (which measure relative inefficiency in UITT) are related to institutional and organizational factors. Following Reifschneider and Stevenson (1991), we assume that the U_i are independently distributed as truncations at zero of the $N(m_i, \sigma_u^2)$ distribution with

$$m_i = Z_i \delta \tag{2}$$

where Z is a vector of environmental, institutional, and organizational variables that are hypothesized to influence efficiency and δ is a parameter vector.[9]

Following Battese and Coelli (1995), we derive maximum likelihood estimates of the parameter vectors β and δ from *simultaneous* estimation of the production function and inefficiency term equations, using the FRONTIER statistical package (Coelli, 1994). Based on these parameter values, we compute estimates of relative productivity.

Our specification of Eq. (1) is based on the knowledge-production function framework developed by Griliches (1979), here extended to university licensing, our proxy for UITT output. We assume a three-factor, log-linear Cobb–Douglas production function, relating

---

[9] Battese and Coelli (1995) have recently extended this model to incorporate panel data.

D.S. Siegel et al./Research Policy 32 (2003) 27–48   33

licensing to three inputs: invention disclosures, TTO staff, and legal expenditures:

$$\ln(\text{LICENSE}_i) = \beta_0 + \beta_1 \ln(\text{INVDISC}_i)$$
$$+ \beta_2 \ln(\text{STAFF}_i)$$
$$+ \beta_3 \ln(\text{LEGAL}_i) + V_i - U_i \quad (3)$$

where LICENSE is the average annual licensing agreements or revenue, INVDISC the average annual invention disclosures, STAFF the average annual TTO employees, and LEGAL denotes the average annual external legal expenditures with the technical inefficiency (U_i) term expressed as:

$$U_i = \delta_0 + \sum_k \delta_k \, \mathbf{ENV}_i + \sum_m \theta_m \, \mathbf{ORG}_i + \mu_i \quad (4)$$

where **ENV** and **ORG** are vectors of environmental and organizational factors, respectively, and μ is a classical disturbance term. As previously noted, we do not have any systematic measures of **ORG**. Nor is it clear from the literature precisely what organizational factors should be measured, even if we had the ability to do so. Thus, the equation we estimate contains only the following environmental/institutional (**ENV**) factors:

$$U_i = \delta_0 + \delta_\text{M} \, \text{MED}_i + \delta_\text{P} \, \text{PUBLIC}_i + \delta_\text{A} \text{AGE}_i$$
$$+ \delta_\text{R} \text{INDRD}_{ij} + \delta_\text{Q} \text{INDOUT}_{ij} + \mu_i \quad (4a)$$

where MED and PUBLIC are dummies denoting whether the university has a medical school and whether it is a public institution, respectively, AGE is the age of the TTO, and INDRD and INDOUT are average annual industry R&D intensity and average annual real output growth in the university's state (j), respectively, during the sample period.[10]

The characteristics of our data and parameter estimates of Eqs. (3) and (4a) are presented in the following section.

4. Data and empirical results

Our primary data source is a comprehensive survey conducted by AUTM, which was completed by TTO

directors at 183 academic institutions for 1991–1996. After eliminating teaching hospitals, research institutes, and Canadian institutions, we have 113 US universities. Our final sample contains 80 out of 89 US "Research 1" institutions.[11]

The AUTM file contains annual data on the number of licensing agreements (LICENSE1), royalty income generated by licenses (LICENSE2), invention disclosures (INVDISC), number of full-time-equivalent employees in the TTO (STAFF), and (external) legal expenditures on UITT (LEGAL).[12] Our data sources for state-level industrial R&D (INDRD) and real output growth (INDOUT) are NSF and the BEA.[13]

There are several difficulties with the output data. First, licensing agreements vary substantially in their significance, making it dangerous to draw inferences about aggregate technology flows based on the *number* of deals.[14] To address this concern, we use licensing revenue as an additional measure of output. Another limitation is that we focus only on two UITT outputs: licensing agreements and royalties. Sponsored research and the formation of startups can also be viewed as UITT outputs. However, startups and sponsored research agreements are often a direct result of licensing agreements. Similarly, one could adopt a broad view of technology transfer and treat patents, invention disclosures, and even students as UITT outputs. Given the uncertainty surrounding this issue, we asked UITT stakeholders to identify the outputs of UITT in our field research.

Descriptive statistics and a correlation matrix for the inputs and outputs of the licensing production function are presented in Table 2. The average university in our sample generates 14 licensing agreements per year, earns US$ 1.8 million in licensing

---

[10] An alternative is to use MSA-level R&D data on industrial innovations and R&D employment, provided in Anselin et al. (1997). Unfortunately, these data (from 1982) do not correspond to our sample period.

[11] Source: Carnegie Foundation for the Advancement of Teaching—to qualify for Research 1 status, a university must award 50 or more doctoral degrees and receive at least US$ 40 million annually in federal research grants.

[12] Unfortunately. AUTM does not ask TTOs to split out information on *exclusive* and *non-exclusive* licenses.

[13] Source: NSF (1991) Research and Development in Industry (1991–1996), US BEA (1999) Gross State Product data reported in *Fixed Reproducible Tangible Wealth*.

[14] A similar problem is encountered with patents. Jaffe et al. (1993), Trajtenberg et al. (1997), and Henderson et al. (1998) weight patents on the basis of the number of citations they receive.

34   D.S. Siegel et al. / Research Policy 32 (2003) 27–48

Table 2
Descriptive statistics and correlation coefficients for inputs and outputs of the stochastic frontier production function (Eq. (3))

Variable name	Description	Mean	Median	Standard deviation
LICENSE1	Average annual licensing agreements	14.3	8	21.4
LICENSE2	Average annual licensing revenue (US$ 000)	1803.7	321	4997.4
INVDISC	Average annual invention disclosures	53.9	24	67.4
STAFF	Average annual TTO employees	9.1	5	16.1
LEGAL	Average annual external legal expenditures on UITT (000)	352.6	129.8	640.1

Variable name	LICENSE1	LICENSE2	INVDISC	STAFF	LEGAL
		Correlation coefficients			
LICENSE1	1.00	0.89	0.66	0.47	−0.39
LICENSE2	0.89	1.00	0.68	−0.03	0.57
INVDISC	0.66	0.68	1.00	0.43	0.48
STAFF	0.47	−0.03	0.43	1.00	0.49
LEGAL	−0.39	0.57	0.48	0.49	1.00

$N = 113$ universities, 1991–1996; source: AUTM (1997).

income, receives 54 invention disclosures, employs nine workers in the TTO, and spends US$ 353,000 on external legal fees to protect its intellectual property. The correlation coefficients generally have the expected signs and magnitudes (e.g. invention disclosures are strongly positively correlated with the number of licensing agreements and revenue).

Note that each variable is computed as an annual average over the sample period. Although it may be desirable econometrically to construct a panel consisting of annual observations, this approach is problematic for two reasons. First, the use of annual data or lagged values to estimate the production function would result in an unbalanced panel, since all universities are not continuous reporters during the sample period. A related concern is that it is desirable to have a large sample of establishments when fitting the production function, given that the precision of this estimation will be highly dependent on the number of establishments used to project the frontier. Computing annual averages over the sample period yields the largest possible number of universities for the econometric estimation.

Table 3 contains two sets of parameter estimates of the stochastic frontier production function and inefficiency models outlined in the previous section (Eqs. (3) and (4a)) for two dependent variables: average annual number of licensing agreements and

average annual licensing revenues, respectively.[15] Columns 1 and 4 present OLS results, which are used to obtain starting values for regression parameters in the SFE model.[16] Columns 2 and 5 contain maximum likelihood estimates of the SFE model without the environmental and institutional variables, while columns 3 and 6 present the coefficients of the "full" version of the SFE model, including the inefficiency model with environmental and institutional variables.

The production function model appears to fit quite well, based on the R^2 values (0.82 and 0.75 for agreements and revenue, respectively). Across all variants, the estimated elasticity of licensing output with respect to invention disclosures is positive and highly significant. It appears that hiring additional TTO staff results in more agreements (columns 1–3), but not additional revenue (columns 4–6). This finding suggests that university administrators have established TTO incentives in a manner that is consistent with the spirit of Bayh–Dole, i.e. to maximize the *number* of licensing agreements.

---

[15] Although there is no direct diagnostic test for multi-collinearity, we do not observe any of the key symptoms of this problem: (1) high R^2 but few significant t ratios; (2) high pairwise and partial correlations among explanatory variables (see Table 2). Thus, we conclude that there does not appear to be a multi-collinearity problem.

[16] Coelli (1994) points out that, except for the intercept term, the OLS estimates are consistent, albeit inefficient.

D.S. Siegel et al./Research Policy 32 (2003) 27–48

Table 3
Maximum likelihood estimates of the stochastic frontier and inefficiency models (Eqs. (3) and (4a))

	Dependent variable					
	Average annual number of licensing agreements			Average annual licensing revenue		
	OLS (1)	SFE1 (2)	SFE2 (3)	OLS (4)	SFE1 (5)	SFE2 (6)
Stochastic frontier						
Intercept	−0.363[a] (0.172)	−0.218[a] (0.108)	−0.297[a] (0.146)	2.210[b] (0.598)	1.948[b] (0.902)	1.501[b] (0.739)
INVDISC	0.669[b] (0.094)	0.657[b] (0.096)	0.649[b] (0.087)	1.295[b] (0.281)	1.386[b] (0.349)	1.316[b] (0.510)
STAFF	0.445[b] (0.087)	0.395[b] (0.119)	0.379[b] (0.095)	−0.219 (0.343)	−0.206 (0.371)	−0.198 (0.299)
LEGAL	−0.061[a] (0.028)	−0.060[a] (0.028)	−0.038[a] (0.018)	0.526[b] (0.110)	0.463[b] (0.129)	0.412[b] (0.145)
Inefficiency model						
MED			0.136 (0.270)			−0.011 (0.126)
PUBLIC			0.012 (0.035)			0.050 (0.067)
AGE			−0.103 (0.189)			−0.115[a] (0.052)
INDRD			−0.125[a] (0.060)			−0.093 (0.071)
INDOUT			−0.044 (0.057)			−0.052 (0.083)
R^2	0.822			0.752		
F statistic for $\beta_1 + \beta_2 + \beta_3 = 1$	1.21			9.95[b]		
log likelihood		−20.79	−19.76		−22.61	−21.41
$\gamma = \sigma_u^2/(\sigma_v^2 + \sigma_u^2)$		0.775[b] (0.173)	0.651[b] (0.259)		816[b] (0.311)	0.716[b] (0.268)
Mean technical efficiency		0.77	0.83		0.76	0.80

Notes: standard errors in parentheses; $N = 113$ universities; SFE1 denotes stochastic frontier estimation excluding environmental/institutional determinants of inefficiency; SFE2 denotes stochastic frontier estimation including environmental/institutional determinants of inefficiency.
[a] Significant at the 5% level.
[b] Significant at the 1% level.

On the other hand, the results imply that spending more on (external) lawyers reduces the number of licensing agreements, but increases licensing revenue. This finding is consistent with the feedback we received from firms in our field research. Several managers reported that it was much more difficult to negotiate with outside attorneys than university administrators, because the lawyers tended to adopt a tougher negotiation stance. Other managers viewed a university's liberal use of outside lawyers as a signal that the institution would be aggressive in exercising its intellectual property rights.

It is difficult to assess the validity of these hypotheses without additional information on the composition of the TTO staff, as substantial external legal expense could actually reflect outsourcing of legal functions or defensive actions in the aftermath of a major lawsuit. Moreover, there could be reverse causality at play, i.e. universities with more lucrative inventions, or those who focus on particularly contentious fields, may be more likely to use outside counsel to protect their intellectual property.[17] These interpretations imply that it is not the *actions* of lawyers that generate higher licensing revenue.

F statistics presented in Table 3 imply that licensing revenue is subject to increasing returns, while licensing agreements are characterized by constant returns to scale. The latter result is consistent with Adams and Griliches (1998), who examined the research productivity of universities (using papers and citations as outputs and R&D expenditures as inputs) and found evidence of constant returns to scale. An implication of increasing returns for licensing revenue is that a university wishing to maximize revenue should spend more on lawyers. Perhaps this would free up TTO staff to spend more time "matching" scientists to firms. Still, this result should be interpreted with caution, as licensing revenue, even when computed over a six-year period, can be a somewhat misleading indicator of current TTO performance, as royalty streams

---

[17] We are indebted to an anonymous referee for this salient point.

36 *D.S. Siegel et al. / Research Policy 32 (2003) 27–48*

may reflect transactions that were consummated many years ago. For instance, the University of Florida has consistently ranked among the top 10 US universities in licensing income due to Gatorade.

Next, we focus on parameter estimates of the "full" SFE model (SFE2), including the inefficiency equation (Eq. (4a)). In general, the coefficients on the environmental and institutional variables have the right signs, but are statistically insignificant. However, the licensing agreement equation (column 3) results indicate that universities in states with higher levels of industrial R&D activity (INDRD) are less inefficient, that is closer to the frontier. This finding implies that there is a positive association between R&D conducted by local firms and UITT productivity at universities in the same state. In the licensing agreement equation (column 6), we find that older TTOs tend to be closer to the frontier, implying that there is a learning effect in university management of intellectual property. Our results are consistent with evidence presented in Mowery et al. (2001), which reports that over time, newer TTOs learn how to raise the quality of their patent portfolios.

Despite the lack of significance of most of the coefficients, the γ values are highly statistically significant, indicating that the (null) hypothesis that inefficiency effects are absent from the model can be decisively rejected in each instance. Further evidence that external factors provide some explanatory power is shown in Table 3, which contrasts the mean technical efficiency in versions of the model excluding (columns 2 and 5) and including (columns 4 and 6) the environmental and institutional variables. The latter set of findings indicate that these external factors explain some of the variation in technical inefficiency across universities, 26.1 and 16.7%, respectively.[18]

In this section, we specified a TTO "production function" where the outputs are the number of licensing agreements (LICENSE1) and licensing revenue (LICENSE2) and the inputs are invention disclosures (INVDISC), employees in the TTO (STAFF), and (external) legal expenditures (LEGAL). These variables are assumed to be under the control of the "producer"

or the TTO director. We also attempted to explain *deviations* from the production frontier (relative inefficiency), which are assumed to be a function of a set of environmental and institutional variables that are outside of the control of the TTO director. These are external factors that could enhance or reduce the rate at which universities transfer technologies to the private sector. Our econometric results suggest that while the TTO production function fits well, deviations from the production frontier *cannot* be completely explained by environmental and institutional factors.

As previously noted, we conjecture that some of the variation in relative productivity can also be attributed to *organizational practices* in university management of intellectual property. These practices could potentially serve to mitigate conflict caused by palpable differences in the motives, incentives, and organizational cultures of scientists, firms, and administrators. Unfortunately, there are no existing data on UITT organizational practices, nor is it even precisely clear what needs to be measured.

Accordingly, we outline our inductive, qualitative approach to the examination of organizational issues in the following section. We also provide detailed description of our qualitative research methods, as most economists are unfamiliar with these techniques. This information may be beneficial to economists who are contemplating fieldwork.

5. Qualitative research methods

Researchers conducting interview-based, field studies confront four methodological issues: sample selection, the nature of the interview questions, procedures for conducting interviews, and qualitative data analysis. Table 4 summarizes how we dealt with these issues.[19] In doing so, we borrow heavily from the fields of management and sociology, where such methods are prevalent. We now briefly consider each of these issues in turn.

We interviewed TTO stakeholders at five US universities in the southwest and southeast. This is

---

[18] That is, the mean technical efficiency is closer to one when we include these variables in the stochastic frontier model ($0.06/(1 − 0.77) = 0.261$ and $0.04/(1 − 0.76) = 0.167$).

[19] This is by no means an exhaustive list of such concerns. For a comprehensive review of qualitative research methods, see Miles and Huberman, 1994 and Yin, 1989.

D.S. Siegel et al. / Research Policy 32 (2003) 27–48

37

Table 4
Four key methodological issues in a field study and how we addressed them

Sample selection	Nature of interview questions	Procedures for conducting interviews	Qualitative data analysis
Convenience sample of five universities from two regions	Semi-structured (some questions were the same for each group, some were tailored to a particular group)	Face-to-face interviews	Tape recording and transcription of interviews by neutral third party
Stratified approach to the selection of interviewees: managers/entrepreneurs, university administrators, university scientists	Open-ended questions	Team approach	Identification of themes from transcripts by multiple assessors
		Neutral probing	Coding of themes
		Pledge of confidentiality	Frequency tables displaying important themes
		Interviewees had prior knowledge of the goals of the study and backgrounds of the researchers	Z tests comparing proportion of responses between stakeholder groups

a convenience sample, due to our familiarity with these institutions and the surrounding regions. Yin (1989) reports that convenience samples are common in inductive, exploratory studies, especially when researchers have limited funding. Although our approach precludes an examination of such hotbeds of UITT activity as Cambridge (MIT, Harvard) or Silicon Valley (Stanford, UC-Berkeley), the schools we visited are probably far more representative of the *modal* university experience with UITT.

The top panel of Table 5 presents some information on the five universities in our field study. These include private and public universities, land grant institutions, and universities with and without a medical school. There is also considerable variation with respect to size and age of the TTO, extent of licensing activity, and technical efficiency.[20] The bottom panel of Table 5 compares mean values of licensing agreements, licensing revenue, TTO staff and age, and technical efficiency for the five institutions we visited and the 113 universities in our econometric analysis. Although these five schools generate below average licensing revenue, they are quite similar to the average AUTM respondent along the other dimensions. These findings lend further

credence to our assertion that the universities in our field study are representative institutions with respect to UITT.

We constructed a stratified sample of interviewees, drawn from each stakeholder group. At each university, we interviewed academic scientists, TTO directors, and top-level research administrators. Within the surrounding region, we also met with entrepreneurs, directors of business development, intellectual property managers and other research executives of large companies, and executives of patent management firms and non-profit organizations with an interest in UITT. All in all, we conducted 55 interviews: 20 managers and entrepreneurs, 15 administrators (including the five TTO directors), and 20 scientists.[21]

Potential respondents were selected in two ways. First, we identified the TTO director and other administrators with UITT responsibilities, such as a Vice Provost, Vice President, or Vice Chancellor for Research.[22] Second, to identify managers/entrepreneurs and scientists, we solicited feedback from two nonpartisan, non-profit organizations that serve as UITT

---

[20] That is, some institutions are close to the frontier, while others are highly inefficient.

[21] Although there were only 55 face-to-face meetings, we actually interviewed 100 individuals, since multiple respondents were present at some meetings (Siegel et al., 2001).

[22] Typically, the TTO director reports to a Vice President, Vice Provost, or Vice Chancellor for Research.

Table 5
Characteristics of the five universities in our field study and comparison of mean values of key variables with full statistical sample of 113 universities

	University A	University B	University C	University D	University E
Organizational status	Private	Public	Public	Public	Public
Medical school	Yes	Yes	No	No	Yes
Land grant institution	No	No	Yes	No	Yes
TTO established in	1984	1985	1982	1985	1988
STAFF	14.2	11.5	11.1	2.9	8.5
LICENSE1	28.1	19.0	26.1	3.4	12.0
LICENSE2	1213.2	773.3	1535.7	382.7	177.0
Technical efficiency	84.1	80.2	87.8	71.3	74.8

Variable name	Description	Five universities in our field study	One-hundred and thirteen universities in our statistical sample		
		Mean values of key variables			
LICENSE1	Average annual licensing agreements	17.7	14.3		
LICENSE2	Average annual licensing revenue (US$ 000)	816.4	1803.7		
STAFF	Average annual TTO employees	9.6	9.1		
AGE	Numbers of years since TTO was established (as of 1996)	11.1	12.5		
Technical efficiency	Estimate of relative productivity based on SFE	79.6	76.9		

facilitators in each region. These facilitators helped us select managers and scientists with different perspectives on UITT.[23]

In formulating our set of questions, we adopted a "semi-structured" approach (Miles and Huberman, 1994), whereby interviewees within each stakeholder category were asked the same questions. According to these authors, the best approach for an inductive study is to ask *open-ended* questions, such as "what are the outputs of UITT?", "what are the barriers to effective UITT?", and "how would you improve the process?" We asked such questions to all stakeholders, although some queries were tailored to a particular group. For example, TTO directors were asked about TTO managerial practices, while administrators were asked broader questions regarding strategic goals for UITT.

Following Sekaran (1992), we conducted *face-to-face* interviews, which the author contends is the

best approach for an inductive study on a controversial topic. We paired economists with management professors, as management professors have much more extensive experience and training in qualitative methods.[24] The use of teams can also enhance the overall effectiveness of a face-to-face interview by increasing the likelihood that a researcher can respond to a clarifying question or establish a rapport with the interviewee. We also employed three tactics (see Waldman et al., 1998) that increase the accuracy of qualitative data: neutral probing of answers, a pledge of confidentiality, and prior knowledge of the goals of the study and backgrounds of the researchers.[25]

Based on the 55 transcripts, we implemented the three stages of qualitative analysis of interview data

---

[23] In one region, a facilitator had published a voluminous report on UITT, which contained the names, phone numbers, and addresses of these potential respondents.

[24] Five professors (two management professors and three economists) conducted the 55 interviews (Siegel, 1999).

[25] According to Yin (1989), this serves two useful purposes. First, it indicates the researchers' concern and respect for the value of the respondent's time. Second, it reduces uncertainty and suspicion regarding the intentions of the researchers.

D.S. Siegel et al./Research Policy 32 (2003) 27–48   39

Table 6
Outputs of UITT as identified by interviewees in our field study

Outputs	Type of interviewee			Z_{12}	Z_{13}	Z_{23}
	Managers/ entrepreneurs (1)	TTO directors/ administrators (2)	University scientists (3)			
Licenses	75.0	86.7	25.0	−1.37	2.14**	3.24*
Royalties	30.0	66.7	15.0	−1.74	0.91	2.61*
Patents	10.0	46.7	20.0	−2.91*	−0.84	2.23**
Sponsored research agreements	5.0	46.7	0.0	−2.72*	0.44	3.33*
Startup companies	5.0	33.3	10.0	−2.07**	−0.56	1.64
Invention disclosures	5.0	33.3	5.0	−2.81*	−0.99	2.28*
Students	25.0	26.7	15.0	−0.22	0.88	1.22
Informal transfer of know-how	70.0	20.0	20.0	2.69*	3.31*	0.03
Product development	40.0	6.7	35.0	2.08**	0.12	−2.01**
Economic development	35.0	20.0	0.0	0.52	2.98*	2.03**
Number of interviews	20	15	20			

Note: the values presented in columns 1–3 are the *percentages* of respondents who identified a particular item as an output of UITT. The values displayed in the last three columns are Z statistics for differences in proportions between each class of interviewee.
** $P < 0.05$.
* $P < 0.01$.

outlined in Miles and Huberman (1994): data reduction, data display, and conclusion drawing/verification (Miles and Huberman, 1994, pp. 10–12). Data reduction involves the selection, simplification, and transformation of raw data (interview responses) into an analyzable form. First, we developed a list of general categories for content analysis. These categories were based on general research questions, such as identifying the barriers to UITT.[26] Next, for each transcript, all comments were independently categorized by at least two members of the research team into four areas: UITT outputs, networks/relationships in UITT, barriers to UITT, and proposed improvements to the UITT process. Researchers' lists of comments within a topic area were then compared and discrepancies discussed, until agreement was reached regarding comments that were pertinent to each category.[27]

Following identification of relevant comments in each topic area, each researcher then worked with five

[26] We also followed the advice of Miles and Huberman (1994) by having *multiple* assessors of interview transcripts. The authors assert that the use of multiple assessors reduces the degree of bias in interpreting such transcripts.

[27] These methods are similar to those employed by Butterfield et al. (1996), who identified unique "thought units" pertinent to their subject of interest (employee discipline).

interview transcripts to generate a list of more specific *themes* within the four categories. The research team then met and discussed the themes that emerged. There was a great deal of similarity in the lists of themes that emerged from the separate samples of comments. After a consensus was reached regarding the themes, we returned to the lists of comments pertinent to each of the four general categories and sorted them into the themes identified for that respective category. For data display purposes, we tabulated frequency counts for each major theme that emerged.

In Tables 6–9, we display *percentages* of respondents who identified a particular theme relating to UITT outputs, relationships/networks, barriers to effective UITT, and suggested improvements to the UITT process. For example, the first column on Table 6 reveals that 75% of the managers/entrepreneurs we interviewed identified licenses as an output of UITT. Note that these analyses are conducted separately for each stakeholder group. Proportion tests of differences (Z tests) were computed to compare whether the proportion of respondents mentioning a theme in a given group differs from the proportion of respondents mentioning a theme in another group. For instance, Z_{12} compares managers/entrepreneurs (Group 1) and TTO directors/university administrators (Group 2).

Table 7
Aspects of relationships/networks in UITT as identified by interviewees in our field study

Relationships/networks	Type of interviewee			Z_{12}	Z_{13}	Z_{23}
	Managers/ entrepreneurs (1)	TTO directors/ administrators (2)	University scientists (3)			
Personal relationships	75.0	66.7	80.0	0.68	−0.42	−1.63
TTO as a facilitator of relationships between scientists and firms	25.0	75.0	40.0	−2.65*	−0.91	1.92
Knowledge transfer from industry to faculty members	25.0	20.0	65.0	0.35	−2.46*	−297*
Conference/expos/town hall meetings on TT issues	35.0	80.0	15.0	−2.34**	1.59	3.56*
Contractual relationships	15.0	6.7	0.0	0.84	1.80	1.02
Number of interviews	20	15	20			

Note: the values presented in columns 1–3 are the *percentages* of respondents who identified a particular item as an aspect of relationships/networks in UITT. The values displayed in the last three columns are Z statistics for differences in proportions between each class of interviewee.

** $P < 0.05$.

* $P < 0.01$.

Table 8
Barriers to UITT as identified by interviewees in our field study

Barriers	Type of interviewee			Z_{12}	Z_{13}	Z_{23}
	Managers/ entrepreneurs (1)	TTO directors/ administrators (2)	University scientists (3)			
Lack of understanding regarding university, corporate, or scientific norms and environments	90.0	93.3	75.0	−0.25	1.19	1.30
Insufficient rewards for university researchers	35.0	60.0	70.0	−1.29	−2.46*	−1.03
Bureaucracy and inflexibility of university administrators	80.0	6.7	70.0	3.96*	0.74	−3.51*
Insufficient resources devoted to technology transfer by universities	35.0	53.3	20.0	−0.95	0.93	2.05**
Poor marketing/technical/negotiation skills of TTOs	55.0	13.3	25.0	2.07**	1.91	−0.71
University too aggressive in exercising intellectual property rights	80.0	13.3	25.0	3.30*	2.94*	−0.91
Faculty members/administrators have unrealistic expectations regarding the value of their technologies	25.0	40.0	10.0	−0.94	1.13	1.90
"Public domain" mentality of universities	40.0	6.7	5.0	1.86	2.60*	0.38
Number of interviews	20	15	20			

Note: the values presented in columns 1–3 are the *percentages* of respondents who identified a particular item as a barrier to UITT. The values displayed in the last three columns are Z statistics for differences in proportions between each class of interviewee.

** $P < 0.05$.

* $P < 0.01$.

D.S. Siegel et al./Research Policy 32 (2003) 27–48   41

Table 9
Suggested improvements to the UITT process, as identified by interviewees in our field study

Improvements	Type of interviewee			Z_{12}	Z_{13}	Z_{23}
	Managers/ entrepreneurs (1)	TTO directors/ administrators (2)	University scientists (3)			
Universities and industry should devote more effort to developing better mutual understanding	80.0	93.3	75.0	−0.96	0.33	1.28
Modify reward systems to reward technology transfer activities	85.0	80.0	80.0	0.35	0.36	−0.00
Universities need to provide more education to overcome informational and cultural barriers	85.0	86.7	60.0	−0.09	1.70	1.74
Universities should devote additional resources to technology transfer	45.0	46.7	60.0	0.11	−1.00	−1.25
Universities should be less aggressive in exercising intellectual property rights	55.0	10.0	15.0	2.52*	2.62*	−0.36
Increase formal and informal networking between scientists and practitioners	35.0	26.7	40.0	0.65	−0.34	−1.09
Universities need greater technical expertise and marketing skills in the TTO	50.0	20.0	25.0	1.76	1.54	−0.37
Number of interviews	20	15	20			

Note: the values presented in columns 1–3 are the *percentages* of respondents who identified a particular item as a suggested improvement to UITT. The values displayed in the last three columns are Z statistics for differences in proportions between each class of interviewee.
  * $P < 0.01$.

6. Qualitative findings

Table 6 demonstrates that licenses and royalties were identified as outputs of UITT by a substantial majority of TTO directors and university administrators. Managers and entrepreneurs also frequently mentioned licenses, but stressed *informal* aspects of UITT a bit more, as well as economic development outcomes. Scientists emphasized product development and surprisingly, failed to mention sponsored research agreements.

Another key finding is that there is considerable heterogeneity in stakeholder perspectives regarding UITT outputs. There appears to be a "Rashomon" effect, as evidenced by the numerous output categories identified by respondents and by the many significant differences between each class of interviewee (16 out of 30 Z statistics are significant at the 5% level).[28] This

[28] For the benefit of *Research Policy* readers who are cinematically deprived, Rashomon is a famous Japanese movie, directed by Akira Kurosawa. It portrays four vastly different views of the same heinous crime. In coining this phrase, we wish to suggest that the three stakeholders (academic scientists, university administrators, and managers/entrepreneurs) may have starkly different perspectives on the same events/process.

is perhaps not surprising, as university management of intellectual property through a TTO is a recent and somewhat controversial development.

This raises the important issue of the tradeoffs associated with stimulating additional UITT, in terms of its impact on the sharing and dissemination of knowledge. Indeed, some interviewees perceived the mission of the TTO (protection and marketing of the university's intellectual property) as being inconsistent with the traditional "public domain" philosophy regarding the dissemination of information that pervades most research universities. This concern was articulated in a recent trenchant essay by Nelson (2001), who asserts that the cost of losing the culture of "open science" that exists at leading universities outweighs any benefits that might arise as a result of more rapid technological diffusion.

Table 7 shows that respondents in each stakeholder category mentioned *personal* relationships in UITT much more often than *contractual* relationships. One scientist said:

I would say right now that I feel that the one-on-one interaction is somewhat more successful in

42 *D.S. Siegel et al. / Research Policy 32 (2003) 27–48*

effectively transferring technology [than is research formally sponsored by a consortium].

This raises the possibility that the formation of "social networks" could be important in UITT. These networks include academic and industry scientists, graduate students and post-doctoral fellows who conduct most of the experimental work in laboratories, former graduate students who have accepted positions in industry, entrepreneurs, and perhaps, university administrators and TTO directors. As defined by Liebeskind et al. (1996), social networks, like markets, involve exchanges between legally distinct entities. However, unlike markets, social networks support these exchanges without using competitive pricing or legal contracting. Instead, they rely on shared norms among the exchange partners, where information is the currency of exchange.[29]

Table 7 also indicates that knowledge transfer appears to work in both directions. For instance, 65% of the scientists noted that interacting with industry has had a positive influence on their experimental work. Some scientists explicitly mentioned that these interactions improved the quantity and quality of their basic research. A representative comment from a scientist was:

> There is no doubt that working with industry scientists has made me a better researcher. They help me refine my experiments and sometimes have a different perspective on a problem that sparks my own ideas. Also, my involvement with firms has allowed me to purchase better equipment for my lab, which means I can conduct more experiments.

This result is consistent with Zucker and Darby (1996), who found an increase in the scholarly output of "star" academic scientists after they were involved in commercialization efforts in biotechnology.[30] This implies that the conventional wisdom regarding the existence of a tradeoff between UITT activity and research performance may be wrong.

As shown in Table 8, all three groups identified a lack of understanding regarding university/corporate/scientific norms as a barrier to effective UITT (90.0, 93.3, and 75.0%). It appears that these cultural and informational barriers are pervasive. That is, university scientists and administrators often do not understand or appreciate the industry environment, and vice versa. An illustrative comment from a scientist was:

> Industry has a lack of understanding of what an academic institution does and a lack of understanding of what a university faculty member's responsibility is to their institution. There are some companies I don't even deal with because their approach to dealing with an academic entity is so poor. They feel that basically we owe them by our position at the university because the state pays our salaries.

Our qualitative evidence is consistent with the view that UITT stakeholders operate under different organizational environments and cultures, implying that they have different norms, standards, and values. For example, Nelson (2001) noted how universities and firms differ in their perspective on the role of knowledge. Managers and entrepreneurs usually do not share the academic values of publishing results and sharing information with colleagues and the general public. Instead, new knowledge and technology is to be kept proprietary and exploited to achieve or sustain a competitive advantage.

Table 8 also indicates widespread belief that there are insufficient rewards for faculty involvement in UITT. Sixty percent of administrators and 70% of scientists reported this as a barrier. In their comments, administrators and scientists specifically referred to tenure and promotion policies and the university's royalty and equity distribution formula. The latter refers to the split in licensing or equity income among the inventor(s), the department or college of the inventor(s), and the TTO or another general research fund within the university. For example, at one school, the formula was 40% inventor, 40% inventor's department, and 20% "invention management fund" which is managed by the TTO.[31] An administrator at

---

[29] Powell (1990) argued that social networks are the most efficient organizational arrangement for sourcing information because information is difficult to price and communicate through a hierarchical structure.

[30] Mansfield (1995) reported similar results for a variety of scientific fields.

---

[31] Jensen and Thursby (2001) surveyed 62 TTOs and found that the mean payout rate to inventors is 40%. See Beath et al., 2000 for an analysis of the optimal payout rate for scientists.

D.S. Siegel et al./Research Policy 32 (2003) 27–48

43

a school with a relatively low payout rate to inventors noted that:

> Some faculty members have complained about the low share of revenue they receive. They may be right. We hope to bring that up to say 40% in the near future. I think we'll have much of a struggle on that one.

The vast majority of interviewees also specifically commented on the fact that tenure and promotion decisions continued to be made almost strictly on the basis of publications and grants. For example, one scientist remarked:

> Technology transfer has not played a role in the performance evaluation process. Performance evaluation is based on publications.

From this scientist's perspective, the existing reward structure at his university is inconsistent with the organizational objective of increasing UITT, a goal that is featured prominently in that university's mission statement and promotional brochures.

Managers/entrepreneurs (80%) and scientists (70%) also frequently pointed to university bureaucracy and inflexibility as barriers to effective UITT. Many scientists and managers provided us with examples of rigid, cumbersome, and unclear policies and procedures that impede UITT. Faculty members who had tried to form startup companies were especially vocal on this point. A typical remark from a scientist was:

> I don't think they understand the flexibility within the framework and what they can do. I think they have a set of forms and a set of ways of doing things, and if it doesn't fit nicely into that, then they make you go through a whole bunch of hoops.

Although some of these complaints may be self-serving, universities that wish to enhance UITT productivity should address such negative perceptions.

Staffing practices in the TTO are also a matter of concern. Recall that a university technology licensing officer is responsible for coordinating the activities that result in a formal agreement between the university (and its scientists) and a firm. Fifty-five percent of the managers and entrepreneurs we interviewed expressed dissatisfaction with the marketing and negotiation skills of TTO personnel. An intellectual property manager stated:

> These guys (TTOs) need to be marketing facilitators rather than lawyers. They need to be able to step into the company and into their customer's shoes and look back.

A lack of requisite business skills and expertise could have a significant deleterious effect on TTO productivity. Other respondents noted that TTOs are either too narrowly focused on a small set of technical areas, or too concerned with the legal aspects of licensing.

There is also a strong belief on the part of industry (80%) that universities are exercising their intellectual property rights too aggressively. One manager stated:

> I think the frustration for commercial licensees who go to a university is that it seems as though the attitude they are hitting at the university is 'oh we've got this wonderful thing and we're going to drag every nickel out of you that we can get for it'.

One interpretation of this perception is that it is self-serving and merely a reflection of the inherently adversarial nature of negotiations. However, this attitude, in conjunction with the concerns raised earlier regarding university bureaucracy and inflexibility, has led some firms to completely avoid working with TTOs. Thus, when an invention is publicly disclosed, some firms will contact scientists and arrange to work with them via informal technology transfer, through consulting or a sabbatical leave. A scientist reported on the attitude of firms he was working with:

> In fact a lot of firms will come to us and say we don't want to go through the university ... we'll just pay you on the side.

Table 9 presents some suggested improvements to the UITT process. These recommendations are fairly consistent with the impediments identified in Table 8. With virtual unanimity, respondents suggested that universities and firms should devote more effort to developing better mutual understanding. Several respondents noted that this could easily be achieved through such events as "Town Hall" meetings involving the three stakeholder groups, as well as by targeting each individual group with additional information to help facilitate UITT. For example, one university scientist pointed out that new faculty orientations at his university did not include a module on UITT issues:

It's appalling that new faculty members don't receive any information on how to get involved in technology transfer at their orientation sessions. What does that tell you about this school's priorities?

Another consistent theme was that universities should align reward systems with UITT goals. Although we lack measures of the intensity of feeling on a particular theme, our analysis of the transcripts reveals that recommendations regarding changes in reward systems were by far the most direct and vivid of the suggested improvements to the UITT process. Many university administrators specifically mentioned the need to reward UITT more in promotion and tenure decisions. One department chair phrased it as follows:

It's the height of hypocrisy for universities to claim that they value technology transfer, or that it's supposed to be a top institutional priority, and then fail to reward it in their promotion and tenure decisions. At some point, we've got to resolve this discrepancy.

Several managers/entrepreneurs and administrators also discussed the need for incentive compensation for TTO staff. A representative comment from a manager was:

The TTO people need to push the deals through .... You've got to look at how they are rewarded. Perhaps if they were paid on the basis of the number of deals they complete or the revenue they generate for the university, you would see more technologies licensed. I guess that they are so terrified of negative publicity if a bad deal goes through, that they're afraid to make this change.

Our respondents noted that some private schools, and even some public ones, such as the University of Washington and Wayne State, recently instituted incentive compensation plans in the TTO. Other schools are contemplating implementing these programs. Such efforts might reduce the high rate of turnover among TTO staff and enhance productivity.[32]

---

[32] Several firms were frustrated by the high rate of turnover in the TTO, which was perceived to be detrimental to relationship building and organizational learning.

Table 9 also demonstrates that, to a lesser extent, there was support for the notion that universities should devote additional resources to UITT, although most of these recommendations were somewhat nebulous. Many respondents also suggested that universities provide more education and/or community outreach to overcome informational and cultural barriers. A predictable recommendation from managers and entrepreneurs is that universities should be less aggressive in exercising intellectual property rights.

7. Conclusions and suggestions for additional research

In this paper, we present quantitative and qualitative evidence on several aspects of UITT. A stochastic production function framework is used to assess the relative productivity of university TTOs. The parameter estimates of the stochastic frontier imply that licensing activity, our proxy for UITT, is characterized by constant returns to scale. The deviations from the frontier, which represent technical inefficiency, are assumed to be a function of a vector of environmental and institutional factors. We find that these variables explain a portion of the variation in relative productivity across universities.

We hypothesize that some of the remaining variation in relative efficiency can be attributed to organizational practices in university management of intellectual property. Unfortunately, this hypothesis cannot be formally tested because there are no systematic measures of these factors. Thus, an analysis of UITT organizational practices is fertile ground for an inductive, exploratory field study. As a first step towards identifying these practices, we conducted 55 face-to-face interviews of 98 key UITT stakeholders at five research universities. This fieldwork also greatly improved our ability to model the UITT process, by providing a critical reality check on the specification of the econometric model. Based on our qualitative evidence, we believe that the most critical organizational factors are reward systems for faculty involvement in UITT, compensation and staffing practices in the TTO, and actions taken by administrators to extirpate informational and cultural barriers between universities and firms. More specifically, it appears that the propensity of faculty members to disclose inventions,

D.S. Siegel et al. / Research Policy 32 (2003) 27–48   45

and thus, increase the "supply" of technologies available for commercialization, will be related to promotion and tenure policies and the university's royalty and equity distribution formula. TTO compensation practices could also be relevant because UITT activity will depend on the efforts of technology licensing officers to elicit invention disclosures and market them effectively to private companies. Thus, we expect that, ceteris paribus, licensing activity will be higher at universities that have implemented some form of incentive compensation plan for technology licensing officers.[33]

Staffing practices in the TTO may also help explain why some universities are more proficient than others in managing intellectual property. According to Parker and Zilberman (1993), TTOs usually hire either a mix of scientists and *lawyers* or a mix of scientists and *entrepreneurs/businessmen*. In the former case, legal functions, such as the adjudication of disputes involving intellectual property rights and the negotiation of licensing agreements, are performed in-house. In the latter case, such functions are usually outsourced. Parker and Zilberman hypothesize that the entrepreneur/business model for TTOs may be more conducive to helping scientists form their own startups. It also seems reasonable to assume that TTOs staffed in this manner would be more effective in the marketing phase of UITT. A substantial percentage of managers suggested that universities hire more licensing professionals with stronger marketing and business skills.

Our findings regarding informational and cultural barriers suggest that "boundary spanning" could be an important skill for university technology licensing officers. Boundary spanning behavior has been studied extensively in the management literature (Katz and Tushman, 1983). In the context of UITT, boundary spanning refers to actions taken by university technology managers to serve as a bridge between "customers" (entrepreneurs/firms) and "suppliers" (scientists), who operate in distinctly different environments. Without effective boundary spanning, the needs of customers may not be adequately communicated to suppliers. Similarly, the capabilities and interests

of suppliers may not be adequately communicated to customers. Effective boundary spanning by a TTO would involve adept communication with both stakeholder groups, in an effort to forge alliances between scientists and firms.

The most natural extension of our exploratory study would be to survey UITT stakeholders at each university in an attempt to measure the organizational factors we have identified.[34] Some variables, such as the university's royalty and equity distribution formula are easy to measure with a survey and may even be available on the worldwide web. Other variables, such as measures of the skills of TTO personnel, tenure and promotion policies, and other policy variables will be more perceptual in nature. In designing these surveys, we need to be mindful of the considerable heterogeneity in stakeholder perspectives on UITT that was revealed in our interviews. This finding underscores the importance of surveying scientists, managers/entrepreneurs, and administrators separately to generate a more accurate and unbiased view of the organizational environment.

Taking stock of organizational practices in university management of intellectual property will be useful in several respects. First, given the somewhat embryonic nature of the TTO enterprise as an organizational form, there is a need to simply document the nature of these practices.[35] Many administrators expressed a strong interest in benchmarking their intellectual property management practices relative to peer institutions. Perhaps the most important benefit of collecting this information is that it can be used to determine the fraction of the variance in relative productivity that can be attributed to organizational factors. We can also identify specific practices that enhance UITT productivity. Finally, these data could be used to assess the performance effects of the adoption of *complementary* organizational practices. Recent theoretical (Athey and Stern, 1998) and empirical (Ichniowski et al., 1997) studies highlight the importance of clusters or "mixes" of complementary organizational practices in enhancing productivity,

---

[33] Lazear (1999) and Ichniowski et al. (1997) report a positive correlation between incentive compensation and worker and plant productivity, respectively.

[34] There is an existing survey instrument to measure boundary-spanning skills (Caldwell and O'Reilly, 1982).
[35] Although TTOs were established many years ago at some elite institutions, our discussion relates to TTOs at more representative universities.

due to interaction effects. It would be interesting to see if such synergies arise in the context of UITT.

Possible extensions to the econometric analysis include adding more environmental and institutional factors as explanatory variables in the inefficiency equation, such as measures of the strictness of state and university technology transfer policies, local venture capital activity, and more detailed data on regional R&D. It might also be useful to employ a more general, "flexible" functional form for the production function, such as the Generalized Leontief specification (see Morrison and Siegel, 1997). Access to more comprehensive data might also allow for an analysis of variation in licensing practices and impediments by technology field (e.g. physical versus life sciences).[36] Another extension to the empirical analysis would involve incorporating multiple outputs of UITT, such as the number of startups and sponsored research agreements resulting from UITT. This requires the use of a "distance" function approach, which has been implemented in recent studies in the stochastic frontier literature.[37]

Acknowledgements

We thank Philippe Aghion, Leanne Atwater, Richard Disney, Jonathan Haskel, Susan Helper, Adam Jaffe, Bruno van Pottelsberghe, Kjell Salvanes, Robert Sauer, Jonathan Silberman, Jerry Thursby, Marie Thursby, Steve Zylstra, three anonymous reviewers, and seminar participants at the NBER, CEPR, Purdue, Rensselaer Polytechnic Institute, CERGI-EI, University of Nottingham, Universite Libre de Bruxelles, Norwegian School of Economics and Business Administration, the 1999 Conference on Comparative Analysis of Enterprise Data (CAED) in The Netherlands, EARIE 2000, the 2000 Strategic Management Society Meetings, and the 2000 International Schumpeter Society Conference for their insightful comments and suggestions. We are also deeply indebted to the many administrators, scientists, managers, and entrepreneurs who agreed to be interviewed. Martha Cobb and Melissa Zidle provided capable research assistance. Financial support from the Alfred P. Sloan Foundation through the NBER Project on Industrial Technology and Productivity is gratefully acknowledged.

References

Adams, J.D., Griliches, Z., 1998. Research productivity in a system of universities. Annals of INSEE 49/50, 127–162.

Aigner, D.J., Lovell, C.A.K., Schmidt, P., 1977. Formulation and estimation of stochastic frontier production functions. Journal of Econometrics 6, 21–37.

Anselin, L., Varga, A., Acs, Z., 1997. Local geographic spillovers between university research and high technology innovations. Journal of Urban Economics 42, 422–448.

Association of University Technology Managers (AUTM), 1997. The AUTM Licensing Survey, Fiscal Year 1996. Norwalk, CT.

Athey, S., Stern, S., 1998. An Empirical Framework for Testing Theories About Complementarity in Organizational Design. NBER Working Paper No. 6600, Cambridge, MA, June 1998.

Audretsch, D.B., Stephan, P.E., 1996. Company-scientist locational links: the case of biotechnology. American Economic Review 86 (2), 641–652.

Bania, N., Eberts, R., Fogarty, M.S., 1993. Universities and the startup of new companies: can we generalize from route 128 and Silicon Valley? Review of Economics and Statistics 76 (4), 761–766.

Battese, G., Coelli, T., 1995. A model for technical inefficiency effects in a stochastic frontier production function for panel data. Empirical Economics 20, 325–332.

Bayh, B., 1996. Keynote Address: Sixteen Years of Bayh–Dole. In: MIT Conference on Intellectual Property Rights: Corporate Survival and Strategic Advantage, Cambridge, MA, 9 December, 1996.

Beath, J., Owen, R., Poyago-Theotoky, J., Ulph, D., 2000. Optimal Incentives for Income-Generation within Universities. Paper presented at the Royal Economic Society Meetings, St. Andrews, Scotland.

Bercovitz, J., Feldman, M., Feller, I., Burton, R., 2001. Organizational structure as determinants of academic patent and licensing behavior: an exploratory study of Duke, Johns Hopkins, and Pennsylvania State Universities. Journal of Technology Transfer 26 (1/2), 21–35.

Butterfield, K., Trevino, L., Ball, G., 1996. Punishment from the manager's perspective: a grounded investigation and inductive model. Academy of Management Journal 39, 1479–1512.

Caldwell, D.F., O'Reilly, C.A., 1982. Boundary spanning and individual performance. Journal of Applied Psychology 67 (1), 124–127.

---

[36] In this regard, Owen-Smith and Powell (2001) report some interesting differences in the perceptions of academics in the physical and life sciences regarding patent outcomes.

[37] As described in Grosskopf et al. (1997), this class of models assumes that the relationship between output and inputs can be represented by a transformation function T, where $0 = T(x, y)$ and y denotes a vector of outputs ($0 = y - f(x)$ for the single output case).

D.S. Siegel et al./Research Policy 32 (2003) 27–48   47

Charnes, A., Cooper, W.W., Lewin A., Seiford, L.M. (Eds.), 1994. Data Envelopment Analysis: Theory, Method, and Applications. Kluwer Academic Publishers, Boston, MA.

Coelli, T., 1994. A Guide to FRONTIER Version 4.1: A Computer Program for Frontier Production and Cost Function Estimation. Mimeo. Department of Econometrics, University of New England, Armidale.

Cohen, W.M., Florida, R., Randazzese, L., Walsh, J., 1998. Industry and the Academy: Uneasy Partners in the Cause of Technological Advance. In: Noll, R.G. (Ed.), Challenges to Research Universities. Brookings Institution Press, Washington, DC.

David, P.A., Hall, B.H., 2000. Heart of darkness: modeling public–private interactions inside the R&D black box. Research Policy 29 (9), 1165–1183.

Gallini, N., Scotchmer, S., 2001. Intellectual Property: When is it the Best Incentive System. In: Jaffe, A., Lerner, J., Stern, S. (Eds.), Innovation Policy and the Economy, Vol. 2. MIT Press, Cambridge, MA.

General Accounting Office (GAO), 1998. Technology Transfer: Administration of the Bayh–Dole Act by Research Universities. General Accounting Office, Washington, DC.

Geroski, P., 2000. Models of technology diffusion. Research Policy 29 (4/5), 603–626.

Griliches, Z., 1979. Issues in assessing the contribution of R&D to productivity growth. Bell Journal of Economics 10, 92–116.

Grosskopf, S., Hayes, K.J., Taylor, L.L., Weber, W.L., 1997. Budget-constrained frontier measures of fiscal equality and efficiency in schooling. Review of Economics and Statistics 79 (1), 116–124.

Henderson, R.M., Jaffe, A.B., Trajtenberg, M., 1998. Universities as a source of commercial technology: a detailed analysis of university patenting 1965–1988. Review of Economics and Statistics 80 (1), 119–127.

Ichniowski, C., Shaw, K., Prennushi, G., 1997. The effects of human resource management practices on productivity: a study of steel finishing lines. American Economic Review 87 (3), 291–313.

Jaffe, A.B., Trajtenberg, M., Henderson, R., 1993. Geographic localization of knowledge spillovers as evidenced by patent citations. Quarterly Journal of Economics 108 (3), 577–598.

Jensen, R., Thursby, M., 2001. Proofs and prototypes for sale: the licensing of university inventions. American Economic Review 91 (1), 240–259.

Katz, R., Tushman, M., 1983. A longitudinal study of the effects of boundary spanning supervision on turnover and promotion in Research and Development. Academy of Management Journal 26, 437–456.

Klette, T.J., Moen, J., Griliches, Z., 2000. Do subsidies to commercial R&D reduce market failures? Microeconometric evaluation studies. Research Policy 29 (4/5), 471–496.

Lazear, E.P., 1999. Personnel Economics: Past Lessons and Future Directions. NBER Working Paper No. 6957. Cambridge, MA. February 1999.

Liebeskind, J.P., Oliver, A.L., Zucker, L.G., Brewer, M.B., 1996. Social networks, learning, and flexibility: sourcing scientific knowledge in new biotechnology firms. Organization Science 7, 428–443.

Mansfield, E., 1995. Academic research underlying industrial innovations: sources, characteristics, and financing. Review of Economics and Statistics 77 (1), 55–65.

Martin, S., Scott, J.T., 2000. The nature of innovation market failure & the design of public support for private innovation. Research Policy 29 (4/5), 437–448.

Meeusen, W., Van den Broeck, J., 1977. Efficiency estimation from Cobb–Douglas production functions with composed errors. International Economic Review 18, 435–444.

Miles, M.B., Huberman, A.M., 1994. Qualitative Data Analysis, 2nd Edition. Sage Publications, Thousand Oaks, CA.

Morrison, C., Siegel, D., 1997. External capital factors and increasing returns in US manufacturing. Review of Economics and Statistics 79 (4), 647–654.

Mowery, D.C., Nelson, R.R., Sampat, B., Ziedonis, A.A., 2001. The growth of patenting and licensing by US universities: an assessment of the effects of the Bayh–Dole Act of 1980. Research Policy 30, 99–119.

National Science Foundation (NSF) Research and Development in Industry, 1991–1994. Government Printing Office, Washington, DC.

Nelson, R.R., 2001. Observations on the post-Bayh–Dole rise of patenting at American universities. Journal of Technology Transfer 26 (1/2), 13–19.

Owen-Smith, J., Powell, W., 2001. To patent or not: faculty decisions and institutional success at technology transfer. Journal of Technology Transfer 26 (1/2), 99–114.

Parker, D.D., Zilberman, D., 1993. University technology transfers: impacts on local and US economies. Contemporary Policy Issues 11 (2), 87–99.

Powell, W.W., 1990. Neither market nor hierarchy: network forms of organization. Research in Organizational Behavior 12, 295–336.

Pressman, L., Guterman, S., Abrams, I., Geist, D., Nelsen, L., 1995. Pre-production investment and jobs induced by MIT exclusive patent licenses: a preliminary model to measure the economic impact of university licensing. Journal of the Association of University Technology Managers 7, 77–90.

Reifschneider, D., Stevenson, R., 1991. Systematic departures from the frontier: a framework for the analysis of firm inefficiency. International Economic Review 32 (3), 715–723.

Sekaran, U., 1992. Research Methods for Managers: A Skill-Building Approach, 2nd Edition. Wiley, New York.

Siegel, D.S., 1999. Skill-Biased Technological Change: Evidence From A Firm-Level Survey. Upjohn Institute for Employment Research, Kalamazoo, MI.

Siegel, D.S., Waldman, D., Atwater, L., Link, A., 2001. Toward a Theory of the Effective Transfer of Scientific Knowledge from Academicians to Practitioners: Qualitative Evidence from the Commercialization of University Technologies. Mimeo. University of Nottingham, Nottingham, August 2001.

Thursby, J.G., Kemp, S., 1998. An Analysis of Productive Efficiency of University Commercialization Activities. Mimeo. Purdue University, Purdue, May 1998.

Thursby, J.G., Thursby, M.C., 2000. Who is Selling the Ivory Tower? Sources of Growth in University Licensing. NBER Working Paper No. 7718. Management Science.

Trajtenberg, M., Henderson, R., Jaffe, A., 1997. University versus corporate patents: a window on the basicness of invention. Economics of Innovation and New Technology 5 (1), 19–50.

US Department of Commerce, Bureau of Economic Analysis, 1999. Fixed Reproducible Tangible Wealth, Computer-Readable Data Set. Government Printing Office, Washington, DC.

Waldman, D., Lituchy, T., Gopalakrishnan, M., Laframboise, K., Galperin, B., Kaltsounakis, Z., 1998. A qualitative analysis of leadership and quality improvement. Leadership Quarterly 9, 177–201.

Yin, R.K., 1989. Case Study Research: Design and Methods, 2nd Edition. Sage Publications, Newbury Park, CA.

Zucker, L.G., Darby, M.R., 1996. Star scientists and institutional transformations patterns of invention and innovation in the formation of the biotechnology industry. Proceedings of the National Academy of Sciences 93, 709–716.

Zucker, L.G., Darby, M.R., Brewer, M.B., 1998. Intellectual human capital and the birth of US biotechnology enterprises. American Economic Review 88 (1), 290–306.

[7]

ELSEVIER

Available online at www.sciencedirect.com

SCIENCE DIRECT•

International Journal of Industrial Organization
21 (2003) 1371–1390

International Journal of
Industrial Organization

www.elsevier.com/locate/econbase

Changes in university patent quality after the Bayh–Dole act: a re-examination

Bhaven N. Sampat[a,*], David C. Mowery[b,d], Arvids A. Ziedonis[c]

[a]*School of Public Policy, Georgia Institute of Technology, 685 Cherry Street, Atlanta, GA 30332, USA*
[b]*Haas School of Business, University of California, Berkeley, CA 94720-1900, USA*
[c]*University of Michigan Business School, University of Michigan, Ann Arbor, MI 48109-1234, USA*
[d]*NBER, Cambridge, MA 02138, USA*

Abstract

The Bayh–Dole Act of 1980 facilitated the retention by universities of patent rights resulting from government funded academic research, thus encouraging university entry into patenting and licensing. Though the Act is widely recognized to be a major change in federal policy towards academic research, surprisingly little empirical analysis has been directed at assessing its impacts on the academy and on university–industry research relationships. An important exception is the work of Henderson et al. [Rev. Econ. Stat. 80 (1998) 119–127] which examined the impact of Bayh–Dole on the quality of university patents, as measured by the number of times they are cited in subsequent patents. The authors found that the quality of academic patents declined dramatically after Bayh–Dole, a finding that has potentially important policy implications. In this paper, we revisit this influential finding. By using a longer stream of patent citations data, we show that the results of the Henderson et al. study reflect changes in the intertemporal distribution of citations to university patents, rather than a significant change in the total number of citations these patents eventually receive. This has important implications not only for the evaluation of Bayh–Dole, but also for future research using patent citations as economic indicators.
© 2003 Elsevier B.V. All rights reserved.

JEL classification: O3

Keywords: Bayh–Dole; University patenting; Patent citations

*Corresponding author. Tel.: + 1-404-894-6822; fax: + 1-404-385-0504.
E-mail addresses: bhaven.sampat@pubpolicy.gatech.edu (B.N. Sampat), mowery@haas.berkeley.edu (D.C. Mowery), azied@umich.edu (A.A. Ziedonis).

0167-7187/03/$ – see front matter © 2003 Elsevier B.V. All rights reserved.
doi:10.1016/S0167-7187(03)00087-0

1372 *B.N. Sampat et al. / Int. J. Ind. Organ. 21 (2003) 1371–1390*

1. Introduction

The Bayh–Dole Act of 1980 created a uniform federal patent policy that allowed universities to retain rights to any patents resulting from government funded research and to license these patents on an exclusive or non-exclusive basis. Prior to the passage of the Act, universities wishing to retain title to patents resulting from federally funded research utilized Institutional Patent Arrangements (IPAs) that were negotiated with individual funding agencies or petitioned these agencies for title on a case-by-case basis. Bayh–Dole was passed in the throes of the 'competitiveness crisis' of the 1970s and 1980s in the belief that the requirement to obtain IPAs or waivers and the frequently inconsistent policies of federal funding agencies regarding these agreements (especially regarding exclusive licensing) impeded technology transfer and commercialization of federally funded research results. In particular, the framers of this legislation argued that if universities could not be granted clear title to patents that allowed them to license rights to patented inventions exclusively, firms would lack the incentive to develop and commercialize university inventions.[1]

The Bayh–Dole Act has been widely cited (on the basis of slim evidence) as an important factor in the 'competitive revival' of the US economy during the 1990s (Association of University Technology Managers, 1998; United States General Accounting Office, 1998; US Congress Joint Economic Committee, 1999), and other countries are currently considering (or have recently enacted) similar legislation.[2] Some observers, however, have expressed concern that the incentives created by Bayh–Dole may have shifted the academic research towards more 'applied' work and away from fundamental research, a development with potentially detrimental long-term effects for US and global welfare (Dasgupta and David, 1994).

One of the few attempts at a rigorous assessment of the effects of the Bayh–Dole Act on university research is the work of Henderson et al. (1995,

---

[1] This argument was based on 'evidence' that government-owned patents had lower utilization rates than those held by contractors, evidence that Eisenberg (1996) has shown to be faulty. The supporters of Bayh–Dole interpreted these data as indicators of the economic impact of academic research, neglecting the range of other formal and informal channels through which firms historically benefited from university research. In opening the Senate hearings, one of the architects of the legislation, Senator Birch Bayh (D. Indiana), cited the low rate of commercialization of government owned patents as evidence of 'very little return on the billions of dollars we spend every year on research and development' (United States Senate Committee on the Judiciary, 1979, p. 2).

[2] A recent report by the Organization of Economic Cooperation and Development (OECD) notes '[I]n nearly all OECD countries there has been a marked trend towards transferring ownership of publicly funded research from the state (government) to the (public or private) agent performing the research. The underlying rationale for such change is that it increases the social rate of return on public investment in research' (Organization of Economic Cooperation and Development, 2002, p. 48).

B.N. Sampat et al. / Int. J. Ind. Organ. 21 (2003) 1371–1390   1373

1998a,b), which examined the impact of Bayh–Dole on the 'quality' of university patents, as measured by the number of times these patents are cited by subsequent patents. The authors found that this measure revealed a decline in the quality of academic patents after Bayh–Dole. In this paper, we show that the post-Bayh–Dole 'quality decline' identified by Henderson and colleagues disappears in analyses that employ patent-citation data covering a longer time period than the data used by these scholars. We find that the 'quality decline' that Henderson et al. (1998a,b) identified in their analysis reflects changes in the intertemporal distribution of citations to university patents, rather than a significant change in the total number of citations these patents eventually receive. Our analysis suggests that during the post-Bayh–Dole period, the lag between application and issue dates for university patents has increased, and citations to university patents occur somewhat later, on average, after issue. These changes may themselves reflect significant differences since 1980 in the content and contributions of university research to innovation.

2. Patent citations and the post-Bayh–Dole 'quality decline'

Henderson et al. (1995, 1998a,b) (hereafter, 'HJT') used publicly available information contained in the front pages of patents assigned to universities during 1965–1988 and in subsequent patents that cited those university patents through the end of 1992 to examine changes in the characteristics of patents issued to US universities before and after Bayh–Dole.

Patent-based measures have been utilized to measure innovative output for several decades (Griliches, 1990). The large variance in the economic and technological significance of individual patents, however, means that simple patent counts are noisy indicators of innovative output. But weighting patents by the number of times they are cited in subsequent patents yields a better measure of the technological importance of these patents (see Trajtenberg, 1990 for one of the first applications of this measure). Citations to one patent by many subsequent patents suggests either that numerous inventions draw on the knowledge embodied in that patent, and/or that this antecedent patent has opened up a significant new field of inventive activity, within which follow-on patents must carefully differentiate their contribution from the prior art represented by this patent and others. Scholars have also used citation-weighted patent counts as measures of the private value of an invention to the patentholder (Hall et al., 2000; Shane and Klock, 1997; Austin, 1994; Harhoff et al., 1999; Sampat and Ziedonis, 2003), and still other empirical work has shown that more heavily cited patents are more likely to be the subject of litigation, another measure of their economic value (Lanjouw and Schankerman, 2001).

1374   *B.N. Sampat et al. / Int. J. Ind. Organ. 21 (2003) 1371–1390*

The work of HJT concluded that expanded patenting by US universities after Bayh–Dole was accompanied by a decline in the quality of these patents, as measured by citations. According to HJT, university patents issued before the passage of the Bayh–Dole Act were significantly more likely to be cited than a 1% random sample of all US patents. But for university patents issued after 1980, this difference diminished and its statistical significance disappeared completely for university patents issued after the mid-1980s.

The meaning of this relative decline in citations to US university patents is open to multiple interpretations. Some authors have interpreted this finding as evidence that research priorities within universities may have shifted towards 'applied research' after Bayh–Dole (e.g. Foray and Kazancigil, 1999).[3] Implicit in this interpretation is the assumption that patents based on 'basic' research would generate a higher level of citations than 'applied' research (cf. Trajtenberg et al., 1997). Alternatively, of course, one could argue that more applied university research should generate more heavily cited patents, based on the utility of these patents for industrial innovation.[4] The different interpretations that can be placed on patent-citation counts underscores the complexities of their economic interpretation.

Although HJT's results attracted considerable attention, further analysis is merited for at least two reasons. First, their analysis relies on citations to university patents only through 1992, although patents in their sample were cited well after 1992. The lack of observations on citations after 1992 thus could introduce a 'truncation bias,' reflecting the fact that earlier patents (those issued further in advance of 1992) enjoy a longer period of potential citation than later patents. Although HJT control for some sources truncation bias, their analysis reveals the most substantial 'quality decline' for the most recent patents in their sample, those for which truncation bias may be most significant. Thus, the nature of their data and results suggest that further analysis employing a longer period for post-issue citations is worthwhile. Second, several recent papers (Mowery and Ziedonis, 2000; Mowery et al., 2002) find no decline in citation-based measures of academic patent quality after 1980, although these analyses employ different control samples and methodologies.

---

[3] Henderson and colleagues also suggested this possible interpretation of the 'quality decline' in an early version of their paper, Henderson et al. (1995).

[4] Henderson et al. (1998a,b) appear to interpret citations in this way, arguing that their results suggest that ' . . . the Bayh–Dole Act and other related changes in federal law and institutional capability have not had a significant impact on the underlying rate of generation of commercially important inventions at universities. Universities either did not significantly shift their research efforts towards areas likely to produce commercial inventions, or, if they did, they did so unsuccessfully' (Henderson et al., 1998b, p. 126).

B.N. Sampat et al. / Int. J. Ind. Organ. 21 (2003) 1371–1390   1375

3. The 'quality decline' revisited

Our analysis utilizes a longer time series of citations to university and industrial patents to further analyze the quality decline reported in Henderson et al. (1998b), but in all other respects is essentially identical to that of HJT. Our dataset consists of all university patents applied for between 1975 and 1988 and granted before 1992, identical to that used by HJT.[5] We also followed HJT in constructing a 1% random sample of all US patents granted during the same period. Although we do not have access to the identical control sample used by HJT, we believe that this control sample is sufficiently similar to theirs for the purposes of this analysis.[6] We collected counts of all citations to the university patents and control sample patents that appeared by the end of 1999, adding 7 years to the citation time series employed in HJT.[7]

3.1. Basic analysis

For purposes of comparison, we create two citation counts for each potentially cited patent, (1) the number of citations generated by the patent through the end of 1992, which covers the period included in the HJT analysis, and (2) the number of citations generated by the patent through 1999. Since we are interested in the overall 'importance' of a patent, we follow HJT in including self-citations in these counts, but our main conclusions are not sensitive to the inclusion or exclusion of self-citations.

Table 1 reports descriptive statistics for patent citation counts in the overall sample of patents, the university patent sample, and the control sample. Increasing the observation period for citations from 1992 to 1999 increased the mean number of citations for patents in all three samples. Regardless of the time-span of citation data collected, university patents are more highly cited than the control patents (4.153 vs. 3.494 using citations as of 1992, and 10.605 vs. 7.047 using citations as of 1999).

Our regressions employ the number of citations to the sample patents as the dependent variable, similarly to HJT. The independent variables include dummy variables for application year, patent class dummies for each of the patent classes

---

[5] Rebecca Henderson kindly provided us with access to the list of university patents used in their analyses.

[6] We checked the sensitivity of our basic results to the use of any particular control sample employed by conducting the analysis discussed below using five different 1% control samples. The results of these analyses are virtually the same as those reported, and are available from the authors upon request.

[7] These data were taken from the Case Western Reserve–NBER Patent Citation database, described in Hall et al. (2000).

Table 1
Descriptive statistics for patent citation counts

Statistic	Mean	Standard Deviation	Minimum	Maximum
Overall sample, $N = 17,996$				
Number of patent citations as of 1992	3.798	5.625	0	126
Number of patent citations as of 1999	8.609	12.038	0	292
University sample, $N = 8,304$				
Number of patent citations as of 1992	4.153	6.549	0	126
Number of patent citations as of 1999	10.605	14.442	0	292
Control sample, $N = 9,692$				
Number of patent citations as of 1992	3.494	4.669	0	81
Number of patent citations as of 1999	7.047	9.195	0	166

included in the university and control patent samples, and application year dummies interacted with a dummy variable indicating whether the patent is a university or control sample patent.[8] More formally, we estimate equations of the form:

$$\text{Citations} = \sum_t \left[\alpha_t \text{APP}_t + \beta_t(\text{APP}_t * \text{UNIV}) \right] + \sum_c \lambda_c \text{CLASS}_c + \epsilon \qquad (1)$$

where the dependent variable is the number of citations to the patent, APP_t is a dummy variable taking on the value of 1 if the patent was applied for in year t ($t = 1975, \ldots, 1988$), UNIV is a dummy variable taking on the value of 1 if patent i is in our university sample, CLASS_c is dummy variable taking on the value of 1 if the patent class is c, and ε is the error term.[9] The coefficients on the interaction terms, β_t, are estimates of the mean differences in the number of citations to university patents and patents from our random sample for a given application year, controlling for technological field effects. Following HJT, we estimate this equation using ordinary least squares (OLS).

The main results are shown in Table 2, which displays the estimated interaction-term coefficients. The first column of the table presents the coefficient estimates from Table 4 of Henderson et al. (1998b). The second column displays the coefficients that we obtained from estimating the specification described in the previous paragraph for patent-citations data through 1992. The magnitude, sign, and statistical significance of the coefficients that we obtain (column 2) are very similar to those from the Henderson et al. (1998b) article (column 1). The results in both columns 1 and 2 indicate that the citation-weighted 'quality' of university

---

[8] The sample analyzed by HJT begins in 1965. Unfortunately, it is difficult to obtain citation information for patents issued prior to 1975, and our sample therefore excludes those patents applied for before 1975. Since the observed 'quality decline' occurs after the mid-1980s, this data limitation does not affect the substance or the conclusions of our analysis.

[9] Our university and control patents span 394 patent classes.

B.N. Sampat et al. / Int. J. Ind. Organ. 21 (2003) 1371–1390 1377

Table 2
Mean difference in number of patent citations, university vs. control samples

Patent application year	Dependent variable		
	1	2	3
	Number of patent citations as of 1992 [HJT, 1998; Table 4]	Number of patent citations as of 1992	Number of patent citations as of 1999
1975	2.54***	2.48***	3.21***
	(0.35)	(0.35)	(0.77)
1976	1.82***	1.67***	2.20***
	(0.34)	(0.35)	(0.76)
1977	1.31***	1.42***	3.02***
	(0.34)	(0.35)	(0.77)
1978	2.04***	2.33***	4.50***
	(0.34)	(0.34)	(0.75)
1979	1.13**	1.34***	2.41***
	(0.31)	(0.32)	(0.71)
1980	1.91***	1.82***	4.01***
	(0.31)	(0.31)	(0.67)
1981	1.68***	1.93***	3.98***
	(0.31)	(0.32)	(0.69)
1982	0.96***	1.49***	3.87***
	(0.31)	(0.31)	(0.68)
1983	0.97***	1.14***	2.89***
	(0.30)	(0.31)	(0.67)
1984	0.47*	0.36	2.22***
	(0.28)	(0.29)	(0.64)
1985	0.40	0.68**	3.41***
	(0.28)	(0.28)	(0.62)
1986	0.06	0.06	2.98***
	(0.27)	(0.27)	(0.60)
1987	−0.07	−0.11	1.90***
	(0.25)	(0.25)	(0.56)
1988	−0.08	−0.16	1.89***
	(0.24)	(0.24)	(0.53)
Year dummies	Significant	Significant	Significant
Patent class dummies	Significant	Significant	Significant
Number of observations	NA	17,996	17,996

*** $p < 0.01$; ** $p < 0.05$; * $p < 0.10$. Standard errors in parentheses.

patents relative to the controls declined after Bayh–Dole; the difference in citations to these two groups of patents is statistically insignificant for patents issued after the mid-1980s. University patents are actually cited less frequently than those in the control sample for patents applied for in 1987 and 1988, although this difference in citation intensity is not statistically significant.

Column 3 of Table 2 presents results from estimating the specification described above with patent citation data that extend through 1999. The results change dramatically—university patents are more highly cited than the controls for patents

1378   *B.N. Sampat et al. / Int. J. Ind. Organ. 21 (2003) 1371–1390*

applied for after as well as before Bayh–Dole, and the difference is statistically significant for all years.[10] Re-estimation of the original HJT specification with a longer time series of citations yields little evidence of a post-Bayh–Dole 'quality decline' in US university patents, something that is illustrated graphically in Fig. 1, which plots the coefficients on the interaction term from both regressions, along with the coefficients from HJT's analysis.[11]

To further test for the possibility of a significant difference between pre- and post-Bayh–Dole academic patents, we regressed citations on a pre-Bayh–Dole and post-Bayh–Dole dummy, each interacted with a university dummy, as well as application year and patent class dummies. When using 'citations through 1992' as the dependent variable, the estimated coefficient on the pre-Bayh–Dole–University interaction term dummy is 1.8 and the estimated coefficient on the post-Bayh–Dole–University interaction term dummy is 0.55. An *F*-test of equality of coefficients rejects the hypothesis that the coefficients are equal. When we use

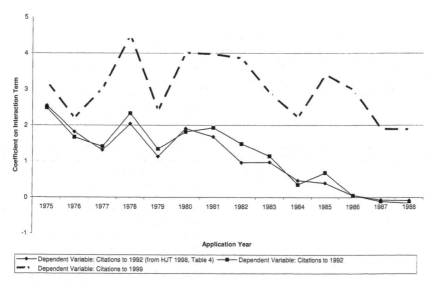

Fig. 1. Coefficients on university*application year interaction term, by application year.

---

[10] At the suggestion of a reviewer, we estimated the quality differences using negative binomial regressions, since the dependent variable (citations) is integer-valued. The results are similar to those obtained via OLS, and are available from the authors upon request.

[11] Henderson et al. also found that the 'generality' of university patents—a measure of the dispersion of citations across technological fields—declined relative to the controls the after the passage of Bayh–Dole. In addition to the results reported above, we calculated generality for the university and control sample patents using citations observed through 1999, and found no evidence of a decline in the generality of university patents. These results are available from the authors upon request.

B.N. Sampat et al. / Int. J. Ind. Organ. 21 (2003) 1371–1390   1379

'citations through 1999' as the dependent variable, however, the estimated pre- and post-Bayh–Dole coefficients are 3.2 and 2.8, respectively, and we cannot reject the hypothesis that they are equal. In other words, the analysis of patent citations through 1999 yields no evidence of a significant change in the quality of university patents relative to the controls after Bayh–Dole.[12]

Based on these results, we conclude that the original HJT findings are sensitive to the number of years of citation data used. The HJT analysis included only 4–7 years of citation data for the patents applied for by universities during 1985–1988, but our longer time series includes 11–14 years of citations for these patents. In other words, the patent 'quality decline' reported by HJT appears to be an artifact of truncation bias.[13] In Section 4, we discuss the nature and effects of truncation in more detail.

4. Truncation bias

The use of a shorter time span of citations could create the impression of a decline in the quality of university patents in at least three ways. First, consider the case in which university patents are more highly cited than the controls across the entire life of the patent and the intertemporal distribution of citations is identical, i.e. at any point in time the same proportion of total citations is observed for patents from each sample. In this case, a shorter 'window' of observations of citations to the two patent samples would produce a smaller cumulative difference

---

[12] In conducting this test of the equality of the coefficients, we are testing the hypothesis that a 'breakpoint' occurs in 1980, the year of passage of the Bayh–Dole Act. A less restrictive test of the structural stability of these coefficients that does not require imposing a specific breakpoint is the residual-based Brown–Durbin–Evans (BDE) test (Link et al., 2002).

[13] It is well known that patent values, like most measures of innovative output, are highly skewed—patents in the upper tail of the patent value distribution account for the bulk of the value of patent portfolio (Harhoff et al., 1999). HJT suggest that their 'quality decline' could reflect increased patenting of 'marginal' inventions by universities after Bayh–Dole, in response to a reduction in the costs of patenting. In this view, Bayh–Dole led US universities to reduce the threshold level of invention quality above which they would file for patent protection. Despite our finding that the 'quality decline' disappears with the addition of additional years of citation data, their threshold hypothesis may still be valid. Because they estimate conditional means, our least-squares regressions are unable to test this hypothesis. We therefore also estimated quantile regressions (which estimate conditional quantiles) to explore changes in 'quality' over time between patents within different quantiles, in order to examine effects of Bayh–Dole on the entire distribution of citations. We estimate these regressions for $q = 0.1$, 0.25, 0.5, 0.75, and 0.9. The results (not reported) show no evidence of a post-Bayh–Dole decrease in the quality of university patents (relative to the controls) in any of the quantiles. Indeed, there is some evidence in these results of an *increase* in quality in the upper quantiles of our university patent sample. These results should be interpreted with caution, however, since in order to obtain convergence, we aggregated the 394 patent class dummies into five broad technological categories using the taxonomy created by Jaffe et al. (1998). These regressions thus do not include complete controls for differences in citation intensity across patent classes.

in citations. Secondly, the intertemporal distribution of citations could differ for the university and control sample patents, with citations to university patents occurring later (on average) than the controls. In this case, a relatively short 'window' of observations for both sets of patents could understate differences in citation-intensity for university and control patents, and this form of truncation bias again would be greater for relatively recent patents. A third possibility is that the intertemporal distribution of citations is changing over time, i.e. citations to university patents are arriving later (relative to citations to the control sample patents) in more recent application years. Since HJT control for the first two forms of potential truncation bias in their analysis, the third may explain the different results that we obtain in using a longer 'window' of observations of citations.

Evidence that citations to university patents occur later on average (relative to citations to patents in the control sample) in more recent application years is provided in Figs. 2–4, which display plots of the cumulative distribution of citations received in 11-year 'windows' following the date of application for university and control patents applied for, respectively, during three periods: 1977–1980, 1981–1984, and 1985–1988. The value of the cumulative distribution function at $t = x$ years after the patent application ($0 \leqslant x \leqslant 11$) is the proportion of total citations during the 11-year period that are observed after x years. Use of an 11-year window enables us to examine the same 'span' of citations for all patents and identify shifts in the intertemporal distribution of citations within that span.

As we noted earlier, the data analyzed by HJT captured only 4 years of citation for the most recently issued patents in their sample, those applied for in 1988 by universities or corporations. The data in Fig. 2 indicate that the 1977–1980 cohort

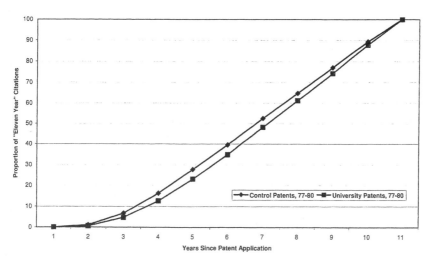

Fig. 2. Cumulative distribution of citation lags, university and control patents, 1977–1980.

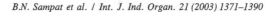
B.N. Sampat et al. / Int. J. Ind. Organ. 21 (2003) 1371–1390   1381

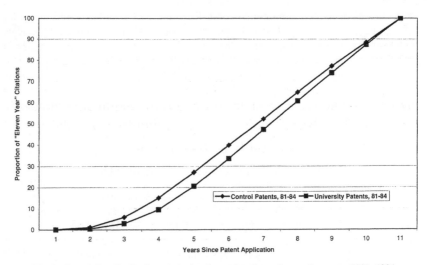

Fig. 3. Cumulative distribution of citation lag, university and control patents, 1981–1984.

of patents in our control sample accumulate 16.3% of their 'total' citations (i.e. citations accumulated within 11 years of the application date) during the first 4 years following their application date. The identical cohort of university patents, however, accumulate 12.6% of their 'total' citations during the first 4 years following their application date. For patents with application dates in the 1981–

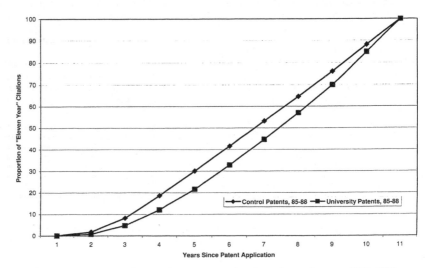

Fig. 4. Cumulative distribution of citation lag, university and control patents, 1985–1988.

1984 period, however, these respective proportions are 15.1% and 9.4%, respectively (Fig. 3), and in Fig. 4, covering 1985–88, these proportions are 18.7 and 12.0%, respectively. A visual comparison of the three figures suggests that the differences between the portion of citations received by university and control sample patents are greater in more recent patent cohorts for several years after $t = 4$ years. That is, citations to university patents in the 1981–84 and 1985–88 cohorts occur later than citations to patents in the control sample by a growing margin.

The data in Figs. 2–4 do not consider differences among technological fields. We therefore estimate two models to analyze changes in the distribution of citation lags for university and control-sample patents that control for patent class. First, we calculate the average lag for forward citations for each cited patent using all citations within 11 years of the application date, and estimate the following equation:[14]

$$\text{Average Citation Lag} = \sum_t [\alpha_t \text{APP}_t + \beta_t (\text{APP}_t^* \text{UNIV})] + \sum_c \lambda_c \text{CLASS}_c + \varepsilon$$

(1)

where the dependent variable is the average lag for all citations to the patent within the 11 year window. We also estimate a similar equation that uses median citation lags as the dependent variable:

$$\text{Median Citation Lag} = \sum_t [\alpha_t \text{APP}_t + \beta_t (\text{APP}_t^* \text{UNIV})] + \sum_c \lambda_c \text{CLASS}_c + \varepsilon$$

(3)

The least squares estimates of the differences in average and median citation lags (the β coefficients) are shown in Table 3. In 8 of the 9 years before 1984, there are no significant differences between the university and controls in the (average or median) lengths of lags to 'forward' citations. In each year after 1984, both the mean and median forward lags are significantly longer for the university patents.

These results indicate that citations to university patents are indeed arriving later relative to citations to the control-sample patents in the 1980s, controlling for technology class, i.e. there is a systematic change in the intertemporal distribution of citations to university patents during the 1980s.

One possible source of this shift is a change in the application-grant lags, or 'pendency' of patents in the university and control samples. In both the HJT analysis and ours, university patents are dated by application year. But since US patent applications historically have not been open to the public, the 'citation clock' for parties other than the patent examiner to cite a patent begins only after

---

[14] The lags in Figs. 2–4 were calculated across each citing-cited pair, but the 'average' and 'median' lags used in these regressions are calculated at the level of the cited patent.

Table 3
Mean difference in average and median patent citation lags, university vs. control samples

Patent application year	Dependent variable	
	1 Average forward citation lag	2 Median forward citation lag
1975	−0.093 (0.13)	−0.127 (0.15)
1976	−0.038 (0.13)	−0.067 (0.15)
1977	0.336** (0.13)	0.295** (0.15)
1978	0.123 (0.12)	0.187 (0.14)
1979	−0.113 (0.12)	−0.135 (0.13)
1980	0.086 (0.11)	0.073 (0.13)
1981	0.152 (0.11)	0.183 (0.13)
1982	0.177 (0.11)	0.156 (0.13)
1983	0.068 (0.11)	0.073 (0.12)
1984	0.221** (0.10)	0.239** (0.12)
1985	0.344*** (0.10)	0.337*** (0.11)
1986	0.502*** (0.10)	0.501*** (0.11)
1987	0.419*** (0.09)	0.481*** (0.10)
1988	0.366*** (0.09)	0.395*** (0.10)
Year dummies	Significant	Significant
Patent class dummies	Significant	Significant
Number of observations	15,299	15,299

*** $p < 0.01$; ** $p < 0.05$; * $p < 0.10$. Standard errors in parentheses.

the patent is issued.[15] Any systematic tendency for the pendency lags for university patents to grow relative to those for patents in the control sample during the 1980s could produce an apparent shift in the intertemporal distribution of forward citations to university patents similar to that observed in our data.

---

[15] Beginning in November 2000, most US patent applications are published 18 months after the filing of the earliest related application.

To examine whether application-grant lags changed between the 1970s and 1980s, we regressed 'pendency lags' on application-year dummies, a university dummy interacted with application-year dummies, and patent class dummies, estimating the following equation:

$$\text{Application Lag} = \sum_t \left[\alpha_t \text{APP}_t + \beta_t (\text{APP}_t^* \text{UNIV}) \right] + \sum_c \lambda_c \text{CLASS}_c + \varepsilon \qquad (4)$$

The coefficients on the interaction terms (β_t) are shown in Table 4 and are plotted in Fig. 5. Before 1983, in all application years but one, the differences between the application-grant lags for the university and control sample patents are not

Table 4
Mean difference in application-grant (pendency) lags, university-control sample

Patent application year	Dependent variable: Application-grant lag
1975	0.110*
	(0.064)
1976	0.087
	(0.063)
1977	0.123*
	(0.064)
1978	0.022
	(0.062)
1979	0.121**
	(0.059)
1980	0.100*
	(0.056)
1981	0.058
	(0.058)
1982	0.074
	(0.057)
1983	0.195***
	(0.056)
1984	0.353***
	(0.053)
1985	0.299***
	(0.051)
1986	0.349***
	(0.050)
1987	0.304***
	(0.046)
1988	0.184***
	(0.045)
Year dummies	Significant
Patent class dummies	Significant
Number of observations	17,996

*** $p < 0.01$; ** $p < 0.05$; * $p < 0.10$. Standard errors in parentheses.

B.N. Sampat et al. / Int. J. Ind. Organ. 21 (2003) 1371–1390   1385

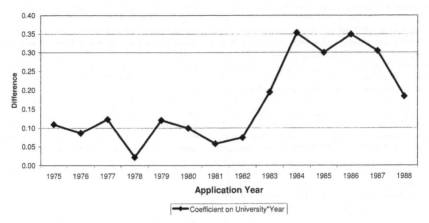

Fig. 5. Mean difference between pendency lags for university/control samples.

statistically significant. But in each application year during 1983–1988, the lags are significantly longer for university patents than for the controls, and this difference appears to be increasing over time (Fig. 5).

Thus university patents take longer to be granted, relative to the controls, for applications filed after 1982. To examine whether this change in average pendency is responsible for the shift in the intertemporal distribution of citations, we re-estimated our average and median citation lag regressions with controls for the application-grant lag of the cited patents. Figs. 6 and 7 plot the estimated coefficients for the interaction terms in these specifications, which capture the mean differences in average and median citation lags for university and control sample patents. The results indicate that after controlling for application-grant lags, the magnitude of the (relative) increase in citation lags decreases but does not vanish. Intertemporal changes in application-grant lags thus provide part of the explanation for the observed changes during the 1980s in the intertemporal distribution of citations. Nevertheless, the changing citation lags reflect more than just longer pendency lags for university patent applications during the 1980s.

Why do university patents take longer to be granted during the 1980s, relative to our control patents? A thorough explanation for this phenomenon is beyond the scope of this paper, although it raises interesting issues for future research. Our analysis does highlight the sensitivity of citation-based analyses of patent characteristics to the techniques used to 'date' the patents. Since the actual date of the invention underlying a patent application necessarily is closer to the application than to the issue date of the patent, the application date is preferable for analyses of the timing of inventive behavior. But the variation in pendency lags noted above provides one argument for employing issue dates in some analyses of patent citations. The ultimate choice of date will depend on the purposes of the

1386   *B.N. Sampat et al. / Int. J. Ind. Organ. 21 (2003) 1371–1390*

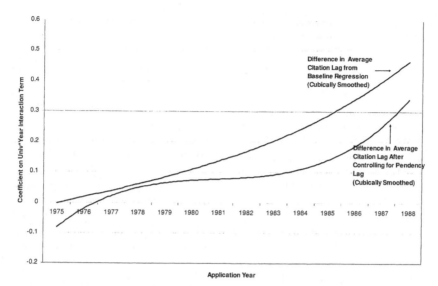

Fig. 6. Difference in average citation lags (university-controls) by application year.

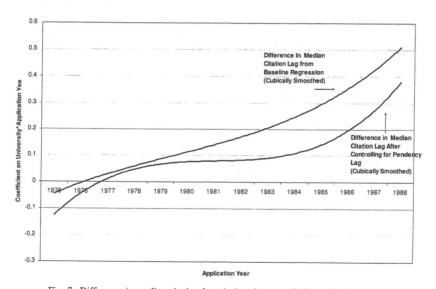

Fig. 7. Difference in median citation lags (university-control) by application year.

B.N. Sampat et al. / Int. J. Ind. Organ. 21 (2003) 1371–1390   1387

analysis. Using issue dates removes one source of intertemporal changes in the distribution of forward citations.

Nevertheless, Figs. 6 and 7 show that even after controlling for changes in application-grant lags, citations to university patents occur later than those to the controls after the mid-1980s. The interpretation of such changes in the intertemporal distribution of citations, however, depends on the meaning of early versus late citations, the topic of several recent empirical studies.

Lanjouw and Schankerman (1999) found that early citations (those observed within 5 years of application date) were highly correlated with their measures of the importance and economic value of patents taken from the application (i.e. number of claims, number of backward citations, number of countries in which patent protection is sought). Later citations were less highly correlated with these measures of patent quality that are based on characteristics of the patent at its issue date. Lanjouw and Schankerman suggest that their finding could indicate that later citations to a patent have a weak relationship to the economic value of the cited patent, perhaps because such citations are simply 'citing the classics.' Alternatively, of course, later citations may be valid measures of patent quality that are uncorrelated with the Lanjouw–Schankerman 'time-zero' measures of patent quality. This interpretation receives some support in the results of Hall et al. (2000), who find that unanticipated future citations (those not predicted by early citations) are the most important correlates of the market value of the firm that is the assignee of the patent.

If later citations to patents are poor indicators of the value or 'quality' of these patents, then the shifts that we observe in the intertemporal distribution of citations to university patents could indicate some decline in the 'quality' of these patents after Bayh–Dole. But if later citations are in fact more accurate measures of the 'quality' of these patents, our results are consistent with an improvement, rather than a decline, in university patent quality.

Still other scholars have interpreted patent citations as (noisy) measures of knowledge 'spillovers,' and a finding that university patents are systematically being cited later suggests that patent-embodied knowledge flows from universities are incorporated into future patents more slowly in the wake of Bayh–Dole. If 'science-based' patents take longer to be cited in subsequent patents, then this longer lag in the citation of university patents might reflect some tendency for US universities to patent 'science' rather than technology in the aftermath of Bayh–Dole.[16] Alternatively, it is possible that the nonpatent 'knowledge complements' resulting from university research (e.g. publications or conference presentations) are being disseminated more slowly as a result of a greater institutional emphasis

---

[16] Examining university patents granted over the 1975–1996 period and a 1% matched control sample, Sampat (2002) found that the number and share of citations in these patents to non-patent prior art increased dramatically beginning in the late 1980s, which may indicate that universities were patenting more 'scientific' than 'technological' research results.

1388 *B.N. Sampat et al. / Int. J. Ind. Organ. 21 (2003) 1371–1390*

on patenting and secrecy in the disclosure of research results before patent applications are filed. Any constriction in the supply of these complementary academic inputs into industrial patenting could slow the rate of exploitation by industrial inventors of academic knowledge, be this patented or unpatented. Either of these possibilities raises serious issues for societal welfare, since they suggest that the 'scientific commons' that underpins the advance of knowledge has been eroded (see Eisenberg and Heller, 1998; Eisenberg and Nelson, 2001).

5. Conclusion

Our analysis of citations to university patents before and after the Bayh–Dole Act suggests that there is no decline in the 'quality' of university patents during the 1980s. The quality decline observed by HJT reflects truncation of the citations data as well as some change in the intertemporal distribution of citations to university patents. These findings are consistent with earlier results (Mowery and Ziedonis, 2000; Mowery et al., 2002) that also used longer citation-data time series than were available to HJT.[17] The sensitivity of these results to truncation and the difficulties in controlling for truncation in the face of shifts in citation lags also highlight the sensitivity of patent-citations analyses to the construction of the relevant datasets.

Finally, the most important questions relating to the effects of the Bayh–Dole Act on US university research and technology transfer cannot be answered solely with patent citation data. Has Bayh–Dole affected the incentives of academic researchers? Does the introduction of commercial incentives into university research threaten the norms of academe? Have universities begun to patent and license 'science' that they previously disseminated freely? Are patents on academic research outputs necessary to facilitate technology transfer? These are important questions that cannot be addressed with patent and patent citation data alone. In addition to paving the ground for subsequent work using patent citation data, another 'spillover' from the paper by Henderson and colleagues is that it has focused attention and stimulated research on the broader issues relating to the effects of Bayh–Dole, an important contribution indeed.

Acknowledgements

We are grateful to Stephen Cameron, Rebecca Henderson, Al Link, Ken Leonard, Frank Lichtenberg, Richard Nelson, John Scott, Don Siegel, Rosemarie

---

[17] Mowery et al. (2002) use only citations observed within 5 years of the issue date of patents, although a median application-grant lag of 2 years that yields approximately 7 years of citation data may be sufficient. The Mowery et al. analysis also uses a different control sample from HJT and excludes self-citations, another feature that may contribute to these differences in results.

B.N. Sampat et al. / Int. J. Ind. Organ. 21 (2003) 1371–1390   1389

Ziedonis, and seminar participants at Columbia University, the Georgia Institute of Technology, the University of North Carolina, and the University of Michigan for comments on earlier drafts. Research for this paper was supported by the Andrew W. Mellon Foundation, Alfred P. Sloan Foundation, and the Mack Center for Technological Innovation at the University of Pennsylvania. All remaining errors are our own.

References

Association of University Technology Managers, 1998. AUTM Licensing Survey, Fiscal Year 1997. Association of University Technology Managers, Norwalk, CT.

Austin, D.H. 1994. 'Patent Citations and Appropriability,' Resources for the Future Working Paper.

Dasgupta, P., David, P.A., 1994. Towards a new economics of science. Research Policy 23, 487–521.

Eisenberg, R., 1996. Accessing and expanding the science and technology knowledge base. STI Review 16, 13–68.

Eisenberg, R., Heller, M., 1998. Can patents deter innovation? The anticommons in biomedical research. Science 280, 698–701.

Eisenberg, R., Nelson, R., 2001. Public versus Proprietary Science: A Fruitful Tension, Draft Manuscript.

Foray, D., Kazancigil, A., 1999. Science, economics and democracy. In: UNESCO World Conference on Science.

Griliches, Z., 1990. Patent statistics as economic indicators: a survey. Journal of Economic Perspectives 28 (4), 1661–1707.

Hall, B.H., Jaffe, A.B., Trajtenberg, M., 2000. Market Value and Patent Citations: A First Look. NBER Working Paper #W7741.

Harhoff, D., Scherer, F.M., Vopel, K., 1999. Citation frequency and the value of patented inventions. Review of Economics and Statistics 81, 511–515.

Henderson, R., Jaffe, A., Trajtenberg, M., 1995. Numbers Up, Quality Down? Trends in University Patenting 1965–1992. Stanford CEPR Draft Manuscript.

Henderson, R., Jaffe, A.B., Trajtenberg, M., 1998a. University patenting amid changing incentives for commercialization. In: Barba-Navaretti, G., Dasgupta, P., Mäler, K.G., Siniscalco, D. (Eds.), Creation and Transfer of Knowledge. Springer, New York.

Henderson, R., Jaffe, A.B., Trajtenberg, M., 1998b. Universities as a source of commercial technology: a detailed analysis of university patenting, 1965–1988. Review of Economics and Statistics 80, 119–127.

Jaffe, A.B., Fogarty, M.S., Banks, B.A., 1998. Evidence from patents and patent citations on the impact of NASA and other federal labs on commercial innovation. The Journal of Industrial Economics 46 (2), 183–205.

Lanjouw, J.O., Schankerman, M., 1999. The Quality of Ideas: Measuring Innovation with Multiple Indicators. NBER Working Paper #7345.

Lanjouw, J.O., Schankerman, M., 2001. Characteristics of patent litigation: a window on competition. RAND Journal of Economics 32 (1), 129–151.

Link, A., Paton, D., Siegel, D., 2002. An Econometric Analysis of Research Joint Ventures, Draft Manuscript.

Mowery, D.C., Sampat, B.N., Ziedonis, A.A., 2002. Learning to patent: experience and the quality of university patents 1980–1994. Management Science 48 (1), 73–89.

Mowery, D.C., Ziedonis, A.A., 2000. Academic patent quality and quantity before and after the Bayh–Dole Act in the United States. Research Policy 31, 399–418.

Organization of Economic Coordination and Development, 2002. Benchmarking Industry–Science Relationships.

Sampat, B.N., 2002. Private parts: patents and academic science in the twentieth century. In: Paper Presented at AAAS/CSPO Research Symposium for the Next Generation of Leaders in S&T Policy.

Sampat, B.N., Ziedonis, A.A. 2003. Cite Seeing: Patent Citations and the Economic Value of Patents, Paper presented at the Conference on Empirical Economics of Innovation and Patenting, Centre for European Economic Research, Mannheim, Germany, March 2003.

Shane, H., Klock, M., 1997. The relation between patent citations and Tobin's Q in the semiconductor industry. Review of Quantitative Finance and Accounting 9, 131–146.

Trajtenberg, M., Henderson, R.A., Jaffe, A.B., 1997. University versus corporate patents: A window on the basicness of invention. Economics of Innovation and New Technology 5, 19–50.

Trajtenberg, M., 1990. A penny for your quotes: patent citations and the value of innovations. Rand Journal of Economics 21, 172–187.

US Congress Joint Economic Committee, 1999. Entrepreneurial Dynamism and the Success of US High-Tech: Joint Economic Committee Staff Report. US Government Printing Office, Washington, DC.

United States General Accounting Office, 1998. Technology Transfer: Administration of the Bayh–Dole Act by Universities, United States General Accounting Report to Congressional Committees. GAO/RCED-98-126. United States Government Printing Office, Washington, DC.

United States Senate Committee on the Judiciary, 1979. The University and Small Business Patent Procedures Act: Hearings on S. 414, May 16 and June 6 in 96th Congress, 1st Session. US Government Printing Office, Washington, DC.

[8]

Pergamon

Journal of High Technology
Management Research 14 (2003) 111–133

THE JOURNAL
OF HIGH
TECHNOLOGY
MANAGEMENT
RESEARCH

Commercial knowledge transfers from universities to firms: improving the effectiveness of university–industry collaboration

Donald S. Siegel[a,*], David A. Waldman[b,1],
Leanne E. Atwater[b,1], Albert N. Link[c,2]

[a]Russell Sage Laboratory, Room 3502, Sage Building, Department of Economics,
Rensselaer Polytechnic Institute, Troy, NY 12180-3590, USA
[b]School of Management, Arizona State University West, Phoenix, AZ 85069-7100, USA
[c]Bryan School of Business and Economics, University of North Carolina at Greensboro,
Greensboro, NC 27412, USA

Accepted 27 November 2002

Abstract

There has been a rapid rise in commercial knowledge transfers from universities to practitioners or university–industry technology transfer (UITT), through licensing agreements, research joint ventures, and start-ups. The purpose of this study was to analyze the UITT process and its outcomes. Based on 98 structured interviews of key UITT stakeholders (i.e., university administrators, academic and industry scientists, business managers, and entrepreneurs) at five research universities in two regions of the US, we conclude that these stakeholders have different perspectives on the desired outputs of UITT. More importantly, numerous barriers to effective UITT were identified, including culture clashes, bureaucratic inflexibility, poorly designed reward systems, and ineffective management of university technology transfer offices (TTOs). Based on this qualitative evidence, we provide numerous recommendations for improving the UITT process.
© 2003 Elsevier Science Inc. All rights reserved.

Keywords: Commercial knowledge transfers; Effectiveness; University–industry collaboration

* Corresponding author. Tel.: +1-518-276-2049; fax: +1-518-276-2235.
E-mail addresses: Sieged@rpi.edu (D.S. Siegel), Waldman@asu.edu (D.A. Waldman),
Leanne.atwater@asu.edu (L.E. Atwater), AL_link@uncg.edu (A.N. Link).
[1] Tel.: +1-602-543-6321; fax: +1-602-543-6221.
[2] Tel.: +1-336-334-5146; fax: +1-336-334-4089.

1047-8310/03/$ – see front matter © 2003 Elsevier Science Inc. All rights reserved.
doi:10.1016/S1047-8310(03)00007-5

112   *D.S. Siegel et al. / Journal of High Technology Management Research 14 (2003) 111–133*

1. Introduction

In the 1970s, American universities were criticized for being more adept at developing new technologies than moving them into private sector applications (US General Accounting Office, 1998). Policymakers asserted that the long lag between the discovery of new knowledge at the university and its use by companies was seriously impairing the global competitiveness of American firms in such key industries as steel, automobiles, televisions, and semiconductors (Marshall, 1985). In 1980, Congress attempted to remove potential obstacles to university to industry technology transfer (UITT) through legislation, which became known as the Bayh–Dole Act (Feldman, Link, & Siegel, 2002). Bayh–Dole instituted a uniform patent policy across federal agencies, removed the restrictions on licensing, and allowed universities to own the patents that arise from federal research grants. Presumably, these changes would give universities greater flexibility in negotiating licensing agreements, and firms would be more willing to engage in them. The framers of this legislation asserted that university ownership and management of intellectual property would accelerate the commercialization of new technologies and promote economic development and entrepreneurial activity.

It appears that Bayh–Dole has indeed brought research universities closer to practitioners and entrepreneurs seeking to commercialize university-based technologies (Jensen & Thursby, 2001). In the aftermath of this legislation, many universities established technology transfer offices (henceforth, TTOs) to manage and protect their intellectual property. The role of the TTO (sometimes referred to as the Technology Licensing Office) is to facilitate commercial knowledge transfers (or technological diffusion) through the licensing to industry of inventions or other forms of intellectual property resulting from university research. There has been an impressive rise in UITT activity, as evidenced by an increase in the number of patents granted to US universities from about 300 in 1980 to approximately 3700 in 1999 and a threefold increase in licensing of university-based technologies to firms since 1991. Annual streams of revenue accruing from these licenses have risen from about US$160 million in 1991 to US$862 million in 1999, now constituting about 2.8% of university R&D expenditures. More importantly, numerous products in a wide variety of key strategic high-technology industries (e.g., computers, pharmaceuticals, agriculture, biotechnology, and instruments) have been developed through UITT. These include internet search engines (e.g., Lycos), the Boyer–Cohen "gene-splicing" technique that launched the biotechnology industry, CAT scanners, diagnostic tests for breast cancer and osteoporosis, music synthesizers, computer-aided design (CAD), and environmentally friendly technologies (US General Accounting Office, 1998).

Despite the potential importance of UITT as a source of financial gain to universities and firms and as an engine of economic growth, there is little systematic understanding of organizational practices in the management of university intellectual property. Furthermore, little attention has been paid to the managerial or private sector implications of UITT. Given that the stakeholders in this process of knowledge transfer (e.g., university faculty, university administrators, private sector managers) have different motives and behaviors and operate in different environments, there is room for considerable disagreement and misunderstanding

D.S. Siegel et al. / Journal of High Technology Management Research 14 (2003) 111–133   113

about the UITT process and how it should be managed. Nevertheless, the "boundaryless organization" philosophy driving change at firms such as General Electric argues for eliminating boundaries vertically down hierarchies, as well as horizontally across departments (Ashkenas, Ulrich, Jick, & Kerr, 1995). Moreover, boundaries between a firm and its customers or suppliers (e.g., universities) should be reduced. In this paper, we present reasons why such boundaries exist between universities and firms and prescribe methods for making such boundaries more seamless.

Thus, the primary goal of this paper is to improve our understanding of UITT so that the managers of the process in universities and industry can enhance its effectiveness. We provide a number of recommendations based on a series of 55 interviews we conducted with 98 UITT stakeholders at five research universities in two regions of the US. These stakeholders included university scientists and administrators, industry scientists, R&D managers at large companies, and entrepreneurs.

The remainder of this paper is organized as follows. In the next section, we analyze the UITT process and examine the goals, motives, and cultures of its major stakeholders. This is followed by an in-depth description of our qualitative methods. We then summarize the field evidence and identify the key outputs of UITT, as well as organizational barriers to the effectiveness of the process. Next, we provide recommendations for technology managers at universities and firms regarding ways to enhance the effectiveness of commercial knowledge transfers between universities and firms. The final section consists of conclusions and reflections on UITT in the 21st century.

2. The UITT process

2.1. Technology transfer in a university setting

Technology transfer is usually thought of as occurring within or across firms, such as the dissemination of information through transfers of employees from one division or country to another (intra-firm transfers of technology). Indeed, much research has focused specifically on the flow of technology transfer within a large R&D organization, or from an R&D subunit to the larger organization (Allen, 1984). In this paper, we focus instead on the UITT process, or commercial transfers of scientific knowledge from universities to firms.

We contend that the key stakeholders in UITT are: (1) university scientists, who discover new technologies, (2) university technology managers and administrators, who serve as liaisons between academic scientists and industry and manage the university's intellectual property, and (3) firms/entrepreneurs, who commercialize university-based technologies. This is by no means an exhaustive list of stakeholders. For example, the federal government, which funds most of these research projects, can also be viewed as a stakeholder.

A general flow model of UITT and stakeholder involvement is shown in Fig. 1. It begins with a discovery by a university scientist in a laboratory or other university setting. The scientist then files an invention disclosure with the TTO. At this point, university officials must decide whether to patent the innovation, in order to protect their intellectual property.

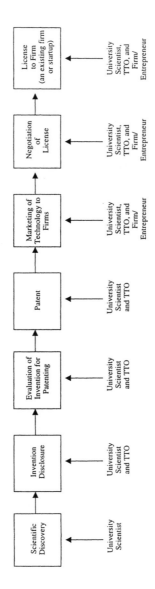

Fig. 1. How a technology is transferred from a university to a firm or entrepreneur (according to theory).

D.S. Siegel et al. / Journal of High Technology Management Research 14 (2003) 111–133   115

This is a somewhat costly decision, so the TTO must evaluate the potential for commercialization. Often, interest in the technology by an industry partner provides sufficient justification for filing a patent. In other cases, the TTO must make a judgement prior to interest being expressed by industry. This is not a trivial decision, since most universities have limited budgets to devote to the filing of patents, which can be quite expensive if the school seeks global patent protection. Schools may choose to apply for domestic patent protection, which safeguards the technology at a much lower cost.

Once the patent has been awarded, the TTO can market the technology, sometimes with faculty input. That is, faculty members can be involved in the process of identifying potential corporate licensees. The next stage involves working with private firms or entrepreneurs (i.e., in the case of start-up firms) to negotiate a licensing agreement for the intellectual property. The agreement could include such benefits to the university as royalty allowances and an equity stake in the case of start-ups. In the fifth and final stage, the technology is converted into a commercialized product. The university may continue its involvement with the firm, for instance, by devoting resources to the maintenance of licensing agreements. Moreover, in the case of start-ups, faculty members may serve as technical advisors or on boards of directors and may also have an equity stake in the start-up.

2.2. Motivation of key stakeholders

A significant aspect of UITT involves the consideration of the actions, motives, and perspectives of scientists, university administrators, and firm/entrepreneurs, which we present in Table 1. A primary motive of university scientists is recognition within the scientific community, which typically emanates from publications in top-tier journals, presentations at prestigious conferences, and research grants. Faculty members may also be motivated by personal financial gain and/or a desire to secure additional funding for graduate students and laboratory equipment.

Table 1
Key stakeholders in the transfer of technology from universities to the private sector

Stakeholder	Actions	Primary motive(s)	Secondary motive(s)	Perspective
University scientist	discovery of new knowledge	recognition within the scientific community—publications, grants (especially if untenured)	financial gain and a desire to secure additional research funding (mainly for graduate students and lab equipment)	scientific
Technology transfer office	works with faculty members and firms/ entrepreneurs to structure deals	protect and market the university's intellectual property	facilitate technological diffusion and secure additional research funding	bureaucratic
Firm/entrepreneur	commercializes new technology	financial gain	maintain control of proprietary technologies	organic/ entrepreneurial

The primary motive of the TTO and university administration is to safeguard the university's intellectual property, while at the same time market that intellectual property to firms. Secondary motives include securing additional research funding for the university via royalties and licensing fees, sponsored research agreements, and an intrinsic desire to promote technological diffusion (the goal of the Bayh–Dole Act). TTO managers, like other university administrators, work within the bureaucratic framework of the university.

The actions and motives of firms and entrepreneurs are relatively straightforward (Siegel, Waldman, & Link, 1999). They seek to commercialize university-based technologies for financial gain. To do so, they desire exclusive rights to the technologies that are generated. Firms and entrepreneurs also express great concern about "time to market," since the ultimate benefits from product and process innovation depend on commercializing the product or perfecting the new production process before competitors do. Finally, firms and entrepreneurs are also concerned about maintaining proprietary control over technologies.

Differences in the actions, motives, and perspectives of the three key players in this process underscore the potential importance of organizational factors in effective university management of intellectual property. One key goal of our field research was to explore these differences so that we could identify a set of organizational and managerial policies and practices to overcome critical barriers to effective technology transfer. In addition, although Bayh–Dole and much of the existing literature stresses commercialization of university-based technologies as the predominant outcome (e.g., licensing and start-up formation) (Bercovitz, Feldman, Feller, & Burton, 2001), we also sought to ascertain how each stakeholder group defines the outputs of UITT.

3. Method

Our results and recommendations are based on semi-structured, in-person interviews with three categories of UITT stakeholders: (1) TTO directors and university administrators, (2) academic scientists, and (3) managers/entrepreneurs. We focused our analysis on five major public and private research universities in Arizona and North Carolina. These universities have relationships with many large and small firms and have also spawned a number of start-up companies. Each of these schools established a TTO soon after the enactment of Bayh–Dole in 1980. Note that we did not examine hotbeds of technology-transfer activity, such as Cambridge/Boston (MIT, Harvard, and Boston University) or the San Francisco Bay area (Stanford and UC—Berkeley). However, the schools we visited are probably far more representative of the average university experience with technology transfer than top-tier schools that have the most favorable environments for stimulating this activity (the best graduate students, an abundance of available venture capital, and a strong entrepreneurial culture). Recall also that the policy initiative, the Bayh–Dole Act, was designed to stimulate UITT at all research universities, not just top-tier institutions.

At each university, we interviewed academic scientists who have transferred technologies, the TTO director, and at least one administrator who oversees the TTO, usually a Vice Provost,

D.S. Siegel et al. / Journal of High Technology Management Research 14 (2003) 111–133 117

Vice President, or Vice Chancellor for Research. Within the surrounding region of the university, we also interviewed founders of start-up companies, directors of business development, intellectual property managers and other research managers at large companies, and executives of patent management firms and nonprofit organizations with an interest in UITT.

Potential respondents were identified from two sources of information. First, we identified the TTO director and consulted each university's organizational chart in the research area to identify the administrator(s) to whom the TTO director reports. Second, to identify managers/ entrepreneurs and scientists, we solicited feedback from two organizations that serve as technology-transfer "facilitators" in each region. By design, these organizations have a balanced view on technology issues. That is, they do not favor one stakeholder group over another. Because facilitators are well connected to many firms, TTOs, and administrators, we used them to identify managers and scientists who had a wide variety of perspectives on UITT and many relationships with TTOs.

In Arizona, we interacted with the High-Technology Industry Cluster (HTIC) of the Governor's Strategic Partnership for Economic Development (GSPED). HTIC includes small and large businesses and has a technology transfer committee, consisting of members who have had both positive and negative experiences with various universities. Thus, we selected members of HTIC to interview, rather than ask university TTOs for a list of firms to contact. In North Carolina, we relied on the North Carolina Biotechnology Center (NCBC) and the Research Triangle Institute (RTI), which are both nonpartisan organizations that provide advice to academics and firms who wish to transfer technologies. NCBC and RTI were also capable of providing connections to individuals and organizations with a broad range of views on UITT.

In sum, a stratified approach was used for the selection of interviewees, so that interviewees would be drawn from the three UITT stakeholder groups. We conducted 55 interviews: 20 managers/entrepreneurs, 15 university administrators (5 TTO directors and 10 other top-level administrators), and 20 university scientists. Our sample included a mix of large and small companies and faculty members in a wide variety of academic disciplines (physics, biology, chemistry, medicine, pharmacology, and engineering). Although there were only 55 face-to-face meetings, we actually interviewed 98 individuals, since more than one person was present at some meetings.

The interviews consisted of a series of open-ended questions that were designed to determine how various stakeholders defined technology transfer and its outputs as well as what they viewed as impediments to successful technology transfer and strategies for improvement. A list of the interview questions used for each group is presented in Appendix A. Note that each stakeholder group was asked to define technology transfer and its outputs, identify impediments to successful technology transfer, and to provide suggestions for improving the process. Questions varied slightly depending on the type of interviewee. For example, only TTO directors and other university administrators were asked to comment on the managerial practices of the TTO. On average, the interviews lasted approximately 1 h and were tape recorded with the consent of interviewees. A typist was hired to transcribe the tapes, in order to ensure a complete and unbiased recording of the interview data.

In order to conduct a quantitative analysis of the qualitative interview data, we employed procedures outlined in Miles and Huberman (1994). First, we simplified and transformed the raw data into an analyzable form, using an initial list of general categories for content analysis purposes. All comments were then independently categorized by two members of the research team into four areas: (1) the nature of UITT outputs, (2) UITT networks and relationships, (3) barriers to UITT, and (4) proposed improvements to the UITT process. The two researchers' lists of comments within a topic area were then compared, and discrepancies were discussed between the two researchers until agreement was reached regarding comments that were pertinent to each category. Similar methods were employed by Butterfield, Trevino, and Ball (1996), who identified unique "thought units" pertinent to their subject of interest (employee discipline).

After a consensus was reached regarding the categories, we returned to the lists of comments pertinent to the each of the four general categories and sorted them into the themes identified for that respective category. For data display purposes, we tabulated the frequencies with which comments emerged for each theme by stakeholder group. For example, Table 2 presents the percentage of respondents who identified themes relevant to barriers to UITT by stakeholder group.

Table 2
Stakeholder perceptions of the barriers to university–industry technology transfer (UITT)

Barriers	Type of stakeholder		
	(1) Managers/ entrepreneurs	(2) TTO directors/ administrators	(3) University scientists
Lack of understanding regarding university, corporate, or scientific norms and environments	90.0	93.3	75.0
Insufficient rewards for university researchers	31.6	60.0	70.0
Bureaucracy and inflexibility of university administrators	80.0	6.6	70.0
Insufficient resources devoted to technology transfer by universities	31.6	53.3	20.0
Poor marketing/technical/negotiation skills of TTOs	55.0	13.3	25.0
University too aggressive in exercising intellectual property rights	80.0	13.3	25.0
Faculty members/administrators have unrealistic expectations regarding the value of their technologies	25.0	40.0	10.0
"Public domain" mentality of universities	40.0	8.3	5.0
Number of interviews	20	15	20

The values presented in columns (1)–(3) are the percentages of respondents who identified a particular item as a barrier to UITT.

D.S. Siegel et al. / Journal of High Technology Management Research 14 (2003) 111–133   119

4. Results and recommendations

In this section, we present our qualitative results regarding stakeholder perceptions on various aspects of UITT. Based on these perceptions and our understanding of how management theories can be applied to UITT, we provide some recommendations for university-based and firm-based improvements in the effectiveness of UITT.

Our interviews revealed that the outputs most frequently mentioned by TTO directors and university administrators were licenses and royalties, which is not surprising since they generate revenue for the university. To a somewhat lesser extent, university administrators also identified patents and sponsored research agreement as outputs of UITT. Although managers and entrepreneurs identified licenses as an output, they also mentioned broader notions of output, such as product development, profit, and economic development. One manager stated:

> For us in business, it [technology transfer] means that we use some of this technology to generate profits for our shareholders. But more importantly, there's a social return which results from the economic development, creation of jobs, the hiring of graduate students.

Indeed, the most frequently mentioned UITT output by managers and entrepreneurs was informal transfer of know-how. An illustrative comment by a manager was:

> So much of what we call technology transfer is information transfer, knowledge transfer. It's not something that could be put immediately into a product. It might be something that is a tidbit of knowledge that will help somebody in their development efforts at one of our companies.

Some university scientists most frequently identified product development and licenses as outputs, although many were reluctant to think of the process in terms of generating "output." They tended to see UITT more as a continuous process rather than one with specific outcomes. Their responses resembled those of UITT managers in that informal transfer of know-how was seen as an output. Our interpretation of this finding is that they could not reach a consensus on the outputs of UITT because they are too focused on their own role in this process and fail to see the "big picture." In this regard, we present the following phrases mentioned by scientists in their discussions of outputs:

> training the engineers who are going to be working with industry

> patents that will be in my name and the graduate students' names

> working with graduate students who are subsequently hired by firms

We also solicited information from stakeholders regarding barriers to effective UITT. All three groups identified a lack of understanding regarding university/corporate/scientific norms as a pervasive barrier to effective UITT. That is, business managers asserted that university scientists and administrators do not understand or appreciate industry goals/culture/ constraints, while university scientists and administrators believe that industry does not understand or appreciate university goals/culture/constraints. Representative comments from university administrators tended to point the finger toward the business community and their lack of appreciation for the university's role and processes:

> Industry has a lack of understanding of what an academic institution does and a lack of understanding of what a university faculty member's responsibility is to their institution. There are some companies I don't even deal with because their approach to dealing with an academic entity is so poor. They feel that basically, we owe them by our position at the university because the state pays our salaries.

> They say to us, you've got all that technology over on the shelf, why aren't you getting it out to the marketplace? They don't understand what we mean by technology. We don't have technology in little boxes on shelves that people can pull out and apply. They think it is like the warehouse at the end of Indiana Jones.

University administrators also questioned the sophistication of university scientists' understanding of the process. In referring to his own faculty members, one university administrator stated:

> Some faculty members have a purely academic orientation and don't have a lot of interest in dealing with private companies...or they don't understand what the motivations of private companies are.

The managers/entrepreneurs in our study commonly perceived that universities are too aggressive in exercising intellectual property rights. This results in a hard line on negotiations, excess concern on the part of university administrators that they will not realize sufficient revenue, and unrealistic expectations. A typical comment was:

> I think the frustration for commercial licensees who go to a university is that it seems as though the attitude they are hitting at the university is 'oh we've got this wonderful thing and we're going to drag every nickel out of you that we can get for it'.

A manager of a biotechnology firm provided this example:

> University scientists look at a technology, maybe it's a petri dish compound that kills fast-dividing cells. Now they can make an extrapolation to an anticancer drug. They look at the market for anticancer drugs and see that they are billions of dollars a year. Therefore, their invention must be worth billions of dollars. When you tell them it's only worth a few hundred thousand dollars they don't understand it is because of the stage of development...all the risk in going forward and whether it really works.

Managers/entrepreneurs and university scientists frequently cited university bureaucracy and inflexibility as barriers to UITT. Essentially, they believe that universities wish to follow rigid procedures that may not fit a particular situation. Furthermore, they noted that these procedures are cumbersome and often not clearly specified. A typical remark from a scientist was:

> I don't think they [the TTO] understand the flexibility within the framework and what they can do. I think they have a set of forms and a set of ways of doing things and if it doesn't fit nicely into that, then you know they make you to through a whole bunch of hoops.

A manager provided this example:

> A lot of technology transfer office people just know what the book says about what the value of this should be commercially, but they don't realize that the value to any given licensee of a very early technology is not what the book says.

University administrators and scientists also cited insufficient rewards for university researchers who are engaged in technology-transfer activities as a barrier to effective UITT. In essence, all groups acknowledged that with few exceptions, university promotion and tenure practices did not value technology transfer. One exception was in engineering, where there was some recognition of this activity. However, the vast majority of interviewees noted that promotion and tenure decisions are based exclusively on publications and federal research grants, with no weight placed on patents and industry partnerships.

Finally, with regard to barriers to technology transfer, firms and entrepreneurs were inclined to point out that the marketing, technical, and negotiation skills of the TTO could be substantially improved. Comments from firms/entrepreneurs included:

> What it takes to be a successful technology transfer officer is being a dealmaker, not an academic.

> These guys [TTOs] need to be marketing facilitators rather than lawyers. They need to be able to step into the company and into their customer's shoes and look back.

Similarly, a scientist remarked:

> In a TTO, they have to know the field. They have to know where they think the technology is moving and then be able to make a decision whether or not to file these patents.

A university administrator also acknowledged:

> The impediment to successful technology transfer at this university was a lack of marketing and skill within the technology transfer office.

In sum, these comments demonstrate the existence of many barriers to effective UITT, including culture clashes, bureaucratic inflexibility, poorly designed reward systems, and ineffective management of TTOs. The end result is a failure to maximize opportunities to transfer technologies, which hurts universities, firms, and ultimately, consumers. In order to avoid such problems in the future, we provide suggestions for improving the UITT process.

The results from the interviews suggest some avenues for improving UITT processes. Many of the interviewees' suggestions for improvement were extremely rich and vivid, given the strong feelings respondents have regarding UITT issues. The consensus that emerged across stakeholder groups regarding suggested improvements was actually quite striking. Although most suggestions were aimed toward universities and their management of the process, a number of comments were also targeted at the private sector. We will divide our below discussion accordingly.

4.1. Recommendations for university-based improvements

Our recommendations for university-based improvements are presented in the top panel of Table 3, which we now consider in turn. The qualitative results suggest that universities need to improve their understanding of the needs of their true "customers," i.e., firms that can potentially commercialize their technologies. Over 75% of all managers, TTO directors, and university scientists agreed that achieving better mutual understanding between universities and industry was needed. While there is strong evidence of cultural misunderstanding on both

Table 3
Suggested university and firm-based improvements to the UITT process

Suggested university-based improvements to the UITT process
◆ Universities need to improve their understanding of the needs of their true "customers," i.e., firms that can potentially commercialize their technologies
◆ Adopt a more flexible stance in negotiating technology-transfer agreements and streamline UITT policies and procedures
◆ Hire licensing officers and TTO managers with more business experience
◆ Switch to incentive compensation in the TTO
◆ Hire managers/research administrators with a strategic vision, who can serve as effective boundary spanners (tie to boundary spanning literature)
◆ Devote additional resources to the TTO and patenting
◆ Increase the rewards for faculty participation in UITT by valuing patents and licenses in promotion and tenure decisions and allowing faculty members to keep a larger share of licensing revenue (as opposed to their department or university)
◆ Recognize the value of personal relationships and social networks, involving scientists, graduate students, and alumni
Suggested firm-based improvements to the UITT process
◆ Be proactive in their efforts to bridge the cultural gap with academia
◆ Hire technology managers with university experience
◆ Explore alternative means for tapping into UITT social networks

sides, it appears that much of the onus lies with universities and academics. One manager stated:

> If I could wave a magic wand over an inventor, I would want them to understand some of the issues I have talked about before. Why does someone want to commercialize your invention? Do you really have a product? What is your goal and how do you want to reach it?

This manager had earlier remarked that he wished scientists and university officials could be more aware of the costs that need to go into an invention before it is marketable and that there are often "good" technologies that are commercial failures.

The mutual articulation of well-defined goals and objectives was frequently mentioned as a way to achieve an understanding of each group's values and needs and reach a common ground. One executive described goals and objectives in this manner:

> There cannot be different objectives in a partnership. The company and the university in a tech transfer agreement have to say 'this is our objective for the tech transfer.' And they have to agree to that set of objectives. It is not sufficient for the university to say 'well our objectives are on the publication side' and have the company say 'our objectives are on the profit side' and then simply not address both objectives in the tech transfer relationship. You can have objectives that are more important to one side or the other, but they all have to be agreed upon and they all have to be worked toward.

Related to the problem of cultural misunderstanding is the need for more flexibility on the part of universities, though this suggestion came primarily from managers/entrepreneurs. Over half of them offered this suggestion. Inflexibility has a negative impact on the TTO's ability to market university-based technologies. More importantly, rigidity significantly impedes the process of negotiating a licensing agreement. Firms repeatedly expressed their frustration at the university's lack of a "deal-making" mentality and aggressive tendencies in exercising their intellectual property rights. In defense of universities, especially public ones, it is important to note that they have a legitimate fear of being accused of "giving away" a technology to a private firm. This can be a public relations nightmare for universities, especially when they are lobbying for additional funding in the state legislature.

Thus, many schools have adopted an extremely conservative negotiation stance, preferring to maximize royalties, even if this significantly reduces the probability of consummating the deal. Nevertheless, a university's risk aversion is especially frustrating for start-ups and other firms that need to respond quickly to changes in the competitive environment. Therefore, we propose that universities adopt a more flexible stance in negotiating technology-transfer agreements and that they streamline UITT policies and procedures.

We also have several recommendations relating to human resource management practices in the TTO. The need for improved marketing expertise within the TTO was commonly mentioned by the managers/entrepreneurs. Our field research revealed that TTOs usually do not actively recruit individuals with marketing skills. More often, they looked for expertise in patent law and licensing or technical expertise. A university administrator (outside of the university's TTO) suggested:

> Someone should be there [in the TTO] who completely understands how to market the product. Mostly the offices are patent attorneys or negotiating attorneys...no one really comes from marketing.

Thus, universities should hire licensing officers and TTO managers with more substantial business experience.

The qualitative evidence also suggests that TTO personnel need to be effective facilitators and negotiators of UITT which means that they should engage in the types of boundary spanning roles so often described in literature on the management of technological innovation (Ancona & Caldwell, 1992; Katz & Tushman, 1983). Unfortunately, many TTOs are not actively recruiting licensing officers who possess such skills or behavioral tendencies. Several respondents who had relationships with many TTOs noted that those managed by directors with substantial business and negotiation experience had a much firmer grasp on how to assess the market potential of a particular technology and create more linkages with firms. They also had a better understanding of the complexity of negotiations and how to be flexible in order to consummate transactions. We suggest that universities should consider the business and negotiation experience of TTO personnel when making hiring decisions.

The notion that reward systems for university technology transfer should be modified was endorsed by over 80% of managers, TTO directors, and university scientists. We conjecture that one change in the rewards system that would improve the effectiveness of UITT is a switch towards incentive compensation in the TTO. This could reduce some of the agency costs associated with university management of intellectual property. As noted in Gomez-Mejia and Balkin (1992: p. 923), "Proponents of agency theory assume that each party acts in its own self interest. This assumption gives rise to the so-called agency problem because the interests of the principal and agent may conflict." While academic scientists receive royalties from patented technologies, TTO officers often have no direct financial incentive to spur technology transfer. That is because most licensing officers are paid strictly on salary. Perhaps if they too received some compensation from "making deals," they would be more motivated to work on the university's behalf. Gomez-Mejia and Balkin (1992) and Eisenhardt (1988) showed that principals may successfully use incentive systems when dealing with non-programmed jobs where direct supervision or monitoring is infeasible.

A consensus also emerged on two additional suggestions for improving UITT. First, universities should devote additional resources to technology transfer and target them more effectively. Resources devoted to UITT will affect the level of patenting. Legal fees must be expended to build a valuable portfolio of university patents. This is quite expensive, especially if universities wish to file for global patent protection, which is more expensive than domestic patent protection. On a similar note, a large TTO staff may be needed to market university-based technologies effectively, especially when the reputation of the university is insufficient to draw unsolicited attention to a school's patent portfolio. That is, non-top-tier institutions must be more proactive in marketing than MIT or Stanford. One company executive summed it up this way:

> It's so easy to see. You look at the TTO and see one full-time person in a 30,000-person university; there is something wrong with that picture. If they are understaffed and underbudgeted, and if there isn't a reasonable budget to protect intellectual property— you can't patent everything. That's why you need more staff.

Second, the upper administration needs to clearly articulate technology transfer as a university priority. That is, leadership is required on the part of upper administration to establish goals and priorities and espouse values pertaining to UITT. One manager of a TTO at a large public university that has achieved remarkable success in recent years underscored the importance of leadership in this quote:

> The fact that our chancellor constantly stresses the importance of technology transfer as a strategic goal has really helped build support from faculty and local firms. More importantly, the upper administration has usually backed me up when a dispute arises, which demonstrates that they are committed to this goal.

The modification of university reward systems is inherently part of establishing a UITT vision and culture. We found a widespread belief that there are insufficient rewards for faculty involvement in UITT. This is especially true for untenured faculty members, who continue to be rewarded within the university almost strictly on the basis of publications and grants. In fact, many senior faculty members look askance at junior faculty members who become involved in UITT. They allege that such activity represents time taken away from fundamental research.

Unfortunately, such reward structures can be viewed as being inconsistent with the stated organizational objective of increasing UITT, which is often advertised prominently in university mission statements and announcements to the external community. Many interviewees in all three groups specifically mentioned that technology-transfer activities should have a greater weight in faculty promotion and tenure decisions. An industry executive said:

> One thing I would do at the university and I think it is being done in some...I would make a patent count toward tenure like any two papers. In fact, in some universities, they count against the researcher.

A university administrator also indicated that incentives were important:

> The way to improve it [tech transfer] is to really provide the very best service you can and incentives for faculty to participate and make sure you have the information support and financial support that it is going to take for them to be successful.

It is also important to consider pecuniary rewards, such as the university's royalty and equity distribution formula. This refers to the split in licensing or equity income among the inventor(s), the department or college of the inventor(s), and the TTO or another general research fund within the university. For example, at one school we visited, the formula was 40% inventor, 40% inventor's department, and 20% "invention management fund," which is managed by the TTO. Adjusting this formula in favor of the scientists could also elicit more faculty involvement in UITT.

Finally, it is important for scientists and university administrators to realize that licenses, royalties, and patents are not the end-all-cure-all of UITT. There is also inherent value in the personal relationships and networks that include the private sector. One scientist put it this way:

> I would say right now that I feel that the one-on-one interaction is somewhat more successful in effectively transferring technology [than is research sponsored by a consortium].

It appears that the formation of social networks is important in UITT processes. These networks include academic and industry scientists, and perhaps, university administrators, TTO directors, and managers/entrepreneurs (Liebeskind, Oliver, Zucker, & Brewer, 1996; Powell, 1990). Social networks that allow knowledge transfer appear to work in both directions. Scientists whom we interviewed noted that interacting with industry enables them to conduct "better" basic research, a finding that has been documented in biotechnology industries (Zucker & Darby, 1996). For example, a scientist commented:

> There is no doubt that working with industry scientists has made me a better researcher. They help me refine my experiments and sometimes have a different perspective on a problem that sparks my own ideas. Also, my involvement with firms has allowed me to purchase better equipment for my lab, which helps me conduct more experiments.

The downside, from a university's perspective, is that too much informal communication between university scientists and managers or entrepreneurs in the private sector may result in a total avoidance of the TTO, i.e., fewer licenses and royalties for the university. That is, when an invention is disclosed (and thus, public information), firms may contact the scientist and arrange to work with him/her and engage in informal commercialization and knowledge transfer, through consulting or a sabbatical leave. As an example, a scientist told us that if asked to develop a piece of software for a firm he would:

> probably do it as a personal consulting job rather than going through the university. Although it is probably easier for me to do it through the university, and it would

D.S. Siegel et al. / Journal of High Technology Management Research 14 (2003) 111–133   127

probably also benefit the students more effectively, it is a hassle to do it. . .it is such a pain in the neck.

Another scientist reported on the attitude of firms he was working with:

> In fact a lot of people will come to us and say we don't want to go through the university. . .we'll just pay you on the side.

However, we believe that such behavior is likely to be problematic only when university inflexibility, mentioned above, reaches such a degree that it frustrates both scientists and firms alike. Only then will university scientists attempt to circumvent more formal UITT processes. As a whole, we encourage more informal interaction between university scientists and managers/entrepreneurs in the private sector.

4.2. Recommendations for firm-based improvements

It may seem odd to propose changes in the behavior of firms/entrepreneurs, since they can be viewed as the customers of UITT, and the conventional wisdom is that the customer is always right. In addition, doesn't the university bear the ultimate responsibility for managing this process? However, we view UITT as a quintessential example of a public–private partnership. Our research suggests that if universities are to manage this partnership successfully, they require some additional input from firms. Thus, we have several suggestions for firms, which we present in the bottom panel of Table 3.

We recommend that firms be proactive in their efforts to bridge the cultural gap with academia. As previously suggested, cultural barriers are pervasive in UITT, given that stakeholders operate under diverse organizational environments and have different norms, standards, and values. For example, universities and firms differ in their perspective on the role of knowledge (Nelson, 2001). Firms typically do not want researchers to publish their results and share information with colleagues and the general public. Instead, they view technology as something to be kept proprietary and used for strategic advantage in the pursuit of profits.

Given the prominence of this difference in perspective, it is critical for companies and entrepreneurs to be make strong efforts to bridge the cultural gap. Indeed, our interviewees generated many interesting suggestions regarding ways to develop better mutual understanding, including technology expositions, formal meetings to discuss technology transfer, and conferences involving scientists, university administrators, and managers/entrepreneurs. An intellectual property manager stated:

> Conferences and expos are critical in establishing relationships with scientists. I also think that the town hall meetings we have had are fruitful in reducing tensions that arise between universities and industry. I know that I have a much healthier relationship with the TTO since attending them on a regular basis.

Another executive provided this suggestion:

> Our institute runs and hosts a workshop, half-day, that has been held for the last 3 years covering the Laws of Science to teach university researchers especially how to think about intellectual property.

In one state that we examined, periodic "town hall" meetings were established to help resolve controversial intellectual property rights issues and to educate firms and universities regarding each other's cultures. In the same state, the TTO director of a major research university often appears before an institutional group representing high-technology firms when intellectual property issues are being considered in the state legislature.

Another way to overcome cultural barriers is through the labor market. Several managers at large firms mentioned that they had achieved better relations with university TTOs when they hired at least one technology manager who had worked at a university or nonprofit organization. Unfortunately, many business development managers, i.e., those often serve as liaison officers between firms and universities, have little experience working with universities. That is why our second recommendation is that firms who engage in substantial UITT activity hire technology managers with university experience.

A third recommendation is that firms take advantage of all avenues to tap into UITT social networks. After all, technology transfer is frequently embodied in the transfer of human capital via graduate students, postdoctoral fellows, or a faculty member on leave or sabbatical from the university. Many entrepreneurs and managers stated that such hiring practices constituted a quite effective form of technology transfer, even though a more tangible form of UITT output, such as a licensing agreement or patent, did not emerge in the short run. In addition, industry should make greater use of these scientists and their laboratories/equipment/talent. Often, managers and entrepreneurs have ideas that can be tested with the sophisticated equipment and talent the university has to offer.

5. Conclusions

In the "new" economy, there is a stronger emphasis on intellectual property, venture capital, and entrepreneurial start-ups. The recent increase in UITT, managed through a TTO, has led to a concomitant rise in the incidence and complexity of research partnerships involving universities and firms. This has led to considerable tension and inefficiency in university management of intellectual property. That is not surprising since formal university management of a portfolio of intellectual property is a relatively new phenomenon, so we are still in a learning phase regarding "best practices."

Our evidence suggests that there is considerable room for enhancing the effectiveness of these commercial knowledge transfers from universities to firms. We find that organizational and managerial behaviors and skills are critical factors in facilitating UITT. Specifically,

D.S. Siegel et al. / Journal of High Technology Management Research 14 (2003) 111–133   129

universities wishing to foster commercialization need to be mindful of the following organizational and managerial factors:

- eradicating cultural and informational barriers that impede the UITT process
- designing flexible university policies on technology transfer
- improving staffing practices in the TTO
- devoting additional resources to UITT, if that is consistent with the university's mission
- enhancing the rewards for engaging in UITT
- encouraging informal relationships and social networks

More generally, our results imply that universities should consider UITT from a strategic perspective. This implies that they must address a set of formulation and implementation issues. We have already noted the critical implementation issues (e.g., changes in HRM and other organizational practices). The key formulation issues are setting institutional goals and priorities for UITT and the related issue of determining the appropriate level of resources to devote to UITT. These choices will affect decisions regarding the set of technologies (e.g., biotechnology) and modes of UITT to stress, i.e., licensing, start-ups, sponsored research, or other UITT mechanisms that are focused directly on stimulating economic development (e.g., science parks).

We have also identified some measures that firms can adopt to facilitate UITT. These include being proactive in their efforts to bridge the cultural gap with academia through frequent meetings and workshops with universities, hiring technology managers who know how to work with universities, and using the labor market to tap into UITT social networks.

US universities have long been known for their scientific breakthroughs and knowledge generation. Only through cooperative efforts with the private sector can the end result of successful commercialization materialize. It is ultimately the responsibility of both universities and firms to ensure such cooperation.

Although we have argued that there should be "thinner" boundaries between universities and firms, there are some potential problems associated with such initiatives that need to be acknowledged. Specifically, they raise concerns regarding how a shift towards commercialization at research universities affects the culture of "open science" (Poyago-Theotoky, Beath, & Siegel, 2002). Open science refers to the free exchange and dissemination of new ideas among faculty members and students. Indeed, Louis, Jones, Anderson, Blumenthal, and Campbell (2001) find that academic scientists engaged in entrepreneurial activities are more likely to deny requests from fellow academics for research results than other faculty members who are not engaged in entrepreneurial activities.

These issues are especially problematic for public universities. An example is the 1998 strategic alliance between the Department of Plant and Microbial Biology at the University of California at Berkeley and Novartis, a Swiss life sciences and pharmaceutical firm. This alliance grants first rights to Novartis to negotiate licenses on approximately one-third of the department's inventions for the next 5 years. Press and Washburn (2000) note that some faculty members and graduate students at Berkeley were concerned that Novartis would attempt to influence the department's research agenda, since the Berkeley administration permitted the company to have two of the five seats on the committee that decides how research money is spent.

Other potential concerns associated with thinner boundaries between universities and firms include a shift from basic to applied research and its influence on education Stephan (2001). For instance, collaborations with industry may shift attention away from fundamental research questions that do not appear likely to generate a commercial payoff. Others have voiced concern that faculty members involved in UITT may spend less time on teaching and service.

It is clear that universities and firms have different perspectives and goals with respect to intellectual property. As these two entities attempt to collaborate, conflicts are inevitable. However, UITT may be one process that can improve our understanding of how convergence can take place between very different organizations. For instance, our qualitative evidence suggests that, contrary to popular wisdom, technology transfer does not flow strictly in one direction, i.e., from firms to universities. We also found that academic scientists may be able to conduct better basic research as a result of their involvement in UITT. This occurs because UITT provides them with access to better equipment and additional financial resources to conduct more experiments, as well as new ideas from industry scientists. Finally, it is conceivable that such alliances could affect the curriculum, as faculty members draw on their experiences with firms to provide instruction that is more relevant and more closely aligned with the needs of high-technology firms (Stephan, 2001).

Acknowledgements

We thank Nicholas Argyres, Susan Helper, Adam Jaffe, Julia Liebeskind, participants at the 1999 Academy of Management meetings in Chicago, and especially, Mike Wright, for their insightful comments and suggestions. We are also deeply indebted to the many administrators, scientists, managers, and entrepreneurs who agreed to be interviewed. Martha Cobb and Melissa Zidle provided capable research assistance. Financial support from the Alfred P. Sloan Foundation and the National Bureau of Economic Research is gratefully acknowledged.

Appendix A. Questions asked of UITT stakeholders

Interview questions for TTO directors:

1. How do you define technology transfer? What are the outputs?
2. How has the process of technology transfer changed over time? Has the relative importance of specific outputs changed over time?
3. What data do you collect to measure the performance of your office?
4. What are the impediments to successful technology transfer?

5. How would you improve the process?
6. Could you describe your managerial philosophy? Are there any specific managerial practices that you utilize in running your office?
7. How much of your time is spent with the business community? With university scientists?
8. What is the nature of these interactions? Do you meet or talk on the phone? What issues do you discuss?
9. Who are the key individuals you network with in order to accomplish your job? What type of communication is involved in such networking? What percentage of your work time is spent in this networking activity?
10. In your role as director, how important is educating firms about the potential value of university technologies? Why do you feel it is important or unimportant?
11. Could you describe the different licensing strategies that you employ?
12. Could you describe the decision-making process regarding whether to patent the invention?
13. Could you describe how you recruit companies who might be interested in the invention?
14. How do you measure the potential commercial viability of a new technology?
15. How much time is spent in your office on renegotiations? Do you have a suggestion for reducing this?
16. What is the most common reason for termination of an agreement?

Interview questions for other university research administrators (e.g., Vice Provost for Research):

1. How do you define technology transfer? What are the outputs?
2. How has the process of technology transfer changed over time? Has the relative importance of specific outputs changed over time?
3. What data do you collect to measure technology transfer performance? Ideally, what would be the best data to collect?
4. What are the impediments to successful technology transfer?
5. How would you improve the process?
6. What is your university's overall strategy for technology transfer?
7. In recent years, has your institution's reward structure changed to promote technology transfer? Do you think it should?

Interview questions for managers and entrepreneurs:

1. How do you define technology transfer? What are the outputs?
2. How do you measure the success of technology transfer?
3. What are the impediments to successful technology transfer?
4. How would you improve the process?
5. How would you characterize your relationships with the TTO?
6. How would you characterize your relationships with university scientists?

7. What individuals do you network with at the university? What type of communication is involved in such networking?
8. How do you measure the potential commercial viability of a new technology?

Interview questions for academic scientists:

1. Please describe your personal experiences with technology transfer.
2. What are the impediments to successful technology transfer?
3. How would you improve the process?
4. How much of your time is spent with the business community? With TTO personnel?
5. How many industry scientists do you interact with? Are these your former graduate students? What is the nature of this interaction? What percentage of your time in devoted to this activity? Has your TTO facilitated these relationships?
6. How much does your university/college/department value technology transfer? Has this changed in recent years?
7. How would you characterize your relationships with the TTO?

References

Allen, T. J. (1984). *Managing the flow of technology: technology transfer and the dissemination of technological information within the R&D organization*. Cambridge, MA: MIT Press.

Ancona, D. G., & Caldwell, D. F. (1992). Bridging the boundary: external activity and performance in organizational teams. *Administrative Science Quarterly, 37*, 634–666.

Ashkenas, R., Ulrich, D., Jick, T., & Kerr, S. (1995). *The boundaryless organization*. San Francisco: Jossey-Bass.

Bercovitz, J., Feldman, M., Feller, I., & Burton, R. (2001). Organizational structure as a determinant of academic patenting and licensing behavior: an exploratory study of Duke, Johns Hopkins, and Pennsylvania State Universities. *Journal of Technology Transfer, 26*, 21–135.

Butterfield, K., Trevino, L., & Ball, G. (1996). Punishment from the manager's perspective: a grounded investigation and inductive model. *Academy of Management Journal, 39*, 1479–1512.

Eisenhardt, K. M. (1988). Agency- and institutional-theory explanations: the case of retail sales compensation. *Academy of Management Journal, 31*, 488–511.

Feldman, M. P., Link, A. N., & Siegel, D. S. (2002). *The economics of science and technology*. Norwell, MA: Kluwer Academic Publishing.

Gomez-Mejia, L. R., & Balkin, D. B. (1992). Determinants of faculty pay: an agency theory perspective. *Academy of Management Journal, 35*, 921–955.

Jensen, R., & Thursby, M. C. (2001). Proofs and prototypes for sale: the licensing of university inventions. *American Economic Review, 91*, 240–259.

Katz, R., & Tushman, M. (1983). A longitudinal study of the effects of boundary spanning supervision on turnover and promotion in research and development. *Academy of Management Journal, 26*, 437–456.

Liebeskind, J., Oliver, A., Zucker, L., & Brewer, M. (1996). Social networks, learning, and flexibility: sourcing scientific knowledge in new biotechnology firms. *Organization Science, 7*, 428–443.

Louis, K. S., Jones, L. M., Anderson, M. S., Blumenthal, D., & Campbell, E. G. (2001). Entrepreneurship, secrecy, and productivity: a comparison of clinical and non-clinical faculty. *Journal of Technology Transfer, 26*, 233–245.

Marshall, E. (1985, April 12). Japan and the economics of invention. *Science*, 157–158.

Miles, M. B., & Huberman, A. M. (1994). *Qualitative data analysis*. (2nd ed.). Thousand Oaks, CA: Sage Publications.

D.S. Siegel et al. / Journal of High Technology Management Research 14 (2003) 111–133   133

Nelson, R. R. (2001). Observations on the post-Bayh–Dole rise of patenting at American Universities. *Journal of Technology Transfer, 26*, 13–19.

Powell, W. W. (1990). Neither market nor hierarchy: network forms of organization. *Research in Organizational Behavior, 12*, 295–336.

Poyago-Theotoky, J., Beath, J., & Siegel, D. (2002). Universities and fundamental research: policy implications of the growth of university–industry partnerships. *Oxford Review of Economic Policy, 18*, 10–21.

Press, E., & Washburn, J. (2000). The kept university. *Atlantic Monthly, 285*(3), 39–54.

Siegel, D., Waldman, D., & Link, A. (1999). Assessing the impact of organizational practices on the productivity of university technology transfer offices: an exploratory study. National Bureau of Economic Research Working Paper No. 7256, July and in press, *Research Policy.*

Stephan, P. (2001). Educational implications of university–industry technology transfer. *Journal of Technology Transfer, 26*, 199–205.

US General Accounting Office. (1998). *Technology transfer: administration of the Bayh–Dole Act by research universities*. Washington, DC: Author.

Zucker, L. G., & Darby, M. R. (1996). Star scientists and institutional transformation: patterns of invention and innovation in the formation of the biotechnology industry. *Proceedings of the National Academy of Sciences, 93*, 709–716.

[9]

Available online at www.sciencedirect.com

SCIENCE ⓓ DIRECT®

ELSEVIER

Research Policy 34 (2005) 369–384

research
policy

www.elsevier.com/locate/econbase

Assessing the relative performance of U.K. university technology transfer offices: parametric and non-parametric evidence[☆]

Wendy Chapple [a,1], Andy Lockett [a,2], Donald Siegel [b,*], Mike Wright [a,1]

[a] *Nottingham University Business School, University of Nottingham, Jubilee Campus, Nottingham NG8 1BB, UK*
[b] *Department of Economics, Rensselaer Polytechnic Institute, 3502 Russell Sage Laboratory, Troy, NY 12180-3590, USA*

Received 3 September 2004; received in revised form 13 December 2004; accepted 20 January 2005
Available online 9 March 2005

Abstract

We present evidence on the relative performance of U.K. university technology transfer offices (TTOs) using data envelopment analysis (DEA) and stochastic frontier estimation (SFE). U.K. TTOs are found to exhibit low-levels of absolute efficiency. There also appear to be decreasing returns to scale, implying that TTOs may need to be reconfigured into smaller units. The development of regionally-based sector focused TTOs is also advised. Consistent with qualitative evidence from U.S. TTOs, we find that there is a need to upgrade the business skills and capabilities of U.K. TTO managers and licensing officers.
© 2005 Elsevier B.V. All rights reserved.

JEL classification: M13; D23; L31; O31; O32

Keywords: Technology transfer office (TTO); Technology licensing; Patents; Data envelopment analysis (DEA); Stochastic frontier estimation (SFE)

1. Introduction

[☆] A previous version of this paper was presented at the September 2004 Technology Transfer Society Meetings in Albany, N.Y. We thank two anonymous reviewers and seminar participants at the University of Nottingham and Rensselaer Polytechnic Institute for their insightful comments and suggestions. The authors thank UNICO for their cooperation in the data collection process and Ajay Vohora for capable clerical assistance.

* Corresponding author. Tel.: +1 518 276 2049.
E-mail addresses: wendy.chapple@nottingham.ac.uk (W. Chapple), andy.lockett@nottingham.ac.uk (A. Lockett), sieged@rpi.edu (D. Siegel), mike.wright@nottingham.ac.uk (M. Wright).
[1] Tel.: +44 115 951 5278.
[2] Tel.: +44 115 951 5268.

In recent years, there has been a rapid rise in the commercialization of intellectual property (IP) at U.S. and U.K. universities. As a result, the generation and exploitation of IP has become a central issue for institutions of higher learning. The successful creation and commercialization of IP can result in pecuniary gains for the university and external benefits for surrounding communities, since new technology-based firms are viewed as a critical source of new job creation.

Licensing has traditionally been the most popular mode of university technology transfer. Field-based,

370   *W. Chapple et al. / Research Policy 34 (2005) 369–384*

qualitative research (e.g. Siegel et al., 2003b) appears to confirm this stylized fact.[3] As a result, studies of the relative performance of U.S. university technology transfer offices (henceforth, TTOs) use the number of licenses or licensing income as "outputs" of technology transfer (Thursby and Kemp, 2002 and Siegel et al., 2003a). These empirical studies were based on data provided by the Association of University Technology Managers (AUTM) and have employed non-parametric (e.g. Thursby and Kemp, 2002) and parametric techniques (Siegel et al., 2003a) to assess the relative performance of universities in this arena.

This paper makes two contributions to the burgeoning literature on university technology transfer. First, we present the first empirical evidence on the relative efficiency of U.K. universities, based on a comprehensive dataset complied by the authors, with the support of the U.K.-based Universities Company Association (UNICO). Second, we compare parametric and non-parametric approaches to productivity measurement.

The U.K. is an interesting country to examine because it is not as advanced as the U.S. in university technology transfer. Therefore, we conjecture that U.K. universities may exhibit higher levels of heterogeneity with respect to relative efficiency than their U.S. counterparts. Such heterogeneity underscores the importance of contrasting parametric (SFE) and non-parametric (DEA) approaches to the measurement of relative performance. DEA generates an efficiency frontier on the basis of individual universities, while SFE yields an efficiency frontier on the basis of average values. Thus, DEA and SFE can generate quite different results, especially when high-levels of heterogeneity and noise are present in the data.

The remainder of this paper is organized as follows. Section 2 describes techniques used to assess the relative efficiency of TTOs. In the following section, we present our econometric models. Section 4 describes the data. Section 5 presents empirical results. The final section consists of conclusions and suggestions for additional research.

---

[3] In recent years, universities spin-outs (USOs) have become a much more popular mode of technology transfer. The importance of licensing was reinforced, however, in the recent Lambert report on university technology transfer (Lambert, 2003).

2. Assessing relative efficiency in university technology transfer

Most studies of the relative efficiency of organizations are based on a production function framework, in which a "best practice" frontier is constructed. The distance from the frontier represents the level of "technical" inefficiency, or the inability of the organization to generate maximal output from a given set of inputs. Two methods are used to estimate these frontiers. One approach is to specify a functional form for the production function and then estimate the production function parameters using regression methods. The parametric approach is useful when there is more interest in estimating average relationships than in identifying outliers for diagnostic purposes. That is, the relationship derived is an "average" production function, so an implicit assumption is that these parameters are the same for all organizations. If the right conditions hold, the parametric approach yields fairly precise estimates. However, many factors can greatly diminish the precision of these parameter estimates, such as multicollinearity, model misspecification and measurement error, the use of multiple outputs, and omitted variables.

Production frontiers are also estimated using non-parametric models, which offer some advantages, relative to the parametric approach. For instance, these methods obviate the need to specify a functional form for the production frontier and also enable us to identify "best practice" universities. Non-parametric techniques can also handle multiple outputs.

Perhaps, the most popular non-parametric estimation technique is data envelopment analysis. The DEA method is essentially a linear-program, which can be expressed as follows:

$$\max h_k = \frac{\sum_{r=1}^{s} u_{rk} Y_{rk}}{\sum_{i=1}^{m} v_{ik} X_{ik}} \tag{1}$$

subject to

$$\frac{\sum_{r=1}^{s} u_{rk} Y_{rj}}{\sum_{i=1}^{m} v_{ik} X_{ij}} < 1; \quad j = 1, \ldots, n, \quad \text{All } u_{rk} > 0,$$

$$v_{ik} > 0 \tag{2}$$

where Y is a vector of outputs; X a vector of inputs; i inputs (m inputs); r outputs (s outputs); n is no. of decision-making units (DMUs), or the unit of observation in a DEA study.

The unit of observation in a DEA study is referred to as the decision-making unit. A maintained assumption of this class of models is that DMUs attempt to maximize efficiency. Input-oriented DEA yields an efficiency "score," bounded between 0 and 1, for each DMU by choosing weights (u_r and v_i) that maximize the ratio of a linear combination of the unit's outputs to a linear combination of its inputs (see Eq. (2)). These scores are often expressed as percentages. A DMU having a score of 1 is efficient, while those with scores of less than one are (relatively) inefficient. Multiple DMUs have scores of 1.

DEA fits a piecewise linear surface to rest on top of the observations. This is referred to as the "efficient frontier." The efficiency of each DMU is measured relative to all other DMUs, with the constraint that all DMU's lie on or below the efficient frontier. The linear programming technique identifies best practice DMUs, or those that are on the frontier. All other DMUs are viewed as being inefficient relative to the frontier DMUs.

Stochastic frontier estimation is a parametric method developed by Aigner et al. (1977) and Meeusen and van den Broeck (1977). SFE generates a production (or cost) frontier with a stochastic error term that consists of two components: a conventional random error ("white noise") and a term that represents deviations from the frontier, or relative inefficiency. Following Battese and Coelli (1995), the stochastic frontier model in cross-sectional form is:

$$Y_i = \exp(x_i\beta + V_i - U_i) \tag{3}$$

where Y_i represents the output or production of the i-th observation ($i = 1, 2, \ldots, N$); x_i is a $(1 \times k)$ vector of values of inputs or resources used in production; and i denotes the i-th firm. β is a $(k \times 1)$ vector of unknown parameters to be estimated. The V_i's are assumed to be iid $N(0, \sigma_V^2)$ random errors, distributed independently of the U_i's. The U_i's are the non-negative random variables associated with technical inefficiency of production, which are assumed to be independently distributed, such that U_i is obtained by truncation (at zero) of the normal distribution with a mean $z_i\delta$ and a variance, σ^2. Z_i is a $(1 \times m)$ vector of explanatory variables associated with technical inefficiency of the production of observations, and finally δ is an $(1 \times m)$ vector of unknown coefficients.

Eq. (3) specifies the stochastic frontier production function in terms of the original production values. In order to explain technical efficiency, this model needs to be extended to make technical efficiency conditional on exogenous variables. Following Battese and Coelli (1995), we can model explanatory variables in a one stage SFE model. That is, the technical inefficiency effects, the U_i's, are assumed to be a function of a set of explanatory variables, the z_i's and the unknown vector of coefficients δ. If all the elements of the δ vector are equal to 0, then the technical inefficiency effects are not related to the z variables, and so the half normal distribution specified in Aigner et al. (1977) is obtained.

The technical inefficiency effect, U_{it}, in the stochastic frontier model (3) can be specified as:

$$U_i = z_i\delta + W_i \tag{4}$$

where the random variable, W_i is defined by the truncation of the normal distribution with zero mean and variance, σ^2.

The method of maximum likelihood is used for the simultaneous estimation of the parameters of the stochastic frontier model and the model for the technical inefficiency effects. The likelihood function is expressed in terms of the variance parameters, $\sigma_S^2 \equiv \sigma_V^2 + \sigma_U^2$ and $\gamma \equiv \sigma_U^2/\sigma_S^2$. Therefore, γ is the ratio of the standard error of technical inefficiency to the standard error of statistical noise, and is bounded between 0 and 1. Note that $\gamma = 0$ under the null hypothesis of an absence of inefficiency, indicating that all of the variance can be attributed to statistical noise. The technical efficiency of production for the i-th observation is defined by:

$$TE_i = \exp(-U_i) = \exp(-z_i\delta - W_i). \tag{5}$$

Choosing between the parametric stochastic frontier estimation and the non-parametric data envelopment analysis is not without controversy (Gong and Sickles, 1993). A main attraction of stochastic frontier analysis is that it allows hypothesis testing and construction of confidence intervals. A drawback of the approach, however, is the need to assume a functional form for the production function and for the distribution of the technical efficiency term. The use of DEA obviates the need to make these assumptions and, as noted earlier, also allows for multiple outputs in the production function. However, a major weakness of DEA is that it is deterministic. Hence, DEA does not distinguish between technical inefficiency and noise.

Thursby and Kemp (2002) and Siegel et al. (2003a) use DEA and SFE, respectively, to analyze the relative productivity of university TTOs. Unfortunately, there has not been any comparison of the two techniques using the same database. We seek to fill this gap in this paper.

There are also statistical issues associated with the use of these techniques to explain technical inefficiency. Generally, two-stage estimation (i.e., calculation of efficiency scores and regression of these scores against exogenous variables) is problematic. In the case of DEA, many authors have estimated OLS or TOBIT regressions on environmental and organizational variables in the second stage. Problems arise with this approach, as there is no consideration of the data generating process, upon which the efficiency scores are conditioned. Another, more serious problem arises when DEA efficiency scores are serially correlated. If this is the case, standard approaches regarding statistical inference are invalid (Simar and Wilson, 2004).

Similarly, with SFE, where the first stage involves the specification and estimation of the stochastic production function and the prediction of technical inefficiency, the assumption is made that inefficiency effects are identically distributed. However, the second stage regression involves estimating a regression of predicted inefficiency values on several independent variables. This contradicts the assumption of identically distributed inefficiency effects with respect to the frontier. Endogeneity is also a major concern when the inputs in the first stage are closely related to the independent variables in the second stage.

For these reasons, we employ the one stage SFE method, outlined in Battese and Coelli (1995). This technique involves the simultaneous estimation of the production frontier and the determinants of relative inefficiency. A DEA version of this model is not available, although theoretical models are currently being developed (Simar and Wilson, 2004).

To assess and explain relative performance in university technology transfer, we must identify outputs, inputs, and the determinants of inefficiency. We follow Siegel et al. (2003a), who conducted field research to specify the arguments of the technology transfer production function. These authors identified two outputs and three inputs. The outputs are (i) the annual number

of licensing agreements consummated by the university and (ii) annual licensing income generated by a university's portfolio of licenses. The inputs are (i) annual invention disclosures, (ii) number of full-time equivalent employees in university TTO, and (iii) external legal costs associated with IP protection and commercialization.

For U.S. universities, invention disclosures are an excellent proxy for the pool of available technologies for licensing or other commercial purposes. In the U.K. context, however, it is more accurate to use total research income as a proxy for a university's stock of technology. This is because there is no U.K. counterpart to the Bayh–Dole act, which was enacted in the U.S. in 1980. As a result, there is no formal requirement in the U.K. for faculty members to disclose inventions. Furthermore, in the U.S. there is some debate as to how effective Bayh–Dole has been, in terms of achieving full invention disclosure. Thursby and Kemp (2002) reported that less than half of faculty inventions with commercial potential are disclosed to the TTO. Some faculty members fail to disclose their inventions because they do not comprehend the commercial potential of their ideas or because they do not want to deal with the university bureaucracy (see Siegel et al., 2003b). They also do not want to delay publication until the technology is patented (or licensed). For these reasons, we estimate our models using invention disclosures and total research income as alternative inputs.

Consistent with Siegel et al. (2003a), we assume that internal (organizational) and external (environmental) factors can explain relative efficiency in university technology transfer. These authors used the following organizational variables: (i) whether the university is private, (ii) whether it has a medical school, and (iii) the age of the technology transfer office. We use (ii) and (iii), but not (i), since almost all U.K. universities are public institutions.

It is important to include regional environmental factors in explaining relative performance, since there may be local technological/agglomeration spillovers from firms to universities, or vice-versa. For example, Bania et al. (1993) find that there is a positive relationship between university R&D and the number of start-ups in the same region. Jaffe et al. (1993) find that patents generated within a region are more likely to be cited by firms in the same region. Therefore, we follow Siegel et al. (2003a) and employ two external factors in

Table 1
Specifications of university technology transfer production functions and determinants of relative efficiency

Outputs, inputs, and determinants of relative efficiency	Production function models			
	1	2	3	4
Output: number of licences or licensing income	✓	✓	✓	✓
Invention disclosures	✓	✓		
Total research income			✓	✓
Number of TTO staff	✓	✓	✓	✓
External legal IP expenditure	✓	✓	✓	✓
Inefficiency model				
Dummy for presence of a medical school		✓		✓
Age of TTO		✓		✓
Regional GDP		✓		✓
Regional R&D intensity		✓		✓

the second stage equation: regional GDP and regional R&D intensity of industrial firms.[4]

3. Empirical models

A summary of our empirical models is presented in Table 1. We estimate numerous variants of a single output, three input production function using DEA and SFE methods, as well as two functional forms for the production function. The first model is DEA-based; the second is a log-linear Cobb–Douglas stochastic production function; the third is a translog stochastic production function.

DEA efficiency scores were computed for each university by solving the following linear programme for each observation:

$$\text{Eff}(y_i, x_i) = \max[\theta : (\theta y_i) \in P^S(x_i)]$$

s.t.

$$\sum_{i=1}^{I} z_i^t y_{im}^t \geq \theta y_m^t, \quad m = 1, \dots, M \tag{6}$$

$$\sum_{i=1}^{I} z_i^t x_{in}^t \leq x_n^t, \quad n = 1, \dots, N$$

$$z_i^t \geq 0, \quad I = 1, \dots, I$$

These efficiency scores show the maximum expansion of outputs (number of licenses [NOLIC] or license income [LICINC]) to the best practice frontier, given

[4] GDP and R&D measures were provided by the U.K. Office for National Statistics. Regional GDP is reported as an index of GDP per capita. R&D expenditure is reported as business R&D expenditure per capita.

the level of inputs (invention disclosure [INVDISC] or total research income [TRESINC], external legal intellectual property spending [LEGAL] and the number of full-time equivalent TTO staff [STAFF]). When invention disclosures are included in the model, this is equivalent to model 1 in Table 1, given that the DEA estimators are not based on environmental variables. Conversely, when total research income is included in the model, this is the equivalent to model 4 in Table 1. If the resulting score is equal to one, the observation is on the frontier and is efficient. In output space, if θ is greater than one, then the observation is said to be inefficient. In this paper, the DEA results are reported as $1/\theta$, for ease of comparison with SFE results.

The SFE models are described as follows. The production function is estimated four ways. Eqs. (7a) and (7b) represent the two alternative model Cobb–Douglas specifications and Eqs. (8a) and (8b) represent the two basic translog specifications:

$$\ln \text{license}_i = \beta_0 + \beta_1 \ln \text{INVDISC}_i + \beta_2 \ln \text{LEGAL}_i$$
$$+ \beta_3 \ln \text{STAFF}_i + V_i - U_i \tag{7a}$$

$$\ln \text{license}_i = \beta_0 + \beta_1 \ln \text{TRESINC}_i + \beta_2 \ln \text{LEGAL}_i$$
$$+ \beta_3 \ln \text{STAFF}_i + V_i - U_i \tag{7b}$$

$$\ln \text{license}_i = \beta_0 + \beta_1 \ln \text{INVDISC}_i + \beta_2 \ln \text{LEGAL}_i$$
$$+ \beta_3 \ln \text{STAFF}_i + 0.5\beta_{11}(\ln \text{INVDISC}_i)^2$$
$$+ 0.5\beta_{22}(\ln \text{LEGAL}_i)^2 + 0.5\beta_{33}(\ln \text{STAFF}_i)^2$$
$$+ \beta_{12}(\ln \text{INVDISC}_i \ln \text{LEGAL}_i)$$
$$+ \beta_{13}(\ln \text{INVDISC}_i \ln \text{STAFF}_i)$$
$$+ \beta_{23}(\ln \text{LEGAL}_i \ln \text{STAFF}_i) + V_i - U_i \tag{8a}$$

374 *W. Chapple et al. / Research Policy 34 (2005) 369–384*

$$\ln license_i = \beta_0 + \beta_1 \ln TRESINC_i + \beta_2 \ln LEGAL_i$$
$$+ \beta_3 \ln STAFF_i + 0.5\beta_{11}(\ln TRESINC_i)^2$$
$$+ 0.5\beta_{22}(\ln LEGAL_i)^2 + 0.5\beta_{33}(\ln STAFF_i)^2$$
$$+ \beta_{12}(\ln TRESINC_i \ \ln LEGAL_i)$$
$$+ \beta_{13}(\ln TRESINC_i \ \ln STAFF_i)$$
$$+ \beta_{23}(\ln LEGAL_i \ \ln STAFF_i) + V_i - U_i \qquad (8b)$$

where license is either annual number of licensing agreements or annual licensing income and the remaining variables are the same as defined earlier. Given that estimates of the production function parameters, and thus, relative efficiency can be quite sensitive to the functional form chosen for the production function, it is useful to present estimates based on both the Cobb–Douglas and translog specifications. Eqs. (7a) and (8a) represent models 1–2 production technology in Cobb–Douglas and translog form, while Eqs. (7b) and (8b) represent the basic production technology for models 3–4 in Cobb–Douglas and translog form (see Table 1).

Following Siegel et al. (2003a), we estimate the following one-stage model to explain the technical efficiency term (U_i):

$$U_i = \delta_0 + \delta_1 MEDSCH_i + \delta_2 AGE + \delta_4 GDP_{ij}$$
$$+ \delta_5 R\&D_{ij} + \mu_i \qquad (9)$$

where MEDSCH is a dummy denoting whether the university has a medical school, AGE the age of the TTO, GDP a regional index measure of GDP per head, and R&D is regional R&D intensity. The estimated coefficients of this equation are presented in models 2 and 4 in Table 1.

4. Data

Our data are derived from a March 2002 survey, consisting of quantitative and qualitative questions. The survey was mailed to the top 122 U.K. universities, as ranked by research income. These institutions were identified using the Higher Education Statistics Agency (HESA) publication entitled *Resources of Higher Education Institutions(2000/2001)*. The remaining 45 universities accounted for just 0.2% (or £3.9 million) of total research grants and contract expenditures by UK universities in financial year 2001.

We received information from 98 of these top 122 universities. Several institutions reported numerous zero values, indicating that the university was not active in the field of technology transfer, and thus, only provided limited information on this activity. Our final sample consists of only those institutions that provided complete information. In total, we obtained data on 50 universities for the different variables. In addition, we

Table 2
Tests for sample response bias

Basis for comparison	N	Mean	S.D.	χ^{2a}
Total research income				
Respondent	50	31.86 m	37972	29.32***
Non respondent	60	7.68 m	12706	
Dummy variable for a medical school				
Respondent	50	0.46	0.50	16.06***
Non respondent	60	0.12	0.32	
Age of TTO				
Respondent	50	9.32	6.71	16.61***
Non respondent	53	5.05	5.49	
Regional GDP				
Respondent	50	98.20	17.06	0.54
Non respondent	60	100.93	18.73	
Regional R&D intensity				
Respondent	50	0.18	0.16	0.21
Non respondent	60	0.17	0.15	

Significance: *$p < 0.1$; **$p < 0.05$; ***$p < 0.01$.
[a] χ^2 with ties.

Table 3
Summary statistics for U.K. universities in our sample

Variable	Variable name	N	Mean	Standard deviation	Minimum	Maximum
Number of licences	NOLIC	47	11.72	13.47	0	58
License income (£)	LICINC	48	0.33 m	543802	0	2.97 m
Invention disclosures	INVDISC	47	28.02	30.62	0	152
Total research income (£)	TRESINC	50	31.86 m	37972	0.62 m	146 m
Number of TTO staff	STAFF	50	6.84	7.33	0	35
External legal IP expenditure (£)	LEGAL	49	0.16 m	265712	0	1.16 m
Medical school	MEDSCH	50	0.46	0.50	0	1
Age of TTO	AGE	50	9.32	6.71	0	31
Regional GDP	GDP	50	98.2	17.06	76	128
Regional R&D intensity	R&D	50	0.18	0.15	0.05	0.54

Table 4
Correlation coefficients

	NOLIC	LICINC	INVDISC	TRESINC	STAFF	LEGAL	AGE	GDP	R&D
NOLIC	1								
LICINC	0.3930	1							
INVDISC	0.6946	0.5546	1						
TREINC	0.6875	0.4728	0.7909	1					
STAFF	0.3983	0.6428	0.6225	0.6158	1				
LEGAL	0.6078	0.3214	0.7265	0.6990	0.4808	1			
AGE	0.1748	0.2385	0.5291	0.4934	0.6248	0.3442	1		
GDP	0.2719	0.1870	0.1249	0.1413	−0.0140	0.1616	−0.2383	1	
R&D	0.5782	0.1107	0.2631	0.3278	0.2110	0.2901	−0.0291	0.3476	1

were able to obtain partial data from the remaining universities in order to test the representativeness of our sample. The results of this analysis are presented in Table 2. These figures reveal that our sample of universities is somewhat skewed towards those institutions that are more active in technology transfer. The universities in our sample have significantly greater total research income ($p < 0.01$), are more likely to have a medical school ($p < 0.01$), and have greater experience, in terms of the number of years the university has been involved in technology transfer activities ($p < 0.01$). No differences were found with respect to the measures of regional GDP index and regional R&D intensity.

Descriptive statistics for the sample of universities are presented in Table 3. The descriptive statistics show that our sample of 50 universities generated a mean of 11.72 licenses and £0.33 m of revenues from licenses in the financial year 2001. There is, however, substantial heterogeneity among the various universities, in terms of the number of licensing agreements and licensing income, as indicated by the high-standard deviations. A similar pattern emerges for the inputs and technical inefficiency measures.

A correlation matrix for all of the variables incorporated in the analysis (with the exception of the binary variable for the presence of a medical school) is presented in Table 4. Not surprisingly, we find some evidence of multi-collinearity, especially in relation to the relationships between INVDISC and TRESINC ($r = 0.79$), which are alternative indicators of technological input, and between both of these measures and the other inputs LEGAL and STAFF.

5. Empirical results

DEA results for the full samples are reported in Table 5, where the inverse of the output oriented scores are shown for comparability with the SFE results.[5] The DEA scores show the average efficiency scores for the whole sample. Technical efficiency, i.e. location on the frontier, is represented by a score of one. A key stylized

---

[5] The inverse of the radial output distance function, under the assumption of strong disposability in outputs and inputs, and under assumptions of constant returns to scale, are equivalent to the radial input distance function.

Table 5
DEA full sample results

	Number of licences		Licensing income	
	INVDISC (model 1)	TRESINC (model 3)	INVDISC (model 1)	INVDISC (model 3)
DEA efficiency	0.188	0.143	0.140	0.133
SFE efficiency	0.260	0.230	0.410	0.290

Note: A university that is fully efficient would have an efficiency score of 1. The inverse of the output efficiency scores are shown for comparability with the SFE scores. The parsimonious SFE efficiency scores from the various output/input combinations are reported.

Table 6
DEA results with outliers omitted

	Dependent variables:			
	Number of licences		Licensing income	
	INVDISC (model 1)	TRESINC (model 3)	INVDISC (model 1)	TRESINC (model 3)
DEA efficiency	0.350	0.266	0.158	0.138
SFE efficiency	0.260	0.230	0.410	0.290

Note: Technical efficiency = 1. The inverse of the output efficiency scores are shown for comparability with the SFE scores. The parsimonious SFE efficiency scores from the various output/input combinations are reported.

fact is that in all models, there is substantial inefficiency present in our sample. For example, the interpretation of the average inefficiency score in the DEA number of licences (1),[6] is that on average, U.K. universities are operating at 18.7% efficiency. In other words, given inputs, U.K. universities could increase the number of licences five-fold. Similarly, when analyzing licensing income (1),[7] on average, U.K. universities are operating at 13.9% efficiency, indicating in terms of licensing income, on average universities could increase licensing income seven-fold. When invention expenditure is substituted for invention disclosure, even lower absolute levels of inefficiency are observed.

It is important to note that the high-level of inefficiency observed could be due to both the DEA process and the structure of the data. An analysis of the standard deviation of the efficiency scores reveals substantial variance. Also, in constructing the efficiency scores, DEA constructs an estimated best practice frontier for each observation, rather than using an average frontier (as in SFE), hence the variation in efficiency scores is likely to be higher. Finally, DEA is deterministic, and thus any noise in the data is treated as inefficiency. Thus, DEA results are highly sensitive to outliers.

To address this issue, we employed Cook's distance test to identify "influential" outliers (see Lichtenberg and Siegel (1991)). The DEA models were then re-estimated with the outliers removed.[8] These results are reported in Table 6. By removing the outliers, the level of efficiency increased substantially. For example, when the number of licensing agreements is used as the proxy for technology transfer output and outliers are removed, the average efficiency score increases from 18.78 to 35.9%. In contrast, only a small increase in efficiency scores is observed when licensing revenue is chosen as the output and outliers are removed. However, when we remove outliers, we also eliminate some leading research universities. That is unfortunate, since by removing leading research institutions, we do not have an accurate and complete projection of the best practice frontier. Thus, we use the DEA scores for the entire sample for our analysis.

Sixteen variations of the stochastic frontier model were estimated (see model specifications 1–4 in Table 1) for two outputs, number of licenses and licensing income, and two specifications of the production function: the Cobb–Douglas and translog functional forms. Maximum likelihood estimates of these models

---

[6] Model 1 uses invention disclosure, staff and IP expenditure as inputs.

[7] Model 2 uses invention expenditure, staff and IP expenditure as inputs.

[8] The outliers are all "redbrick" universities, or established eminent research institutions.

Table 7
Hypothesis tests (nested models)

Null hypothesis		$-\ln[L(H_0)]$	$-\ln[L(H_1)]$	λ	Critical $\chi^2_{0.95}$ value[a]	Decision
Output is number of licenses with invention disclosures as an input[b]						
Cobb–Douglas frontier is an adequate representation	$H_0 : \beta_{ij} = 0, \quad i \le j = 1, \ldots, 3$	-34.76	-37.77	6.01	14.07	Accept H_0
There is no technical inefficiency	$H_0 : \gamma = 0$	-37.77	-42.67	9.8	7.05	Reject H_0
Output is number of licenses with total research income as an input[c]						
Cobb–Douglas frontier is an adequate representation	$H_0 : \beta_{ij} = 0, \quad i \le j = 1, \ldots, 3$	-37.75	-41.92	8.34	14.07	Accept H_0
There is no technical inefficiency	$H_0 : \gamma = 0$	-41.92	-47.20	10.56	7.05	Reject H_0
Output is licensing income with invention disclosures as an input[d]						
Cobb–Douglas frontier is an adequate representation	$H_0 : \beta_{ij} = 0, \quad i \le j = 1, \ldots, 3$	-64.76	-75.98	22.44	14.07	Reject H_0
There is no technical inefficiency	$H_0 : \gamma = 0$	-64.76	-74.27	19.02	7.05	Reject H_0
Output is licensing income with total research income as an input[e]						
Cobb–Douglas frontier is an adequate representation	$H_0 : \beta_{ij} = 0, \quad i \le j = 1, \ldots, 3$	-70.93	-72.35	2.84	14.07	Accept H_0
There is no technical inefficiency	$H_0 : \gamma = 0$	-72.35	-79.21	13.72	7.05	Reject H_0

[a] The critical values for $\gamma = 0$ are obtained from Table 1 of Kodde and Palm (1986) due to the mixed χ^2 distribution. All other test use regular χ^2 distributions. The degrees of freedom are $q + 1$, where q is the number of parameters, which are specified to be zero.

[b] The starting model for the hypothesis testing for the number of licenses model with invention disclosure is the full translog specification including inefficiency effects, model 2.

[c] The starting model for the hypothesis testing for the number of licenses model with total research income is the full translog specification including inefficiency effects, model 4.

[d] The starting model for the hypothesis testing for the licensing income model with invention disclosure as an input is the full translog specification including inefficiency effects, model 2.

[e] The starting model for the hypothesis testing for the licensing income model with total research income as an input is the full translog specification including inefficiency effects, model 4.

are shown in the Appendix A (Tables A.1–A.4).[9] In the first stage of the analysis, we assess the appropriate functional forms and specification of these models.

Following Battese and Broca (1997), log-likelihood ratios were used to formally test the correct model specification and functional form. The log-likelihood ratio models are used because of the nested nature of the models. These results are shown in Table 7. The base models for hypothesis testing were models 2 and 4, i.e. those including technical inefficiency effects.

---

[9] The parameters were estimated using FRONTIER Version 4.1 (Coelli, 1994). The log-likelihood function for this model is presented in Battese and Coelli (1995), as the first partial derivatives of the log-likelihood function with respect to the parameters of the model.

The first null hypothesis, $H_0 : \beta_{ij} = 0$, $i \le j = 1, \ldots,$ 3, is that the Cobb–Douglas is the appropriate functional form for the data. For the number of licensing agreement version of the model with invention disclosures as an input, we failed to reject the null hypothesis, implying that the Cobb–Douglas functional form is appropriate. This was also the case when total research income was substituted for invention disclosure (model 4). Therefore, in each variant of the models using the number of licensing agreements as the output of technology transfer; the Cobb–Douglas is the appropriate functional form.

Note that when licensing income is used as an output, the null hypothesis was rejected for model 2, but we fail to reject the null hypothesis for model 4. Therefore, when invention disclosures are included as

Table 8
AIC model selection (non-nested model section)

Output	Number of licenses		Licensing income	
	INVDISC (model 2)	TRESINC (model 4)	INVDISC (model 2)	TRESINC (model 4)
Functional form	Cobb–Douglas	Cobb–Douglas	Translog	Cobb–Douglas
Log-likelihood	−37.77	−41.92	−64.76	−72.35
AIC	93.54	101.84	165.52	162.70

Table 9
Elasticities of mean output under different model specification

Inefficiency model	Number of licences	Licensing income
Model	Model 2	Model 4
Functional form	Cobb–Douglas	Cobb–Douglas
ε INVDISC (model 2); ε TRESINC (model 4)	0.537^{***} (0.131)	0.461^{***} (0.019)
ε STAFF	0.136^{***} (0.077)	0.367^{***} (0.0187)
ε LEGAL	−0.03 (0.07)	0.093^{***} (0.005)
Returns to scale parameter	0.643	0.930

Standard errors are in parentheses. Significance: $^{*}p < 0.1$; $^{**}p < 0.05$; $^{***}p < 0.01$.

an input to licensing revenues, it is not appropriate to use the Cobb–Douglas functional form, and thus the translog functional form is preferred. This highlights the importance of testing the functional form where different variables are included, as the "one size fits all" approach may lead to the use of an inappropriate functional form, and thus incorrect inferences regarding relative performance.

The second null hypothesis, $H_0 : \gamma = 0$ is that universities are fully efficient, i.e. that there is no technical efficiency. If this were the case, it would be appropriate to model the technology using the traditional mean response function. This hypothesis was decisively rejected in all cases, which supports the use of technical efficiency models 2 and 4.

The final stage of the model selection process involves the choice between invention disclosures or total research income as an input (models 2 and 4) for the two outputs. Because these models are not nested unlike the previous tests, the aikaike information criterion (AIC)[10] is used to determine which input

[10] The aikaike information criteria (AIC) can be estimated by $-2 \times$ log-likelihood $+ 2 \times p$, where p is the number of parameters estimated in the models. This way the AIC scores are adjusted for the number of parameters involved in the model, allowing the comparison between the Cobb–Douglas and translog functional forms. The models with the lowest AIC score were chosen as the best fitting models.

is appropriate for each output. These results are presented in Table 8. The models with the lowest AIC scores were chosen, and hence when output is the number of licensing agreements, model 2 was chosen, with invention disclosure as an input. For the model with total research income as an output, model 4 with invention expenditure was chosen.

Therefore, the two models that we will focus on in our discussion of results are model 2 with the Cobb–Douglas functional form for number of licences, and model 4 with the Cobb–Douglas functional form for licensing income.

Estimates of the output elasticities of the various inputs are displayed in Table 9. In model 2, the coefficient on invention disclosures is positive and highly significant, as is the coefficient on total research income in model 4. Therefore, higher levels of invention disclosure or total research income lead to a higher number of licences or higher licensing income. Similarly, the significant positive elasticity for number of staff, suggests that hiring more staff, leads to both a higher number of licences and higher licensing revenues. It appears as though external legal IP expenditure has a negative, but not significant, influence on the number of licenses, but is positive and significant in determining licensing income in most models. The protection of licences, therefore, is important in gaining revenue from licenses, or inversely, universities with more lucrative inventions

Table 10
Estimated average technical efficiency: parsimonious model

Output	Number of licences	Licensing income
Model	Model 2	Model 4
Functional form	Cobb–Douglas	Cobb–Douglas
Estimated technical efficiency	0.26	0.29

Table 11
Technical efficiency effects: parsimonious model

Inefficiency model	Number of licences	Licensing income
Model	Model 2	Model 4
Functional form	Cobb–Douglas	Cobb–Douglas
MEDSCH	−0.077 (0.267)	3.127** (1.769)
AGE	0.027* (0.019)	0.12 (0.127)
GDP	−0.03 (0.009)	−0.125*** (0.057)
R&D	−2.27** (1.217)	0.433 (1.072)

Standard errors are in parentheses.
* $p < 0.1$.
** $p < 0.05$.
*** $p < 0.01$.

are more likely to use external IP protection. This finding is consistent with findings reported in Siegel et al. (2003a) for U.S. university TTOs.

A closer inspection of the elasticities indicates that in both models there are decreasing returns to scale. This could be an indicator of "x-inefficiency" in larger TTOs, in terms of generating licensing agreements and licensing income. An alternative interpretation of this finding is that the strategies of larger institutions are different, whereby the focus is on only licensing lucrative inventions. This results in fewer licensing agreements and time delays in realising the licensing revenues from the aforementioned lucrative licenses, which lead to less licensing income.

Turning to the technical efficiency scores (Table 10), both model specifications provide low, but consistent average technical efficiency scores. For model 2, employing the number of licenses as the output, technical efficiency is reported at 26%, whereas for licensing income, average technical efficiency is reported at 29%. These indicate the potential for universities to improve their output 3–4-fold, given their inputs.

When compared to the estimated DEA scores, it can be seen that the SFE efficiency measures are much higher (18.8 and 13.3% versus 26 and 29%). This, however, is a function of the deterministic nature of DEA, and the noise component. In SFE, the noise component is separated from the inefficiency term, whereas in DEA, all noise is treated as inefficiency. In both of the SFE models, the estimate for the variance parameter, γ is significant and close to 1, indicating that we can decisively reject the absence of inefficiency in the data.[11] The end result is that we are justified in estimating the full stochastic frontier model with inefficiency effects, as some (albeit a relatively small amount) noise

is present. DEA does not incorporate noise, and hence will have a tendency to over estimate inefficiency levels.

The technical inefficiency model results for the parsimonious models are shown in Table 11. In model 2, using the number of licenses as the dependent variable, the coefficient on age of the TTO is positive and statistically significant ($p < 0.10$), implying that older TTOs are less efficient than comparable TTOs. This finding is contrary to findings presented in Mowery et al. (2001) and Siegel et al. (2003a). However, we conjecture that this result could reflect diseconomies of scale, as age is strongly correlated with the size (invention disclosures and number of TT office staff), see Table 4. Alternatively, older U.K. universities may employ a different licensing strategy, such as maximising licensing revenue, as opposed to newer institutions, which might have a strategy of maximizing the number of licenses.

Note also that the coefficient on regional R&D intensity is negative and significant ($p < 0.01$), as reported in Siegel et al. (2003a). It appears as though universities in regions with a higher R&D intensity are more efficient in generating new licences. This finding could be due to spillover effects from private R&D, through collaboration and partnerships or due to R&D agglomeration effects.

Turning to the licensing income model, the presence of a medical school is found to be positive and significant ($p < 0.05$), which suggests that U.K. universities with medical schools have higher levels of technical inefficiency. This finding is contrary to evidence on U.S. universities presented in Siegel et al. (2003a). We hypothesize that this result may be due to differences

---

[11] Note that if $\gamma = 0$, deviations from the frontier are entirely due to noise, and the model reduces to a traditional mean response model, where technical efficiency is assumed.

between product markets for health care in the U.K. and U.S. The health care market is substantially larger in the U.S. than in the U.K. We also find that universities in areas with higher economic activity (regional GDP) are more effective.

In sum, it appears as though there are strong regional effects, both in terms of economic (GDP) and R&D activity. This could be because of agglomeration effects (e.g. high-tech industries being clustered in certain regions), which may have important implications for government policy on commercialisation of research.

6. Conclusions

This paper extends previous research on the relative performance of U.S. university TTOs by Thursby and Kemp (2002) and Siegel et al. (2003a). We report the first analysis of the relative productivity of U.K. university TTOs and also simultaneously present parametric and non-parametric evidence, which was reported separately in the U.S.-based papers.

A striking feature of the U.K. data is the substantial heterogeneity in relative performance. This heterogeneity is present in both the non-parametric DEA and parametric SFE approaches. We eschew the DEA findings because they are shown to be much more sensitive to the presence of outliers. In general, the production function parameters have the expected signs and reasonable magnitude. That is, the inputs have positive marginal products.

However, in contrast to the U.S., we find decreasing returns to scale to licensing activity, using both output measures and alternative functional forms from the production frontier. This could be a timing issue, since it is conceivable that more substantial payoffs to technology transfer by larger universities may be just a few years down the road. It is important to note that many universities have just begun gearing up for this activity (Wright et al., 2003).

In each variant of the model, we also strongly reject the absence of inefficiency effects. In fact, the SFE analysis reveals that average levels of technical efficiency for the SFE analysis are approximately 26–29%. This indicates that substantial improvements can be made with respect to the efficiency of U.K. technology transfer offices.

It might also be useful to analyze organizational and institutional practices in the U.S. that have been successful in enhancing UITT effectiveness. For example, Link and Siegel (2005) find that universities having more attractive incentive structures for technology transfer, i.e. those that allocate a higher percentage of royalty payments to faculty members, tend to be more efficient in technology transfer activities. This has resonance with survey evidence from the U.K. that identifies incentive problems as a barrier to the transfer of technology (Wright et al., 2003). Thursby and Thursby (2002) suggest, vis-à-vis licensing by universities in the U.S., the possibility of learning by doing effects on the ability of technology transfer officers to facilitate transactions.

With respect to evidence on the determinants of relative inefficiency, we find that having a medical school has a negative effect on efficiency. Older TTOs appear to be less efficient, suggesting an absence of learning effects. Universities located in regions with higher levels of R&D and GDP appear to be efficient in technology transfer, implying that there may be regional spillovers in technology transfer.

These findings may have a number of significant policy implications. First, the *x*-inefficiency observed in larger TTOs may be the result of the broad-based nature of their research, as opposed to smaller more specialized universities. That is, TTOs in larger universities have to provide commercialization services for a wide range of industries. Existing research has demonstrated that different industry sectors require diverse types of knowledge and diverse business models (Druilhe and Garnsey, 2004). Owen Smith and Powell (2001) have shown that technology transfer in the life sciences is substantially different than technology transfer in the physical sciences. Larger offices may suffer from the problem of being generalists rather than specialists. Therefore, an improvement in the performance of university TTOs may require the creation of smaller, more specialist TTOs at universities rather than just increasing the size of technology transfer offices per se.

It may be appropriate for generalist universities to adopt different approaches according to the type of technology being transferred (Clarysse et al., 2005). Bearing in mind that generalist universities may engage in a wide range of technology transfer activities, this may indicate a need to reconfigure the management of technology transfer into a differentiated approach, whereby one or more divisions focus on particular high-tech sectors with high-revenue generation prospects, while others focus on activities designed to meet broader objectives.

Second, the strong regional effects lead us to suggest that in some regions, due to lower levels of R&D and economic activity, universities will be less efficient in the commercialisation of technology. In these instances, government might use such regional TTOs to offer additional assistance to both universities and business. A potential advantage to organizing TTOs on a regional basis is that it may facilitate the emergence of specialist teams for different industry sectors. It might also enable the development of a critical mass of expertise and experience. Of course, such an approach may need to address potential differences in the relative strengths and objectives of the universities involved.

Our findings also have implications for policy initiatives to redress the balance in university technology transfer between spin-outs and licensing (see, e.g.

Lambert, 2003; HM Treasury, 2004). The magnitude of TTO inefficiency suggests that without emphasis on the development of skills of TTOs, a shift of emphasis towards licensing may not necessarily have the desired effects in respect of revenue creation for universities. To date, the policy focus has been on start-up formation. However, policymakers should also be mindful of the expertise required to ensure that licensable inventions are identified and that there be an appropriate balance licensing and start-up activity. It is also critical that optimal licensing arrangements are made, both in terms of the legal delineation and protection of IP, as well as establishing and strengthening links with the most suitable industry partners. This again emphasizes the need to recruit and train technology licensing officers with the appropriate skills and capabilities.

Appendix A

See Tables A.1–A.4.

Table A.1
Measure of output: number of licenses, Cobb–Douglas

Results: unbalanced	Maximum likelihood estimates of the stochastic frontier and inefficiency equation			
Dependent variable	Number of licensing agreements: Cobb–Douglas			
Model	1	2[a]	3	4[b]
Stochastic frontier				
Intercept	0.995^* (0.612)	2.217^{***} (0.708)	-3.861 (4.368)	-1.515 (1.906)
INVDISC	0.568^{***} (0.123)	0.537^{***} (0.131)		
TRESINC			3.410^{***} (0.127)	0.338^{***} (0.128)
STAFF	0.104^* (0.070)	0.136^{**} (0.077)	0.128^* (0.085)	0.180^{***} (0)
LEGAL	-0.003 (0.060)	-0.030 (0.070)	$0.015(0.313)$	-0.036 (0.077)
Inefficiency model				
Intercept		1.965^{**} (0.998)		2.954^{***} (0.986)
MEDSCH		-0.077 (0.267)		0.0385 (0.344)
AGE		0.027^* (0.019)		0.023 (0.022)
GDP		-0.03 (0.009)		-0.012^* (0.008)
R&D		-2.27^{**} (1.217)		-2.375^{***} (0.749)
Log-likelihood	-42.67	-37.77	-47.20	-41.92
σ^2	0.948	0.463	0.622	0.522
γ		0.999^{***}		0.999^{***}
Average technical efficiency		0.26		0.23
N	40	40	40	40

Standard errors are in parentheses. Significance: $^*p < 0.1$; $^{**}p < 0.05$; $^{***}p < 0.01$.
[a] Preferred model for *Number of Licenses frontier*, with invention disclosure as an input.
[b] Preferred model for *Number of Licenses frontier*, with total research income as an input.

Table A.2

Measure of output number of licenses translog

Results: unbalanced	Maximum likelihood estimates of the stochastic frontier and inefficiency equation			
Dependent variable	Number of licensing agreements: translog production function			
Model	1	2	3	4
Stochastic frontier				
Intercept	2.51(3.331)	2.227 (2.648)	2.200 (2.231)	7.138 (35.14)
INVDISC	−0.118 (1.918)	1.636 (1.813)		
TRESINC			−0.982 (3.020)	−2.375 (2.727)
STAFF	−1.015 (1.661)	−1.818 (1.583)	0.038 (2.746)	1.976 (2.489)
LEGAL	−0.036 (0.190)	−0.045 (0.187)	0.851 (2.165)	2.363* (1.947)
INVDISC*INVDISC	0.000 (0.332)	0.427 (0.330)		
TRESINC*TRESINC			0.142 (2.278)	0.338* (0.256)
STAFF*STAFF	0.029 (0.069)	0.145** (0.071)	0.069 (0.119)	0.174* (0.108)
LEGAL*LEGAL	−0.032 (0.063)	0.008 (0.065)	0.063 (0.105)	0.137* (0.094)
INVDISC*STAFF	0.110 (0.219)	−0.275* (0.210)		
TRESINC*STAFF			−0.038 (0.213)	−0.175 (0.189)
INVDISC*LEGAL	0.059 (0.228)	−0.17 (0.218)		
TRESINC*LEGAL			−0.093 (0.197)	−0.236* (0.178)
STAFF*LEGAL	0.103 (0.180)	0.255* (0.175)	0.071 (0.176)	0.105 (0.163)
Inefficiency model				
Intercept		1.394 (1.113)		3.927 (18.126)
MEDSCH		−0.261 (0.304)		0.116 (0.311)
AGE		0.0573*** (0.023)		0.0461*** (0.020)
GDP		0.004 (0.008)		0.001 (0.008)
R&D		−1.75** (0.889)		−2.144*** (0.832)
Log-likelihood	−41.475	−34.764	−44.897	−37.749
σ^2	0.465	0.336	0.552	0.386
γ		0.999***		0.986
Average technical efficiency		0.17		0.20
N	40	40	40	40

Standard errors are in parentheses. Significance: $^*p < 0.1$; $^{**}p < 0.05$; $^{***}p < 0.01$.

Table A.3

Measure of output: licensing revenue Cobb–Douglas

Results: unbalanced	Licensing revenue: Cobb–Douglas			
Dependant variable	Number of licensing revenue: Cobb–Douglas			
Model	1	2	3	4[a]
Stochastic frontier				
Intercept	10.149***	9.776*** (0.102)	7.190 (0.753)	4.357*** (0.293)
INVDISC	0.735***	0.772*** (0.247)		
TRESINC			0.314 (0.085)	0.461*** (0.019)
STAFF	0.257**	0.234*** (0.092)	0.461 (0.142)	0.367*** (0.0187)
LEGAL	0.081*	0.107*** (0.033)	0.0611 (0.123)	0.093*** (0.005)
Inefficiency model				
Intercept		0.726 (0.780)		4.305** (2.582)
MEDSCH		0.219 (0.978)		3.127** (1.769)
AGE		0.124 (0.115)		0.12 (0.127)
GDP		−0.041*** (0.020)		−0.125*** (0.057)
R&D		0.21 (0.978)		0.433 (1.072)
Log-likelihood	78.63	−75.98	−79.21	−72.35
σ^2	0.845	10.53	11.2	15.45
γ		0.999***		0.999***
Average technical efficiency		0.28		0.29
N	43	43	43	43

Standard errors are in parentheses. Significance: $^*p < 0.1$; $^{**}p < 0.05$; $^{***}p < 0.01$.

[a] Preferred model for *licensing income* frontier, with total research income as an input.

W. Chapple et al. / Research Policy 34 (2005) 369–384 383

Table A.4
Measure of output: licensing revenue translog

Results: unbalanced	Licensing revenue: translog			
Dependent variable	Number of licensing revenue: translog			
Model	1	2[a]	3	4
Stochastic frontier				
Intercept	4.447*** (1.698)	2.818 (7.66)	2.253*** (0.996)	1.884** (1.002)
INVDISC	5.266*** (1.688)	3.81*** (1.26)		
TRESINC			−1.247*** (0.517)	−3.718*** (1.111)
STAFF	−1.32*** (0.386)	−1.477 (2.12)	−4.930*** (1.081)	1.847 (2.740)
LEGAL	0.220 (0.417)	0.724*** (0.32)	4.343*** (0.833)	6.181*** (1.260)
INVDISC*INVDISC	−2.124*** (0.732)	−1.14 (1.23)		
TRESINC*TRESINC			0.325*** (0.097)	0.657*** (0.176)
STAFF*STAFF	−0.230*** (0.102)	−0.210 (0.248)	−0.266*** (0.056)	0.081 (0.084)
LEGAL*LEGAL	−0.017 (0.100)	−0.537** (0.031)	0.304** (0.148)	0.403*** (0.128)
INVDISC*STAFF	0.807*** (0.347)	0.527 (0.716)		
TRESINC*STAFF			0.369*** (0.065)	−0.023 (0.148)
INVDISC*LEGAL	0.037 (0.239)	−0.016*** (0.621)		
TRESINC*LEGAL			−0.437*** (0.123)	−0.610*** (0.147)
STAFF*LEGAL	−0.046 (0.070)	0.0277 (0.112)	−0.038 (0.059)	−0.078** (0.048)
Inefficiency model				
Intercept		2.78 (8.34)		7.478** (4.158)
MEDSCH		3.72*** (11.6)		10.125*** (4.297)
AGE		0.031 (0.71)		0.364*** (0.114)
GDP		−0.110*** (0.055)		−0.321*** (0.126)
R&D		−0.698 (2.36)		−1.846 (1.451)
Log-likelihood	−74.27	−64.76	−77.356	−70.93
σ^2	7.922	11.959	7.47	17.62
γ		0.999***		0.964***
Average technical efficiency		0.41		0.49
N	43	43	43	43

Standard errors are in parentheses. Significance: *$p < 0.1$; **$p < 0.05$; ***$p < 0.01$.

[a] Preferred model for *licensing income* frontier, with invention disclosure as an input.

References

Aigner, D., Lovell, C.A.K., Schmidt, P., 1977. Formulation and estimation of stochastic frontier production function models. Journal of Econometrics 6 (1), 21–37.

Bania, N., Eberts, R., Fogarty, M.S., 1993. Universities and the start-up of new companies: can we generalize from route 128 and Silicon Valley? Review of Economics and Statistics 76 (4), 761–766.

Battese, G., Broca, S., 1997. Functional forms of stochastic frontier production functions and models for technical inefficiency effects: a comparative study for wheat farmers in Pakistan. Journal of Productivity Analysis 8, 395–414.

Battese, G., Coelli, T., 1995. A model for technical inefficiency effects in a stochastic frontier production function for panel data. Empirical Economics 20, 325–332.

Clarysse, B., Wright, M., Lockett, A., van de Elde, E., Vohora, A., 2005. Spinning out new ventures: a typology of incubation strategies from European research institutions. Journal of Business Venturing 20 (2), 183–216.

Coelli, T. 1994. A Guide to FRONTIER Version 4:1: A Computer Program for Stochastic Frontier Production and Cost Function Estimation. Mimeo, Department of Econometrics, University of New England, Armingdale.

Druilhe, C., Garnsey, E., 2004. Do academic spin-outs differ and does it matter? Journal of Technology Transfer 29 (3/4), 269–285.

Gong, B., Sickles, R., 1993. Finite sample evidence on performance of stochastic frontiers using panel data. Journal of Econometrics 51, 259–284.

HM Treasury, 2004. Science and Innovation Investment Framework 2004–2014. HM Treasury/dti/department for Education and Skills.

Jaffe, A.B., Trajtenberg, M., Henderson, R., 1993. Geographic localization of knowledge spillovers as evidenced by patent citations. Quarterly Journal of Economics 108 (3), 577–598.

Kodde, D., Palm, F., 1986. Wald criteria for jointly testing equality and inequality restrictions. Econometrica 54, 1243–1248.

Lambert, R., 2003. Lambert Review of Business-University Collaboration. HMSO, London.

Lichtenberg, F., Siegel, D., 1991. The impact of R&D investment on productivity—new evidence using linked R&D-LRD data. Economic Inquiry 29 (2), 203–229.

Link, A.N., Siegel, D.S., 2005. Generating science-based growth: an econometric analysis of the impact of organizational incentives on university-industry technology transfer. European Journal of Finance, forthcoming.

Meeusen, W., van den Broeck, J., 1977. Efficiency estimation from Cobb–Douglas production functions with composed error. International Economic Review 18, 435–444.

Mowery, D.C., Nelson, R., Sampat, B., Ziedonis, A., 2001. The growth of patenting and licensing by U.S. universities: an assessment of the effects of the Bayh–Dole Act of 1980. Research Policy 30, 99–119.

Owen Smith, J., Powell, W.W., 2001. To patent or not: faculty decisions and institutional success in technology transfer. Journal of Technology Transfer 26 (1-2), 99–114.

Siegel, D.S., Waldman, D., Link, A., 2003a. Assessing the impact of organizational practices on the relative productivity of university technology transfer offices: an exploratory study. Research Policy 32 (1), 27–48.

Siegel, D.S., Waldman, D., Atwater, L., Link, A., 2003b. Commercial knowledge transfers from universities to firms: improving the effectiveness of university-industry collaboration. Journal of High Technology Management Research 14, 111–133.

Simar, L., Wilson, P., 2004. Estimation and Inference in Two Stage, Semi-parametric Models of Production Process. Department of Economics, University of Texas, Mimeo.

Thursby, J.G., Kemp, S., 2002. Growth and productive efficiency of university intellectual property licensing. Research Policy 31, 109–124.

Thursby, J.G., Thursby, M., 2002. Who is selling the ivory tower? Sources of growth in university licensing. Management Science 48 (1), 90–104.

Wright, M., Binks, M., Vohora, A., Lockett, A., 2003. Annual Survey of Commercialization of University Technology. UNICO/NUBS/AURIL, Nottingham.

Part II
Science Parks and Incubators

[10]

Omega, Int. J. Mgmt Sci. Vol. 23, No. 4, pp. 345–360, 1995
Copyright © 1995 Elsevier Science Ltd
Printed in Great Britain. All rights reserved
0305-0483/95 $9.50 + 0.00

0305-0483(95)00021-6

Links Between Higher Education Institutions and High Technology Firms

P WESTHEAD

DJ STOREY

University of Warwick, UK

(Received February 1995; accepted after revision April 1995)

Universities and other higher education institutions (HEIs) are an important resource network for high technology firms. In order to develop stronger links with industry HEIs have established Science Parks. To ascertain 'added-value' of a Science Park location in the UK the formal and informal links developed with local HEIs by independent Science Park firms are compared with the links made by a comparable group of independent high technology firms not located on a Park. Analysis of the combined sample of on and off-Park firms revealed having a link with a local HEI in 1986 was associated with survival over the 1986–1992 period. However, on the downside, empirical evidence collected in 1992/93 from firms in a follow-on sample (originally interviewed in 1986) as well as a 'new sample' study (independent firms that had located on a Science Park between 1986 and 1992) both revealed that the vast majority of links developed with local HEIs are generally informal ones. The policy implications of the research findings are discussed.

Key words—high technology firms, higher education institutions, links, Science Parks, policy implications

1. INTRODUCTION

HIGH TECHNOLOGY firms are a source of structural change altering the mix of products, industries and jobs in an economy [37, p. 26]. Their prime contribution, however, is as a source of innovation which:

> "...depends on people, their accumulated knowledge and capabilities gained through experience, and the information and contact networks on which they draw..." [37, p. 158].

Further, a co-operation/network strategy between a firm and other businesses (customers as well as suppliers) or other external organisations can lead to an efficient use of R&D resources for that firm [4, 16, 17, 19]. Håkansson [18] has presented a 'network' model (covering three elements—actors, resources and activities) in order to explain how firms handle their technological development. Most notably, he has shown in Sweden that collaborative relationships evolve organically and informally and are of strategic importance to technology-based firms.

Universities and other higher education institutions (HEIs) are an important source of new scientific knowledge. Industry can gain access to this knowledge or resource by developing formal and/or informal links with HEIs [44, 45].

> "Although some may question the historical importance of universities in transferring technology to the commercial sector, few can question that universities are increasing their technology transfer activities.... Universities see linkages to

345

industry as providing financial and practical support for their larger knowledge creation, dissemination, and retention missions" [5, p. 60].

The development of HEI-industry links is, therefore, assumed to encourage innovation and production. Hence locales with highly interlinked HEI and industry are expected to have enhanced levels of wealth creation and job generation [37, p. 117]. As a result, the commercialization of academic research (in the form of Science Parks or incubator centres, HEI companies, independent spin-off enterprises, licensing agreements and collaboration and joint ventures) has been identified:

"... as a panacea for reversing industrial decline and promoting innovation in many Western countries" [35, p. 27].

This paper reviews the evidence for these statements. It begins with a review of the existing research surrounding the relationship between HEIs and high technology firms, deriving hypotheses which are formally tested later in the paper. The data upon which the analysis is conducted is described. Results are then presented. The final section speculates upon some of the policy implications of the findings.

2. LINKS BETWEEN HEIs AND HIGH TECHNOLOGY FIRMS

2.1. Industry links with a local HEI

Porter [47, p. 115] has asserted that,

"The local environment creates potential for competitive success, but firms must sense and respond to it".

In addition, Lorenzoni and Ornati [32] have suggested that firms located in 'constellations' (or in new industrial spaces such as a Science Park) are more willing to seek information from outside sources such as HEIs, consultants and community entrepreneurs than other types of firms. Further, they assert that a supportive environment with a leading central organization (e.g. a HEI/Science Park) is crucial not only to new firm formation but also to organizational survival and development.

Segal Quince & Partners [51] found Cambridge University had indirectly been the ultimate origin of all 261 high technology firms in

the Cambridge area. A later study in Cambridge found 46% of local high technology firms claimed to have informal as well formal R&D links with the university [25, p. 162]. Similarly, Bishop [6, p. 161] in a study of 79 high technology establishments in the three Travel-to-Work-Areas of Bristol, Plymouth and Exeter in south-west England found 39 establishments (49%) had some links with an academic institution. Firms with over 100 workers were significantly more likely to have a link with an academic institution than firms with less than 50 employees (a similar relationship has been identified by Lawton-Smith [28, p. 130] in Oxfordshire). With regard to the types of link:

"... 32 of the 39 firms with linkages had industrial research linkages, whilst only just over half had linkages in management training" [6, p. 161].

Rothwell and Beesley [50, p. 26] also explored the types of inter firm linkages recorded by 102 innovative manufacturing firms in the UK. They found that sponsorship and placement of students in HEIs provided useful means of gaining access to state of the art research and knowledge. For example, 31% of surveyed firms had sponsored students at educational establishments and a further 39% of firms had provided placements for sandwich students. They concluded,

"In general, external expertise acts as a complement to, rather than as a substitute for, internal expertise" [50, p. 29].

However, a lower incidence of academic–industry linkage has been reported along the M4 Corridor in southern England [7]. Lawton-Smith [28, 29] presented evidence surrounding the growth of high technology spin-off firms around Oxford University. Here the spin-off between university and industry was minimal [28, p. 132]. The importance of informal contacts between industry and HEIs has been questioned by MacDonald [36]. Sceptical views of HEI–industry relationships are also provided by Lowe [34], Senker [52], Miller and Cote [40], Joseph [23] and Shachar and Felsenstein [53]. In addition, Howells [21] explored the regional economic development potential of encouraging HEI–industry links but found no clear connection. This was principally because the most important links developed were often made

Omega, Vol. 23, No. 4 347

across long distances and with a small number of prestigious institutions. A study of high technology firms located on Science Parks in Belgium and Holland by van Dierdonck *et al.* [58, p. 122] also observed 'rather sparse' HEI–industry linkages. Thirty-four (83%) surveyed firms in Holland and 46 firms (68%) in Belgium reported the existence of contacts with a local university. But only 17 Belgian firms (25%) and 12 Dutch firms (29%) had collaborative R&D arrangements with a local university. These researchers went on to further argue,

> "... a science park is not necessarily the most effective way to become involved in industrial science and technology. A multitude of other mechanisms exist" [58, p. 122].[1]

Overall, the evidence surrounding linkages between HEIs and technology-based firms in the locality seems mixed. In the UK the links are clearly present in Cambridge but less so in Oxford and elsewhere. Roberts [49] has found a similar pattern in the USA with Massachusetts Institute of Technology (MIT) being the dominant source of technology-based entrepreneurs not only in Boston, but also even dwarfing the contribution of Stanford in its own 'backyard' of northern California.

We, therefore, propose the following hypotheses:[2]

H_{1a} *Independent Science Park firms are more likely to use the resources of a local HEI than independent off-Park firms.*

H_{1b} *Independent Science Park firms will have*

more links with a local HEI than independent off-Park firms.

2.2. HEI links and organization survival

Low and MacMillan [33] argue that ventures can shape their own survival by building networks. Founders with dense and varied personal and business networks of contacts can gain access to information to overcome business development problems. Organizations which have gained access to a wide and diverse relevant knowledge base through contacts with professional advisers may be more likely to survive.

HEIs are an important element of local infrastructure and can act as a vehicle for the sponsorship of high-technology firms through the use of grants, contracts and sponsored research [13, p. 146].

> "Sponsorship is a deliberate attempt to make available a significantly higher and more stable level of resources to selected firms ... [and] ... When organizations are sponsored, their environment is enriched, providing legitimacy ... to their birth and early survival" [13, p. 129, 131].

Associated with this trend has been a rapid growth in the number of Science Parks in the UK the function of which is to encourage the formation, survival and growth of high-technology firms. The United Kingdom Science Park Association (UKSPA) has asserted that Park firms

> "... would not have survived if they had located off-park" and the support for new businesses on Science Parks has been the "... salvation of the academic entrepreneur ..." [15, p. 120].

Linkages are, however, one of many factors influencing the survival/non-survival of businesses. To assess the impact of linkages it is necessary to take account of those elements such as age, sector and employment size of the business.[3]

We therefore, propose the following hypotheses:

H_{2a} *Independent firms which have a link with a local HEI are more likely to survive.*

H_{2b} *Surviving independent firms will have more links with a local HEI than non-survivors.*

---

[1]"Indeed Science Parks only represent one particular mechanism to stimulate technology transfers between academia and industry; multiple other mechanisms exist, e.g. research consortia, joint ventures, contract research, etc." [58, p. 111].

[2]Eighteen alternative hypotheses are presented each of which suggests the apparent relationship in the sample accurately reflects the relationship in the population. The null hypothesis in each case is that the apparent relationship found in the sample is not representative of a relationship in the population from which the data have come from. Further, in each case the null hypothesis is the opposite of what the researcher would like to believe (i.e. there is no difference).

[3]Multivariate logistic regression models have isolated the *combination* of influences associated with the survival/non-survival of independent technology-based firms located on and off Science Parks in the UK [60].

2.3. HEIs as growth poles for high technology firms

For several reasons HEIs are important as facilitators for growth:

- First, HEIs concentrate in one location a critical mass of scientifically sophisticated individuals who can generate new technologies [12]. Innovative ideas (and technological knowledge) generated in a HEI can be channelled and diffused by new commercial ventures. Supporting this view Jaffe's empirical study of patent activity in the USA revealed,

  "... university research causes industry R&D and not vice versa. Thus, a state that improves its university research sys-

tem will increase local innovation both by attracting industrial R&D and augmenting its productivity" [22, p. 968].[4]

- Second, the technical expertise available in HEIs can be used by existing local businesses to solve production process problems [30, p. 28] and to supplement their commercial advantage [28, p. 128]. As a result, local firms can become more technologically sophisticated thus enhancing their competitive performance.

- Third, HEIs have computing, testing and analysis and library facilities which are an incentive for engaging in a HEI–industry based relationship [30, p. 28].

- Fourth, HEIs are increasingly seen as a crucial source of skilled graduates whom local businesses can employ after graduation [30, p. 28; 27, pp. 171–172].

- Fifth, the development of a centre of academic excellence in a certain field can create or enhance a favourable public image and reputation. As a result, additional jobs can be created not only in the HEI, but also in the wider community surrounding the HEI, because of its enhanced economic and social status [37, p. 305].

In addition, other groups have an interest in fostering cooperation between HEIs and industry [3, 8, 9, 31, 39, 57].[5] First, since 1979, the UK Government has encouraged the higher education sector to become more flexible and business-minded, through reduced dependency on public funding [46, p. 207]. A number of HEIs have turned directly to industry for additional external funding and established mechanisms to commercially exploit research conducted within the HEI. HEIs have themselves encouraged industry links because of a belief that exposure of academics to industrial environments improves the quality of teaching within the HEI. As a result,

  "HEIs are less 'ivory towered' in attitude than they might have been in the past; academics are more willing to negotiate for industrial sponsorship for their research and/or move into industry and

---

[4] On the downside, Jaffe [22, p. 968] also found, "There is only weak evidence that spillovers are facilitated by geographic coincidence of universities and research labs within the state". This latter assertion has recently been questioned. Acs *et al.* [1, p. 306], in their study of innovations (rather than the number of patented inventions) recorded in the USA in 1982, interestingly found corporate innovation activity responded positively to commercial spillovers from university research.

[5] A variety of factors influence the development of HEI–industry links, most notably, culture, individual motivations, institutional stimuli and structural conditions [57, p. 344; 31, pp. 18–20]. In addition, operational characteristics may act as barrier. Recently, Bell [3, p. 317–318] has identified a number of perceived problems and obstacles surrounding academic–industrial collaborative arrangements. For example, the HEI research agenda could be set by industrial rather than academic interests; academics will have less freedom to publish and discuss their findings; in order to minimize risk and uncertainty the innovatory research process in HEIs could be replaced by hierarchial and bureaucratic managerial procedures; industry can change its research needs and, hence, there is the danger that industry can take a cynical attitude towards the value of research and regard it as a vehicle for training and motivating their scientific and technical labour forces; industry can change the research agenda faster than is conducive to academic progress; there are dangers in socialising students only for industry; common technology transfer practices may disadvantage small firms who can not pay a local HEI the same level of remuneration as a large firm; there are also significant ownership issues and patent right obligations, particularly when new technology has been developed and supported by a multiplicity of sources (both from the public and private sectors); businesses complain about the high initial option and licence fees and royalty rates demanded by HEIs for embryonic technology; and finally, valuation disputes are not uncommon with HEIs reportedly tending to overvalue their technology, either because they overlook the development issues or because they are unfamiliar with the production process or market environment into which their technology is to be inserted.

Omega, Vol. 23, No. 4 349

other sectors of the economy in order to further their careers. Academics and the HEIs that employ them want to exploit their assets more effectively to generate revenue..." [3, p. 308].

Second, industry facing stiff competition, has appreciated the need to increase its knowledge base. Technology-driven competition is technically difficult and expensive to counter. Links with HEIs enable industry to gain early access to scientific or technological knowledge, access to unique research skills and cost reductions, through delegation of selected activity.

Third, local and national Governments view the high technology sector as a source of direct and indirect employment opportunities, and HEIs are seen as crucial to facilitating the growth of the local high technology sector.

We, therefore, propose the following hypotheses:

H_3 *Young independent firms which have a link with a local HEI are more likely to survive.*

H_4 *Small employment sized independent firms which have a link with a local HEI are more likely to survive.*

2.4. Development of Science Parks in the UK

The phenomenal growth in the number of high technology firms (and resultant new employment) around, for example, Stanford University in Palo Alto and MIT in Boston in the USA was a role model for the development of Science Parks in the UK. It encouraged many British universities to seek to upgrade the technological capability of firms in their local communities by establishing or expanding regional innovation centres adjacent to the HEI.

Property developments, linked with a local HEI, were planned to become 'growth poles' in which clusters of high technology firms would interact with each other and with the 'host' HEI [58, p. 111], enabling both applied research and businesses to achieve their full potential. As a result, in recent years Science Parks have been established around most British HEIs to formalize these linkages between academics and industry. Science Parks are property-based initiatives which [41, p. 64; 38, p. 28]:[6]

- have formal and operational links with a university, other HEI or research centre and thus improve the take-up of ideas to new products or processes;

- were designed to encourage the formation and growth of knowledge-based businesses and other attendant organizations normally resident on site;

- have a management function which actively encourages the transfer of technology and business skills between the organizations on site and the local HEI; and

- can create employment opportunities and promise a 'sunrise' future which replaces a 'sunset' in a potentially depressed local economy.

Science Parks reflect an assumption that technological innovation stems from scientific research and that Parks can provide the catalytic incubator environment for the transformation of 'pure' research into production. Adherents of this so-called 'linear model' assume there is a chain of successive interrelated activities. These begin with basic scientific research, pass through applied and more developmental research activities, the development of new product and process ideas, the evolution and testing of proto-types, to commercial production and finally to diffusion [38, p. 56]. Information channels are seen as central to the transfer of knowledge from person to person, from HEI to firm, and from firm to firm. As a result, a Science Park can encourage local synergistic linkages between an HEI and high technology firms [26, p. 212].

As early as 1985, however, the Science Park movement in the UK was criticised by Oakey [43, p. 59] who questioned the presumed 'role

---

[6]Few HEIs in the UK have developed Science Parks on their own (a detailed summary of the rapid growth in the number of Science Parks in the UK has been detailed by Monck *et al.* [41, pp. 70–78] and Grayson [15]). In the main, Science Parks have been established by a variety of external partners, generally a regional development agency, a local authority (particularly those located in declining urban areas) or a private sector group (usually including a financial institution). These various parties all anticipate numerous wealth creation and job generation benefits associated with the development of a cluster of high technology firms in their locale. Also, in the UK it has been appreciated that, "...there is no single model to be followed" [41, p. 67]. Nevertheless, the UK Science Park model is much closer to American Innovation Centres than to the US-style Science Parks [41, p. 70].

models' of American university developments being transferred to a British university setting. He warned:

> "... without the generation of production to create the critical mass of technical production skills, the new science parks are unlikely to reach a stage where the full critical mass of research and development and production economies allow the self-sustained growth of the development. A degree of 'ivory towerism' is inherent in the superficial social responsibility apparent in the setting up of science parks" [43, p. 46].

He went on further to argue:

> "The current eagerness of university bodies to establish science parks is less based on a thorough understanding of how they might best create and nurture high technology industrial production, and more on a pragmatic attempt to come to terms with the current political climate" [43, p. 66].

Later, Massey *et al.* [38, pp. 76–85] argued the linear model of innovation reflected in Science Parks was too simplistic. They identified alternative theories of innovation but suggested there was no single model of how innovation occurred. They also claimed the conceptualisation of Science Parks intrinsically entailed social inequality.

Nevertheless, Science Parks can provide a range of key benefits to tenant firms. Most notably,

- close proximity to an HEI,

- the opportunity for HEI academics to exploit their business ideas,

- high quality accommodation,

- management facilities,

- the opportunity for links between firms, and

- the opportunity for inter-trading between firms.

Through these benefits, firms on Science Parks might be expected, in some sense, to out-perform otherwise comparable businesses not located on a Park. Some evidence for this is provided by Hauschildt and Steinkühler [20, p. 190]. They found new technology-based firms (NTBFs) located on Science and Technology Parks in Germany had on average a greater ability to survive and grow than high technology firms forced to develop in the open market.[7]

We, therefore, propose the following hypotheses:

H_{5a} *Over time independent Science Park firms will be more likely to have a link with a local HEI.*

H_{5b} *Over time independent Science Park firms will be more likely to have more links with a local HEI.*

H_{6a} *Over time independent off-Park firms will be more likely to have a link with a local HEI.*

H_{6b} *Over time independent off-Park firms will be more likely to have more links with a local HEI.*

H_{7a} *Over time surviving independent Science Park firms will be more likely to have a HEI link than independent off-Park firms.*

H_{7b} *Over time surviving independent Science Park firms will have more HEI links than independent off-Park firms.*

H_{8a} *Recently established independent Science Park firms are more likely to have a link with a local HEI than independent Science Park firms had in the past.*

H_{8b} *Recently established independent Science Park firms will have more links with a local HEI than independent Science Park firms had in the past.*

H_{9a} *Recently established independent off-Park firms are more likely to have a link with a local HEI than independent off-Park firms had in the past.*

H_{9b} *Recently established off-Park firms will have more links with a local HEI than independent off-Park firms had in the past.*

H_{10a} *Recently established independent Science Park firms are more likely to use the resources of the local HEI than recently established independent off-Park firms.*

---

[7]Hauschildt and Steinkühler [20, p. 190] also found, "... the strong companies have a much better opportunity to develop, and the weak firms are given better chances of survival".

Omega, Vol. 23, No. 4   351

H_{10b} *Recently established independent Science Park firms will have more links with a local HEI than recently established independent off-Park firms.*

3. DATA COLLECTED

3.1. Data collected in 1986

To test these hypotheses data are derived from a longitudinal study which explored the characteristics and performance of firms located on and off Science Parks in the UK [59]. Data were originally collected through a face-to-face questionnaire survey of organisations located in 1986 on Science Parks and with comparable off-Park firms [41].

In total, 284 direct face-to-face interviews were conducted in 1986 (most frequently with the owner-managers of independent and subsidiary organizations) (row 1 in Table 1), of which 183 were on a Science Park and 101 were not on a Park. This constituted 53% of all tenants on UK Science Parks at that time, with Heriot Watt the only significant location omitted. Monck *et al.* [41, pp. 110–111] argued,

"... that the firms in this survey do provide an adequate sample of Britain's new high technology industries, providing adequate geographical, technological, sectoral and ownership coverage".

The Science Park firms were thus 'matched' with 101 firms which were not on a Park but which were in similar sectors, of similar age, of similar ownership pattern and in comparable areas of the UK. The matching was successful with regard to three out of the four categories, the exception being that of the off-Park firms tended to be somewhat older than the Science Park firms. This paper will chart the formation of links over the 1986–1992 period between HEIs and the 135 independent Science Park organizations as well as the 101 independent off-Park organizations first interviewed by Monck *et al.* [41] in 1986 (row in Table 1).

3.2. Data collected in 1992—follow-on sample

In 1990 a follow-on pilot study of 35 Science Park organizations (rows 2 and 3 in Table 1) was conducted by Storey and Strange [55]. The pilot longitudinal study did not attempt any contact with the off Park 'control' group sample of high-technology organizations. During 1992/93 empirical evidence from a second, and much more extensive, longitudinal follow-on survey of independent and subsidiary organizations located on and off Science Parks in 1986 was collected [59]. It was decided not to re-survey those organizations contacted in 1990.

The survival of organizations surveyed in 1986 was ascertained by contacting Science Park managers and by searches through the Companies House register of limited liability companies in the UK, telephone listings, telephone and local trade directories. The following

Table 1. Survival and closure of high technology organizations over the 1986–1992 period*

	Science Park sample†			Off-Park sample		
	Total	Ind	Sub	Total	Ind	Sub
1. Number of surveyed organizations in 1986	183	135	48	101	92	9
Sample of 35 organizations selected for interview in 1990 during the pilot follow on survey but excluded from the 1992/93 follow on survey						
2. Survived—either original or new address by the end of 1992	24	17	7			
3. Confirmed closure by the end of 1992	11	6	5			
4. Survived—interview completed during 1992/93	59	49	10	50	44	6
5. Survived—either original or new address, 1992	31	26	5	19	18	1
6. Confirmed closure by the end of 1992	46	25	21	21	19	2
7. Organisation has no telephone listing/not recorded in telephone or trade directory by the end of 1992	12	12	0	11	11	0
8. Total sample closure rate (including no telephone listings) over the 1986 to 1992 period		43 (32%)			30 (33%)	
9. Number of organizations in the valid 1992/93 follow on sample (excluding those 23 independent Science Park organizations re-interviewed in 1990 and the organizations that had closed over the 1986 to 1992 period)		75			62	
10. Valid response rate to interview survey, 1992/93		65%			71%	

*The 'tracking' of Science Park organizations was more successfully achieved because information was more extensive from Science Park managers surrounding organization name changes and/or organization relocations.
†Nine surveyed firms located on a Science Park in 1986 have subsequently survived and moved to an off-Park location.
Ind, independent organization in 1986. Sub, subsidiary organization in 1986.

definition of independent organization closure was used:

> "An independent business is regarded as a closure if, in 1992, it is no longer identifiable as a trading business. An independent business which moves locations but continues as a trading business is *not* regarded as a closure. If the business is a subsidiary or a branch plant then it is regarded as having ceased if it no longer trades at its previous location" [59, p. 25].[8]

A similar definition has been utilized elsewhere [10, p. 17; 24 p. 144; 14, pp. 185–186].

Table 1 also shows that out of the 135 independent organizations interviewed in 1986 which located on a Science Park, 92 (68%) remained in business in 1992 (rows 2, 4 and 5). Over the same period 62 off-Park independent organizations (67%) remained in business (rows 4 and 5).

Rows 3 and 6 in Table 1 indicate 31 independent Science Park organizations were closures. For untraced organizations additional evidence from direct fieldwork was gathered from individuals adjacent to the original location of the organization surrounding its current status and location (a similar method was used by Reid [48, p. 547]). Twelve independent Science Park organizations could not be traced and did not appear in any identifiable form (row 7). This

latter group of organizations were also regarded as closures. Hence the total number of independent Science Park closures was 43 (row 8). With regard to the off-Park sample, 19 were closures (row 6) and a further 11 could not be traced (row 7). Hence 43 (32%) independent Science Park organizations closed over this 6-year period compared with 30 (33%) independent off-Park organizations (row 8).

Row 9 in Table 1 shows 75 independent surviving Science Park organizations in the valid 1992/93 follow-on sample (excluding the 17 surviving independent organizations re-interviewed in 1990 and 43 independent organization closures) and a further 62 independent off-Park organizations (excluding the 32 independent organization closures). Questionnaire responses surrounding current links with a local HEI were collected from surviving independent organizations (in 1986) during late 1992 and early 1993. Row 4 in Table 1 indicates 49 follow-on interviews were conducted with independent Science Park organizations (65% valid response rate—row 10) and a further 44 interviews were conducted with independent off-Park organizations (71% valid response rate—row 10).[9]

3.3. Data collected in 1992—new sample

HEI–industry links were examined by Westhead and Storey [59]. All 448 organizations located on Science Parks in the UK between 1986 and 1992 were identified. From this list 110 organizations were randomly selected covering Science Parks in Government designated 'assisted' and 'non-assisted' areas. Seventy-one interviews were conducted with these independent and subsidiary firms (65% response rate).

To ascertain the 'added value' of a Science Park location, high technology firms not located on a Park were also interviewed. Science Park firms were 'matched' with off-Park firms by industry, ownership type of the organization, age of the organization and location of the business. Seventy-one off-Park firms were identified (for a full discussion see [59]). Face-to-face interviews were conducted both with Science Park tenants and with 'comparable' firms not located on a Park.[10] This paper will explore the extent to which the 47 surveyed independent Science Park firms and the 48 independent off-Park firms in the 'new sample' utilized their local HEI resource networks.

---

[8]The key justification for this definition relates to the purpose of the study conducted by Westhead and Storey [59]. "Our objective is to be able to track and compare over a six-year period the on-Park firms interviewed in 1986 with the off-Park firms. A definition of closure needs to be chosen which enables a valid and direct comparison to be made between the two groups of firms. It also needs to recognise that the quality of information about the off-Park firms is weaker than that for Science Park firms. A definition therefore has to be employed which the researchers can be confident ensures that both groups of firms are treated comparably" [59, p. 25].

[9]Responses to the follow-on survey was examined for non-response bias [59, pp. 33–39]. No marked differences between the 1986 and the 1992 follow-on survey returns were recorded with regard to ownership characteristics, sectoral or geographical coverage or the age of surveyed businesses.

[10]The Science Park and the off-Park samples were perfectly matched with regard to sectoral composition. In addition, no statistically significant difference was recorded between the two new samples with regard to ownership characteristics and the age of surveyed firms. However, the 'matching' of surveyed Science Park and off-Park firms was not successful according to location. Relatively more Science Park firms were located in Scotland and the West Midlands of England whilst markedly more off-Park firms were in South East England.

Table 2. Links with the local university, polytechnic or institute of higher education (HEI) in 1986 by independent Science Park and off-Park firms

Link with HEI	Science Park firms, 1986		Off-Park firms, 1986		Total		χ^2 statistic significance level
	No.	%	No.	%	No.	%	
1. No	16	12.1	20	23.0	36	16.4	0.05
2. Yes	116	87.9	67	77.0	183	83.6	

$\geqslant 1$ link with HEI
Science Park firms—1986 $\bar{x} = 4.66$ $\sigma = 2.79$ $n = 116$ median = 4
Off-park firms—1986 $\bar{x} = 3.73$ $\sigma = 2.97$ $n = 67$ median = 3

$t = 2.09$, d.f. = 181, statistically significant difference at the 0.05 level of significance (one-tailed test)

Type of HEI link for those firms with $\geqslant 1$ link							
1. Informal contact with academics	82	70.7	42	62.7	124	67.8	NS
2. Employment of academics on a part-time basis/consultancy basis	43	37.1	24	35.8	67	36.6	NS
3. Sponsor research trials or projects	19	16.4	14	20.9	33	18.0	NS
4. Access to specialist equipment	52	44.8	25	37.3	77	42.1	NS
5. Test/analysis in HEI	17	14.7	12	17.9	29	15.8	NS
6. Student projects	33	28.4	23	34.3	56	30.6	NS
7. Employment of recent graduates	39	33.6	25	37.3	64	35.0	NS
8. Training by HEI	7	6.0	6	9.0	13	7.1	NA
9. Assistance by business in HEI teaching programme	9	7.8	10	14.9	19	10.4	NS
10. Other formal links	29	25.0	6	9.0	35	19.1	0.05
Use of facilities:							
11. Computer	67	57.8	17	25.4	84	45.9	0.001
12. Library	41	35.3	5	7.5	46	25.1	0.001
13. Recreation	19	16.4	9	13.4	28	15.3	NS
14. Conferences	34	29.3	4	6.0	38	20.8	0.001
15. Dining	14	12.1	2	3.0	16	8.7	0.1
16. Audio-visual	3	2.6	5	7.5	8	4.4	NA
17. University as a customer	22	19.0	16	23.9	38	20.8	NS
18. Other	12	10.3	6	9.0	18	9.8	NS
Valid cases	116		67		183		

NS, χ^2 statistic not statistically significant at the 0.05 level of significance.
NA, due to the assumptions of the χ^2 test it was not possible to calculate a coefficient.

4. TESTING THE HYPOTHESES

4.1. Links with a local HEI by independent Science Park and off-Park firms in 1986

H_{1a} *Independent Science Park firms are more likely to use the resources of a local HEI than independent off-Park firms.*

H_{1b} *Independent Science Park firms will have more links with a local HEI than independent off-Park firms.*

As hypothesized (H_{1a}), the top section of Table 2 shows, in 1986, independent Science Park firms were significantly more likely than independent off-Park firms to have a link with

a local HEI (87.9 and 77.0% of Science Park and off-Park firms, respectively). The second section of the table shows, for those firms having a link, there was no significant difference between the two samples with regard to the *number* of links with a local HEI in 1986 (means of 4.7 and 3.7 links for Science Park and off-Park firms, respectively).[11,12] As a result, hypothesis H_{1b} cannot be supported.

The third section of Table 2 identifies eighteen different separate links. The most frequently specified link for firms in both samples was informal contact with academics (70.7 and 62.7% of Science Park and off-Park firms, respectively).[13] Science Park firms were significantly more likely to have developed other formal links (25.0% compared with 9.0%), have used HEI computer facilities (57.8% compared with 25.4%), as well as library (35.3% compared with 7.5%), conference (29.3% compared with 6.0%) and dining facilities (12.1% compared with 3.0%). This suggests that for links, in general, there was little difference between on and off-Park firms. The Science Park firms were,

[11] Those with one or more links with a HEI in 1986.
[12] A general necessity for the t-test is data normality (the assumption that the observations are randomly drawn from a normal distribution with the same variance), although it is tolerant of a surprising degree of skewness [42, B-9].
[13] Percentages relate to valid responding cases (or independent firms that had established one or more links with a HEI).

Table 3. Links with the local university, polytechnic or institute of higher education (HEI) in 1986 by independent business survival over the 1986–1992 period

Link with HEI	Independent business non-survival		Independent business survival		χ^2 statistic significance level
	No.	%	No.	%	
1. No	17	24.6	19	12.7	0.05
2. Yes	52	75.4	131	87.3	

⩾1 link with HEI
Independent business non-survival $\bar{x} = 4.10$ $\sigma = 2.83$ $n = 52$ median = 3
Independent business survival $\bar{x} = 4.41$ $\sigma = 2.91$ $n = 131$ median ≈ 3
$t = -0.68$, d.f. = 181, no statistically significant difference at the 0.05 level of significance (one-tailed test).

not surprisingly, much more likely to use HEI facilities than the off-Park firms.

4.2. Survival of independent Science Park and off-Park firms, 1986–1992

H_{2a} *Independent firms which have a link with a local HEI are more likely to survive.*

H_{2b} *Surviving independent firms will have more links with a local HEI than non-survivors.*

Hypothesis H_{2a} suggests independent firms (in a combined sample of Science Park and off-Park firms) with links in 1986 would be more likely to survive until 1992 than those without. The top half of Table 3 shows this is the case. The lower half of the table shows that it is *whether* the firm had a link, rather than the *number* of links which is associated with firm survival. Hence, hypothesis H_{2b} is rejected. Also, no

statistically significant differences were recorded between both groups of firms with regard to the types of links made in 1986.

H_3 *Young independent firms which have a link with a local HEI are more likely to survive.*

Table 4 suggests having an HEI link overcomes some of the 'liability of newness' [2, 54] for independent high technology firms. As hypothesized, young firms (<3 years of age in 1986) with an HEI link (in 1986) were more likely to survive over this 6 year period, although not in a statistically significant direction (58.3% of 'non-surviving' firms had a link compared with 71.4% of 'surviving' firms). Only weak support for hypothesis H_3, however, is provided.

H_4 *Small employment sized independent firms which have a link with a local HEI are more likely to survive.*

Table 5 tentatively suggests some of the 'liability of small employment size' [1] can be offset by having a link with a local HEI. 'Surviving' firms in the 1 to 2 employment size category (in 1986) were more likely to have established an HEI link than 'non-surviving' firms (75.0% of 'non-surviving' firms had a link compared with 90.9% of 'surviving' firms). Therefore, some weak support for hypothesis H_4 is provided.

Table 4. Independent business survival over the 1986–1992 period by age of the firm in 1986 and a link with a HEI in 1986

Age in 1986	Non-survival				Survival				Total			
	Link		No link		Link		No link		Link		No link	
	No.	%	No.	%	No.	%	No.	%	No.	%	No.	%
1–2	7	58.3	5	41.7	10	71.4	4	28.6	17	65.4	9	34.6
3–5	26	81.3	6	18.8	35	87.5	5	12.5	61	84.7	11	15.3
6–10	6	75.0	2	25.0	24	92.3	2	7.7	30	88.2	4	11.8
⩾11	2	66.7	1	33.3	21	87.5	3	12.5	23	85.2	4	14.8

Table 5. Independent business survival over the 1986–1992 period by the employment size of the firm in 1986 and a link with a HEI in 1986

Employment size of the firm in 1986	Non-survival				Survival				Total			
	Link		No link		Link		No link		Link		No link	
	No.	%	No.	%	No.	%	No.	%	No.	%	No.	%
1–2	6	75.0	2	25.0	10	90.9	1	9.1	16	84.2	3	15.8
3–25	29	76.3	9	23.7	85	85.9	14	14.1	114	83.2	23	16.8
26–50	1	50.0	1	50.0	14	87.5	2	12.5	15	83.3	3	16.7
⩾51	1	100.0	0	0.0	7	100.0	0	0.0	8	100.0	0	0.0

Omega, Vol. 23, No. 4 355

Table 6. Links with the local university, polytechnic or institute of higher education (HEI) by surviving surveyed independent Science Park Firms in 1986 and 1992

Link with HEI	Science Park firms, 1986		Science Park firms, 1992		χ^2 statistic significance level
	No.	%	No.	%	
1. No	4	8.7	0	0.0	NA
2. Yes	42	91.3	46	100.0	

$\geqslant 1$ link with HEI
Science Park firms—1986 $\bar{x} = 4.98$ $\sigma = 3.02$ $n = 42$ median $= 5$
Science Park firms—1992 $\bar{x} = 5.80$ $\sigma = 4.13$ $n = 46$ median $= 5$

$t = -1.07$, d.f. $= 86$, no statistically significant difference at the 0.05 level of significance (one-tailed test).
NA, due to the assumptions of the χ^2 test it was not possible to calculate a coefficient.

Table 7. Links with the local university, polytechnic or institute of higher education (HEI) by surviving surveyed independent off-Park firms in 1986 and 1992

Link with HEI	Off-Park firms, 1986		Off-Park firms, 1992		χ^2 statistic significance level
	No.	%	No.	%	
1. No	4	13.8	0	0.0	NA
2. Yes	25	86.2	29	100.0	

$\geqslant 1$ link with HEI
Off-Park firms—1986 $\bar{x} = 4.40$ $\sigma = 3.29$ $n = 25$ median $= 3$
Off-Park firms—1992 $\bar{x} = 3.38$ $\sigma = 2.26$ $n = 29$ median $= 3$

$t = 1.31$, d.f. $= 52$, no statistically significant difference at the 0.05 level of significance (one-tailed test).
NA, due to the assumptions of the χ^2 test it was not possible to calculate a coefficient.

4.3. Development of HEI links by independent Science Park and off-Park firms, 1986–1992

H_{5a} *Over time independent Science Park firms will be more likely to have a link with a local HEI.*

H_{5b} *Over time independent Science Park firms will be more likely to have more links with a local HEI.*

Table 6 shows in 1992 all 46 surviving surveyed Science Park firms had at least one link with a local HEI, compared with 42 firms in 1986. Hypothesis H_{5a} is, therefore, confirmed. The second part of the table shows that surviving Science Park firms had *more* links with their local HEI in 1992 than they had in 1986 (means of 5.0 and 5.8 links for surviving surveyed Science Park firms in 1986 and 1992, respectively), although not in a statistically significant direction.[14] This confirms hypothesis H_{5b}. Although not shown in the table it was found, over this 6 year period, the prime growth in links was in the greater use of HEI library (38.1% compared with 71.7%) and recreation

facilities (16.7% compared with 37.0%). In addition, Science Park firms had increasingly commercialized their activities by selling their own skills and services to HEIs (21.4% compared with 41.3%). Interestingly, presumably due to the rapid growth in the use of personal microcomputers Science Park firms reported a marked reduction in their use of HEI computer facilities (down from 59.5% to 26.1% of firms).

H_{6a} *Over time independent off-Park firms will be more likely to have a link with a local HEI.*

H_{6b} *Over time independent off-Park firms will be more likely to have more links with a local HEI.*

Table 7 shows all 29 surviving off-Park firms in 1992 reported at least one link with a local HEI. For 4 firms this link was new since 1986. As a result, hypothesis H_{6a} is supported. Contrary to expectation (H_{6b}), off-Park firms with at least one link in 1992 suggested they had fewer links with the HEI in 1992 than they had in 1986 (means of 4.4 and 3.4 links for surviving surveyed off-Park firms in 1986 and 1992, respectively). Although not shown in detail, it was found that there were falls (but not in a statisti-

[14]Linkages were explored over a period covering an economic boom (1986–1988) as well as a recession (1989–1992) in the UK.

Table 8. Links with the local university, polytechnic or institute of higher education (HEI) in 1992 by surviving surveyed independent Science Park and off-Park firms

Link with HEI	Science Park firms, 1992		Off-Park firms, 1992		Total		χ^2 statistic significance level
	No.	%	No.	%	No.	%	
1. No	0	0.0	0	0.0	0	0.0	NA
2. Yes	46	100.0	29	100.0	75	100.0	

⩾1 link with HEI
Science Park firms—1992 $\bar{x} = 5.80$ $\sigma = 4.13$ $n = 46$ median = 5
Off-park firms—1992 $\bar{x} = 3.38$ $\sigma = 2.26$ $n = 29$ median = 3

$t = 3.28$, d.f. = 73, statistically significant difference at the 0.005 level of significance (one-tailed test).
NA, due to the assumptions of the χ^2 test it was not possible to calculate a coefficient.

cally significant direction) in the proportion of firms reporting informal contact with academics and also the use of HEI computer facilities.

H_{7a} *Over time surviving independent Science Park firms will be more likely to have an HEI link than independent off-Park firms.*

H_{7b} *Over time surviving independent Science Park firms will have more HEI links than independent off-Park firms.*

The links in 1992 developed by the 46 surviving Park and the 29 off-Park firms are compared in Table 8. At that time, all firms had developed at least one link with a local HEI. Hypothesis H_{7a} is, therefore, not confirmed. However, as found with the total sample of surveyed firms in 1986 (Table 2) Table 8 indicates surviving Science Park firms had significantly more HEI links in 1992 than their off-Park counterparts (means of 5.8 and 3.4 links for surviving Science Park and off-Park firms in 1992). As a result, hypothesis H_{7b} is supported.

Examining the individual links, four statistically significant differences emerged between the two groups of firms. As found in 1986, Science Park firms continue to be significantly more

likely to use the computer (26.1% compared with 3.4%), library (71.7% compared with 34.5%) and dining facilities of a local HEI (26.1% compared with 3.4%). In addition, by 1992, Science Park firms were significantly more likely to utilize the recreation facilities of a local HEI (37.0% compared with 3.4%).

4.4. Development of HEI links by independent Science Park and off-Park firms in the new sample

H_{8a} *Recently established independent Science Park firms are more likely to have a link with a local HEI than independent Science Park firms had in the past.*

H_{8b} *Recently established independent Science Park firms will have more links with a local HEI than independent Science Park firms had in the past.*

Table 9 shows that over 86% of independent Science Park firms in both the Monck *et al.* sample and the Westhead and Storey new sample had contacted a local HEI. Hypothesis

Table 9. Links with the local university, polytechnic or institute of higher education (HEI) by independent science park firms surveyed by Monck *et al.* in 1986 and Science Park firms in the new sample surveyed by Westhead and Storey in 1992

Link with HEI	Monck *et al.* Science Park sample, 1986		Westhead and Storey Science Park new sample, 1992		χ^2 statistic significance level
	No.	%	No.	%	
1. No	16	12.1	6	12.8	NS
2. Yes	116	87.9	41	87.2	

⩾1 link with HEI
Monck *et al.*, Science Park $\bar{x} = 4.66$ $\sigma = 2.79$ $n = 116$ median = 4
  sample—1986
Westhead and Storey Science $\bar{x} = 5.73$ $\sigma = 3.80$ $n = 41$ median = 5
  Park new sample—1992

$t = -1.65$, d.f. = 155, statistically significant difference at the 0.05 level of significance (one-tailed test).
NS, χ^2 statistic not statistically significant at the 0.05 level of significance.

Omega, Vol. 23, No. 4 357

Table 10. Links with the local university, polytechnic or institute of higher education (HEI) by independent off-Park firms surveyed by Monck *et al.* in 1986 and off-Park firms in the new sample surveyed by Westhead and Storey in 1992

Link with HEI	Monck *et al.* off-Park sample, 1986		Westhead and Storey off-Park new sample, 1992		χ^2 statistic significance level
	No.	%	No.	%	
1. No	20	23.0	12	25.0	NS
2. Yes	67	77.0	36	75.0	

$\geqslant 1$ link with HEI
Monck *et al.*, off-Park sample—1986 $\bar{x} = 3.73$ $\sigma = 2.97$ $n = 67$ median $= 3$
Westhead and Storey off-Park new sample—1992 $\bar{x} = 3.56$ $\sigma = 2.51$ $n = 36$ median $= 3$

$t = 0.31$, d.f. $= 101$, no statistically significant difference at the 0.05 level of significance (one-tailed test).
NS, χ^2 statistic not statistically significant at the 0.05 level of significance.

H_{8a} is, therefore, not supported. However, as hypothesized (H_{8b}), independent Science Park firms in the new sample had more links in 1992 than independent Science Park firms interviewed by Monck *et al.* in 1986 (means of 4.7 and 5.7 links for Monck *et al.*, Science Park firms and Westhead and Storey's new sample Science Park firms, respectively).

Examining the individual links it appears that Science Park firms in the new sample were significantly more likely to indicate their businesses had assisted the HEI in a teaching programme (26.8% compared with 7.8%). Moreover, significantly more new sample firms had used HEI library (78.0% compared with 35.3%), recreation (43.9% compared with 16.4%) and dining facilities (36.6% compared with 12.1%). In marked contrast, new sample firms were significantly less likely to have contacted a HEI to use its computer facilities (9.8% compared with 57.8%).

H_{9a} *Recently established independent off-Park firms are more likely to have a link with a local HEI than independent off-Park firms had in the past.*

H_{9b} *Recently established off-Park firms will have more links with a local HEI than independent off-Park firms had in the past.*

Table 10 shows that in both the Monck *et al.* sample and the Westhead and Storey new sample over 74% of independent off-Park firms had contacted a local HEI. Firms with links in both samples also mentioned developing a similar number of links with their local HEI (means of 3.7 and 3.6 links for Monck *et al.* off-Park firms and Westhead and Storey's new sample off-Park firms, respectively). As a result, neither hypothesis H_{9a} nor H_{9b} can be confirmed.

H_{10a} *Recently established independent Science Park firms are more likely to use the*

Table 11. Links with the local university, polytechnic or institute of higher education (HEI) by independent new sample Science Park and off-Park firms surveyed by Westhead and Storey in 1992

Link with HEI	Westhead and Storey Science Park new sample, 1992		Westhead and Storey off-Park new sample, 1992		χ^2 statistic significance level
	No.	%	No.	%	
1. No	6	12.8	12	25.0	NS
2. Yes	41	87.2	36	75.0	

$\geqslant 1$ link with HEI
Westhead and Storey Science Park new sample—1992 $\bar{x} = 5.73$ $\sigma = 3.80$ $n = 41$ median $= 5$
Westhead and Storey off-Park new sample—1992 $\bar{x} = 3.56$ $\sigma = 2.51$ $n = 36$ median $= 3$

$t = 3.00$, d.f. $= 75$, statistically significant difference at the 0.005 level of significance (one-tailed test).
NS, χ^2 statistic not statistically significant at the 0.05 level of significance.

resources of the local HEI than recently established independent off-Park firms.

H_{10b} *Recently established independent Science Park firms will have more links with a local HEI than recently established independent off-Park firms.*

Finally, Table 11 shows that independent Science Park new sample firms interviewed in 1992 were not significantly more likely to have contacted a local HEI than new sample off-Park firms. However, Science Park firms were likely to have significantly more links than off-Park firms (means of 5.7 and 3.6 links for Westhead and Storey's new sample Science Park and off-Park firms, respectively). Hypotheses H_{10a} is, therefore, rejected but hypothesis H_{10b} is accepted. In addition, to only three types of links were statistically significant between firms in the two groups. Science Park firms had a significantly greater propensity, in 1992, to have used HEI library (78.0% compared with 27.8%), recreation (43.9% compared with 0.0%) and dining facilities (36.6% compared with 0.0%).

5. CONCLUSIONS AND IMPLICATIONS

This research has explored the informal and formal linkages made by technology-based firms located on and off Science Parks in the UK with HEIs. In 1986, a number of firms suggested they had located their businesses on a Science Park in order to be close to an HEI. However, the extent to which these HEI-industry links existed was less than anticipated [41]. To some extent this was rationalized at that time on the grounds that most of the firms, and many of the Science Parks, were relatively new. It was felt the building up of links would take place only over a lengthy period of time.

In 1986, firms located on a Science Park were significantly more likely to have a link with a local HEI and have more links than off-Park firms. However, the key result of this paper is that independent high technology organizations in the combined sample (irrespective of location) with a link [irrespective of the number and/or type of link(s)] with a local HEI in 1986 (and access to the HEI resource network) were significantly more likely to survive to the end of 1992. Also, the liabilities of newness and small employment size can to some extent be alleviated if organizations 'tap-into' local HEI

resource networks. This research has, therefore, shown that the survival of new and small independent high technology organizations can be enhanced if organization decision-makers, network gatekeepers (such as Science Park managers and HEI industrial liaison officers) as well as academics in HEIs, appreciate the potential benefits of HEI-industry co-operation. Most notably, they should appreciate an appropriately structured 'hands-on' support to new NTBFs,

> "... can have a positive effect in enabling viability and survival, if not growth, of such enterprises" [26, p. 215].

Both Science Park and off-Park firms were more likely to use the resources of a local HEI in 1992 than in 1986. However, off-Park firms with at least one link with a local HEI in 1992 reported they had fewer links in 1992 than they had in 1986. We are not clear why this should be the case.

By 1992, surviving surveyed Science Park as well as off-Park firms had appreciated the advantages of a HEI link. Science Park firms had generally increased their links with the local HEI, whereas the off-Park firms had reduced the number of links with a local HEI. Nevertheless, it would be unwise to assume off-Park firms had little contact with a local HEI in 1992 since 59% of off-Park firms claimed to have informal contact with academics and 48% claimed to have employed recent graduates.

It is also interesting that firms in the 1992 new sample were not significantly more likely to have an HEI link than firms in 1986. In part, this is because more than 86% of Science Park firms in both samples had a link with a local HEI in 1986 as well as 1992. Similarly, over 74% of off-Park firms in both 1986 and 1992 had established at least one HEI link.

Even so, contact with a local HEI is vital. Science Park managers and HEI industrial liaison officers have an important role here not only establishing links but also encouraging the development of more formal links over time. In part, the higher incidence of HEI-industry linkage in the Science Park new sample than in the off-Park new sample may be due to the activities of Science Park managers and HEI industrial liaison officers actively attempting to link Park firms with their local HEI.

Interestingly, additional empirical analysis (summarized in [59, pp. 118–123]) revealed a 'latent demand' for contact and liaison with HEIs, both amongst Science Park and off-Park firms. Firms, irrespective of location, claimed the HEI should make greater efforts to ensure its services and facilities are made more accessible to businesses. It is, therefore, disconcerting to note that Science Park firms were no more likely to have received a visit from a representative of an HEI to discuss its facilities than off-Park firms. It may be that HEI personnel felt the responsibility for initiating this contact lay with the Science Park manager, but the assumption that Science Park firms are well informed about research in the HEI does not seem valid. In addition, technology-based firms in general felt links with HEIs could be improved and that, perhaps by implication, the first move had to be made by HEIs to set the process in motion. Respondents also suggested there was a lot of information within HEIs which would be useful to business if only it were able to access it appropriately. From the businesses' perspective, however, they found the 'searching out' of information extremely time-consuming and believed it was the responsibility of the HEI to foster better links with the business community. In reality, both parties have a responsibility of ensuring a successful academic/industry network [11, p. 312].

The evidence here suggests the role of industrial liaison officers within HEIs needs to be strengthened [56, p. 147]. Science Park managers and industrial liaison officers need to become even more proactive and establish systems which actively link individuals in specific firms with individuals in appropriate HEI departments (and other high technology firms located on and off the Science Park).

We also believe HEIs should appreciate, in order to maximise the contribution of a Science Park, the necessity of having an effective (but not extravagant) managerial structure designed to 'add value' to tenant firms. There is a 'happy medium' between, on the one hand, a solely property-based initiative which happens to be located adjacent to a HEI and, on the other, what is perceived by tenant firms as an over-staffed bureaucracy which they are funding from their rental payments. The happy medium is a lean central unit which both manages property aspects efficiently and is an effective

conduit to the HEI and other sources of business information and resources. This role can be exercised with regular contact between Science Park management and tenant firms.

In 1988, Monck *et al.* [41] pointed to the need for HEIs to enter into flexible relationships with members of their staff wishing to commercialize their research ideas. The evidence from this survey is that these (generally informal) arrangements have only developed very modestly and, given the need to increase the number of high technology businesses, this is another area which HEIs should look at more closely.

ACKNOWLEDGEMENTS

We would like to thank the Department of Trade and Industry, National Westminster Bank, KPMG Peat Marwick and the United Kingdom Science Park Association (UKSPA) for their financial sponsorship. The views expressed here do not necessarily reflect those of the sponsors, but have benefitted considerably from the comments received from two anonymous referees.

REFERENCES

1. Acs ZJ, Audretsch DB and Feldman MP (1992) Real effects of academic research: comment. *Am. Econ. Rev.* **82**, 363–367.
2. Aldrich H and Auster ER (1986) Even dwarfs started small: liabilities of age and size and their strategic implications. *Research in Organizational Behavior* (Edited by Staw B and Cummings LL), Vol. 8, pp. 65–198. JAI Press, Greenwich, Conn.
3. Bell ER (1993) Some current issues in technology transfer and academic-industrial relations: a review. *Technol. Anal. Strategic Mgmt* **5**, 307–321.
4. Bidault F and Fischer WA (1994) Technology transactions: networks over markets. *R&D Mgmt* **24**, 373–386.
5. Bird BJ, Hayward DJ and Allen DN (1993) Conflicts in the commercialization of knowledge: perspectives from science and entrepreneurship. *Entrepreneurship Theory Pract.* **17**, No. 4, 57–77.
6. Bishop P (1988) Academic-industry links and firm size in south west England. *Reg. Stud.* **22**, 160–162.
7. Boddy M and Lovering J (1986) High technology industry in the Bristol sub-region: the aerospace defence nexus. *Reg. Stud.* **20**, 217–231.
8. Bonaccorsi A and Piccaluga A (1994) A theoretical framework for the evaluation of university-industry relationships. *R&D Mgmt* **24**, 229–247.
9. Bower DJ (1992) *Company and Campus Partnership: Supporting Technology Transfer.* Routledge, London.
10. Cooper AC and Bruno A (1977) Success among high technology firms. *Busin. Horiz.* **20**, No. 2, 16–22.
11. Cromie S and Birley S (1994) Relationships among small business support agencies. *Entrepreneurship Reg. Dev.* **6**, 301–314.
12. Florax R (1992) *The University: a Regional Booster?* Avebury, Aldershot.
13. Flynn DM (1993) A critical exploration of sponsorship, infrastructure, and new organizations. *Small Business Econ.* **5**, No. 3, 129–156.
14. Garnsey EW and Cannon-Brookes A (1993) The 'Cambridge phenomenon' revisited: aggregate change

360   *Westhead, Storey—HEIs and High Technology Firms*

among Cambridge high-technology companies since 1985. *Entrepreneurship Reg. Dev.* **5**, 179–207.

15. Grayson L (1993) *Science Parks: an Experiment in High Technology Transfer.* The British Library, London.

16. Håkansson H (1987) (Ed.) *Industrial Technological Development: a Network Approach.* Croom Helm, London.

17. Håkansson H (1989) *Corporate Technological Behaviour: Co-operation and Networks.* Routledge, London.

18. Håkansson H (1990) Technological collaboration in industrial networks. *Eur. Mgmt J.* **8**, 371–379.

19. Håkansson H and Laage-Hellman J (1984) Developing a network R&D strategy. *J. Prod. Innov. Mgmt* **1**, 224–237.

20. Hauschildt J and Steinkühler RH (1994) The role of science and technology parks in NTBF development. *New Technology-based Firms in the 1990s* (Edited by Oakey R), pp. 181–191. Chapman, London.

21. Howells J (1986) Industry-academic links in research and innovation: a national and regional development perspective. *Reg. Stud.* **20**, 472–476.

22. Jaffe AB (1989) Real effects of academic research. *Am. Econ. Rev.* **79**, 957–970.

23. Joseph RA (1989) Technology parks and their contribution to the development of technology-oriented complexes in Australia. *Envir. Plan. C* **7**, 173–192.

24. Kalleberg AL and Leicht KT (1991) Gender and organizational performance: determinants of small business survival and success. *Acad. Mgmt J.* **34**, 136–161.

25. Keeble D (1989) High technology industry and regional development in Britain: the case of the Cambridge phenomenon. *Envir. Plan. C* **7**, 153–172.

26. Keeble D (1994) Regional influences and policy in new technology-based firm creation and growth. *New Technology-based Firms in the 1990s* (Edited by Oakey R), pp. 204–218. Chapman, London.

27. Laranja M (1994) How NTBF's acquire, accumulate and transfer technology: implications for catching-up policies of less developed countries such as Portugal. *New Technology-based Firms in the 1990s* (Edited by Oakey R), pp. 169–180. Chapman, London.

28. Lawton-Smith H (1990) Innovation and technical links: the case of advanced technology industry in Oxfordshire. *Area* **22**, 125–135.

29. Lawton-Smith H (1991) The role of incubators in local industrial development: the cryogenics industry in Oxfordshire. *Entrepreneurship Reg. Dev.* **3**, 175–194.

30. Link AN and Rees J (1990) Firm size, university based research, and the returns of R&D. *Small Bus. Econ.* **2**, 25–31.

31. López-Martinez RE, Medellin E, Scanlon AP and Solleiro JL (1994) Motivations and obstacles to university industry cooperation (UIC): a Mexican case. *R&D Mgmt* **24**, 17–31.

32. Lorenzoni G and Ornati OA (1988) Constellations of firms and new ventures. *J. Bus. Venturing* **3**, 41–57.

33. Low MB and MacMillan IC (1988) Entrepreneurship: past research and future challenges. *J. Mgmt* **14**, 138–161.

34. Lowe J (1985) Science parks in the UK. *Lloyds Bank Rev.* **156**, 31–42.

35. Lowe J (1993) Commercialization of university research: a policy perspective. *Technol. Anal. Strategic Mgmt* **5**, 27–37.

36. MacDonald S (1987) British science parks: reflections on the politics of high technology. *R&D Mgmt* **17**, 25–37.

37. Malecki EJ (1991) *Technology and Economic Development: the Dynamics of Local, Regional and National Change.* Longman, London.

38. Massey D, Quintas P and Wield D (1992) *High Tech Fantasies: Science Parks in Society, Science and Space.* Routledge, London.

39. McMullan WE and Melnyk K (1988) University

innovation centres and academic venture formation. *R&D Mgmt* **18**, 5–12.

40. Miller R and Cote M (1987) *Growing the Next Silicon Valley.* Lexington Books, Lexington, Mass.

41. Monck CSP, Porter RB, Quintas P, Storey DJ and Wynarczyk P (1988) *Science Parks and the Growth of High Technology Firms.* Croom Helm, London.

42. Norusis MJ (1990) *SPSS/PC + Advanced Statistics V2.0.* SPSS, Chicago.

43. Oakey R (1985) British university science parks and high technology small firms: a comment on the potential for sustained industrial growth. *Int. Small Bus. J.* **4**, 58–67.

44. OECD (1981) *The Future of University Research.* Organisation for Economic Co-Operation and Development, Paris.

45. OECD (1993) *Small and Medium-sized Enterprises: Technology and Competitiveness.* Organisation for Economic Co-Operation and Development, Paris.

46. Palfreyman D (1989) The Warwick way: a case study of entrepreneurship within a university context. *Entrepreneurship Reg. Dev.* **1**, 207–219.

47. Porter ME (1991) Towards a dynamic theory of strategy. *Strategic Mgmt J.* **12**, 95–117.

48. Reid GC (1991) Staying in business. *Int. J. Ind. Org.* **9**, 545–556.

49. Roberts EB (1991) *Entrepreneurs in High Technology: Lessons from MIT and Beyond.* Oxford University Press, New York.

50. Rothwell R and Beesley M (1988) Patterns of external linkages of innovative small and medium-sized firms in the United Kingdom. *Piccola Impresa/Small Business* **1**, No. 2, 15–31.

51. Segal Quince & Partners (1985) *The Cambridge Phenomenon: the Growth of High Technology Industry in a University Town.* Brand Brothers, London.

52. Senker JM (1985) Small high technology firms: some regional implications. *Technovation* **3**, 243–262.

53. Shachar A and Felsenstein D (1992) Urban economic development and high technology industry. *Urban Stud.* **29**, 839–855.

54. Stinchcombe AL (1965) Social structure and organizations. *Handbook of Organizations* (Edited by March JG), pp. 142–193. Rand McNally, Chicago.

55. Storey DJ and Strange A (1992) Where are they now? some changes in firms located on UK science parks in 1986. *New Technology, Work and Employment* **7**, 15–28.

56. Tsipouri LJ (1991) The transfer of technology issue revisited: some evidence from Greece. *Entrepreneurship Reg. Dev.* **3**, 145–157.

57. van Dierdonck RV and Debackere K (1988) Academic entrepreneurship at Belgian universities. *R&D Mgmt* **18**, 341–353.

58. van Dierdonck RV, Debackere K and Rappa MA (1991) An assessment of science parks: towards a better understanding of their role in the diffusion of technological knowledge. *R&D Mgmt* **21**, 109–123.

59. Westhead P and Storey DJ (1994) *An Assessment of Firms Located On and Off Science Parks in the United Kingdom.* HMSO, London.

60. Westhead P, Storey DJ and Cowling M (1994) An exploratory analysis of the factors associated with the survival of independent high-technology firms in Great Britain. *Small Firms: Partnerships for Growth* (Edited by Chittenden F, Robertson M and Marshall I), pp. 63–99. Chapman, London.

ADDRESS FOR CORRESPONDENCE: *Paul Westhead, Centre for Small and Medium Sized Enterprises, Warwick Business School, The University of Warwick, Coventry CV4 7AL, UK.*

[11]

ELSEVIER

Research Policy 25 (1996) 325–335

research
policy

Assessing value-added contributions of university technology business incubators to tenant firms

Sarfraz A. Mian

School of Business, State University of New York, Oswego, NY 13126, USA

Final version received January 1995

Abstract

This paper assesses the value-added contributions of university technology business incubators (UTBIs) to their new technology-based tenant firms. The business incubator is widely believed as providing a nurturing environment for new business start-ups. However, the role played by university relationships in supporting the development of new technology-based firms (NTBFs) has escaped systematic review in the US due to a lack of historical data. To fill this gap, this article presents empirical data on UTBIs by focusing on their value-added dimensions which include typical incubator services along with university-related inputs. The study is based on a national survey of six representative UTBI facilities, providing an insight into the value-added aspects as perceived by the clients. It concludes that several UTBI services, specifically some of the university-related inputs such as university image, laboratories and equipment, and student employees add major values to the client firms, making the UTBI a viable strategy for nurturing NTBFs.

1. Introduction

The university technology business incubator (UTBI) is a modern enterprise development tool employed by some entrepreneurial universities to provide support for nurturing new technology-based firms (Mian, 1994a). The incubation concept seeks to link effectively talent, technology, capital and know-how to leverage entrepreneurial talent, accelerate the development of new companies, and thus speed the commercialization of technology (Smilor and Gill, 1986). Three major groups of elements have been identified as providing the infrastructure for supporting the development of new technology-based firms: business, technical, and social inputs (Miller and Marcel, 1987). The UTBI's efforts in providing these in-frastructure elements in the form of a variety of incubator services and other inputs from the surrounding university environment are aimed at providing a milieu for technological entrepreneurship (Bullock, 1985; Mian, 1994b).

The term value-added, employed in this paper, has become part of the lexicon of the technology business incubation industry, which corresponds to the provision of the aforementioned three major groups of elements sought for nurturing new technology-based ventures. In the incubator industry, value-added refers to those specific ways that an incubator program enhances the ability of its tenants to survive and grow in business (Allen and Bazan, 1990). To accomplish these firm survival and growth objectives a typical business incubator program provides shared office services

326   *S.A. Mian / Research Policy 25 (1996) 325–335*

and business assistance including affordable rent and fostering connections with firms inside the incubator and in the local economy. In the case of UTBIs, these value-added components are further supplemented by the provision of various university-related inputs such as university image, student employees, faculty consultants, and the institutional support provided by the R & D community in and around the university.

This article assesses university technology business incubators in the US by exploring their value-added contributions to technology-based start-ups. The study is based on six cases of UTBIs representing a population of 30 5-year

and older facilities in the US. The paper attempts to answer questions such as: What contributions do university incubators make to new technology-based start-ups in the form of various services provided? What additional benefits accrue from the university relationships? What are some of the implications for technology-based firms?

2. Relevant literature and study framework

With the popularity of the business incubation concept starting in the early 1980s, numerous

Table 1
University technology business incubator perspective: major studies

Author(s), year	Research sample	Study context	Key findings/contribution
Allen, 1985	70 incubators (UTBIs 15%, response 66%) 910 firms (response 56%)	Institute of Public Administration, Pennsylvania State University, University Park, PA and the US Department of Commerce, Washington DC	This study pointed out the potential of incubators for regional development. It helped to defined incubator organization types based on sponsorship, and service categories provided to the tenants. The concept of incubator was described as: a network of organizations providing skills, knowledge and motivation, real estate experience, provision of business and shared services
Smilor and Gill, 1986	117 incubators (UTBIs 10%, response 43%) 211 firms (response NA)	IC² Institute, University of Texas at Austin, TX	The findings of this research supported much of what was already known and provided new data about the age, education, and salary of incubator managers. Using the four incubator organization types identified earlier the study further identified their measures of success
Campbell et al., 1988	13 incubators (UTBIs 21%, case study) 294 firms (response 55%)	H. Humphrey Institute, University of Minnesota, Minneapolis, MN	In this case study, the features identified contributing to the incubator effectiveness were: low cost developing and operating; and quality management of facilities
Mian, 1991, 1994a	6 incubators (UTBIs 100%, case study) 150 firms (response 32%)	School of Business & public Management, George Washington University, Washington DC	As the first UTBI focused work, the study supported the assertion that university incubators appear to provide the resource base and environment conducive to the development of NTBFs. It provided a chicklist for successful facilities and developed an assessment framework for UTBIs
Rice, 1993	9 incubators (56% UTBIs, case study) 36 firms (selected)	School of Management, Renselaer Polytechnic Institute, Troy, NY	The study contended that managerial intervention is the key in incubation support, and success is measured by proactive direct intervention. Factors limiting the effectiveness of direct intervention were identified as the availability of time and lack of responsiveness of the firms

S.A. Mian / Research Policy 25 (1996) 325–335 327

studies have been conducted to assess the emerging incubator industry across the nation (Allen, 1985; Allen and Levine, 1986; Smilor and Gill, 1986; Campbell et al., 1988; Mian, 1991; Rice, 1993). Most of these studies are primarily descriptive, generally covering various types of incubator models. Table 1 provides a summary of the major studies including UTBI perspective. As shown, only a handful of the studies were comprehensive enough to include the role of university-related facilities in providing business incubation support. And with the exception of one study (Mian, 1991) none of the other studies specifically focused on the university technology incubator, generally understood to provide a resource base necessary for the development of new technology based firms (NTBFs) (Allen and Levine, 1986; Mian, 1991, 1994a,b)

From the incubation business literature reviewed (Allen, 1985; Allen and Levine, 1986; Smilor and Gill, 1986; Campbell et al., 1988; Mian, 1991; Rice, 1993) it is clear that most of the incubator-related knowledge does not have a sound theoretical base of its own and is by and large anecdotal in nature. Hence, our understanding of the business incubation function in general and the university-sponsored business in-cubation support for developing new technology-based firms, in particular, remains fairly rudimentary. Consequently, there is no consensus on what makes up the content of successful UTBI management practices in providing an optimal set of technology and business incubation services and how the value-added contributions of these services may be enhanced (Allen and Levine, 1986; Deutriaux, 1987).

The UTBIs' value-added dimensions employed in this research along with the authors who used these dimensions in various studies are summarized in Table 2. These dimensions are derived from parallel but separate incubator and university–industry interaction studies reported in the literature (Mian, 1991). As shown, there are two main categories of services: (a) typical incubator services which include shared office services, business assistance, access to capital, business networks, and rent breaks; and (b) the university-related services including faculty consultants, student employees, university image conveyance, library services, labs/workshops and equipment, mainframe computers, related R&D activity, technology transfer programs, employee education and training, and sports and other social activity. The determination of the provision

Table 2
Summary of the literature on value-added contributions of UTBI services

Contribution	Used by
Typical incubator services and their impact	
1. Shared office services	Allen and Rehman (1985), Smilor (1987), Hisrich and Smilor (1988)
2. Business assistance	Allen and Bazan (1990), Smilor (1987)
3. Access to capital	Plosila and Allen (1985), Smilor (1987)
4. Business networks	Smilor (1987), Lichtenstein (1992)
5. Rent breaks	Hisrich and Smilor (1988), Allen and Bazan (1990)
University-related services and their impact	
1. Faculty consultants	Allen and Levine (1986), Smilor et al. (1988), Udell (1990)
2. Student employees	Same as above
3. University image	Smilor (1987), Scheirer et al. (1985)
4. Library services	Smilor (1987), Allen and Levine (1986)
5. Labs and workshops	Brown (1985), Smilor (1977), Doutriaux (1987)
6. Mainframe computers	Bullock (1985), Hisrich and Smilor (1988)
7. Related R & D activity	Allen and Levine (1986), Smilor et al. (1988) Doutriaux (1987)
8. Technology transfer programs	Allen and Levine (1986), Smilor (1987), Hisrich and Smilor (1988), Abetti and Stuart (1985)
9. Employee education and training	Allen and Levine (1986), Hisrich and Smilor (1988), Udell (1990)
10. Sports and social activity	Allen and Levine (1986), Smilor (1987)

328   *S.A. Mian / Research Policy 25 (1996) 325–335*

Table 3

Selected UTBIs' background, institutional support, and their client firms' survey data

Incubator facility, sponsoring university (year established)	Facility background	Programs institutions providing R & D and other support services to client firms	No. of client firms contacted	No. of client firms responded
(1) Technology Advancement Program (TAP), University of Maryland – a state university (1984)	TAP rents 15 700 square feet² space to a group of 15 to 19 tenants at a rate of $7.5 foot⁻², which is about 30% less than the market rate	– Technology initiatives program – Maryland ind'l partnerships – Technology extension service – Dingman entrepr. center – Law and enterpr. program	25	10
(2) Advanced Technology Development Center (ATDC), Georgia Tech – a state university (1980)	ATDC rents 15 700 feet² space at its main facility on Georgia Tech campus, at a rate of $9.50 foot⁻², which is more than 30% cheaper than the market rate	– Georgia Tech res. inst. – Georgia Tech res. corp. – Manufacturing res. center – Industral extension service – Georgia capital network	37	9
(3) The Ben Craig Center (BCC), University of North Carolina at Charlotte – a state university (1986)	BCC's 87 000 feet² rentable space at its newly built facility is available at $10.50 foot⁻², which is slightly cheaper (0 to 15%) than the market rate	– Small business tech. dev. center – Univ. tech. transfer center – International bus. dev. program – Univ. res. park	17	8
(4) Technology Innovation Center (TIC), Northwestern University – a private university (1986)	TIC rents its 33 000 feet² of rentable space at its new facility at a rate of $14.75 foot⁻², which is market competitive	– Small bus. dev. corp. – Evanston bus. investment corp. – Basic ind'l research lab. – Basic ind'l research inst. – Inst of learning sciences	31	7
(5) Ben Franklin Technology, Incubator (BFTI), Lehigh University – a private university (1983)	BFTI rents 21 900 feet² of its rental space in four different buildings. The rental rates vary from $5.00 to $15.00 foot⁻². These rates are about 30% less than the market rate	– Technical assistance program – Business assistance program – Challenge grants program – Seed grants program – Univ. tech. transfer office	29	9
(6) Edison Technology Incubator (ETI), Case Western Reserve University – a private university (1984)	ETI rents 13 000 feet² of its space in its multistory building. The rental rate varies from $4.50 to $12.50 foot⁻². These rate are about from 15 to 30% less than the market rates	– Edison biotechnology center – Cleveland adv. manuf. program – University tech. trans. office – Marketing services associates	11	4
Total			150	47 (32%)

Table 4
Client firms' use and value-added contributions of incubator services (values in percent)

Incubator service/item	Reported frequency of use				Value added contribution				Rel. between use and value-added: correlation coefficient (significant?)
	Daily/ weekly	Monthly/ yearly	Only at inception	Never	No value	Minor value	Moderate value	Major value	
A. Shared office services									
1. Photocopier	83	5	10	2	2	10	35	53	0.31 (yes)
2. Telephone	61	3	9	27	14	7	31	48	0.76 (yes)
3. Facsimile (Fax)	66	13	8	13	11	8	34	47	0.66 (yes)
4. Conference room	40	50	7	3	3	15	37	45	0.47 (yes)
5. Security	83	0	3	14	9	13	38	40	0.55 (yes)
6. Receptionist	61	3	9	27	22	19	19	40	0.75 (yes)
7. Custodial/ maintenance	94	0	3	3	3	19	39	39	0.35 (yes)
8. Personal computer	47	14	14	25	26	3	39	32	0.76 (yes)
9. Shipping/receiving	46	20	8	26	18	27	24	31	0.68 (yes)
10. Mail sorting	72	0	3	25	10	30	33	27	0.48 (yes)
11. Word processing/ clerical	19	31	9	41	23	26	32	19	0.62 (yes)
12. Cafeteria/lunch room	57	0	4	39	33	11	48	8	0.17 (no)
B. Business assistance and networks									
1. Govt. grants and loans	9	32	12	47	38	14	10	38	0.68 (yes)
2. Business plan	0	39	28	33	12	21	35	32	0.56 (yes)
3. Legal/govt. regulations	3	40	6	51	28	30	14	28	0.20 (no)
4. Tax assistance	0	27	6	67	36	16	20	28	0.20 (no)
5. Accessing outside capital	5	34	16	45	40	24	9	27	0.46 (yes)
6. Marketing	5	35	11	49	32	19	23	26	0.64 (yes)
7. Accounting	3	33	11	53	26	35	16	23	0.39 (yes)
8. Personnel recruiting	3	38	9	50	35	35	15	15	0.24 (no)
9. Business connections outside the incubator	17	66	3	14	6	21	32	41	0.59 (yes)
10. Business connections between tenants	24	68	3	5	10	24	37	29	0.43 (yes)
11. Rent breaks	–	–	–	–	41	8	8	43	–

and tenant firms' perceived value-added contributions of these UTBI services forms the basis of this study.

This framework captures most of the key UTBI services described in the literature and is able to address the major aspects of the UTBI value-added dimensions. The following sections employ this framework to analyze the selected six cases.

3. Methodology and sample

In this study a multiple-case design with an embedded survey of the client firms was em-

ployed (Mian, 1991). For data collection on-site interviews were conducted with the incubator managers and their staff, and these were supplemented by information obtained through mail surveys administered to the client firms [1] of the following six selected UTBI cases:

● Technology Advancement Program (TAP),
● Advanced Technology Development Center (ATDC),
● The Ben Craig Center (BCC),

---

[1] Client firms include both tenant firms as well as graduate firms.

330 *S.A. Mian / Research Policy 25 (1996) 325–335*

Table 5
Client firms' use and value-added contributions of university-related services (values in percent)

University related service/item	Firm's degree of involvement in (or use of) services/items			Value added by each of these factors/items				Rel. between use and value added: (significance?)
	No involvement	Occasional involvement	High involvement	No value	Minor value	Moderate value	Major value	
1. University image	18	40	42	19	12	28	40	0.80 (yes)
2. Labs/workshops and equipment	40	38	22	33	16	18	33	0.85 (yes)
3. Student employees	15	53	32	13	20	35	32	0.76 (yes)
4. Faculty consultants	23	63	14	20	28	26	26	0.79 (yes)
5. Library resources	21	62	17	19	26	29	26	0.80 (yes)
6. Related R & D activity	55	30	15	49	9	20	22	0.92 (yes)
7. Education and training	80	18	2	69	9	13	9	0.73 (yes)
8. Tech. transfer programs	73	25	2	59	23	12	6	0.86 (yes)
9. Sports and social activities	68	22	10	56	29	9	6	0.87 (yes)
10. Mainframe computer	85	12	3	73	15	9	3	0.89 (yes)

● Technology Innovation Center (TIC),
● Ben Franklin Technology Incubator (BFTI),
● Edison Technology Incubator (ETI).

Table 3 provides a list of the six selected cases, their sponsoring universities, facility background, institutional support, and their client firms' survey data. As shown, the six UTBIs studied were chosen (from a sampling frame of 30) to represent programs which [2]: (a) were sponsored by a 'major' university in the US; (b) represented both public and private university types; (c) were generally viewed as successful or otherwise unique; (d) were at least 5 years old. Out of the total 150 client firms contacted 47 responded to the survey (a response rate of 32%). [3]

---

[2] Fourteen of the most highly respected experts in the field were interviewed personally during the annual professional conference (with extended telephone follow-ups). These experts were asked to verify the selection criteria and help identify a representative sample for the case study. Based on a summation of their responses a total of seven UTBI facilities were identified out of which six allowed access.
[3] Mail reminders, and help from the respective facility management was sought to encourage response without bias and selectivity. None the less, most of the non-respondents were found to be relatively newer tenants and were not dissimilar to the responding tenants in terms of industry type and/or size.

4. Provision of services and infrastructure support

University technology business incubators are multi-tenant buildings, in and around university campuses, which provide affordable, flexible space and a variety of typical incubator and university-related services for a select group of technology-based tenant firms.

Tables 4 and 5 (column one) list the type of services provided by the six UTBI facilities included in the survey. As shown in Table 4, essential shared office services were provided by almost all of the six facilities studied. Business assistance services were also generally available but with different arrangements. At ATDC, business and management consulting was provided by in-house consultants, while at BCC, TIC, BFTI, and ETI the services were available through resident private firms. No such formal arrangement was reported at TAP, where the incubator manager and the staff seemed to have assisted entrepreneurs in business/management problems.

Most of the typical university-related services were available at all the six facilities (Table 5). Access to a student labor pool, related R & D activity, technology transfer programs, mainframe computers, and library/information database fa-

S.A. Mian / Research Policy 25 (1996) 325–335 331

cilities were reported across the board. However, with the exception of TAP, access to the remaining services (see Table 5) was not equally emphasized.

Table 3 (column 3) depicts the institutional support system available to the clients in each of the six facilities surveyed. As shown, tenants from all six programs can take advantage of their respective university research and development activities including technology transfer programs, technology and business development assistance centers, and research institutes. Two of the land grant institutions, [4] that is, University of Maryland and Georgia Institute of Technology, have technology/industrial extension services which provide the necessary technology transfer environments. Both Georgia Institute of Technology and Northwestern University have established industrial research laboratories and institutes for contractual applied research. As for certain specialized areas, Northwestern University and Case Western Reserve University both have established biotechnology centers/institutes. Georgia Institute of Technology has recently established an information technology center. Only the Ben Craig Center at University of North Carolina at Charlotte has a focused international program to help develop US subsidies of foreign businesses.

5. Use and value-added contributions of the services

The individual case-by-case data on the UTBI services show considerable variation in the frequency of use and their client-perceived value-added contributions. [5] In this section the case-wide data is aggregated ($N = 47$) and analyzed as de-

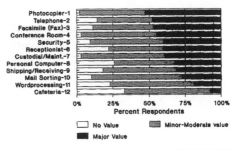

Fig. 1. Perceived value-added of shared office services.

picted in Tables 4 and 5. As shown, against each of the service, client reported frequency of use, the value-added contributions, and the relationship between these two variables are delineated. Furthermore, Figs. 1 to 3 provide details of the value-added contributions, which are rank ordered (in each figure) according to the percentage of respondents assigning major value-added contributions to each of the service reported. Table 4 shows the client firms' response data on typical incubator services which include 12 shared office services and 11 business assistance and network services including rent breaks.

In the shared office services category, the data show that a majority (more than 50%) of the

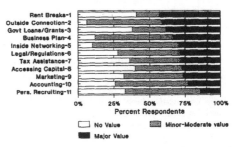

Fig. 2. Perceived value-added of business assistance/networking services.

---

[4] Land-grant institutions are American colleges and universities initially given federal aid in 1870s, especially by land grants, they are now supported by the individual states, with supplementary federal funds.
[5] Value-added contributions of the services provided were assessed through tenant's perceptions recorded on a 4-level scale, with 0 as no value-added, 1 as minor value-added, 2 as moderate value-added, and 3 as major value added.

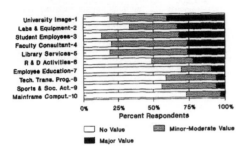

University Image-1
Labs & Equipment-2
Student Employees-3
Faculty Consultant-4
Library Services-5
R & D Activities-6
Employee Education-7
Tech. Trans. Prog.-8
Sports & Soc. Act.-9
Mainframe Comput.-10

0%   25%   50%   75%   100%
Percent Respondents

☐ No Value   ▨ Minor-Moderate Value
■ Major Value

Fig. 3. Perceived value-added of university-related services.

respondents reported using eight out of 12 services frequently (daily/weekly); these include: mail sorting (72%), photocopier (83%), receptionist (61%), facsimile/fax (66%), custodial maintenance (94%), cafeteria/lunch room (57%), security (83%), and telephone (61%). Infrequent use (monthly/yearly) of a conference room was reported by 50% of the respondents. For wordprocessing, 41% reported they never used this service, while 31% reported infrequent use (monthly/yearly). In the case of personal computer services 47% reported frequent use (daily/weekly) while 25% reported they never used this service. For shipping and receiving, 46% reported frequent use (daily/weekly) and 26% reported they never used the service. In sum, almost all of the services had some use, with the majority being used frequently. On the value-added side of the table, a majority (67% or more) of the respondents reported that all 12 services had some value-added contribution (minor to major) to their firms.

As shown in Fig. 1, the 12 shared office services were ranked in terms of the percentages of respondents assigning a major value to these services. The figure shows that nearly half of the respondents assigned a major value to photocopier, telephone, and fax services.

In the business assistance set of services depicted in Table 4 section B (1–8), a majority or near majority of the respondents (45% or more) replied that they never used seven out of the available eight services. In fact, only one service, i.e. business plan assistance was used at inception by 67% of the respondents. On the value-added side of the Table 4, a majority of the respondents assigned some value (minor or major) for all of the 11 services. This means that although they are not using these services, they do not consider them to be valueless. In business networking set of services (Section B9, 10), a majority of the respondents (66%–68%) reported monthly/yearly use of the assistance available in providing business connections among tenants and business connections outside the incubator. In rent breaks (Section B11), there was a major split between no value-added (41%) and major value-added (43%) responses. This seems obvious due to the fact that two out of six UTBIs (i.e. TIC and BCC) charged market competitive rents, while the remaining tend to subsidize rents.

As shown in Fig. 2, the 11 business assistance and other networking services are ranked in terms of the percentages of respondents assigning major values to these services. The figure shows that at least one quarter of the respondents assign a major value to nine out of the 11 services. These findings support the earlier work on the value-added contributions of Pennsylvania's business incubators (Allen and Bazan, 1990).

Similarly, the individual case-by-case data analyses on value-added contributions of university-related services show considerable variation in the frequency of use and the client-perceived value-added contribution. As stated earlier, here too the case-wide data was aggregated for the analysis. The results are shown in Table 5 which provide UTBI-wide data on the reported use and perceived value-added patterns of the university-related services ($N = 47$).

In terms of use, a majority (50% or more) of the respondents answered involvement/use (occasional to high) with five (out of ten) services frequently used, namely: student employees (85%), university image conveyance (82%), labs/workshops and sophisticated equipment (60%), library/information databases (79%), and faculty consultants (77%). No involvement was reported by 50% or more respondents in the remaining five service areas, namely: mainframe computers (85%), technology transfer programs (73%), employee education and training (80%), and sports and other social activity (68%).

In terms of value-added contributions (see Fig. 3) more than one half of the respondents assigned some value to six out of the ten university-related services. These findings generally support the earlier work on the university and technology-based firms linkages (Allen and Levine, 1986).

A review of the study results show that, while most of the above services were provided at each of the six facilities studied, their modes of delivery differed. There is insufficient data to suggest that any one of the modes is better than any other, and these different modes apparently suited to the individual UTBI needs.

6. Relationships between the frequency of use and value-added of the services

Tables 4 and 5 (last columns) list the strength of relationships between the frequency of use and the value-added contributions of the UTBI services, as indicated by the Pearson correlation coefficients.

As shown in Table 4, the measure of association between the frequency of use and value-added contributions show significant relationships (with Pearson correlation coefficients varying from 0.31 to 0.76) in 11 out of the 12 shared office services. The only exception is the cafeteria/lunch room service, where there is low positive relationship (Pearson correlation coefficient 0.17) which is not significant either.

In business assistance, relationships were significant (with Pearson correlation coefficient varying from 0.39 to 0.68) in five out of the eight services. Assistance in legal/government regulations, personnel recruiting, and tax matters did not show any significant association between their use and value-added contributions. In providing inside as well as outside business networks these associations were found significant (with Pearson correlation coefficient of 0.43 and 0.59, respectively).

In the case of university-related services the measures of association between the frequency of use and value-added contributions show a high positive relationship (with Pearson correlation coefficients varying from 0.73 to 0.92) in all of the ten university-related services. All these relationships were found significant. The highest relationship (0.92) was revealed in the use of related R & D activity, which means that if the client's business related R & D activities are in progress, then it becomes highly valuable for the client firm to locate in the UTBI and make use of the available knowledge. Same is true with respect to the remaining services where high positive relationships were found between the frequency of use and the values they add to the client firms. In sum, this analysis showed that the firms who needed and used these services valued them highly.

7. Summary and conclusion

The above findings indicate that the UTBI concept seems to provide a nurturing environment for the development of NTBFs through a combination of much needed university-related inputs and other typical incubator services. Furthermore, the vast majority of the respondents believed that the UTBI services they received were adding value to their fledgling firms. Thus, it can be concluded that the UTBI in the US does contribute to the growth and survival of their tenants making it a viable system for nurturing NTBFs. When compared with previous fragmented research findings (Allen and Levine, 1986; Allen and Bazan, 1990), these findings not only confirm that the incubators add value to their client firms, but go a step further to establish that UTBIs are specifically suitable for developing NTBFs.

In interpreting these conclusions on the client reported value-added contributions, there is, however, a need for caution. Some previous authors (Allen and Bazan, 1990) have commented on the generally modest perceptions of value-added components by incubator tenants saying that,

334 *S.A. Mian / Research Policy 25 (1996) 325–335*

"entrepreneurs are not a particularly appreciative group, and their high degree of autonomy and self-esteem shade their perceptions of how much they are really being helped". This further strengthens the findings.

In spite of the fact that the tenant response rate was only around one third and the plausibility that a majority of the respondents may have been 'successful' tenants, the overall conclusion would remain the same. Furthermore, the contributions reported here may not have fully accounted for some of the softer value-added aspects such as: (a) the psychological support the tenants draw from each other (Lichtenstein, 1992), (b) managerial interventions which may provide critical know-how and the sharing of entrepreneurial skills (Rice, 1993), and (c) miscellaneous other programs the UTBIs offer, for example, seminars and meetings and mentoring with local entrepreneurs etc.

From the NTBF entrepreneur's viewpoint, the implications of these findings are obvious. The UTBI's university linkage plays an important role in providing the infrastructure support necessary for nurturing their firms (Mian, 1994b). From the university point of view, the UTBIs' contributions in their work with university-related clients (faculty, students, and alumni) is equally important in developing entrepreneurs from within at the same time enhancing the prospects for university technology commercialization (Abetti and Sheart, 1985; Doutriaux, 1987).

In a broader sense, what makes the UTBI's value-added contributions justifiable from a university policy perspective is the continuing evidence that an entrepreneurial university is broadening its mission in addressing the technology-based economic development needs of their regions. While this preliminary effort has provided useful insights into the value added contributions of UTBIs, several challenges remain. To make the UTBI tool more attractive to the entrepreneurial university, perhaps more self-sustainable models will have to be developed. Additionally, from entrepreneur's point of view the relative merits of the UTBI compared to the classic intrapreneurial model for new venture creation, or the traditional independent NTBF de-

velopment mode need to be probed. These areas including a better accounting of the aforementioned softer value-added components need further research.

References

Abetti, P. and R. Stuart, 1985, Entrepreneurship and technology transfer: key factors in the innovation process, in: D.L. Sexton and R.W. Smilor (Editors), The Art and Science of Entrepreneurship (Ballinger Publishers, Cambridge, MA).

Allen, D., 1985, Small business incubators and enterprise development, report prepared for the US Department of Commerce (Pennsylvania State University, University Park, PA).

Allen, D. and E. Bazan, 1990, Value-added contribution of pennsylvania's business incubators to tenant firms and local economies, report prepared for Pennsylvania Department of Commerce (Pennsylvania State University, University Park, PA).

Allen, D. and V. Levine, 1986, Nurturing advanced technology enterprises: emerging issues in state and local economic development policy (Prager, New York).

Allen, D. and S. Rehman, 1985, Small business incubators: a positive environment for entrepreneurship, Journal of Small Business Management (July), 12–24.

Brown, W., 1985, A proposed mechanism for commercializing university technology, Technovation 3, 19–25.

Bullock, M., 1985, Cohabitation: small research-based companies and the universities, Technovation 3, 27–38.

Campbell, C., D. Berge, J. Janus and K. Olsen, 1988, Change Agents in the New Economy: Business Incubators and Economic Development (University of Minnesota, Minneapolis, MN).

Coopers, A., 1985, The role of incubator organizations in the founding of growth oriented firms, Journal of Business Venturing 1, 75–86.

Doutriaux, J., 1987, Growth patterns of academic entrepreneurial firms, Journal of Business Venturing 2, 285–297.

Hisrich, R. and R. Smilor, 1988, The university and business incubation: technology transfer through entrepreneurial development, Technology Transfer (fall), 14–19.

Lichtenstein, G., 1992, The significance of relationships in entrepreneurial development: a case study of the ecology of enterprise in two business incubators, unpublished dissertation (University of Pennsylvania, PA).

McMullan, W., W. Long and J. Graham, 1986, Assessing economic value-added by university-based outreach programs, Journal of Business Venturing (spring), 225–240.

Mian, S., 1991, An assessment of university-sponsored business incubators in supporting the development of new technology-based firms, unpublished doctoral dissertation (The George Washington University, Washington, DC).

Mian, S., 1994a, U.S. university-sponsored technology incubators: an overview of management, policies, and performance, Technovation 14, 515–528.

Mian, S. 1994b, Are university technology incubators providing a milieu for technology-based entrepreneurship? Technology Management 1, 86–93.

Miller, R. and C. Marcel, 1987, Growing the Next Silicon Valley, (Lexington Books, Lexington, MA).

Plosila, W. and D. Allen, 1985, Small business incubators and public policy: implications for states and local development strategies, Policy Studies Journal 13, 729–734.

National Business Incubation Association, 1992, The State of the Business Incubation Industry – 1991 (NBIA, Athens, OH).

Rice, M., 1993, Intervention mechanisms used to influence the critical success of new ventures: an exploratory study, unpublished doctoral dissertation (Renssalaer Polytechnic Institute, Troy, NY).

Scheirer, M.A., V. Nieva, G. Gaetner, P. Newman and V. Ramsey, 1985, Innovation and enterprise: a study of NSF's innovation centers program, report prepared for the National Science Foundation (Washington, DC).

Smilor, R., 1987, Managing the incubator system: critical success factors to accelerate new company development, IEEE Transactions on Engineering Management 34(3), 146–155.

Smilor, R. and M.Gill, 1986, The New Business Incubator: Linking Talent, Technology and Know-How (Lexington Books, Lexington, MA).

Smilor, R., W. Kozmetsky and D. Gibson (Editors), 1988, Creating the Technopolis (Ballinger Publishing, Cambridge, MA).

Udell, G., 1990, Academe and the goose that lays its golden eggs, Business Horizon (Mar–Apr), 29–37.

[12]

ELSEVIER

Research Policy 31 (2002) 1103–1122

www.elsevier.com/locate/econbase

How effective are technology incubators?
Evidence from Italy

Massimo G. Colombo*, Marco Delmastro

Università di Pavia, Dip. Informatica e Sistemistica, Via Ferrata 1, 27100 Pavia, CIRET-Politecnico di Milano, Pza Leonardo da Vinci 32, 20133 Milan, Italy

Received 25 January 2001 ; received in revised form 14 March 2001 ; accepted 12 October 2001

Abstract

In spite of the diffusion of science parks in Europe, it is still unclear whether they have been successful in fostering the establishment and growth of new technology-based firms (NTBFs). This paper aims to contribute to answer such question. For this purpose, a sample composed of 45 Italian NTBFs which at the beginning of 2000 were located on technology incubator within a park is compared with a control sample of off-incubator firms. Aspects considered in the study include the personal characteristics of founders of NTBFs, the motivations of the self-employment choice, the growth and innovative performances of firms, propensity towards networking, and access to public subsidies. In the comparison, we use a larger set of indicators than in previous studies. The empirical results confirm the conventional wisdom that input and output measures of innovative activity are only marginally different between on- and off-incubator firms. Nonetheless, they also show that Italian parks managed to attract entrepreneurs with better human capital, as measured by educational attainments and prior working experience. In addition, on-incubator firms show higher growth rates than their off-incubator counterparts. They also perform better in terms of adoption of advanced technologies, aptitude to participating in international R&D programs, and establishment of collaborative arrangements, especially with universities. Lastly, they find it easier to get access to public subsidies. Altogether, such findings support the view that science parks are an important element of a technology policy in favor of NTBFs. This holds true especially in a country like Italy which is characterized by a rather weak national innovation system. © 2002 Elsevier Science B.V. All rights reserved.

JEL classification: J23; L86; L63

Keywords: NTBFs; Science parks; University industry relations

1. Introduction

It is common wisdom among policy makers that a dynamic new technology-based firm (NTBF) sector is a key element to assure innovation and creation of new jobs in the economic system. It is also widely accepted that NTBFs face greater obstacles than other firms, and so deserve support from governmental institutions.

The economic literature has provided two rationales for such view.

Firstly, it is claimed that there are severe market failures that prevent NTBFs from fair access to key inputs. Such reasoning especially applies to finance. It is argued that banks generally lack the technical expertise required to assess the quality of a new business in a high-technology sector, whereas new firms do not have track records on which banks may base their lending decisions. In addition, banks may simply perceive the projects of high-technology en-

* Corresponding author.
E-mail address: massimo.colombo@polimi.it (M.G. Colombo).

1104 *M.G. Colombo, M. Delmastro/Research Policy 31 (2002) 1103–1122*

trepreneurs as too risky (Hall, 1989; Storey, 1994; Oakey, 1995). Therefore, new firms suffer from credit rationing (Stiglitz and Weiss, 1981); the presence of other financial intermediaries that are more sensitive to the requirements of NTBFs such as venture capital firms, is not sufficient to close the gap. A number of empirical studies have provided evidence consistent with the argument that capital market constraints negatively affect the behavior of entrepreneurs. First of all, the likelihood of entering self-employment is shown to increase with the net worth of an individual and his family (see Evans and Jovanovic, 1989; Evans and Leighton, 1989). Furthermore, changes over time of founders' net worth, for instance due to receipt of an inheritance (Holtz-Eakin et al., 1994a,b) or to a rise of the value of housing equity (Black et al., 1996), are found to influence new business formation, the amount of capital committed by founders to the new ventures, and business survival. Nonetheless, other studies question the robustness of such results. Cressy (1996) suggests that the correlation between survival and financial capital may be spurious; as assets are explained by human capital, the observed correlation may be indicative of the human capital deficiencies of unsuccessful entrepreneurs rather than of failures of capital markets. According to data provided by Levenson and Willard (2000) on small business in the USA in the 1980s, the extent of credit rationing appears to be fairly limited, even though smaller, younger firms are relatively more constrained.[1]

Secondly, a strong case for public support to NTBFs hinges on the peculiar role they play in promoting dynamism in advanced economies. Advocates of public intervention in favor of NTBFs point out that such firms often are a source of radical innovations based on unconventional technical approaches.

Such innovations challenge existing technological paradigms dominated by large, established industry leaders, and have the potential of revolutionizing industries, opening up new industry segments. As the benefits to society arising from the innovative activity of NTBFs largely exceed those that can be appropriated by them, such positive externality justifies governmental support (see for instance Oakey, 1995).

It is important to emphasize that the view that NTBFs deserve favorable treatment by governments is not unanimously shared by the economic profession. While reviewing standard efficiency and equity criteria for the provision of public support to small business and entrepreneurial firms, Holtz-Eakin (2001) casts serious doubts on the presence of positive externalities and capital market imperfections that may justify such supporting measures. In addition, Jovanonic's (1982) seminal paper highlights that the creation of a new firm may be the result of the subjective erroneous evaluation by the founder of his(her) own capabilities. In Jovanovic's model, new firms entering the market do not exactly know their level of efficiency; they learn it over time observing the profits they make, with competition leading to exit of inefficient firms. It follows that a technology policy that indiscriminately protects NTBFs may slow down the selection effect of market competition, thus negatively affecting economic efficiency. Such effect may be amplified if overconfidence leads to excess of entry on the part of "unfitted" individuals who mistakenly opt for the self-employment choice (see Camerer and Lovallo, 1999); this is likely to happen above all in the early stages of the life cycle of a new industry (see for instance Colombo and Delmastro, 2001).

In spite of the controversial nature of governmental intervention in this domain, in Europe, a series of policy measures based on a variety of schemes has been adopted by national governments and the EC to create a supportive environment for NTBFs (see Storey and Tether, 1998). At the same time, such measures have often been considered as a means to revitalize depressed or declining European regions through the development of new high-technology ventures. Among such schemes, a prominent role has been played by the creation of science parks (SPs) and business innovation centers (BICs). In general terms, these can be defined as property-based initiatives, aimed at supporting innovative firms through the provision of

---

[1] Market failures may also relate to other inputs to the activity of NTBFs. In particular, NTBFs generally face difficulties in acquiring the services of external consultants in fields such as technology, business strategy, staff recruiting, marketing, advertising, public relations, and administrative and legal affairs. From the one side search costs including the opportunity cost of entrepreneurs' time, are deemed excessive by small young firms in comparison with expected benefits. From the other side, consultant firms often lack focus on the special requirements of NTBFs. Note, however, that the above mentioned difficulties largely remain speculative. For instance, Robson and Bennet (2001) document that recourse to external advice is now rather widespread among UK small and medium enterprises.

M.G. Colombo, M. Delmastro / Research Policy 31 (2002) 1103–1122   1105

logistic, technological and other business services. More specifically, the presence within a park of a technology incubator is regarded as a crucial factor to nurture the formation and growth of NTBFs.[2]

European parks have often been established through a partnership between national and local governmental institutions, private firms and local universities, and were intended to replicate earlier US success stories.[3] Since the early initiatives in the late 1960s and early 1970s,[4] their number has been growing rapidly in the 1980s and 1990s in all European countries (see again OECD, 1997; Storey and Tether, 1998). The rationale for their creation can be synthesized as follows (Massey et al., 1992; Quintas et al., 1992; Westhead and Storey, 1994, 1995; Westhead, 1997; Westhead and Batstone, 1998; Storey and Tether, 1998). First of all, proximity to university laboratories and other research centers provides firms located on park with easier access to scientific expertise and research results, thus, facilitating transfer of research into commercial applications.[5] Such argument relies on evidence that in the US, spillovers from university research has favored the innovative activity of local firms. Jaffe (1989) and Acs et al. (1992), using patent and innovation count data, respectively show that there is a positive correlation at the state level between innovative activity and university research, especially when university and industrial research activity within a state are closely located. Acs et al. (1994) find that such spillover effects are more pronounced for small

firms. Secondly, the existence of a technology incubator makes it easier for academic personnel to exploit knowledge-based business ideas, thus lowering the barriers that inhibit direct commercial application of the results of university research.[6] Furthermore, park firms benefit from agglomeration economies, due to the fact that numerous high-technology enterprises are clustered in a relatively small area, especially if they operate in the same sector (or in closely connected sectors). The networking opportunities of tenant firms are also widened, basically for the same reason. Lastly, the park acts as a bridging institution providing tenant firms with suitable accommodations on flexible terms and technical and business services which are particularly valuable to new high-growth enterprises. Nonetheless, some authors are critical of the effectiveness of parks. For instance, Macdonald (1987) suggests that the premise that high-technology firms gain competitive advantage through location alongside a university because of the information flows from the university, is flawed. He also questions the existence of the agglomeration economies permitted by on-park location.

Indeed, in spite of the diffusion of parks in Europe, whether they have been successful or not in supporting NTBFs still is unclear. One of the problem is the lack of large scale longitudinal empirical evidence on the characteristics and performances of incubated firms, with the partial exception of the UK.[7] In addition, the few studies which have compared on- and off-park firms through the analysis of matched pairs sample have provided mixed results. First, as concerns input and output innovative measures, there is no clear evidence that independent park firms outperform comparable firms located off park. In an early study of UK firms, Monck et al. (1988) find that the percentage of qualified scientists and engineers out of the total workforce and the R&D intensity, measured by the ratio of R&D expenses to sales, of tenant firms were higher than those of firms in a control sample; however, such results are not replicated in a later study (Westhead, 1997), which finds such differences to be statistically insignificant. Similarly, no

---

[2] In this section, the term "park" will be used to refer indistinctly to both SPs and BICs. A more precise definition and a discussion of the differences between such two kinds of initiatives are postponed to Section 2. A "business incubator" is generally defined as a property-based venture which provides entrepreneurs and start-ups with physical facilities and technical and business services (see OECD, 1997). A "technology incubator" is a business incubator specifically oriented towards NTBFs.

[3] The first US parks (the Stanford Research Park around Stanford University and the Research Triangle Park in North Carolina) were established during the 1950s (in 1951 and 1959, respectively). By the mid 1990s, firms located on them had about 60,000 employees (see Storey and Tether, 1998).

[4] The Sophia Antipolis park, in Southern France, was created in 1969, while the establishment of the Cambridge Science Park and the Heriot–Watt Park in the UK dates back to 1972.

[5] The above reasoning applies in particular to parks that in addition to university research laboratories, are able to attract other knowledge intensive units, such as the research laboratories of established firms not otherwise connected with the park.

[6] Strictly speaking, this argument only holds true for parks that develop a close collaborative linkage with an academic institution.

[7] Such lack of robust empirical findings extends to the US. For evidence of the effectiveness of US technology incubators based on case studies of "success stories", see Mian (1996).

1106 *M.G. Colombo, M. Delmastro / Research Policy 31 (2002) 1103–1122*

statistically significant difference emerges between on- and off-park firms as to the number of patents and copyrights (see also Westhead and Storey, 1994). Nor tenant firms outperform firms located off-park as regards the number of new products and services launched to both existing customers and new markets (Westhead, 1997). Conversely, Westhead and Storey (1994) show that over the period 1986–1992, UK independent park firms had consistently higher growth rates than their off-park counterparts. Their results also indicate that parks were able to attract more qualified entrepreneurs. Lastly, whether the establishment of parks contributes to close the gap between NTBFs and the scientific community also is questionable. On the one hand, the available evidence supports the view that in the UK, linkages with academic institutions are more robust for tenant firms than for other firms, with all else being equal. On the other, a closer look at the nature of such linkages shows that they mainly are of informal or practical nature. In particular, there is a remarkable similarity between on- and off-park firms as to the extent of the employment of academic personnel, the sponsorship of research contracts, the use of test and analysis services provided by universities, the employment of graduates, and the launch of student projects. The only notable difference is the larger number of tenant firms that mention having informal contacts with academic personnel and having made use of university facilities such as computers, libraries, and conference premises (see Monck et al., 1988; Quintas et al., 1992; Westhead and Storey, 1994, 1995. Along the same lines see the studies by Felsenstein, 1994 on Israeli SPs and Von Dierdonck et al., 1991 on Belgian and Dutch SPs).

The aim of the present paper is to contribute to ascertain the added value to NTBFs of location on a park's technology incubator. For this purpose, we compare a sample of 45 Italian independent NTBFs that at the beginning of 2000 were located on technology incubator with a matched sample of 45 similar off-incubator firms. All the firms considered were established after 1980 and operate in one of the following sectors: aerospace, biotechnology, pharmaceuticals, electronics, computers, software, Internet services, and multimedia content.[8] The study tries to

extend the above mentioned empirical literature in three respects. First, we explicitly focus on independent NTBFs. Second, we consider a more comprehensive set of indicators than previous studies. In particular, we compare on- and off-incubator firms according to:

- the characteristics of their founders, in terms of educational background, prior working experience, and motivations of the entrepreneurial choice;
- the growth and innovative performances of firms, and their propensity towards networking: again with respect to earlier work we use a wider set of indicators, including adoption of new technologies and establishment of formal collaborative relations with other institutions (both universities and business firms);
- the access to external financing in the form of public subsidies.

Third, for the first time extensive coverage is provided of the park movement in Italy, and of the characteristics of Italian incubated firms.[9] In our opinion, this is an important addition to the literature on this issue. In fact, Italy is a very interesting case. On the one hand, propensity towards enterprenneurship is especially high in Italy (see for instance Blanchflower and Oswald, 1999) and small firms account for a disproportionately high share of total employment.[10] On the other hand, Italy exhibits a poor performance in high-technology industries, with the ratio of research expenditures to GNP being close to 1%, that is less than half the value of France, Germany, the UK and other northern European countries. Creation of new enterprises is heavily concentrated in low-technology mature sectors. In addition, as has been highlighted elsewhere by the authors (see Colombo and Delmastro, 2001), the characteristics of Italian NTBFs

---

[8] Note that all park firms in our sample either were born on park or moved to the park location in the very early stage of their life.

[9] To our knowledge, systematic evidence on Italian parks is almost absent. For an initial attempt to address such issue, see Cesaroni and Gambardella (1998).

[10] In 1992, in Italy manufacturing firms with less than 20 employees accounted for 38.7% of employment in manufacturing, a value that is five times as large as that of the US and about three times as large as that of France, Germany and the UK (see OECD, 1998, pp. 10–12; data are from the OECD SME database and Eurostat). As regards total employment in Italy (i.e. employment in agriculture, manufacturing and services), in 1996, the share of firms with less than 20 employees was 58%; that of firms with less than 10 employees was 47% (see Istat, 1996).

M.G. Colombo, M. Delmastro/Research Policy 31 (2002) 1103–1122   1107

differ substantially from the pattern prevailing in the above-mentioned European countries, with Italian high-technology entrepreneurs being less educated and having less prior sector-specific working experience than their European counterparts. As was pointed out above, the establishment of parks and technology incubators aims to deal with market failures relating to knowledge and other inputs of the innovative process (i.e. technical and business services, including real estate services; access to external financing) which negatively influence the formation of NTBFs and their post-entry performances. Accordingly, such initiatives are expected to play a relatively more important role in those situations where such market failures are more pronounced. This is more likely to be the case of Italy, which is characterized by a rather inefficient national innovation system (see for instance Malerba, 1993), than of other technologically more advanced European countries, where the supply of such inputs to NTBFs is relatively more developed.

The remaining of the paper is organized as follows. In Section 2, the characteristics of Italian SPs and BICs are briefly described. In Section 3, the methodology of the field analysis of NTBFs incubated on-park is presented. The empirical evidence on such firms is illustrated in Section 4, which is devoted to the characteristics of firms' founders, and Section 5, which analyzes the growth and innovative performances of firms, their propensity towards networking, and their ability to obtain public subsidies. A discussion of the results, highlighting implications for technology policy in Section 6 concludes the paper.

2. Science parks and business innovation centers in Italy

We define a "science park" as a property-based initiative which (i) has formal operational links with centers of knowledge creation, such as universities and (public and/or private) research centers, (ii) is designed to encourage the formation and growth of innovative (generally science-based) businesses, and (iii) has a management function which is actively engaged in the transfer of technology and business skills to "customer" organizations.[11] Characteristics that

are generally associated with a SP are the presence of a business incubator and the localization on site of research laboratories, that may belong to the park, to partner (academic or non-academic) institutions, to other non-profit organizations, or to business firms. At the end of 1999, there were 17 SPs in Italy that matched the above definition.[12]

The notion of "business innovation center" is linked to the set-up by the EC, through the DG XVI, in 1984 of the European Business Innovation Network, with the aim of supporting innovation and the creation of new firms, especially in depressed European regions. In spite of the lack of a precise definition, a BIC shares most of the key characteristics of a SP. It is a property-based venture for the establishment and growth of firms, provides customer firms with technical and business services, and is aimed at strengthening the networking capabilities of firms, promoting the establishment of cooperative relations among them and between these and research institutions. However, a BIC differs from a SP in two important aspects. First, it is less focused on innovation and science-based activities, with relatively greater attention being devoted to the creation of new firms in low-technology sectors. Second, the linkage with academic and research institutions is generally weaker than in a SP (or even absent). Our survey found 24 BICs in Italy.

In January 2000, a questionnaire was mailed to the 17 SPs and 24 BICs. The questionnaire was followed by interviews by phone or on a face-to-face basis with SPs' and BICs' management. The requested information concerned the year of establishment and a number of characteristics describing the organization of the initiative and the activities performed. The results of the survey are briefly summarized in the next

---

[11] Such definition corresponds quite closely with the one adopted by the UK Science Park Association for eligibility to join the

association (see UKSPA, 1998). In the literature, a distinction is sometimes made between science parks and technology parks, the main difference being the larger size of these latter (see for instance OECD, 1997). For the purpose of the present paper, such difference can be neglected. Note also that in accordance with the above definition, the activities of a SP are mainly, but not exclusively oriented towards firms that operate in high-technology industries.

[12] Actually, the number of members of the Italian Association of Scientific and Technological Parks (APSTI) was higher (24). However, some members were excluded either because they had no building space and physical facilities (i.e. they were "virtual" parks) or because they had no formal operational link with a knowledge creating institution.

1108 *M.G. Colombo, M. Delmastro/Research Policy 31 (2002) 1103–1122*

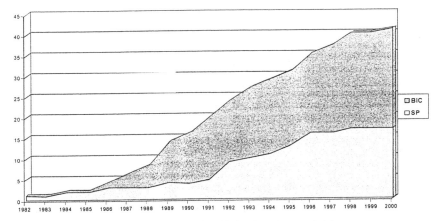

Fig. 1. Number of science parks and business innovation centers in Italy.

two sections, devoted to SPs and BICs, respectively. SPs and BICs also provided the list of companies that (i) at the beginning of 2000 were located on site, and (ii) were in a high-technology industry.[13] We will come back to this list in Section 3.

Fig. 1 shows the evolution over time of the number of Italian SPs and BICs. In comparison with other European countries, Italy has been a laggard in the development of such initiatives. The first Italian SP, the Area science park in Trieste, was created in 1982. Furthermore, the SP movement did not take off until the early 1990s: between 1990 and 1995 the number of SPs rose from 4 to 13, and then continued to grow though at a much lower rate. In spite of a later start (in 1986), the number of BICs grew more rapidly: at the end of the 1980s, there already were 10 of them. Growth continued at fast rate in the first half of the 1990s and leveled off in the second half. As concerns the localization of Italian SPs and BICs, 59% of the former, but only 39% of the latter are situated in northern regions. The higher percentage of BICs in central and southern regions is in line with the view according to which such initiatives are instrumental

to the restructuring and rejuvenation of disadvantaged regions.[14]

2.1. The characteristics of Italian Science Parks

There is considerable heterogeneity across Italian SPs as to characteristics such as their size, the nature of the activities performed, and the ability to attract external knowledge-intensive units. In general, the size of Italian SPs is rather small. Altogether, at the beginning of 2000 in the 17 surveyed parks, there were 364 tenant organizations with 4021 employees. Out of these, 198 were independent firms with 1794 employees (see Table 1). There also were 144 research laboratories, almost equally subdivided between the "privately owned", "State-owned"[15] and "park-owned" categories. The four largest parks (the Area science park in Trieste, the RAF science park in Milan, the VEGA park in Venise, and the Environment park in Turin) accounted for more than 50% of the

---

[13] Remember that according to the definition adopted in this work, high-tech industries include the following ones: aerospace, biotechnology, pharmaceuticals, electronics, computers, software, Internet services, and multimedia content.

[14] The greater availability of subsidies from the national government (laws 46/82, 64/86, 181/89, 488/92) and the EC (through the European Structural Funds and the European Social Fund) in Central and Southern Italy has obviously influenced the localization of SPs and BICs.

[15] The "State-owned" category also includes research labs owned by non for profit organizations such as research foundations.

M.G. Colombo, M. Delmastro / *Research Policy 31 (2002) 1103–1122*

Table 1
Tenant organizations on Italian Science Parks and Business Innovation Centers at the beginning of 2000

	Science parks				Business innovation centers			
	Units		Employees		Units		Employees	
	Numbers	%	Numbers	%	Numbers	%	Numbers	%
Independent firms	198	54.4	1794	44.6	390	91.8	2536	89.4
Subsidiaries	22	6.0	189	4.7	31	7.3	283	10.0
Private research laboratories	47	12.9	811	20.2	1	0.2	5	0.2
Public research laboratories[a]	55	15.1	843	21.0	2	0.5	10	0.4
Park-owned research laboratories	42	11.5	384	9.5	1	0.2	4	0.1
Total	364	100.0	4021	100.0	425	100.0	2838	100.0

[a] This category also includes research laboratories owned by non for profit research organizations.

total number of tenant companies. Concentration was even higher in terms of number of employees of tenant companies, with the two largest parks accounting for 50% of total employment. In addition, if one focuses attention on independent companies, only 57.5% of them turned out to be in a high-technology sector[16] and about 25% were in high-technology services (software, Internet services, and multimedia content). Note also that in general, Italian SPs have a rather small internal staff; if one neglects two outliers (Tecnopolis in Bari and Pastis-CNRSM in Brindisi, which altogether have 315 employees), the average number of direct employees in the remaining 15 parks is below 20 units. However, there were 314 external consultants collaborating with the parks on a regular basis. To sum up, the Italian SP movement is less developed and Italian SPs are much smaller than those of other European countries.[17]

Furthermore, there is great heterogeneity as regards the nature of the activities performed by Italian SPs and their ability to attract external research ventures. From this standpoint, a distinction can be made between SPs that have internalized to a substantial extent the R&D function, and are thus equipped with an internal R&D staff, and other parks which prevalently emphasize coordination of external (that is, nonpark-owned) knowledge-intensive activities. Actually, while more than half of parks' direct employees were in R&D, seven parks possessed no R&D facilities; moreover, three parks (Tecnopolis, Abruzzo science park and Pastis) accounted for about 75% of parks' R&D employees. As regards external R&D laboratories, 82 out of the 102 surveyed were situated in two parks (Area and RAF science parks); both such parks had very limited direct involvement in R&D activities.

Lastly, it is quite interesting to analyze the nature of the services provided by the surveyed parks. While all SPs provide services of scientific and/or technical nature (R&D support, technology transfer, promotion of technological collaborations) and most of them provide professional training, quite surprisingly less than 50% provide financial services. The same applies to marketing and other commercial services, while the figure is even lower for administrative and legal services (18%).

2.2. The characteristics of Italian Business Innovation Centers

The characteristics of Italian BICs are relatively more uniform than those of SPs. At the beginning of

---

[16] The fact that a non-negligible number of independent tenant firms is in low-tech sectors does not violate the definition of SPs given above. In fact, in all SPs emphasis is placed on innovative activities, be they in high- or low-tech sectors. In addition, informal discussion with parks' managers suggested that their attention is catalyzed by high-tech activities.

[17] For instance, according to data provided by the UKSPA, in the UK in 1997, the number of tenant organizations amounted to 1414, with 27,371 employees; out of these 61% were independent companies, while the remaining ones were subsidiaries of other firms (32%), units of high education institutions (3%), and non for profit organizations (4%) (see UKSPA, 1998). In France, in 1995, there were 7160 firms located on park, employing a workforce of 145,834 units. The 4381 firms with more than 65,000 employees, were situated in the four largest parks—Sophia Antipolis, Tetrapole Grenoble, Nancy Brabols Innovation, and Villeneuve d'Ascq (see Storey and Tether, 1998).

2000, we found 425 organizations located on BIC, with only 2838 employees. The large majority (390 units with 2536 employees) were independent firms. Only 30% of them were in a high-technology sector. As it was the case for SPs, out of these latter a conspicuous number was in services. We only surveyed four research laboratories, of which only one was owned by a BIC. Italian BICs generally have a very agile organization, with a small number of employees. Altogether, at survey time the 24 BICs had 290 employees and 358 external consultants. These findings witness the large recourse to service outsourcing on the part of Italian BICs, with emphasis being placed on the coordination of activities and services performed by third parties. They also show that in comparison with SPs, BICs are less focused on innovation-led activities and the knowledge creating stages of the corporate value chain.

That BICs are less oriented towards R&D and technology intensive activities is also evident if one considers the services they provide. Actually, 78.3% of BICs provides professional training, 78.3% marketing and other commercial services, and 65.2% internationalization support services. Administrative and legal, financial advisory and fund search services are also more frequent than is the case for SPs: they are provided by 52.2, 69.6 and 56.5% of BICs, respectively. On the contrary, BICs providing scientific and technical services are less numerous than SPs: 52.2% of BICs is involved in technology transfer activities and only 39.1% in R&D services.

3. Methodology of the field analysis on firms located on a technology incubator

The main objective of this paper is to provide original empirical evidence on how effective are Italian technology incubators that are situated within SPs and BICs. For this purpose, we compare along a series of dimensions which will be defined in detail later, a sample of independent NTBFs which were incubated on a SP or a BIC with a similar sample composed of off-incubator firms. The starting point for the analysis was the list of independent high-technology firms which at the beginning of 2000 were located on a SP or a BIC (see Section 2). Such list comprised 232 enterprises.

A questionnaire was mailed to such firms inquiring about their characteristics and those of their founders, their growth and innovative performances, the cooperative agreements they established, and whether they got public subsidies. In particular, firms were asked to provide the following information:

- year of establishment of the firm;
- number of employees at start-up and at the end of 1999;
- whether the firm was a corporate spin-off[18] or not;
- measures of innovative activity: these include traditional input and output measures (number of researchers out of the total workforce in 1999, patents and copyrights granted to the firm in the period 1996–1999). We also measured the skill level of the workforce by the number of graduates out of the total 1999 workforce. In addition, we considered whether the firm had adopted advanced information and communication technologies by 1999, a dimension of innovative activity that has been neglected by previous studies on this issue, and indicators of access to external knowledge resources (i.e. participation in R&D programs promoted by the EC, purchase of the R&D services of universities and research centers);
- measures of relational capabilities: establishment of formal collaborative agreements with other firms and universities, and nature of the agreements concluded;
- whether the firm obtained public subsidies in the course of its life;
- age of each founder, educational attainments, main motivation of the self-employment choice, and nature of the previous working experience in terms of functional activity (R&D, production, sale, etc.), hierarchical position, and characteristics of the firm (or other organization) by which he was employed before becoming an entrepreneur.

The questionnaire was followed by direct and/or phone interviews with firms' owner-managers conducted by instructed personnel. The aim of the interviews was to complete the questionnaire (if necessary),

---

[18] In this study a "corporate spin-off" is defined as a newly created independent company which at start-up time, benefited from tangible and/or intangible assets (physical equipment, brand, know how) provided by an established firm (the "mother" firm).

M.G. Colombo, M. Delmastro / Research Policy 31 (2002) 1103–1122   1111

Table 2
Industry and geographical composition of NTBFs on and off technology incubator

	On-incubator		Off-incubator	
	Numbers	%	Numbers	%
Sector of operation				
Aerospace	2	4	2	4
Biotechnology and pharmaceuticals	7	16	7	16
Electronics	8	18	8	18
Computers	2	4	2	4
Internet (ISP, e-commerce)	12	27	12	27
Software	12	27	12	27
Multimedia content	2	4	2	4
Total sample	45	100	45	100
Area of firm's localization				
North	35	78	35	78
Center/south	10	22	10	22
Total sample	45	100	45	100

and to verify the accurateness of the answers. We obtained back 45 valid fully filled questionnaires concerning firms that had been established after 1980. Out of the 45 incubated NTBFs included in the sample, 26 are in services (software, Internet services, and multimedia content). The majority of firms are located in northern Italy. The distribution of the sample firms by industry and geographic area is presented in Table 2.

The sample firms were then matched with 45 independent NTBFs that were not located on technology incubator, but were in similar sectors, in similar geographic areas, and of similar age. In order to find firms that complied with the above mentioned criteria, we resorted to the RITA database. Developed by CIRET-Politecnico di Milano, RITA provides information on a sample of Italian high-technology start-ups established after 1980 and on their founders. The present release of the database includes almost 400 firms and 1000 entrepreneurs. The matching strategy was successful as concerns both industry and geographic area. As was the case in most previous empirical studies on this issue, the only exception was the age criterion, with off-incubator firms being somewhat older than those located on a technology incubator. However, the difference between the average age of the two categories of firms is less than 1 year (5 against 6 years).

Due to the fact that firms in both the on- and off-park samples were surveyed at a particular date (i.e. the beginning of 2000), the question arises whether the data relating to such firms suffer from sample selection problems and what may be the implications for the empirical analysis. For one thing, one may presume that survival rates are higher among on-park firms in comparison with their off-park counterparts; actually the former enjoy a more protected situation, due to the seedbed role played by the park.[19] Furthermore, innovative firms may be more prone to risk taking and may be characterized by higher early mortality rates than other firms if they are not protected. So they may be relatively less numerous in the control sample than in the sample of incubated firms. Note, however that it may be less innovative, under-performing firms that mostly benefit from the protection offered by location on park. Then the sample selection bias would turn in the opposite direction: more innovative firms would be underrepresented in the on-park sample. In addition, a major reason for voluntary abandonment of on-park location is lack of space. Such situation more often applies to successful, innovative, high-growth firms which again may be relatively less numerous in the on-park sample. Altogether, it is fair to recognize that our data are probably affected by sample selection biases. Nevertheless, opposed forces are at work; therefore, we are quite confident that the empirical

---

[19] Note, however that the available evidence seems not to support such presumption. See for instance Westhead (1997, p. 50).

results that are presented in the following sections are largely independent of such biases. Of course, a sounder methodological approach would have been to identify all firms that were ever incubated in a SP or BIC—and not only those located on park at the date of the survey, to draw a sample from such population, and to track them over time up to the year 2000 if they were still on park at that time, or up to exit time, with exit being the consequence of bankruptcy, take over or the decision of the firm to leave the park for another location. Such sample could then be matched with a control sample chosen in accordance with criteria similar to those mentioned above (i.e. same sector, region, year of establishment, and age). Unfortunately, such research design turned out not to be viable in practice, as Italian SPs and BICs did not systematically keep track of the necessary information.

An additional problem might arise due to the fact that the on-park sample is likely to be affected by a self-selection bias, and thus, may not be representative of the target population. In fact, incubated firms which are performing well may be more willing to provide information about themselves; so they are likely to be over-represented in the on-park sample. Nonetheless, the same self-selection bias does affect the control sample, as data from the RITA database were collected through a similar survey. It follows that the selection procedure is unlikely to have biased the comparison between on- and off-park firms.

The sample of incubated firms was compared with the control sample along a series of dimensions through statistical tests (*t*-tests, binomial and multinomial Chi-squared tests). The findings of the statistical analysis are presented in the following two sections. Section 4 is devoted to the characteristics of firms' founders, while the growth and innovative performances of firms, the establishment of collaborations with other firms and universities, and access to public subsidies are considered in Section 5.

4. Characteristics of founders of NTBFs located on and off technology incubators

This section is devoted to the analysis of the characteristics of founders of NTBFs located on and off SPs and BICs. Data regard 241 entrepreneurs; 129 of them are founders of firms located on incubating

structures and 112 are entrepreneurs of firms located off parks.

Table 3 presents evidence on the characteristics of high-technology entrepreneurs in terms of age (at the date of firm's establishment), educational attainments and prior working experience. In order to evaluate the statistical significance of differences between the two categories of NTBF founders (i.e. the on- and off-incubator categories), we have proceeded to compute *t*-tests (for continuous and discrete variables), binomial Chi-squared tests (for dummy variables) and multinomial Chi-squared tests (for categorical variables). Overall, results show that founders of NTBFs located on technology incubators have a different education and working profile with respect to other high-technology entrepreneurs. At the date of firm start-up on-incubator entrepreneurs are only marginally younger (35 years old against 36 of other founders), with the difference between the two categories being statistically insignificant. More interestingly, they have a considerably richer educational background.[20] As is evident from Table 3, the percentage of founders of tenant firms with a post-graduate degree is significantly greater (at the 1% level) than that of off-incubator entrepreneurs: 10% of the individuals in the former category has a Ph.D. degree against only 1% in the latter category of entrepreneurs. Not only on-park entrepreneurs have a better post-graduate education, but among them the proportion of individuals with a graduate degree also is significantly (at 1%) higher (59% against 40%). In particular, 16% of them has a degree in engineering against 12% of the founders of NTBFs located off incubators, and 29% has a degree in other scientific or technical fields such as computer science, mathematics, physics and chemistry, against 12% of the other category. Italian SPs and BICs seem, therefore, able to attract a more educated category of entrepreneurs, who are relatively more specialized in scientific and technical branches. Given the low propensity of Italian technical graduates towards the self-employment choice (see again Colombo and Delmastro, 2001), our

---

[20] Note that there are remarkable differences as regards Italian and European graduate and post-graduate programs. For a more detailed discussion of such issue and for a comparison of the educational attainments of Italian NTBF founders with those of other European high-tech entrepreneurs see Colombo and Delmastro (2001).

M.G. Colombo, M. Delmastro / Research Policy 31 (2002) 1103–1122   1113

Table 3
Characteristics of NTBF founders: age, education and prior working experience

	On-incubator			Off-incubator		
	Minimum	Mean	Maximum	Minimum	Mean	Maximum
Age at firm's foundation[a]	20	34.71	61	19	36.17	70
	No. of observations		%	No. of observations		%
Education						
Ph.D.[b]	13[c]		10.08	1[c]		0.89
Graduate degree[b]	76[c]		58.91	45[c]		40.18
Engineering	21		16.28	13		11.61
Other technical degree[d]	37		28.68	13		11.61
Economics	11		8.53	8		7.14
Other graduate degree	7		5.42	11		9.82
Prior working experience[e]						
First working experience	10		7.75	11		9.82
Consultant	51		39.53	47		41.96
University and other R&D organization	12		9.30	4		3.57
High-technology firm[f]	40		31.01	35		31.25
Other firm	16		12.40	15		13.39
Total sample	129		100	112		100
Spin-off[b]	37		66.07	34		68.00

[a] *t*-Test between the two categories (on- and off-incubator) of NTBF founders.

[b] Binomial Chi-squared test between the two categories (on- and off-incubator) of NTBF founders.

[c] Significance level greater than 1%.

[d] Graduate degree in: computer science, mathematics, physics, chemistry and biology.

[e] Multinomial Chi-squared test between the two distributions (on- and off-incubator) of NTBF founders.

[f] Aerospace, biotechnology, pharmaceuticals, computer, electronics, software, Internet services, multimedia content.

findings suggest that technology incubators may play a pivotal role in fostering technological enterpreneurship in a country which is a laggard in science-based sectors. At the very least, they act as a catalyst for technologically educated entrepreneurs.

A (partial) confirmation of this claim comes from data of Table 3 concerning the prior working experience of NTBF founders. Even though the two categories of entrepreneurs under scrutiny do not show significant differences as regards working background by a multinomial Chi-squared test, the only exception regards the percentage of entrepreneurs being previously employed by a university or another research organization: this percentage is as high as 9.3% for the sample of entrepreneurs working on incubators, but is only 3.6% for founders of NTBFs located off parks. Turning to the other categories of working background and focusing only on entrepreneurs of incubated firms, 8% of them had no prior working experience before founding the firm and 40%

worked as an external consultant. Of entrepreneurs with a working experience within a business company (43%), some 71% was previously employed by a high-technology firm, and the remaining 29% by a firm operating in a low-technology industry.

In Table 4, we present results on the characteristics of the prior working experience of the NTBF founders that before starting the new enterprise were working in a business organization. The two samples reduce to 56 and 50 founders for the on- and off-incubator categories, respectively. In particular, we concentrate on the founder's position and function and the size of the firm by which he was formerly employed. Multinomial Chi-squared tests between the two distributions of NTBF founders show that differences always are significant at conventional levels. In particular, among founders of incubated firms those that worked in a medium or large firm (i.e. a firm with more than 100 employees), had a top or middle management position, and were assigned to technological functions

1114   M.G. Colombo, M. Delmastro / Research Policy 31 (2002) 1103–1122

Table 4
Prior working experience of NTBF founders: position, function and firm size[a]

	On-incubator		Off-incubator	
	No. of observations	%	No. of observations	%
Position[b]				
Top and middle manager	20	35.71	9	18.00
Other managerial position	23	41.07	28	56.00
Other	13	23.22	13	26.00
Total sample	56[c]	100	50[c]	100
Function[b]				
R&D	12	21.43	2	4.00
Design and engineering	11	19.64	8	16.00
Information systems	11	19.64	5	10.00
Production	10	17.86	10	20.00
Sales	5	8.93	20	40.00
Administration/finance	7	12.50	5	10.00
Total sample	56[d]	100	50[d]	100
Size[b]				
Small firm (<100 employees)	27	48.21	33	66.00
Medium firm (100–500)	19	33.93	10	20.00
Large firm (>500)	10	17.86	7	14.00
Total sample	56[c]	100	50[c]	100

[a] Characteristics observed only for founders with previous working experience within a firm.
[b] Multinomial Chi-squared test between the two categories (on- and off-incubators) of NTBF founders.
[c] Significance level greater than 5%.
[d] Significance level greater than 1%.

such as R&D, design and engineering, and information systems are relatively more numerous than in the control sample. Namely, 52% of on-incubator entrepreneurs worked in a firm with more than 100 employees against 34% in the off-incubator category, 36% had a middle or high managerial position against only 18% in the other category, and 61% was previously employed in R&D, design and engineering, and information systems departments against 30%. On the contrary, before the self-employment choice founders of firms located off incubators had mostly low managerial positions within small firms (with less than 100 employees) and were prevalently assigned to commercial functions. So, even though the proportion of founders with working experience in (high-technology and other) firms is quite similar for the on- and off-incubator categories (43.4 and 44.6%, respectively, see Table 3), their profile turns out to be very different one from another.

Finally, the interviewed entrepreneurs were asked to choose out of four kinds of motivations the one which

has been the most important to shape the start-up decision.[21] Selected motivations are of the following four types. First, entrepreneurs may be induced to start a new business because of the negative prospect of other alternatives. Following existing literature (see for instance Arrighetti and Vivarelli, 1999), we call this situation as 'defensive motivation'. Second, the self-employment decision may be mainly driven by psychological factors such as willingness to autonomously manage working time and aversion to hierarchical corporate culture. By following the income choice approach (see for instance Blanchflower and

_____
[21] Actually, we allowed for seven motivations and then, for exposition matters, we aggregated them into four categories. In particular, the defensive motivation category includes three factors: skepticism about prospects of the mother firm, concern about future career developments, and no job alternatives. The personal motivation category comprises two factors: aversion to hierarchical corporate culture and desire to self-manage working time. Instead, the other two motivations (i.e. belief in introducing an innovation and perceive potential for higher income) have been unchanged.

M.G. Colombo, M. Delmastro / Research Policy 31 (2002) 1103–1122   1115

Table 5
Founding motivations of NTBF founders

Motivations[a]	On-incubator		Off-incubator	
	No. of observations	%	No. of observations	%
Belief in introducing an innovation	66	51.16	40	35.71
Perceive potential for higher income	17	13.18	31	27.68
Personal motivation	25	19.38	19	16.96
Defensive motivation	21	16.28	22	19.64
Total sample	129[b]	100	112[b]	100

[a] Multinomial Chi-squared test between the two categories (on- and off-incubators) of NTBF founders.
[b] Significance level greater than 1%.

Oswald, 1998), we also include motivations regarding an expected increase in the entrepreneurs' income by becoming self-employed. Lastly, entrepreneurs may be of a Schumpeterian type, being mainly motivated by the belief in introducing an innovation.

Table 5 reports results for the two categories of NTBF founders. First, the difference between the two distributions of motivations is found to be statistically significant at the 1% level by a multinomial Chi-squared test. Second, while personal and defensive motivations score similar percentages for the two categories of entrepreneurs, economic and innovation factors obtain very different results. In particular, entrepreneurs of incubated high-technology start-ups are mainly motivated by innovation-related factors: 51% of them indicates this motivation as the major determinant of the self-employment choice, while this percentage reduces to 36% for founders of NBFTs located off-incubators.

To sum up, Italian entrepreneurs of firms incubated on SPs and BICs present distinctive characteristics with respect to other Italian high-technology entrepreneurs. First, founders of incubated NTBFs are on average more educated and are more likely to come from universities and other research organizations. Moreover, when their prior working experience is in a business organization they are more likely to come from technological units (such as R&D laboratories). These features are also mirrored by the founding motivation: they are more likely to start-up a new high-technology venture driven by the willingness of introducing a technological innovation. In addition, they usually hold a higher position in the managerial hierarchy of the firm where they were previously employed, and such firm usually is of larger size. We can therefore, conclude that Italian technology incubators

appear to attract educated individuals with quite sophisticated technological and managerial skills, who in Italy, for reasons examined elsewhere by the authors (see again Colombo and Delmastro, 2001), are quite unlikely to take the self-employment choice.

5. Characteristics of firms located on- and off-technology incubators

In this section, we compare the characteristics of the sample firms located on SPs and BICs with those of the off-incubator control sample.

Let us start with firm size. In Table 6, we illustrate the estimates of two simple econometric Tobit models, given the left-truncated nature of the depen-

Table 6
Start-up size and post-entry growth (logarithm of the number of employees), Tobit models

Variables	Start-up size	Size in 1999
Constant	−0.1667 (0.5743)	0.9960 (0.5785)
On-incubator	0.0539 (0.1539)	0.3173 (0.1584)[a]
Corporate spin-off	0.4787 (0.2245)[a]	0.3962 (0.2489)
Start-up size	–	0.3016 (0.0721)[b]
Firm's age	–	0.1156 (0.0194)[b]
Number of founders	0.1372 (0.0404)[b]	0.0669 (0.0419)
Education	0.0346 (0.0340)	−0.0272 (0.0346)
Working experience	0.0282 (0.0090)[b]	0.0030 (0.0096)
Observations	90	86[c]
Log-likelihood function	−94.1970	−90.2202

[a] Significance level greater than 5%. Standard errors are in parentheses.
[b] Significance level greater than 1%. Standard errors are in parentheses.
[c] Four firms which were founded in 1999 could not be included in the regression.

dent variables (i.e. logarithm of the number of employees at start-up and at 31 December 1999), one for start-up size and the other for post-entry growth. The aim is to highlight the influence exerted by firm location (i.e. on-park versus off-park) upon the start-up size and the post-entry growth performances of firms, after controlling for the role played by both founders' skills and constraints due to the lack of financing and other key resources. In particular, "On-incubator" is a dummy variable which is one whenever the firm is located on a SP or a BIC. Control variables include the following ones. "Corporate spin-off" is a dummy which indicates whether the firm at start-up time benefited from tangible and/or intangible assets provided by an established firm;[22] "Number of founders" is the number of firm's owners at start-up. The former variable takes into account financial and/or physical support provided by a mother company at start-up, while the latter is a proxy of both the internal financial resources provided by founders and heterogeneities of capabilities. "Working experience" is the average number of years of founders' working experience before firm's foundation; such variable provides information not only on founders' professional skills, but also on their average earnings level at start-up. Turning to entrepreneurs' competencies, the variable 'Education' is the average number of years they spent on educational programs. Finally, in the post-entry growth regression, we also included 'Start-up size' and 'Firm's age' as control variables.

Let us firstly consider the size of firms at start-up. As a preliminary remark, note that the average number of employees at firm's foundation is 4.8 for NTBFs embedded in a technology incubator and 5.7 for those located off such structures. However, the estimates of the start-up size model show that after controlling for factors other than location, such difference vanishes. Indeed, the variable "On-incubator" turns out to have no impact on the number of employees at firm's foundation. Conversely, the coefficients of variables which provide information on the resources (e.g. financial) that at start-up were at disposal of founders, i.e. "Corporate spin-off" and "Number of founders", are pos-

itive and significant at conventional levels. In this respect, the detected positive and significant (at 1%) impact of "Working experience" would seem to confirm the importance of the role played by financial resources rather than founders' skills. Accordingly, the variable "Education plays,, no role in affecting firm's size at start-up.

Let us now turn attention to the determinants of firms' post-entry growth.[23] As was mentioned earlier, in order to assess whether localization on incubator affects growth, we have regressed the logarithm of the number of employees in 1999 on embedness within an incubating structure, controlling for start-up size, firm's age and a series of variables that capture human capital of firms' founders and financial resources at start-up time. Again results are presented in Table 6. Location on SPs and BICs turns out to positively influence the post-entry growth of NTBFs: the coefficient of "On-incubator" is positive and significant at 5%. Other things being equals (i.e. with start-up size,[24] firm's age and other explanatory variables being evaluated at their mean value), the average annual growth rate is 55% for incubated firms and 30% for firms in the off-park sample: incubated high-technology firms start with a size which is similar to that of other NTBFs, but thereafter, they tend to grow at a faster pace.[25] Note finally that variables that take into account financial

---

[22] It is worth noticing that there are three corporate spin-offs in the two samples: one in the incubated firm sample and two in the control sample. See footnote 18 for the definition of "corporate spin-off" that we have adopted in this work.

[23] It is worth mentioning that for some firms, we also have information on turnover at the survey date. However, data on this variable are often missing so that it is not possible to estimate an econometric model using turnover as a proxy of firm size.

[24] Note that since the coefficient of start-up size is significantly lower than 1, Gibrat law does not hold for this sample of Italian NTBFs (see Audretsch et al., 1999).

[25] Note that the growth model suffers from two shortcomings, related to sample attrition problems (see Section 3). First, we do not take survival rates into account. As has long been highlighted by the literature on the post-entry performances of firms (for a survey, see for instance Sutton, 1997; Caves, 1998), failure to adjust for the likelihood of survival affects growth rates, as we only observe the growth rates of surviving firms. However, as was said earlier, there is no robust evidence suggesting that survival rates should substantially differ between on- and off-incubator firms. Second, there is an additional sample selection problem due to the fact that all else being equal, rapidly growing firms are more likely to abandon their on-incubator location; in that case, they would be missed by our survey. This means that with all else being equal, the on-incubator sample is likely to underestimate firms' actual growth rates. This however provides further support to our findings.

M.G. Colombo, M. Delmastro/Research Policy 31 (2002) 1103–1122   1117

Table 7
Measures of innovative activity

	On-incubator	Off-incubator
Researchers[a] (%)	13.31	14.19
Employees with graduate degree[a] (%)	52.26[b]	29.51[b]
Firms involved in EU R&D projects[c] (%)	24.44[b]	8.89[b]
Firms that have purchased R&D services from universities or other research laboratories[c] (%)	28.89[b]	13.33[b]
Firms with patent activity[c] (%)	17.78	13.33
Firms with copyright[c] (%)	11.11	8.89
Number of PC per firm[a]	11.04	10.31
Number of workstation per firm[a]	4.60[b]	2.22[b]
Firms with LAN[c] (%)	97.78[b]	80.00[b]

[a] *t*-Test between the two categories (on- and off-incubator) of NTBFs.

[b] Significance level greater than 1%.

[c] Binomial Chi-squared test between the two categories (on- and off-incubator) of NTBFs.

constraints and educational attainments seem to play no additional role in the post-entry growth regression.

We further investigated the characteristics of NTBFs by looking at various measures of innovative activity (see Table 7). In order to assess the statistical significance of the detected differences, we have again proceeded to run binomial Chi-squared tests and *t*-tests between the two categories of firms. In accordance with the studies mentioned in Section 1, we found no significant difference between on- and off-park firms in the share of R&D employees out of the total workforce.[26] However, employees of incubated firms turned out to be on average more educated: 52% of them has a graduate degree against 29% of the workforce of firms located off incubators, with the difference being significant at the 1% level. In addition, incubated firms are more likely to exploit links with universities and other research institutions. Indeed, 24% of them has been involved in EU R&D projects (against only 9% of firms off incubators, with

the difference being significant at conventional levels) and 29% has acquired R&D services from universities and/or other research laboratories (against 13%; the difference is again significant). Furthermore, there is evidence that firms located on SPs and BICs produce a (marginally) higher innovation output than firms in the control sample: 18% of them has patented a new product and/or process against 13% of the sample of NTBFs located off incubators[27] and 11% has been granted a copyright against 9%. Nonetheless, such differences are small and statistically insignificant at conventional levels. Lastly, the data presented in Table 7 show that incubated firms are more likely to adopt information and communication technologies than off-incubator firms: the average number of PCs per firm is 11 against 10 of the off-incubator sample, the average number of workstation is 4.6 against 2.2, and the percentage of LAN users is 98% against 80%, with the two latter differences being statistically significant at the 1% level.

To sum up, our findings basically confirm previous evidence that the R&D intensity (an input measure) of firms located on incubator is similar to that of comparable off-incubator firms, and that the former firms have only a slightly greater innovative output than the latter. Nonetheless, our results also show that incubated firms have a more educated workforce, a significantly greater probability of adopting technological innovations, a greater aptitude to participating in international collaborative R&D projects and getting access to R&D output of research centers. This documents a direct and/or indirect positive impact of on-incubator location. From one side, SPs' and BICs' staff provides useful technological brokerage services, which increase the capabilities of NTBFs to leverage their internal knowledge resources. From the other, the greater educational achievements and professional skills of both entrepreneurs and employees

---

[26] Unfortunately, due to missing data, we were unable to compute the R&D to sales ratio. So, in order to measure innovative input, we had to rely only on R&D employees. However, it is also worth mentioning that the intensity of R&D expenses has been the subject of much criticism when it is applied to NTBFs (see for instance Hansen, 1992).

[27] We have also measured the average number of patents for the two sample of firms. This value is close to 0.4 for both samples (i.e. 0.38 for incubated firms and 0.42 for off-park firms), and the difference between the two values is found to be statistically insignificant by a Wilcoxon rank test. Note, however, that given the very low percentage of firms involved in patent activity these values should be taken with caution. Indeed, they are deeply influenced by outliers: in fact, the marginally higher value of the off-park sample is mostly due to the activity of one NTBF which has been granted eight patents.

Table 8
Cooperative activity: firms that have stipulated formal agreements (%)

	On-incubator	Off-incubator
Total[a] (%)	77.78[b]	57.78[b]
Commercial agreements[a] (%)	64.44[c]	51.11[c]
Technological agreements[a] (%)	57.78[b]	28.89[b]
Technological agreements with		
Clients and/or suppliers[a] (%)	24.44	15.56
Other firms[a] (%)	11.11	8.89
Universities[a] (%)	48.89[b]	13.33[b]

[a] Binomial Chi-squared test between the two categories (on and off-incubator) of firms.

[b] Significance level greater than 1%.

[c] Significance level greater than 5%.

of incubated start-ups clearly increase the "absorptive capacity" (Cohen and Levinthal, 1989) of these firms, thus, leading to the same outcome.

This analysis is confirmed by results on the cooperative activity of firms. Indeed, Table 8 shows that firms incubated on SPs and BICs are significantly more likely to engage in formal agreements with other units: 78% of them has stipulated commercial and/or technological agreements against 58% of the sample of NTBFs located off incubators. This difference is significant even when we look separately at commercial agreements (64% against 51%; the difference is significant at the 5% level) and technological agreements (58% against 29%, significant at 1%). While incubated firms have a higher, but not significantly so, probability of engaging in technological agreements with business partners (both clients, suppliers and other firms), the difference is large and significant (at the 1% level) when we concentrate on agreements with universities: 49% of incubated NTBFs has stipulated a formal agreement with one (or more) university while this percentage declines to only 13% for the sample of NTBFs located off incubators.[28]

---

[28] Note that greater recourse to external R&D services and collaborative arrangements on the part of incubated firms may simply substitute for internal R&D, thus, explaining failure of this study (and of most previous studies) to detect any difference in R&D intensity according to firms' location on and off incubator. Alternatively, closer collaborative linkages with universities and other firms may increase the productivity of incubated firms' R&D; under such circumstances the fact that innovative output is only marginally higher in the on-incubator category might be due to the well known shortcomings of indicators based on patent activity.

Table 9
Access to State funds: firms that have received financial subsidies from public institutions (%)

	On-incubator	Off-incubator
Total[a] (%)	51.11[b]	33.33[b]
National institutions[a] (%)	20.00	15.56
Local institutions[a] (%)	42.22[b]	28.89[b]

[a] Binomial Chi-squared test between the two categories (on- and off-incubators) of firms.

[b] Significance level greater than 5%.

Finally, Table 9 shows that NTBFs located on SPs and BICs had easier access to public financial funds: 51% of on-incubator firms received public subsidies compared with 33% of the off-incubator sample, with the difference being statistically significant at 5%. The larger difference concerns subsidies granted by local institutions. Such evidence confirms the enabling role played by on-incubator location. With a few exceptions, empirical studies on new firms (see Section 1) point to the financial constraints to which such firms are subject. In addition, in Italy there are no policy schemes that specifically target NTBFs, and lack of public subsidies is considered by entrepreneurs in high-technology activities as one of the main obstacle to innovation and growth (see Calderini et al., 2000). Therefore, the support offered by SPs and BICs in this domain appears of great value. Note also that the easier access to public subsidies allowed by on-incubator location may have the additional beneficial effect of inducing risk-averse individuals (in particular, older individuals with greater human capital and higher income) to take the self-employment choice. Such argument is coherent with the detected differences between founders of on- and off-park firms illustrated in Section 4.

6. Discussion and policy implications

The main objective of this paper was to contribute to ascertain the added value to NTBFs of location within a SP or a BIC. In fact, in spite of the popularity of such institutions and their rapidly growing number in Europe over the 1980s and 1990s, it is still doubtful whether they have been successful in supporting the establishment and post-entry development

M.G. Colombo, M. Delmastro / Research Policy 31 (2002) 1103–1122   1119

of NTBFs. For this purpose, we have compared a sample composed of 45 Italian NTBFs that at the beginning of year 2000 were situated in a technology incubator within a SP or a BIC with a control sample of similar off-incubator firms (in terms of age, sector of activity, and geographical location). The comparison concerned the characteristics of firms' founders (i.e. educational attainments, prior working experience, and motivations of the self-employment choice), the innovative and growth performances of firms, the establishment of cooperative relations with other firms and universities, and the ability to have access to public subsidies.

This work differs from the empirical literature on this issue in two respects. First, a more comprehensive set of indicators was used than in previous studies. Second, the analysis of the Italian case is an interesting addition to the literature, which so far mainly focused attention on northern European countries. On the one hand, the supply of entrepreneurs is larger in Italy than in other European countries. On the other hand, most Italian new firms are in mature industries, the country is a laggard in high-technology sectors, and the national innovation system is rather weak; in particular, the provision of key inputs to firms' innovative activities such as technical, financial, and other business services, suffers from serious market failures. Under such circumstances, one would expect SPs and BICs to play a relatively more important role in supporting the NTBF movement.

The results of the paper confirm such intuition. From one side, Italian SPs and BICs have been rather successful in attracting entrepreneurs with high quality human capital, thus, playing a positive selection role. On average founders of on-incubator firms have a richer educational background, especially as regards scientific and technical studies, than their off-incubator counterparts: entrepreneurs with a Ph.D. degree and those with a graduate degree in engineering or in other scientific and technical fields account for a significantly higher percentage in the on-incubator category than in the off-incubator one. As concerns prior working experience, a larger number of founders of SP and BIC firms was employed by a university or another research organization. When attention is focused on entrepreneurs that were previously employed by a business firm, those that worked in medium or large firms, had a top or middle management position,

and were assigned to a technological function (i.e. R&D, design and engineering, and information systems) turned out to be relatively more numerous in the on-incubator sample than in the control sample. In accordance with such evidence, on-incubator entrepreneurs mention innovation-driven motivations as the main driver of the self-employment choice to a much larger extent than entrepreneurs in the control sample. Our findings also show that on-park firms have easier access to public subsidies. From this standpoint, the selection function performed by SPs and BICs has the beneficial effect of channeling those subsidies to relatively more promising ventures (i.e. those established by individuals with richer human capital). Of course, the question arises whether SPs and BICs have simply promoted the geographical clustering of high quality new technology-based businesses, or they also have encouraged the creation of businesses which otherwise would not have been established. The data we have do not provide any direct evidence relating to such aspect. Its analysis would be an interesting extension of the findings illustrated in the present paper.

From the other side, the post-entry performances of NTBFs turned out to differ according to their location status. The empirical findings illustrated in the paper conform to previous evidence relating to the UK situation in that the R&D intensity of firms, an indicator of innovative input, is not significantly different between the on- and off-incubator categories; the difference as regards innovative output measured by patent activity also is negligible. Nonetheless, the evidence that on-incubator location favors firm's growth is also replicated. After taking into account a series of control variables (i.e. the number of a firm's founders, the characteristics of their human capital, their ability to finance the new venture with their own resources, whether the new firm is a corporate spin-off, start-up size and firm age), incubated firms exhibit a significantly larger number of employees at survey date, all else being equal. In addition, the results of the empirical analysis show that SP and BIC firms outperformed off-incubator firms according to a number of other indicators, including the education of the workforce, the adoption of innovative information and communication technologies, participation in research projects sponsored by the EU, and the ability to take advantage of the scientific and technical services provided by research organizations. Incubated

1120 *M.G. Colombo, M. Delmastro / Research Policy 31 (2002) 1103–1122*

firms also showed a greater likelihood of establishing formal cooperative relations, both of commercial and technical nature; the difference between the on- and off-incubator samples was especially remarkable as concerns technical collaborations with universities.

Altogether, the empirical findings illustrated in the paper suggests a more positive view of SPs and BICs than the one offered by most previous studies.[29] A possible explanation may reside in the fact that Italy is a laggard in high-technology activities. In situations were there are substantial market failures as regards the provision of essential inputs to NTBFs (including finance, real estate, technical and other business services), the presence of bridging institutions such as SPs and BICs may be relatively more beneficial than in countries where the national innovation system is more advanced. For technology policy, this is an interesting result which is waiting for confirmations relating to other laggard countries.

Nonetheless, it is fair to recognize that in order to shed new light on the support to NTBFs offered by parks, much remains to be done. In this paper, we have shown that incubated firms have superior post-entry performances than non-incubated ones, especially as regards growth rates. The econometric estimates suggested that such result could not be explained by the superior human and financial capital of the founders of tenant firms. In other words, there seems to be an added value provided by SPs and BICs. However, the small number of observations hindered use of a more robust methodology, capable of disentangling more effectively the effects due to selection biases from those that can genuinely be attributed to location on-park.[30]

In addition, we still ignore whether the added value of on-park location illustrated by our findings is attributable to the quality of the services provided by parks to tenant firms, the agglomeration economies associated with such location, or the easier access to external resources, especially in the technical and financial spheres (i.e. collaborations with universities

and other knowledge creating institutions, public subsidies). Of course, being able to distinguish between such effects has important policy implications. For this purpose, one needs to specify and estimate a more general growth model than the one considered here, a task which is high in our research agenda.

Furthermore, we mentioned in Section 2 that there is considerable heterogeneity among Italian SPs and BICs; differences concern important characteristics such as overall size, the ability to attract external knowledge creating units, the nature of the sponsoring institutions, the presence of a dedicated manager, and the internalization of the provision of R&D and other technical services. This situation is common to other countries (for the UK, see for instance Massey et al., 1992). So the question of whether there exists a successful organizational model for SPs and BICs naturally arises. Westhead and Batstone (1999) have explored the benefits to NTBFs of location on a managed park, that is a park with a full-time manager on site. They have showed that the impact of a pro-active management function generally is positive. This is an important initial result. The informal and qualitative evidence that we have collected gives some further interesting indications. In particular, it seems to suggest that key success factors for parks include a lean and agile internal organization, and effective coordination of the services provided by third parties, with the emphasis being placed on the brokerage and gate-keeping function carried out by parks. The fact that in the selection of tenant units, especially in the early period after establishment of a park, priority be given to the R&D laboratories of large firms so as to increase the attractiveness to NTBFs of on-park location, also appears to play a crucial role. Unfortunately, the number of incubated firms in our data set is too small to obtain robust quantitative evidence on these issues. More generally, additional data need to be gathered to provide further insights into the drivers of parks' success and to draw out the consequent implications for technology policy.

Acknowledgements

The support of University of Pavia 2000 FAR funds, MURST 2000 funds, and a grant from CNR (CNRC00E3AF) are gratefully acknowledged. We are

---

[29] For evidence relating to Germany of the positive impact of on-incubator location on NTBFs, see Sternberg (1990).

[30] Storey (1998) highlights two sources of selection biases. First, as far as firms that choose to be located on park differ from other firms there is a self-selection bias. Second, there also is an administrative selection bias, as park officials accept some applicants, but reject others. Both biases may have inflated the observed positive impact of on-park location on firms' growth.

indebted to Mario Calderini, Paola Garrone, Sergio Mariotti, David Storey, Marco Vivarelli, participants in the 28th EARIE Conference and in a seminar held at Politecnico di Milano, and three anonymous referees for helpful comments. We are also grateful to Marco Mantegazza and Andrea Re Depaolini for research assistance. Responsibility for any errors lies solely with the authors. The authors are jointly responsible for the work. However, Sections 1–3 have been written by Massimo G. Colombo, and Sections 4–6 by Marco Delmastro.

References

Acs, Z.J., Audretsch, D.B., Feldman, M.P., 1992. Real effects of academic research: comment. American Economic Review 81, 363–367.

Acs, Z.J., Audretsch, D.B., Feldman, M.P., 1994. R&D spillovers and innovative activity. Managerial and Decision Economics 15, 131–138.

Arrighetti, A., Vivarelli, M., 1999. The role of innovation in the post-entry performance of new small firms: Evidence from Italy. Southern Economic Journal 65, 927–939.

Audretsch, D.B., Santarelli, E., Vivarelli, M., 1999. Start-up size and industrial dynamics: some evidence from Italian manufacturing. International Journal of Industrial Organization 17, 965–983.

Blanchflower, D., Oswald, A., 1998. What makes an entrepreneur? Journal of Labor Economics 16, 26–60.

Blanchflower, D., Oswald, A., 1999. Measuring latent entrepreneurship across nations, mimeo, University of Warwick, Warwick.

Black, J., de Meza, D., Jeffreys, D., 1996. House prices, the supply of collateral, and the enterprise economy. The Economic Journal 106, 60–75.

Calderini, M., Colombo, M.G., Delmastro, M., Garrone, P., Mariotti, S., 2000. Il sistema innovativo italiano nelle tecnologie dell'informazione e della comunicazione, CIRET-Politecnico di Milano (in Italian).

Camerer, C., Lovallo, D., 1999. Overconfidence and excess of entry. American Economic Review 89, 306–318.

Caves, R., 1998. Industrial organization and new findings on the turnover and mobility of firms. Journal of Economic Literature XXXVI, 1947–1982.

Cesaroni, F., Gambardella, A., 1998, "Dai "contenitori" ai "contenuti": i parchi scientifici e tecnologici in Italia". In: Proceedings of the Conference on "Ripensare l'innovazione tecnologica: nuovi paradigmi, nuove politiche", Fondazione Giovanni Agnelli (in Italian).

Cohen, W.M., Levinthal, D.A., 1989. Innovation and learning: the two faces of R&D. The Economic Journal 99, 569–596.

Colombo, M.G., Delmastro, M., 2001. Technology-based entrepreneurs: does Internet make a difference? Small Business Economics 16, 177–190.

Cressy, R., 1996. Are business startups debt rationed? The Economic Journal 106, 1253–1270.

Evans, D.S., Jovanovic, B., 1989. An estimated model of entrepreneurial choice under liquidity constraints. Journal of Political Economy 97, 808–827.

Evans, D.S., Leighton, L.S., 1989. Some empirical aspects of entrepreneurship. American Economic Review 79, 519–535.

Felsenstein, D., 1994. University-related science parks: "seedbeds" or "enclaves" of innovation? Technovation 14, 93–110.

Hall, G., 1989. Lack of finance as a constraint on the expansion of innovative small firms. In: Barber, J.L., Metcalfe, J.S., Porteous, M. (Eds.), Barriers to Growth in Small Firms. Routledge, London.

Hansen, J.A., 1992. Innovation, firm size and firm age. Small Business Economics 4, 37–44.

Holtz-Eakin, D., 2001. Public policy toward entrepreneurship. Small Business Economics 15, 283–291.

Holtz-Eakin, D., Joulfaian, D., Rosen, H.S., 1994a. Sticking it out: entrepreneurial decisions and liquidity constraints. Journal of Political Economy 102, 53–75.

Holtz-Eakin, D., Joulfaian, D., Rosen, H.S., 1994b. Entrepreneurial decisions and liquidity constraints. Rand Journal of Economics 25, 334–347.

Istat, 1996. Censimento intermedio.

Jaffe, A.B., 1989. Real effects of academic research. American Economic Review 79, 957–970.

Levenson, A.R., Willard, K.L., 2000. Do firms get the financing they want? Measuring credit rationing experienced by small businesses in the US. Small Business Economics 14, 83–94.

Macdonald, S., 1987. British science parks: reflections on the politics of high-technology. R&D Management 17, 25–38.

Malerba, F., 1993, The National System of Innovation: Italy. In: Nelson, R.R. (Ed.), National Innovation Systems: A Comparative Analysis. Oxford University Press, Oxford, pp. 230–259.

Massey, D., Quintas, P., Wield, D., 1992. High-Tech Fantasies: Science Parks in Society, Science and Space. Routledge, London.

Mian, S.A., 1996. Assessing value-added contribution of university technology business incubators to tenant firms. Research Policy 25, 325–335.

Monck, C.S.P., Porter, R.B., Quintas, P., Storey, D., Wynarczyk, P., 1988. Science Parks and The Growth of High-Technology Firms. Croom Helm, London.

Oakey, R., 1995, High-Technology New Firms: Variable Barriers to Growth. Chapman & Hall, London.

OECD, 1997, Technology incubators: nurturing small firms. OCDE/GD, (97) 202.

OECD, 1998, Small businesses, job creation and growth: facts, obstacles and best practices, http://www.oecd.org/dsti/sti/industry/smes/prod/smes.pdf

Quintas, P., Wield, D., Massey, D., 1992. Academic-industry links and innovation: questioning the science park model. Technovation 12, 161–175.

Robson, P.J.A., Bennet, R.J., 2001. SME growth: the relationship with business advice and external collaboration. Small Business Economics 15, 193–208.

Sternberg, R., 1990. The impact of Innovation centers on small technology-based firms: the example of the Federal Republic of Germany. Small Business Economics 2, 105–118.

Stiglitz, J.E., Weiss, A., 1981. Credit rationing in markets with imperfect information. American Economic Review 71, 393–410.

Storey, D.J., 1994. Understanding the Small Business Sector. Routledge, London.

Storey, D.J., 1998. Six steps to heaven. Evaluating the impact of public policies to support small businesses in developed countries. Warwick Business School, WP 59.

Storey, D.J., 1998. Public policy measures to support new technology-based firms in the European Union. Research Policy 26, 1037–1057.

Sutton, J., 1997. Gibrat's legacy. Journal of Economic Literature 11, 40–59.

UKSPA, 1998. Annual report.

Von Dierdonck, R.V., Debackere, K., Rappa, M.A., 1991. An assessment of science parks: towards a better understanding of their role in the diffusion of technological knowledge. R&D Management 21, 109–123.

Westhead, P., 1997. R&D "inputs" and "outputs" of technology-based firms located on and off science parks. R&D Management 27, 45–62.

Westhead, P., Batstone, S., 1998. Independent technology-based firms: the perceived benefits of a science park location. Urban Studies 12, 2197–2199.

Westhead, P., Batstone, S., 1999. Perceived benefits of a managed science park location. Entrepreneurship and Regional Development 11, 129–154.

Westhead, P., Storey, D.J., 1994. An assessment of firms located on- and off-science parks in the UK. HMSO, London.

Westhead, P., Storey, D.J., 1995. Links between higher education institutions and high-technology firms. Omega International Journal of Management Science 23, 345–360.

[13]

ELSEVIER

Available online at www.sciencedirect.com

SCIENCE DIRECT®

International Journal of Industrial Organization
21 (2003) 1323–1356

International Journal of
Industrial
Organization

www.elsevier.com/locate/econbase

U.S. science parks: the diffusion of an innovation and its effects on the academic missions of universities

Albert N. Link[a], John T. Scott[b],*

[a]*Department of Economics, University of North Carolina at Greensboro, Greensboro, NC 27402, USA*
[b]*Department of Economics, Dartmouth College, Hanover, NH 03755, USA*

Abstract

The paper is an exploratory study of science parks in the United States. It models the history of science parks as the diffusion of an innovation that was adopted at a rapid and increasing rate in the early 1980s, and since then at a decreased rate. It models the growth of a science park once established, showing significant effects on growth for the proximity to universities and other resources. The paper also reports university administrators' perceptions about the impact of their science parks on the academic missions of their universities. Statistical analyses show there is a direct relationship between the proximity of the science park to the university and the probability that the academic curriculum will shift from basic toward applied research.
© 2003 Elsevier B.V. All rights reserved.

JEL classification: I2; L31; O32; R1

Keywords: Science parks; Innovation; University/industry relationships

1. Introduction

While there is a growing body of knowledge regarding university–industry

---

*Corresponding author. Tel.: +1-603-646-2941; fax: +1-603-646-2122.
E-mail addresses: al_link@uncg.edu (A.N. Link), john.t.scott@dartmouth.edu (J.T. Scott).

0167-7187/03/$ – see front matter © 2003 Elsevier B.V. All rights reserved.
doi:10.1016/S0167-7187(03)00085-7

1324   *A.N. Link, J.T. Scott / Int. J. Ind. Organ. 21 (2003) 1323–1356*

research partnerships,[1] there are few studies of university–industry strategic alliances in science parks. In this paper, we first describe the establishment and growth of a prominent sample of science parks that were among those operating in the United States at the end of the twentieth century. We then characterize, using survey data collected from a sample of major research universities in the United States, the perceptions of university administrators about the impact of science parks on various dimensions of the academic mission of a university. We relate those data about perceptions statistically to university and science park characteristics. Those characteristics include the distance of the park from the university and the formality of the relationship between the park and the university. Other characteristics are the R&D budget of the university and the percentage of its faculty engaged in research with science park organizations, the percentage of total academic R&D financed by industry, whether the university is public or private, the age of the park, and the technologies pursued by faculty associated with the park.

Surprisingly, given their long history in the United States as well as in other countries, there is no generally accepted definition of a science park. One definition has been posited by the Association of University Related Research Parks (AURRP).[2] As stated in their *Worldwide Research & Science Park Directory, 1998* (AURRP, 1997, p. 2):[3]

---

[1] Much of this literature is reviewed in Hall et al. (2000, 2003), forthcoming) and in the papers in Siegel et al. (2001). Formal university participation in industrial research joint ventures has increased steadily since the mid-1980s (Link, 1996), the number of university–industry R&D centers has increased by more than 60 percent during the 1980s (Cohen et al., 1997), and a recent survey of U.S. science faculty revealed that many desire even more partnerships with industry (Morgan, 1998). Mowery and Teece (1996, p. 111) contend that such growth in strategic alliances in R&D is indicative of a "broad restructuring of the U.S. national R&D system."

[2] In 2002, the Association was renamed the Association of University Research Parks (AURP).

[3] More narrowly, the U.S. General Accounting Office (GAO, 1983, p. ii) defines university-related research parks as "clusters of high technology firms or their research centers located on a site near a university, where industry occupancy is limited to research-intensive organizations." The lack of a standard definition of a science park is not unique to the United States. As Monck et al. (1988, p. 62) point out: "There is no uniformly accepted definition of a Science Park [in Britain] and, to make matters worse, there are several terms used to describe broadly similar developments—such as 'Research Park,' 'Technology Park,' 'Business Park,' 'Innovation Centre,' etc." The United Kingdom Science Park Association (UKSPA, 1985, p. ii) defines a science park in terms of the following features: "A science park is a property-based initiative which: has formal operational links with a university or other higher education or research institution; is designed to encourage the formation and growth of knowledge-based businesses and other organizations normally resident on site; has a management function which is actively engaged in the transfer of technology and business skills to the organizations on site."

A.N. Link, J.T. Scott / Int. J. Ind. Organ. 21 (2003) 1323–1356   1325

The definition of a research or science park differs almost as widely as the individual parks themselves. However, the research and science park concept generally includes three components:

- A real estate development
- An organizational program of activities for technology transfer
- A partnership between academic institutions, government and the private sector.

'Science park' has evolved to become a generic term which refers to parks with some or all of the foregoing characteristics. Included under this rubric are—and these designations are subjective—research parks with a majority of tenants that are heavily engaged in basic and applied research. As well, science parks include technology parks with a majority of tenants that are heavily engaged in applied research and development. Technology or innovation parks often house new start-up companies and incubator facilities.[4] Finally, commercial or industrial parks typically have tenants that add value to R&D-based products through assembly or packaging, rather than do R&D. However, we prefer the generic term science park since each of the classifications above does include some of the characteristics noted in the AURRP definition.

Fig. 1, based on the 1998 *Directory*, the most complete directory published by AURRP to date, illustrates the historical growth for the AURRP's U.S. science parks, as defined by the date at which each park was founded.[5] The AURRP *Directory*'s set of parks is just one sample of U.S. science parks.[6] Notable in Fig. 1 are the following parks: Stanford Research Park (established in 1951), Cornell Business & Technology Park (established in 1952), and the Research Triangle Park of North Carolina (established in 1959). We examine the foregoing set of science parks that have been formed in the United States since 1950—the AURRP membership—to establish a few simple facts about the establishment and growth of science parks.

---

[4] Incubator facilities house pre-start-up companies. Often, when the science park is tied to a state university, the state underwrites the cost of operating the incubator facility as part of a regional economic development strategy.

[5] Year of establishment is only one metric for dating the age and subsequent growth of science parks in the United States. It, like other metrics, is less than perfect since the date of establishment of a park may not be the date at which the first organization established itself in the park. In the case of the Research Triangle Park of North Carolina, the first tenant committed to the Park in 1965 (Link, 1995, 2002; Link and Scott, 2003) six years after the Park was formally established.

[6] Without an accepted definition of what a park is, without the complete population, and without a field-tested taxonomy of science parks, however, we do not know if the characterization of the establishment and growth of science parks that comes from examining the AURRP membership is a characterization of science parks more generally.

1326   *A.N. Link, J.T. Scott / Int. J. Ind. Organ. 21 (2003) 1323–1356*

Science Parks in the United States from 1951-1998

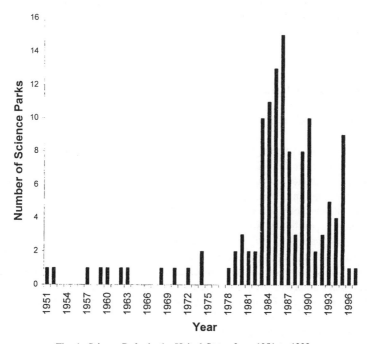

Fig. 1. Science Parks in the United States from 1951 to 1998.

Few scholars or researchers have studied science parks in any systematic manner.[7] A number of studies have examined the influence of being in a science

---

[7]There have, however, been a number of important and carefully done historical studies of the formation and/or growth of science parks. Castells and Hall (1994) and Saxenian (1994) describe the Silicon Valley (California) and Route 128 (around Boston) phenomenon; Luger and Goldstein (1991), Link (1995, 2002), and Link and Scott (2003) detail the history of Research Triangle Park (North Carolina); Gibb (1985), Grayson (1993), Guy (1996a,b), and Vedovello (1997) summarize aspects of the science park phenomenon in the United Kingdom; Gibb (1985) also chronicles the science park phenomenon in Germany, Italy, Netherlands, and selected Asian countries; and Chordà (1996) reports on French science parks, Phillimore (1999) on Australian science parks, and Bakouros et al. (2002) on the development of Greek science parks.

A.N. Link, J.T. Scott / Int. J. Ind. Organ. 21 (2003) 1323–1356   1327

park on various aspects of firm performance (e.g., growth and R&D productivity).[8] However, after describing the U.S. experience with the establishment and growth of the modern science park, this paper provides, in an exploratory manner, the first systematic insights into the influence of industry in science parks on the academic missions of universities.

2. Emergence and growth of U.S. science parks

2.1. Diffusion of the science park innovation

If the cumulative total for the science parks shown in Fig. 1 is plotted against time, the familiar logistic curve results.[9] In this section we offer an analytical model to characterize the 'lazy-S,' S-shaped pattern of the cumulative total of parks through time. We argue that the observed pattern of the establishment of science parks should be interpreted in terms of a model of the adoption of an innovation. Specifically, we posit the appearance of a new park as a new adoption of the innovative environment of a science park. We demonstrate that the establishment of science parks can be seen in terms of a simple model of diffusion, thereby offering support for this conceptualization and for how one might think of, and possibly forecast, the growth of the numbers of science parks in existence.

We have chosen a Gompertz survival-time model for our analytical demonstration because the model is quite simple and yet more general than a model using the exponential distribution that has a constant hazard rate. Geroski (2000)

---

[8] See Monck et al. (1988); Sternberg (1990); Westhead and Storey (1994); Westhead and Cowling (1995); Westhead et al. (1995); Westhead (1997); Westhead and Batstone (1998); Löfsten and Lindelöf (2002); and Siegel et al. (2003). Implicitly, policy makers assume that science parks do add value to firm performance, as well as to local community development, as evidenced by the recent National Research Council studies of the proposed Sandia Science Park and Ames Research Center (Wessner, 1999, 2001). As Massey et al. (1992, p. 56) point out, the 'environmental focus' that others have taken has merit:

At the core of the science-park phenomenon lies a view about how technologies are created. This view is that scientific activities are performed in academic laboratories [and Massey et al. assume that at the core of a science park is a university] isolated from other activities. The resulting discoveries and knowledge are potential inputs to technology. Science provides break-throughs from which new technological goods may spring. ... The argument goes that universities have many brilliant people making new discoveries but that they lack the means or the will to reach out to the market. *Science parks constitute a channel by which academic science may be linked to commerce* [emphasis added]. Thus science parks are there to promote, not 'science,' but its application in technology.

[9] Danilov (1971) attributes the relatively long period from about 1960 to the early 1970s, during which the science park movement seemingly stalled, to a number of park efforts that failed as well as to restraints on corporate R&D growth because of a lackluster economy.

discusses many distinct reasons for S-shaped diffusion curves, and he observes that different reasons suggest different distributions for describing adoptions of innovation. For example, when there are asymmetries in the speed of diffusion among different groups in the population of adopters, the Gompertz distribution has been used.[10] The Gompertz survival-time model allows the data to represent a monotonically increasing or decreasing hazard rate for the adoption of the innovation—the appearance of a group of research companies in the innovative environment of a new science park. We hypothesize that as understanding of the science park innovation and the importance of interaction between industry and university science increased over the last half century, the hazard rate (described fully below) for adopting the science park innovation has increased.

The Gompertz model we estimate describes the adoption of the science park innovation as a stochastic diffusion process with an increasing hazard rate. Alternatively, the Weibull distribution could be used with the survival time model and also allow estimation of a hazard rate that increases or decreases through time. The log–normal or log–logistic distributions could be used for data with hazard rates that initially increase and then decrease, and the generalized gamma model would allow for even more flexibility in the hazard function.[11] For our purposes, the Gompertz model offers the appropriate flexibility with a simple functional form to describe the S-shaped diffusion curve where the hazard rate for the population of adopters of the innovative environment increased over time.[12]

Our time series of adoptions of the science park innovation, for our sample of AURRP members in the United States, runs from 1951 when the first park was established until the most recent adoptions in our data that occurred in 1997. In the absence of any particular event that precipitated the awareness of the concept of a science park, we assume that in 1950 potential adopters of the science park concept are made aware of the possibilities. Then, through time science parks appear with appearances being most likely in the environments most favorable to the success of a science park.

The probability that an adoption of the innovation—the establishment of a

---

[10] See Geroski (2000); in particular, see his discussion there of Dixon (1980) and Davies (1979).

[11] StataCorp (2001), pp. 343–75) describes the alternative distributions, and the implementation of the Gompertz distribution for use as an estimable parametric survival-time model. Rather than using maximum likelihood techniques to estimate survival-time models using various distributions as we do here, the early literature on the diffusion of innovations imposed the logistic S-curve for the diffusion of an innovation using appropriate transformations to reach a functional form that could be estimated with relatively simple estimation techniques. See Geroski (2000) for a tracing of the literature from the pioneering studies to the later ones that have modeled hazard rates.

[12] The implementation of the Gompertz distribution for use as an estimable parametric survival model is described in StataCorp (2001, p. 351–2), and we provide a brief explanation here as well. Our estimation uses the procedures and software described in StataCorp (2001, pp. 343–75).

A.N. Link, J.T. Scott / Int. J. Ind. Organ. 21 (2003) 1323–1356   1329

science park—will have occurred by time t is:

$$F(t) = 1 - S(t). \tag{1}$$

$S(t)$ is the probability that for a particular adopter, the adoption has not occurred by time t:

$$S(t) = e^{(-e^{\lambda}/\gamma)(e^{\gamma t} - 1)} \tag{2}$$

The hazard rate for the adoption is:

$$h(t) = F'(t)/(1 - F(t)), \tag{3}$$

where

$$F'(t) = -S'(t) = e^{(\lambda + \gamma t) - (e^{\lambda}/\gamma)(e^{\gamma t} - 1)}. \tag{4}$$

Substituting (1), (2), and (4) into (3), the hazard rate for adoption is then:

$$h(t) = e^{\lambda + \gamma t} = e^{\lambda} e^{\gamma t}, \tag{5}$$

and the hazard rate is increasing, decreasing, or constant as γ is $>$, $<$, or $= 0$.

The hazard rate is the conditional probability density for adoption of the science park innovation. Conditional on an incipient group of potential investors not yet having adopted the innovative environment of a science park, the probability that it will adopt the innovation and establish a park during the small interval of time dt is given by $h(t)$dt. The parameter λ determines the base level of the hazard rate throughout the history of the second half of the twentieth century, while the parameter γ determines the rate at which that base level grows through time. The survival-time model that we use to describe the history of science parks as the diffusion of an innovation treats the parameter λ as a constant plus a linear combination of explanatory variables that have had an impact on the diffusion of science parks.

For the Gompertz diffusion model that we estimate, we have a proportional hazard model where the hazard $h(t_j)$ for the jth adopter is:

$$h(t_j) = e^{x_j \beta} e^{\gamma(t_j)}. \tag{6}$$

The vector of explanatory variables for the jth observation is denoted as $\mathbf{x}_j$. The parameters in the vector $\boldsymbol{\beta}$ and the ancillary parameter γ are estimated from the data with a maximum likelihood estimator. We find that the ancillary parameter γ is significantly greater than zero; thus, the hazard rate for adoption has increased throughout the fifty-year period.

Using the data provided in AURRP (1997), we estimate the model to describe the historical experience in the United States. The presence of a medical center or the park having aerospace/aeronautics among its technologies has a significant positive effect on the hazard rate. Park technology in the biotechnology/bio-

1330   *A.N. Link, J.T. Scott / Int. J. Ind. Organ. 21 (2003) 1323–1356*

medical area significantly reduces the hazard rate, reflecting the historical fact that while aerospace emerged relatively early in the half century of science park emergence, biotechnology emerged as an important area for industrial investment more recently. On the whole, the hazard rate for a park in the South or the Northeast exceeded that for a park in the West or the Midwest.[13]

To help intuition about the model, we present the results of the model as hazard ratios for each variable. The hazard ratio for an explanatory variable shows the effect on the hazard rate given a one-unit change in the variable while all other variables remain unchanged. From Eq. (6), the hazard ratio for variable z among the several in $\mathbf{x}_j$ is then:

$$(h(t_j|z+1) = e^{x_j\beta}e^{\gamma(t_j)}e^{\beta_z})/(h(t_j) = e^{x_j\beta}e^{\gamma(t_j)}) = e^{\beta_z} \tag{7}$$

The model is estimated using the 77 science parks for which data about the technologies were available. The model is estimated with robust standard errors, accounting for the fact that the same 'subjects' appear repeatedly in the pools of 'subjects at risk'.[14] With the interpretation we provide, the statistics in Table 1 show the historical picture for the emergence of science parks. Note that the z

Table 1
Gompertz survival time model of the diffusion of science parks[a]

Explanatory Variable	Hazard Ratio	Robust Std. Error	z[b]	Prob. $> |z|$[b]
Medical Center	1.93	0.519	2.45	0.014
t1	1.74	0.467	2.08	0.038
t4	0.649	0.157	−1.79	0.073
South	1.36	0.302	1.37	0.170
Northeast	1.61	0.465	1.66	0.097
gamma	0.180	0.0215	8.35	0.000

Number of subjects = 77, number of observations = 77, number of failures = 77, time at risk = 2607, Wald chi-squared (5) = 10.6, log likelihood = 8.38, probability > chi-squared = 0.0594.

[a] The dependent variable or outcome is analytical time of the establishment of the park ('failure time' or 'analysis time when record ends'—thus, for the model, analysis time begins in 1950, and a science park that was established in 1983 has an analytical time of establishment of 33). The term 'failure' refers to traditional applications of the survival-time model and the 'survival' function, S. As long as a 'subject at risk' has not adopted the innovation by establishing a science park, it 'survives' in the data, but on adoption it ceases to 'survive' and leaves the set of potential adopters. t1 = aerospace/ aeronautics; t4 = biotechnology/biomedical; the remaining technology categories (in the intercept here in Table 1) provided in AURRP (1997) are provided in the note to Table 2 below where they are used.

[b] The z statistics and probability statements are for each of the underlying coefficients, rather than for the hazard ratios.

---

[13] The U.S. Census definitions for regions of the United States were used to assign states to one of the four regions—West, Midwest, South, and Northeast.

[14] StataCorp (2001, p. 281, p. 345).

A.N. Link, J.T. Scott / Int. J. Ind. Organ. 21 (2003) 1323–1356 1331

statistics and probability statements are for each of the underlying coefficients in β, the vector of coefficients, rather than for the hazard ratios that are formed using those coefficients.[15]

The hazard ratios in Table 1 show that holding other things constant the hazard rate increases by 1.9 times if a medical center is present and by 1.7 times given aerospace/aeronautics technology. Reflecting its emergence later in the history of science parks, the hazard rate is 65 percent as great if biotechnology/biomedicine is indicated, other things the same. Because the model is estimated over the entire half of the century of the science park experience, the technology effects on the hazard rate, for the long-term historical S-curve for the diffusion of science parks, reflect the fact that aerospace investments were more likely earlier in the history, while biotechnology is more likely to be reported by parks formed later in the history. The model also shows that over the entire half of the century, the hazard rates for science parks are about 1.4 times as great in the South and 1.6 times as great in the Northeast as in the West and the Midwest. The AURRP (1997) data of course provide much more information about technologies and various other characteristics of parks, but for our statistical summary of the history, we have reported a very simple specification with just the effects that are statistically significant (or, in the case of the geographic effects, somewhat significant) in the presence of other effects. Our purpose at this point is not to document all of the detail of the history, but to use the simple model to provide a formal description that illustrates science parks as an innovation that diffused throughout the second half of the twentieth century.

The graph shown in Fig. 2 uses the estimated model to predict, for a science park with the characteristics of the average park in our sample, the probability that the innovation (the science park) will not have occurred by time t, where time is measured along the x-axis in analytic time from 0 to 47 which corresponds to calendar time from 1950 to 1997. Fig. 3 shows the predicted hazard rate for the park with average characteristics.[16] Subtracting from 1 the probability shown in Fig. 2 gives the probability that the innovation (the science park) has occurred by each time.[17] Multiplying that probability by the number of science parks in our population gives the model's fitted logistic curve, shown in Fig. 4, that corresponds to the actual curve that could be plotted by cumulating the appearance of the parks as shown in Fig. 1. Instead of the actual result, the model is predicting the expected number of parks at each time, illustrating that their appearance has

---

[15] StataCorp (2001, pp. 354–355).

[16] The statistics show that the gamma parameter is significantly greater than zero, so the hazard rate is increasing over time. Thus, the Gompertz model is appropriate rather than the simple exponential model where the hazard rate is constant. The plot of the hazard rate against time for the average science park is shown in Fig. 3.

[17] Using the model's average estimation of lambda, -8.43 is the average for the sample of the linear combination of the estimated coefficients and the explanatory variables, and gamma, estimated to be 0.180, we then have the probability of occurrence for the average park through time.

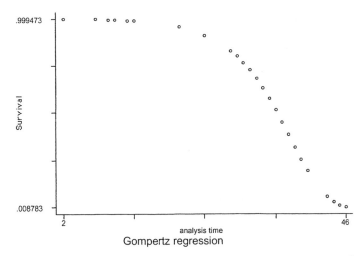

Fig. 2. The probability that the average science park would not have appeared by time *t* for *t* from 1950 to 1997.

followed the S-shaped logistic curve often associated with the diffusion of an innovation.

Using the date at which each new science park is established, we have a list of the 77 parks' arrival times starting with the earliest ones appearing in the early

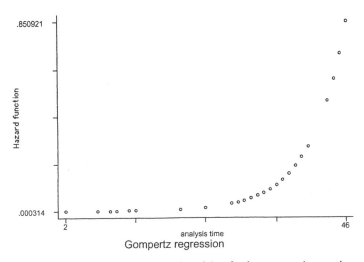

Fig. 3. Plot of the hazard rate as a function of time for the average science park.

A.N. Link, J.T. Scott / Int. J. Ind. Organ. 21 (2003) 1323–1356   1333

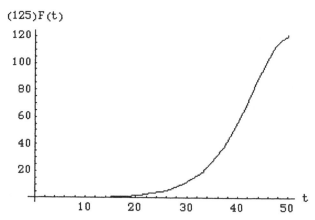

Fig. 4. The expected cumulative number of science parks by time *t* for last half of the twentieth century.

1950s, and ending with those appearing in the late 1990s. With that information, we were able to estimate λ and γ for the diffusion model showing the adoption of the science park research environment by successive groups of investors. On average for those groups, the model shows that λ is estimated to be -8.43 and γ is estimated to be 0.18 for the diffusion of the innovation—the science park. Thus, from Eq. (5), in 1950 at $t=0$ the hazard rate on average across the 77 groups of investors is $e^{-8.43}=0.00022$, and the hazard rate grows at the rate of 18 percent per year.

Fig. 4 raises a question that is important for the formation of technology policy. Has the adoption of the innovation of the science park run its course? Would public policy make possible the beginning of a new logistic curve, rising from the flat portion that both actual adoptions in Fig. 1 and the simulated ones in Fig. 4 suggest has followed half of a century of growth?[18] The actual establishments of research parks as shown in Fig. 1 as well as our diffusion model's tracking of the history as shown in Fig. 4, suggest that public policy can have a large impact on the formation of science parks. From both Fig. 1 and Fig. 4, we see that the acceleration in the formation of science parks occurred after the passage of several technology initiatives in the early 1980s. These policies included, in chronological order, the Bayh–Dole Act of 1980 which reformed federal patent policy by providing increased incentives for the diffusion of federally-funded innovation results; the research and experimentation (R&E) tax credit of 1981 which underwrote, through tax credits, the internal cost of increases in R&E in firms; and

---

[18] Price (1963, Chapter 1) provides a seminal discussion of the appearance of new logistic curves in the history of science.

1334 *A.N. Link, J.T. Scott / Int. J. Ind. Organ. 21 (2003) 1323–1356*

the National Cooperative Research Act of 1984 which encouraged the formation of research joint ventures, as well as numerous state policies that coincided with the adoption of science parks.[19] These technology policies, and others, were a public sector reaction to both the productivity growth slowdown that began in the early 1970s and to the associated precipitous decrease in the competitive position of many U.S. technology-based industries. Of course, the public policies, being more or less coincident with the growth in science parks, could reflect public policies that followed the actions of industry rather than policies that stimulated those actions.

New public policies that encouraged interactions between universities and industry could stimulate a new logistic curve, perhaps even a new fifty-year cycle of growth for science parks. Would such public policy be desirable? The answer is not obvious, but any new policies that foster partnerships between universities and research organizations—private, public, or non-profit—would certainly enhance the environment conducive for partnering within science parks. As for the social desirability of such an environment, that depends on the costs of the new policies and on the size of the net benefits from cooperation, benefits that might include shortened research time and reduced research costs. Are the effects of newly directed commercial interests within science parks in the public interest? The answer will require developing understanding of the sources of growth for science parks, the effects that the parks have on both the economy and on the academic missions of universities, and the role of science parks in the U.S. innovation system.

2.2. Growth of science parks

Science parks are an innovation that reorganizes the method of applying scarce research resources to the production and application of knowledge by combining university and industry resources in a new way. As discussed in the introduction, Fig. 1 shows the adoption of science parks—reflecting the establishment and formation of the science park concept—throughout the last half of a century. We have modeled that adoption as the diffusion of an innovation, with the model estimating the logistic curve in Fig. 4.

In this section, we address the question: Once each park is established, how can we explain its growth over time? In particular, we are interested in developing initial stylized facts about the growth of science parks. To that end, we estimate a model describing the growth of a science park once the basic innovation of the park for combining and applying research resources has been adopted.

Our growth model is:

$$y(t) = ae^{gt}e^{\varepsilon} \tag{8}$$

---

[19] These initiatives are discussed in detail in Audretsch et al. (2002).

A.N. Link, J.T. Scott / Int. J. Ind. Organ. 21 (2003) 1323–1356   1335

where $y(t)$ is the science park's employment t years after it was established, a is the minimum efficient start-up scale for a science park, g is the annual growth rate of the park, and ε is random error.

The growth rate for the park is a function of various explanatory variables, x_1 to x_k:

$$\frac{\dot{y}}{y} = g = b_0 x_0 + b_1 x_1 + \cdots + b_k x_k \tag{9}$$

We then have:

$$\ln y(t) = \ln a + gt + \varepsilon \tag{10}$$

Substituting, we have an estimable model:

$$\ln y(t) = \ln a + b_0 t + b_1 x_1 t + \cdots + b_k x_k t + \varepsilon \tag{11}$$

Estimation of the growth model for the U.S. data is presented in Table 2. The coefficient on t (the length of time that a park has been in existence) shows the annual growth rate for science parks to be 0.084 or 8.4 percent for the parks in the Northeast when none of the qualitative variables in our model are 'turned on'. The annual growth rates for the West, Midwest, and South do not differ significantly, ceteris paribus.

The coefficient on each of the remaining variables (each being the interaction of an explanatory variable and the time that the science park has existed) gives the variable's effect on the annual growth rate. The growth rate of science parks has varied with technologies and with park characteristics. There are controls for all technology effects (leaving 'other technologies' in the intercept) and all regional effects (leaving Northeast in the intercept).[20]

The variable tp is a dummy variable that equals 1 if a park was established in 1980 or later during the period of technology policy initiatives. Thus, the coefficient on its interaction with the time a park has been in existence shows the difference in the annual average rate of growth for parks established after the passage of the aforementioned new technology policies. The coefficient is statistically significant and equal to 0.102; parks established after the passage of the new technology policies have annual growth rates that are higher by 10.2 percentage points, other things being the same.

Three park characteristics are robustly significant. (1) A knowledge environment variable: the driving distance (in miles) between the park and the nearest university, which has a negative effect on growth. For smaller mileage, the growth rate per year falls by the amount of about 10 percentage points for every 100 miles distance between the park and the nearest university. The effect diminishes as

---

[20] The technology areas are those reported to the AURRP, and the regional areas are again those described by the Census for the U.S.—Northeast, West, Midwest, and South.

1336   A.N. Link, J.T. Scott / Int. J. Ind. Organ. 21 (2003) 1323–1356

Table 2
Explaining the growth of science parks*

Variable	Coefficient (standard error)
t	0.0842 (0.0480)*
$t \times West$	− 0.0194 (0.0358)
$t \times Midwest$	− 0.0302 (0.0385)
$t \times South$	0.00800 (0.0309)
$t1 \times t$	− 0.0433 (0.0373)
$t2 \times t$	− 0.0837 (0.0458)*
$t3 \times t$	0.0635 (0.0354)*
$t4 \times t$	0.0160 (0.0350)
$t5 \times t$	− 0.148 (0.0415)***
$t6 \times t$	−0.0346 (0.0275)
$t7 \times t$	0.0875 (0.0385)**
$t8 \times t$	0.00817 (0.0252)
$t9 \times t$	0.121 (0.0313)***
$t10 \times t$	0.0331 (0.0394)
$t11 \times t$	− 0.0266 (0.0305)
$t12 \times t$	0.0113 (0.0445)
$t13 \times t$	− 0.0236 (0.0304)
$t14 \times t$	0.115 (0.0383)***
$t15 \times t$	− 0.0309 (0.0313)
$t16 \times t$	− 0.00146 (0.0341)
$t17 \times t$	0.0796 (0.0310)**
$Lease \times t$	− 0.0662 (0.0258)**
$Venture\text{-}capital \times t$	0.0692 (0.0284)**
$Miles \times t$	− 0.00104 (0.000374)***
$Miles^2 \times t$	1.29×10^{-6} (6.99×10^{-7})*
$tp \times t$	0.102 (0.0363)***
constant	3.21 (0.604)***

Number of observations = 51; $F(26, 24) = 5.14$***; $R^2 = 0.848$; adjusted $R^2 = 0.683$.
*The dependent variable, ln *emp*, is the natural logarithm of employment. The observations are for all science parks in the U.S. for which the data were available. The park technology categories are from AURRP (1997): $t1$ = aerospace/aeronautics; $t2$ = agriculture; $t3$ = animal science; $t4$ = biotechnology/biomedical; $t5$ = chemical; $t6$ = communication; $t7$ = computer; $t8$ = electronics/microelectronics; $t9$ = engineering; $t10$ = environmental; $t11$ = information technology; $t12$ = food processing; $t13$ = life science; $t14$ = medical related; $t15$ = pharmaceutical; $t16$ = software; $t17$ = telecommunications; $t18$ = other. Significance levels are denoted by * (10 percent), ** (5 percent), and *** (1 percent).

mileage increases.[21] (2) A financial environment variable: 1 if venture capital funds are available and 0 otherwise, which has a positive effect on growth. The

---

[21] The negative sign on mileage and the positive sign on mileage squared imply the negative effects on growth of more miles bottoms out (and then turns up, but we believe the upturn is really outside the range of anything interesting or sensible). With $y = a + bx + cx^2 + \ldots$, the first order condition $dy/dx = b + 2cx = 0$ implies that the negative effect will bottom out at $-b/2c$ miles. So, for the growth model in Table 2, the strong negative effect for low mileage gradually diminishes until miles = 0.00104/0.0000026 = 400 miles. There is only one observation among the 51 observations in the model for which a science park is more than 400 miles from the associated university.

A.N. Link, J.T. Scott / Int. J. Ind. Organ. 21 (2003) 1323–1356   1337

growth rate per year increases by the amount of 6.9 percentage points per year if the park reports that venture capital funds are available. (3) A real-estate management variable: having sites for lease only ($=1$) as contrasted with having sites for sale and lease ($=0$), which has a negative effect on growth. The annual growth rate is lower by 6.6 percentage points when parks report sites are leased rather than leased and sold.

Additionally, there are technology effects. Across technologies reported by the AURRP, the strongest statistically significant growth has come from computers, engineering, medical, and telecommunications technologies. The technologies showing the most pronounced negative growth rates are agriculture and chemicals.

The model also provides a stylized fact for the base size for a park. The constant term gives a stylized, initial estimate of the log of the minimum efficient start-up scale for a research park. Looking at the model in that way, we see that the minimum efficient scale is a park with 25 employees (the base to the natural logarithms raised to the power 3.21).

These are exploratory results; future research should consider other explanatory variables such as the extent and nature of faculty and university administration involvement with the university-related science park and whether clusters of universities affect the performance of science parks. Further, growth is just one metric for the success of a park, but it is probably not a bad metric for success. Presumably growth would be correlated with many other metrics for success that would be less easy to quantify (positive externalities affecting the regional economy or the entire economy, successful transfer to industry of university research, placement of university graduates, and so on).

3. Science parks and the academic missions of universities

3.1. Sample of U.S. universities and the data collection process

The population sample of U.S. universities selected for this study consists of the 88 academic institutions that are categorized *both* in the top 100 academic institutions as measured by R&D expenditures and as defined by the National Science Board (2000), and in the Carnegie extensive classification of doctoral/research universities (Carnegie Foundation, 2001). Our priors were that this sample would contain a large segment of academic institutions located in or near science parks that have a research or technology park character, and that have significant interactions with park organizations. The population sample is shown in Table 3.

A brief survey was designed, pretested, and then sent electronically in 2001 to the provost's office at each of these 88 universities. The purpose of the 10 percent pretest ($n=9$) was to ensure that a provost could answer our survey questions in

1338   *A.N. Link, J.T. Scott / Int. J. Ind. Organ. 21 (2003) 1323–1356*

Table 3
Sample of U.S. universities ($n = 88$)

Auburn U	SUNY Buffalo	NYU
U of Alabama at Birmingham	SUNY Stony Brook	U of Rochester
U of Arizona	North Carolina State	Yeshiva U
UC-Berkeley	U of North Carolina	Duke
UC-Davis	Ohio State	Case Western
UC-Irvine	U of Cincinnati	Carnegie Mellon
UCLA	U of Oklahoma	U of Pennsylvania
UC-San Diego	Oregon State	Vanderbilt
UC-Santa Barbara	Penn State	
Colorado State	U of Pittsburgh	
U of Colorado	Clemson U	
U of Connecticut	U of Tennessee	
Florida State	Texas A&M	
U of Florida	U of Texas-Austin	
U of South Florida	U of Utah	
Georgia Tech	Utah State	
U of Georgia	U of Virginia	
U of Hawaii	Virginia Tech	
U of Illinois, Chicago	U of Washington	
U of Illinois, Urbana-Champaign	Washington State	
Indiana U	U of Wisconsin	
Purdue U	Cal Tech	
Iowa State	Stanford	
U of Iowa	U of Southern California	
U of Kansas	Yale	
U of Kentucky	Georgetown	
LSU	U of Miami	
U of Maryland, Baltimore County	Emory U	
U of Maryland, College Park	Northwestern	
U of Massachusetts	U of Chicago	
Michigan State	Tulane	
U of Michigan	Johns Hopkins	
Wayne State	Boston U	
U of Minnesota	Harvard	
Mississippi State	MIT	
U of Missouri	Tufts	
U of Nebraska	Washington U	
Rutgers	Princeton	
New Mexico State	Columbia	
U of New Mexico	Cornell	

an informed manner and to ensure that questions were phrased in an unambiguous manner. Follow-up telephone surveys were made to all non-respondents.

A variety of information was requested (discussed below), but the primary goal of the survey was to collect qualitative information regarding the provost's

A.N. Link, J.T. Scott / Int. J. Ind. Organ. 21 (2003) 1323–1356   1339

perception of the impact of the university's involvement with science parks on the following six academic missions:[22]

- research output, measured in terms of publications
- research output, measured in terms of patents
- extramural research funding
- applied versus basic nature of the curriculum
- placement of doctoral graduates
- ability of the university to hire preeminent scholars.

Motivating this inquiry is not only the conspicuous void of information about science parks in general and about technology flows from organizations into universities in particular, but also the need to understand how those flows affect fundamental academic behavior. Nelson (2001), for example, has asked if universities can take on the role of 'commercial enterprises' (e.g., licensing and patenting) without jeopardizing their more traditional roles such as their commitment to publish in the public domain and contribute to public science.

We received 47 responses (electronic and telephone), representing an initial response rate of 53.4 percent. However, 18 universities responded that they currently have no relationship with a science park and that the survey was therefore not relevant to them. Our final sample, which is analyzed in this paper, consists of the remaining 29 of the 47 responding universities, representing an overall usable response rate of 33.0 percent. Each of the 29 science parks is either a research park or a technology park, using the taxonomy above.

Table 4 shows the distribution of responses to statements about the influence of science parks on the academic missions of the university. Two general patterns are clear from the distribution of responses. First, there is more agreement than disagreement (e.g., more 4 and 5 responses than 1 and 2 responses) that involvement with a science park positively affects the research output and extramural research funding of universities. Second, there is more disagreement than agreement that such involvement affects the placement of doctoral graduates and improves the ability of the university to hire preeminent scholars.

---

[22] A concern prior to administering the survey was whether a provost (including the resources the provost could draw upon) could meaningfully provide such information. During the pretest phase of the study we specifically explored this issue and found in all cases that there was institutional knowledge about the university–science park relationship, even in cases where the provost was only recently appointed. Further, during the follow-up telephone interviews, each respondent was asked whether non-response to the electronic survey was in any way because of ambiguity in the survey or an inability to respond accurately to the survey statements. Also, we discussed with the provosts involved in the pretest stage the appropriateness of the six academic mission statements.

1340   *A.N. Link, J.T. Scott / Int. J. Ind. Organ. 21 (2003) 1323–1356*

3.2. Quantitative analysis of the impact of science parks on the academic missions of universities

To address the general question of how a science park relationship affects the academic missions of a university, we estimated six ordered probit models using the data collected from our survey. The left-hand-side variable in each of the models is a Likert-scale response variable; hence, the ordered probit model is the appropriate statistical technique. Each model was specified to explain inter-university differences in the extent to which provosts agreed or disagreed with the academic mission statements referenced in Table 4. Greater agreement with a mission statement is associated with a higher score; for example, a higher score for the first question means greater enhancement of the university's academic mission of creating research publications. The extent of agreement is modeled as a function of characteristics of both the university and the science park with which the university is affiliated.

Our models initially focused on the same set of independent variables as represented in the model:

$$academic\ mission = f\ (relationship, mileage, rd, \mathbf{X}) \tag{12}$$

where *academic mission* represents each provost's response to each of the six academic mission statements, and where the independent variables will be discussed below. Thus, we estimated six versions of Eq. (12), one corresponding to each survey statement summarized in Table 4.[23]

Regarding the independent variables in Eq. (12), *relationship* dichotomizes the structure of each university's relationship with its science park. The variable *formal* equals one when the relationship is formal, and it equals zero if it is informal. Two questions on the survey quantify this: "Does your university have a *formal* relationship with a science park? (By 'formal' we intend any institutionally recognized arrangements, such as contractual arrangements of various sorts between your university and the science park.)"[24] Or, "Does your university have an *informal* relationship with a science park? (By 'informal' we intend individual rather than institutional relationships, for example, contract research between faculty members and the science park that is not contracted through the university

---

[23] Alternative econometric approaches to the general question of how a university's relationship with organizations in a science park affects the academic missions of the university were considered. Those alternatives are discussed in the Appendix.

[24] Following this question we asked: If YES, what is the name of the science park and what is the nature of your formal relationship (e.g., joint research with selected organizations, joint appointments of faculty at a research institute, own the land the park is on, lease buildings to research companies in the park, etc.)?

A.N. Link, J.T. Scott / Int. J. Ind. Organ. 21 (2003) 1323–1356   1341

Table 4
Percent distribution of responses by provosts to mission statements (n = 29)

Mission statement	Response scale (1 = 'strongly disagree' and 5 = 'strongly agree')				
	1	2	3	4	5
'As a result of my university's involvement with organizations in a science park, the ... '					
overall research output, measured in terms of publications, by faculty has increased.	28%	7%	21%	21%	24%
overall research output, measured in terms of patents, by faculty has increased.	24%	10%	21%	24%	21%
overall extramural research funding by faculty has increased.	21%	10%	28%	17%	24%
research curriculum has become more applied.	24%	10%	31%	7%	28%
placement of doctoral graduates has improved.	24%	14%	28%	28%	7%
ability of the university to hire preeminent scholars has improved.	24%	28%	21%	17%	10%

Note: The rows may not add to 100% due to rounding.

1342   *A.N. Link, J.T. Scott / Int. J. Ind. Organ. 21 (2003) 1323–1356*

but treated as individual consulting.)"[25] We hypothesize that a formal relationship between a university and a science park leads to greater control over the interaction between faculty and the organizations in the park, much like in a centralized decision-making firm. Thus, where formal relationships exist the university may be able to exercise greater influence over the entrepreneurial direction that faculty take and how organizations in the park interact with the university as a whole. To the extent that a formal relationship overcomes barriers to faculty–organization interactions, it may reveal itself as greater faculty research output, greater placement of doctoral graduates, and a greater ability for the university to hire preeminent scholars.

The variable *mileage*—the miles between a university and its associated science park—quantifies the geographical relationship between the university and the science park.[26] Adams and Jaffe (1996) suggest that communication costs related to collaborative R&D activity increase with distance. Wallsten (2001) shows that geographical proximity to other successful innovative firms, as evidenced by the firm receiving a Small Business Innovation Research (SBIR) award, is associated with a firm's own success. These papers, as well as the works of Feldman (1999), Feldman and Lichtenberg (2002), and Adams (2002) motivate the inclusion of the variable *mileage*; we hypothesize that the closer a science park is to the university the more innovative the university. In the context of our model, *mileage* should thus enter negatively in the research output and extramural research equations. We also expect it to enter negatively in the curriculum equation, expecting a closer science park to have a bigger impact on a university's applied research since that is the research area common to both the university and the organizations in the park.

The variable *rd* is a scale variable, distinguishing universities in terms of their total research and development budget in millions of dollars.[27] Following Cohen and Levinthal (1989), we conjecture that more R&D-active universities may have a greater capacity to absorb the knowledge gained through research relationships with organizations in a science park. Thus, we hypothesize that such universities will benefit, in a research sense, relatively more from a relationship with a science park, and this absorption will show itself in more basic research and related research output.

Vector **X** controls for other university and firm characteristics. Two technology dummy (i.e., set to equal either one or zero) variables are included in the empirical

---

[25] Following this question we asked: If YES, what is the name of the science park and what is the nature of your informal relationship (e.g., joint research or faculty members who have consulting positions with selected businesses or a research institute; have an incidental, real estate relationship with the science park but no formal joint effort between the university and the tenants to develop the park in ways that integrate the tenants' activities with the university's research resources; etc.)?

[26] Data on mileage between a university and its named science park came from Internet information about the university or about the park.

[27] These data came from National Science Board (2000, p. A-315).

A.N. Link, J.T. Scott / Int. J. Ind. Organ. 21 (2003) 1323–1356   1343

specifications. Each provost was asked on the survey what technology(ies) are being investigated by faculty involved in research with science park organizations. The variable *dIT* equals 1 if information technology was mentioned, and *dbiotech* equals 1 if biotechnology was mentioned. Multiple technologies were generally mentioned; however, no significance was given to the order in which they were mentioned.

Provosts were also asked to approximate the percentage, *perinresrch,* of faculty who are routinely involved in research with science park organizations. That percentage is a scale variable approximating the proportion of faculty who could be the recipients of a reverse knowledge flow from industry into the university. The reverse flow of knowledge could have an impact on the university's academic missions.

The variable *agepark* is the age of the science park with which each university interacts, measured as the number of years between the time of the survey (in late 2000 with telephone follow-ups well into 2001) and the year that the named science park was formed.[28] This variable is designed to control for the development over time of park organizations with which the university could interact as well as the development of the quality of the interactions—a process that takes time. However, it is an imperfect control for this purpose, although no better information is available, since a park may not begin to have organizations enter immediately upon its formation.

In addition to the university and park characteristics described above, we also control for response bias. As seen in Table 5, the sample of 29 responding and reporting universities does not perfectly mirror the population sample of 88 universities in terms of the selected key characteristics. To control for differences in the probability of responding to the survey, we estimated the probability of responding and completing the survey, that is, the probability of selection into the

Table 5
Selected mean values, by sample of universities

University characteristics	Population sample ($n = 88$)	Responding sample ($n = 29$)
Park on campus (*parkoncampus*)	54.55%	65.52%
Total academic R&D (*rd*)	$198.41M	$207.07M
% of total academic R&D from industry (*indrd*)	13.57%	15.00%
% public universities (*pubpriv* = 1 if public; 0 otherwise)	69.32%	79.31%

---

[28] In 27 of 29 parks we could identify the year the park was formed using information from the Internet and from AURRP (1997).

1344   A.N. Link, J.T. Scott / Int. J. Ind. Organ. 21 (2003) 1323–1356

sample of 29, *prob*8829.[29] That probability is then used as a control variable in Eq. (12).[30] We believe that this variable is doing more than simply controlling for the effect of a correlation in random errors in the model of response and complete models of the provosts' perceptions about the effects of science parks on academic missions. Our model of perceptions is exploratory and unlikely to be complete with just the variables other than *prob*8829. We view the variable *prob*8829 as capturing substantive effects of the complete model that otherwise would be left in the error term and that are related to the probability of responding to the survey.

Table 6 shows the econometric results for the six ordered probit models to assess the determinants of inter-university differences in the impact of science park relationships on the academic missions of universities. The specifications presented are for the parsimonious models that include (apart from the response control) only the explanatory variables that had coefficients at least as great as their standard errors when each model was estimated with all of the explanatory variables. As we have presented in the conference versions of this paper, remarkably (given the small number of observations and the large number of explanatory variables) the full specifications with every one of the explanatory variables included show essentially the same results regarding the significant variables presented in Table 6. The variables omitted in Table 6 had insignificant coefficients, but their inclusion in the all-inclusive models did not eliminate the significance or change the signs of the other variables as presented in Table 6's parsimonious models. Given the small number of observations and the exploratory

---

[29] The probit estimates used to calculate *prob*8829 came from a model of the probability of selection into the sample of 29 respondents among the 88 universities surveyed. The explanatory variables for the probit model of selection were *parkoncamp*, *indrd*, and *pubpriv*. Each explanatory variable had a positive impact on the probability of response to the survey. Although the coefficients were not very significant individually, the probabilities predicted by the model are important in explaining the provosts' responses to some of the mission statements.

[30] Alternatively, the hazard rate from the probability of response model can be used to control for systematic components in the error that are associated with selection into the sample. Results are similar using the hazard rate rather than the probability of selection. We prefer to control for the possibility that something in the error is associated with the selection into the sample by using the probability of response directly. The specifications for our models are exploratory, and Maddala (1983, p. 269) points to evidence "that the normal selection-bias adjustment is quite sensitive to departures from normality." The use of the probability of response rather than the hazard rate has straightforward, intuitive meaning that is not dependent on an assumption of joint normally distributed disturbances for the response probit and the ordered probit models. Further, the standard approach to selection bias of course depends on complete models for response and for the substantive model of interest—here the model of university administrators' perceptions. The response term in the later model then captures the effect of correlation in the random errors in the two models. As discussed in the text, we view the variable *prob*8829 as completing our substantive model, capturing systematic effects on the academic missions that vary with characteristics of universities that are associated with the probability of response. Those ultimate causal characteristics may not be those in our response model, but rather associated with them and therefore with response.

A.N. Link, J.T. Scott / Int. J. Ind. Organ. 21 (2003) 1323–1356   1345

nature of the models, our preferred specifications are the parsimonious ones shown in Table 6.

Ceteris paribus, universities with a formal relationship with a science park realize greater benefits from that relationship as quantified through increased publication and patenting activity, greater extramural funding success, and through an enhanced ability to hire preeminent scholars and to place doctoral graduates.

The closer geographically a university is to the science park, ceteris paribus, the greater the university's success obtaining extramural funding, the greater the influence of park tenants on the applied versus basic research nature of the university's curriculum, and the greater the ability of the university to place its doctoral graduates. The effects are stronger the closer the university and the science park are to one another, and the attenuation of the effect associated with increasing mileage should be considered for ranges reasonably near the sample means. The finding about the applied research curriculum is revisited below.[31]

The total R&D budget of the university, *rd*, enters significantly in three cases. It enters positively in the patenting equation meaning that, ceteris paribus, more R&D-active universities have their patenting activity positively influenced by their association with a science park, supporting the hypothesis about absorptive capacity. It enters negatively in the extramural funding equation, as well as in the hiring equation. We interpret the latter two findings to suggest that the R&D activity of the university, rather than its science park affiliation, drives its academic reputation as reflected through enhanced funding and hiring. The effect of *rd* is explored further below.

The results in Table 6 also suggest (keeping in mind the caveats associated with *agepark*) that older parks have an applied influence on the university's research curriculum, perhaps also explaining the positive effect of age on patenting. Older parks are also more likely to have a positive influence on the hiring of preeminent scholars. The percentage of faculty engaged in university/science park activities, which like *rd* is a scale variable, also enters significantly in the publications equation.

The probability of responding to the academic mission statements, *prob*8829, enters somewhat significantly in the publications model, the patents model, and the

---

[31] Note that there are two models with the nonlinear mileage effect, and the negative effect in the first case—for extramural funding—bottoms out at $0.0951/0.005 = 19$ miles, but recall that the sample mean for the sample of responding firms is only 5.7 miles. For the range around the mean where it is sensible to simulate the effect, the effect is negative. In the second case, the effect bottoms out at $0.942/0.034 = 28$ miles. The effect estimated is negative and diminishing. Think of a negatively sloped curve that gradually bottoms out and approaches an asymptote. It is very sensible that as distance gets bigger, the marginal negative effect would diminish, but we think that mathematical upturn is not of interest empirically given the sample means. Just 4 of the 29 responding parks are further than 19 miles and just 2 of the 29 (and of the 27 used in the applied research model) are further than 28 miles.

Table 6
Ordered probit estimates of agreement with mission statements

Variable	Mission statement coefficient (robust standard error)					
	Publications	Patents	Extramural research funding	Applied research curriculum	Placement of doctoral graduates	Hiring of preeminent scholars
formal	3.31 (0.832)***	2.57 (0.753)***	1.01 (0.618)*	1.39 (0.601)**	1.10 (0.622)*	1.92 (0.644)***
mileage		− 0.0354 (0.0293)	− 0.0951 (0.0573)*	− 0.942 (0.176)***	− 0.0327 (0.0257)	
mileage^2			0.00252 (0.00125)**	0.0175 (0.00369)***		
rd		0.0120 (0.00541)**	− 0.00431 (0.00267)#	− 0.00618 (0.00506)		− 0.00510 (0.00307)*
dIT	− 2.33 (0.807)***		− 1.09	− 1.06 (0.603)*		
dbiotech						− 0.798 (0.441)*
perinresrch	0.159 (0.0714)**					
agepark		0.0301 (0.0190)#		0.0876 (0.0288)***	0.0236 (0.0173)	0.0455 (0.0195)**
prob8829	5.77 (3.21)*	6.67 (3.15)**	3.19 (3.07)	− 6.96 (3.95)*	0.131 (1.58)	1.70 (2.65)
Number of observations	28	27	29	27	27	27
Log likelihood	− 19.99	− 24.21	− 35.72	− 17.30	− 34.59	− 32.46
Pseudo-R^2	0.519	0.420	0.212	0.569	0.157	0.231
Wald Chi-squared (df)	20.0 (4) ***	36.2(5)***	24.8 (6)***	62.8 (7)***	14.1 (4)***	23.6 (5)***
cut1	2.16 (1.04)	5.33 (1.48)	− 0.779 (1.34)	− 6.75 (1.98)	0.030 (0.613)	0.192 (1.06)

A.N. Link, J.T. Scott / Int. J. Ind. Organ. 21 (2003) 1323–1356   1347

cut2	2.47 (1.12)	5.99 (1.55)	−0.141 (1.42)	−4.19 (1.79)	0.682 (0.622)	1.59 (1.04)
cut3	4.42 (1.36)	7.30 (1.65)	0.909 (1.52)	−1.38 (1.51)	1.62 (0.704)	2.46 (1.14)
cut4	6.20 (1.64)	8.77 (1.83)	1.49 (1.54)	−0.988 (1.60)	2.91 (0.895)	3.41 (1.28)
Mean *formal* (n = 29)	0.655					
Mean *mileage* (n = 29)	5.741					
Mean *rd* (n = 29)	207.07					
Mean *dIT* (n = 29)	0.345					
Mean *dbiotech* (n = 29)	0.414					
Mean *perinresrch* (n = 28)	3.750					
Mean *agepark* (n = 27)	19.185					
Mean *prob8829* (n = 29)	0.363					

Notes: Significance levels denoted by #(15 percent), *(10 percent), **(5 percent), ***(1 percent). From the sample of 29 responding universities, 2 listed science parks for which we were unable to determine the year in which the park began, thus we were unable to calculate the variable *agepark*, defined as (2000 − year started). Also, a third university did not report a value for *perinresrch*.

1348 *A.N. Link, J.T. Scott / Int. J. Ind. Organ. 21 (2003) 1323–1356*

applied research model. It remains an open question whether the effect reflects a substantive effect of unobserved explanatory variables associated with response, or instead is simply the result of correlation of the errors in the model of response and the models of university administrators' perceptions.

3.3. Interpretation of statistical results for perceptions of science parks' effects on academic missions of universities

Universities seek external research relationships in an effort to enrich both the knowledge in their research base and the financial value of that knowledge. Herein, we explored how university research relationships with clusters of industrial firms in a science park affect six academic missions. While our sample is relatively small and the information collected from university provosts is qualitative, this study is, to our knowledge, the first to address such impacts in a systematic manner.

The statistical relationships that we found are interesting for a general understanding of science parks and associated knowledge flows. However, the relationships also show how universities that are considering establishing a science park might benchmark their planned activities and structure their relationship with their science park to control the influence of the relationship on academics at the university. Our survey did not apply to 18 of the 47 universities that returned our survey. Five of those 18 universities reported that they are currently planning a science park or are in the process of building one. While we may not see a resurgence of the creation of new science parks as observed in the mid- to late 1980s (see Fig. 1), our survey data and informal discussions with science park directors suggest that the science park phenomenon is again on the rise. Put differently, in terms of our model as illustrated in Fig. 4, a new logistic curve may be taking off from the plateau attained after the first half century of science park growth. As university administrators deal with collaborative research relationships in science parks, our results suggest the following expectations.

First, the organizational nature of the university–park relationship is important. Our measures of a formal versus an informal relationship apparently capture important differences in how universities form a research relationship with their science park. When the relationship is formal, specific impacts will follow including enhanced research output (e.g., publications and patents), increased extramural funding, and improvements in hiring and placement capabilities.

Second, proximity of the science park to the university has an impact on various aspects of the university's academic mission. Proximity, other things held constant, increases success in obtaining extramural funding. Further, other factors held constant, a science park located on or very close to the university campus confers greater employment opportunities for doctoral graduates. But, this nexus

A.N. Link, J.T. Scott / Int. J. Ind. Organ. 21 (2003) 1323–1356   1349

also has a curricular influence by causing a more applied research curriculum other things being the same.[32]

Third, ceteris paribus, more R&D-active universities are more likely to report that their interaction with science park organizations positively affects their propensity to patent. They are less likely to report science park effects on their extramural funding activity or on their ability to hire preeminent scholars. The R&D activity within the university is considered in more detail below.

Fourth, as measured by the percentage of faculty, the intensity with which university faculty are engaged in research with science park organizations appears to have little measurable impact on the effect of science parks on the academic missions of universities except on publications.

Fifth, the influence of university-park research interactions may change over the life of the interaction. Over time, the impact that science parks have on academic missions changes. Initially, that impact may not influence patenting activity or curriculum, but over time it will. Similarly, over time the reputation of the science park will confer a hiring advantage to the university, ceteris paribus.[33]

Reemphasizing the caveats associated with this study, namely that we rely on the provosts' perceptions of effects (rather than time-series data about the effects) and that our sample is small, the results in Table 6 may nevertheless be useful for guiding aspects of university decision making. The results may inform the decision making of universities that have science parks and are trying to understand the full extent of the university–park relationship. Also, the results may inform universities that are contemplating establishing a science park or planning one. We illustrate this with two examples, both focusing on the effect of a university's involvement with a science park on the applied nature of the university's research curriculum. That dimension of curricular focus has gained attention in recent years. As noted previously, Nelson (2001) has warned that as universities take on commercial activities, often in conjunction with industry, their commitment to public science may be endangered. Stephan (2001) as well has noted that there is the potential that technology transfer activities—likely to occur from university/science park interactions—will divert faculty away from students and curriculum and towards commercial activities such as the quest for extramural research funding. If such funding comes from industrial firms, then it is reasonable to be concerned that commercial influences will spill over to influence the character of the university's research and hence its research curriculum.

---

[32] Nelson (2001) is concerned that commercialization of university research may have a detrimental effect on its 'public science.' Stephan (2001) observes that university/industry research partnerships have a potential to have a detrimental affect on the university's basic research curriculum. This issue is discussed in more detail in Poyago-Theotoky et al. (2002).

[33] We did investigate the possibility of a nonlinear age of park effect, but that variable never entered at even a marginally significant level.

First, consider a university that has an ongoing relationship with organizations in a science park; consider also the ordered probit results presented in Table 6 for the applied research curriculum mission of the university. Ceteris paribus, as *rd* increases, there is a decrease in the probability of agreement with the mission statement that the university's research curriculum has become more applied as a result of its involvement with organizations in a science park. The point is that university R&D activity is an instrument that the university can use to control the impact that its involvement with its science park has on its curricular mission. As well, university R&D activity is an instrument useful in predicting, in a benchmarking sense, what impact to expect from its science park involvement. Interpreted slightly differently, the research culture of the university—and we suggest that the 'strength' of that culture may be related to the intensity of the university's R&D activity—that also confers an academic reputation on the university, offsets outside (e.g., through science park relationships) influences that push the academic curriculum away from basic research toward applied research.

Second, consider a university planning a science park. Again, using the estimated coefficients in Table 6, ceteris paribus, for a reasonable range around the sample mean, as mileage increases, the probability of agreement with the mission statement that the university's research curriculum has become more applied as a result of its involvement with organizations in a science park decreases. Proximity does matter. When planning an on-campus science park, *mileage* = 0, provosts should expect over time a significant applied influence in the research curriculum from that relationship. Ceteris paribus, the probability of such an influence decreases rapidly when the cluster of industrial firms is off campus.

4. Conclusions

There is much to be learned about science parks, in general, and their influence on university activity, in particular. This exploratory paper is only a first step in the new learning about science parks and their effects on the academic missions of universities. We have in our paper modeled the appearance of science parks throughout the last half of a century as the diffusion of an innovation—the innovation of the modern science park. With the model, we could describe the hazard rate for the appearance of new science parks through time, and we could observe the initial increase in the rate of new park formations about the time of the Bayh–Dole Act's passage, the enactment of the R&E tax credit, and the rise in research joint venture activity encouraged through the National Cooperative Research Act, and then the eventual decline in that rate. Understanding the determinants of the rate of formation can inform public policy toward science parks as we enter a new era of growth in the formation of science parks. We have provided initial insights about the forces that stimulate the growth of a science

A.N. Link, J.T. Scott / Int. J. Ind. Organ. 21 (2003) 1323–1356   1351

park once it has been established. We tentatively identified sources of growth from knowledge, financial, and real estate resources, holding constant the types of technologies associated with the science park and its geographic region and the apparent effect of the technology policies. Further development of the model will be important to inform public policy toward science parks. Finally, we surveyed university administrators to discover their perceptions about the impacts of science parks on their universities' academic missions. Formal association with a science park tends to be perceived by the university administrators as increasing research outputs as measured by publications and patents, as increasing extramural funding, as improving their universities' prospects for hiring preeminent scholars and for placing doctoral graduates. Proximity to a science park improves success in obtaining extramural funding, and proximity improves a university's doctoral graduates' prospects for jobs. However, the applied nature of the university's research curriculum increases with such proximity; R&D spending at the university reduces that impact.

Future research can extend and develop the findings of this exploratory paper. Regarding the diffusion of the innovation of science parks, the underlying determinants of our model's gamma and lambda can be further developed and explored with data describing the resources available in the geographical environments that host the science parks. For future research about adoptions of the science park concept, samples should include not only established science parks, but as well entrepreneurial groups considering establishment of a park yet never adopting the science park innovation within the sample period. That is, the sample would include entrepreneurial groups that 'survive' throughout the sample period—hence do not 'fail' in the language of the survival time model—and do not adopt the science park innovation. Further, the samples could include parks that were established—adopted the science park concept—but then failed as science parks. Our preliminary work with the growth of science parks once they are established suggests the importance of the knowledge, financial, and real estate resources available to a science park, but future research is needed to develop our exploratory findings.

Our initial look at the perceptions of university administrators is only a beginning in developing understanding about the impact of science parks on the academic missions of universities. The sample size is necessarily small when the unit of observation is the university itself, and a useful extension of our exploratory study could focus on multiple respondents for each university. Multiple respondents could be developed with interviews of faculty members as well as university administrators, and with respondents representing industry participants in the science park. The multiple responses—combined with additional data (including data about the geographic and economic areas in which the parks are located and including qualitative historical data) about the universities and the science parks—will allow future research to develop further the understanding of the interactions between the university and the associated science park.[34] In particular, our findings suggest that the proximity of the science park to the university has no discernable impact on two of the six dimensions of the academic mission. We expect that the reason may simply be the small size of our sample, but future research should explain why, and it should also develop the timing of science park impacts on the academic missions of universities.

Further, in addition to working with the perceptions of those involved with the university/science park interactions, quantitative measures of the interactions' effects should be evaluated in future research. For example, future work could attempt to assess quantitatively a university's success in basic research as a function of the degree of involvement with a science park, measuring success with citation counts or ranking of graduate programs in science and engineering. Additionally, our exploratory study focused on the experience in the United States with its patent law, its mix of public and private universities, and so forth; one expects different experiences in different countries, and future research will develop those differences and thereby increase knowledge about the science park/university interactions.

Acknowledgements

Earlier versions of parts of this paper were presented at the University of Nottingham's Institute for Enterprise and Innovation/National Academy of Sciences' Board of Science, Technology and Economic Policy Collaborative Conference on "Policies to Promote Entrepreneurship in a Knowledge-Based Economy: Evaluating Best Practices from the U.S. and U.K," September 18–19, 2000; at the Industrial Organization Society's session on "Innovations in Industrial Organization of R&D and Technology Transfer" at the Allied Social Sciences Association's meetings in New Orleans, January 5, 2001; at the Georgia Institute of Technology Roundtable for Engineering Entrepreneurship Research Conference, March 21–23, 2002; and at two workshops at the University of North Carolina at Greensboro — the National Science Foundation Workshop on Science Park Indicators, November 14, 2002, and the Workshop on the Economics of Intellectual Property at Universities, November 15, 2002. We appreciate comments from the participants at those conferences, especially those from Irwin Feller and Donald Siegel, as well as comments from Richard Arnott regarding the directions

---

[34] The details that distinguish science parks may be crucial to understanding the perceptions that we have documented in our exploratory study. Future research should develop those details. Richard Arnott has suggested (personal correspondence, July 26, 2002) questions such as the following ones. "Do most faculty who have an association with a research park consult or are they part owners of start-up companies? If a professor develops a product in a science park that derives from basic research performed at the university, who has the patent rights? Do the professor's research students at the university routinely get involved in their science park activities?"

A.N. Link, J.T. Scott / Int. J. Ind. Organ. 21 (2003) 1323–1356   1353

for future research. We also appreciate the generous funding provided by the National Science Foundation to conduct this study.

Appendix A

In this Appendix, we discuss alternative econometric approaches to the question of how a university's relationship with a science park affects the academic missions of the university. One alternative to exploring inter-university differences in perceived effects of a science park on academic missions would have been to collect quantitative data on aspects of university activity (e.g., publications, patents, extramural funds, curriculum, student placements, and hiring) and estimate for each university a time series model, controlling for the date that the university began its relationship with the science park. Such a model as

$$\text{academic activity}_{t=0 \text{ to } t=n} = f\ (\text{science park interaction}_{t=0 \text{ to } t=n}) \qquad \text{(A.1)}$$

has the benefit of relying on objective data to quantify academic activity on the left. However, the error in the equation may be correlated (causing biases in the estimates of the model's coefficients) with the errors in the observations of the independent variables—errors that may be severe because there is no meaningful way to date when a university began to have relationship with a park. Parks evolve over time from a concept to a development project to an infrastructure housing research partners. Research Triangle Park is a case in point. Faculty from Duke University, University of North Carolina, and North Carolina State University (then State College) were involved with the Park before the Park became a park. That is, faculty were integrally involved in research relationships with companies as far back as the late 1950s, although the first tenant did not commit to the Park until 1965 and began research operations more than a year later. In other cases, there have been long standing relationships between the university and the park, but the park has yet to move from a land development corporation to one with research tenants. Or, we could have created a matched sample of universities with and without a science park relationship and compared the performance of each group of universities. Such a model as

$$\text{academic activity}_{\text{university A vs. university B}}$$

$$= f\ (\text{science park interaction}_{\text{university A vs. university B}}) \qquad \text{(A.2)}$$

also has the advantage of objective data on the left, but there is not a meaningful (as opposed to systematic) way to create a matched sample of universities that do not have a science park relationship. Again, we expect correlation between the error in equation and the errors in the explanatory variables. There are two main reasons for those errors. One, the relationship between a university and park is an evolving one, as just discussed, and, even controlling for age of park, the sample of universities with park relationships would still have a degree of heterogeneity that could not be matched in the sample of universities without park relationships. And two, we would have had no way to hold constant in such an experiment other industry influences on the university that occurred as a result of research or other interactions outside of the geographic park setting. As compared with our approach, the alternative approaches represented by Eqs. (A.1) and (A.2) have some advantages despite the potentially bias-inducing errors in variables difficulties we have identified. Just as clearly, however, our approach has its own advantages, and the perceptions of the universities' provosts about the effects of the science park affiliations on the universities' missions are important in themselves. Although the dependent variables in the versions of Eq. (12) that were estimated clearly reflect perceptions, we are convinced, as a result of our pretests, that provosts reported well-informed perceptions. And, given that the dependent variable reflects perceptions, ordered probit is the appropriate econometric technique. The alternative models noted above would also have contained judgmental information, but would have done so in a manner that would be likely to create an important errors in variables problem. Although there are econometric approaches to dealing with the errors in variables problem, the errors introduced in the two alternative models would be central to the time series investigation and especially intractable.

References

Adams, J.D., 2002. Comparative localization of academic and industrial spillovers. Journal of Economic Geography 2, 253–278.

Adams, J.D., Jaffe, A.B., 1996. Bounding the effects of R&D: An investigation using matched establishment-firm data. Rand Journal of Economics 94, 700–721.

Association of University Related Research Parks (AURRP), 1997, Worldwide Research & Science Park Directory 1998. BPI Communications.

Audretsch, D.B., Bozeman, B., Combs, K.L., Feldman, M.P., Link, A.N., Siegel, D.S., Stephan, P.E., Tassey, G., Wessner, C., 2002. The economics of science and technology. Journal of Technology Transfer 27, 155–203.

Bakouros, Y.L., Mardas, D.C., Varsakelis, N.C., 2002. Science park, a high tech fantasy?: An analysis of the science parks of Greece. Technovation 22, 123–128.

Carnegie Foundation for the Advancement of Teaching, 2001. The Carnegie Classification of Institutions of Higher Education, 2000 Edition. Carnegie Foundation, Menlo Park, California.

Castells, M., Hall, P., 1994. Technopoles of the World. Routledge, London.

Chordà, I.M., 1996. Towards the maturity state: An insight into the performance of French technopoles. Technovation 16, 143–152.

Cohen, W.M., Levinthal, D.A., 1989. Innovation and learning: The two faces of R&D. Economic Journal 99, 569–596.

Cohen, W.M., Florida, R., Randazzese, L., Walsh, J., 1997. Industry and the academy: Uneasy partners in the cause of technological advance. In: Noll, R. (Ed.), Challenge to the University. Brookings Institution Press, Washington, D.C.

A.N. Link, J.T. Scott / Int. J. Ind. Organ. 21 (2003) 1323–1356   1355

Danilov, V.J., 1971. The research park shake-out. Industrial Research 13, 1–4.

Davies, S., 1979. The Diffusion of Process Innovations. Cambridge University Press, Cambridge.

Dixon, R.J., 1980. Hybrid corn revisited. Econometrica 48, 145–146.

Feldman, M., 1999. The new economics of innovation, spillovers and agglomeration: A review of empirical studies. Economics of Innovation and New Technology 8, 5–25.

Feldman, M., Lichtenberg, F., 2002. Innovation, imitation and distance in the pharmaceutical industry. Mimeograph, Johns Hopkins University.

Geroski, P.A., 2000. Models of technology diffusion. Research Policy 29, 603–625.

Gibb, M.J., 1985. Science Parks and Innovation Centres: Their Economic and Social Impact. Elsevier, Amsterdam.

Grayson, L., 1993. Science Parks: An Experiment in High Technology Transfer. The British Library Board, London.

Guy, I., 1996a. A look at Aston Science Park. Technovation 16, 217–218.

Guy, I., 1996b. New ventures on an ancient campus. Technovation 16, 269–270.

Hall, B.H., Link, A.N., Scott, J.T., 2000. Universities as research partners. NBER Working Paper 7643.

Hall, B.H., Link, A.N., Scott, J.T., 2003. Universities as research partners. Review of Economics and Statistics 85, 485–491.

Link, A.N., 1995. A Generosity of Spirit: The Early History of the Research Triangle Park. University of North Carolina Press for the Research Triangle Park Foundation, Research Triangle Park.

Link, A.N., 1996. Research joint ventures: Patterns from Federal Register filings. Review of Industrial Organization 11, 617–628.

Link, A.N., 2002. From Seed To Harvest: The History of the Growth of the Research Triangle Park. University of North Carolina Press for the Research Triangle Park Foundation, Research Triangle Park.

Link, A.N., Scott, J.T., 2003. The growth of Research Triangle Park. Small Business Economics 20, 167–175.

Löfsten, H., Lindelöf, P., 2002. Science parks and the growth of new technology-based firms—Academic-industry links, innovation and markets. Research Policy 31, 859–876.

Luger, M.I., Goldstein, H.A., 1991. Technology in the Garden. University of North Carolina Press, Chapel Hill.

Maddala, G.S., 1983. Limited Dependent and Qualitative Variables in Econometrics. Cambridge University Press, Cambridge.

Massey, D., Qunitas, P., Wield, D., 1992. High-tech Fantasies: Science Parks in Society, Science and Space. Routledge, London.

Monck, C.S.P., Porter, R.B., Quintas, P., Storey, D.J., Wynartczyk, P., 1988. Science Parks and the Growth of High Technology Firms. Croom Helm, London.

Morgan, R.P., 1998. University research contributions to industry: The faculty view. In: Blair, P., Frosch, R. (Eds.), Trends in Industrial Innovation: Industry Perspectives & Policy Implications. Sigma Xi, The Scientific Research Society, Research Triangle Park, pp. 163–170.

Mowery, D.C., Teece, D.J., 1996. Strategic alliances and industrial research. In: Rosenbloom, R., Spenser, W. (Eds.), Engines of Innovation: U.S. Industrial Research at the End of an Era. Harvard Business School, Boston, pp. 111–129.

National Science Board, 2000. Science & Engineering Indicators—2000. National Science Foundation, Arlington, Virginia.

Nelson, R.R., 2001. Observations on the post-Bayh–Dole rise of patenting at American universities. Journal of Technology Transfer 26, 13–19.

Phillimore, J., 1999. Beyond the linear view of innovation in science park evaluation: An analysis of Western Australian Technology Park. Technovation 19, 673–680.

Poyago-Theotoky, J., Beath, J., Siegel, D.S., 2002. Universities and fundamental research: Reflections on the growth of university–industry partnerships. Oxford Review of Economic Policy 18, 10–21.

Price, D.J. de Solla, 1963. Little Science, Big Science. Columbia University Press, New York.

Saxenian, A.L., 1994. Regional Advantage. Harvard University Press, Cambridge.

Siegel, D.S., Thursby, J.G., Thursby, M.C., Ziedonis, A.A., 2001. In: Symposium On Organizational Issues in University–Industry Technology Transfer. Journal of Technology Transfer, Vol. 1–3.

Siegel, D.S., Westhead, P., Wright, M., 2003. Science parks and the performance of new technology-based firms: A review of recent U.K. evidence and an agenda for future research. Small Business Economics 20, 177–184.

StataCorp, 2001. Stata Statistical Software: Release 7.0, Vol. 3. Stata Corporation, College Station, Texas.

Stephan, P.E., 2001. Educational implications of university–industry technology transfer. Journal of Technology Transfer 26, 199–205.

Sternberg, R., 1990. The impact of innovation centres on small technology-based firms: The example of the Federal Republic of Germany. Small Business Economics 2, 105–118.

United Kingdom Science Park Association (UKSPA), 1985. Science Park Directory. UKSPA, Sutton Coldfield.

U.S. General Accounting Office, 1983. The Federal Role in Fostering University–Industry Cooperation. GAO, Washington, D.C.

Vedovello, C., 1997. Science parks and university–industry interaction: Geographical proximity between the agents as a driving force. Technovation 17, 491–502.

Wallsten, S., 2001. An empirical test of geographic knowledge spillovers using geographic information systems and firm-level data. Regional Science and Urban Economics 31, 571–599.

Wessner, C.W. (Ed.), 1999. A Review of the Sandia Science and Technology Park Initiative. National Research Council, Washington, D.C.

Wessner, C.W. (Ed.), 2001. A Review of the New Initiatives at the NASA Ames Research Center: Summary of A Workshop. National Research Council, Washington, D.C.

Westhead, P., 1997. R&D 'inputs' and 'outputs' of technology-based firms located on and off science parks. R&D Management 27, 45–62.

Westhead, P., Batstone, S., 1998. Independent technology-based firms: The perceived benefits of a science park location. Urban Studies 35, 2197–2219.

Westhead, P., Cowling, M., 1995. Employment change in independent owner-managed high-technology firms in Great Britain. Small Business Economics 7, 111–140.

Westhead, P., Storey, D.J., 1994. An Assessment of Firms Located On and Off Science Parks in the United Kingdom. HMSO, London.

Westhead, P., Storey, D.J., Cowling, M., 1995. An exploratory analysis of the factors associated with the survival of independent high-technology firms in Great Britain. In: Chittenden, F., Robertson, M., Marshall, I. (Eds.), Small Firms: Partnerships For Growth. Paul Chapman, London, pp. 63–99.

[14]

The Growth of Research Triangle Park

Albert N. Link
John T. Scott

ABSTRACT. In light of the history of Research Triangle Park, we develop an analytical model to characterize the Park's growth. The model is based on the hypothesis that the Park's growth can be thought of as the adoption of an innovation, where the innovation is the new innovative environment created by the Park and its infrastructure.

I. Introduction

> In the heart of North Carolina there exists one of the Nation's most important industrial resources . . . the Research Triangle (Link, 1995, p. 1).

Over the past fifty years the term "Research Triangle" has been used in a number of ways, but generally it has been used to refer to the geographic area defined by Duke University in Durham, North Carolina State University in Raleigh,[1] and the University of North Carolina at Chapel Hill.[2,3] Within Research Triangle is Research Triangle Park, a well-defined area of 6,900 acres, and within its incorporated boundaries are 137 organizations with over 41,600 employees, including 104 research companies with over 40,000 research employees. Certainly the largest research park in the United States both in terms of employees and acreage, and arguably the most

Albert N. Link
Department of Economics
University of North Carolina at Greensboro
Greensboro, NC 27412
U.S.A.
E-mail: al_link@uncg.edu

and

John T. Scott
Department of Economics
Dartmouth College
Hanover, NH 03755
U.S.A.
E-mail: john.t.scott@dartmouth.edu

notable, the Park began with only a vision, survived financially turbulent times, and then it slowly grew toward its current eminent status.

The remainder of this paper is outlined as follows. In the following Section II, we briefly chronicle the history of Research Triangle Park.[4] In Section III, we develop an analytical model to characterize the growth of the Park over time. We hypothesize that the growth of the Park can be thought of as the adoption of an innovation as new companies adopted over time the Park's innovative environment. Our model fits the data quite well. Then, in Section IV, we set forth one explanation for why the Park has grown as successfully as it has. There, we hypothesize the Park's successful growth may have been because of the continuity of entrepreneurial leadership that the Park enjoyed for more than 30 years. Section V of the paper offers some concluding observations.

II. A brief history of Research Triangle Park

After World War II, the North Carolina economy was very unstable. Historically, the state's economy had relied almost exclusively on three traditional industries: furniture, textiles, and tobacco. The furniture industry was leaving the state and expanding into the northeastern United States; the textile industry was beginning to face growing competition from Asian producers; and tobacco manufacturing employment was on the decline, in part because of automation and in part because of decreasing demand.

North Carolina's per capita income had long been one of the lowest in the Nation,[5] and the decline in its traditional industries made it even more difficult for the state to employ its own college graduates. During the early 1950s, the academic community was becoming increasingly concerned about the out migration of its better

 Small Business Economics **20**: 167–175, 2003.
© 2003 *Kluwer Academic Publishers. Printed in the Netherlands.*

college graduates and began a dialogue with the state's economic development leaders about ways to attract new industries to North Carolina. The idea of using the three triangle universities to attract research companies into a park area central to the universities quickly emerged from the dialogue.

In early 1954, Brandon Hodges, the state treasurer of North Carolina, Robert Hanes, the president of Wachovia Bank and Trust Company, and Romeo Guest, a Greensboro building contractor who some say gave birth to the idea of a research park in the triangle area, met to discuss North Carolina's need for industrial growth. Hanes, an extremely influential citizen, was not immediately sold on the idea. In the fall of 1954, Hodges and Guest enlisted the support of key deans and faculty at North Carolina State, and in December 1954, the group convinced Chancellor Carey Bostian to take the triangle idea to Governor Luther Hodges. While the governor, like Hanes, did not immediately see the potential of the idea for North Carolina, he was willing to commission a concept report. The 10-page document, written by William Newell, director of the Textile Research Center at North Carolina State, was delivered to the governor on January 27, 1955, and soon thereafter the triangle idea became known as the "Governor's Research Triangle" (Link, 1995, p. 20).

In April 1955, having solicited the support of Gordon Gray, president of the University of North Carolina, and Hollis Edens, president of Duke University, Governor Hodges organized the Research Triangle Development Council with Hanes as chairman.[6] During the next year the Council and its various subcommittees agreed that the Research Triangle project should be maintained as a private effort and that the universities, "by the research atmosphere that their very existence creates," will act as a magnet to attract industry "by providing a wellspring of knowledge and talents for the stimulation and guidance of research by industrial firms" (Link, 1995, p. 29). Soon thereafter, George Simpson, professor of sociology at Chapel Hill, agreed to take a one-year leave of absence to be director of the organization that, on September 25, 1956, would be named the Research Triangle Committee, Inc. His task was to attract research companies to the triangle.

While the leaders in the state believed that the Research Triangle was a good idea, a number of obstacles immediately stood in the way. First, North Carolina was in the South, although it did have a progressive reputation; it had reacted relatively well to the Supreme Court's 1954 *Brown v. Board of Education* decision. Second, there was a tendency for large companies to maintain their research facilities near their manufacturing sites. And third, there was a folk wisdom that Route 128 around Boston and Stanford Research Park were not planned but rather just happened, so there was no clear path to follow.

Simpson realized that university cooperation would be essential for the park idea to succeed, so he assembled a team of faculty to develop brochures documenting the research expertise of the three universities in selected fields and to travel to visit companies and tell them about the park idea.[7] By the end of 1957, over 200 companies were visited, but the faculty really had nothing to "sell" but a concept. Land would be needed.

As early as January 1957, Governor Hodges, anticipating the need for land, had tried to identify investors in North Carolina in the Research Triangle but had not been successful. However, William Saunders, director of the state's Department of Conservation and Development, had the idea to approach New Yorker, Karl Robbins. Robbins had retired to New York in the 1950s, but because he had previously owned textile mills in North Carolina he was familiar with the areas and was a friend of Guest's. Robbins was interested and made a commitment to invest up to $1 million but began with an investment of only $30,000.

Separate and apart from the planning and marketing of the Research Triangle Committee, Guest took the lead in creating a private land venture. By July 1957, he and those helping him had acquired options to purchase nearly 800 acres at an average price of $161 per acre in what would eventually become Research Triangle Park. Operating secretly and without fanfare, Guest and his associates had acquired options under the name of Pinelands, Inc. for 3,430 acres of an identified 4,000 acres by September when the press began to publicize the park idea. Most of the options were due at the end of November, but Robbins was reluctant to invest any more than the $109,000 he had invested to date because no North Carolinians had yet invested.

By early 1958, Pinelands, the private land development group, and the Research Triangle Committee, the state and university planning and marketing group, realized that there were problems and that they could no longer rely on Robbins for sufficient financial capital to assemble the land while the Committee tried to identify and attract research companies to the area. In August 1958, Governor Hodges and Hanes approached Archibald (Archie) Davis, also of Wachovia Bank and Trust, to help attract North Carolina investors for the Pinelands Company. Davis recognized that the Research Triangle had the potential to be extremely important for the future economic direction of the state, and he realized that if the Triangle was designed for public service rather than for private gain it would be much easier to raise money from corporations and institutions that were interested in serving the state of North Carolina. Thus, he agreed to raise contributions, as opposed to solicit financial investments, under the condition that the pledged funds would be used to pay the Pinelands Company's borrowed debt ($415,000), to finance the establishment of a research institute ($500,000 estimated), and to construct a building ($250,000 estimated). In October, Davis presented this proposal to the Committee and it was accepted. He began his fund raising efforts on December 1, and on January 9, 1959, Governor Hodges announced that Davis had raised $1.425 million and that these funds would be used to acquire the land assembled by Pinelands and to pass control of this enterprise to the recently constituted nonprofit Research Triangle Foundation of North Carolina. Further, the funds would be used to establish as a centerpiece for the Park the Research Triangle Institute for the purpose of doing contract research for business, industry, and government as well as for a building to house the Foundation and Institute in the center of the Research Triangle Park.

The Park moved forward rather slowly. In May 1959, Chemstrand Corporation announced its decision to relocate from Decatur, Alabama, to the Park. Thus, Chemstrand and the Research Triangle Institute became the anchors for the Park. But, for the next five years the Foundation had little success in attracting companies. In fact, the Foundation borrowed $1.3 million to redeem outstanding shares in Pinelands, to purchase additional tracts of land, and to sustain Park operations.

Nineteen hundred and sixty five marked the turning point for the Park. On January 6, Governor Terry Sanford announced that the U.S. Department of Health, Education, and Welfare had selected the Research Triangle Park for its $70 million National Environmental Health Sciences Center. And, on April 14, Governor Dan Moore announced that IBM would locate a 600,000-square foot research facility on 400 acres in the Park.[8] As clearly seen from Figure 1 and Figure 2, the sustained growth of the Park began in that year.

While new tenants continued to enter the Park over the ensuing decades, there was one key event that distinguishes the Park from all other science parks both in the United States and in other countries.[9] In early 1974, Davis, in his role as president of the Foundation, charged the leadership of Duke University (President Terry Sanford) and the University of North Carolina (President William Friday) to formulate a plan to ensure the continued presence of the three sister institutions in the Park, for the Park began with those institutions at its core and their continued presence would be needed for its ultimate prosperity. What evolved from committee discussions was the decision to set aside a campus of approximately 120 acres, to be donated by the Foundation, for the purpose of housing organizations that could bring together faculty from the three universities and Park scientists to work collaboratively. The "park within a park" was to be called the Triangle Universities Center for Advanced Studies, Inc. (TUCASI).

Thanks to the vision of Davis and his leadership and that of Sanford and Friday (and others over the years), there are today six organizations on the TUCASI campus: the National Humanities Center, the Microelectronics Center of North Carolina, the North Carolina Biotechnology Center, Sigma Xi, the National Institute of Statistical Sciences, and the Burroughs Wellcome Fund. These organizations are an outward reflection of the universities' core values and as such, TUCASI is an intangible asset that makes

Albert N. Link and John T. Scott

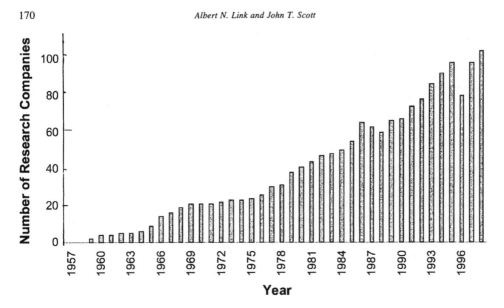

Figure 1. Number of research companies in Research Triangle Park from 1957 through 1998.

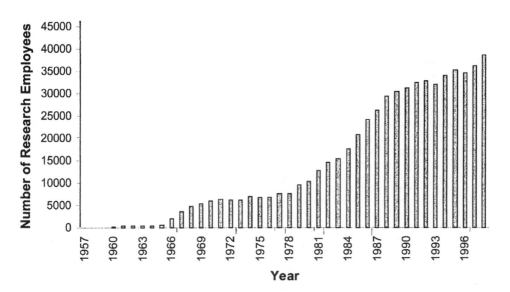

Figure 2. Number of research employees in Research Triangle Park from 1957 through 1998.

Research Triangle Park unique and helps to attract new organizations into the area.

III. Characterizing the growth of Research Triangle Park

In this section we offer an analytical model to characterize the seemingly S-shaped pattern of growth in the Park as illustrated in Figure 1.[10] We argue that the observed pattern of growth in the Park can be interpreted in terms of a model of the adoption of an innovation. Specifically, we posit the appearance of a new research company in the Park as another company adopting the Park's innovative environment. As such, we demonstrate below that we can indeed estimate the Park's growth in terms of a simple model of diffusion, thereby offering support for this conceptualization and for how one might think of, and possibly forecast the growth of, a science park in general.

We have chosen a Gompertz survival-time model for our analytical demonstration because the model is quite simple and yet more general than a model using the exponential distribution that has a constant hazard rate. Geroski (2000) discusses many distinct reasons for S-shaped diffusion curves, and he observes that different reasons suggest different distributions for describing adoptions of innovation. For example, when there are asymmetries in the speed of diffusion among different groups in the population of adopters, the Gompertz distribution has been used.[11] The Gompertz survival-time model allows the data to represent a monitonically increasing or decreasing hazard rate for the adoption of the innovation – the appearance of research companies in the innovative environment of the Research Triangle Park. We hypothesize that as understanding of the science park innovation and the importance of interaction between industry and university science increased over the last half century, the hazard rate (described fully below) for adopting the science park innovation has increased.

The Gompertz model we estimate describes the adoption of the Research Triangle Park by research companies as a stochastic diffusion process with an increasing hazard rate. Alternatively, the Weibull distribution could be used with the survival time model and also allow estimation of a hazard rate that increases or

decreases through time. The lognormal or log-logistic distributions can be used for data with hazard rates that initially increase and then decrease, and the generalized gamma model allows for even more flexibility in the hazard function.[12] For our purposes, the Gompertz model offers the appropriate flexibility with a simple functional form to describe the S-shaped diffusion curve where the hazard rate for the population of adopters of the innovative environment increased over time.

The time series of adoptions of the science park innovation in the United States begins in 1951 when the first park was established. In the absence of any particular event that precipitated the awareness of the concept of a science park, we assume that in 1950 potential adopters of the science park concept are made aware of the possibilities. Then, through time, science parks appear with appearances being most likely in the environments most favorable to the success of a science park. The first research companies appeared in the Research Triangle Park in 1959, and starting with two research companies in that year, the Park grew to include 104 research companies by 1998.

Implementing the diffusion model, the probability that the establishment of a particular research company in Research Triangle Park will have occurred by time t is:

$$F(t) = 1 - S(t). \tag{1}$$

$S(t)$ is the probability that for a particular adopter, the adoption has not occurred by time t:

$$S(t) = e^{(-e^{\lambda/\gamma})(e^{\gamma t}-1)}. \tag{2}$$

Deriving the hazard rate for the model explains the descriptive roles for the two parameters of the model, lambda (λ) and gamma (γ). The hazard rate for the adoption is:

$$h(t) = F'(t)/(1 - F(t)) \tag{3}$$

where

$$F'(t) = -S'(t) = e^{(\lambda+\gamma t)-(e^{\lambda/\gamma})(e^{\gamma t}-1)}. \tag{4}$$

Substituting (1), (2), and (4) into (3), the hazard rate for adoption is then:

$$h(t) = e^{\lambda+\gamma t} = e^{\lambda}e^{\gamma t} \tag{5}$$

and the hazard rate is increasing, decreasing, or constant as γ is >, <, or = 0.

The hazard rate is the conditional probability density for adoption. Conditional on a company not yet having adopted the innovative environment of Research Triangle Park, the probability that it will adopt the innovation and move into the Park during the small interval of time dt is given by $h(t)dt$. The parameter lambda determines the base level of the hazard rate throughout the history of Research Triangle Park, while the parameter gamma determines the rate at which that base level grows through time. The survival-time model could treat the parameter lambda as a constant plus a linear combination of explanatory variables, but here we just estimate the constant term to establish our point that the entry of research companies into Research Triangle Park can be described as the diffusion of an innovation.

We have data on the net number of research companies in Research Triangle Park in each year. Using the time at which each net arrival of a research company occurs, we have a list of the 104 research companies' arrival times starting with company one and company two appearing in 1959, and ending with companies 99 through 104 appearing in 1998. With that information, we can estimate λ and γ for the diffusion model showing the adoption of the Research Triangle Park environment by research companies. Table I provides the estimates. We see that λ is estimated to be -6.30 and γ is estimated to be 0.109 for the diffusion of research companies into the Research Triangle Park. Thus, from equation (5), in 1950

at $t = 0$ the hazard rate is $e^{-6.30} = 0.00184$, and the hazard rate grows at the rate of 10.9 percent per year.

Figures 3, 4 and 5 use the estimates of lambda and gamma and the number of companies as of 1998 and simulate the hazard rate, the probability of entry, and the expected number of research companies in the Research Triangle Park over the period 1950 through 2010. Figure 3 shows the hazard rate increasing exponentially; Figure 4 shows that the probability of entry follows an S-shaped curve; and Figure 5 shows the model's estimation of the diffusion path for research companies entering Research Triangle Park. Clearly the only historically accurate part of the description is for the period through 1998, but the projection for the additional few years shows the S-shaped diffusion curve clearly.

From the analytical exercise of fitting the Gompertz survival-time model, we conclude that it is reasonable to characterize the growth of Research Triangle Park as research companies adopting the Park's innovative environment. An alternative approach, and one that would work very well with a set of explanatory variables to show the determinants of lambda across different companies rather than simply describing the overall diffusion path, would be to define a set of potential entrants to the Park a priori. Then, the model would be estimated not just with the set of firms that actually entered, but with the entire population of potential entrants. Not all subjects

TABLE I
Gompertz diffusion model for research companies entering Research Triangle Park

Gompertz Regression – log relative-hazard form*

No. of subjects = 104
No. of observations = 104
No. of "failures" = 104
Time at risk = 3391
Log likelihood = −34.340818

	Coefficient	Std. error	z	$P > |z|$	95% Confidence interval	
Lambda	−6.297894	0.3369615	−18.690	0.000	−6.958327	−5.637462
Gamma	0.1091215	0.0098872	11.037	0.000	0.089743	0.1284999

* Estimated using Stata (1999). The term "failure" refers to traditional applications of the survival-time model and the "survival" function, S (see Stata, 1999). As long as a company has not adopted the Park's innovative environment, it "survives" in the data, but on adoption it ceases to "survive" and leaves the set of potential adopters.

The Growth of Research Triangle Park   173

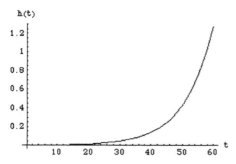

Figure 3. Estimated hazard rate for research companies entering Research Triangle Park from 1950 through 2010.

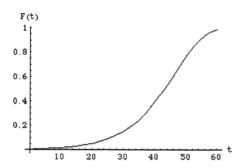

Figure 4. Estimated probability that the typical research company has entered Research Triangle Park by year *t* from 1950 through 2010.

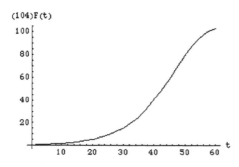

Figure 5. Estimated expected number of research companies in Research Triangle Park in year *t* from 1950 through 2010 using just the population of established companies as of 1998.

would enter, and we would have a model illustrating not just the diffusion path for the actual entrants, but a model explaining the selection of potential entrants as actual entrants over time.

IV. Entrepreneurial leadership and the growth of Research Triangle Park[13]

Why has Research Triangle Park grown as successfully as it has? We set forth in this section the idea that the successful growth of the Park may have been because of the continuity of entrepreneurial leadership that the Park has enjoyed for more than 30 years.

What is entrepreneurial leadership? The answer rests of course on who an entrepreneur is and what an entrepreneur does. The history of economics holds diverse opinions on the nature and role of the entrepreneur. Contemporary economic theory recognizes the entrepreneur as an independent factor of production that is important for producing outputs just as the factors land, labor, and capital are important.

The entrepreneur has been associated with many roles as intellectual thought about entrepreneurship has developed. At least twelve themes, often overlapping, have surfaced in the literature over the years:

1. The entrepreneur is the person who assumes the risk associated with uncertainty.
2. The entrepreneur is the person who supplies financial capital.
3. The entrepreneur is an innovator.
4. The entrepreneur is a decision maker.
5. The entrepreneur is an industrial leader.
6. The entrepreneur is a manager or superintendent.
7. The entrepreneur is an organizer and coordinator of economic resources.
8. The entrepreneur is the owner of an enterprise.
9. The entrepreneur is an employer of factors of production.
10. The entrepreneur is a contractor.
11. The entrepreneur is an arbitrageur.
12. The entrepreneur is an allocator of resources among alternative uses.

Theories of entrepreneurship may be either static or dynamic, but only dynamic theories of entrepreneurship deal directly with change and uncertainty. For example, the role of the entrepreneur as a superintendent would be consistent with a static environment, but the role of the entrepreneur as innovator brings the dynamic environment important for understanding the history of the Research Triangle Park to the fore.

Dismissing static theories as irrelevant for understanding the successful growth of Research Triangle Park, the taxonomy of entrepreneurial theories can be condensed into three major intellectual traditions, each tracing its origin to Cantillon (c. 1680–1734). These traditions are the German Tradition (Thünen and Schumpeter), the Chicago Tradition (Knight and Schultz), and the Austrian Tradition (Mises, Kirzner, and Shackle).

Without tracing the development of the ideas that underlie these three traditions, one synthesis of these bodies of thought would define an entrepreneur as an individual *who perceives opportunity and has the ability to act upon it*. Given this definition, one could embrace the idea that the history of Research Triangle Park has been a history of entrepreneurial leadership guided primarily by one individual, Archie Davis.

Recall that it was Davis who perceived the importance of the Park developing not as a for-profit company (i.e., Pinelands) but rather as a nonprofit organization designed for the common weal. And, guided by that generosity of spirit, Davis was able within 30 days to raise nearly $1.5 million dollars for the betterment of the Park and the state. While this event does combine *perception* and *action*, Davis' vision and energies continued to influence the growth of the Park for more than 30 years. It was Davis who best understood the importance of there being a research institute in the Park. The institute would be a symbol to the corporate research community that the Research Triangle leaders had enough faith in the park concept to establish first their own research facility. And, it was Davis who raised the initial money for an institute and encouraged the Foundation to allocate increasing amounts of land for it. Finally, it was Davis' vision that lead to the creating of the TUCASI campus, and it was Davis who was instrumental in persuading the American Academy of Arts and Sciences to locate their National Humanities Center there.

In other words, time and time again, Davis provided the entrepreneurial leadership that guided the growth and development of Research Triangle Park. He not only demonstrated perception about what the Park could become, but also he was directly active in bringing those visions to reality.

V. Concluding observations

Arguably Research Triangle Park is the most notable and successful of all science parks in the United States, and that success suggests questions. Why has Research Triangle Park grown successfully?[14] Can other parks (existing parks or new parks) imitate its successful growth? Certainly, the Park has a number of obvious advantages such as three outstanding universities,[15] a world-class research institute, and a favorable geographic location and climate. But also, the Park has benefited from the continuity of entrepreneurial leadership by Archie Davis.

While we are only now in the process of documenting the historical development of the growth of other notable science parks and investigating why other science parks transformed themselves into industrial parks,[16] our preliminary opinion is that:

> The most successful science parks are those that have benefited from a continuity of entrepreneurial leadership. Thus, companies are eager to adopt the park's innovative environment and as a result the park grows.

Acknowledgements

An earlier version of this paper was presented at the University of Nottingham's Institute for Enterprise and Innovation/National Academy of Sciences' Board of Science, Technology and Economic Policy Collaborative Conference on "Policies to Promote Entrepreneurship in a Knowledge-Based Economy: Evaluating Best Practices from the U.S. and U.K.," September 18–19, 2000 at the University of Nottingham.

Notes

[1] North Carolina State College became North Carolina State University in 1965.
[2] North Carolina State and the University of North Carolina at Chapel Hill are part of the consolidated University of North Carolina.
[3] It is traditional when referring to these three sister institutions to list them alphabetically.

[4] The historical discussion of the Research Triangle Park draws on Link (1995, 2002).

[5] In 1952, only two states, Arkansas and Mississippi, had per capita incomes lower than that of North Carolina.

[6] The minutes of the first formal meeting of the Council on May 27, 1955, record that the members agreed on an important vision statement: "Research Triangle is an effort to make use of the triangle educational institutions . . . in the development of a research center which will attract business investment and which will give aid to North Carolina industry."

[7] Five brochures were developed to emphasize expertise in pharmaceuticals, chemistry, electronics, engineering, and forestry.

[8] IBM had been courted for seven years, and much of that process had been kept a secret.

[9] Herein, we use the term science park and research park synonymously.

[10] This section of the paper was supported by a research grant from the National Science Foundation, Division of Science Resources Studies.

[11] See Geroski (2000); in particular, see his discussion there of Dixon (1980) and Davies (1979).

[12] Stata (1999, pp. 432–454) describes the alternative distributions, and the implementation of the Gompertz distribution for use as an estimable parametric survival-time model is described in StataCorp (1999, p. 439). Rather than using maximum likelihood techniques to estimate survival-time models using various distributions as we do here, the early literature on the diffusion of innovations imposed the logistic S-curve for the diffusion of an innovation using appropriate transformations to reach a functional form that could be estimated with relatively simple estimation techniques. See Geroski (2000) for a tracing of the literature from the pioneering studies to the later ones that have modeled hazard rates.

[13] This section draws directly from Hébert and Link (1988, 1989).

[14] We realize that tenant growth is only one metric by which to measure the success of a science park. Attendant regional economic growth and development is yet another important metric, but we have not addressed it in this paper.

[15] There are no other science parks in the United States that are juxtaposed with three major research universities. We have anecdotal evidence that there are important research synergies among the three universities that not only enhance the reputation of the Park but also serve to attract research companies to the area. However, the primary vehicle that enhances these synergies is the TUCASI campus and the interactions that occur there.

[16] We are pleased to acknowledge the support of the National Science Foundation's Research and Development Statistics Program for this project.

References

Davies, Stephen, 1979, *The Diffusion of Process Innovations*, Cambridge, England: Cambridge University Press.

Dixon, Robert J., September 1980, 'Hybrid Corn Revisited', *Econometrica* **48**, 145–146.

Geroski, Paul A., April 2000, 'Models of Technology Diffusion', *Research Policy* **29**, 603–625.

Hébert, Robert F. and Albert N. Link, 1988, *The Entrepreneur: Mainstream Views and Radical Critiques*, Second edition, New York: Praeger Publishers.

Hébert, Robert F. and Albert N. Link, 1989, 'In Search of the Meaning of Entrepreneurship', *Small Business Economics* **1**, 39–49.

Link, Albert N., 1995, *A Generosity of Spirit: The Early History of the Research Triangle Park*, Research Triangle Park: The Research Triangle Foundation of North Carolina.

Link, Albert N., 2002, *From Seed to Harvest: The Growth of Research Triangle Park*, Research Triangle Park: The Research Triangle Foundation of North Carolina.

StataCorp, 1999, *Stata Statistical Software: Release 6.0*, vol. 3, College Station, TX: Stata Corporation, pp. 432–454.

[15]

ELSEVIER

Available online at www.sciencedirect.com

SCIENCE  DIRECT®

International Journal of Industrial Organization
21 (2003) 1357–1369

International Journal of
Industrial
Organization

www.elsevier.com/locate/econbase

Assessing the impact of university science parks on research productivity: exploratory firm-level evidence from the United Kingdom

Donald S. Siegel[a,*], Paul Westhead[b], Mike Wright[b]

[a]*Department of Economics, Rensselaer Polytechnic Institute, 110 8th Street, 3502 Russell Sage Laboratory, Troy, NY 12180-3590, USA*
[b]*Nottingham University Business School, Nottingham NG8 1BB, UK*

Abstract

University science parks are alleged to stimulate technological spillovers. However, there is virtually no empirical evidence on the impact of these facilities on research productivity. We begin to fill this gap by examining whether companies located on university science parks in the United Kingdom have higher research productivity than observationally equivalent firms not located on a university science park. The preliminary results appear to be consistent with this hypothesis and are robust to the use of alternative econometric procedures to assess relative productivity.
© 2003 Elsevier B.V. All rights reserved.

JEL classification: O32; O33; O38; L31

Keywords: ; Science parks; R&D; Productivity; University technology transfer

1. Introduction

In recent years, there has been substantial growth in university technology transfer. A burgeoning academic literature has emerged that seeks to assess the

*Corresponding author. Tel.: +1-518-276-2049; fax: +1-518-276-2235.
E-mail addresses: sieged@rpi.edu (D.S. Siegel), paul.westhead@nottingham.ac.uk (P. Westhead), mike.wright@nottingham.ac.uk (M. Wright).

0167-7187/03/$ – see front matter © 2003 Elsevier B.V. All rights reserved.
doi:10.1016/S0167-7187(03)00086-9

1358   *D.S. Siegel et al. / Int. J. Ind. Organ. 21 (2003) 1357–1369*

antecedents and consequences of the rapid rise in patenting, licensing, and the formation of entrepreneurial startups at universities. An aspect of university technology transfer that has not attracted as much scholarly attention is the science park.

According to the United Kingdom Science Park Association (UKSPA, 1996), science parks have three fundamental features. They are designed to foster the creation and growth of R&D-intensive firms, provide an environment that enables large companies to develop relationships with small, high-tech companies, and promote formal and operational links between firms, universities, and other research institutions (e.g., federal research labs). Thus, science parks are expected to provide access to critical human and physical capital for innovative companies. Furthermore, the clustering of high-tech firms should serve to stimulate technology transfer and the acquisition of key business skills, such as the ability to develop new products.

All UK science parks are located on or near universities. The university environment could be especially conducive to enhancing the ability of firms to conduct R&D.[1] In OECD nations, two policy initiatives are alleged to have accelerated the rate of knowledge transfer from universities to firms: targeted legislation designed to stimulate research joint ventures between universities and firms (e.g., the European Union Framework Programmes) and a major shift in the intellectual property regime in favor of universities (e.g., enactment of the Bayh–Dole Act of 1980 in the USA). It appears that these trends have resulted in a rapid rise in all forms of university–industry research relationships (e.g., licensing, co-authoring of academic articles by university and industry scientists, and sponsored research). This includes property-based institutions that foster university technology transfer, such as engineering research centers, industry–university cooperative research centers (see Adams et al., 2001), and science parks.[2]

Despite the potential importance of university science parks as a mechanism for stimulating technological spillovers, there is no direct empirical evidence on the impact of these facilities on the research productivity of firms. The purpose of this paper is to fill this gap. This analysis could have important policy implications, since university science parks are typically supported by public funds. One measure of the "success" of such facilities, from a public policy perspective, is whether they stimulate higher research productivity. This can be viewed as one dimension of the social return to public investment in R&D. Our empirical analysis of these returns is based on a rich, firm-level UK dataset. These data

---

[1] Link and Scott (2002) attempt to show that there is a reverse flow of knowledge and influence from the park to the university.

[2] Mowery et al. (2001) provide a cautionary note on a causal interpretation of the effects of Bayh–Dole on university technology transfer. See Poyago-Theotoky et al. (2002) for a broader consideration of the economic and managerial implications of the rise of university–industry research relationships.

D.S. Siegel et al. / Int. J. Ind. Organ. 21 (2003) 1357–1369 1359

allow us to assess the difference between the average research performance of firms that are located on university science parks and observationally equivalent firms that are not located on these facilities.

The remainder of this paper is organized as follows. Section 2 provides background information on university science parks and reviews the limited empirical evidence on other aspects of the performance of science park firms. Section 3 outlines the econometric models used to assess research productivity. Data and empirical findings are presented in Section 4. The final section consists of preliminary conclusions, caveats, and suggestions for additional research.

2. Background information and brief literature review

We begin with some stylized facts. In 1972, the first UK science parks were established in Cambridge and Heriot-Watt. By 1992 (the year our survey was conducted), there were 32 parks in operation, as most of the older UK universities had adopted this organizational innovation. Over time, more "polytechnics" or "new" universities also established such a facility, so that by 1999, there were 46 fully operational university science parks in the UK.

As noted earlier, in contrast to the US (see Link and Scott, 2002), *all* science parks in the UK are *university* science parks, located at the institution or within close proximity. The UKSPA (1999) also reports that 80% of the science park firms have fewer than 15 employees and that over half of the firms located on these facilities are engaged in R&D and/or new product development. Some of these companies are attempting to commercialize leading-edge technologies, most notably, biotechnology, materials, computers/telecommunications, and technologies with environmental, energy, and industrial applications.

There is limited empirical evidence on some dimensions of the relative performance of firms on UK science parks.[3] A major breakthrough in this literature was the creation of a longitudinal dataset containing performance indicators for firms located on parks and a control group of firms not located on parks. These data were originally collected by Monck et al. (1988) and updated and extended by Westhead and Storey (1994). Our empirical analysis will also be based on this file. In Section 4, we will describe the construction of this dataset in great detail.

In a series of studies, Westhead and Storey (1994) and Westhead (1997) used this file to compute differences in the mean values of several performance indicators for science park and non-science parks firms. The authors reported statistically insignificant differences in the probability of survival, job creation, R&D expenditures, the number of scientists and engineers, the number of patents and copyrights, and the creation of new products.[4]

---

[3] See Siegel et al. (2003b) for a more comprehensive review of this evidence.
[4] See Westhead and Storey (1994) and Westhead (1997).

1360   *D.S. Siegel et al. / Int. J. Ind. Organ. 21 (2003) 1357–1369*

Although these findings are useful, they do not allow us to make inferences regarding relative research *productivity*, i.e., whether firms located on science parks are more *efficient* in conducting R&D. In the following section, we outline several variants of an econometric model that enables us to address this issue.

3. Econometric models

Three econometric strategies are used to test whether science park firms have higher research productivity than observationally equivalent non-science park firms. We specify an R&D production function (Griliches, 1998) with three possible R&D "outputs" and two R&D "inputs":

NEWPRODS, PATENTS, or COPYRIGHTS

$$= f(\text{RDEXP, RDSCI, SCIPARK}), \tag{1}$$

where NEWPRODS is the number of new products/services, PATENTS is the number of patents applied for or awarded, COPYRIGHTS is the number of copyrights, RDEXP is the R&D expenditures, RDSCI is the number of scientists and engineers, and SCIPARK is a dummy variable which is 1 if a firm is located on a science park and 0 otherwise

A key parameter in Eq. (1) is the coefficient on SCIPARK, which will have a positive sign if location on a science park is associated with better research performance. However, the inclusion of SCIPARK in Eq. (1) raises concerns regarding endogeneity, since it is conceivable that the location decision and R&D output could be jointly determined.[5]

The existence of an endogeneity bias could cloud the accuracy of estimates of the impact of university science parks on the research productivity of firms. To address this concern, we estimate a variant of the model that includes an additional equation:

$$\text{SCIPARK} = g\left(\text{RADICAL, TECH,} \sum_m Z_m\right), \tag{2}$$

where RADICAL is a dummy variable denoting whether the firm is engaged in research on a "radical" innovation, TECH is a categorical variable classifying the nature of the firm's *existing* technology (i.e., whether it is "leading edge," advanced, or established), and Z is a vector of m control variables. We conjecture that firms engaged in "radical" innovation (i.e., firms developing a major

---

[5] Another econometric concern, which often arises in production function studies, is simultaneity. As shown in Olley and Pakes (1996), there are ways of dealing with this problem with panel data. The cross-sectional nature of our data limits our ability to address this problem.

D.S. Siegel et al. / Int. J. Ind. Organ. 21 (2003) 1357–1369 1361

technological breakthrough) could be more likely to locate on a science park.[6] That is because establishing a physical presence on (or near) campus could enable them to benefit more directly from knowledge spillovers arising from cutting-edge university research. The location decision could also be related to the extent to which a firm's *existing* technology is state-of-the-art.

In each variant of the regression model, we will report the coefficient on SCIPARK, with and without controlling for the possibility of an endogeneity bias. In the latter case, we will use a two-stage estimation procedure for a count variable. An alternative to the use of a dummy variable as a regressor involves splitting the sample into science park and non-science park firms and estimating separate R&D production function regressions. This approach yields separate estimates of the marginal product of R&D, which could be higher for firms located on university science parks if such facilities do indeed foster technological spillovers.

The final method we use to assess relative research performance is stochastic frontier estimation (henceforth, SFE), which generates a production frontier with a stochastic error term consisting of two components: a conventional random error ("white noise") and a term that represents deviations from the frontier, or relative inefficiency.[7] Siegel et al. (2003a) used SFE to assess the relative efficiency of university technology transfer offices.[8]

In SFE, a production function of the following form is estimated:

$$y_i = X_i \beta + \epsilon_i, \tag{3}$$

where the subscript i refers to the ith firm, y denotes an R&D output (e.g. the number of new products), X is a vector of R&D inputs, β is the unknown parameter vector, and ϵ is an error term with two components, $\epsilon_i = V_i - U_i$, where U_i represents a non-negative error term to account for technical inefficiency, or failure to produce maximal output, given the set of inputs used. V_i is a symmetric error term that accounts for random effects. A standard assumption in SFE (see Aigner et al., 1977) is that the U_i and V_i have the following distributions:

$$U_i \sim \text{i.i.d.} \ N^+(0, \sigma_u^2), \ U_i \geq 0,$$

$$V_i \sim \text{i.i.d.} \ N(0, \sigma_v^2).$$

---

[6] Hall et al. (2000) report that firms often invite universities to join an RJV in order to help them understand basic research results.

[7] See Aigner et al. (1977) and Meeusen and Van den Broeck (1977). SFE can be contrasted with data envelopment analysis (DEA), a non-parametric estimation technique that has been used extensively to compute relative productivity in service industries. See Charnes et al. (1994).

[8] Thursby and Kemp (2002) use DEA to study the same phenomenon.

1362   *D.S. Siegel et al. / Int. J. Ind. Organ. 21 (2003) 1357–1369*

That is, the inefficiency term (U_i) is assumed to have a half-normal distribution; i.e., firms are either "on the frontier" or below it.[9]

SFE models have been developed that allow the technical inefficiency or relative productivity term to be expressed as a function of a vector of additional variables (e.g., organizational and environmental characteristics). Consistent with Reifschneider and Stevenson (1991), we assume that the U_i are independently distributed as truncations at zero of the $N(m_i, \sigma_u^2)$ distribution with

$$m_i = Z_i \delta, \tag{4}$$

where Z is a vector of additional variables that are hypothesized to influence relative productivity and δ is a parameter vector.[10]

Following Battese and Coelli (1995), we derive maximum likelihood estimates of the parameter vectors β and δ from simultaneous estimation of the production function and relative inefficiency equations, using the FRONTIER statistical package (see Coelli, 1994). The first equation is the following (single output) translog production function:

$$
\begin{aligned}
\ln(\text{NEWPRODS}_i) = {} & \beta_0 + \beta_1 \ln(\text{RDEXP}_i) + \beta_2 \ln(\text{RDSCI}_i) \\
& + \gamma_{11} \ln(\text{RDEXP}_i)^2 + \gamma_{22} \ln(\text{RDSCI}_i)^2 \\
& + \gamma_{12} \ln(\text{RDEXP}_i) \ln(\text{RDSCI}_i) + V_i - U_i.
\end{aligned}
\tag{5}
$$

The second equation describes the determinants of relative productivity:

$$
\begin{aligned}
U_i = {} & \text{RELPROD} \\
= {} & \delta_0 + \delta_S \, \text{SCIPARK} + \delta_T \, \text{TOTEMP}_i + \delta_R \, \text{REVENUE}_i + \delta_P \, \text{PROFIT} + \mu_i,
\end{aligned}
\tag{6}
$$

where SCIPARK is a dummy variable denoting whether a firm is located on a university science park, TOTEMP refers to total firm employment, REVENUE is annual revenue, and PROFIT is a dummy variable denoting whether a firm generated a profit in the previous fiscal year.[11]

4. Data and empirical results

As noted earlier, our primary data source is a UK firm-level survey constructed by researchers at the Centre for Small and Medium Size Enterprises at the

---

[9] An important parameter in this model is $\gamma = \sigma_u^2/(\sigma_v^2 + \sigma_u^2)$, the ratio of the standard error of technical inefficiency to the standard error of statistical noise, which is bounded between 0 and 1. Note that $\gamma = 0$ under the null hypothesis of an absence of inefficiency, signifying that all of the variance can be attributed to statistical noise.

[10] Battese and Coelli (1995) extend this model to incorporate panel data, although we only have cross-sectional data.

[11] Unfortunately, we do not have a continuous measure of profitability.

D.S. Siegel et al. / Int. J. Ind. Organ. 21 (2003) 1357–1369 1363

University of Warwick in the late 1980s. The file was then updated and extended by Paul Westhead and David Storey, who analyzed the data in several papers in the late 1990s. The first objective in constructing the dataset was to generate a random sample of science park firms. This was not too difficult, since the UKSPA provided the Warwick researchers with information on the universe (population) of companies located on such facilities. A more onerous task was to generate a random sample of "comparable" non-science park companies.

To facilitate generalization, interviews were conducted with representative firms in many science parks. Also, structured questionnaires were implemented in 1986 and 1992 to gather information from owner-managers of science park firms. In-person interviews with the owner-managers of science park firms were conducted (in 1986 and 1992), to ensure a high response rate and more accurate information. In order to control (albeit imperfectly) for sample selection bias, data were collected in both years from observationally equivalent firms (a control group of similar firms not located on a science park). Samples of science park and off-park firms were matched, in 1986, along the following dimensions: age of firm, industry, ownership status, and region.

This matching process is highly dependent on the ability to identify privately-held companies, since many firms on a university science park are in emerging industries. Many companies in such sectors have not yet gone public. Fortunately, it is easier to collect information on the characteristics of privately-held firms in the UK than in the US, due to the existence of the Inter-corporate (ICC) and Financial Analysis Made Easy (FAME) databases. However, it is difficult to know whether we have a random sample of science park firms, since there are no population statistics to compare our final sample with.

A notable feature of the Westhead and Storey sample design is that the authors decided to survey only "independent" science park firms. This precludes an assessment of large firms with smaller R&D units on such facilities. Thus, we cannot examine *intra-firm* spillovers that might arise when a firm located on a science park benefits from R&D conducted by its parent company (perhaps at a corporate R&D facility) at other locations. On the other hand, it does allow for a cleaner analysis of the impact of the science park on research productivity. The bottom line is that it was obviously much easier to construct a "matched pairs" sample using this criterion.

Our final sample contains 177 firms, consisting of 89 science park firms and 88 non-science park firms, reporting information for 1992. Descriptive statistics for the inputs and outputs of the R&D production function are presented in Table 1. The average firm in our sample generated approximately five new products or services, at least one patent and copyright, spends about £345K on R&D, and employs over seven scientists or engineers. Although it appears as though science park firms generate slightly more patents and new products, *t*-tests of differences in means for all three R&D output measures were insignificant. It is important to note, however, that such comparisons do not simultaneously take account of input

Table 1
Descriptive statistics for the inputs and outputs of the R&D production function ($n = 177$ firms, 1992)

Variable	Description	All firms		Science park firms		Firms not located on science parks	
		Mean	S.D.	Mean	S.D.	Mean	S.D.
NEWPRODS	Number of new products or services	5.2	9.1	5.6	10.3	4.9	8.9
PATENTS	Number of patents applied for or awarded	1.4	2.3	1.7	2.5	1.5	2.2
COPYRIGHTS	Number of copyrights	1.2	1.5	1.1	1.6	1.3	1.4
RDEXP	R&D expenditures (£000)	345.2	874.8	338.9	855.9	353.4	888.6
RDSCI	Number of scientists and engineers	7.2	11.4	7.5	10.3	7.1	12.8

Source: Westhead and Storey (1994) survey of independent science park and non-science park firms in the UK.

usage, as we will do in our econometric analysis of research productivity equations.

Note that our three R&D output measures are count variables and there are some zero values. Therefore, we considered Poisson and negative binomial (generalized Poisson) specifications, which were estimated using LIMDEP.[12] Given that the Poisson specification was decisively rejected, based on values of the χ^2 statistic, we present only the negative binomial results.[13]

Table 2 contains the first set of econometric findings. Recall that we have three R&D output measures: the number of new products and services, patents, and copyrights. We present two sets of results for each of the three R&D outputs. Columns (1), (3), and (5) contain negative binomial parameter estimates with no controls for endogeneity bias, while columns (2), (4), and (6) contain "two-step" negative binomial estimates (see Greene, 1995), which control for possible endogeneity bias associated with the science park dummy variable (SCIPARK).

Several interesting patterns emerge from this table. First, for two out of three output measures, the model appears to be fit fairly well. Most of the coefficients on the R&D inputs have the expected (positive) signs, and some are statistically significant. To assess whether firms on university science parks are more "productive" in research, we focus our attention on the coefficients on SCIPARK. These parameter estimates are positive and statistically significant for new products and services and patents. Note, however, that the magnitudes of these

---

[12] Since the seminal paper by Hausman et al. (1984), Poisson models are quite commonly employed in empirical studies of count variables (especially patents).

[13] The Poisson results, which do not differ much from the negative binomial estimates, are available upon request from the authors.

Table 2
Maximum likelihood estimates of negative binomial (NB) and "two-step" negative binomial (TSNB) regressions of the determinants of R&D outputs (Eq. (1))

Coefficients on independent variables	Dependent variables: proxies for R&D output					
	New products/services		Patents		Copyrights	
	NB (1)	TSNB (2)	NB (3)	TSNB (4)	NB (5)	TSNB (6)
INTERCEPT	1.028*** (0.389)	−1.214*** (0.368)	−1.236*** (0.508)	−1.215*** (0.567)	−1.623*** (0.780)	−1.424*** (0.568)
RDEXP	0.362** (0.184)	0.320** (0.159)	0.276** (0.130)	0.201** (0.093)	0.069 (0.058)	0.058 (0.046)
RDSCI	0.111 (0.066)	0.108 (0.070)	0.190** (0.094)	0.093 (0.058)	0.123** (0.061)	0.078 (0.061)
SCIPARK	0.150** (0.072)	0.122** (0.060)	0.140** (0.067)	0.110** (0.052)	0.074 (0.048)	0.081 (0.060)
Log likelihood	−144.24	−146.21	−143.99	−147.02	−157.51	−159.23
Chi-squared	20.20	18.38	19.87	17.96	17.43	14.05

Notes: Heteroskedastic-consistent standard errors are reported in parentheses. ***Significant at the 1% level, **significant at the 5% level. Columns (1), (3), and (5)—NB-negative binomial estimation. Columns (2), (4), and (6)—TSNB-"two-step" negative binomial estimation (see Greene, 1995, p. 581).

Table 3
Estimates of the elasticity of R&D output with respect to R&D expenditure

	Proxies for R&D output		
	New products/ services (1)	Patents (2)	Copyrights (3)
All firms (N = 177)	0.429*** (0.185)	0.318** (0.159)	0.069 (0.048)
Firms located on university science parks (N = 89)	0.569*** (0.154)	0.453*** (0.212)	0.051 (0.042)
Firms not located on university science parks (N = 88)	0.263** (0.131)	0.223** (0.108)	0.123 (0.079)
F Statistic for *difference* in elasticity estimates between firms located on university science parks and firms not located on university science parks	5.78**	5.03**	1.58

Notes: Heteroskedastic-consistent standard errors are reported in parentheses. ***Significant at the 1% level, **significant at the 5% level.

Table 4
Maximum likelihood estimates of the determinants of relative inefficiency (Eq. (6))

Determinants of relative productivity	Dependent variables: proxies for R&D output		
	New products/ services	Patents	Copyrights
SCIPARK	−0.072** (0.034)	−0.062** (0.029)	0.028 (0.033)
TOTEMP	−0.121** (0.058)	−0.103* (0.044)	−0.036 (0.024)
REVENUE	−0.042 (0.025)	−0.037 (0.023)	−0.073 (0.071)
PROFIT	0.020 (0.057)	−0.128** (0.062)	−0.055** (0.027)
Log likelihood	−31.67	−29.64	−33.02

Notes: Maximum likelihood estimates of the parameter vector δ from simultaneous estimation of the production function and relative inefficiency equations, using the FRONTIER statistical package (see Coelli, 1994). Standard errors in parentheses. ***Significant at the 1% level, **significant at the 5% level.

coefficients are fairly small. It appears that these findings hold even when we control for the possibility of endogeneity bias, although the "two-step" estimates are considerably lower.

Table 3 presents estimates of the output elasticity or marginal product of R&D

D.S. Siegel et al. / Int. J. Ind. Organ. 21 (2003) 1357–1369 1367

for the entire sample of 177 firms (row 1), the 89 science park firms (row 2), and the 88 non-science park firms (row 3). We also report test statistics for differences in these elasticity estimates between science park and non-science park firms. Our findings are similar to those contained in the previous table, in the sense that, for two of the three R&D output measures (new products and patents), the output elasticities of R&D are positive and statistically significant. More importantly, the significant *F* statistics in the first two columns imply that the marginal product of R&D is higher for firms located on university science parks.

Table 4 contains maximum-likelihood estimates of the determinants of relative productivity (Eq. (6)), based on stochastic frontier analysis for those firms with non-zero research outputs.[14] The results imply that these variables have some explanatory power. The negative and significant coefficient on TOTEMP indicates that larger firms may be more productive in research (less inefficient, in the stochastic frontier framework). On the other hand, the coefficient on REVENUE, which is also sometimes used as a proxy for firm size in empirical studies of the Schumpeterian hypothesis, is insignificantly different from zero. We also find that firms generating a profit tend to be closer to the frontier. More importantly, the estimated coefficients on SCIPARK (for new products/services and patents) appear to confirm our previous results indicating that science parks firms are more productive in research.

5. Conclusions, caveats, and extensions

Our preliminary results suggest that firms located on university science parks have slightly higher research productivity than observationally equivalent firms not located on university science parks. These impacts are not as strong when we control for endogeneity bias, or the possibility that location on a university science park and the generation of research output are jointly determined. However, they do appear to be robust to alternative econometric specifications, including testing for a shift factor (the use of a dummy variable), an examination of differences in the marginal product of R&D, and stochastic frontier analysis.

The notion that location on a university science park is associated with higher research productivity presents an opportunity for analysis of the factors underlying this difference in research performance. Aside from some vague notion of technological/knowledge spillovers from universities to firms, it would be interesting to examine the connection between the productivity differential and the "closeness" of the relationship between the science park firm and the university. For this, we need a direct measure of contact between these companies and academics and graduate students. The role of distance also needs to be explored.

---

[14] The full set of parameter estimates of the translog production frontier is available upon request from the authors.

Several caveats should be noted. One concern, which is common to studies of patents, is that we have *count* measures, as opposed to estimates of the *values* of these technology flows. A more accurate measure of research performance ("true" research productivity) would be based on properly deflated R&D outputs, where, for example, patents would be weighted by citations (Hall et al., 2001). Another limitation of our empirical analysis is that it is based on data that is a decade old. This is problematic, since it is conceivable that the returns to being located on a science park may have shifted over time.

We also hope to pursue several extensions of this research. Further exploration of the heterogeneity across different types of science parks might also be useful. That is, it is conceivable that our results could be masking important differences in the returns to different *types* of science parks. For instance, the UKSPA (1999) distinguishes between "managed" and "non-managed" science parks. A managed science park has a full time, on-site manager, who may prove useful in terms of facilitating knowledge spillovers from universities to firms and among companies located on the same science park. It might also be useful to conduct international comparisons of the returns to location on university science parks.

Acknowledgements

Comments from Irwin Feller, Al Link, John Scott, Jerry Thursby, and participants at the 2002 Georgia Tech Roundtable for Entrepreneurship Research (REER), the session on "International Trends in the Transfer of Academic Research" at the 2002 American Association for the Advancement of Science (AAAS) Meetings in Boston, and the IJIO Special Issue workshop at UNC-Greensboro are greatly appreciated.

References

Adams, J.D., Chiang, E.P., Starkey, K., 2001. Industry–university cooperative research centers. Journal of Technology Transfer 26 (1/2), 73–86.

Aigner, D.J., Lovell, C.A.K., Schmidt, P., 1977. Formulation and estimation of stochastic frontier production functions. Journal of Econometrics 6, 21–37.

Battese, G., Coelli, T., 1995. A model for technical inefficiency effects in a stochastic frontier production function for panel data. Empirical Economics 20, 325–332.

Charnes, A., Cooper, W.W., Lewin, A., Seiford, L.M. (Eds.), 1994. Data Envelopment Analysis: Theory, Method, and Applications. Kluwer Academic, Boston, MA.

Coelli, T., 1994. A guide to FRONTIER version 4.1: a computer program for frontier production and cost function estimation. Mimeo, Department of Econometrics, University of New England, Armidale.

Greene, W., 1995. LIMDEP—Version 7.0 Users Manual. Econometric Software, Inc, Bellport, NY.

Griliches, Z., 1998. R&D and Productivity: The Econometric Evidence, National Bureau of Economic Research for the University of Chicago Press. University of Chicago Press, Chicago.

Hall, B.H., Jaffe, A.B., Trajtenberg, M., 2001. The NBER patent citations data file: lessons, insights, and methodological tools. NBER Working Paper #8498.

Hall, B.H., Link, A.N., Scott, J.T., 2000. Universities as research partners. NBER Working Paper No. 7643 and forthcoming, Review of Economics and Statistics.

Hausman, J., Hall, B.H., Griliches, Z., 1984. Econometric models for count data with an application to the patents–R&D relationship. Econometrica 52, 909–938.

Link, A.N., Scott, J.T., 2002. Science parks and the generation of university-based knowledge: an exploratory study. International Journal of Industrial Organization, forthcoming.

Meeusen, W., Van den Broeck, J., 1977. Efficiency estimation from Cobb–Douglas production functions with composed errors. International Economic Review 18, 435–444.

Monck, C.S.P., Porter, R.B., Quintas, P., Storey, D.J., Wynarczyk, P., 1988. Science Parks and the Growth of High Technology Firms. Croom Helm, London.

Mowery, D.C., Nelson, R.R., Sampat, B., Ziedonis, A.A., 2001. The growth of patenting and licensing by U.S. universities: an assessment of the effects of the Bayh–Dole Act of 1980. Research Policy 30, 99–119.

Olley, S.G., Pakes, A., 1996. The dynamics of productivity in the telecommunications equipment industry. Econometrica 64 (6), 1263–1297.

Poyago-Theotoky, J., Beath, J., Siegel, D.S., 2002. Universities and fundamental research: reflections on the growth of university–industry partnerships. Oxford Review of Economic Policy 18 (1), 10–21.

Reifschneider, D., Stevenson, R., 1991. Systematic departures from the frontier: a framework for the analysis of firm inefficiency. International Economic Review 32 (3), 715–723.

Siegel, D.S., Waldman, D., Link, A.N., 2003a. Assessing the impact of organizational practices on the productivity of university technology transfer offices: an exploratory study. Research Policy 32 (1), 27–48.

Siegel, D.S., Westhead, P., Wright, M., 2003b. Science parks and the performance of new technology-based firms: a review of recent U.K. evidence and an agenda for future research. Small Business Economics 20 (2), 177–184.

Thursby, J.G., Kemp, S., 2002. Growth and productive efficiency of university intellectual property licensing. Research Policy 31 (1), 109–124.

UKSPA, 1996. UKSPA 96: The United Kingdom Science Park Association Annual Report 1996. The United Kingdom Science Park Association, Birmingham.

UKSPA, 1999. 15th Anniversary 1984–1999. The United Kingdom Science Park Association, Birmingham.

Westhead, P., 1997. R&D "inputs" and "outputs" of technology-based firms located on and off science parks. R&D Management 27, 45–62.

Westhead, P., Storey, D.J., 1994. An Assessment of Firms Located On and Off Science Parks in the United Kingdom. HMSO, London.

[16]

Science Park Location and New
Technology-Based Firms in Sweden –
Implications for Strategy and Performance

Peter Lindelöf
Hans Löfsten

ABSTRACT. One logical way to assess the performance of Science Parks is to compare the performance of their firms to similar firms not located there. A total of 273 new technology-based firms (NTBFs) were surveyed, of which 134 were on a Science Park and 139 were not on a park. There were significant differences in the means of strategy dimensions between the on-Park and off-Park firms. It can be seen that the NTBFs who located in Science Parks showed significantly greater emphasis on firm characteristics as innovation ability, competitor- and market-orientation, sales and employment growth, high profits etc. The differences indicates a slight advantage for the Science Park firms. The off-Park sample reported proximity to other firms to be of higher importance than the on-Park sample in their choice of location. However, these differences do not show any clear pattern, making it difficult to understand if NTBFs who locate on Science Parks are systematically looking for something different in their location.

1. Introduction

Westhead (1997) claims that *Science Parks* reflect an assumption that technological innovation stems from scientific research and that parks can provide the *catalytic incubator* environment for the transformation of "pure" research into production. A

Final version accepted on November 19, 2001

Peter Lindelöf
School of Economics
University of Göteborg
Department of Business Administration
SE-405 30 Göteborg
Sweden
E-mail: peter.lindelof@handels.gu.se

Hans Löfsten
Chalmers University of Technology
Department of Industrial Dynamics
SE-412 96 Göteborg
Sweden
E-mail: halo@mot.chalmers.se

key role of NTBFs (new technology-based firms) is to accelerate diffusion of technology and so enhance the competitive position of users. The importance of new technology-based firms on Science Parks is related to their performance: they are expected to perform better than the average firm. Science Parks provide an important resource network for new technology-based firms. Government and other organisations (Swedish Board for Industrial and Technical Development) has introduced regionally targeted measures to provide an appropriate *physical infrastructure* to encourage economic development in deprived and depressed localities. Central government has a long history of providing support for R&D, the transfer of technology and its diffusion into industry.

Local authorities in Sweden have developed a range of local economic initiatives designed to create new employment opportunities. Local authorities also have played a key role in encouraging universities to take a more active role in the revival of local economies. Does Science Park location make for more innovative firms, or do the more innovative tend to cluster in Science Parks? Science Parks are invariably associated with more than just a role in promoting innovation and entrepreneurialism, and a successful Science Park is viewed as more than an innovation-generating environment. There must therefore be a further aspect of the seedbed environment that is related to behavioural factors and is also important in understanding the relationship between Science Park location and innovation.

It is difficult to appraise the effectiveness of Science Parks because the objectives of the different partners in the parks may differ considerably (Monck et al., 1988). A university may be interested in achieving a satisfactory level of income from the park by promoting business activities closely linked to its own research interests. Private sector organisations, such as banks, are likely to have a more strictly commercial set of objectives towards investments in the park or its constituent firms. Monck et al. (1988) say that despite the performance and contribution of NTBFs to the economy, the survey identified several constraints on the ability of NTBFs in general to fulfil their economic potential. These included management capacity, finance and weakness in sales and marketing. Monck et al. (1988) claim that in order to understand the "added value" of a Science Park location there is need for detailed research exploring the characteristics and performance of firms located on a variety of Science Parks.

The main purpose in this study is to explore the characteristics (motivations of location, strategies, collaborations and performance) between NTBFs who locate on Science Parks and those who locate elsewhere.

2. Review of literature and analytical framework

2.1. *Motivations of Science Park location*

To confirm the "added value" of a Science Park location the innovativeness of independent technology-based Science Park firms are compared with the levels recorded by a comparable group of firms not located on a Park (Westhead, 1997). Monck et al. (1988) showed that when a direct comparison was made, and taking account of the different ages of the firms, those on Science Parks had achieved somewhat lower levels of employment by a given age than otherwise comparable firms located off-Parks. This might suggest that parks were actually hindering the development of such firms. Further analysis indicated a more plausible explanation, which was that almost one-fifth of businesses on Science Parks were founded by academics and ex-academics, and it was those businesses which under-performed, in terms of employment growth, compared with other businesses. Mian (1996) says that the term "value-added" has become a part of the lexicon of the technology business incubation industry, which corresponds to the provision of the three

major groups of elements (business, technical and social inputs). In the incubator industry, value added refers to those specific ways that an incubator program enhances the ability of its tenants to survive and grow in business (Allen and Bazan, 1990).

Felsenstein (1994) examines the role of Science Parks as "seedbeds" for innovation. Felsenstein makes the distinction between spatial and behavioural conceptions of the seedbed metaphor. The paper surveys the evidence related to the limited interaction effects between Science Park firms on the one hand and their neighbouring park firms, local universities and off-Park firms on the other hand. This suggest that Science Parks might be functioning as "enclaves" of innovation rather than seedbeds. Felsenstein claims that the "seedbed" hypothesis is supported only under certain conditions. In common, with other empirical evidence (Massey et al., 1992; and MacDonald, 1987) the level of interaction between firms located on Science Parks and local universities is generally low.

Westhead (1997) says that there is a growing literature surrounding the relationship between a firm's environment and its ability to innovate (Kleinknecht and Poot, 1992; Feldman, 1994; Goss and Vozikis, 1994; and Pfirrmann, 1994). Monck et al. (1988) and Westhead and Storey (1994) claim that some firms have moved to Science Parks simply because of the "image and overall prestige of the site" rather because of "access to facilities of the HEI (Higher Education Institute)/centre of research" and the "prestige of being linked to the HEI/centre of research". To maintain rental income some park managers have relaxed their "selection" criteria for tenants (Westhead, 1997).

Mian (1994) focused on a sample comprising three state university-sponsored and three private university-sponsored facilities, generally viewed as being successful. The university-sponsored technology incubators practices and performance are explored using several key dimensions: organisational design, tenant performance review, funding sources, targeted technologies, strategic operational policies, services and their value-added component and growth of the client firms. A comparative review of these dimensions reveals that there are no significant differences based on the type of sponsorship – state or private. It is concluded that, given the fuller utilization of university resources by the application of sound policies and business-management practices, the university-sponsored technology incubators appear to provide an environment conducive to the development of NTBFs. Mian (1997) provides a conceptual framework for assessing and managing the university technology-based incubator as a tool for new venture creation. The article concludes with a set of elements identified for evaluating university technology-based incubators under three performance dimensions (program sustainability and growth, tenant firm's survival and growth and contributions to the sponsoring university's mission) providing measurement indicators.

With the popularity of the business incubation concept starting in the early 1980s, numerous studies have been conducted to assess the emerging incubator industry across the nation (Mian, 1996). Most of these studies are primarily descriptive, generally covering various types of incubation models. To accomplish these firms survival and growth objectives a typical business incubator program provides shared office services and business assistance including affordable rent and fostering connections with firms inside the incubator and in the local economy (Mian, 1996).

The attitudes and motivation of the firm founders and managers is another key factor in the ability to raise funds and achieve high growth and profitability. Those firms with dynamic and positive leadership which are seeking strong growth are much more likely to be successful. This contrasts with those founders who are less aggressive and are unwilling to assume the risks associated with rapid growth. They may well have development opportunities open (and the added value of a Science Park) to them but prefer a more relaxed life-style and, therefore, do not appeal to investors seeking high growth and high returns (Monck et al., 1988).

2.2. Management of technology and firm strategy

According to many, the strategy concept has one of its main values, for both profit-seeking and non-profit-seeking organisations, in determining how an organisation defines its relationship to its environment in the pursuit of its objectives (Bourgeois, 1980). Organisational environment includes such dimensions as uncertainty, directness, change, dynamism, homogenity and complexity. Danila (1989) claims that managers have discovered that technology and strategy are inseparable. The most important reason is that management of technology seems to be closer and closer to strategy and to the firm's competitive success. For a long time the study of strategy and more specifically the study of corporate strategy have been distinct from the study of technology. Miller (1987) claims that organizational structures and strategy-making processes are highly interdependent and must be complementary in many ways to ensure good performance under challenging conditions.

According to Acs and Audretsch (1988) a strategy of product innovation can at least partially compensate for the inherent size disadvantage of small firms. They found that the innovative strategy explains a significant proportion of the variation in the presence of small firms. Van der Auwera and Eysenbrandts (1989) compiled a set of specific advantages of small versus medium/large NTBFs in Belgium. Small NTBFs have a greater job flexibility and less hierarchy. The flow of information between management and production is faster and they have a better view over the innovation process. Small firms also have a direct relationship with suppliers and customers and they respond more rapidly to direct demand from abroad.

Miller (1987) claims that organisational structures and strategy-making processes are highly interdependent and must be complementary in many ways to ensure good performance under challenging conditions. An empirical analysis of 97 small and medium-sized firms showed that a structural formalization and integration were related to the levels of interaction and proactiveness among decision making: analysis of decisions, planning, systematic scanning of environments and explicitness of strategies. In firms that must often perform complex innovations, structure alone is insufficient; interactive and rational decision-making must complement it to facilitate both identification of emerging market threats and opportunities and collaboration among diverse specialists, who must simultaneously consider the repercussions of innovation for marketing, R&D, and production (Khandwalla, 1977).

It may be hypothesized that a successful strategic (technology) partnership constitutes an optimization of the potential synergies and the dynamic complementarities between large, established firms and small – new technology-based firms (Segers, 1993). With respect to technology, Hagedorn and Schakenraad (1990) limit strategic partnering to interfirm technology cooperation, i.e. those firms of inter-firm collaboration for which joint development of new technologies and or agreements aimed at improved innovative performance are at least a part of the agreement. In that context, strategic partnering is defined as those agreements that focus on a long-lasting effect on the product-market positioning of the participating companies (Segers, 1993).

Segers (1993) underlines that there is an increased emphasis on NTBFs (Rothwell, 1983, 1984; Oakey et al., 1988) and on strategic partnerships or alliances (Doz, 1988). According to Doz (1988), partnerships usually offer large firms a channel to tap into the innovative and entrepreneurial potential of smaller companies. Rothwell (1983) states that the main advantage of small firms are "people embodied", while those of large firms are "resource embodied". Segers (1993) claims that NTBFs often enjoy the advantage of dynamic, entrepreneurial management embodied in the system that is flexible and highly respon-

sive to change, and who are willing to accept financial, technological and marketing risk.

Assessments of the technical and commercial success uncertainties provide the basis for deciding whether or not the organisation can afford the risks of failure and how these risks will be handled (see Baker, 1974; Souder et al., 1974; and Souder and Mandakovic, 1986). Yap and Souder (1993) claim that an organisation with a long history of research commitments and successes will generally have a better chance of attracting talented researchers than its less committed rivals.

2.3. *Analytical framework*

To fulfil the development ambitions the NTBFs will be faced with normal management problems associated with rapid growth. The problem of management development associated with entrepreneurial growth is a well-known phenomenon. The conceptual model (see Figure 1) is going to serve as the analytical framework for this study and analysis. These dimensions are presented in Figure 1. The application of the framework will provide an opportunity to synthesize information from different sources and better understand the Science Parks performance in its context (on the firm-level).

The importance of NTBFs on Science Parks is related to their performance: they are expected to "perform better" than the average firm. Further,

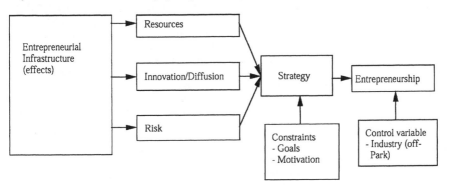

Source: Löfsten and Lindelöf (2001, p 319).

Figure 1. Analytical framework for studies on the firm-level.

analysis of the empirical and theoretical basis for Science Parks, drawing on current understanding of the innovation process and the relationship between academic research and industrial activity, suggests that the Science Park model itself is problematic (Löfsten and Lindelöf, 2001). Researchers have missed the important link and interaction between the firm's resources, innovation/diffusion, risk and *strategy* in our Science Park Model (Entrepreneurial Infrastructure effects).

We argue that independent Science Parks (NTBFs) will have a higher entreprenurial capability than independent off-Park sample (NTBFs). There is however, a need for caution. Allen and Bazan (1990) have commented on the generally modest perceptions of value-added components by incubator tenants saying that, "entrepreneurs are not a particularly appreciative group, and their high degree of autonomy and self-esteem shade their perceptions of how much they are really being helped". For the majority of Science Park firms undertaking R&D, the ultimate purpose is the launch of new products and markets. When comparing differences between on and off-Park NTBFs, observed differences could reflect the motivations of the NTBFs as well as the added value of a Science Park location (see Figure 1, constraints).

Many firm's low performance is the result of poorly performing assets (businesses). Strategic controls focus on long-term performance: managers in firms that emphasize strategic controls evaluate the strategies business-level managers formulate and the strategic actions they take rather than their outcomes. Firms in which strategic controls are used often are more focused and emphasize the long-term development of their core businesses. Use of strategic controls helps establish a norm of risk sharing between corporate and business-level managers. Business-level managers are more likely to undertake risky projects because they feel that corporate managers understand their strategic proposals. Business-level managers believe they will be rewarded for the quality of their strategies rather than for short-term financial outcomes (Hitt et al., 1990).

3. Method and sample

3.1. *Data collected*

Sample

The total number of "Science Parks" in Sweden are 23 (see Swedepark; the Swedish Science Park Association). We initially chose to limit our study to ten Science Parks. The main participants establishing Science Parks in Sweden, such as universities, local authorities and development agencies, have encouraged the formation of a heterogeneous group of parks. We excluded 13 of the Parks in this study because the parks are brand new or acting as a "firm hotel". The total number of firms in the ten parks were 477 with a technological base. Much emphasis is placed on high technology industries, and so a workable definition would seem to be essential. These include (Monck et al., 1988): new knowledge-based, leading edge, and R&D intensive industry. Science Parks contain not only independent, entrepreneurially managed firms but also firms which may be part of a group and where the ultimate ownership is outside the park. In order to make valid comparisons both between this study and other studies, only single-plant independent firms are included (joint-stock firms, trading companies, limited partnership companies etc.). As expected, the new and emerging technologies such as information and software technology and electronics dominated the ten Science Parks.

The on-Park sample ($N = 265$ NTBFs) is a random sample of 477 independent NTBFs located on Science Parks in Sweden, and were drawn on a stratified basis from the total number of on-Park from locations. To identify the off-Park NTBFs CD-rom business data bases were used and a database of new, Swedish, technology-based firms that have been developed within the CREATE group at the Department of Industrial Dynamics at Chalmers University of Technology. The database includes all Swedish firms that fulfill certain criteria of size, year of foundation, independence at start and industry (Rickne and Jacobsson, 1999). 1,126 firms were identified as fulfilling this criteria.

The off-Park random sample consists of 500 independent firms and were drawn on a stratified basis (branches, according to weightings from

Science Park firms, step by step). 200 firms were excluded according to technology base etc. However, defining what is and what is not high technology is problematic. The identification of comparable off-Park firms was a time-consuming project and off-Park selection problems were compounded due to name changes, changes of location and business closures. Science Park firms were then "matched" with a similar group of off-Park firms based on the selection criteria (Westhead and Storey, 1994): industry, ownership type of the firm, age of the firm and location of the firm.

Questionnaire and variables

A survey study was selected in order to give information about the factors that explain any differences in performance (on- and off-Park). Questionnaire responses were collected from independent organisations (respondent: manager/director) during early 1999 and in the middle of 1999. After two remainders (and one remainder by telephone) in springtime, 283 firms had responded to the survey. Of those firms that had responded to the survey, about ten were wrongly classified. Of the firms that had not responded to the survey, some could not be localised or had no activity and some said they did not have time to answer the questionnaire. The questionnaire included questions about:

- Motivations of location (11 variables)
- Strategies (19 variables)
- Collaborations (4 variables)
- Performance (18 variables)

Firm managers were asked to report, on a 5-point scale, how their firms performed over the last three years in terms of profits and sales relatively competitors etc. Differences are statistically significant at the 5 percent level. A range of questions in our survey were intended to provide an indication of the technological capability of the NTBFs. The forthcoming section 4 reports the responses of firms to questions about the four categories of variables – motivations of location, strategies, collaborations and performance – information about the factors which may explain any differences in firm growth. We are interested in finding any differences between NTBFs who have

chosen to locate on Science Parks compared to those who have chosen to locate elsewhere.

Means and frequencies

It is necessary to subdivide the firms not solely between those located on and off the Science Park, but also in a number of other ways – such as branch, whether or not they are located in the north of Sweden (region) etc. The branches are software/information technology, technology consultants, electronics/electrical, pharmacology and pharmaceutical preparation, mechanics and industrial chemistry/plastics. A total of 273 NTBFs were surveyed, of which 134 were on a Science Park and 139 were not on a park. This section is devoted to a description of the broad characteristics of the firms involved (see Table I). Most of the businesses are rather youthful (mean; 7.19 and 9.00 years), probably reflecting the fact that small firms tend to be younger than medium- or large-sized firms. The tracking of NTBFs on Swedish Science Park organisations was successfully achieved because information was more extensive from Science Park managers surrounding organisation name changes and/or organisation changes.

There is some conflicting evidence of differential performance of firms of a Science Park. This should not come as a surprise since off-Park firms were specifically chosen to be "comparable" with those on the park. The fact that areas in which NTBFs are concentrated also experience an "above-average" performance in their conventional sectors can be explained in two ways (Monck et al., 1988). The first is that the high-tech sector "leads" economic development and that the conventional sectors benefit from the additional purchasing power generated. The second explanation is that the type of "environment" which includes the establisment and growth of NTBFs is also one likely to lead to growth amongst conventional business.

Westhead and Storey (1994) found few statistically significant differences between the NTBFs located in Science Parks and those located off-Park. They found that firms in Science Parks were younger than the off-Park firms (mean age of 9.6 years versus 12.4), and were also slightly smaller (19 versus 23 employees). The main difference between our groups (Science Park and off-Park)

TABLE I
Means and frequencies of surveyed high technology organisations over the 1996–1998 period

1. Response rate:

	On-Park sample	Off-Park sample
N	265	300
n	134	139
No valid firms	5	5
Response rate (%)	52.1	48.0

2. Variables – Means and frequencies:

	On-Park sample				Off-Park sample			
	Response		No response		Response		No response	
	Mean	Std dev.	Mean	Std dev.	Mean	Std dev.	Mean	Std dev.
Growth (%)								
Sales	38.75	66.62	31.31	43.35	11.19	31.01	12.54	31.11
Employment	27.94	66.19	25.76	65.06	4.20	25.21	6.84	20.60
Profitability	2.97	21.99	1.56	24.85	6.51	12.71	6.07	15.26
Start								
Sales[a]	9,292.4	16,360.7	10,658.8	16,540.2	11,532.7	16,054.5	12,101.0	13,023.4
Employment	10.37	19.19	10.35	13.96	11.72	14.67	11.49	12.77
Branch[b]	3.29	2.06	3.31	2.00	3.42	2.02	3.28	2.02
Age	7.19	2.94	8.37	2.19	9.00	1.83	9.17	1.55
Region[c]	120.40	256.77	101.13	224.89	123.94	217.06	74.55	140.26

3. Branch – frequencies (%)

	On-Park sample		Off-Park sample	
	Response	No response	Response	No response
Software/information technology	34.3	30.0	29.7	30.7
Technology consultants	25.4	23.6	26.1	24.8
Electronics/electrical	11.9	16.4	13.0	13.9
Pharmacology and pharmaceutical preparation	14.2	15.5	13.0	13.9
Mechanics	9.7	10.9	11.6	11.9
Industrial chemistry/plastics industry	4.5	3.6	6.5	5.0
Sum	100.0	100.0	100.0	100.0

[a] 1000 SEK.
[b] Branch (6 branches), different weightings.
[c] Region (10 regions), different weightings.

could be apparent with regard to stated technology structure and R&D intensity. A number of firms are leading edge firms undertaking R&D. Others are less sophisticated, undertaking little R&D, and essentially are involved in downstream commercial activities.

Löfsten and Lindelöf (2001) used a compara-

tive evaluation approach and has taken into consideration NTBFs in nine Swedish Science Park organisations over the 1994–1996 period. The hypotheses are empirically tested on the basis of 263 new technology-based firms in Sweden located both on and off-Park. The pilot study endeavoured to cover joint-stock firms located on the nine target Science Parks (163 firms). The remainder of the NTBFs were drawn from off-Park locations (100 firms). The study showed a general trend in sales growth (NTBFs on Science Parks, yearly averages 1994–1996: 45.60% and NTBFs, off-Park: 12.93%), employment growth (On-Park: 27.95% and Off-Park: 10.17%) and profitability (On-Park: 4.70% and Off-Park: 9.63%). The collected data cover all three years of the NTBFs operational life. The findings on Science Parks performance suggest that the parks milieu appear to have a positive impact on their firms growth as measured in terms of sales and jobs. However, there was no evidence of a direct relationship between Science Park location and profitability. Monck et al. (1988) say that it is curious that data on profitability performance of high-tech firms is very different from that on the other measures of performance and the low proportion of firms on a Science Park making profits in their early years of life are also attributable to the fact that many actually start without any formal product to sell.

3.2. Characteristics of surveyed firms and matching criteria

New technology-based firms

Little (1979) settled on the following characteristics of an NTBF: (1) it must not have been established for more than 25 years (2) it must be a business based on potential invention or one having substantial technological risks over and above those of normal business (3) it must have been established by a group of individuals – not as a subsidiary of an established company (4) it must have been established for the purpose of exploiting an invention or technological innovation. Bollinger et al. (1983) describe a number of factors and policies that are most critical for countries that wish to encourage the growth of NTBFs:

- Regional policy;
- Sector differences and product versus process innovation;
- Technology-oriented complexes;
- Other factors such as information flow, existence of financial markets and capital

constraints and government or large firm procurement procedures.

Oakey et al. (1988) define new technology-based firms (NTBFs) as "small firms with a higher inherent innovative potential than large firms and small firms in general". Small firms often play an important role in industries characterized by a particularly high rate of growth and technological change. Roure and Keely (1989) identified the following factors of technology availability or market opportunities in the process of creation of NTBFs:

- The presence of "incubator" type companies in the area;
- Attractive potential market, preferably, near;
- Universities with a strong interaction with firms;
- Government purchase contracts, research projects and incentives or subsidies to innovation.

NTBF characteristics refer in our study to the firm's number of patents, licenses and education level. Patents are often used as an indicator of technological development, although the propensity to patent varies between sectors, between firms and countries (Taylor and Silberston, 1973). Over the years there have been a number of surveys of entrepreneurs which have investigated the question of whether higher levels of education are associated with smaller firms that have a better performance than otherwise comparable firms which are owned by less educated individuals. However, the results have been somewhat inconsistent (see Pickles and O'Farrell, 1987).

Comparative evaluations

One logical way to assess the performance of Science Parks is to compare the performance of their tenants to similar firms not located there. Previous research has shown this approach has its limitations (Mian, 1991): (1) there is no reliable and cost-effective way to identify a comparison group because of poor data sources on small start-up firms (2) there is no reliable way to identify a comparison group because of a strong selection bias of university technology business incubator (3) lack of control on firm variables and (4) the effects of university technology business incubators are not limited to their tenant firms. It is difficult to say if the combined on- and off-Park sample can be regarded as a representative sample of all NTBFs in Sweden 1996–1998. The Science Park sample, however, was reasonably representative of all NTBFS located on parks.

Weiss (1972) has suggested three conditions that experience suggests particularly recommend the use of comparative evaluations: (1) when the issues are real and policy-makers are faced with vital decisions among alternative strategies for action; (2) when the alternative programs are relatively well defined, with substantially similar aims and (3) when there is a preliminary evidence that programs have the viability and strength to offer some likelihood of success. However, the use of "matched samples" has become widely appreciated and utilized in the small firms and entrepreneurship research fields (according to O'Farrell and Hitchens, 1988).

4. Identifying strategy and performance variables for NTBFs located on and off Science Parks

4.1. *Variables – motivations of location and strategies*

Universities and other higher education institutions are an important source of new scientific knowledge. Industry can gain access to this knowledge or resources by developing formal and informal links with higher education institutes (OECD, 1981, 1993). The development of higher education institute links is, therefore, assumed to encourage innovation and production (Westhead and Storey, 1994). Hence locales with highly interlinked higher education institutes are expected to have enhanced levels of wealth creation and job generation (Malecki, 1991). We might expect Science Park firms to be more active receivers of research results and maybe more active partners in research and education projects.

The factors reported to be most important to the surveyed firms are, in descending order (on-Park): nearness to universities, nearness to customers and importance for new customers. The off-Park sample reported proximity to other firms to be of higher importance than the on-Park sample in their choice of location. When it comes to the importance of other factors in the location decision,

off-Park NTBFs put more value on nearness to customers/new customers. Information on the location of customers shows whether firms are linked to local, national or international markets, and thereby their potential for growth. Given the short product life-cycle of many technology-based products and services, there is a requirement to reach a large international market quickly to exploit the profit potential of the product.

Strategy as a means for achieving competitive advantage takes into account both the positioning analysis of what business to be in and where to compete and the resource-based analysis of how to compete. The competitive advantage is the result of a thorough understanding of the external and internal forces that strongly affect an organisation. The process of strategy formulation requires managers/decision-makers to address issues of growth, diversification etc and the NTBFs competitive domain refers to the organisation's choice of economic mission (Gilmore, 1971). As it is shown in Table II, there were significant differences in the means of eight strategy dimensions between the on-Park and off-Park firms. Looking first at the strategy dimensions, it can be seen that the NTBFs who located in Science Parks showed significantly greater emphasis on firm characteristics as innovation ability, action-orientation, competitor- and market oriented, sales and employment growth, high profits etc. The differences indicates a slight advantage for the Science Park firms. Science Parks is probably attracting a more motivated group of entrepreneurs than off-Park locations.

4.2. *Variables – collaborations and performance*

One of the important arguments in favor of Science Parks is the claimed networking benefits. By providing a Science Park location that is proximal to important customers, suppliers, researchers and other businesses/organisations it is assumed that the NTBFs will be able to build networks that support their development. The assessing of academic knowledge and expertise by businesses located on site is a key principle of Science Parks. One might expect a discrepancy between Science Park NTBFs and off-Park NTBFs over-all importance with their location. Science Park proponents have claimed that Science Parks

Peter Lindelöf and Hans Löfsten

TABLE II
Variables – motivations of location and strategies

Variables	Mean		F	Significant	p-value	Std. dev.		Scale[c]
	1[a]	0[b]				1	0	
Motivations of location								
Significant								
Nearness to universities	3.16	2.54	6.50	0.01	0.00*	1.38	1.56	1–5
Importance for new customers	2.14	2.79	20.56	0.00	0.00*	1.33	1.68	1–5
Nearness to customers	2.45	2.89	0.00	0.93	0.01*	1.36	1.43	1–5
Non-significant								
Rent for the premises	2.61	2.83			0.14			1–5
Nearness to well-known firms	2.04	2.23			0.25			1–5
Nearness to competitors	1.32	1.44			0.27			1–5
Transportation/means of communication	3.05	3.22			0.33			1–5
Attractive/expansive region	2.77	2.61			0.36			1–5
Community-related advantages	1.92	2.06			0.38			1–5
Nearness to firms/partners	1.69	1.63			0.67			1–5
Recruitments	3.54	3.60			0.74			1–5
Strategies								
Significant								
Conservative – innovative and action-oriented	4.17	3.70	1.41	0.24	0.00*	1.05	1.14	1–5
Competitor- or market-oriented	4.00	3.45	6.15	0.01	0.00*	0.98	1.15	1–5
Sales growth – not important–important	4.15	3.53	5.95	0.02	0.00*	1.02	1.20	1–5
Employment growth – not important–important	2.91	2.38	0.16	0.69	0.00*	1.28	1.22	1–5
Firm actions – cautiousness–rapidity	3.13	2.72	0.04	0.85	0.01*	1.23	1.20	1–5
High profits – not important–important	3.50	3.21	0.88	0.35	0.04*	1.09	1.24	1–5
Sales development relatively competitors	2.01	1.58	0.60	0.44	0.04*	1.80	1.68	1–5
Competitors – elimination–co-operation	2.74	2.42	0.08	0.78	0.04*	1.22	1.22	1–5
Non-significant								
Product development (rate)	3.20	2.91			0.08			1–5
Technology development	3.52	3.54			0.10			1–5
Price (low–high)	2.95	2.75			0.13			1–5
Price competition	2.72	2.91			0.23			1–5
Competition (general)	3.33	3.14			0.29			1–5
New products/quality	3.17	3.00			0.30			1–5
Milieu	1.70	1.85			0.31			1–5
Decreasing demand	2.83	3.01			0.33			1–5
Price – market based	2.93	2.87			0.74			1–5
Price – cost-based	2.56	2.60			0.84			1–5
Competitor behaviour	2.76	2.79			0.84			1–5

* Significance 5%-level (p-value < 0.05).
[a] On-Park.
[b] Off-Park.
[c] 1 = very poor, 5 = very high, Yes = 1, No = 0.

offer NTBFs an environment that supports network formation and meets the operational needs of NTBFs. Our survey results did not show a consistent advantage in favor of firms located on Science Parks.

Science Park managers have an important role not only establishing links, but also encouraging the development of more formal links over time. Westhead and Storey (1995) believe higher education institutions should appreciate the necessity of having an effective managerial structure designed to "add value" to tenant firms. The linkage between Science Park NTBFs and the university is fundamental to the concept of Science Parks. In different universities certain institutes or departments strongly relate to industry.

The level of inter-firm linkage is heavily contingent on factors exogenous to the Science Park, such as firm organisational structure and market structure. Science Parks characterized by branch plants are likely to have less local producer – supplier relations than parks composed of independent, single-facility units (Hagey and Malecki, 1986). Market structure is likely to dictate the level of local linkage (Felsenstein, 1994). Customized production rather than mass production is more likely to have a local seeding effect in terms of external linkages and spin-offs (Glasmeier, 1988).

In general, the comparison between significant and non-significant variables by category would emphasize the result that on-Park firms have different motivations but not different performance than off-Park firms (see Table III). The most obvious observation is how apparently similar off-Park firms responses were to those of on-Park firms regarding performance (see Table III). One measure of output (performance) is the level of patenting activity in firms. However, patenting is not affected by Science Park locations.

5. Conclusions

We conducted the analysis using 273 respondent NTBFs, assuming the NTBFs on and off-Park to be a sufficiently homogenous group. This study applies especially to small high technology-based business organisations – those most likely to face the challenges of increasing scale, market scope

and administrative complexity. Informal and highly centralized structures and the intuitive and individualistic modes of strategymaking that usually occur within them become inadequate; more formal, specialized and more rational modes of strategy making emerge. The present research indicates that important relationships among the variables composing strategy making and growth. These variables often have crucial implications for growth.

(1) The analysis showed some differences between the experience of firms on-Park and off-Park in respect of motivations of location and strategy issues. We found significant differences in the importance of co-operation with firms being close to other firms in the industry. There were also significant differences with regard to the degree of importance with proximity to customers and nearness to universities (Motivations of location). However, these differences do not show any clear pattern, making it difficult to understand if NTBFs who locate on Science Parks are systematically looking for something different in their location. When comparing differences between Science Park and off-Park firms, observed differences could reflect the motivations of the firms as well as the benefits of a Science Park location. Science Parks is probably attracting a more motivated group of entrepreneurs than off-Park locations. There is therefore, some conflicting evidence of differential performance.

(2) No statistically significant differences between Science Park NTBFs and off-Park NTBFs were recorded with regard to patents/products launched in the last three years (Performance – patents/products). One finding from this research is that Science Park NTBFs are not able to channel investments into greater R&D outputs than comparable off-Park firms. The number of patents registered by a firm remains a widely used output measure of the level of technology diffusion. Monck et al. (1988) found that a larger proportion of Science Park firms had lodged at least one patent in the last two years than had off-Park firms (the significance was not statistically significant). Further research should investigate whether the lack of difference in R&D output levels (patents/products) is due to the management activities of Science Park managers.

(3) On-Park firms collaborate less than off-Park

TABLE III
Variables – collaborations and performance

Variables	Mean		F	Significant	p-value	Std. dev.		Scale[c]
	1[a]	0[b]				1	0	
Collaboration								
Significant								
Co-operation regarding production								
activities	1.25	2.37	145.29	0.00	0.00*	0.76	1.67	1–5
Co-operation of marketing activities	1.22	1.82	52.19	0.00	0.00*	0.72	1.31	1–5
R&D co-operation	1.30	1.76	30.20	0.00	0.00*	0.81	1.21	1–5
Co-operation of administration								
services	1.24	1.50	24.79	0.00	0.04*	0.81	1.23	1–5
Performance								
Non-significant profits								
Market value of the firm								
(more or less than competitors)	1.60	1.30			0.18			1–5
Profit margin								
(not satisfying–satisfying)	2.44	2.57			0.44			1–5
Cash flow (negative–positive) on								
comparison with competitors	1.22	1.08			0.49			1–5
Bigger profits than competitors								
(smaller–bigger)	1.48	1.46			0.91			1–5
Business organisation								
Change of business organisation								
last 12 months								
(small changes–big changes)	1.80	1.44			0.09			1–5
Change of business organisation								
last 12 months	0.60	0.50			0.13			Yes/no
Planning								
Long-range planning of investments	1.80	1.57			0.09			1–5
Long-range planning of technology								
development	1.94	1.77			0.24			1–5
Changed products (last 12 months)	0.80	0.74			0.42			Yes/no
Analysis of consumer behaviour	2.54	2.66			0.49			1–5
Patents/products								
New products (before competitors)	0.62	0.68			0.34			Yes/no
Patents	0.32	0.36			0.56			Yes/no
Excluding products and services	0.23	0.25			0.76			Yes/no
Licenses	0.23	0.18			0.33			Yes/no
Patents	0.04	0.07			0.25			Yes/no
Franchising	0.03	0.04			0.70			Yes/no
Other	0.02	0.02			0.99			Yes/no
Share of turnovers (licenses,								
patents, franchising and others)	7.39	4.23			0.13			Procent

* Significance 5%-level (p-value < 0.05).
[a] On-Park.
[b] Off-Park.
[c] 1 = very poor, 5 = very high, Yes = 1, No = 0.

firms and their technological and economic performance (Table III) do not significantly differ from the latter. The variables used to support an advantage of on-Park firms are motivation variables and not performance indicators. However, the results obtained in earlier sections (Section 3: employment growth and sales growth) show that NTBFs on Science Parks have a rate of job creation and sales growth which is substantially higher than that for NTBFs in general (see also Löfsten and Lindelöf, 2001). The commercial pressures upon Science Park managers may have influenced the presented results. For many NTBFs it is likely to be several years before such firms achieve high profitability (Section 3: on-Park: 2.97% and off-Park: 6.51%) and this is incompatible with many providers of finance who require a very short-term pay-back.

(4) No single university will provide the full range of scientific or management skills required by the park NTBFs (Motivations of location: nearness to universities). There may be park-based firms which have the majority of their formal links with universities. Science Parks are a particularly suitable location for new businesses and opportunities exist for Park managers to develop training and business placing programs to assist potential entrepreneurs. Opportunities also exist for park managers to develop "added value" networks with similar organisations. Complementing this picture is the empirical evidence pointing to the generally low level of collaboration and performance. Some questions can be raised about the extent of research links and the basis for the Science Park strategy as a means to achieve linkage.

The significant finding here is that innovation (patents/products, product development and technology development) were no more evident than off-Park firms. In general, academic research is focused on basic research rather than applied research and Science Park NTBFs are not in a position to undertake long-term R&D. Maybe Science Parks represent more centers of learning than innovation and it's difficult to say whether they can be effective only in those areas in which innovation is science-based and less in areas in which innovation is based on the development of new products and markets. Those policy-makers seeking to support academic-industry links with a

view to promoting technological innovation would better achieve their objectives by looking beyond Science Parks. Some of these results confirm the critique to the efficiency of Science Parks and the difficulty of measuring their benefits for innovation. Science Parks is just one of a collection of policy instruments that aim to encourage the development of innovation and is often uncritically accepted.

References

Acs, Z. J. and D. B. Audretsch, 1988, 'Entrepreneurial Strategy and the Presence of Small Firms', *Small Business Economics* 1(3), 193–274.

Allen, D. and E. Bazan, 1990, *Value-added Contribution of Pennsylvania's Business Incubators to Tenant Firms and Local Economies*. Report prepared for Pennsylvania Department of Commerce (Pennsylvania State University, University Park, PA).

Baker, N. R., 1974, 'R&D Project Selection Models: An Assessment', *IEE Transactions on Engineering Management* E-M-21(4), 165–171.

Bollinger, L., K. Hope and J. Utterback, 1983, 'A Review of Literature and Hypotheses on New Technology-based Firms', *Research Policy* 12, 1–4.

Bourgeois, L. J. I., 1980, 'Strategy and Environment: A Conceptual Integration', *Academy of Management Review* 5(1), 25–39.

Danila, N., 1989, 'Strategic Evaluation and Selection of R&D Projects', *R&D Management* 19(1), 47–62.

Doz, Y. L., 1988, 'Technology Partnerships between Larger and Smaller Firms: Some Critical Issues', in F. J. Contractor and P. Lorange (eds.), *Cooperative Strategies in International Business: Joint Ventures and Technology Partnerships between Firms*. Boston: Lexington Books.

Feldman, M. P., 1994, *The Geography of Innovation*. Dordrecht: Kluwer Academic.

Felsenstein, D., 1994, 'University-related Science Parks – "Seedbeds" or "Enclaves" of Innovation?', *Technovation* 14(2), 93–110.

Gilmore, F. F., 1971, 'Formulating Strategy in Smaller Companies', *Harvard Business Review* 49(3), 71–81.

Glasmeier, A., 1988, 'Factors Governing the Development of High Tech Industry Agglomerations: A Tale of Three Cities', *Regional Studies* 22(4), 287–301.

Goss, E. and G. S. Vozikis, 1994, 'High Tech Manufacturing: Firm Size, Industry and Population Density', *Small Business Economics* 6, 291–297.

Hagedoorn, J. and J. Schakenraad, 1990, 'Inter-firm Partnerships and Co-operative Strategies in Core Technologies', in C. Freeman and L. Soete (eds.), *New Explorations in the Economics of Technical Change*. London: Frances Pinter.

Hagey, M. J. and E. J. Malecki, 1986, 'Linkages in High Technology Industries: A Florida Case Study', *Environment and Planning A* 18, 1477–1498.

Hitt, M. A., R. E. Hoskisson and R. D. Ireland, 1990, 'Mergers and Acquisitions and Managerial Commitment to Innovation in M-form Firms', *Strategic Management Journal* **11** (special issue), 29–47.

Khandwalla, P. N., 1977, *The Design of Organizations*. New York: Harcourt Brace Jovanovich.

Kleinknecht, A. and T. P. Poot, 1992, 'Do Regions Matter for R&D?', *Regional Studies* **26**, 221–232.

Little, A. D., 1979, *New Technology-based Firms in the U.K. and Federal Republic of Germany*. London: Wilton House Publications.

Löfsten, H. and P. Lindelöf, 2001, 'Science Parks in Sweden – Industrial Renewal and Development?', *R&D Management* **31**(3), 309–322.

MacDonald, S., 1987, 'British Science Parks: Reflections on the Politics of High Technology', *R&D Management* **17**(1), 25–37.

Malecki, E. J., 1991, *Technology and Economic Development: the Dynamics of Local, Regional and National Change*. London: Longman.

Massey, D., P. Quintas and Wield, 1992, *High Tech Fantasies: Science Parks in Society, Science and Space*. London: Routledge.

Mian, S., 1991, *An Assessment of University-sponsored Business Incubators in Supporting the Development of New Technology-based Firms*. Unpublished doctoral dissertation. George Washington University, Washington DC.

Mian, S. A., 1994, 'U.S. University-sponsored Technology Incubators: An Overview of Management, Policies and Performance', *Technovation* **14**(9), 515–528.

Mian, S., 1996, 'Assessing Value-added Contributions of University Technology Business Incubators to Tenant Firms', *Research Policy* **25**, 325–335.

Mian, S. S., 1997, 'Assessing and Managing the University Technology Business Incubator: An Integrative Framework', *Journal of Business Venturing* **12**, 251–285.

Miller, D., 1987, 'Strategy Making and Structure: Analysis and Implications for Performance', *Academy of Management Journal* **30**(1), 7–32.

Monck, C. S. P., R. B. Porter, P. Quintas, D. J. Storey and P. Wynarczyk, 1988, *Science Parks and the Growth of High Technology Firms*. London: Croom Helm.

Oakey, R., R. Rothwell and S. Cooper, 1988, *The Management of Innovation in High Technology Small Firms*. London: Frances Pinter.

OECD, 1981, *The Future of University Research. Organisation for Economic Co-Operation and Development*, Paris.

OECD, 1993, *Small and Medium-sized Enterprises: Technology and Competitiveness. Economic Co-Operation and Development*, Paris.

O'Farrell, P. N. and D. M. W. N. Hitchens, 1988, 'The Relative Competitiveness and Performance of Small Manufacturing Firms in Scotland and the Mid-west of Ireland: An Analysis of Matched Pairs', *Regional Studies* **22**, 339–415.

Pickles, A. R. and P. N. O'Farrell, 1987, 'An Analysis of Entrepreneurial Behaviour from Male Work Histories', *Regional Studies* **21**(5), 425–444.

Pfirrmann, O., 1994, 'The Geography of Innovation in Small and Medium-sized Firms in West Germany', *Small Business Economics* **6**, 41–54.

Rickne, A. and Jacobsson, S., 1999, 'New Technology-based Firms in Sweden – A Study of Their Direct Impact on industrial Renewal', *Economics of Innovation and New Technology* **8**, 197–223.

Rothwell, R., 1983, 'Innovation and Firm Size: A Case For Dynamic Complementarity: Or, is Small Really so Beutiful?', *Journal of General Management* **8**(3), 5–25.

Rothwell, R., 1984, 'The Role of Small Firms in the Emergence of New Technologies', *OMEGA – The International Journal of Management Science* **12**(1), 19–29.

Roure, J. B. and R. H. Keely, 1989, 'Comparison of Predicting Factors of Successful High Growth Technological Ventures in Europe and U.S.A.', in S. Birley (ed.), *European Entrepreneurship: Emerging Growth Companies*. Cranfield: European Foundation for Entrepreneurship Research.

Segers, J. P., 1993, 'Strategic Partnering between New-technology Based Firms and Large Established Firms in the Biotechnology and Micro-electronics Industries in Belgium', *Small Business Economics* **5**, 271–281.

Souder, W. E. and T. Mandakovic, 1986, 'R&D Project Selection Models – The Dawn of a New Era', *Research Management* **29**(4), 36–42.

Souder, W. E., P. M. Maher, C. R. Shumway, N. R. Baker and A. H. Rubenstein, 1974, 'Methodology for Increasing the Adoption of R&D Project Selection Models', *R&D Management* **4**(2), 75–83.

Taylor, C. and A. Silberston, 1973, *The Economic Impact of the Patent System*. Cambridge: Cambridge University Press.

Van der Auwera, F. and D. Eysenbrandts, 1989, *High Tech Firms in Flanders*. Brussels: BBM.

Weiss, C. H., 1972, *Evaluation Research*. Englewood Cliffs, NJ: Prentice Hall.

Westhead, P., 1997, 'R&D "Inputs" and "Outputs" of Technology-based Firms Located on and Off Science Parks', *R&D Management* **27**(1), 45–62.

Westhead, P. and D. J. Storey, 1994, *An Assessment of Firms Located On and Off Science Parks in the United Kingdom*. London: HMSO.

Westhead, P. and D. J. Storey, 1995, 'Links Between Higher Education Institutions and High Technology Firms', *OMEGA – International Journal of Management Science* **23**(4), 345–360.

Yap, C. M. and W. E. Souder, 1993, 'A Filter System for Technology Evaluation and Selection', *Technovation* **13**(7), 449–469.

[17]

Science Parks and the Development of NTBFs—
Location, Survival and Growth

Richard Ferguson[1]
Christer Olofsson[2]

ABSTRACT. This study investigates survival and growth of NTBFs located on and off two Swedish science parks. We find that firms located on science parks have significantly higher survival rates than off-park firms. However, we observe insignificant differences in sales and employment. Wider variation in the growth rates of firms located on parks together with the better survival suggests that the science parks may be providing favorable locations for NTBFs in a range of development phases. The image benefit associated with a science park location is not helpful in explaining growth, whereas a location benefit associated with cooperation with universities is positively associated with growth.

JEL Classification: D92, L25, L32, O32

1. Introduction

The formation, survival, and growth of new technology-based firms (NTBFs) has been a policy issue for some time now. Firms exploiting emerging technologies are seen as a means to realize returns on academic research, and are recognized for their high-growth potential as significant contributors in the general economy. This perception has motivated national and local policy initiatives aimed at supporting the growth and development of NTBFs. Establishing science parks is one such local action.

Science parks have been defined as property-based ventures with clear links to university or

[1]SLU, Department of Economics
Swedish University of Agricultural Sciences
Box 7013
S-750 07 Uppsala, Sweden
E-mail: richard.ferguson@ekon.slu.se
[2]SLU, Department of Economics
Swedish University of Agricultural Sciences
Box 7013
S-750 07 Uppsala, Sweeden
E-mail: richard.ferguson@ekon.slu.se

other research institutions, where firms can be offered well-suited facilities from which to conduct their business (Monck *et al.*, 1988). While in practice the services offered to tenants by different parks ranges from full-time management consulting to not much more than one might expect from any business hotel, science park initiatives share the idea that a special location environment will support the development of NTBFs.

Clear evidence of exactly what and how firm development is being supported through a science park location, however, has been difficult to find. The science park rhetoric asserts that park locations offer firms distinct advantages over off-park locations. Yet, research has found few consistent benefits beyond a "prestigious address" (Westhead and Storey, 1994), "social signaling" (Felsenstein, 1994), or "image effects" (Ferguson, 1999). Other claimed science park advantages—such as proximity to research and access to management support services—have not been substantiated.

If we give science parks the benefit of the doubt, the so-called image effects may indeed be supporting firms' development: In providing firms with a high-image place of business, science parks may contribute to firms' legitimacy, helping them to attract new customers and establish new network ties. If this is the case, we might expect to see an impact from these image effects on firms' survival and development.

In 1995, we conducted a survey of a population of Swedish NTBFs located both on and off science parks in two city areas. With the aim of learning more about the role science parks play in the development of NTBFs, we asked firms for their reasons for locating where they did and what benefits they perceived in their choice. Findings showed few conclusive differences between science park and off-park firms with the significant

Journal of Technology Transfer, 29, 5–17, 2004
© *2004 Kluwer Academic Publishers. Manufactured in The Netherlands.*

exceptions that firms on science parks were on average younger and slightly smaller, and reported receiving greater "image benefits" from their location (Ferguson, 1999; Ferguson and Olofsson, 1998).

In a deeper qualitative study of some of the surveyed firms, we learned that there were two dimensions to the firms' perceived image benefits. On the one hand, image benefits were realized through external social signaling, where the firms felt that potential customers and other actors in the environment perceived the firm in a more advantageous light due to their science park location; and on the other hand, firms reported an internal image benefit, where by being located in a high standard, "real" place of business, firm founders and employees from academic and research backgrounds felt more encouraged to play the part of the business entrepreneur (Ferguson, 1999).

Based on these findings, we hypothesized that the image factor could be of particular value to NTBFs: With both their young age and new technology, these firms face a particularly high "liability of newness". If firms receive a positive image benefit from their location, we reasoned, it could help them to gain legitimacy in the marketplace and thereby contribute to their survival and growth.

To test this posit, we have gathered data on the location, survival, sales, and employment over the course of 1991 through 2000 for the group of NTBFs who participated in our 1995 survey. This data allows us to compare the survival and growth of the studied firms over a 10 year period.

Our results show that the firms located on science parks have a significantly greater rate of survival, though only a marginally greater, and wider ranging rate of growth than comparable firms located off of science parks. This indicates that firms in different phases of development are finding ways to meet their survival needs in science park locations.

In the remainder of this section, we will develop two hypotheses which support the science park and NTBF literature. We follow this with a section that presents our methodology and includes a description of the study sample. We then present our analysis in three parts, covering firm survival, firm growth, and correlations

between claimed location advantages, and survival and growth.

NTBFs and science parks

Storey and Tether (1998) raise four criteria that researchers may include in defining NTBFs: age, size, independence, and technology. Some NTBF studies follow quite closely the definition proposed by Little (1977), where NTBFs are said to be independent firms founded not more than 25 years ago, that are based on the exploitation of an invention or technological innovation, implying substantial technological risk. Many studies of NTBFs, however, show varying rigidity in the adherence to these criteria. For example, neither Rickne (2000) nor Storey and Tether (1998) include the criterion of independence. Autio (1994) and Klofsten (1994) open the technology criterion to include all firms with advanced technological know-how that is exploited in products and services. Finally, we can see variation in the criterion of size, where some researchers assume NTBFs to be a subset of small and medium-sized enterprises (e.g. Oakey *et al.*, 1988; Storey and Tether, 1998), where as others clearly state that size is not a criterion (e.g. Rickne, 2000).

We use the term NTBFs here to indicate relatively young, small firms whose core technology is dependent upon a high degree of state-of-the-art knowledge.

Monck *et al.* (1988) define science parks based on four criteria: Science parks are (1) property-based ventures, (2) with links to university or other academic research institutions, (3) designed to encourage the formation and growth of knowledge-based businesses, and (4) have management functions to support the transfer of technology and business skills to tenant firms. As with the NTBF definition, however, researchers have emphasized each of these criteria in varying degrees.

Of the four criteria identified by Monck *et al.* (1988), the science park managerial functions show a particular variation from park to park. Grayson (1993) identifies three types of management agreements: informal teams, single on-site managers, and on-site management companies. Parks working with informal teams provide management services to tenants by offering guidance in finding appropriate third-party business support actors. In contrast, parks with single on-site managers or on-site management companies directly provide management support to tenants.

Parks operating under these latter two types of management agreements have been referred to as "managed science parks", whereas park with informal teams have been referred to as non-managed science parks (Westhead and Batstone 1999; Westhead and Storey 1994). The distinguishing characteristic between the managed and non-managed science parks is whether in-house development services are offered to tenants, as opposed to management services being provided by third-party actors.

There is some evidence suggesting regional differences in the management approach science parks take. Westhead and Batstone (1999) reported a greater share of managed science parks in northern U.K. than in the south. Bengtson and Löwegren (2001), in a comparison of Swedish and Finnish science parks, found that Finnish parks worked from a "competence center approach", offering their tenants substantial in-house business advice, whereas Swedish parks more often used an "agent approach", helping tenants find suitable network partners rather than providing direct development support.

Both Westhead and Batstone (1999) and Weathead and Storey (1994) found that business closure rates were lower in non-managed science parks than in managed science parks. They suggested that this could be due to different selection criteria used by park management in selecting tenant firms, with managed parks being more willing to accept weaker firms as tenants. In support of this explanation, they noted that the tenants on managed science parks tended to be smaller and younger—factors that have been negatively associated with survival (further discussed below),

We use the term science parks here to indicate property-based ventures, with links to universities and/or other academic research institutions, that aim to support technology-based businesses and the transfer or development of new technology through the provision of a high quality, full service business location. As science parks in Sweden—where our study was conducted—tend to provide

business and technology development services to tenants through third-party actors (Bengtson and Löwegren, 2001), we further limit our use of the science park term in this study to include only so-called "non-managed" science parks.

NTBF survival

The fact that NTBFs are small and new suggests that they face a "liability of newness" (Stinchcombe, 1965). Stinchcombe used this term to explain the higher rate of failure among young firms, which he attributed to the difficulties new firms have in securing the resources they need for survival. This liability arises at least in part because young firms have less of the legitimacy needed to gain trust and support from other actors (Singh *et al.*, 1986).

To develop legitimacy, firms need to gain recognition as actors who follow the prevailing norms of the system (DiMaggio and Powell, 1991). NTBFs may face a particular challenge in this sense, as they are not only new players in the game, but come with new ideas and/or products. They need to prove themselves to be worthy business partners, just as any new firm must do, but they also need to teach the environment the meaning and value of their new products and/or services.

A number of science park studies have found that one of the most distinguishing attractions of science parks is an image benefit or prestigious address (Ferguson, 1999; Westhead and Storey, 1994). Felsenstein (1994) discusses a "social signaling" associated with science parks, where science parks are perceived as "enclaves of innovation". If other actors in the environment share these perceptions of science parks, we might expect NTBFs to gain legitimacy through a science park location, easing the liability of newness, and thereby having a greater chance of survival.

Hypothesis 1: Firms located on science parks will show higher survival rates that firms located off science parks.

NTBF growth and science parks

Researchers have sought to identify key underlying issues in small firm growth, and a number of factors have repeatedly been linked to firms' performance. Storey (1994) makes the distinction between "firm-specific", "founder-specific", and "external" factors that have been found in various studies to influence growth. Of the factors that Storey lists, firm age and size, ownership, founders' background/skills, industry sector, and regional location have been found to be useful in modeling business growth (Almus and Nerlinger, 1999; Davidsson *et al.*, 2002; Evans, 1987).

With regard to firm-specific growth factors, firm size (usually in combination with firm age) has been one of the more significant and consistent factors in explaining firm growth (Almus and Nerlinger, 1999; Davidsson *et al.*, 2002; Evans, 1987). This has been explained by the need for small firms to grow to certain minimum sizes in order to survive (Almus and Nerlinger, 1999; Audretsch, 1995; Geroski, 1995).

Many science park studies based on a comparison of on- and off-park firms have found that firms located on science parks tend to be younger and slightly smaller (Ferguson, 1999; Löfsten and Lindelöf, 2001; Westhead and Storey, 1994). In light of the fore-mentioned growth research, we might therefore expect the on-park firms to show better growth than off-park firms.

With regard to founder-specific growth factors, technical and business competencies have been found to be significant in business development. Klofsten found that, though the balance of skills differ between different types of small firms, both technical and business skills are needed to establish a stable business platform for continued growth and development (Klofsten, 1994; Klofsten *et al.*, 1988). Almus and Nerlinger (1999) included an aspect of founders' competence or skills in their growth model, considering both technical skills and business skills. Oddly, Almus and Nerlinger found a positive growth effect from business skills and technical skills independently, but no effect when they were combined. Whether this is an anomaly of their data set or a reflection of focused management attention (business development or technical development) leading to more aggressive behavior is a question for further research.

A number of comparative science park studies have found that founders of firms located on science parks tend to have a higher degree of education than off-park firm founders, and that the science park firm founders are less likely to have prior business experience (Löfsten and Lindelöf, 2001; Westhead and Storey, 1994). This suggests that the firms located on science parks have a higher technology competence, but may need support in business competence. Applying the line of reasoning in Klofsten *et al.* (1988), if science parks help firms with "management functions to support the transfer of technology and business skills to tenant firms" (Quintas *et al.*, 1992), then we might again expect to see stronger development and growth.

Hypothesis 2: Firms located on science parks will tend to have higher growth rates than firms located off science parks.

Westhead and Storey (1994) report some evidence of better growth in firms located on science parks. They conducted a follow-up study of Monck *et al.* (1988), comparing firms located in science parks to firms located off-park in the United Kingdom. They found that a park location did not seem to influence firm survival, though the group of surviving firms located in science parks showed a greater average growth rate over the course of the studied six years. However, Westhead and Storey note that the average growth (as indicated by growth in employment) in both the on- and off-park groups was significantly influenced by the very strong performance of relatively few firms.

Löwegren (2003) found that different types of management teams explained some "perceived growth" differences. Firms being managed by founders tended to report weaker perceived growth than firms with recruited management and firms with parent-company management. This suggests the need for considering different science park effects in different tenant sub-groups when investigating firm growth.

Olofsson and Wahlbin (1993) studied the growth patterns of firms started by university researchers in Sweden. Many of these firms stay small, showing very moderate growth over the 10 years studied, yet continued in existence. This weak growth reflects a large share of "part-time" firms, where founders continue to hold university employment and thus reducing the need for income from the firm. In contrast, firms showing strong growth were found more often to be run by entrepreneurs who made a full-time commitment to develop successful businesses.

Olofsson and Wahlbin (1993) found that university spin-offs, in spite of their frequent slow growth, made significant contributions in the research and development of their customers. This may explain why the firms continued to survive in lack of better growth performance: The immediate economic value created by the academic spin-offs may be quite small compared to the value generated once the products or services are put into use by customers. This latent value may provide customers with the incentive to build and maintain relationships with the academic spin-offs despite their weak business performance.

Lindström and Olofsson (2002) note that technology-based firms may prolong an "establishing phase" of development to continue the development of the technology and/or business concept before entering a commercial growth phase. To survive this extended establishing phase—where there is little generated revenues—firms gain the support of actors who are willing to provide the necessary resources in exchange for a share of anticipated future returns. Thus, some NTBFs may show extended periods of relatively weak commercial growth, eventually followed by relatively high growth in the successful cases.

The findings of Lindström and Olofsson (2002) and Olofsson and Wahlbin (1993) make clear the need for treating survival and growth independently. While literature on small firm growth (e.g. Almus and Nerlinger, 1999; Audretsch, 1995; Geroski, 1995) and Stinchcomb's (1965) "liability of newness" suggest a need for strong early growth in order to reach a minimum size to assure survival (linking survival to growth), some potentially successful firms may survive for many years without showing significant growth.

To summarize then, our knowledge of the growth of NTBFs and the character of firms located in science parks suggests that we should see higher growth in firms located in science parks compared to off-park firms. At the same time, we find evidence in the literature that some NTBFs may survive for extended periods with little growth by gaining support from actors who are willing to provide the resources necessary for the firm to continue its development. Thus, commercial

growth is not the only means of overcoming the liability of newness.

2. Methodology

To test the hypotheses that NTBFs located on science parks have a greater rate of survival and a stronger rate of growth than NTBFs in off-park locations, we examine a group of 66 NTBFs who participated in a 1995-survey study (Ferguson, 1999). The firms are from two Swedish "university cities" in south-central Sweden. Both the city areas have dynamic technology-based industries, and each has an established, "non-managed" science park. The survey sample was drawn from local business address registers owned and maintained by NTBF support actors in each city. These registers are used to target business development activities and disseminate information to local NTBFs. Postal codes were used to ensure selected firms were from within the metropolitan areas, and stratified sampling was used to attain similar sized groups of firms located on and off of science parks.

This method of compiling a sample should provide a better basis for the comparative study of location effects on firm development than the often-used matched sampling (where one sample of science park NTBFs is "matched" to another sample of NTBFs taken from a different source using criteria such as firm size, age, and industry. See, for example, Löfsten Lindelöf, 2001; Monck et al., 1988; Westhead and Storey, 1994). While matched-sampling can provide good general representativeness of the individual comparative groups (a representative sample of firms on science parks and a representative sample of firms located outside parks), there is a risk of differing sampling bias. It is difficult to know whether observed differences between the groups being compared are associated with the issue being studied, or a result of different samplings.

While the nature of the address registers we drew our sample from most likely means that very new firms are under-represented, and that development-oriented firms are over-represented, these biases should be independent of the sub-groups, thereby giving our results high reliability. Any similarities and differences we find between the sub-groups should reflect genuine differences within NTBFs. At the same time, the general validity of our findings extends only to the relative comparison of the sub-groups we study. The actual survival and growth values reported in this study will reflect any biases in the population from which our sample was drawn.

The study sample

Seventy-six firms replied to the 1995 survey, which was 58% of the final sample population. Of these, 71 had a legal business form requiring them to send their annual report to the Swedish Patent and Registration Office (partnerships and corporations), providing us with access to archival survival and growth data.

Of the 71 firms, seven reported zero employees at the time of the survey. Of those seven, five were still reporting zero employees in 2000. As our interest lies in the survival and development of "genuine" businesses, and extended periods of zero employment suggest more "convenience-oriented" firms (tax shelters, holding companies, etc.), we have removed these firms from our sample. The result is a study sample of 66 firms, 30 of which were located on science parks at the time of the survey, and 36 who were located off-park.

The survey administered in 1995 was first reported in Ferguson (1999). The purpose of the survey was to study the role that science parks were playing in the development of NTBFs. Respondents provided information on their perception of the location benefits they were receiving.

Operationalization of firm survival and growth

Both firm survival and firm growth can be interpreted and measured in different ways. We have chosen here to base "survival" on the continued legal existence of the firm, and to base "growth" on changes in employment and gross sales. While this approach ignores the fate of the business ideas and other resources of non-surviving firms, and does not consider other measures of growth (such as research and development, capital asset growth, or returns on investment), similar indicators have been used by others (Almus and Nerlinger, 1999; Davidsson *et al.*, 2002; Evans,

1987; Löfsten and Lindelöf, 2001; Westhead and Storey, 1994), and provide a readily obtainable and highly comparable measure. These measures also directly reflect the underlying political goals of public science park policy, namely business and job creation, and economic activity.

We obtained our survival and growth data from the Swedish Patent and Registration Office. This agency collects annual reports from all incorporated business in Sweden, and maintains status and address information. We extracted gross annual sales and number of employees from the firms' annual reports as submitted. While these figures will reflect any "creative book-keeping" that firms may engage in for tax reasons or other purposes, they accurately represent what the firms are officially presenting to the public.

3. Results

The firms located on science parks in our study tended to be both younger and smaller in number of employees and sales than their off-park counterparts (see Table I). This is consistent with the results of other comparative studies (e.g. Löfsten and Lindelöf, 2001; Westhead and Storey, 1994), and with the way our sample has been drawn, strongly supports the notion that science parks tend to house firms that are younger and smaller off-park locations.

It is also quite clear in our sample that firms located on science parks report a greater image benefit than the off-park firms (see Table II).

We also have compared the firms who were located on science parks in 1995 to the off-park firms with regard to industry (IT, biotech, "other", and "multiple"), the background of the founding group ("business", "research/technical", and "other"), and type of majority product ("services" and "goods"), and found no significant, or even marginally, noteworthy differences between the location groups. This supports our assumption that the groups of NTBFs located on parks and off parks in our sample are from a common larger population.

Firm location

Firm location is a dynamic variable in this study. In our data set, we have location information at

Science Parks and the Development of NTBFs 11

Table I
Sales, employment and age in 1995, by location

		Location in 1995	
		Science park	Off-park
Sales in 1995**	Mean	4.33 MSEK	10.24 MSEK
	Median	0.24 MSEK	5.41 MSEK
	Std Dev.	4.26	11.75
	n =	29	36
Employees in 1995*	Mean	6.5	11.4
	Median	4	7
	Std Dev.	10.0	11.8
	n =	30	36
Age in 1995**	Mean	6.1	9.9
	Median	6	9
	Std Dev.	4.3	5.4
	n =	30	36

Notes: *Significant difference, $p \leq 0.1$; **Significant difference, $p \leq 0.01$.

three different times: at the start-up of the firm (which is not the same point in time for different cases); in 1995; and in 2002. Firms indicated the type of location they had "at start-up" and "currently" in the 1995 survey. We verified firms' postal code to be a reliable indicator of a science park location, as both of the parks in the study have their own unique code, and used Swedish Patent and Registration Office address information to determine location in 2002.

As shown in Figure 1, in 1995 the sample was fairly evenly divided between science park and off-park locations (30 and 36 firms, respectively). A third of the sample had started their business in a science park location, the remaining two-thirds starting off-park. Of the firms who started on science parks, nearly three-quarters remained in 1995. Fourteen of the original 22 start-ups were still in their park locations in 2002. Of the 44 firms who started off-park, two-thirds were still in off-

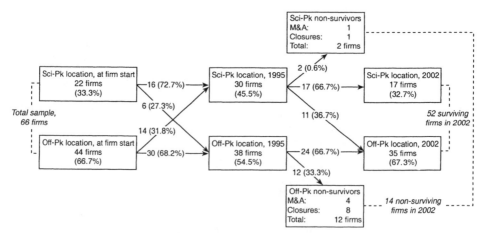

Figure 1. Firm location and relocation.

Table II
Number of firms (percent of location group) reporting image benefits, grouped
by firm location in 1995

		Location, 1995		
		Science Park	Off-park	Total
Reported image benefit	Low	7 (25.0%)	22 (62.9%)	29 (46.0%)
	High	21 (75.0%)	13 (37.1%)	34 (54.0%)
	Total	28 (100.0%)	35 (100.0%)	63 (100.0%)

Note: $x^2 = 8.97$; d.f. = 1; significant level = 0.003.

park locations in 1995, all remaining off-park through 2002.

In 2002, there were a total of 17 firms located in science parks, and 35 firms located off-park. The other 14 of the 66 studied firms had closed by the end of 2002 (reported in more detail below).

Firm survival

Businesses in Sweden are required to report all changes in legal status to the Swedish Patent and Registration Office. This includes changes between sole proprietorship, partnership and corporate business forms, as well as notice of formal inactivity, merger or acquisition, liquidation, and bankruptcy. Based on this reported information, we defined surviving firms in this study as those firms who were still in operation under their 1995 entity number. Non-surviving firms include firms that have "failed", ending in liquidation or bankruptcy, as well as those that have "succeeded", ending in merger or acquisition. We will call the non-surviving group of firms that has ended in liquidation or bankruptcy closures, and the group that has ended in merger or acquisition M&A.

Of the 66 firms in our 1995 sample, 14 were no longer registered as operating businesses, resulting in a 79% overall survival rate. Of the 30 firms located on science parks in 1995, 28 firms (93.3%) were still in operation in 2002, compared to only 24 of the 36 off-park firms (66.7%). Kaplan-Meier survival analysis shows this difference in survival to be statistically significant at the 99%-level (see Table III).

It is also noteworthy that half of the non-surviving firms from the science park group are in the M&A sub-group, compared to only a third of the non-surviving off-park firms. Though the actual

number of firms is very low, the pattern suggests that the firms on science parks are more apt to develop a commercially attractive business idea.

We can note that all five of the M&A firms are considered to be success cases in the local business communities. These firms had all successfully developed a product or services with strong market potential, which was transferred together with personnel and other production resources into another business for marketing and/or continued development. We followed up on four of the nine closures, and confirmed that they had failed to develop an economically attractive product. For example, one firm developed an expensive scientific instrument with a highly specific and limited use in basic research. While its technical merit was unchallenged, its market was insufficient in both size and ability to pay.

If we consider the non-surviving firms' starting location, we can see in Figure 1 that three of the closed firms started in a science park location (13.6%), though all three had moved off-park by 1995. Eleven of the non-surviving firms started in off-park locations (25.0%), though two had moved into science parks by 1995. With the relatively small numbers, this difference does not have high statistical significance, though it again suggests better survival for firms in science parks.

We can also note that all of the 16 firms who started in science parks and were still in science parks in 1995 survived through 2002, whereas only three of the six firms who started in science parks and moved off-park by 1995 survived. This indicates that firms tend to move from science park locations prior to ultimate closure. While this might explain some of the science park group's better survival, the fact that 12 of the 14 firms who moved into science parks after a start off-park survived, versus 21 of the 30 firms who started off-

Table III
Firm survival analysis, 1995–2002, grouped by location in 1995
(number of firms and percent of location group)

	Location, 1995*		
	Science Park	Off-park	Total
*Surviving***	28	24	52
	93.3%	66.7%	78.8%
M&A	1	4	5
	3.3%	11.1%	7.6%
Closed	1	8	9
	3.3%	22.2%	13.6%
Total	30	36	66
	100.0%	100.0%	100.0%

Notes: *Table $x^2 = 7.065$; d.f. = 2; significant level = 0.029.
**Kaplan-Meier, log rank = 6.68; d.f. = 1; significant level = 0.009.

park and were still off-park in 1995, though statistically marginal, again suggests a survival–advantage in a science park location.

Firm growth

Our data set included sales and employment data from firms' annual reports for the years 1991, 1993, 1995, 1998, and 2000 (at the time of compilation in 2002, 2000 was the last year with relatively full data). These years where chosen to balance our interest in capturing the early growth of entering firms with the time and cost involved in extracting the data from the archive. The series results in up to four periods in which we can calculate annual average growth for each firm by

dividing the change in sales during the period by the sales in the first year of the period, and then divide this by the total number of years in the period:

$$\frac{(sales_2 - sales_1)/sales_1}{\text{yrs in period}}.$$

And likewise for employment:

$$\frac{(empl_2 - empl_1/empl_1)}{\text{yrs in period}}.$$

Firms founded after 1991 naturally had missing values for some of the years, as did some firms who did not submit annual reports as required. The calculated annual sales growth rates ranged from 0.50 up to 5.72, with one exception.[1] The calculated annual growth in employment ranged from -0.50 to 3.25. Firms' growth in sales and growth in employment are highly correlated in all periods, with the cumulative averages showing a Pearson correlation of 0.702 ($p < 0.10$).

Looking at the growth rate differences in location group means shown in Table IV, we can see a marginal tendency for better growth in firms located on science parks. This holds true for all of the measured periods for both growth in employment and growth in sales, except for the 1995–1998 period, where the off-park group shows marginally better growth. This marginal difference becomes even less if we look at the median growth rates, indicating that the possible better performance in

Table IV
Range and average of annual growth in employment and sales in science park and off-park firms for measured periods

		Science park					Off-park			
		Min.	Max.	Mean	Median		Min.	Max.	Mean	Median
Employment 1991–1993	$n = 16$	-0.41	0.50	0.07	0.00	$n = 18$	-0.25	0.38	0.06	0.00
Employment 1993–1995	$n = 22$	-0.38	2.00	0.41	0.26	$n = 21$	-0.25	3.25	0.29	0.11
Employment 1995–1998	$n = 25$	-0.33	1.33	0.16	0.00	$n = 24$	-0.33	3.08	0.30	0.13
Employment 1998–2000	$n = 23$	-0.50	2.69	0.18	0.00	$n = 23$	-0.50	0.83	0.11	0.10
Sales 1991–1993	$n = 17$	-0.25	5.72	0.56	0.13	$n = 19$	-0.21	0.93	0.12	0.03
Sales 1993–1995	$n = 24$	-0.42	3.93	0.61	0.23	$n = 21$	-0.13	3.03	0.54	0.29
Sales 1995–1998	$n = 27$	-0.33	1.17	0.24	0.23	$n = 24$	-0.18	2.98	0.45	0.17
Sales 1998–2000	$n = 26$	-0.50	37.24*	1.81	0.07	$n = 24$	-0.50	0.77	0.25	0.21

Notes: *See footnote 1 for details. No mean differences are statistically significant at the 0.10-level or better (Mann–Whitney test for independent samples).

Table V
Total average annual growth rates in science park and off-park firms

		Science park	Off-park	Total
Average annual growth in employment				
	n =	27	24	51
	Mean	0.2662	0.2070	0.2384
	Std Dev.	0.5555	0.3814	0.4778
	Median	0.14	0.10	0.12
Average annual growth in sales				
	n =	27	24	51
	Mean	0.5254	0.3475	0.4417
	Std Dev.	0.6841	0.3674	0.5599
	Median	0.37	0.23	0.25

the science park group is due to a few high-performing firms. Westhead and Storey (1994) noted a similar pattern in their study population.

In all of the measured periods, the science park group showed greater variation. This can be clearly seen in the differences in standard deviation shown in Table V. Much of this variation is due to high-performing outliers among the science park firms, however the science park group also often included the weakest growers in the different measured periods. The greater range and variation in growth performance together with the greater rate of survival in the firms located on science parks suggests that these firms are in some way less dependant upon growth for their survival.

Reported location advantages and firm growth

In the 1995 survey, firms reported their perceived benefits of location on a one-to-five scale for a number of different aspects. In comparing the response of all 66 sampled firms to those of only the 52 surviving firms, we can note some differences.

First, there is a general decline in the share of firms reporting a "high" or "very high" benefit in nearly all of the categories, in both the science park and off-park groups. This indicates that the non-surviving firms generally reported greater benefits from their location.

Second, the relative difference between the location groups in the reported location benefit in cooperation with universities increases, becoming statistically significant at the $p \leq 0.1$-level. Similarly, the relative difference in the reported

unique location benefits (the general benefit variable) also increase, again with firms in science parks reporting the greater benefit.

In checking for association between the possible benefits of location and firms' growth, five of the benefits included in the survey, "recruiting", "cooperation with universities", "access to new customers", "positive image", and "unique advantages", are noteworthy.

Firms that found a high recruiting advantage in their location showed weakly significant better total average growth in sales ($p \leq 0.10$; $eta^2 = 0.063$). This relationship is even more pronounced in firms' earlier growth, though high variation in the data leads to only a marginal improvement in the test scores. This makes logical sense, as firms who can recruit the necessary new employees, especially when they are young, can then grow. At the same time, while Table VI shows that firms on science parks reported higher recruiting advantages in their location than off-park firms, the difference is not significant at even the 0.10-level.

Firms reporting benefits from their location in cooperation with universities tended to have higher average annual growth rates ($p \leq 0.10$; $eta^2 = 0.062$). This relationship was much less apparent in firms' early growth in sales ($eta^2 = 0.027; 0.10 < p$).

Growth rates do not vary significantly with firms' perception of location benefits associated with access to new customers, nor image. Neither does the general benefit variable show a significant relationship with growth.

We can see in Tables VI and VII that, of all the location benefits measured, only "cooperation

Table VI
Percent of firms reporting high or very high advantages of their location

Reported high location benefits	All 66 firms (n = 58–63)		Surviving 52 firms (n = 47–50)	
	Sci. pk (%)	Off-park (%)	Sci. pk (%)	Off-park (%)
Access to research	20.0	34.3	13.0	25.0
Recruiting benefits	55.6	42.9	52.0	33.3
Cooperation in R&D	43.5	40.0	38.1	29.2
Cooperation with university	57.7	40.0	54.2*	29.2
Access to new customers	32.1**	8.8	30.8**	4.2
Access to equipment	22.2	8.6	24.0	8.3
Image benefits	75.0***	37.1	73.1**	37.5
Unique location benefits	65.4*	42.9	66.7**	37.5

Notes: * significant location group difference, $p \leq 0.1$. ** significant location group difference, $p \leq 0.05$. *** significant location group difference, $p \leq 0.01$.

Table VII
Average annual growth in sales for different perceptions of location benefits

Location benefit		Average annual growth in sales			
		N	Mean	Std dev.	Median
*Recruiting benefits**					
	Low benefit	27	0.3287	0.4648	0.1778
	High benefit	21	0.6161	0.6627	0.4181
*Cooperation with universities**					
	Low benefit	28	0.3356	0.4286	0.1945
	High benefit	20	0.6209	0.7059	0.4180
Access to new customers					
	Low benefit	40	0.4459	0.6043	0.2391
	High benefit	9	0.5049	0.3744	0.5338
Image benefits					
	Low benefit	22	0.3195	0.4356	0.2133
	High benefit	27	0.5686	0.6401	0.3953
Advantages from location					
	Low benefit	22	0.3212	0.4146	0.1945
	High benefit	25	0.5769	0.6774	0.3658

Note: *Significant difference at the 0.10-level.

with universities" is both significantly different between the science park and off-park groups *and* shows a significant relationship with growth. In other words, firms located on science parks are more apt to report strong benefits in cooperation with universities from their location, and firms that claim such benefits tend to have better growth. While we should be cautious in assuming causality, firms located in science parks appear to benefit from greater cooperation with universities, leading to stronger growth, than off-park counterparts.

4. Conclusions

Our results show that the firms located on science parks in our study had a better rate of survival than the off-park firms between 1995 and 2002. At the same time, growth in employment and sales during 1991–2000 was not significantly different in the firms on and off of the parks. This is particularly noteworthy considering that the firms on science parks tended to be smaller and younger: Recent research on growth in NTBFs shows that smaller, younger firms tend to have higher growth rates, reflecting their need to increase in size to offset their liability of newness (Almus and Nerlinger, 1999; Audretsch, 1995; Geroski, 1995). If the smaller, younger firms in science parks are surviving better than their larger, older off-park counter parts without showing significantly better growth, we need to turn to other factors to find a possible explanation.

Before discussing explanations of the pattern described above, we should recall that the group of firms in science parks had greater variation in their growth rates than the off-park firms, reflecting that parks host both high growth firms and firms that are showing weak growth: There are both more high-growth outliers, as well as more weak-growth firms. This suggests that the firms located in science parks are in a wide range of development phases and are apt to have different needs. At the same time, the higher survival rate of the firms on science parks suggests that the range of needs is being met.

Of the location benefits firms report receiving, the greater benefits in cooperation with universities reported by firms in science parks may be supporting the firms in ways that offset the need for early growth, and at the same time bed the way for subsequent high growth. To test this, we need to investigate more closely how firms are cooperating with universities, and what the fruits of the cooperation are.

The firms located on science parks also reported a higher image benefit. Though we hypothesized that such a benefit would help firms overcome the liability of newness, and thereby improve the chances of survival, we found no clear relationship between perceived image benefits and survival and/or growth. This suggests that an image benefit needs to be accompanied by other factors if it is to be realized by the firm, and that it is not a guarantee to overcoming a liability of newness in and of itself.

Our findings in this study confirm some of the prevailing understanding of firms located on science parks with a sampling method that offers high reliability: Firms located on science parks tend to be younger and smaller than off-park counter parts, and science park locations are more often perceived to offer an image benefit to firms. Our finding also show that the firms on science parks have a greater rate of survival, despite a

greater range—though not significantly higher on average—of growth in sales and employment. This indicates the need for further study to increase our understanding of firm survival independent of growth. The studied firms show that small young firms do not necessarily need to grow more rapidly to overcome the liability of newness.

Acknowledgments

The authors would like to thank the two anonymous reviewers, editor Donald Siegel and Mike Wright for their helpful comments on earlier versions of this paper.

Notes

1. One firm reported exceptional sales in 2000, resulting in a 3,724% average annual growth rate for the 1998–2000 period. This was preceded by three periods of negative growth. Further investigation showed that this very high rate was attained after business restructuring, when another business gained ownership in the firm. After this restructuring, the firm began marketing the new owner's product. Though the sales in 2000 appear to be related to the firm's earlier activities, the unusual pattern reflects extenuating circumstances that cannot be said to represent normal NTBF development.

References

Almus, M. and E. Nerlinger, 1999, 'Growth of New Technology-Based Firms: Which Factors Matter?,' *Small Business Economics* 13, 141–154.

Audretsch, D.B., 1995, 'Innovation, Growth and Survival,' *International Journal of Industrial Organization* 13, 441–457.

Audretsch, D.B., L. Klomp, and A. Thurik, 2002, 'Gibrat's Law: Are the Services Different?,' Working paper, Rotterdam: Erasmus University Rotterdam.

Autio, E., 1994, 'New, Technology-Based Companies as Agents of R&D and Innovation,' *Technovation* 14 (4), 259–273

Bengtsson, L. and M. Löwegren, 2001, 'Internationalisation in Science Parks—The Case of Finland and Sweden,'. Paper presented at the *2001 Swedish Network for European Studies in Economics and Business Conference* in Mölle, Sweden, May 14–16.

Davidsson, P., 1989, *Continued Entrepreneurship and Small Firm Growth*, Dissertation, Stockholm: Stockholm School of Economics.

Davidsson, P., B. Kirchhoff, A. Hatemi-J, and H. Gustavsson, 2002, 'Empirical Analysis of Business Growth Factors using Swedish data,' *Journal of Small Business Management* 40 (4), 332–349.

Davidsson, P., C. Olofsson, and L. Lindmark, 1996, *Närings-slivsdynamik under 90-talet (Business Dynamics in the 90s)*, Stockholm: NUTEK.

DiMaggio, P. and W. Powell, 1991, 'Introduction', in W. Powell, and P. DiMaggio (eds.), *The New Institutionalism in Organizational Analysis*, Chicago: The University of Chicago Press.

Drew, R., P. Dew, C. Leigh, D. Morris, and J. Curson, 1996, 'The Virtual Science Park,' *British Telecommunications Engineering* 15 (4), 322:329.

Evans, D.S., 1987, 'The Relationship Between Firm Growth, Size, and Age: Estimates for 100 Manufacturing Industries,' *Journal of Industrial Economics* 35 (4), 567–581.

Felsenstein, D., 1994, 'University-Related Science Parks—'Seedbeds' or 'Enclaves' of Innovation?,' *Technovation* 14 (2), 93–110.

Ferguson, R., 1999, *What's in a Location? Science Parks and the Support of New Technology-Based Firms*, Agraria 137 (dissertation), Uppsala: Swedish University of Agricultural Sciences.

Ferguson, R. and C. Olofsson, 1998, *Science Parks and the Location of NTBFs—A Survey*, working paper, Uppsala: CEF.

Geroski, P.A., 1995, 'What Do We Know About Entry?' *International Journal of Industrial Organization* 13, 421–440.

Grayson, L., 1993, *Science Parks: An Experiment in High Technology Transfer*, London: The British Library.

Klofsten, M., 1994, 'Technology-Based Firms: Critical Aspects of their Early Development,' *Journal of Enterprising Culture* 2 (1), 535–557.

Klofsten, M., P. Lindell, C. Olofsson, and C. Wahlbin, 1988, 'Internal and External Resources in Technology-Based Spin-Offs: A Survey,' in B. Kirchhoff, W. Long, E. McMullan, K. Vesper, and W. Wetzel (eds.), *Frontiers of Entrepreneurship Research*, Wellesley: Babson College.

Lindholm Dahlstrand, Å., 1999, 'British and Swedish Science Parks and Incubators for Small Technology-Based Firms,' in During, W., R. Oakey, and S.-M. Mukhtar, (eds.), *New Technology-Based Firms in the 1990s*, Volume VI, Elsevier Science.

Lindström, G. and C. Olofsson, 2002, *Affärsänglar och teknik-baserade tillväxtfoöretag* (Business angels and technology-based growth firms), Stockholm: SNS förlag.

Little, A., 1977, *New Technology-Based Firms in the United Kingdom and the Federal Republic of Germany*, London: Wilton House.

Löfsten, H. and P. Lindelöf, 2001, 'Science Parks in Sweden—Industrial Renewal and Development?,' *R&D Management* 31 (3), 309–322.

Löwegren, M., 2003, *New Technology-Based Firms in Science Parks: A Study of Resources and Absorptive Capacity*, Lund Studies in Economics and Management 76 (dissertation), Lund: Lund Business Press.

Monck, C., P. Quintas, P. Porter, D. Storey, and P. Wynarczyk, 1988, *Science Parks and the Growth of High Technology Firms*, London: Croom Helm.

Oakey, R., R. Rothwell, and S. Cooper, 1988, *The Management of Innovation in High-Technology Small Firms: Innovation and Regional Development in Britain and the United States*, London: Printer Pub.

Olofsson, C. and C. Wahlbin, 1993, 'Firms Started by University Researchers in Sweden—Roots, Roles, Relations, and Growth Patterns,' Paper presented at the *1993 Babson Entrepreneurship Research Conference*, Houston, TX, March 25–27.

Quintas, P., D. Wield, and D. Massey, 1992, 'Academic-Industry Links and Innovation: Questioning the Science Park Model,' *Technovation* 12 (3), 161–175.

Rickne, A., 2000, *New Technology-Based Firms and Industrial Dynamics: Evidence from the Technological System of Biomaterials in Sweden, Ohio and Massachusetts* (dissertation), Gothenberg: Department of Industrial Dynamics, Chalmers University of Technology

Singh, J., D. Tucker, and R. House, 1986, 'Organizational Legitimacy and the Liability of Newness,' *Administrative Science Quarterly* 3 (1), 171–193.

Stinchcomb, A., 1965, 'Social Structure and Organizations,' in J. March (ed.), *Handbook of Organizations*, Chicago: Rand McNally.

Storey, D., 1994, *Understanding the Small Business Sector*, London: Internaitonal Thompson Business Press.

Storey, D. and B. Tether, 1998, 'New Technology-Based Firms in the European Union: An Introduction,' *Research Policy* 26, 933–946.

Westhead, P. and S. Batstone, 1999, 'Perceived Benefits of a Managed Science Park Location,' *Entrepreneurship and Regional Development* 11 (2), 129–155.

Westhead, P. and S. Batstone, 1998, 'Independent Technology-Based Firms: The Perceived Benefits of a Science Park Location,' *Urban Studies* 35 (12), 2197–2219.

Westhead, P. and D. Storey, 1994, *An Assessment of Firms Located on and off Science Parks in the United Kingdom*, London: HMSO.

[18]

Available online at www.sciencedirect.com

SCIENCE ⓓ DIRECT®

Research Policy 34 (2005) 305–320

ELSEVIER

research
policy

www.elsevier.com/locate/econbase

University–incubator firm knowledge flows: assessing their impact on incubator firm performance

Frank T. Rothaermel[a] *, Marie Thursby[b]

[a] College of Management, Georgia Institute of Technology, Atlanta, GA 30308-0520, USA
[b] Georgia Institute of Technology and NBER, USA

Received 20 June 2004; received in revised form 25 October 2004; accepted 29 November 2004
Available online 17 March 2005

Abstract

Technology incubators are university-based technology initiatives that should facilitate knowledge flows from the university to the incubator firms. We thus investigate the research question of how knowledge actually flows from universities to incubator firms. Moreover, we assess the effect of these knowledge flows on incubator firm-level differential performance. Based on the resource-based view of the firm and the absorptive capacity construct, we advance the overarching hypothesis that knowledge flows should enhance incubator firm performance. Drawing on longitudinal and fine-grained firm-level data of 79 technology ventures incubated between 1998 and 2003 at the Advanced Technology Development Center, a technology incubator sponsored by the Georgia Institute of Technology, we find some support for knowledge flows from universities to incubator firms. Our evidence suggests that incubator firms' absorptive capacity is an important factor when transforming university knowledge into firm-level competitive advantage.
© 2005 Elsevier B.V. All rights reserved.

Keywords: Knowledge flows; Localized spillovers; Resource-based view of the firm; Absorptive capacity; Incubator firm performance

1. Introduction

How do technology ventures access university knowledge and how does it affect their performance? Knowledge produced in universities has been studied extensively, as has its impact on industry. Yet, we know

* Corresponding author. Tel.: +1 404 385 5108;
fax: +1 404 894 6030.
E-mail address: frank.rothaermel@mgt.gatech.edu
(F.T. Rothaermel[a]).

little about knowledge flows at the firm level, either in terms of the flows themselves or effects thereof. In part, this is because of the inherent difficulty tracking knowledge created for the public domain, but in part, it is because the firm has not been a common unit of analysis. Moreover, there is mounting empirical evidence that local knowledge spillovers produced by university research are not "free," but depend on contractual agreements. Thursby and Thursby (2002) and Zucker and Darby (1996, 1998) document this. Moreover, Cockburn and Henderson (1998) demon-

0048-7333/$ – see front matter © 2005 Elsevier B.V. All rights reserved.
doi:10.1016/j.respol.2004.11.006

306   *F.T. Rothaermel, M. Thursby / Research Policy 34 (2005) 305–320*

strate that firms must exhibit substantial absorptive capacity to capture and appropriate rents to publicly available knowledge. Cohen and Levinthal (1989) advance the notion of absorptive capacity, which is understood as a firm's ability to recognize, value, and assimilate new external information.

Herein, we attempt to address the two-pronged research question of (1) how knowledge flows from universities to incubator firms and (2) how these flows affect the performance of new technology ventures. As part of the first question, we identify and analyze the effects of different mechanisms through which knowledge flows from universities to incubator firms: university license, and patent backward citations to university research, academic journals, research by the incubator-sponsoring university, and research from other universities than the sponsoring university. Embedded in the second research question is the search for an appropriate performance metric for nascent technology ventures, a significant methodological challenge, which has clearly retarded empirical research in this important area as emphasized by Phan et al. (2004).

Given the dearth on empirical research investigating university knowledge flows and their effect on incubator firm performance, we develop two explorative hypotheses that we subsequently examine econometrically. Firstly, we argue that exclusive knowledge flows in terms of a university license can endow the start-up with a unique resource. Important theoretical work in the strategic management literature has argued that valuable, rare, inimitable, and non-substitutable resources may endow a firm with a competitive advantage that translate to superior performance (Barney, 1991). Secondly, we suggest that university backward patent citations are indicative of a start-up's absorptive capacity that enables it to recognize public knowledge flows emanating from a university, assimilate them internally, and then to apply them to commercial ends (Cohen and Levinthal, 1989). This in turn should lead to a variance in performance among technology ventures with a venture's absorptive capacity being positively correlated with venture performance.

We test these two tentative hypotheses on a sample of 79 incubator firms incubated in the Advanced Technology Development Center (ATDC) at the Georgia Institute of Technology (Georgia Tech (GT)). We follow these firms over the 6-year time span between 1998 and 2003. The use of an annual repeat survey enables us not only to collect fine grained data for nascent technology ventures, but also aids us in overcoming a survivor bias common to research on new technology ventures. Moreover, we attempt to enhance the robustness of the analysis by applying four different performance measures: total revenues, total funds obtained, venture capital (VC) funding obtained, and failure or graduation from the incubator. Applying different outcome variables might aid in identifying an appropriate outcome measure in the new venture context, in particular, when attempting to capture the performance implications of university knowledge flows.

This paper has the following outline. Section 2 reviews prior research on university–industry knowledge flows, and Section 3 develops the hypotheses regarding university licenses, patent citations, and new venture performance. Section 4 discusses the methodology applied, Section 5 presents the empirical results, while Section 6 concludes this paper with a discussion of the results, limitations as well as implications for future research and public policy.

2. University–industry knowledge-flows—prior research

Early work on the industrial impact of academic research includes Adams (1990), who showed that academic knowledge, as measured by publications, was a major contributor to productivity growth for 18 of 20 two-digit U.S. manufacturing industries from 1943 to 1983, albeit with a substantial lag times which varied from 0–10 years for applied sciences and engineering to 20 years for basic science publications. Jaffe (1989) classic study of the real effects of academic research showed that university research had significant effects on the generation of industrial patents at the state level.

With the exception of the work by Zucker and Darby (1996, 1998) and Zucker et al. (2002), which we discuss below, the focus of research in this area is not overall firm performance but the effect of university research on industry R&D output. Even when data were collected by firm, the questions of interest have been variations in the relevance of university research by industry and academic field. For example, both the 1983 Yale Survey and the 1994 Carnegie Mellon Survey of R&D managers asked the relevance of university research

F.T. Rothaermel, M. Thursby / Research Policy 34 (2005) 305–320 307

for technical progress in their industry (Klevorick et al., 1994; Cohen et al., 1998). Mansfield's survey of R&D executives of 66 firms examined the perceived impact of university research on the firm's ability to develop new processes and products in a timely fashion (Mansfield, 1995). Not surprisingly, all of this work finds the most pervasive effects of university research are in the drug, chemical, and electronics industries.

This prior research demonstrates that knowledge flows from universities tend to be mitigated by geographic distance, which of course suggests that academic publications alone cannot be the sole means by which firms gain access to university knowledge. Researchers have used a variety of methods to examine the channels by which university knowledge is transferred to industry, including interviews and survey research, citations to academic publications and patents, collaboration patterns in academic publications and patents, as well as information on formal contracts such as licenses or sponsored research. The most comprehensive survey in this regard is the Carnegie Mellon Survey of 1478 R&D laboratories which asked R&D managers the importance to them of 10 channels of knowledge flow (patent, publications, meetings or conferences, informal channels, hires, licenses, joint ventures, contract research, consulting, and personal exchange). Of these publications, public meetings and conferences, informal and personal information channels, and consulting contracts appear to be the four most important channels, suggesting a complementarity between publication and other mechanisms involving personal contact (Cohen et al., 1998). The results on consulting support the results from Mansfield (1995) that show a complementarity between consulting and the research agendas of university scientists working with industry.

The use of citation data, either to academic publications or patents, in economics has a rich tradition, not only for examining knowledge flows from universities, but also R&D spillovers in general (Griliches, 1992). With regard to flows from universities, a series of important studies examine a variety of measures of citations to university patents in order to examine issues of localization as well as the importance of university patents (Jaffe et al., 1993; Trajtenberg et al., 1997; Henderson et al., 1998). Branstetter (2004) examines patent citations to academic publications and shows an increasing trend for industrial patents to cite academic science. This work complements that of Agrawal and

Henderson (2002) and Murray and Stern (2004) which examines the interaction of academic and industry collaboration and citation patterns. Here, one underlying assumption is that knowledge spillovers tend to be localized, and that being located close to the knowledge source enhances the efficiency and effectiveness of the knowledge transfer. When studying the performance of U.S. university research parks, for example, Link and Scott (2004) found that parks located closer geographically to a research university grew significantly faster.

While much of this literature focuses on knowledge flows as spillovers, some authors have focused on market transactions involving university industry collaboration. Prominent in this stream is the work of Zucker and Darby (1996, 1998) who examine the role of star university scientists in the formation and performance of new firms in biotechnology. Their work points to the importance of star scientist collaboration in the transfer of information to nascent firms. Similarly, Thursby and Thursby (2004) also examine collaboration between scientists and firms but their sample is comprised of firms that license university technologies and their focus is on contractual mechanism of transfer.

3. Knowledge flows and incubator firm performance

In this paper, we build on the ideas from this literature and hypothesize that both contractual and noncontractual mechanisms are important for understanding university–firm knowledge flows and the effects on incubator firm performance.

3.1. University licenses and incubator firm performance

Since the early 1990s, licensing activity in U.S. research universities has increased considerably. Analyzing the growth of university licensing, Thursby and Thursby (2002) draw on data from a survey by the Association of University Technology Managers (AUTM) and state that in 1998 alone, the 132 research universities responding to the survey reported more than 9500 disclosures, more than 4100 new patent applications, and more than 3000 licenses and options executed.

308   *F.T. Rothaermel, M. Thursby / Research Policy 34 (2005) 305–320*

The university licensing process starts with a faculty member disclosing a discovery to the university's office of technology transfer. Some universities, like Georgia Tech, do not wait for faculty to take the first step of disclosing an invention but rather proactively monitor university faculty research and encourage faculty to disclosure inventions. Once a discovery is disclosed, the office of technology transfer evaluates the commercial potential of this invention. If there is some commercial potential and expected licensees are anticipated, the office of technology licensing applies for a patent. Note that not all technology licenses go along with patent protection because many inventions are protected by copyright, for example, software. Yet, university technology licenses are generally exclusive. As a case in point, all of the licenses granted by Georgia Tech to the incubator firms in this study are exclusive.

We suggest that exclusive licenses endow the incubator firm with a unique resource. In a seminal article that laid the theoretical foundation for the resource-based view of the firm, an important framework in strategic management research, Barney (1991, pp. 105–106) posited that for firm resource to have the potential to be the basis of a competitive advantage, "(a) it must be valuable, in the sense that it exploits opportunities and/or neutralizes threats in a firm's environment, (b) it must be rare among a firm's current and potential competitors, (c) it must be imperfectly imitable, and (d) there cannot be strategically equivalent substitutes for this resource that are valuable but are neither rare or imperfectly imitable." Competitive advantage is defined as "a value creating strategy not simultaneously being implemented by any current or potential competitors" (Barney, 1991, p. 102).

We thus posit that a technology license fulfills the attributes discussed by Barney as it is valuable because it allows the firms to exploit a technological opportunity; it is rare because the license is exclusive and contains novel technology; it is generally imperfectly imitable, often protected by legal barriers like patents or copyrights; and there are generally no readily available substitutes. Thus, holding a technology license should aid an incubator firm in achieving superior performance because it can implement a strategy based on this unique resource that its existing or potential competitors cannot readily imitate.

3.2. Patent citations, absorptive capacity, and incubator firm performance

Backward patent citations are references made to prior art in a patent application. Patent backward citations are bibliometric fossils that identify the ideas on which an incubator firm draws when applying for a patent. Being able to draw on past research, albeit public in nature, demonstrates that the incubator firm is endowed with some degree of absorptive capacity which enables it to recognize, assimilate, and exploit external knowledge. Here, it is important to note that university knowledge, albeit publicly available, is far from costless. Firms must build internal capabilities to evaluate external research and apply it to commercial ends (Cohen and Levinthal, 1990). This is often done through hiring intellectual human capital in the form of star scientists (Zucker and Darby, 1996, 1998), through participation in the broader scientific community through journal publications (Henderson and Cockburn, 1994; Cockburn and Henderson, 1998), and/or through strategic alliances with providers of the new technology (Rothaermel, 2001). A firm's absorptive capacity has been shown to enhance a firm's innovative capability (Cohen and Levinthal, 1989), which in turn improves firm performance especially in highly dynamic industries (Rothaermel and Hill, 2005).

We thus suggest that backward patent citations to university research are indicative of an incubator firm's absorptive capacity to recognize, assimilate, and apply university knowledge flows to commercial ends. This is because many capabilities like absorptive capacity cannot be observed directly. Godfrey and Hill (1995) argued that unobservable constructs lie at the core of a number of influential theories in strategic management research. Given this serious challenge impeding empirical research, they suggested that "what scholars need to do is to theoretically identify what the observable consequences of unobservable resources [capabilities] are likely to be, and then go out and see whether such predictions have a correspondence in the empirical world. The analogy here is with quantum mechanics, which has been confirmed *not* by observing subatomic entities (since they are unobservable) but by observing the trail left by subatomic entities in the cloud chambers of linear accelerators" (Godfrey and Hill, 1995, p. 530, italics in original).

F.T. Rothaermel, M. Thursby / Research Policy 34 (2005) 305–320 309

We suggest that a firm's absorptive capacity, while an important construct, is not directly observable. Thus, we resort to proxying for absorptive capacity by patent backward citations, which can be understood as indicating the existence of firm-level absorptive capacity deep within the firm. Moreover, absorptive capacity is a firm-level capability that is expected to be heterogeneously distributed among firms and thus should lead to variance in performance. In summary, we suggest that backward patent citations to university research should positively enhance incubator firm performance.

4. Methodology

4.1. Research setting—Georgia Tech's Advanced Technology Development Center

The research setting of this study is the Advanced Technology Development Center, a technology incubator sponsored by the Georgia Institute of Technology. The incubator is located adjacent to the Georgia Tech main campus in midtown Atlanta as part of a US$ 250 million state-of-the-art building complex that houses Georgia Tech's Business School and Economic Development Institute, among others. Besides being sponsored by Georgia Tech, the ATDC also receives legislative and financial appropriations from Georgia's Governor and the General Assembly of the state.

The ATDC was founded in 1980 as one of the first technology incubators in the U.S., and has since generated a cumulative of 4100 jobs and US$ 352 million in total revenues as of December 31, 1998. During our study period, the ATDC member firms had a total of US$ 12 million in annual revenues in 1998, US$ 19 million in 1999, and US$ 18 million in 2000. In the late 1990s, Georgia Tech's ATDC was voted as one of the top incubators in the U.S. based on a survey of peer incubators conducted by *Inc.* magazine (Rosenwein, 2000). The ATDC focuses on incubating early stage companies (0–3 years), with the company's founding date generally coinciding with the firm's admission to membership into the incubator.

The ATDC managers actively solicit applications from new ventures, and admitted, during our study period, between 10 and 20% of their applicants after a fairly stringent, two-staged review process. It is not necessary that the technology underlying the new ven-

ture is related to Georgia Tech; yet, it must be proprietary in nature. During the last few years, the size of the full-time professional staff of the ATDC remained, despite turnover, fairly constant at 22 managers. These managers assist the commercialization efforts of the ATDC member firms.

4.2. Sample and data

The sample consists of the population of member firms in the ATDC for the years 1998–2000. A total of 79 firms were tenants of the ATDC during this 3-year time frame. The year 1998 marks the first year detailed data were collected for the firms in the incubator. We drew our sample based on the years 1998–2000 to be able to follow each firm for a minimum of 4 years to assess the performance of the incubator firms. Employing multiple performance measures, we assessed the performance of the newly formed ventures over or at the time period $t + 1$, where $t \leq 3$ years. This time window appears to be a conservative one given the fact that incubator tenants tend to graduate from public incubators within 2 years and from private incubators within 1 year (Rosenwein, 2000). While the ATDC has no explicit graduation policy, it attempts to graduate their members in a timely fashion. In the year $t + 1$, the technology venture could fall into one of three categories: (1) failure, i.e., the firm ceased to exist due to bankruptcy or liquidation; (2) firm remains in the incubator; and (3) successful graduation, i.e., the firm is a stand-alone going concern or was acquired. We included acquisitions as part of successful graduation based on qualitative assessments made by ATDC managers.

Data for the 79 firms were collected annually for the 6-year time period between 1998 and 2003 through a survey instrument that was administered to all firms in the sample in the spring of every year to collect data for the prior year. Accordingly, data collection began in the spring of 1999 and ended in the spring of 2004. This longitudinal, repeat survey approach allowed us to obtain multiple, ubiquitous performance outcomes for all 79 firms in the initial sample. Thus, our results are not prone to a survivor bias, frequently observed in studies focusing on new venture creation and their early performance.

For the subset of firms based on Georgia Tech technologies, the Georgia Institute of Technology's Office of Technology Licensing provided us with data on relevant patents and founding dates. We augmented the collection of the quantitative data through semi-structured interviews with managers of the ATDC, the Institute's Vice Provost for Economic Development and Technology Ventures, the Institute's Director of the Technology Licensing Office, and the Institute's Director of its VentureLab, a center founded to identify commercializable technologies within the Institute.

A third source of data was the patent database maintained by the U.S. Patent and Trademark Office, an agency of the U.S. Department of Commerce. Here, we accessed all patents awarded to the incubator firms in this sample.

4.3. Measures

4.3.1. Incubator firm performance

Incubator firm performance is the dependent variable of this study. Clearly, assessing the performance of entrepreneurial start-ups, and incubator firms in particular, is a thorny problem retarding empirical research in this important area (Phan et al., 2004). Based on the annual repeat survey instrument underlying the data collection for this study, we are fortunate to assess the performance of incubator firms on multiple dimensions including revenues, total funds raised, venture capital funding obtained, and whether the firm graduated, failed, or remained in the incubator. Assessing the performance of incubator firms along several performance dimensions is particularly salient in this context because the most appropriate performance metrics for nascent technology ventures are less than clear.

4.3.1.1. Revenues. One of the performance metrics we employed is total cumulative revenues obtained by the incubator firms. To enhance the validity of this measure, we did assess it as cumulative revenues accrued over the time period including $t + 1$ to avoid dependence on single observations often characterized by high annual fluctuations. While revenues are an accepted performance metric for more mature firms, it is less clear if this measure is suitable for the incubator context. We attempt to shed some more light on this issue. We applied a logarithmic transformation to enhance the normality of this variable.

4.3.1.2. Total funds raised. A second performance metric used is the total amount of cumulative funding the new ventures obtained over the time period including $t + 1$. We constructed the *total funds raised* variable by leveraging fine-grained data pertaining to the different financing sources: family and friends, angel investors, venture capitalists, private placements, equity investments, and grants.

4.3.1.3. VC funding. One important milestone in the development of a nascent technology venture is obtaining venture capital funding (Shane and Cable, 2002; Shane and Stuart, 2002). Funding obtained from venture capitalists takes on an important signaling role as it often bestows legitimacy upon the new venture (Stuart et al., 1999). Moreover, some universities, albeit not the focal institution of this study, make obtaining a university license contingent upon having received venture capital. We assessed whether the incubator firms in this sample have obtained venture capital during the time period including $t + 1$ by a bivariate indicator variable taking on the value of 1 if the incubator firm received venture capital funding, and 0 otherwise.

4.3.1.4. Failure, graduation, and remain in incubator. As discussed in detail in Rothaermel and Thursby (2005), one of the important milestones in the development of incubator firms is the timely graduation from the incubator. On an average, private incubators expect their tenants to graduate within 1 year, while public incubators expect their tenants to graduate within 2 years (Rosenwein, 2000). To be conservative, we assessed the state of incubator firms in $t + 1$, where $t \leq 3$ years. In the year $t + 1$, an incubator venture could fall into one of three categories: (1) failure, i.e., the firm ceased to exist due to bankruptcy or liquidation; (2) firm remains in the incubator; and (3) successful graduation, i.e., the firm is a stand-alone going concern or was acquired. We subsumed acquisitions under successful graduation because the few cases in which incubator firms were acquired in this sample (three firms or 4%) reflect successes rather than failures based on the evaluations by ATDC managers. We coded the performance of the new technology ventures in $t + 1$ as a multinomial variable with three categories: failure, graduation, and remaining in incubator. Remaining in the incubator serves as reference category.

4.3.2. Knowledge flows from university to incubator firms

The key independent construct of this study concerns knowledge flows from the university to the incubator venture. Here, we hypothesized that exclusive knowledge flows in terms of a university license can endow the start-up with a unique resource that should lead to a superior performance (Barney, 1991). Moreover, we suggested that university backward patent citations are indicative of a start-up's absorptive capacity that enables it to recognize public knowledge spillovers emanating from the university, assimilate them internally, and then to apply them to commercial ends (Cohen and Levinthal, 1989). To obtain a comprehensive and fine-grained assessment of knowledge flows from the university to incubator firms, we employed five distinct variables proxying for different mechanisms through which knowledge may flow from the university to an incubator firm. In particular, we proxied for knowledge flows from the sponsoring university as well as more general university knowledge flows emanating from the broader university community.

4.3.2.1. GT license.
One mechanism through which knowledge can flow from a university to an incubator firm is through a licensing agreement. Here, we assessed potential knowledge flows from the sponsoring university, Georgia Tech, to the incubator firms by including a variable that tracks whether the firm in the sample was founded to commercialize a technology invented at Georgia Tech and subsequently licensed it from the Institute's Office of Technology Licensing ($1 = GT$ *license*). These licenses are exclusive in the sense that they are only given to one firm.

4.3.2.2. Backward citations to university research.
A second area where knowledge flows from universities to incubator firms should manifest themselves is in the incubator firm's patent citations because all prior art must be credited in the patent application. Patents reflect inventions because they are only granted to processes or products that are novel, non-obvious, and industrially useful as judged by someone possessing proficient knowledge in the relevant technical area (Acs and Audretsch, 1989).

Here, assessing knowledge flows from a university to an incubator firm can be accomplished by analyzing the backward citations to university research in a technology venture's patent portfolio. To do this, we secured copies of all patents that the start-ups in the sample had obtained. We then counted all backward citations to university research in an incubator firm's patent portfolio. University research is defined as either citations to patents granted to universities or citations to academic journals publishing research results. In the final step, we took the ratio of an incubator firm's patent backward citations to university research over its total number of patent backward citations to assess the magnitude to which the new venture is drawing on university research in their own inventions. This measure can be considered as a proxy for knowledge flows from universities to incubator start-ups.

4.3.2.3. Backward citations to academic journals.
We suggest that research findings published in academic journals tend to be more embryonic and basic in nature than research that is explicated in university patents, which tend to be more developed and explicit. In general, university faculty tend to first publish research results in academic outlets prior to the university applying for a patent. For example, in 1973, Stanley Cohen (then a professor at Stanford) and Herbert Boyer (then a professor at the University of California, San Francisco) first published their scientific breakthrough in recombinant DNA in the *Proceedings of the National Academy of Sciences of the United States of America* (Cohen et al., 1973). The patent on recombinant DNA, however, was granted 7 years later in 1980, and assigned to Stanford University with Cohen and Boyer listed as inventors (U.S. Patent 4,237,224). Therefore, to assess the potential flow of early stage, basic knowledge to incubator firms, we included a ratio of an incubator firm's patent backward citations to academic journals over its total number of patent backward citations.

4.3.2.4. Backward citations to GT research.
Besides highlighting a technology license of the sponsoring university as one possible mechanism through which knowledge from the sponsoring university can flow to an incubator firm, we also assessed the impact of knowledge flows from the sponsoring university by including a ratio of the firm's patent backward citations to Georgia Tech research over its total number of patent backward citations. This measure indicates how much the incubator firm draws on localized knowledge. Georgia Tech research is defined as either citations to patents

312   *F.T. Rothaermel, M. Thursby / Research Policy 34 (2005) 305–320*

granted to Georgia Tech or citations to research published by Georgia Tech faculty members.

4.3.2.5. Backward citations to non-GT research. Besides focusing on knowledge flows from the sponsoring university, we also consider the impact of knowledge flows from research universities that are not directly linked to the focal incubator under consideration. Here, we assess the impact of the ratio of firm's patent backward citations to non-GT research over its total number of patent backward citations. Non-GT research is defined as either citations to patents granted to any university other than GT or citations to research published by any person that is not a GT faculty member. Please note that the sum of *backward citations to GT research* and *backward citations to non-GT research* equates to *Backward Citations to University Research,* the first backward citation measure introduced above.

4.3.3. Control variables

We included a number of control variables that theoretically could impact new venture performance.

4.3.3.1. Firm size. When assessing the performance of incubator firms, it is critical to control for their firm size. Because the important assets of incubator firms tend to be intangible in nature, it is more appropriate to use the number of employees as a proxy for firm size (*employees*) as done in prior research focusing on high-technology ventures (Rothaermel, 2002; Rothaermel and Deeds, 2004).

We controlled for firm size effects through the number of employees up to the year prior to which the outcome variable was assessed. Moreover, because newly created ventures tend to be quite small, we collected data not only on the number of full-time employees, but also on the number of part-time employees. Each full-time employee was counted as one employee, while one part-time employee was counted as one-half of a full-time employee.

4.3.3.2. Industry effects. When assessing new venture performance, it is pertinent to control for industry effects. We tracked each incubator firm's industry based on their Standard Industry Classification (SIC) codes. About 60% of the firms were active either in the software industry or the in telecommunications industry. To control for these two most prevalent industries, we inserted two indicator variables in the regression models. The first indicator variable takes on 1 if the incubator firm is a *software* company, and 0 otherwise. The second indicator variable takes on 1 if the incubator firm is a *telecom* company, and 0 otherwise.

4.3.3.3. Time in incubator. While the sample is not prone to a survivor bias, we are faced with the problem of left censoring because the ATDC technology incubator was in existence prior to 1998, the first year of our annual data collections. To ameliorate this problem, we recorded the year that each firm was admitted into the incubator, which generally coincides with the firm's founding date, and the last year the firm remained in the incubator. These two data points enabled us to construct the *time in incubator* variable, which is the number of years the firm remained in the technology incubator, to account for left censoring.

4.3.3.4. Non-GT university link. When assessing the effect of university knowledge flows on incubator firm performance, it is prudent to control for university linkages that the ATDC ventures may have to other, non-sponsoring universities. In fact, the sample firms listed linkages to 11 other U.S. research universities besides Georgia Tech. To isolate the effect of different knowledge flow mechanisms on the performance of ATDC ventures, we created an indicator variable that takes on the value of 1 if the firm had a link to a university other than Georgia Tech. Some ATDC firms in the sample, for instance, maintained a link to a university other than Georgia Tech but did not have a link to Georgia Tech.

4.3.4. Estimation procedures

When assessing the performance of incubator firms, we focus on four different outcome variables: revenues, total funds raised, venture capital obtained, and graduation, failure, or remaining in the incubator. These different dependent variables indicate different estimation procedures. The regression models with revenues and total funds obtained as dependent variables were estimated using ordinary least squares (OLS).

Venture capital obtained is a binary variable taking on 1 if the incubator firm received venture capital, and 0 otherwise. This model indicates logit regression. The outcome variable, $\hat{Y}$, is the probability of the venture receiving or not receiving venture capital based

F.T. Rothaermel, M. Thursby / Research Policy 34 (2005) 305–320   313

on a non-linear function with two outcomes. The logit model is estimated with a maximum likelihood procedure and has the following specification:

$$\ln\left(\frac{\widehat{Y}}{1-\widehat{Y}}\right) = \alpha + \sum \beta_j X_{ij},$$

where X_{ij} is a vector of independent variables.

The last performance variable employed in this study can take on three categories: failure, remaining in incubator, and successful graduation. This indicated application of a multinomial logistic regression, estimated with a maximum likelihood procedure. The outcome variable, P_j, is the probability of falling into one of the outcome categories based on a non-linear function with three outcomes (Maddala, 1983):

$$P_j = \frac{e^{\beta_j x}}{D} \quad (j = 1, 2, \ldots, m-1)$$

and

$$P_m = \frac{1}{D}$$

where

$$D = 1 + \sum_{k=1}^{m-1} e^{\beta_j x}.$$

5. Results

We assessed the effect of university–incubator firm knowledge flows on 79 firms incubated in the Georgia Tech's ATDC over the 6-year time period between 1998 and 2003. We employed multiple performance measures to reflect the multi-dimensional nature of incubator firm performance. In particular, we assessed the performance of the newly formed ventures over or at the time period $t + 1$, where $t \leq 3$ years. Relying on a repeat sample method, we were able to obtain ubiquitous outcome variables on all 79 firms, thus overcoming a potential survivor bias.

We tracked incubator firm performance on four different dimensions. In total, the 79 incubator firms raised over US$ 404 million in funding, with a US$ 193 million (48%) thereof being VC funding. The average incubator firm had revenues of US$ 1.6 million and had raised a total of US$ 5.1 million in funding. Notable is also the high variance in these performance variables.

While some incubator firms did not generate any revenues or raised any funding, one firm accrued over US$ 39 million in revenues and another firm raised a total of US$ 36.5 million in funding. Almost one-half of the sample incubator firms (46%) obtained VC funding. In the year $t + 1$, 23 firms (29%) had graduated successfully, 15 firms (19%) remained in the incubator, while 41 firms (52%) had failed.

The key independent variables of this study proxy for university–incubator firm knowledge flows. We find that 11 firms (14%) were founded based on a Georgia Tech license. Of the 79 incubator firms, 13 firms (16.5%) had rights (either through a Georgia Tech license or as an assignee themselves) to a total of 35 patents from the U.S. Patent and Trademark Office. It is important to note that the firms founded on GT licenses in comparison to non-GT start-ups that were assigned patents did not differ with respect to the total number of patents granted or any of the four different patent backward citations measures used in this study. This implies that the analysis of university–incubator firm knowledge flows based on patent citation measures is unbiased with respect to the firm having obtained a GT license or not.

Overall, these 35 patents contained 978 citations, splitting into 766 backward citations and 212 forward citations.[1] The 766 backward citations split into 627 non-university (i.e., industry) backward citations (82%) and 139 (18%) university backward citations. Of the latter, 22 (16%) were backward citations to Georgia Tech research.

At the firm level, about 3.3% of all patent citations referenced university research in general, while 2.4% of all patent citations were traced back to academic journals in particular. When dividing the university backward citations in citations to the sponsoring university and citations to other non-sponsoring university research, we find that 0.7% of all backward citations are to Georgia Tech research, while 2.6% of all backward citations are to non-GT university research. The average patent citations to university research are

---

[1] When analyzing the backward citations, we also coded whether the citation was added by the inventor or by the examiner. Since 2001, patent citations added by the examiner are marked by an asterisk. In this sample, there were 397 backward citations since 2001. We found that only six of these citations (0.15%) were added by the patent examiner. We are thus confident that the results are not materially influenced by patent citations added by the patent examiner.

314   *F.T. Rothaermel, M. Thursby / Research Policy 34 (2005) 305–320*

quite low because most incubator firms (66 firms or 83.5%) did not obtain any patents. Thus, our econometric estimates for university patent citation ratios on incubator firm performance are quite conservative, and potentially biased downward. When assessing the prevalence of university patent backward citations among the firms that have been granted patents, we found that 18% of all their patent citations was to university research, which split into 14% to non-Georgia Tech research and 4% GT research. When considering the more narrow set of academic journal citations, we find that among these firms, 12% of all patent citations are to academic journals. Indeed, some of the firms exhibited very high university backward citations in their patent portfolios. For example, the maximum ratio for overall university backward citations was 83%, for backward citations to academic journals it was 79%, and for backward citations to Georgia Tech research it was 32%.

Noteworthy is also the discriminant validity of the different knowledge flow measures employed in this study. When excluding bivariate correlations that share by definition a significant amount of common variance,[2] and which are not inserted in the same regression models, we find that the bivariate correlations among the different knowledge flow measures are well below the suggested cut-off point of $R = 0.70$, suggesting satisfactory discriminant validity (Cohen et al., 2003).

The control variables reveal that the average incubator firm had about 14 employees and spent 2.4 years in the ATDC. The majority of firms are either active in the software industry (34 firm or 43%) or in the telecommunications industry (13 firms or 17%).[3] A little more

---

[2] That is, backward citations to university research and backward citations to academic journals; backward citations to university research and backward citations to non-GT research; backward citations to academic journals and backward citations to non-GT research.

[3] In total, the 79 firms fall into 14 different industries based on four-digit SIC codes. Besides software and telecommunications, there are six firms each in manufacturing and communications (8%), five in healthcare (6%), three Internet businesses (4%), two firms each in agriculture, biotechnology, environmental services, and general services (3% each), and one firm each in microelectronics, paper industry, robotics, and video industry (1% each). We suggest that the results presented below appear not to be directly influenced by the Internet boom and bust during the late 1990s and early 2000s because only three firms in the sample are Internet firms.

than 20% of the firms had a linkage to a research university other than Georgia Tech. Table 1 depicts the descriptive statistics and bivariate correlation matrix, while Table 2 presents the regression results.

We advanced two exploratory hypotheses. We argued that exclusive knowledge flows in terms of a university license can endow the start-up with a unique resource, which can lead to a competitive advantage (Barney, 1991). We also suggested that university backward patent citations are indicative of a start-up's absorptive capacity that enables it to recognize public knowledge flows emanating from a university, assimilate them internally, and then to apply them to commercial ends (Cohen and Levinthal, 1989). A new venture's absorptive capacity is hypothesized to positively affect its performance.

Each of the four different performance measures was assessed in three different regression models. The four different performance dimensions are revenues, funds obtained, venture capital, and graduation from the technology incubator. In the first model of each three-model block, we added the effect of backward citations to university research on incubator firm performance. In the second model, we evaluated the impact of a somewhat more stringent knowledge flow measure, backward citations to academic journals, on incubator firm performance. In the last model of each block, we split the backward citations to university research into backward citations to research by the sponsoring university, Georgia Tech, and backward citations to research by other universities. Each regression model, however, contains the proxy for a GT license.

Models 1–3 evaluate the effect of the five different knowledge flow mechanisms on incubator firm performance proxied by revenues. Here, we find that none of the knowledge flow proxies reach significance. This might be indicative of the fact that revenues is not the most appropriate measure when assessing the performance of nascent technology ventures.

Models 4–6 assess the impact of the different knowledge mechanisms on the total amount of funds raised by the incubator firms. All three models are overall highly significant ($p < 0.001$), and exhibit R^2 values of around 0.36. With respect to individual coefficients, the regression results reveal that backward citations to university research (Model 4), backward citations to academic research (Model 5), and backward citations to non-GT research (Model 6) are each positive and

F.T. Rothaermel, M. Thursby / Research Policy 34 (2005) 305–320 315

Table 1
Descriptive statistics and bivariate correlation matrix

		Mean	S.D.	1	2	3	4	5	6	7	8	9	10	11	12	13	14	15
1.	Revenues	1,654,023	5,338,124															
2.	Total funds raised	5,116,468	7,779,855	0.05														
3.	VC funding	0.456	0.501	0.01	0.32													
4.	Failure	0.519	0.503	−0.29	−0.28	−0.19												
5.	Graduation	0.291	0.457	0.25	0.35	0.14	−0.67											
6.	Remain in incubator	0.190	0.395	0.08	−0.05	0.08	−0.50	−0.31										
7.	Employees	13.734	16.152	0.23	0.50	0.41	−0.07	0.30	−0.26									
8.	Software	0.430	0.498	0.03	0.24	0.18	0.02	0.06	−0.09	0.17								
9.	Telecom	0.165	0.373	0.07	0.05	0.21	−0.05	0.09	−0.04	0.25	−0.39							
10.	Time in incubator	2.430	2.164	0.24	−0.33	−0.23	−0.03	−0.28	0.37	−0.25	−0.19	−0.07						
11.	Non-GT university link	0.203	0.404	−0.09	−0.14	−0.02	0.17	−0.32	0.16	−0.14	0.13	−0.22	0.02					
12.	GT license	0.139	0.348	0.05	−0.01	0.00	−0.20	−0.10	0.36	−0.14	−0.28	0.02	0.26	−0.02				
13.	Backward citations to university research	0.033	0.123	−0.03	0.00	0.05	−0.25	−0.07	0.40	−0.11	−0.22	−0.12	0.24	0.30	0.38			
14.	Backward citations to academic journals	0.024	0.101	−0.09	0.01	0.09	−0.19	−0.11	0.37	−0.10	−0.18	−0.10	0.17	0.31	0.24	0.95		
15.	Backward citations to GT research	0.007	0.038	0.10	−0.08	−0.09	−0.19	−0.07	0.32	−0.10	−0.16	−0.08	0.28	0.24	0.36	0.56	0.44	
16.	Backward citations to non-GT research	0.026	0.107	−0.07	0.03	0.09	−0.22	−0.06	0.35	−0.09	−0.20	−0.11	0.17	0.26	0.32	0.96	0.94	0.29

N = 79.

Technological Entrepreneurship

F.T. Rothaermel, M. Thursby / Research Policy 34 (2005) 305–320

Table 2
Regression results assessing the impact of university–incubator firm knowledge flows on incubator firm performance

	Model 1 Revenues	Model 2 Revenues	Model 3 Revenues	Model 4 Funds raised	Model 5 Funds raised	Model 6 Funds raised	Model 7 VC funding	Model 8 VC funding
Constant	3.683**** (0.300)	3.683**** (0.299)	3.683**** (0.301)	5.11E06**** (7.36E05)	5.11E06**** (7.36E05)	5.11E06**** (7.42E05)	-0.184 (0.278)	-0.183 (0.280)
Employees	0.803*** (0.337)	0.803*** (0.334)	0.794*** (0.338)	0.410**** (0.106)	0.414**** (0.106)	0.411**** (0.107)	0.919*** (0.396)	0.934*** (0.398)
Software	0.171 (0.369)	0.142 (0.365)	0.178 (0.370)	0.210** (0.116)	0.206** (0.116)	0.209** (0.117)	0.638** (0.329)	0.644** (0.326)
Telecom	0.086 (0.360)	0.075 (0.356)	0.090 (0.360)	-0.007 (0.115)	-0.014 (0.113)	-0.007 (0.109)	0.610*** (0.318)	0.600*** (0.317)
Time in incubator	0.930*** (0.326)	0.939*** (0.324)	0.885*** (0.331)	-0.247*** (0.103)	-0.243*** (0.102)	-0.243** (0.105)	-0.469* (0.334)	-0.417* (0.336)
Non-GT university link	-0.112 (0.332)	-0.061 (0.329)	-0.151 (0.336)	-0.152* (0.105)	-0.152* (0.104)	-0.148 (0.106)	-0.005 (0.293)	-0.027 (0.294)
GT license	-0.108 (0.342)	0.111 (0.325)	0.056 (0.348)	0.109 (0.108)	0.131 (0.103)	0.114 (0.110)	0.230 (0.293)	0.291 (0.290)
Backward citations to university research	-0.163 (0.362)			0.155* (0.114)			0.441* (0.306)	
Backward citations to academic journals		-0.315 (0.336)			0.150* (0.107)			0.500* (0.340)
Backward citations to GT research			0.233 (0.348)			0.019 (0.110)		
Backward citations to non-GT research			-0.260 (0.344)			0.146* (0.109)		
R^2	0.159	0.167	0.168	0.355	0.356	0.356	0.353	0.363
F-stat	1.921*	2.035*	1.767*	5.586****	5.616****	4.833****		
−2 log likelihood							84.665****	83.859****

	Model 9 VC funding	Model 10 Fail	Model 10 Graduate	Model 11 Fail	Model 11 Graduate	Model 12 Fail	Model 12 Graduate
Constant	-0.193 (0.282)	1.097* (0.676)	1.346** (0.686)	0.749* (0.553)	0.021** (0.564)	3.335** (1.593)	3.610** (1.597)
Employees	0.920*** (0.394)	-0.612* (0.419)	-0.334 (0.486)	-0.466 (0.385)	-0.268 (0.439)	-0.949** (0.533)	-0.667 (0.603)
Software	0.629** (0.328)	-0.483 (0.394)	-0.357 (0.439)	-0.349 (0.372)	-0.316 (0.408)	-0.651* (0.468)	-0.548 (0.517)
Telecom	0.603** (0.318)	-0.300 (0.315)	-1.272*** (0.502)	-0.344 (0.290)	-1.147*** (0.480)	-0.469 (0.379)	-1.608*** (0.583)
Time in incubator	-0.420 (0.333)	0.079 (0.347)	-2.039*** (0.860)	0.136 (0.332)	-1.350* (0.643)	0.023 (0.408)	-5.380*** (2.162)
Non-GT university link	0.031 (0.297)	-0.334 (0.365)	-0.514 (0.421)	-0.373 (0.360)	-0.255 (0.383)	-0.929** (0.494)	-1.069* (0.624)
GT license	0.275 (0.302)	-5.620**** (1.496)	0.507 (0.481)	-4.850**** (1.534)	0.147 (0.950)	-18.036*** (6.244)	1.375 (1.175)
Backward citations to GT research	-0.207 (0.542)						
Backward citations to non-GT research	0.509* (0.334)						
R^2	0.363	0.546		0.468		0.654	
−2 log likelihood	83.837****	119.663****		129.753****		103.452****	

Standard errors in parentheses.

* $p<0.10$.
** $p<0.05$.
*** $p<0.01$.
**** $p<0.001$.

F.T. Rothaermel, M. Thursby / Research Policy 34 (2005) 305–320   317

significant ($p < 0.10$) in predicting incubator firm performance.

The results of the logit estimations, predicting the probability of obtaining VC funding, are displayed in Models 7–9. The results for obtaining VC funding are basically identical to the results when applying total funds raised as dependent variable. All three models are overall highly significant ($p < 0.001$), and exhibit R^2 values of around 0.36. Here again, backward citations to university research ($\exp(\beta) = 1.554$, Model 7), backward citations to academic research ($\exp(\beta) = 1.649$, Model 8), and backward citations to non-GT research ($\exp(\beta) = 1.663$, Model 9) are each positive and significant ($p < 0.10$) in predicting incubator firm performance.

Models 10–12 display the results when assessing the impact of the different knowledge flows on the incubator firm's probability of failure and graduation, while remaining in the incubator serves as reference category. Each of the three models is statistically significant ($p < 0.01$ or smaller), and the R^2 ranges between 0.47 and 0.65. Holding a GT license reduces the probability of outright failure (Model 12: $\exp(\beta) = 0.395, p < 0.05$), but also retards timely graduation from the incubator (Model 12: $\exp(\beta) = 0.343$, $p < 0.05$). With respect to backward patent citations, we find that backward citations to university research (Model 10: $\exp(\beta) = 0.004$, $p < 0.001$), backward citations to academic journals (Model 11: $\exp(\beta) = 0.008$), and backward citations to GT research (Model 12: $\exp(\beta) = 1.47\mathrm{E}{-8}$, $p < 0.01$), each significantly reduces the probability of outright failure.

Some of the results for the control variables are also noteworthy. Firms that grow faster in terms of employees perform significantly better along all the different performance metrics used to assess incubator firm performance in this study. Yet, these faster growing firms are also somewhat more likely to fail. The results also manifest consistent industry effects. Software firms tend to perform significantly higher when considering the amount of funding raised, the probability of obtaining VC funding, and exhibit a lower likelihood of outright failure. Telecom firms are significantly more likely to obtain VC funding and less likely to experience failure. Firms that remain longer in the incubator tend to raise fewer funds, are less likely to obtain VC funding, and are less likely to graduate in a timely fashion. Firms that stay longer in the incuba-

tor, however, tend to generate significantly higher revenues. Incubator firms that maintain linkages to other research universities than Georgia Tech tend to raise significantly fewer funds and are less likely to graduate within 3 years or less.

5.1. Robustness checks

We checked if multi-collinearity could bias the results when applying OLS estimations (Models 1–6). Here, we found that the maximum variance inflation factor was 1.5, well below the suggested cut-off point of 10 (Cohen et al., 2003). Multi-collinearity, however, did appear to affect the results when including an additional control variable for an incubator firm's total number of patents received or a binary indicator variable whether the firm received a patent or not. The results for the probability of obtaining VC funding and the results with respect to failure or graduation remained robust; however, the results for predicting the total amount of funding raised do not reach significance. The overall somewhat weaker results can be explained by the fact that the variable *total number of patents received* and the indicator variable *patent received* (=1) are highly significantly correlated with each of the four backward patent citation measures employed in this study (at $p < 0.01$ or smaller). This high correlation is expected because the firms that obtain patents are the only ones that can cite university research in their patents. Therefore, it appears prudent to not include the patent count or indicator variables thereof simultaneously with the backward patent citations measures in the regression estimations.

6. Discussion

One of the arguments for incubators associated with universities is that knowledge flows from universities should enhance performance of high-technology ventures and that access to this knowledge is not "free," despite the publication norms of science. In this paper, we examined two mechanisms by which incubator firms can access this knowledge. One, which is available to new ventures based on Georgia Tech inventions, is a license to develop and use a university invention. In the case of ATDC firms, all of the licenses to Georgia Tech inventions were exclusive so that the

318 *F.T. Rothaermel, M. Thursby / Research Policy 34 (2005) 305–320*

resource-based view of the firm suggested that these licenses provide a unique, performance-enhancing resource (Barney, 1991). The other mechanism we explored was citations to university research found in the patents associated with incubator firms. We argued that this mechanism reflects not only a non-exclusive means for firms to access university knowledge, but also that it reflects the ability of the new venture to utilize university knowledge, and thus could be seen as a proxy for absorptive capacity (Cohen and Levinthal, 1990). We argued that both licenses and backward citations should be positively related to incubator firm performance. A secondary purpose of this study was to examine different performance metrics for evaluating the performance of nascent technology ventures.

We found little support for the unique resource hypothesis because the license variable was in general not significant. Holding a Georgia Tech license had a significant effect only on performance measured by failure and graduation, and then only when the citation ratios were split between Georgia Tech and non-Georgia Tech citations. This result is interesting because this is also the only model for which the localized citation variable, the ratio of citations to Georgia Tech research to all citations, is significant.

We found more consistent support for the absorptive capacity hypothesis as backward citations to university research positively affect three of the performance measures. This was the case both for all university citations and citations to academic publications alone. Notice that the variable backward citations to university research is, ceteris paribus, one minus the ratio of citations to industry patents to all citations (abstracting from non-university and non-industry citations). Thus, the coefficient for the university research variable is the opposite of the coefficient had we entered the ratio of industry citations. A natural interpretation of the university citation variable is that it is a measure, not only of absorptive capacity, but also of how basic are the patents of the new venture. According to this interpretation, our results of citations on the probability of obtaining VC funding suggest that venture capitalists tend to be more likely to back basic inventions rather than those whose prior art arises primarily in industry.

With respect to evaluating different performance metrics for technology ventures, in particular in the context of university knowledge flows, we found that revenues were a poor measure for incubator firm perfor-

mance. The revenue models explain the lowest amount of variance, and none of the individual proxies for knowledge flows reaches statistical significance. It is not surprising that revenues appear to be an inappropriate measure for assessing the performance of incubator firms because the firms are very young (less than 3 years old) and compete in the high-technology space, where many firms do not generate much revenues initially as they invest to develop the new technology. More promising performance metrics appear to be the total amount of funding obtained, whether the firm was backed by VC funding, and whether the firm graduated from the incubator in a timely manner or failed altogether. The last variable should be applied with caution in future research because many incubators tend to have an explicit graduation policy (not the ATDC) and encourage or expect timely graduation. Thus, total funds obtained or VC funding are market mechanisms that appear to assess the performance of new technology ventures in a satisfactory manner.

6.1. Limitations and future research

One of our more important assumptions underlying this research was that patent citations reflect knowledge flows. While this assumption is based on a long tradition in economics, some recent research has suggested that patent citations may not reflect knowledge flows, since citations are often added by attorneys and patent examiners (Jaffe et al., 2000; Alcacer and Gittelman, 2004; Sampat, 2004). While this is a fundamental challenge to the research relying on patent data when attempting to capture knowledge flows, the recent practice of publishing examiner cites mitigates this problem. Moreover, if patent citations indeed do not truly reflect knowledge flows, future research needs to develop alternate metrics that capture knowledge flows more effectively.

We suggested that firms with a higher ratio of university citations in their patent portfolio achieve higher performance because these firms are based on more basic invention with a greater potential of making a commercial breakthrough. While the ratio of university citations to total citations was a positive predictor of incubator firm performance, especially with respect to total amount of funding obtained and the probability of obtaining VC funding, we need to emphasize that the relationship between the ratio of university ci-

F.T. Rothaermel, M. Thursby / Research Policy 34 (2005) 305–320 319

tations to total patent citations on firm performance may not be positive and linear because the average firm in this sample exhibited a low level of university citations among its patents. Future research could investigate a potentially diminishing marginal or even diminishing total returns hypothesis for the relationship between university backward citations and firm performance.

Clearly, future research should also address the generalizability of our findings. While we find some support for the absorptive capacity hypothesis, we need to emphasize that our research setting is somewhat unique. While it enabled us to empirically assess interfirm performance differentials among incubator firms, we were limited to firms incubated in the ATDC sponsored by Georgia Tech, a research institute with a clear focus on engineering sciences. Some researchers have begun to compare incubator differential performance (Mian, 1996; Colombo and Delmastro, 2002); however, studies on interfirm differential performance of incubator firms are rare. We hope that future research will be able to apply a repeat survey approach similar to the one used in this study in order to collect fine-grained, longitudinal data on incubator firms across different technology incubators.

6.2. Implications for public policy

The results presented in this study seem to indicate that knowledge does flow, via different mechanisms, from universities to incubator start-up firms. While the negative impact of having a link to a research university other than the sponsoring university on firm performance seems to indicate some benefits of being closely located to the sponsoring university, other measures for localized spillovers did generally not reveal significant results. One area of public policy concern could therefore be the enhancement of localized spillovers because many public incubators and other university-based technology initiatives are formed to improve the economic performance of the region. Siegel et al. (2003), for example, showed, when examining the effect of university science parks in the UK on firm research productivity, that firms associated with science parks were more productive than those not so located. The question of how localized spillovers from universities to incubator firms can be enhanced is an interesting one and opens up another promising avenue for future research.

Acknowledgements

We thank Tony Antoniades (of the ATDC), George Harker (Director, Office of Technology Licensing, Georgia Institute of Technology), and H. Wayne Hodges (Vice Provost for Economic Development and Technology Ventures, Georgia Institute of Technology) for their generous support and invaluable input, Stuart Graham for comments and suggestions, and Shanti Dewi for research assistance. A prior version of this paper was presented at the 2004 Technology Transfer Society (T2S) Conference. We thank the special issue editors and the session attendants for valuable input. All remaining errors and omissions are entirely our own. Thursby gratefully acknowledges research support from NSF SES 0094573.

References

Acs, Z., Audretsch, D.B., 1989. Patents as a measure of innovative activity. Kyklos 42, 171–180.

Adams, J., 1990. Fundamental stocks of knowledge and productivity growth. Journal of Political Economy 98, 673–702.

Agrawal, A., Henderson, R., 2002. Putting patents in context: exploring knowledge transfer from MIT. Management Science 48, 44–60.

Alcacer, J., Gittelman, M., 2004. How do I know what you know? Patent examiners and the generation of patent citations. Working Paper. New York University.

Barney, J., 1991. Firm resources and sustained competitive advantage. Journal of Management 17, 99–120.

Branstetter, L., 2004. Is academic science driving a surge in industrial innovation? Evidence from patent citations. Working Paper. Columbia University.

Cockburn, I.M., Henderson, R.M., 1998. Absorptive capacity, coauthoring behavior, and the organization of research in drug discovery. Journal of Industrial Economics 46, 157–182.

Cohen, S.N., Chang, A.C.Y., Boyer, H.W., Helling, R., 1973. Construction of biologically functional bacterial plasmids in vitro. Proceedings of the National Academy of Sciences of the United States of America 70, 3240–3244.

Cohen, J., Cohen, P., West, S.G., Aiken, L.S., 2003. Applied Multiple Regression/Correlation Analysis for the Behavioral Sciences. Erlbaum, Mahwah, NJ.

Cohen, W.M., Levinthal, D.A., 1989. Innovation and learning: the two faces of R&D. Economic Journal 99, 569–596.

Cohen, W.M., Levinthal, D.A., 1990. Absorptive capacity: a new perspective on learning and innovation. Administrative Science Quarterly 35, 128–152.

Cohen, W.M., Florida, R., Randazzes, L., Walsh, J., 1998. Industry and the academy: uneasy partners in the cause of technological advance. In: Noll, R. (Ed.), Challenges to Research Universities. The Brookings Institution, Washington, DC, pp. 171–200.

Colombo, M.G., Delmastro, M., 2002. How effective are technology incubators? Evidence from Italy. Research Policy 31, 1103–1122.

Griliches, Z., 1992. The search for R&D spillovers. Scandinavian Journal of Economic 94, 29–47.

Godfrey, P.C., Hill, C.W.L., 1995. The problem of unobservables in strategic management research. Strategic Management Journal 16, 519–533.

Henderson, R., Cockburn, I., 1994. Measuring competence? Exploring firm effects in pharmaceutical research. Strategic Management Journal 15, 63–84 (winter special issue).

Henderson, R., Jaffe, A., Trajtenberg, M., 1998. Universities as a source of commercial technology: a detailed analysis of university patenting. Review of Economics and Statistics 80, 119–127.

Jaffe, A.B., 1989. Real effects of academic research. American Economic Review 79, 957–970.

Jaffe, A.B., Trajtenberg, M., Fogarty, M., 2000. The meaning of patent citations: report on the NBER/Case Western Research Survey of Patentees. NBER Working Paper 6507.

Jaffe, A.B., Trajtenberg, M., Henderson, R.M., 1993. Geographic knowledge spillovers as evidenced by patent citations. Quarterly Journal of Economics 108, 577–598.

Klevorick, A.K., Levin, R., Nelson, R., Winter, S., 1994. On the sources and significance of interindustry differences in technological opportunities. Research Policy 24, 195–206.

Link, A.N., Scott, J.T., 2004. U.S. university research parks. Working Paper. University of North Carolina at Greensboro.

Maddala, G.S., 1983. Limited-Dependent and Qualitative Variables in Econometrics. Cambridge University Press, Cambridge, UK.

Mansfield, E., 1995. Academic research underlying industrial innovations: sources, characteristics, and financing. Review of Economics and Statistics 77, 55–65.

Mian, S.A., 1996. Assessing value-added contributions of university technology business incubators to tenant firms. Research Policy 25, 325–335.

Murray, F., Stern, S., 2004. Do formal intellectual property rights hinder the free flow of scientific knowledge? Evidence from patent–paper pairs. Working Paper. MIT.

Phan, P.H., Siegel, D.S., Wright, M., 2004. Science parks and incubators: observations, synthesis and future research. Journal of Business Venturing 20, 165–182.

Rosenwein, R., November 2000. The idea factories. In: Inc.

Rothaermel, F.T., 2001. Complementary assets, strategic alliances, and the incumbent's advantage: an empirical study of industry and firm effects in the biopharmaceutical industry. Research Policy 30, 1235–1251.

Rothaermel, F.T., 2002. Technological discontinuities and interfirm cooperation: what determines a start-up's attractiveness as alliance partner? IEEE Transactions on Engineering Management 49, 388–397.

Rothaermel, F.T., Deeds, D.L., 2004. Exploration and exploitation alliances in biotechnology: a system of new product development. Strategic Management Journal 25, 201–221.

Rothaermel, F.T., Hill, C.W.L., 2005. Technological discontinuities and complementary assets: a longitudinal study of industry and firm performance. Organization Science 16, 52–70.

Rothaermel, F.T, Thursby, M., 2005. Incubator firm failure or graduation? The role of university linkages. Research Policy 34, in press.

Sampat, B., 2004. Examining patent examination: an analysis of examiner and applicant generated prior art. Working Paper. Georgia Institute of Technology.

Shane, S., Cable, D., 2002. Network ties, reputation, and the financing of new ventures. Management Science 48, 364–381.

Shane, S., Stuart, T., 2002. Organizational endowments and the performance of university start-ups. Management Science 48, 154–170.

Siegel, D.S., Westhead, P., Wright, M., 2003. Assessing the impact of science parks on the research productivity of firms: exploratory evidence from the United Kingdom. International Journal of Industrial Organization 21, 135–169.

Stuart, T.E., Hoang, H., Hybels, R.C., 1999. Interorganizational endorsements and the performance of entrepreneurial ventures. Administrative Science Quarterly 44, 315–349.

Thursby, J., Thursby, M.C., 2002. Who is selling the ivory tower? Sources of growth in university licensing. Management Science 48, 90–104.

Thursby, J., Thursby, M., 2004. Are faculty critical? Their role in university–industry licensing. Contemporary Economic Policy 22, 162–178.

Trajtenberg, M., Henderson, R., Jaffe, A., 1997. University versus corporate patents: a window on the basicness of invention. Economic Innovation and New Technology 5, 19–50.

Zucker, L.G., Darby, M.R., 1996. Costly information—firm transformation, exit, or persistent failure. American Behavioral Scientist 39, 959–974.

Zucker, L.G., Darby, M.R., 1998. Intellectual human capital and the birth of U.S. biotechnology enterprises. American Economic Review 88, 290–306.

Zucker, L.G., Darby, M.R., Armstrong, J., 2002. Commercializing knowledge: university science, knowledge capture, and firm performance in biotechnology. Management Science 48, 138–153.

Part III
University-Based Startups

[19]

UNIVERSITIES AND THE STARTUP OF NEW COMPANIES: CAN WE GENERALIZE FROM ROUTE 128 AND SILICON VALLEY?

Neil Bania, Randall W. Eberts, and Michael S. Fogarty*

Abstract—In order to increase the commercialization of basic research, policy makers have tried to foster closer ties between university research and industry R&D. To empirically test whether there is a link between commercialization and university research, this paper models firm startups during 1976–78 for six 2-digit manufacturing industries located in 25 metropolitan areas. The findings are mixed: the relationship between university research and firm births in the electrical and electronic equipment industries (SIC 36) is positive and statistically significant, while in the instruments and related industries (SIC 38) the relationship is statistically insignificant.

Pointing to U.S. industry's failure to commercialize its research, policy makers expect that forming closer ties between basic research (mostly at universities) and industry R&D will increase innovation (National Academy of Sciences, 1986).[1] An important question is whether commercialization depends on geographic proximity. One reason is that states have seized on the experiences of Boston's Route 128 and Silicon Valley as models for economic development, resulting in a dramatic growth in state science and technology (S&T) programs. An underlying assumption of state S&T programs is that universities create local technology spillovers, which are then captured either within a state or metropolian region. (Technology spillovers are externalities associated with the production of knowledge created by R&D. Local spillovers are more likely if the mechanisms for transmitting technological information require personal contact.) Some fraction of a university's contribution to innovation through spillovers is captured locally as new companies.[2] This paper focuses on the importance of universities in explaining the opening rate of new manufacturing establishments in metropolitan areas. If spillovers are not captured locally, the benefits from state S&T investments will be quickly diffused to other regions and countries.

I. Local Technology Spillovers

Firms invest in R&D to increase innovation and productivity growth (Griliches and Lichtenberg, 1984), but also to appropriate information from other firms'

Received for publication July 2, 1990. Revision accepted for publication June 23, 1992.

* Case Western Reserve University, W. E. Upjohn Institute for Employment Research, and Case Western Reserve University, respectively.

The authors are grateful for the helpful comments of Patricia Beeson, Adam Jaffe, and two anonymous referees.

[1] Examples of such federal efforts to foster closer university-industry ties include 18 NSF Engineering Research Centers, 50 NSF Industry-University Cooperative Research Centers, 11 NSF Science and Technology Centers, and 5 NIST technology transfer centers.

[2] One recent study documented 198 new companies, two-thirds of which are located in Boston, started by MIT alumni between 1980 and 1988 (Bank of Boston, 1989).

and other institutions' R & D efforts, including universities (Cohen and Levinthal, 1989). Geographic proximity may facilitate the capturing of spillovers and shorten the time between invention and innovation.[3]

Local firms benefit from a region's technical infrastructure in various ways: by hiring graduates from local universities, by using faculty as consultants, by becoming sponsors of joint university-industry research centers, by using local universities for education and training of their workforce, and by utilizing university facilities such as laboratories, libraries, specialized equipment, and by attending seminars.[4] The clearest and most visible mechanism creating spillovers is the hiring of local university graduates whose education and training embodies some of the fruits of academic research. Because an educated and skilled workforce facilitates the diffusion of technology (Bartel and Lichtenberg, 1986; Wozniak, 1987), we would expect to observe more localization of spillover benefits in places with greater concentration of skilled workers, such as scientists and engineers.

Without considering the influence of geographic proximity, Jaffe (1986) found that a firm's R & D productivity is increased by its own R & D as well as by technologically similar R & D performed by other firms. Jaffe (1989) also finds state-level evidence that geographic proximity between university research and industry R & D increases corporate patenting activity within a state.[5] Henderson, Jaffe, and Trajtenberg (1991) use patent citations to trace the geographic distribution of spillovers from university and corporate research; they find that spillovers are more likely to come from nearby universities.

II. Modeling Openings

We follow Carlton (1979, 1983) in modeling openings. The opening (birth) rate is measured as the number of new establishments within an industry divided by the number of "potential" entrepreneurs available to start a new business. Since the birth of new establishments is a discrete and infrequent event, the business formation process is characterized as a Poisson probabilistic model. Let l_i represent the probability of an establishment opening in a particular industry and metropolitan area and X_i a vector of economic

characteristics hypothesized to influence the probability. We assume that

$$\ln l_i = \ln X_i \beta + \epsilon_i \tag{1}$$

where ϵ_i is an error term consisting of the Poisson process variance and a random error. Although the probability of starting a new establishment is not directly observed, we estimate l_i consistently from

$$l_i = N_i / BP_i \tag{2}$$

where N_i is the observed number of establishment births and BP_i is potential births, which we approximate with SMSA employment (the pool of potential entrepreneurs). We use weighted least squares, with weights equal to the standard error of the process, which as Carlton (1979) shows, provide consistent and asymptotically efficient estimates of β in (1).

Data

Our statistical analyses focus on two sets of factors determining opening rates: (1) traditional economic factors including labor costs, degree of unionization, price of capital, taxes, and energy costs; and (2) technical infrastructure, which we measure with total university research, the number of research universities, and the percent of employed workers who are scientists or engineers. The analysis is based on 87 4-digit manufacturing industries in 25 large metropolitan areas (SMSAs) for 1976–78.[6]

The statistical tests focus on two groups: small, independent manufacturing firms (firms with 100 or less employees) and all manufacturing firms. The opening of small businesses are generally thought to reflect entrepreneurship; openings among all businesses include branch plants. The Establishment Longitudinal Microdata (USELM) file used in this paper includes data for 1976–78 and 1980–82 (Harris, 1983). We chose to analyze the 1976–78 data in order to emphasize openings during a period of growth. (1980–82 was a major recessionary period.)

The appropriate labor cost variable controls for workforce quality, which is correlated with productivity. Therefore, we use a skill-adjusted labor cost differential based on national-level earnings regressions to correct wages for differences in worker characteristics across metropolitan areas (Eberts and Stone, 1986). Unionization is measured by the percent of SMSA workers unionized (Freeman and Medoff, 1979). In addition to unions' effect on wages, the union variable may capture the effects of work rules, work stoppages, and differences in productivity. Because we expect

---

[3] Closer geographic ties, which suggests greater personal contact, may alter the composition of university research, increasing its commercial potential.

[4] The importance of spillovers is further indicated by the magnet effect universities have on the location of R & D labs (Lund, 1986; Bania, Calkins, and Dalenberg, 1992; Jaffe, 1989).

[5] In his surveys of research managers, Richard Nelson (1986) found that innovation in some industries, especially those associated with the biological sciences, was linked to university research.

[6] We are limited to using twenty-five SMSAs because the price of capital and the degree of unionization are only jointly available for these 25 places.

unions' effect on wages to vary with degree of unionization, the regressions also include a variable which interacts the percent unionized and the skill-adjusted wage.

The SMSA manufacturing capital stock was estimated using a perpetual inventory method (Fogarty and Garofalo, 1982). Following Field and Grebenstein (1980), the price of capital is estimated for each metropolitan area using data on its four components: the rate of return on capital, the rate of net depreciation (including the discard rate of capital), the local property tax rate, and the state income tax rate. The price of capital varies across metropolitan areas because depreciation varies with the age distribution of capital and because property and state income taxes vary by metropolitan area.

Energy prices were computed from energy usage data published in the 1977 *Census of Manufactures.* The variable measures the average price of natural gas by dividing the total cost by the quantity consumed by SMSA manufactures.

We utilize a measure of business taxes developed by Wheaton (1983) for 1977. Wheaton calculates the legal tax liability for businesses at the state level by adding taxes for which area businesses are liable and dividing the sum by his estimate of net business income.

We measured each metropolitan area's technical infrastructure with three variables: total university research, the number of universities, and the percent of employed scientists and engineers in each SMSA. University research was obtained by identifying each metropolitan area's universities and summing university research expenditures in 1978 across institutions located in each SMSA.[7] Because university research may be less effective in creating new companies if the research is spread across a number of institutions, we have included the number of institutions as a variable to control for this effect.[8] The percent of employed scientists and engineers is used as a proxy for the technical composition of the SMSA workforce. The simple correlation between university research and the percent employed scientists and engineers is 0.01, indicating a weak geographic association.[9]

The relative importance of firm startup determinants is likely to vary across industries. For example, the startup rate of businesses in high-technology industries would be most affected by spillovers from university research and the technical composition of the workforce. We have chosen to use 4-digit rather than 2-digit industries because the broader industry categories mask important differences within the industry. For example, transportation equipment (SIC 37) consists mostly of auto-related industries in Ohio metropolitan areas, while in California it consists mostly of aerospace industries.

We have estimated separate regressions for 2-digit industries when there exist sufficient 4-digit level data within each 2-digit industry category. The data were stratified into six 2-digit industries. In order to estimate the model separately for broad industries, we used firm startup data on 87 4-digit industry categories.[10] For estimation, we grouped these 87 4-digit industry categories into 6 broad 2-digit categories: Primary Metals (SIC 33, 10 4-digit industries), Fabricated Metal products (SIC 34, 17 4-digit industries), Non-electrical Machinery (SIC 35, 28 4-digit industries), Electrical and Electronic equipment (SIC 36, 19 4-digit industries), Transportation Equipment (SIC 37, 8 4-digit industries), and Instruments and Related products (SIC 38, 5 4-digit industries). The Electrical and Electronic Equipment (SIC 36) and the Instruments and Related products (SIC 38) industries consist mostly of high-technology industries. Within each 2-digit category, we use dummy variables to allow for differences in the startup rate across 4-digit industry categories.

To allow for the possibility that additional unmeasured conditions correlated with metropolitan size (agglomeration economies) might affect new business formation rates, we include 1970 SMSA population in the regressions.

III. Regression Results

The regression results for all firms and small firms for two of the selected 2-digit industries are reported in table 1 (SIC 36, which is Electrical and Electronic Equipment, contains nineteen 4-digit industries; SIC 38, which is Instruments and Related Products, contains five 4-digit industries).[11] The twenty-four 4-digit industries used in our analysis are identified in the appendix.

In general, the results support the view that the startup rate is reduced by high labor costs. Moreover, this result is consistent across both firm-size categories, so the following comments apply to small and large

---

[7] University research funding was obtained from NSF, *Surveys of Academic Science and Engineering Statistics Survey* tape, 1978.

[8] Jaffe (1989) suggests that states with research concentrated in fewer institutions are more successful in attracting research funding.

[9] The simple correlation between university research and the total number of scientists and engineers is 0.69.

[10] USELM data are available for 20 2-digit, 17 3-digit, and 109 4-digit manufacturing industries. We could not analyze the other 22 4-digit industries because the data are spread across nine 2-digit industry categories, thus there were insufficient degrees of freedom to estimate a separate regression for each 2-digit category.

[11] The regression results for the other 4-digit data (stratified into four 2-digit industry categories), as well as the variable means, are available from the authors on request.

TABLE 1.—REGRESSION RESULTS

| Variable | Electrical and Electronic Equipment (SIC 36) | | | | Instruments and Related Products (SIC 38) | | | |
| | Small Firms | | All Firms | | Small Firms | | All Firms | |
	Coefficient	t-statistic	Coefficient	t-statistic	Coefficient	t-statistic	Coefficient	t-statistic
INTERCEP	−0.784	−1.083	−1.224	−1.973[b]	−3.532	−2.721[c]	−4.351	−3.971[c]
QWAG74	−0.188	−2.845[c]	−0.498	−2.217[b]	−0.303	−2.573[b]	−0.923	−2.508[b]
FMUNION	−0.049	−2.125[b]	−0.200	−2.567[b]	−0.001	−0.026	−0.004	−0.036
UNWAG	0.007	3.385[c]	0.021	2.868[c]	0.012	3.061[c]	0.038	3.116[c]
LPK	−3.190	−2.385[b]	−10.201	−2.325[b]	−7.493	−3.353[c]	−26.933	−4.005[c]
LTAX	0.645	1.832[a]	1.167	0.977	0.220	0.388	−0.092	−0.052
LNGPRICE	0.872	1.592	3.151	1.701[a]	−0.137	−0.169	−0.528	−0.209
LSPOP70	−1.262	−4.287[c]	−3.464	−3.574[c]	−1.201	−2.625[b]	−3.458	−2.503[b]
LFUND	0.271	2.177[b]	0.699	1.653[a]	−0.039	−0.213	−0.373	−0.655
PSE80	−19.348	−1.201	−45.818	−0.836	−38.502	−1.532	−126.274	−1.600
NUMINST	−0.066	−1.291	−0.170	−0.995	0.003	0.037	−0.064	−0.267
SIC3622	−0.361	−0.687	−1.039	−0.581				
SIC3623	0.682	0.920	3.422	1.354				
SIC3624	0.909	1.027	2.305	0.752				
SIC3629	−0.069	−0.108	−0.889	−0.403				
SIC3641	0.182	0.262	2.192	0.927				
SIC3651	1.486	2.867[c]	5.172	2.933[c]				
SIC3652	1.552	2.753[c]	5.056	2.633[c]				
SIC3661	−0.686	−1.147	−1.618	−0.796				
SIC3662	−0.681	−1.340	−1.626	−0.939				
SIC3671	2.905	2.102[b]	8.595	1.818[a]				
SIC3672	2.406	2.291[b]	7.221	2.013[b]				
SIC3673	1.728	2.164[b]	5.306	1.916[a]				
SIC3674	1.180	2.249[b]	4.533	2.539[b]				
SIC3675	−0.293	−0.208	−2.428	−0.493				
SIC3677	1.088	1.575	3.355	1.416				
SIC3678	1.991	1.931[a]	7.240	2.058[b]				
SIC3679	−0.140	−0.291	0.195	0.118				
SIC3693	0.449	0.906	2.949	1.752[a]				
SIC3823					−0.074	−0.166	−0.590	−0.421
SIC3825					0.058	0.129	0.595	0.424
SIC3842					0.128	0.290	0.242	0.176
SIC3861					0.251	0.547	1.119	0.779
Observations:	234		234		95		95	
Adjusted R-square	0.358		0.320		0.168		0.23	

Notes: Small firms are those with 100 or fewer employees.
[a] Significant at the 10% level.
[b] Significant at the 5% level.
[c] Significant at the 1% level.

businesses except where noted. The conclusion regarding the importance of business costs is especially true with respect to quality-adjusted wages and the price of capital, where the coefficients are negative and significant in both high-technology industry categories. Therefore, unless offset by other factors, high wages and a high price of capital appear to reduce the startup rate of new manufacturers.

A high degree of unionization also appears to reduce firm opening rates, although the effect is significant only for Electrical and Electronic Equipment industries. However, the variable measuring the interaction between unionization and wages is positive and significant in all of the regressions, suggesting labor quality characteristics associated with unions are not fully accounted for by the quality-adjusted wage.

The tax and energy variables give disappointing results. The coefficient on the tax variable, which mea-

sures business taxes as a proportion of business income, is typically positive and sometimes significant. One possible explanation may be that the tax variable measures the overall tax rate rather than an industry-specific rate. A second possibility is that the price of capital, which includes tax rates among its components, is picking up the effect of taxes, thereby mitigating the effect of the tax variable. Finally, we were unable to construct a reasonable measure of government-provided services to business.[12]

The energy cost variable also gives mixed results. The only significant coefficient was positive; this was

[12] The coefficient on taxes could be positive if there are net benefits to industry from government services. See Carlton (1979) and Modifi and Stone (1990) for a discussion of issues concerning metropolitan-level business taxes and government expenditures.

for all firms in Electrical and Electronic Equipment industries. The variable may be capturing other important influences which are correlated with regional differences.

Our results with respect to the influence of university research on the firm opening rate are interesting and suggestive, but mixed. The contribution of university research is positive and statistically significant for Electrical and Electronic Equipment industries; in contrast, the results are insignificant for the second group of high-technology industries in the Instruments and Related Products category. (The effect of university research was insignificant in four other 2-digit industries.) The finding of a positive and statistically significant relationship between university research and the startup rate of new manufacturers for Electrical and Electronic Equipment industries is certainly consistent with the view that universities have played a central role in the development of the nation's microelectronics industry.

Although the coefficient on the number of universities has the expected negative sign in three of the four regressions, the variable is always insignificant. Therefore, there is no evidence that the contribution of the research to startups is diminished as the number of institutions in an SMSA increases.

Somewhat surprisingly, no evidence was found that a more technical workforce (a higher percentage of scientists and engineers) increased the startup rate.[13] The percent scientists and engineers was insignificant in all 4-digit level regressions.[14] The overall measure may simply be inadequate for capturing the effect of a technical workforce on the formation of new manufacturing firms in very detailed high-technology industries. For example, the startup rate of firms in the Electrical and Electronic Equipment industries may depend more on the concentration of electrical engineers than on all engineers.

IV. Conclusions and Implications

The evidence presented in this paper suggests that states cannot generalize from the Route 128 and Silicon Valley experiences. In analyzing eighty-seven 4-digit manufacturing industries within six 2-digit industry categories, the only consistent evidence concerning the effect of university research on new business startups was found for 19 prominent high-technology

industries in Electrical and Electronic Equipment.[15] The significance of university research for this particular group of industries is consistent with the view that universities have been especially important in the development of the nation's microelectronics industry.

Recent studies of technological spillovers show a strong geographic association between university research and corporate patenting activity (Jaffe, 1989; Henderson, Jaffe, and Trajtenberg, 1991). Therefore, without diminishing the significance of this finding, one broad conclusion would have to be that the pipeline between university research and local commercialization, as measured by a higher startup rate of new firms, has substantial leaks. One potentially promising avenue of research on the commercialization issue would involve developing a better understanding of the mechanisms that create technological spillovers leading from university research to new firms. For example, even though investments in biotechnology research at a number of universities may increase the inventive activity of R & D laboratories located within the same metropolitan region, any resulting new products or processes will frequently be developed in other locations.

Interestingly, Jaffe (1989) found the strongest evidence of geographically mediated technological spillovers for research related to drugs and chemicals, and a smaller effect for electronics-related research. If universities are especially important for emerging industries, then we might expect that the effect of university research was more important for the emerging electronics industry in the late 1970's (corresponding to our data), while the impact on the newly emerging biomedical industries became more important in the mid-1980's (corresponding to Jaffe's data). One explanation of this effect may be that university research is probably more important for product rather than process R & D and therefore is likely to provide that greatest benefits for new businesses in infant industries.

Finally, is this a national issue? Although we might be pleased to see Michigan succeed in commercializing more of the research performed at the University of Michigan, it needn't be a national issue. However, it could become a national issue if further study were to indicate that the nation produces less innovation by locating many of its major research universities in smaller cities, geographically removed from concentrations of key industries (Krugman, 1991). Another way to ask the question is: Would MIT have had a smaller effect on innovation and created fewer new companies if it were located in Pittsfield rather than Boston? Policies to address the concern about U.S. industry's

---

[13] In contrast with our results, Carlton (1979) found that the effect of engineers on firm openings was positive and significant. One explanation for this difference might be that his model did not include university research. Our results with regard to energy prices, wages, and taxes were similar to Carlton's findings.

[14] This result is unchanged if the percent scientists and engineers is replaced with the total number of scientists and engineers.

[15] The firm startups in the nineteen 4-digit industry categories represent roughly 21% of the total startups in the 4-digit industries available for testing.

failure to commercialize the nation's research requires more knowledge about the role geographic proximity plays in fostering innovation.

REFERENCES

Bania, Neil, Lindsay N. Calkins, and Douglas R. Dalenberg, "The Effects of Regional Science and Technology Policy on the Geographic Distribution of Industrial R & D Laboratories," *Journal of Regional Science* 32 (May 1992), 209–228.

Bank of Boston, *MIT: Growing Business for the Future* (Boston: Economics Department, Bank of Boston, 1989).

Bartel, Ann, and Frank Lichtenberg, "The Comparative Advantage of Educated Workers in Implementing New Technology," this REVIEW 69 (Feb. 1986), 1–11.

Carlton, Dennis, "The Location and Employment Choices of New Firms: An Econometric Model with Discrete and Continuous Endogenous Variables," this REVIEW 65 (Aug. 1983), 440–449.

_____, "Why New Firms Locate Where They Do: An Econometric Model," in William Wheaton (ed.), *Interregional Movement and Regional Growth* (Washington, D.C.: Urban Institute, 1979).

Cohen, Wesley M., and Daniel A. Levinthal, "Innovation and Learning," *The Economic Journal* 99 (Sept. 1989), 569–596.

Eberts, Randall W., and Joe A. Stone, "Metropolitan Wage Differentials: Can Cleveland Still Compete?," *Federal Reserve Bank of Cleveland Economic Review* 22 (Quarter 2 1986), 2–8.

Field, Barry C., and Charles Grebenstein, "Capital-Energy Substitution in U.S. Manufacturing," this REVIEW 62 (May 1980), 207–212.

Fogarty, Michael S., and Gaspar Garofalo, "Capital Stock Estimates for Metropolitan Areas, 1957–77," in *Proceedings of the Thirteenth Annual Pittsburgh Conference on Modeling and Simulation* (Pittsburgh: University of Pittsburgh, 1982).

Freeman, Richard B., and James L. Medoff, "New Estimates of Private Sector Unionism," *Industrial and Labor Relations Review* 32 (Jan. 1979), 143–174.

Griliches, Zvi, and Frank Lichtenberg, "R & D and Productivity Growth at the Firm Level: Is There Still a Relationship?" in Z. Griliches (ed.), *R & D Patents and Productivity* (Chicago: University of Chicago Press, 1984).

Harris, Candee S., *U.S. Establishment an Enterprise Microdata (USEEM): A Data Base Description* (Washington, D.C.: The Brookings Institution, 1983).

Henderson, Rebecca, Adam Jaffe, and Manuel Trajtenberg, "Telling Trails out of School: Geographic Localization of Knowledge Spillovers as Evidenced by Patent Citations," Working Paper (Cleveland: Center for Regional Economic Issues, Case Western Reserve University, 1991).

Jaffe, Adam B., "Technological Opportunity and Spillovers of R & D: Evidence from Firms' Patents, Profits, and Market Value," *American Economic Review* 76 (Dec. 1986), 984–1001.

_____, "Real Effects of Academic Research," *American Economic Review* 79 (Dec. 1989), 957–970.

Lund, Leonard, "Location of Corporate R & D Facilities," Conference Board Report No. 892 (New York: Conference Board, 1986).

Mofidi, Ala, and Joe A. Stone, "Do State and Local Taxes Affect Economic Growth?" this REVIEW 72 (Nov. 1990), 686–691.

National Academy of Sciences, *New Alliances and Partnerships in American Science and Engineering* (Washington, D.C.: National Academy Press, 1986).

Nelson, Richard, "Institutions Supporting Technical Advance in Industry," *American Economic Review* 76 (May 1986), 186–189.

Wheaton, William, "Interstate Differences in the Level of Business Taxation," *National Tax Journal* 36 (Mar. 1983), 83–94.

Wozniak, Gregory D., "Human Capital, Information, and the Early Adoption of New Technology," *Journal of Human Resources* 22 (Winter 1987), 101–112.

APPENDIX

SIC Code	Description
SIC3621	Motors and Generators
SIC3622	Industrial Controls
SIC3623	Welding Apparatus, Electric
SIC3624	Carbon and Graphite Products
SIC3629	Electrical Industrial Apparatus
SIC3641	Electric Lamp Bulbs and Tubes
SIC3651	Household Audio and Video Equipment
SIC3652	Phonograph Records and Prerecorded Audio Tapes
SIC3661	Telephone and Telegraph Apparatus
SIC3662	Radio and TV Communications Equipment
SIC3671	Electron Tubes, Receiving Type
SIC3672	Cathode Ray Television Picture Tubes
SIC3673	Electron Tubes, Transmitting
SIC3674	Semiconductors and Related Devices
SIC3675	Electronic Capacitors
SIC3677	Electronic Coils, Transformers, and Other Inductors
SIC3678	Electronic Connectors
SIC3679	Electronic Components
SIC3693	X-ray Apparatus and Tubes
SIC3811	Engineering and Scientific Industries
SIC3823	Industrial Instruments for Measurement, Display, and Control
SIC3825	Instruments for Measuring and Testing of Electricity
SIC3842	Orthopedic, Prosthetic, and Surgical Appliances and Supplies
SIC3861	Photographic Equipment and Supplies

[20]

Organizational Endowments and the Performance of University Start-ups

Scott Shane • Toby Stuart

R. H. Smith School of Business, University of Maryland, College Park, Maryland 20742
Graduate School of Business, University of Chicago, 1101 East 58th Street, Chicago, Illinois 60637
sshane@rhsmith.umd.edu • toby.stuart@gsb.uchicago.edu

The question of how initial resource endowments—the stocks of resources that entrepreneurs contribute to their new ventures at the time of founding—affect organizational life chances is one of significant interest in organizational ecology, evolutionary theory, and entrepreneurship research. Using data on the life histories of all 134 firms founded to exploit MIT-assigned inventions during the 1980–1996 period, the study analyzes how resource endowments affect the likelihood of three critical outcomes: that new ventures attract venture capital financing, experience initial public offerings, and fail. Our analysis focuses on the role of founders' social capital as a determinant of these outcomes. Event history analyses show that new ventures with founders having direct and indirect relationships with venture investors are most likely to receive venture funding and are less likely to fail. In turn, receiving venture funding is the single most important determinant of the likelihood of IPO. We conclude that the social capital of company founders represents an important endowment for early-stage organizations.
(*Entrepreneurship; Social Capital; Financing*)

Introduction

At inception, founders endow the organizations they create with certain resources. In this article, we ask: How do initial resource endowments affect the performance of new ventures? A number of organizational theorists have posited that initial resource stocks may have enduring effects on organizational performance (Stinchcombe 1965, Baron et al. 1996, Hannan 1998), perhaps evincing a positive feedback dynamic in the resource accumulation process in which initial advantages amplify over time. Other researchers have challenged this view, asserting that resource endowments—and the advantages they engender—often dissipate quickly (Bruderl and Schussler 1990, Fichman and Levinthal 1991).

The debate about the influence of initial resource endowments on organizational life chances has continued because systematic evidence on the subject has been elusive. One reason for this is the difficulty

researchers have encountered in obtaining the information needed to explore endowment effects. The most significant obstacle has been that the study of initial endowments cannot proceed without detailed information on the earliest days of an organization's existence. Unfortunately, new organizations often fail before they are recognized in industry directories and by the popular press, which means that there are few data sets describing initial resource endowments in nonselected samples. As a result, inferences regarding the effects of endowments on organizational performance have, for the most part, been drawn from analyses of indirect relationships, such as the pattern of age dependence apparent in studies of organizational failure rates.

In this article, we analyze a unique data archive describing the life histories of 134 high technology firms founded to exploit MIT-assigned inventions during the period from 1980 to 1996. The start-ups in

MANAGEMENT SCIENCE © 2002 INFORMS
Vol. 48, No. 1, January 2002 pp. 154–170

0025-1909/02/4801/0154$5.00
1526-5501 electronic ISSN

this population were founded specifically to commercialize technologies licensed from MIT. In addition to documenting the date of founding in a complete and nonselected organizational population, these data also include archival records and in-depth interviews with company founders. The data describe (i) whether company founders had (pre-existing) social relations with venture investors at the time they launched the new company, (ii) the prior industry and start-up experience of company founders, (iii) the technological assets of the company at founding, and (iv) characteristics of the industries that the new ventures entered. We also collected event histories describing the performance milestones achieved by each firm. Therefore, our analyses enable comparisons of the relative influences of social capital, human capital, technological resources, and market conditions at founding on the subsequent performance of new technology firms.

Because extant studies have established that organizational outcomes are affected by new ventures' human capital endowments (Bruderl et al. 1992), their stocks of technical assets (Stuart et al. 1999), and the environmental and market conditions at the time of founding (Hannan and Carroll 1992), we concentrate on the relationships between founders' social capital at the time of founding and later-life outcomes. An additional reason for this focus is that the organization building process is hampered by widespread information problems that make it likely that founders' social capital influences new venture performance, particularly in the case of technology-based ventures. Therefore, we concentrate the theoretical development on the social capital argument, but our analytical strategy will treat the relative influence of the endowments of these four categories of resources on organizational outcomes as an empirical question to be unraveled in the analysis. Moreover, we perceive the contribution of this article to lie in the evidence linking different types of resource endowments to organizations' critical, early-stage performance milestones.

Founders' Social Capital and Resource Acquisition

Creating new organizations involves allocating resources to novel uses. But because the entrepreneurs who discover opportunities for new ventures often do not control the resources needed to pursue them, they must enlist the patronage of outside investors. The founders of early-stage ventures vary in their ability to obtain the support of resource holders, and this variance likely has a salient effect on venture performance (Aldrich and Zimmer 1986, Stuart et al. 1999, Stuart 2000). The conjecture we explore here is that entrepreneurs' social capital contributes to new venture performance, in large part because of its effect on founders' ability to secure external financing to pursue the opportunities they discover.

A resource holder's decision to support an entrepreneurial enterprise depends on his or her appraisal of the attractiveness of the opportunity identified by an entrepreneur.[1] However, researchers in the areas of finance, economic sociology, transaction costs economics, and entrepreneurship have observed that a set of uncertainties and information asymmetries encumber the evaluation of new ventures and complicate the process of contracting between resource holders and new ventures. The contention that we make is that the presence of these factors elevates the significance of the social capital of the founding team as a basis for making investment decisions.

Uncertainty about the quality of start-ups in part arises from the simple fact that young companies have very short performance track records, and thus do not lend observable histories to the task of evaluating their quality. Stated differently, the information that resource providers would ideally use to assess a venture's quality is not observable until after the entrepreneur has obtained resources, established a

---

[1] Throughout the article, we will use the terms "resource holder" and "investor" as synonyms. Although we develop the social capital argument specifically in terms of the decision of the suppliers of financing to invest in an early-stage venture, the argument is qualitatively generalizable to the case of a potential supplier's or customer's decision to transact with a new organization or a potential employee to work for a particular startup.

SHANE AND STUART
Organizational Endowments and the Performance of University Start-ups

functioning organization, and started down the path of developing products (Arrow 1974).

Uncertainty about the future prospects of young organizations is likely to be particularly high among those enterprises established to commercialize new technologies (Aldrich and Fiol 1994). Technology companies may require large resource commitments to conduct exploratory development projects, and hoped-for revenues and profits often lie far in the future. Moreover, new technology is intrinsically unpredictable. Emerging markets progress along unforeseeable paths, incompatible technologies compete for market acceptance, and technical roadblocks routinely derail once promising development projects (Tushman and Rosenkopf 1992). For these reasons, a lengthy time period and large resource outlays may stand between an early-stage technology company and the resolution of the uncertainty about its long-term viability. Thus, the quality of embryonic technology companies, the magnitude of the underlying market opportunities that venture founders wish to exploit, and the level and duration of the investment required to nurture early-stage companies elude precise delineation in ex ante evaluations.

Information asymmetries also obscure evaluations of new ventures. Relative to outside evaluators, entrepreneurs are privy to more information about the prospects of their ventures and the abilities and level of commitment of the founding team. This increases the risk borne by investors in new companies because entrepreneurs may exploit their superior knowledge of their company's position to gain concessions from investors, for example, by extracting a higher valuation or larger resource commitment than a fully (or more) informed investor would provide. Like the level of uncertainty, information asymmetries may be particularly acute in the case of early-stage technology companies. In these instances, firm founders are often the leading experts in the relevant area of technology, and therefore are the best informed about the feasibility of a proposed technology.

Prior research identifies two types of responses from resource holders when the decision to invest is complicated by the presence of uncertainty and information imbalances. The economics literature emphasizes the design of contracts—particularly the allocation of control rights between trading partners—that minimize agents' capacities to behave opportunistically vis-à-vis their transaction partners when one party in a deal has more information than the other and unforeseeable contingencies obfuscate the future terms of the relationship (Gompers and Lerner 1999, Kaplan and Stromberg 1999).[2]

However, contractual controls rarely succeed at fully eliminating the entrepreneur's ability or incentive to take actions that conflict with the interests of outside investors (Venkataraman 1997, Arrow 1974). Moreover, when there is high uncertainty about how an early-stage business might evolve, it is very difficult to design contracts that attend to all possible, future contingencies that might impact the terms of the relationship between entrepreneurs and their investors. As a result, the agreements between entrepreneurs and investors are often subject to ex-post opportunism (Williamson 1975).

Whereas the economics literature has focused on how formal contracts and the allocation of control rights between the parties in an exchange can minimize transactional risks under conditions of uncertainty and information asymmetry, the sociological literature on the subject has emphasized the implications of these conditions for the selection of exchange partners. Sociologists observe that when the circumstances surrounding a transaction preclude an actor from entering a relationship without the risk that his partner will behave opportunistically, he often chooses to conduct business only with exchange partners he knows (Macaulay 1963, Granovetter 1985, Bradach and Eccles 1989, Coleman 1990, Stuart and Robinson 2000).

The sociological argument distills to the contention that actors rely on social networks to select transaction partners who they believe will behave reliably, even when a partner is not contractually obligated to do so. In general, networks serve two functions

---

[2] Types of opportunistic behavior that investors may be exposed to include failure on the part of entrepreneurs to exert promised effort to develop a new company, entrepreneurs undertaking actions that yield private gains at the company's expense, and company founders holding up investors by threatening to depart.

that facilitate, respectively, the enforcement of implicit contracts and the selection of reliable partners. First, the network is a mechanism for sanctioning actors who behave opportunistically; second, it delineates the pathways through which information is relayed about its members. Because information about actors' conduct in previous transactions diffuses through the connections in a network, actors will know of the past behavior of the other members of the network within their information spheres, and they will have the power to sanction their transaction partners by disseminating negative information about them in the event of malfeasant behavior (Granovetter 1985, Raub and Weesie 1990).

These functions of the network may influence the resource holder's decision to support the entrepreneur. When an investor evaluates a new venture, she produces estimates of the expected value of the investment under different scenarios. Because opportunistic behavior on the part of the entrepreneur reduces the expected payoff from the investment, investors will be less likely to finance projects in which they question the reliability of the entrepreneur. Ceteris paribus, as the probability that an exchange partner will behave opportunistically declines, the expected value of transacting with that partner increases.

One of the more robust findings in the literature on intercorporate and interpersonal relations is that actors with established trading histories are likely to trust one another. This is because past partners are of known character, and the counterparties in an ongoing relationship have an incentive to behave with good faith to preserve the health of the relationship for future exchanges. Further, a history of past exchanges often produces feelings of obligation between exchange partners, in part because the relationship may double as a friendship. We therefore posit, *new ventures with founding teams that have pre-established relationships with venture investors are more likely to acquire external funding for their ventures.*

Just as a history of direct exchange reduces the perceived threat that a partner will behave opportunistically, indirect ties between two parties may facilitate exchange by increasing the level of trust in the relationship. When ties to a mutual third party link two

actors, the third party may play the role of "intermediary in trust" (cf. Coleman 1990). In this situation, the relationship between would-be trustor and trustee is facilitated when the trusting party has confidence in the advisor's judgment, who, in turn, has confidence in the ability of the trustee.[3] In effect, the intermediary certifies the counterparties in a potential transaction by relaying subject evaluations about qualities like an actor's reliability. This process suggests that *new ventures with founding teams that have pre-established relationships with third parties who are connected to venture investors are more likely to acquire external funding for their ventures.*

There is one additional factor that may reinforce the role of direct and indirect ties in increasing the likelihood of an investment: Ties between investors and entrepreneurs may also affect investors' assessments of the quality of the entrepreneur's project when uncertainty is high (e.g., when the new venture aims to develop an unproven technology). By definition, uncertainty increases the problem of identifying quality. As the task of assessing competence becomes increasingly imprecise, evaluators' appraisals of quality are opened to the influence of indirect signals, such as the social status of the actors under scrutiny and the prestige of their affiliates (Podolny 1994, Stuart et al. 1999). To the extent that the social structural proximity of other actors becomes a basis for making quality inferences, the estimates of the potential value of an investment opportunity, in addition to expectations of the trustworthiness of entrepreneurs who propose the project, are also positively influenced when a potential investor and entrepreneur are near in social space. Consistent with this view, Wilson (1985) emphasizes the importance of referrals

---

[3] In this case, the advisor's incentives are linked to the credibility of his advice. If his advice proves incorrect, he loses the confidence of those he has advised, and his position as a trusted intermediary is compromised. There are a number of perspectives on the interests of the intermediary in three party systems, most of which build from Simmel's (1950) analysis of triad structures. For example, in Blau's (1964) exchange theory, advice is exchanged for deference and thus the intermediary's incentives are also linked to the accrual of status. Burt's (1992) discussion of the *tertius* role stresses that intermediaries can extract "profit" by brokering the direct relationship between two disconnected parties.

to signal quality to venture capitalists, as does a survey performed by Tyebjee and Bruno (1984).

Endowments: A Shadow Over the Future

The preceding section outlined arguments for why we expect new ventures with founders who are within the social circles of venture investors to be advantaged in the resource acquisition process. Before presenting the empirical analysis, we return briefly to the question of how long this and similar initial advantages are likely to persist. Although the notion of a "liability of adolescence," in which organizational mortality rates increase as new ventures deplete their initial resource endowments, has found some empirical substantiation in the ecology literature (Bruderl and Schussler 1990, Fichman and Levinthal 1991), others argue that early resource endowments set a new venture on the path toward the establishment of long-term, robust positions (cf. Hannan 1998).

In support of Stinchcombe's (1965) imprinting argument, a number of recent papers exploring the evolution of technology companies have produced some of the strongest evidence yet that the early decisions made by organizations persist for considerable periods of time (Sorensen and Stuart 2000, Baron et al. 2001). To the extent that endowment levels directly constrain organizational decision making, the level of initial resource endowments may position organizations on different developmental trajectories. For example, a lack of resources at founding might compel an organization to adopt a set of decision rules aimed at cost minimization, such as "buying cheap materials" or "avoiding high salary employees" (Swaminathan 1996, Burderl et al. 1992). A resource shortage may also discourage employees from investing in organization-specific skills because they are doubtful of their employer's viability and thus their ability to recoup investments in firm-specific knowledge (Swaminathan 1996). Similarly, resource-poor start-ups may have weak bargaining positions with their customers and suppliers (Stinchcombe 1965). This can be a particularly severe disadvantage in high technology industries, where a lack of resources may

force young firms to cede to alliance partners significant rights to future products and technologies in exchange for assistance in supporting a research program (cf. Lerner and Tsai 1999).

All of these factors combine to suggest that new ventures lacking initial resource endowments might develop inferior structures, internal processes, and human resources relative to their competitors, and thus may develop a reputation for low quality that can be extremely difficult to escape. We therefore believe that initial resource endowments are likely to be parlayed into sustainable advantage, and we present suggestive evidence to this effect.

Methodology

Sample and Data Sources

The data set we analyze includes the population of 134 firms founded to exploit inventions assigned to the Massachusetts Institute of Technology between 1980 and 1994.[4] Like many other research universities, the institute often takes title to commercially useful inventions that are developed by faculty, staff, or students and that emerge from work making material use of MIT resources (e.g., laboratory facilities). MIT then attempts to commercialize some of these discoveries. The study population was identified from the records of the MIT Technology Licensing Office (TLO), to which we were permitted access to perform this analysis. The TLO's mission is to commercialize MIT technology. Although many of the enterprises licensing MIT's intellectual property are established companies, a subset of these licensees includes new ventures founded to develop the institute's technology. We examine these entities here.

The TLO archives describe the contracts between MIT and its licensees, characteristics of the licensed intellectual property, and start-ups' business plans. In addition, the TLO tracked the sales growth and

---

[4] This paper examines the MIT-originated start-ups from the point of incorporation forward. Shane and Khurana (2000) and Shane (2001, 2002) exploit data from the MIT TLO to explain why some patented inventions are more likely than others to be exploited by new firms. The analysis here begins where those studies end: at the point of firm formation.

financing obtained by its licensees. To supplement the TLO data, we conducted unstructured interviews with company founders and consulted online databases including Lexis/Nexis, Diolog Business Connection, and ABI Inform. These sources were used to verify information and fill in gaps in the TLO records. Finally, we obtained additional information on the venture capital financing received by the TLO firms from the Venture Economics and Venture One databases. All variables were coded from these data sources. The objective of the data collection effort was to create detailed profiles of all firms at the time of founding, along with a (retrospective) life history for each firm in the data set.

Although MIT-based start ups clearly do not constitute a representative sample of all technology-based companies, these data have two important advantages relative to other samples of new ventures. The most important feature of these data is that the TLO has a record of *every* company established to commercialize MIT's intellectual property since 1980. As a result, the TLO data are free from survivor bias—a sample selection problem that is endemic to studies of early-stage companies. Sample selection bias is rampant in research on new ventures because archival data sources rarely record the existence of companies that fail at a very young age. In fact, the data we utilize evince the general difficulty of obtaining a nonselected sample of startup companies: A number of the firms in the TLO sample fail before they are acknowledged in any publicly available database. Although we possess information on these organizations from the TLO archives and interviews with company principals, it would not have been possible to learn about them from secondary sources. Moreover, interviews with founders and TLO staff indicated that many of these failures occurred because companies were unable to obtain financing from external sources, thus demonstrating the limitations of explaining how initial endowments affect new venture performance in samples that exclude early failures.[5]

[5] Of course, there is still a selection process that operates on these data: The TLO, MIT inventors, and entrepreneurs all influence which MIT technologies will be licensed to start-up companies. All new organizations emerge from an opportunity identification

A second advantage of the TLO data is that there are no left censored firm histories (i.e., all firms in the sample are observed from the time of incorporation until a performance outcome is recorded, or until the observation is right censored at the end of calendar 1996). Because we employ event history methods to analyze firm performance, we require a sample without left censored observations to obtain reliable parameter estimates.

Method

The events we model include receiving venture capital funding, IPO, and failure.[6] As a general rule, the most desirable type of liquidity event (from the perspective of the owners of the firm) is an initial sale of securities on the public equity markets. From the perspective of company founders and owners, selling equity to the public often generates much-needed capital and the opportunity for equity holders to exchange stock for cash. We analyze the three organizational transitions (financing, IPO, and failure) in terms of the instantaneous transition rate, r, defined as

$$r_k(t) = \lim_{\Delta_t \downarrow 0} \frac{\Pr(t \leq T < (t + \Delta t), D = k \mid T \geq t)}{\Delta t},$$

where k refers to one of three mutually exclusive destinations in D (the performance events). The variable T measures the time spent at risk of making one of these possible transitions, and the probability Pr refers to the likelihood of experiencing one of these transitions during the small interval from t to $(t + \Delta t)$, conditional on a start up being at risk of making a

process that precedes the incorporation of the firm, but these data are once again unique in allowing this issue to be examined empirically (see Shane and Khurana 2000, Shane 2001, 2002).

[6] Although we possess data on angel financings, the time-to-VC-funding regressions are limited to the first occurrence of financing from a VC firm. Because the sample consists entirely of early-stage technology companies, traditional performance metrics such as accounting-based indicators of profitability are inappropriate for these data. For example, many of the firms in the sample are in the biotechnology industry, and these organizations can have highly successful IPOs even with no revenues from the sale of internally developed products. For this reason, we analyze performance in terms of the rate of occurrence of a set of important milestones for new ventures.

transition as of time t (Tuma and Hannan 1984). The waiting time clock in the firm event histories turns on at the time of incorporation.

The transition to IPO and failure are treated as "competing risks" and are modeled using the approach discussed in Kalbfleisch and Prentice (1980). These events are terminal in the sense that the occurrence of either of them obviates the possibility that the other transition will take place within our observation window, so an organization exits the risk set after experiencing either event.[7] The hazard of receiving venture financing is estimated in a separate set of regressions because we model only the first occurrence of this event. Although VC funding could be treated as a repeatable event and included as a competing risk in the models of the other two performance-related transitions, our interest in how initial conditions affect performance outcomes makes the first round of venture financing the milestone of greatest significance to us.[8] In both the time-to-VC funding and the IPO/ failure rate models, we create

annual spells to update the values of the time changing covariates. Each spell ends in censoring unless an event occurs within the focal firm-year observation.

We specify each rate as varying according to the piecewise-exponential functional form

$$r_k(t) = \exp[\gamma_p + B'X_t],$$

where γ_p includes three duration-period effects, X_t contains independent variables (some of which vary over time), and B are the parameters to be estimated. We adopt the piecewise specification of duration dependence because it permits the rate to vary flexibly with duration (in this case, firm age) without requiring strong parametric assumptions. The age pieces we include are less than four years old, four to seven years old, and greater than seven years old; the baseline rate is assumed to be constant within each period, but is unconstrained across periods. The transition rate models were estimated using TDA (Blossfeld and Rohwer 1995).

Covariates

Endowments-Social Capital. Our first prediction is that company founders with pre-established ties to angel investors or venture capitalists will be more likely to obtain external funding for their fledgling companies and also are more likely to achieve an IPO. We measure the presence of a direct tie as a dummy variable denoting that at least one member of the founding team had a direct business or social relationship with a venture investor prior to the founding of the firm.[9] To ensure against the risk that this variable may be miscoded in the affirmative for firms that

---

[7] Twenty-two firms in the sample were acquired. In the hazard rate models, we handle acquisition by censoring the event histories of acquired companies at the time of the deal. In unreported regressions, we have estimated the rate of acquisition as an additional competing risk, but chose not to report the acquisition models both to conserve space and because the meaning of an acquisition varies across events. This variance occurs because some of the firms in the sample were acquired at relatively high valuations, whereas others were acquired at low valuations or when a venture was on the verge of liquidation. The former type of acquisition was in all likelihood construed by company principals as a successful exit, whereas the latter type of acquisition would be viewed as a failure. Unlike some researchers, we opted to not categorize acquisitions as "successful" or "unsuccessful" and include the successful acquisitions with IPOs and unsuccessful acquisitions with firm failures. That approach would introduce subjectivity into our measurement of the dependent variable.

[8] The reason for this is that venture capitalists typically fund their portfolio companies in a series of financing rounds (Lerner 1994). Thus, a new venture must receive a first round of funding to be eligible for a second round, and market conditions and the development of the firm between rounds should be the predominant determinants of second- and later-stage financing rounds. This illustrates the path dependencies in the VC funding process, but also suggests that initial conditions may not play a substantial role in later-stage funding decisions net of their effect on the occurrence of the first financing round.

[9] This variable indicates simply whether a relationship between a founder and an investor predated the founding of a company; it does not necessarily indicate a pre-established tie to the specific investor(s) who funded a focal venture (if the company did receive funding at some point in the future). Obviously, coding the variable as 1 if a founder had a tie with the investor that ultimately funded the company would be tantamount to using the dependent variable (in the case of funding) to predict itself (i.e., the direct tie variable would be 1 for all companies that received funding, and 0 for all other firms). For more direct evidence of the effect of a pre-established relationship between an entrepreneur and an investor on the likelihood that a VC funds a new venture, see Shane and Cable (1998) and Sorenson and Stuart (2001).

SHANE AND STUART
Organizational Endowments and the Performance of University Start-ups

did receive venture funding but may not have had a relationship with investors that predated the time of funding, we coded direct ties as a 1 only when another data source confirmed that the relationship existed prior to the time of firm founding.[10]

The second contention we make is that founders with ties to third parties who in turn have relationships with angels or venture capitalists are more likely to obtain external funding for their companies and also are more likely to achieve positive performance milestones.[11] We measure indirect ties as a dummy variable denoting whether at least one member of the founding team had a business or social tie to a third party who had a direct tie with a venture capitalist or angel investor prior to the founding of the firm. As in the case of direct ties, we required documentation from at least two information sources to code this variable in the affirmative.

Endowments-Human Capital. New ventures with founders that have previous experience in the industry of the start-up are likely to perform well relative to companies with management teams that lack industry familiarity. Founders with industry experience presumably have knowledge of effective strategies and customer preferences, as well as valuable contacts with customers, suppliers, and other industry participants (Bruderl et al. 1992, Gimeno et al.

1997). We therefore create a dummy variable, industry experience, which is coded 1 if at least one member of the founding team had previous experience in the new firm's industry.

Companies founded by individuals with previous start up experience also may have an advantage relative to organizations created by first-time entrepreneurs. Start-up experience enhances entrepreneurs' understanding of how to staff and lead early-stage organizations, to develop new products, and to manage relationships with investors, employees, suppliers, and customers (Bruderl et al. 1992). We construct a dummy variable, start-up experience, which is coded 1 if at least one member of the founding team had previously launched a new company.[12]

Endowments-Technical Assets. All firms in our sample were established to commercialize MIT inventions, but they vary in the magnitude and quality of their technical endowments. The strength of a new firm's intellectual property position is thought to be an important determinant of its success, particularly because new firms, by definition, do not have complementary assets in place (Merges and Nelson 1990, Teece 1986). We include a number of measures of the technological strength and quality of the firms in the sample *at the time of founding*. First, we define a variable, patent stock, to designate the number of MIT patents that were licensed to the new venture at founding (many of the firms in the sample license more than one MIT-assigned patent). We also coded a second variable, exclusive license, which indicates whether the new venture has an exclusive right to use MIT technology in a particular field of use.[13]

---

[10] In the modal case, the two information sources were interviews with a company founder and the TLO archives. For example, the direct tie variable would be coded 1 when (i) a company founder stated that he had a pre-existing professional relationship with a venture capitalist, and (ii) the TLO record for the founder's company contained a memo from a licensing officer indicating that the firm would target a particular venture capitalist for funding because one of the founders had previously conducted technical due diligence work for that venture capitalist.

[11] Our analysis excludes indirect ties to investors created by the TLO officers. Shane and Cable (1998) report that university technology licensing officers often introduce entrepreneurs to venture investors. Although this process operates in the setting we examine, we cannot explore it with our data because this source of referrals is likely invariant across the firms in the sample. Measuring the effect of variation in ties between licensing officers would be problematic because MIT's licensing officers specialize by technology and industry. As a result, variation in social ties across licensing officers would be confounded with differences across industries and technologies.

---

[12] In unreported models, we included continuous measures of founders' human capital, including the total number of start ups previously begun by all members of the founding team and the total number of years of industry experience possessed by all founders. In both cases, the model fit was improved when we included the dichotomous human capital proxies.

[13] In addition to patent stock and exclusive license, we included in unreported regressions the following proxies for the technological endowments of the firms in the sample: the total number of international patent classes in which a new venture's patents were listed, the total number of claims made by all patents licensed to a start up, the total number of inventors associated with all licensed

We also include a variable that measures the highest rank obtained by any of the MIT inventors of the technology licensed by the new venture. This variable represents the prestige of the scientists on whose knowledge the venture is based. The right to use an invention often does not imply access to all of the information necessary to commercialize it, nor does it convey the knowledge necessary to develop subsequent (follow-on) technologies. In many instances, the new ventures in our sample negotiate access to the MIT personnel who developed the licensed technology (either on a full-time or consulting basis). We suspect that potential investors may favor firms with access to experienced and high status investors because having well-known affiliates is often considered a signal of new venture quality (cf. Stuart et al. 1999). As a proxy for the status and depth of knowledge of the MIT inventors who developed a licensed technology, we measure for each firm the highest university rank achieved by any member of the team of inventors that created the technology licensed by the firm. We coded this variable as follows: student $= 0$, research associate $= 1$, assistant professor $= 2$, untenured associate $= 3$, tenured associate $= 4$, full professor $= 5$, department chair or research center director $= 6$, and institute professor $= 7$.[14]

Endowments-Industry Attractiveness. The new ventures in our sample are in a variety of industries, which differ significantly in terms of the competitive environment and growth prospects they present. We include two variables reflecting industry conditions at the time of founding (and an additional set of time-changing covariates, which we discuss below, that capture changes in industry circumstances). First,

we include the size of the industry each organization enters measured in the year that the new venture is founded. The size measure, obtained from the Census of Manufacturers, is the total value of shipments in the industry. Large industries may offer superior growth chances to new ventures, because start ups in large industries may grow without securing a large market share.

The strength of intellectual property protection afforded by patents varies greatly by industry. This variance will influence new firms' abilities to protect their technology from imitators, and thus to attract investments and grow. To capture this heterogeneity, we include the Levin et al. (1987) measure of patent effectiveness, which is obtained from a survey of R&D managers and gauges the extent to which patents are perceived to be successful at protecting intellectual property.

Control Variables—Industry Level. Technology-intensive industries are notoriously cyclic, bouncing between "hot" and "cold" periods (Ritter 1984). The cycles in high technology industries largely reflect shifts in the openness and enthusiasm of the public equity markets for new security issues in an industry, and almost surely affect the general munificence of the resource environment faced by high technology startups. In hot periods, investment capital is often (relatively) plentiful; in cold periods, it may be very scarce. We therefore include two time-changing measures of the resource richness of the industry occupied by each venture in the sample. The first variable, the industry IPO rate, is the percentage of all VC-backed firms in an industry-year that have IPOs in the year (i.e., the number of private, venture-backed companies that have IPOs in an industry year, divided by the total number of VC-backed firms at risk of an IPO in the industry year; this variable was coded from the full Venture Economics database). In addition to the IPO rate, we also include for each start up-year observation a simple count of the number of venture-backed firms that had IPOs in the start up's industry in the focal year. We chose to include the count and the rate because, while the rate better reflects actual market conditions, the IPO count

---

patents, and a variety of citation-based indicators of the importance and radicalness of the patents licensed to each new venture. In the innovation literature, all of these variables have been proposed as measures of the value of patents, but none had significant effects in any of the models we estimated. For the sake of parsimony, we exclude these measures from the reported regressions.

[14] Highest inventor rank could also be construed as a measure of a firm's human and social capital endowment. Presumably, inventor rank and technical competence are positively correlated, as is rank and the extensiveness of an individual's contact network.

is more readily observable and thus may be a better measure of the salience of successful outcomes for early-stage companies in an industry.

Net of the industry attractiveness endowment variables and the time-changing measures of the industry-specific state of the equity markets, we found few industry effects and thus report models without industry dummies. However, we did include an indicator for the semiconductor industry in the VC funding regressions because the semiconductor firms in the sample has a very high rate of receiving venture funding. By including this dummy variable, we reduce the likelihood that a time-invariant industry effect is misattributed to another (correlated) covariate.

Control Variables—Firm Level. Although our primary focus is on how initial conditions affect new venture performance, we report some regressions accounting for firms' development over time. In the models of IPO and failure, we include a number of variables that reflect the financial status of each firm. First, we include the annually updated, cumulative amount of venture financing received, reflecting our expectation that firms with more funding are able to quickly progress through the development process and are more likely to IPO. In addition to VC funding, some of the firms in our sample obtained funding from two other sources: Small Business Investment Research (SBIR) grants and MIT. Thus, we include for each firm an annually updated, cumulative total of the amount of SBIR funds received. We indicate an investment from MIT with a dummy variable denoting the presence of equity funding from the institute. Finally, we include the cumulative sales generated by each new venture, which is again updated on an annual basis. The sales variable is a proxy for the extent to which a venture has progressed through the product development cycle.

Results

Table 1 reports results from the piecewise constant models of the hazards of IPO and failure. The first model in the table serves as a baseline for statistical tests and includes only the age periods for the IPO

and failure models. The pattern of duration dependence varies somewhat across the two outcomes. In the IPO model, it is highest during the middle age period (four to seven years); in the mortality analysis, the baseline failure rate increases in each successive period. The pattern of duration dependence in the failure rate may be consistent with that of a liability of adolescence, in which the rate initially rises and later declines, but this would depend on a subsequent decline in the failure rate beyond the time period covered by these data.

Model 2 in the table adds the technology endowment variables. The number of patents licensed, the highest rank of the MIT inventor associated with the licensed intellectual property, and whether or not the license was exclusive all have positive coefficients in the IPO regressions, and both the patents stock and inventor rank variables are statistically significant. In the failure rate model, both the patent stock and inventor rank variables significantly reduce the hazard of mortality. On balance, the regressions suggest that firms with large initial technology endowments are more likely to IPO and less likely to fail at an early age.

The third model in the tables reports the effects of the human capital endowment proxies. The signs of these variables are consistent with expectations: Positive in the time-to-IPO model and negative in the mortality analysis, but only the industry experience variable in the IPO regression approaches statistical significance.

Model 4 reports the effects of industry characteristics on the two performance measures. The Table 1 coefficients show that startups in large industries (recall that industry size is measured in the year of founding and is not updated over time) and those in industries with stronger patent protection are more likely to IPO. Although industry size does not affect the likelihood of failure, the high technology start ups in the sample in industries with effective patent protection are less likely to fail.

The two social capital variables are displayed in Column 5 of Table 1. Both the measures of direct and indirect ties to investors have statistically significant, economically meaningful, negative effects on the probability of failure. For example, if a member of a

SHANE AND STUART
Organizational Endowments and the Performance of University Start-ups

Table 1 Piecewise Constant Models of the Hazard of IPO and Mortality

Variable	Model 1		Model 2		Model 3		Model 4		Model 5		Model 6		Model 7	
	IPO	Failure	IPO	Failure	IPO	Failure	IPO	Failure	IPO	Failure	IPO	Failure	IPO	Failure
Age < 4 year	−3.231** (12.92)	−3.295** (12.76)	−5.570** (5.04)	−1.935* (4.55)	−3.613** (9.77)	−3.003** (10.17)	−6.014** (5.17)	−0.911 (0.79)	−3.263** (7.78)	−2.443** (7.86)	−7.886** (4.77)	0.040 (0.03)	−7.280** (3.18)	−0.32 (0.19)
Age 4–7 years	−3.100** (6.93)	−2.917** (7.14)	−5.482** (4.74)	−1.457* (2.78)	−3.467** (6.66)	−2.620** (6.03)	−5.784** (4.82)	−0.507 (0.42)	−3.101** (5.61)	−2.057** (4.59)	−7.549** (4.66)	0.655 (0.54)	−7.618** (3.34)	0.586 (0.35)
Age > 7 years	−3.423** (5.92)	−2.730** (6.68)	−5.696** (4.80)	−1.089* (1.85)	−3.670** (5.83)	−2.436** (5.46)	−6.019** (4.93)	−0.374 (0.31)	−3.449** (4.92)	−1.518** (2.93)	−7.379** (4.59)	1.277 (1.01)	−7.160** (3.12)	1.701 (0.95)
Technology endowment														
Patent stock @ founding			0.045* (1.93)	−0.119* (1.70)							0.044* (1.66)	−0.099 (1.42)	0.047 (1.37)	−0.143* (1.72)
Highest rank of MIT inventor			0.204* (1.70)	−0.253** (2.82)							0.199 (1.51)	−0.210* (2.25)	0.087 (0.63)	−0.153 (1.53)
Exclusive license dummy			1.495 (1.43)	−0.450 (1.05)							1.205 (1.08)	0.203 (0.36)	0.898 (0.75)	0.180 (0.26)
Human capital endowment														
Founder has industry experience					0.713 (1.62)	−0.500 (1.09)					0.921* (1.92)	−0.292 (0.61)	1.127* (1.95)	−0.155 (0.28)
Founder has startup experience					0.021 (0.04)	−0.420 (0.91)					−0.180 (0.38)	−0.001 (0.00)	0.105 (0.19)	−0.121 (0.20)
Initial industry conditions														
Industry size @ founding							0.001** (3.20)	−0.000 (0.16)			0.001** (3.30)	0.000 (0.00)	0.001** (2.31)	0.000 (0.35)
Patent effectiveness							0.696** (2.47)	−0.688** (2.04)			0.569* (1.79)	−0.526 (1.41)	0.445 (0.81)	−0.372 (0.73)
Social capital endowment														
Direct tie to investor									−0.321 (0.70)	−1.082** (2.24)	−0.628 (1.17)	−0.861* (1.72)	−0.256 (0.41)	−0.847 (1.62)
Indirect tie to investor									0.205 (0.46)	−1.247** (2.98)	−0.079 (0.15)	−1.127* (2.43)	−0.861 (1.36)	−1.326** (2.63)
IPO rate in industry-year													−0.055 (0.15)	−0.227 (0.65)
IPO count in industry-year													0.002 (0.47)	−0.002 (0.65)
Cumulative VC funds raised													0.010* (5.18)	−0.016 (1.24)
MIT invested dummy													0.51 (0.98)	1.558** (2.86)
Cumulative SBIR funding													0.000 (0.64)	−0.000 (0.80)
Log of cumulative revenues													0.006 (0.09)	−0.168 (1.60)
[3pt] Log likelihood	−211.8		−199.26		−208.78		−204.6		−205.1		−187.34		−164.88	

Note. Analysis file consists of 134 firms. 644 spells. 28 IPOs, and 34 failures. *t* statistics in parentheses. *$p < 0.10$, **$p < 0.05$ (two-sided tests).

new venture's founding team had an existing relationship with a venture investor that predated the time her firm was founded, she could anticipate an approximately 70% lower chance of failure. Although ties to venture investors appear to forestall failure, neither of the social capital variables has a significant effect on the hazard of IPO.

The sixth model in Table 1 reports regressions including all of the endowment effects together. The results in the Model 6 regressions remain virtually unchanged from earlier models. It is important that the social capital effects persist in the failure rate models even when the measures of founders' industry and start-up experience are included in the same model, because founders with past industry and start-up experience may be more likely to have relationships with venture investors. Thus, the effects of human and social capital may be confounded in regressions that do not include both sets of variables.

The fully specified model including all endowment effects and control variables is reported in Model 7 of Table 1. Among the newly added variables, the cumulative amount of venture capital funding has by far the greatest effect on the rate of IPO. The results indicate that a one standard deviation increase in the cumulative amount of VC raised multiplies the rate of IPO by a factor of two. Unreported models show that the VC effect is obtained simply by including a dummy variable denoting the presence of VC funding, and these models also show this to be the single largest determinant of IPO.[15]

The control variables generally have negligible effects in the failure rate models, with two significant exceptions. One exception is the negative coefficient on the log of cumulative firm revenues, indicating that firms that have developed and sold products are less likely to fail. On the other hand, the MIT invested dummy variable is positive and significant. One possible explanation for this is that MIT often exchanges

an equity position in a start-up for the up-front licensing fee it normally charges licensees. It may be that founders who capitalize patent costs by granting an equity stake in their companies to the Institute are less willing or able to bear the costs associated with developing their ventures; stated differently, the MIT invested dummy may increase the hazard of mortality because it is correlated with the scarcity of resources at the new venture.

The endowment effects in the full models are fairly consistent with the previous specifications and hold up surprisingly well. Recall that all of the endowment effects are measured at organizational inception and the covariates are not updated over time. It is therefore notable that many of the endowment effects continue to have explanatory power in the full model, despite being causal in intermediate outcomes such as the amount of funding and revenues obtained by the firms in the sample, which are accounted for in the full models. The patent stock, the industry experience of the founding team, and the size of the industry at founding are the three covariates that continue to have positive influences on the hazard of IPO. In the failure rate models, inventor rank and the social capital effects dominate; firms that license patents created by high status inventors and those with founders having pre-established ties to investors fail at a lower rate.

The Table 1 results suggest obtaining VC funding has a very substantial influence on the likelihood of IPO, which in turn implies that much of the variance in new venture performance is attributable to the factors that affect the likelihood of VC funding. The regressions of time-to-VC funding are presented in Table 2. The baseline model in Column 1 includes only the age pieces and a semiconductor dummy variable. As in the other regressions, we include three age (duration) periods, but because venture funding typically occurs at a much earlier organizational age than does failure or IPO, the age pieces in the VC funding models are defined over shorter intervals. The coefficients on the age pieces exhibit a consistent pattern throughout the table: The baseline rate declines sharply as organizations age. If new firms do not

---

[15] When we include VC funding as a dummy variable (coded 1 in all firm spells after an organization first receives venture capital funding) rather than as a cumulating total of the dollar amount of money raised, the coefficient on the dummy is 2.18 ($p < 0.001$). This translates to a rate multiplier of exp(2.18) or 8.8. In other words, new ventures that obtain VC funding experience a hazard of IPO that is 8.8 times greater than the other firms in the population.

SHANE AND STUART
Organizational Endowments and the Performance of University Start-ups

Table 2   Piecewise Constant Models of the Time Until Venture Capital Funding

Variable	Model 1	Model 2	Model 3	Model 4	Model 5	Model 6
Age <1 years	−1.621**	−1.911**	−2.013**	−3.981**	−2.499**	−5.204**
	(7.87)	(4.16)	(7.15)	(4.89)	(6.57)	(4.06)
Age 1–3 years	−2.401**	−2.685**	−2.753**	−4.694**	−3.254**	−5.601**
	(9.88)	(5.65)	(9.14)	(5.82)	(8.18)	(4.47)
Age >3 years	−4.241**	−4.554**	−4.476**	−6.553**	−4.476**	−6.90**
	(8.54)	(7.02)	(8.54)	(7.10)	(8.54)	(5.23)
Semiconductor dummy	1.984*	1.984*	1.853*	2.443*	1.871*	2.556*
	(3.773)	(3.19)	(3.03)	(3.85)	(3.85)	(3.46)
Technology endowment						
Patent stock		0.026				0.027
		(1.11)				(1.04)
Highest university rank of an inventor		0.038				−0.116
		(0.537)				(1.38)
Exclusive license dummy		0.068				−0.801
		(0.158)				(1.61)
Human capital endowment						
Founding team industry exp. dummy			0.979**			0.379
			(3.06)			(1.04)
Founding team startup exp. dummy			−0.337			−0.662*
			(1.01)			(1.82)
Initial industry conditions						
Size of industry, year of founding				0.001**		0.001
				(2.04)		(1.63)
Effectiveness of patents in industry				0.615**		0.572*
				(3.05)		(1.71)
Social capital endowment						
Direct tie to VC or angel investor					0.452	1.016**
					(1.56)	(2.78)
Indirect tie to VC or angel investor					1.025**	1.513**
					(2.86)	(3.67)
Control variables						
Rate of IPO in industry-year						0.264
						(1.25)
Count of IPOs in industry-year						0.005*
						(1.84)
MIT invested dummy						0.175
						(0.43)
Log of cumulative sales						0.175
						(0.43)
Cumulative SBIR funding						−0.002
						(1.46)
Log of cumulative sales						−0.135**
						(2.25)
Log likelihood	−141.18	−140.30	−136.46	−135.98	−135.64	−112.17

Note.   Analysis file consists of 134 firms and 47 funding events. *t* statistics in parentheses. *$p < 0.10$, **$p < 0.05$ (two-sided tests).

attract VC funding in the initial years after founding, they are unlikely to do so in the future.[16]

Column 2 includes the technology endowment variables, none of which has a significant effect on venture capital funding. As Model 3 shows, one of the human capital variables affects the hazard of VC funding: The rate is increased by a factor of 2.6 for new ventures with founding teams that possess prior experience in the industry of the start-up. Model 4 demonstrates that industry attributes factor into the VC funding decision. New ventures launched in large industries and those in industries that afford stronger patent protection are more likely to receive venture funding.

Model 5 reports the effects of the two social capital variables. Although the coefficient is just shy of statistical significance, the presence of a direct tie to a venture capitalist prior to firm founding has a positive influence on the rate of VC funding. The existence of an indirect tie to a venture investor prior to firm founding very sharply increases the hazard of receiving venture financing; the rate of VC funding increases by a factor of 2.8 for firms with founders that have a relationship with a third party who can refer them to a venture investor. Moreover, the social capital endowments result in a greater improvement in model fit in Table 2 than does the introduction of any of the other variables capturing differences in initial endowments.

The Column 6 regression includes all of the endowment effects together, as well as the two time-changing measures of the openness of the IPO market

---

[16] One potential problem with modeling the time-to-VC funding is that very high quality start-ups may prefer to delay venture funding because companies that are funded later often are in stronger positions when negotiating with investors. To address this issue, we ran a simple logit model of the probability of obtaining venture funding without taking into account the timing of funding. In this analysis, we excluded all companies that were founded in the last two years of the observation period and that had yet to receive venture funding (these organizations were excluded because there is some chance that they received funding after the point of right censoring). Start-ups were coded as 1 if they received venture funding prior to failing, going public, or being acquired, and 0 otherwise. The coefficients on the endowment variables in this analysis almost exactly mirrored those in Model 6 of Table 2, confirming that similar results are obtained in analyses that ignore the timing of the investment.

to new issues in the industry of each new venture. Both the IPO rate and the IPO count in an industry-year increase the hazard of VC funding. At least with regard to high technology firms striving to commercialize relatively basic technology, VCs appear to be highly sensitive to current equity market conditions when they decide how to allocate their capital to projects in different industries. Although current market conditions have a large effect on the likelihood of VC funding, the social capital variables continue to have statistically strong effects, and in fact, the net effects of the two variables are even greater in the model that controls for market conditions than they are in the paired-down specification. For the most part, the other endowment effects remain intact, with the measures of industry conditions at founding continuing to have a large impact on the rate of obtaining funding.

The final model in Table 2 includes the MIT invested dummy, the cumulative amount of SBIR funding received, and the log of cumulative revenues. The MIT dummy has no effect on the likelihood of funding, but the SBIR variable has a negative and almost significant effect. One possible justification for this is that the negative coefficient on SBIR funding is that it is capturing unobserved differences between the technologies being pursued by the firms in the sample, with SBIR grants perhaps going to more speculative technologies. Although it may seem counterintuitive, cumulative sales also has a negative effect on the hazard of VC funding. The likely explanation for this effect is that firms with substantial sales that have not yet received VC funding (and thus already exited the risk set) may not be actively looking for funding from venture capitalists because they are able to support their operations with internally generated cash flows.

Putting the results from the two tables together, the factors that increase the likelihood of an IPO also positively impact the hazard of venture funding and negatively influence the probability of firm failure. This is as we would expect; since dissolutions and IPOs are at opposite ends of the performance continuum and the aim of venture investors is to liquidate their positions in start-ups via public stock offerings, we should observe that venture investors are drawn to companies with high likelihoods of achieving public offerings. The primary exception to this pattern concerns the technology endowment variables; although these increase the propensity to IPO and reduce hazard of failure, they have no statistical effect on obtaining venture funding. Although we cannot definitively rule out the possibility that some firms with significant technology endowments simply opted not to pursue venture funding, the findings that the technology endowment has an insignificant effect on VC funding, but experienced founding teams and start-ups in more attractive industries are more likely to receive venture backing, is consistent with the common claim in the popular press and the entrepreneurship literature that VCs often place the greatest weight on the management team and the market opportunity in making investment decisions. Because evaluations of industry conditions and founders' experiences are relatively precise as compared to assessments of early stage technology, this pattern of results is perhaps unsurprising.

Discussion and Conclusion

This study has examined the influence of start-ups' initial resource endowments on the incidence of critical, early-life performance milestones. Particular emphasis was placed on how founders' social capital endowments affect the development of entrepreneurial ventures. Analyzing the population of new firms founded to exploit MIT-assigned inventions during the 1980–1996 period, we show that two measures of founders' social capital—the presence of direct and indirect ties to venture investors prior to firm founding—sharply decrease the hazard of mortality and increase the likelihood that start-ups obtain external funding. Moreover, comparing the effects of many different firm and industry characteristics, we find that the presence of venture capital funding is the single largest contributor to the likelihood that a start-up undergoes an IPO. We interpret these results to mean that social capital endowments, through their impact on the fund-raising process, have long-term, positive influences on the performance of new ventures.

One important shortcoming of the present analysis arises from collecting retrospective data. Although the TLO sample offered a unique opportunity to overcome the sample selection biases that draw into question the findings of many of the existing studies of organizational endowments (as well as the indirect evidence on the subject gleaned from analyses of age dependence in organizational populations), the fact that the measures of founders' social capital had to be collected after the time of start-up precluded precise measurement of the construct. Because we could not be certain that entrepreneurs would have accurate memories of the relationships they had during the past, we were only comfortable creating dichotomous indicators of the presence of ties to venture investors, and even then we required verification of a relationship from a second information source. Moreover, there is always potential for recall bias in retrospective data. For example, founders who did not receive venture funding may have been less likely to remember their contacts to venture investors than founders who received venture funding. This would lead to an overestimate of the actual effects of the social capital variables on the likelihood of receiving venture financing.

Our inability to specify the details of entrepreneurs' social network creates two related problems in addition to the (probably) less significant one of measurement error. First, the dichotomous tie variables offer an indirect test of the social mechanisms that we believe underlie them; namely, that trust emerges from a history of past direct and indirect relationships, and thus entrepreneur-investor dyads situated within such a network are likely to represent trusting relationships. Because the measures of entrepreneurs' social networks are so coarse, it was not possible for us to be very precise about elucidating the particular mechanisms at work. For example, do investors who are relationally proximate to entrepreneurs perceive company founders to be more competent? Do they anticipate greater transactional reliability from close contacts, and thus perceive less risk even though they have less information than do company founders? Or, are investors more confident because mutual third parties confirm their opinions about an entrepreneur? Moreover, the dichotomous tie variables obviously do not capture any dimension of relationship strength, either social structural (i.e., the level of embeddedness of the cited relationships) or affective (i.e., the strength of the bonds between entrepreneurs, referrers, and investors).

A related limitation arising from the imprecision in the measurement of entrepreneurs' social capital is unobserved heterogeneity. The binary measures of direct and third-party ties to venture investors are potentially correlated with other characteristics of founders' backgrounds, such as founding team size, start-up experience, areas of technical specialty, previous work experiences, financial status, and so on. Although we are aware of a number of the potential correlates of the social capital variables and include these in the regressions, we clearly cannot take into account all such possibilities given available information. For example, while we do measure the prior start-up and industry experience of the founding team, we cannot measure entrepreneurial talent. Not only would fine-grained measures of the quality differences between founders be costly to collect, some dimensions, like the founder's charisma, might be virtually unmeasurable. Unfortunately, if entrepreneurs who have a keen eye for indentifying new business opportunities or who are charismatic are more likely to be in contact with venture investors than entrepreneurs who lack these characteristics, the social capital effects may be biased upwards because they correlate with entrepreneurial talent. As the delineation of founders' network position becomes more exact, however, the likelihood of correlation with unobserved factors diminishes, as does the possibility of more precisely distinguishing between potential mechanisms. Thus, more detailed network measures permit more convincing empirical demonstrations, and we therefore consider the results of the present to be suggestive rather than conclusive.

We do, though, view the results as a step in the direction of developing the literature on the social context of entrepreneurial finance. While there is a large literature in entrepreneurial finance addressing the information and agency problems in financial contracting, explicit contracts often cannot completely redress possible incentive problems and, moreover, meticulous financial contracts have only been used for the last half century and only in developed economies. Furthermore, although elaborate contracts are now used regularly in venture capital, they are less frequently employed in angel finance. For these reasons, we believe that network-based theories have much to contribute to our understanding of entrepreneurial finance (cf. Shane and Cable 1998, Sorenson and Stuart 2001).

Acknowledgments

We would like to thank Don Kaiser, Lita Nelsen, and Lori Pressman at the MIT Technology Licensing Office (TLO) for access to the data on MIT patents and for answering many questions about the data and TLO policies and procedures. We would also like to thank David Hsu for extensive comments on an earlier draft of this paper. An earlier version of this paper was presented at the Georgia Tech-Management Conference on University Entrepreneurship and Technology Transfer, December 7–9, 2000. Alvin Klevorick and Richard Nelson generously provided the Yale data on innovation. Stuart would like to thank the University of Chicago Graduate School of Business and the Center for Entrepreneurial Leadership at the Ewing Kauffman Memorial Foundation in Kansas City, MO for financial support. Authorship on this paper is alphabetical.

References

Aldrich, H., M. Fiol. 1994. Fools rush in? The institutional context of industry creation. *Acad. Management Rev.* 19(4) 645–670.

——, C. Zimmer. 1986. Entrepreneurship through social networks. D. Sexton and R. Smilor, eds. *The Art and Science of Entrepreneurship.* Ballinger, Cambridge, MA.

Arrow, K. 1974. *The Limits of Organization.* W.W. Norton, New York.

Baron, J., M. Burton, M. Hannan. 1996. The road taken: Origins and evolution of employment systems in emerging companies. *Indust. Corporate Change* 5 239–275.

——, M. Hannan, M. Diane Burton. 2001. Labor pains: Organizational change and employee turnover in young, high-tech firms. *Amer. J. Soc.* 106(4) 960–1012.

Blau, P. 1964. *Exchanche and Power in Social Life.* Wiley, New York.

Blossfeld, H., G. Rohwer. 1995. *Techniques of Event-History Modeling: A New Approach to Casual Analysis.* Erlbaum, Mahwah, NJ.

Bradach, J., R. Eccles. 1989. Price, authority, and trust: From ideal types to plural forms. *An. Rev. Soc.* 15 97–118.

Bruderl, J., P. Preisendorfer, R. Ziegler. 1992. Survival chances of newly founded business organizations. *Amer. Soc. Rev.* 57 227–242.

——, R. Schussler. 1990. Organizational mortality: The liabilities of newness and adolescence. *Admin. Sci. Quart.* 35 530–547.

Burt, R. 1992. *Structural Holes.* Harvard University Press, Cambridge, MA.

Coleman, J. 1990. *Foundations of Social Theory.* Belknap Press, Cambridge, MA.

Fichman, M., D. Levinthal. 1991. Honeymoons and the liability of adolescence: A new perspective on duration dependence in social and organizational relationships. *Acad. Management J.* **16** 442–468.

Gimeno, J., T. Folta, A. Cooper, C. Woo. 1997. Survival of the fittest? Entrepreneurial human capital and the persistence of under-performing firms. *Admin. Sci. Quart.* **42** 750–783.

Gompers, P., J. Lerner. 1999. *The Venture Capital Cycle.* MIT Press, Cambridge, MA.

Granovetter, M. 1985. Economic action and social structure: The problem of embeddedness. *Amer. J. Soc.* **91** 481–510.

Hannan, M. 1998. Rethinking age dependence in organizational mortality: Logical formalizations. *Amer. J. Soc.* **104** 126–164.

——, G. Carroll. 1992. *The Dynamics of Organizational Populations.* Oxford University Press, New York.

Kaplan, S., P. Stromberg. 1999. Financial contracting meets the real world: An empirical analysis of venture capital contracts. Working paper, University of Chicago, Chicago, IL.

Kalbfleisch, J. D., R. L. Prentice. 1980. *The Statistical Analysis of Failure Time Data.* Wiley, New York.

Lerner, J. 1994. The syndication of venture capital investments. *Financial Management* **23**(3) 16–27.

——, A. Tsai. 1999. Do equity financing cycles matter? Evidence from biotechnology alliances. Working paper, Harvard Business School, Boston, MA.

Levin, R., A. Klevorick, R. Nelson, S. Winter. 1987. Appropriating the returns from industrial R&D. *Brookings Papers Econom. Activity* **3** 783–831.

Macaulay, S. 1963. Noncontractual relations in business: A preliminary study. *Amer. Soc. Rev.* **28** 55–67.

Merges, R., R. Nelson. 1990. On the complex economics of patent scope. *Columbia Law Rev.* **90**(4) 839–916.

Podolny, J. 1994. Market uncertainty and the social character of economic exchange. *Admin. Sci. Quart.* **39** 458–483.

Raub, W., J. Weesie. 1990. Reputation and efficiency in social interactions: An example of network effects. *American J. Sociology* **96** 626–654.

Ritter, J. 1984. The "hot issue" market of 1980. *J. Bus.* **57** 215–240.

Shane, S. 2001. Technology opportunity and firm formation. *Management Sci.* **47**(2) 205–220.

——. 2002. Selling university technology: Patterns from MIT. *Management Sci.* **48**(1).

——, D. Cable. 1998. Social relationships and the financing of new

ventures. Working paper, Massachusetts Institute of Technology, Cambridge, MA.

——, R. Khurana. 2000. Career experience and firm founding. Working paper, University of Maryland, College Park, MD.

Simmel, G. 1950. *The Sociology of Georg Simmel.* Free Press, Glencoe, IL.

Sorensen, J., T. Stuart. 2000. Aging, obsolescence, and organizational innovation. *Admin. Sci. Quart.* **45**(1) 81–112.

Sorenson, O., T. Stuart. 2001. Syndication networks and the spatial distribution of venture capital investments. *Amer. J. Soc.* **106**(6) 1546–1588.

Stinchcombe, A. 1965. Social structure and organizations. J. March, ed. *Handbook of Organizations.* Rand McNally, Chicago, IL.

Stuart, T. 2000. Interorganizational alliances and the performance of firms: A study of growth and innovation rates in a high-technology industry. *Strategic Management J.* **21** 791–811.

——, H. Huang, R. Hybels. 1999. Interorganizational endorsements and the performance of entrepreneurial ventures. *Admin. Sci. Quart.* **44** 315–349.

——, D. Robinson. 2000. The emergence of interorganizational networks: Probation until reputation. Working paper, University of Chicago GSB, Chicago, IL.

Swaminathan, A. 1996. Environmental conditions at founding and organizational mortality: A trial-by-fire model. *Acad. Management J.* **39**(5) 1350–1377.

Teece, D. 1986. Profiting from technological innovation: Implications for integration, collaboration, licensing, and public policy. *Res. Policy* **15** 286–305.

Tuma, N., M. Hannan. 1984. *Social Dynamics: Models and Methods.* Academic Press, San Francisco, CA.

Tushman, M., L. Rosenkopf. 1992. Organizational determinants of technological change: Toward a sociology of technological evolution. *Res. Organ. Behavior* **14** 311–347.

Tyebjee, T., A. Bruno. 1984. A model of venture capital investment activity. *Management Sci.* **30** 1051–1066.

Venkataraman, S. 1997. The distinctive domain of entrepreneurship research: An editor's perspective. J. Katz, R. Brockhaus, eds. *Advances in Entrepreneurship, Firm Emergence and Growth,* Vol. 3. JAI Press, Greenwich, CT, 119–138.

Williamson, O. 1975. *Markets and Hierarchies: Analysis and Anti-Trust Implications.* Free Press, New York.

Wilson, R. 1985. Reputations in games and markets. A. Roth, ed. *Game Theoretic Models of Bargaining.* Cambridge University Press, New York, 65–84.

Accepted by David C. Mowery and Scott Shane; received December 2000. This paper was with the authors 9 months for 1 revision.

[21]

Equity and the Technology Transfer Strategies of American Research Universities

Maryann Feldman • Irwin Feller • Janet Bercovitz • Richard Burton

Whiting School of Engineering, Johns Hopkins University, Baltimore, Maryland 21218
Department of Economics, Pennsylvania State University, University Park, Pennsylvania 16802
The Fuqua School of Business, Duke University, Durham, North Carolina 27708
The Fuqua School of Business, Duke University, Durham, North Carolina 27708
maryann.feldman@jhu.edu • iqf@psu.edu • janetb@duke.edu • rmb2@mail.duke.edu

A merican universities are experimenting with new mechanisms for promoting the commercialization of academic research and generating revenue from university intellectual property. This paper discusses mechanisms available to universities in managing the commercialization of intellectual property, considering equity as a technology transfer mechanism that offers advantages for both generating revenue and aligning the interests of universities, industry and faculty. Employing data from a national survey of Carnegie I and Carnegie II institutions, we document the recent rise in university equity holdings. We present and estimate a model that considers the university's use of equity to be a function of behavioral factors related to the university's prior experiences with licensing, success relative to other institutions, and the organization of the technology transfer office, as well as structural characteristics related to university type.

(*University-Industry Relationships; Equity Financing; Academic Patents; Licensing; Technology Transfer*)

Introduction

American universities are experimenting with new mechanisms for promoting the commercialization of academic research and generating revenues from university intellectual property. The 20 years since the passage of the Bayh–Dole Act have witnessed a search to optimize, or, more pragmatically, to balance the objectives of managing intellectual property rights, developing new revenue sources, and accommodating faculty interests while simultaneously maintaining norms related to the conduct of academic research and the dissemination of research findings. Based on their own experiences with patent and licensing activities as well as from lessons learned from the experiences of other institutions, universities have experimented with, and embraced, alternative mechanisms of intellectual property transfer.

Equity positions in companies, as a payment for the use of university intellectual property, are one emerging mechanism. Agreements in which a university takes an equity interest in a company in exchange for providing the company the right to use university intellectual property is becoming common.[1] The Association of University Technology Managers (AUTM) first reported on this trend in 1995. In 1999, 79 of 190 institutions responding to the AUTM survey had

---

[1] This paper is not about direct monetary investment in companies or investments in venture capital firms, some of which in turn may invest in start-up firms based on university-based research (Desruisseaux 2000).

0025-1909/02/4801/0105$5.00
1526-5501 electronic ISSN

MANAGEMENT SCIENCE © 2002 INFORMS
Vol. 48, No. 1, January 2002 pp. 105–121

FELDMAN, FELLER, BERCOVITZ, AND BURTON
Equity and Technology Transfer Strategies of American Research Universities

taken equity positions in 243 firms (AUTM 1999). Our survey of research universities, conducted in Spring 2000 shows that 1978 was the earliest date reported for an equity deal. By 1992, 40% of our respondents were taking equity in companies licensing their technology, and, in 2000, 70% had participated in at least one equity deal (see Figure 1). While equity was initially conceived as a last resort means of accepted payment reserved for cash-starved start-up firms, the use of equity now extends to more established companies as part of a diversified compensation scheme.

The number of universities using equity licensing transactions, coupled with the emergence of equity in a more diversified set of bargaining situations, suggests some strategic net advantages. By net advantages, we mean comparisons of the costs and benefits of equity positions relative to the costs and benefits of alternative technology transfer revenue-generating options. University technology transfer operations have multiple objectives as determinants of intellectual property strategy. Faculty retention, closer university–industry linkages, enhanced university prestige, and, more generally, enhanced and accelerated technology transfer for the social and economic benefit of the national or regional economy are core objectives named by university respondents (Thursby et al. 2001). As no single technology transfer mechanism may ideally suit these multiple objectives, universities are experimenting with different mechanisms.

In this paper, we describe three advantages to taking equity positions in lieu of licensing fees that interviewees cited as important from the perspective of the university. First, equity provides a university with options or financial claims on a company's future income streams. The attractiveness of the option is consistent with the uncertainty associated with the technical and economic characteristics of academic patents and with the experience-based assessment that the opportunity cost of foregone license and royalty revenue is generally low. Second, equity deals, in which the university becomes part owner of the company, are reported by our interviewees to align the interests of the university and the firm towards the common goal of commercializing the technology. Equity also may mitigate the potential for disputes and litigation about intellectual property between the university and the industry and the potential for conflicts of interest that can arise if a faculty member shifts loyalty away from the university and towards the company developing their intellectual property (Jensen and Thursby 2001). Third, according to our interviewees, equity may serve a certification function that provides a signal to relevant third parties. From the perspective of the university, taking equity may signal to the outside world that the university is entrepreneurial. For the firm, an equity deal may signal to other investors that the firm has received a valuable technology from the university and that the university is confident in the value of technology that

Figure 1   More Universities Take Equity Interests: Year of First University Equity Deal ($n = 67$)

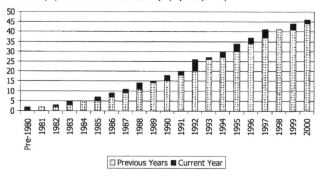

MANAGEMENT SCIENCE/Vol. 48, No. 1, January 2002

the firm holds. This may enhance the firm's ability to receive additional funding.

Interviewees also noted the risks and negative aspects of taking equity besides those associated with low or zero economic payoff. On many campuses, the decision to take equity occurred only after considerable debate about the propriety of extending the university involvement in the commercialization of academic knowledge into holding direct ownership stakes in firms. Some critics saw equity holdings as increasing the risk that the university might be held liable or suffer from adverse publicity for product defects. The claimed benefit of improved alignment with the interests of a firm was also seen as lending credence to charges that the university was losing sight of its traditional role as a generator of knowledge as a public good and as an independent societal source of expertise on complex scientific and technical issues. The following discussion of the relative attractiveness of equity and licensing as compensation mechanisms abstracts from these considerations.

Cataloguing the pros and cons of alternative mechanisms, however, is essentially a static task. Technology transfer officials expressed many of these same assessments about the relative attractiveness of equity and licensing in the mid-1980s (Feller 1990). Few, however, entered into equity arrangements at that time. Drawing on data from a survey of Carnegie I and II research universities, we offer a set of findings about the spread of equity holdings among universities and the patterns that exist among universities in their willingness to use the equity mechanism. The conceptual model we develop treats the move to equity as an adaptation to the problems and inadequacies of traditional licensing agreements. Our inquiry is cast in terms of a model of institutional change and adaptation conditioned by learning and the diffusion of best practices, and organizational incentives and behavior.

Why Equity Has Emerged As a Technology Transfer Mechanism

The provisions of the Bayh–Dole Act established universities' property rights over federally funded inventions and encouraged universities to actively promote the transfer of those inventions to commercial use. The initial university response was to create technology transfer offices to secure intellectual property rights through patents, and endeavor to sell rights to use those patents to firms. Three patterns have emerged. First, the number of patents received by universities increased to the point where 3,151 patents— 5%, of the U.S. total patents in 1998—were granted to universities. Second, the number of universities receiving patents has increased (Henderson et al. 1998, Mowery and Ziedonis 1999). This corresponds to an increase in the number and size of university technology transfer offices (Association of American Universities 1986, Seigel et al. 1999, Rogers et al. 2000, Thursby et al. 2001). Third, and most important to this inquiry, the mechanisms used to transfer technology and to attain revenue from intellectual property rights have changed and evolved. These changes reflect the greater sophistication and learning that have come with the experience derived from each university's own involvement in patent and licensing as well as lessons learned from the experience of other institutions. The purpose of the next section is to consider university experience with traditional licensing agreements and then evaluate the reasons for the growing adoption of equity deals.

Licensing Reconsidered

Licensing agreements typically involve selling a company the rights to use a university's inventions in return for revenue in the form of upfront fees at the time of closing the deal, and annual, ongoing royalty payments that are contingent upon the commercial success of the technology in a downstream market. The terms of the licensing agreement depend upon the assessment of the value of the technology in a product market that is often uncertain and thus difficult to evaluate. While there are some standards, many provisions of the royalty agreement are negotiated. Bray and Lee (2000) report that license issue fees typically range from $10,000 to $50,000 but may be as high as $250,000, while royalty rates are typically 2% to 5% but may be as high as 15%.[2] The bargaining power of the two parties may be very

---

[2] This is the same range reported by Feller (1990).

FELDMAN, FELLER, BERCOVITZ, AND BURTON
Equity and Technology Transfer Strategies of American Research Universities

uneven depending upon such factors as their relative sophistication, experience and resources, established industry-specific yardsticks, and the perceptions of the attributes of the technology, such as its commercial promise and distance to market. As a result, the deals negotiated between one firm and several universities or between one university and its licensees may be very different.

There are many positives to university technology licensing. First, an active license program has both substantive and symbolic importance: It attests to the capabilities of universities to advance technology and to serve as an engine of growth for both national and local economies. Second, an active technology transfer organization (TTO) with a large number of active licenses has become an instrument that the university can use in recruiting and retaining faculty.[3] Interviews with TTO officials at several universities indicate that some prospective faculty seek meetings with these officials to determine if the university is a congenial home to their prospective entrepreneurial activities.

Current trends in patents and licensing suggest mixed patterns, however. The continuing upward annual trend in patents, licenses, and license revenues reported in the AUTM 1999 survey suggests that academic licensing still is growing, with most institutions reporting more licensing revenue than they did the previous year.[4] Still, there is evidence that despite these rising totals, traditional licensing as a technology transfer mechanism has not yielded major financial returns for most institutions.

Efforts by universities to secure revenues from licensing have been hindered by the fact that the standards for securing patents for intellectual property are not equivalent to the requirements for commercial success.[5] In a recent survey of technology transfer officers, Jensen and Thursby (2001) found that only about 12% of the licensed technology is ready for commercialization. The majority of licensed technology requires significant developmental work and ongoing cooperation by faculty to realize commercial success.

Only a small subset of invention disclosures generate any licensing interest; of those that do, very few generate sizeable net returns. The rule of thumb in university technology transfer is that for every 100 invention disclosures, 10 patents and 1 commercially successful product result (Blake 1993). The distribution of licensing revenues is highly skewed with a few big commercial successes generating large returns for a small number of universities. Well-known licenses. such as the Cohen Boyer gene splicing technique (University of California and Stanford), Gatorade (University of Florida), Cisplatin (Michigan State), Fax technology (Iowa State), or Taxol (Florida State University) are the exceptions rather than the rule.[6]

Finally, biomedical invention accounts for a substantial share of academic licenses (Mowery et al. 1999, Feller et al. 2000), and commercialization of these products requires navigating the U.S. Food and Drug Administration approval process, which takes an average of 10 years. Considering that additional development is needed to convert the licensed technology into a viable product before a firm even can begin the long approval process, long lag times exist before the receipt of any royalties by the university.[7] Equity, in contrast, may provide a financial return in

---

[3] The right of faculty to share in the licensing revenue was a provision of the Bayh–Dole Act. Although substantial royalty windfalls have been reported for a small number of faculty, the after-tax return to faculty from royalties in general has been reported as relatively disappointing, comparing unfavorably with the revenue that faculty earn from consulting (Blake 1993).

[4] For the 82 recurrent respondents that reported data for the period FY 1991–FY 1999, the total increased from $149 million to $655 million. These revenues, while small in comparison with other university revenue sources, are not insignificant.

[5] The basic principle is well known. For example, as articulated by Niels Reimers, formerly of the Office of Technology Licensing, Stanford University: "The bad news is that the technology is underdeveloped and unproven, and a significant investment is required by the company for development and ultimately may be unsuccessful for market or technological reasons. The good news is that often a basic patent position will be available" (Reimers 1989).

[6] Taxol, for example, the patent owned by the Florida State University, has worldwide annual sales worth $1.2 billion and is expected to yield $60 million in licensing revenue this year (Zacks 2000).

[7] Indeed, several of our survey respondents expressed frustration with licensing as a transfer mechanism due to this time lag.

the case of an Initial Public Offering or an acquisition by another firm.

Further, there is evidence that licensing has not been an entirely satisfactory mechanism from the industry perspective, either. In a survey of industry licensing executives, Thursby and Thursby (2000a) found that 66% (199 business units out of a total of 300) had not licensed intellectual property from universities. The reasons given included the feeling that university research is generally at too early a stage of development (49%); that universities rarely engage in research in a related line of business (37.4%); university refusal to transfer ownership to company (31%); university policies regarding delay of publication are too strict (20%); and concerns about obtaining faculty cooperation for further development of the technology (16%).[8] In sum, there is evidence of industry reluctance to licensing.

Equity Considered

In the immediate post-Bayh–Dole period, university technology transfer offices generally considered equity-based licenses to be a compensation mechanism of last resort reserved for cash-starved, start-up firms. "Start-ups rarely have a positive cash flow during their first years of operation; therefore, taking equity in such start-ups partially in lieu of cash fees is an important technique to conserve the company's cash for investment in product development" (AUTM 1999, p. 17.) Although relative to the fixed upfront fees and standard royalty rates of traditional licenses, equity held the promise of enabling the university to share in potentially larger revenues if a licensee flourished as a result of use of the university's patents, these revenues were perceived to be highly uncertain. The high failure rate of new firms was well known. Acting as would be predicted by the well-established certainty effect (Kahneman and Tversky 1979, Tversky and Kahneman 1992), technology transfer officers valued the relatively certain expected revenues accruing from traditional licenses more than the uncertain, though potentially higher, expected revenues associated with equity deals.

With the exception of a few universities such as MIT that made equity a core part of its technology transfer and licensing portfolio, most universities at first accepted equity deals in those cases where the university believed that a patent had economic value but no established firm was able to pay the required fees and royalties of a traditional license.[9] Even if the expected returns did not materialize, the university might still realize value by advancing its objectives of disseminating knowledge, getting the technology out for commercialization, and, in some cases, accommodating the interests of the faculty inventors.[10]

Our interviews with technology transfer officers suggest that this perception of equity as the mechanism of last resort has changed. Three main factors appear to underlie this evolution. The first is the increased experience of TTOs with traditional licensing. This has resulted in a greater understanding of the limitations of this transfer mechanism in terms of a downward revision in expectation about licensing's revenue-generating potential.[11] In contrast, equity is perceived to offer an advantage as the potential return

---

[8] Twenty-eight percent of the respondents indicated some other difficulty such as "general attitude is poor," "complexity of deal and... weird expectations," "too cumbersome" and "high licensing fees" Thursby and Thursby (2000a).

[9] JHU took its first equity deal in 1993 for the use of intellectual property that was licensed to a firm called CardioLogic. Larger firms had been approached but were not interested in the technology, which faculty and TTO staff believed was an important invention. The only mechanism that would allow the technology to be licensed was an equity deal with a start-up firm.

[10] Duke University's involvement in one of early equity deals in 1987 follows such a scenario. Though the faculty inventor expressed strong interest in taking the technology to a start-up of his own, the university insisted on first trying to license it to an established firm. They were successful in this. However, the license was subsequently reacquired from the initial licensee—a large, established pharmaceutical company—due to the company's failure to move the technology forward. At that point, the university still chose to spend an additional year seeking to make a deal with another established firm before accepting a license-for-equity deal with the firm established by the inventor.

[11] The earliest university licenses were granted on an exclusive basis that provided no limits on the company's use of the intellectual property. Exclusive licenses gave the company total control over the INTELLECTUAL PROPERTY in all potential applications, markets and adaptations. However, our interviews revealed that increasingly licenses are nonexclusive with stipulated limits on technology application, geographic scope or terms of use.

FELDMAN, FELLER, BERCOVITZ, AND BURTON
Equity and Technology Transfer Strategies of American Research Universities

is based on the total assets of the firm, which is expected to be greater than the return to any individual product. Second, TTOs, as well as firms, have begun to appreciate the mutual benefits of equity in aligning university-firm interests. Third, interviewees believe that equity more so than licensing provides prestige and legitimacy for both the university and the firm. We discuss these arguments within the context of pertinent theoretical frameworks in the sections below.

The Upside Revenue Potential of Equity

In discussing the advantages of equity-based licenses, many of our respondents cited the upside potential of this transfer mechanism. Through equity, the university has the opportunity to benefit from future products or processes that increase the technical and economic value of the firm. This view of equity is not new; however, for several reasons the perceived value of equity has increased over the past 10 years compared to the value ascribed to traditional licensing. First, as discussed, many universities have been disappointed by the revenue-generating performance of their traditional licenses. Not only have relatively fewer inventions resulted in licenses than had been hoped, but also the majority of these licenses have provided only moderate, if any, returns. The opportunity cost of taking an equity option is the forgone revenues that the university could receive had it negotiated a traditional license with upfront fees, milestone payments, and running royalties. Given that universities have learned from their own experiences and the experiences of other universities that this opportunity cost is, on average, relatively low, the decision to trade traditional licensing revenues for equity holdings has become more attractive.

Second, many respondents noted that equity has the advantage in providing the university with an opportunity to share in the fortunes of a firm rather than just in the fortunes of a technology that may have contributed to the development of the firm but did not directly result in a commercial product. While traditional licensing agreements are specific to the use of a particular patent, equity deals provide a means for the university to share in the company's success even in the event that no licensing royalties accrue

to the original technology. The technology covered by university patents and licenses are typically far away from the commercial market and may not result in a viable commercial product. However, a firm's experience with the licensed technology may provide knowledge that is incorporated into subsequent products and materially contribute to the company's ultimate commercial success. Equity deals permit the university to capture at least some of the returns associated with such knowledge transfer. In the worst-case scenario—where the original technology proves to be completely worthless—the university still can benefit from an equity deal if the selected partner proves viable. Equity holdings yield a portfolio that captures a broad range of potential futures. In this respect, equity has come to be perceived as being less risky than traditional licenses.

Third, there is a broader recognition that holding an equity position permits the university to buy time, waiting to exercise its option (i.e., sell its equity) until uncertainty about the economic value of its patent holdings is reduced (Vonortas and Hertzfeld, 1998). Again, academic patents typically are early-stage technological developments characterized by high degrees of technical and market uncertainty. To bring the technology under an academic patent to market often requires considerable follow-on research, as well as additional costs for approval (in the case of drugs), production, and distribution. With a traditional license, the university has little option but to negotiate the upfront fees, milestone payments, and fixed royalty rates in the shadow of this uncertainty. To deal with such uncertainty, the universities tend to adopt standard industry-specific running royalty rates, or to rely on technology licensing officials with expertise in selected technological fields. The first technique drives the institution's negotiating position to the average rate of return for licenses in a field, while the latter entails additional administrative costs. In fact, the latter is feasible only for those institutions with sizeable numbers of patents, clustered into discernible utility or industry classes. Employment of either of these techniques effectively reduces overall licensing returns. In comparison, equity deals look relatively more attractive. If the company has an Initial Public Offering or is acquired before achieving

110

a marketable product equity may provide a shorter time horizon to revenue realization.

Finally, it must be noted that for most of the 1990s—the period when university equity holding increased—the performance of the stock market, and of technology stocks in particular, had been quite positive.[12] University personnel, evaluating the potential of equity against this backdrop, were likely to perceive the returns of equity to be quite promising.

The Incentive Alignment Value of Equity

Another recurring theme that emerged from our discussions with technology-transfer officers was the view that equity more so than licensing was a means to align the interests of the university and the licensing firm. Three aspects of alignment were stressed: (1) common goals related to the appreciation of the value of the firm and the commercialization of the technology; (2) relative ease of initial contractual negotiations; and (3) provision for ongoing, within agreement, decision-making and adjustment. Each of these is discussed in turn.

Several technology transfer officers emphasized the benefits provided by equity-based licenses by aligning the long-term interests of the firm and the university. With equity, both parties gain as the total value of the licensed technology, as well as the firm as a whole, increases. As such, it is in the best interests of both parties to take actions that enhance the probability of the firm's commercial success. TTO officials view this goal alignment as smoothing existing and future university-firm technology transfer transactions. As noted by one respondent, a firm that has executed an equity-based license can expect to find the going much easier in subsequent negotiations to sponsor research with, or acquire additional technology rights from, the university. Rather than play hardball in hopes of structuring the best possible one-time, stand-alone deal, the university—evaluating the new deal in light of its existing ties—is more likely to strive to expedite the transaction in a manner that enhances firm viability.

A number of respondents also highlighted the comparative ease of constructing an equity-based licensing agreement as compared to the challenge of negotiating a traditional license. Traditional licenses are, in essence, contracts that specify price, detailed by level of royalty rates and upfront fees, performance requirements as reflected in milestone payment terms, and enforcement rights executed through the courts. An equity-based license changes the focus from contracting on price and performance to agreeing on ownership shares (i.e., how much stock does the university receive for the right to use the technology?).

Our interviewees suggest that it is easier to agree on the latter than the former.[13] Specifically, equity agreements are easier to write as they center on the delineation of property rights and do not involve the specification of the large number of contingency terms that a traditional license does. Equity also is reported to have an advantage over traditional licensing in that it reduces the potential for litigation relating to the firm's use of the licensed technology. Consider a case in which a firm draws upon a university license in its evolving efforts to develop a commercially viable product, all the while modifying, scrapping, and extending elements of the technology. Each modification opens up new potential for legal conflicts about the extent to which the final product makes use of the licensed technology. As the original contract rarely completely (or even significantly) anticipates these developments, there are seldom payment and/or performance terms on point. To resolve disputes, the university and firm may attempt to renegotiate in good faith. However, such renegotiations, given the zero-sum nature of royalty payments, may be contentious, break down, and lead to litigation. In an equity deal, contribution disputes are less likely to produce this outcome as both players share in all value created.

---

[12] Interviews were conducted in Summer 2000 before the sharp decline in the stock market in the second half of the year market.

[13] Though prior to taking a first equity deal, there is often contentious debates at the university about the proper role of the university and the general framework for all future equity deals, these deliberations generally come before the university sits down to negotiate with an individual firm. Interviewees tell us those subsequent firm–university negotiations, given the focused nature of the negotiation on a particular deal, is generally straightforward.

The example of The Pennsylvania State University and AbioMed illustrates this point. Penn State took equity in AbioMed, a 19-year-old biomedical firm in Boston, in exchange for giving the company the rights to use artificial heart technology developed at the Hershey Medical School. AbioMed was working on a product that would have inevitably been a competitor to the Hershey Heart. Equity became the preferred compensation mechanism for both parties because it facilitated the integration of the company's on-going research and development work with Penn State intellectual property while avoiding potential future legal complications.

The Legitimacy Value of Equity

A final benefit of equity-based licenses cited by respondents is the belief that it provides legitimacy and or prestige for both the firms and the university. In discussing why firms seek equity deals, several of the technology transfer officers interviewed noted that beyond the obvious benefit of conserving cash, firms believe university equity holding enhanced their credibility.[14] Lerner (1999) concludes that firms participating in the government Small Business Innovation Research (SBIR) program grew significantly faster than comparable firms and were more likely to attract venture capital financing indicating the government funding conferred a halo effect. A similar halo may be generated by a university ownership position. Specifically, our interviews reveal that a university's willingness to accept equity in lieu of up-front fees and/or royalties is believed to provide a

signal to capital markets and potential strategic partners that the university has made a positive evaluation of the worthiness of the technology and the firm's development competencies. If this signal is perceived as valuable, it may give the university some advantage in the equity share negotiations and thus enhance its returns.

Perhaps more salient for our goal of understanding universities' use of the equity mechanism is the prestige value that technology transfer personnel believe that having active licenses conveys to the university. The university's willingness to take equity lowers the cost of licensing the technology and this may generate more licensing activity. We therefore might expect that universities with low levels of licensing activity, both in absolute and relative terms, to adopt taking equity as a means to increase their measured level of technology transfer activity. Further, there is also a perceived halo effect of university equity positions. Universities with a high number of equity deals generally gain an affirmative reputation for being progressive and entrepreneurial.

In conclusion, equity appears to provide an improved mechanism for university technology transfer. Although equity options are not without problems, our interviews reveal that university officials find that equity offers some advantages over traditional licensing agreements based on up-front fees and royalty payments. The next section develops a set of hypotheses that relate university characteristics to the adoption of equity and presents data that we will use to test these hypotheses.

---

[14] Evidence about the existence and direction of legitimacy effects of equity holdings is indirect and mixed. Shane (2000) in a study of MIT patents however points to a negative relationship between university equity holdings and the successful commercialization of the technology covered by the relevant license. The reasoning behind this finding involves a restatement of the mainstream motivation for why universities take equity: No existing firm believes that the patented technology is commercially profitable. Start-up firms that seek to commercialize such technologies are inherently highly risky enterprises. Our focus in this paper does not displace these dynamics. The belief, on the part of the firm, that having a university as an equity partner adds legitimacy to the firm's ventures is not a guarantee that the firms will succeed. Exuberant spirits may exist on both sides of the bargaining table.

Hypotheses and Data

Writing just after Johns Hopkins University took its first equity interest, David Blake, Senior Associate Dean of the School of Medicine, wrote "Most universities and their trustees are quite comfortable with accepting royalty payments and sharing them with faculty inventors under approved formulas. They are much less comfortable with holding stock in a company that is commercializing a university discovery (Blake 1993, p. A52)." As noted previously. we have seen a recent increase in the use of equity in technology transfer. Logically, one can attribute this increase in the number of equity transactions to the perceived attractiveness of this mechanism, as described above. However, substantial variation exists in both the timing of first equity deals and the intensity of equity involvement across the universities in our sample. The remaining question, and the one we tackle in this section, is what factors explain these differing adoption strategies?

We propose a model in which the intensity of a university's equity involvement is related to a set of behavioral and structural variables. The behavioral variables relate to intra- and interinstitutional learning and adaptation that come with time and experience. The control variables include the Carnegie Classification of the university, the status as a public or private entity, and the affiliation with a medical school.

Direct Technology Transfer Office Attributes: Experience and Structure

One strong association that emerged from our interviews was that of the relationship between technology-transfer experience and the perceived attractiveness of equity as a technology transfer mechanism. In general, we observed that experience with traditional licensing give rise to dissatisfaction with this technique and subsequent experimentation with new mechanisms. Hands-on experience seemed to expose previously unconsidered limits of traditional licensing. As TTOs gained experience with traditional licensing mechanisms, they appear to also become more skeptical about the expected returns accruing to this transfer mechanism. This greater understanding of potential limits led to a downward revision of the transfer mechanism's relative attractiveness, which, in turn, appears to create a willingness to experiment with alternative transfer mechanisms, such as equity-based licenses.

In addition, universities that have more experience with industry-sponsored research are expected to have a greater commitment to technology transfer and to be more willing to experiment with new mechanisms that appear to offer perceived benefits. As TTOs gain experience with industry through sponsored research they appear to be more willing to attempt to facilitate increased interaction in technology transfer. Thus, the following hypothesis.

HYPOTHESIS 1. *The greater a university's experience with technology transfer, the more likely the university will be to adopt equity-based transfer mechanisms.*

Along with licensing experience, we argue that the budgetary policy of the technology transfer office may also influence equity involvement. While we hypothesize that greater experience leads to greater dissatisfaction with traditional licensing, and thus greater interest in equity-based transfer deals, willingness to make this trade-off may be constrained, or secondary, to immediate budgetary needs. Traditional licenses generate both certain and uncertain revenue streams. Up-front fees, the required payments at the origin of a licensing deal, are immediate and certain. Upon completion of negotiations, the university can expect to receive these fees. Specifically, transfer offices that are required to be self-supporting may rely on the immediate and certain revenues coming form the up-front fees of traditional licenses. As noted by March and Shapira (1987), managers are much less likely to take risks when organizational survival is at stake. Thus, the following hypothesis.

HYPOTHESIS 2. *The expectation that the technology-transfer office should be self-supporting reduces the propensity for the university to adopt equity-based transfer mechanisms.*

Technology Transfer Experience Relative to Other Institutions

While direct experience is expected to be an important influence in the decision to adopt alternative transfer mechanisms, we also argue that the experience of others also comes in to play. Many of the technology-transfer officers we spoke with volunteered that they commonly benchmark their university's performance against the performance of other similar institutions. The average performance of a cohort comes to represent the minimal acceptable performance level—to either the TTO or those that are evaluating the TTO.

March and Shapira (1987) and March (1988) argue that aspirations or performance targets affect risk-taking behavior. This may be extended to reflect the expected influence of traditional license-related performance benchmarks on a university's propensity to enter equity-based licenses. Though expected value may be high, equity deals are generally perceived to be more risky than traditional licenses. Equity is riskier because of its relative novelty—few institutions have had any significant experience with this mechanism. In addition, there is greater potential return variance associated with equity. While traditional license returns are somewhat narrowly bound between up-front fees and a percentage of product sales, equity returns vary more broadly from zero, if the firm fails, to some percentage of the firm's total worth.

March and Shapira (1987, p. 1413) argue that managers that are near a performance target will be relatively risk averse. These individuals are expected to avoid a risky action that may cause performance to fall below target. However, when performance exceeds the target by a substantial amount, managers are more likely to engage in risky behavior in hopes of capturing the potential up-side benefit. Thus, the following hypothesis:

HYPOTHESIS 3. *Leading performers, those performing substantially above the benchmarked target, will be more likely than average pwformers to adopt equity-based transfer mechanisms.*

For decision-makers who have not been successful to date—those performing substantially below target levels—the desire to reach the target will cause them to focus on opportunities associated with the risky action (March and Shapira 1987). Any action that may get them closer to the target is attractive. Because, these managers are currently doing poorly, they do not have much to lose if the gamble fails to play out to their advantage. Thus, these individuals are expected to have a predilection for risk-prone behavior:

HYPOTHESIS 4. *Lagging universities, performing substantially below their cohorts, will be more likely than average performers to adopt equity-based technology transfer mechanisms.*

Description of Survey Data
The most cited source on university technology transfer, the AUTM annual survey, first reported data on university equity agreements in 1995. Over the course of the survey's history, however, AUTM has changed data collection items, adding and dropping variables

in response to changes in university practices. The changes limit the usefulness of these surveys to discern trends. As a result, researchers interested in more focused questions have used mail and telephone surveys to collect original data on the equity aspects of university technology transfer activities. Bray and Lee (2000), for example, have compared the amount of revenue received from equity positions versus licensing fees, while Di Gregorio and Shane (2000) have looked at equity as one dimension in considering why some universities generate more start-up firms than others. Our interest is in understanding equity as part of a general examination of the evolving character of university–industry relationships. Thus, as with these other recent studies, our research involved a series of telephone interviews with university technology licensing and transfer officials.

In Summer 2000, we conducted a survey of the 124 Carnegie I and II research universities that have active technology transfer operations.[15] The letter that introduced the survey was addressed to the head of the TTO as identified by AUTM or the university's web page. We contacted each university official at least three times to attempt to set up the survey interview. The interview protocol asked about university practices related to equity, among other questions related to the organization and function of the TTO. The majority of the 124 institutions (76%) participated in the AUTM survey on a regular basis.

We received 67 responses, for a response rate of 54%. Comparison of the respondents with the total universe of universities indicates no biases in terms of structural characteristics (e.g., Carnegie Classification, public/private, land grant/non–land grant, medical school/no medical school). Our model estimation is based on 62 observations. Lack of data on some of

---

[15] Under the Carnegie classification, Research Universities I award 50 or more doctorates each year and annually receive $40 million or more in federal research support. Research Universities II are the same as Research I universities except that they receive between $15.5 million and $40 million annually in federal research support. This classification system will be undergoing major changes in the near future. Only one institution, Howard University, did not have an office of technology transfer or some individual whom we were able to identify as being assigned technology transfer as their primary responsibility.

the independent variables from sources other than our survey necessitated omitting five institutions from our econometric estimation. Again, we do not find evidence that the estimation sample is biased with respect to any measurable characteristics.

In describing the characteristics of our respondents, we draw upon the full sample of 67. Of the TTO respondents, 76% indicated that their university had taken equity in a company. Our findings are similar to those from Thursby et al. (2001), who found that 82% of their 62 responding universities had taken equity as part of a licensing deal. The similar number of respondents is a coincidence, as the sampling frame of our respondents differ. The lower rate of universities taking of equity in our sample may be a result of the greater institutional diversity in our sample frame.

Thirteen universities (19% of our respondents), each a public university, were prohibited from taking equity in companies because of state statutes that limit their range of activity. These legislative restrictions do not limit the universities' initiatives to be in a legal position to accept equity, however. Of these universities, 10 formed independent 501(c)3 entities to manage their intellectual property and to take equity

holdings.[16] To date, seven of these entities have taken equity in lieu of licensing fees for a university invention. Three of the independent entities had not taken equity at the time of our interview.

University officials were asked the total number of equity deals in which they had participated. Our respondent set of 67 universities participated in 679 equity deals. The distribution of the number of deals is highly skewed as shown in Figure 2. The mean number of equity transactions was 10.3, the median was 5 and the mode was 0. The maximum number of equity deals was 90.

Dependent Variable. The dependent variable for our study is the intensity of equity involvement. We measure this variable as the total number of a university's equity interests divided by the number of the university's active licenses for 1998. Active licenses are the cumulative number of licenses that had not terminated by the end of the 1998.

The total number of equity deals is from our survey, verified against the AUTM survey. The number of active licenses is from the 1998 AUTM survey. For universities that did not routinely participate in

Figure 2   Diversity in Experience with Equity Deals ($n = 67$)

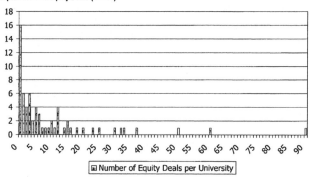

[16] An example is the Ohio State University Research Foundation. Other institutions that have not been subject to statutory limitations have formed this type of entity to serve as a bridging mechanism. For example, the University of Illinois system formed Illinois Ventures as an intermediary institution to focus on commercializing university intellectual property.

FELDMAN, FELLER, BERCOVITZ, AND BURTON
Equity and Technology Transfer Strategies of American Research Universities

Figure 3   Distribution of the Intensity of the Use of Equity: Equity Deals As a Percentage of All Active Licensing Agreements

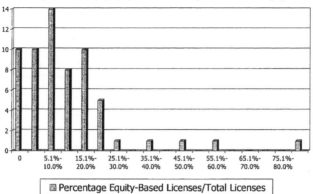

AUTM, we gathered data on the number of active licenses from web pages or from our interviews.

There is variation in the use of equity deals as a percentage of all intellectual property licenses (see Figure 3). For our respondents, the percentage of equity deals accounted for a mean value of 14.4%, and a median of 8.5%. The maximum use of equity was 88.1% indicating that this respondent used equity for the vast majority of their intellectual property agreements. This last statistic is an artifact of the relatively small number of licensing agreements at this university, as well as to other universities in the upper tail of the distribution. To adjust for this skewnesss, we weight our regression model to mitigate the effect of outliers who appear to have made high use of equity simply because they did not have many licensing opportunities.

Independent Variables. The technology transfer experience of the university provides the independent variable for Hypothesis 1. We use three measures of experience: (1) age of the technology transfer office; (2) cumulative number of executed licenses (1991–1998); and (3) the log of the cumulative amount of industrial research support received (1991–1998). These data are from the annual AUTM surveys, verified and augmented by our survey and institutional data from the National Science Foundation's Com-

puter Aided Science Policy Analysis and Research (CASPAR) database.

For Hypothesis 2, the budgetary structure of the technology transfer office is the independent variable of interest. Using our survey data, we construct a dummy variable equal to 1 if the expectation is that the technology-transfer office will be self-supporting, 0 otherwise. Roughly, half (47%) of the respondent offices in our survey had expectations of being self-supporting.

The university's technology transfer experience relative to others is the independent variable for the final two hypotheses. Our interviews revealed that TTOs are sensitive to the amount of intellectual property activity they have relative to a cohort of similar institutions. Our interviews revealed that status, as either a public or private institution, the presence of a medical school, and some measure of the level of intellectual property income relative to an institution's total R&D expenditures were considerations in defining one's cohort. Accordingly, we grouped institutions into four cohorts based on status as either a public or private institution and the presence or absence of a medical school: public/with medical school; public/no medical school; private/with medical school; private/no medical school. To construct the cohort variable of licensing income relative to R&D expenditures we calculated the total annual licensing rev-

116

FELDMAN, FELLER, BERCOVITZ, AND BURTON
Equity and Technology Transfer Strategies of American Research Universities

Table 1   Summary of Hypotheses

Hypothesis	Dependent Variable	Independent Variable	Operational Independent Variable	Predicted Sign
Hypothesis 1	Equity envolvement intensity:	Own experience	Age of technology transfer office	+
	Total # of equity interests *Ave. annual active licenses*		Cumulative number of licensing deals Average annual industrial research support	+
Hypothesis 2	Equity involvement intensity:	Budgetary structure	Expectation of TTO self-sufficiency Yes = 1 No = 0	−
	Total # of equity interests *Ave. annual active licenses*			
Hypothesis 3	Equity involvement intensity:	Relative experience	Leading cohort	+
	Total # of equity interests *Ave. annual active licenses*			
Hypothesis 4	Equity Involvement intensity:	Relative experience	Lagging cohort	+
	Total # of equity interests *Ave. annual active licenses*			

enues from 1991–1998 relative to the university's total research budget. Considering the distribution of similar institutions,[17] we classify institutions greater than one standard deviation above the category average as leading their cohort (Hypothesis 3). Similarly, institutions with average annual licensing revenue that was more than one standard deviation below the category mean are classified as lagging their cohort (Hypothesis 4).

Control Variables. In addition to the independent variables, we add controls for university type. Specifically, we create three dummy variables (each with 1 = Yes, 0 = No) to delineate whether a university (1) has a medical school; (2) is private; and (3) is classified as a Carnegie I Research Institution.

Table 2 provides descriptive statistics for the variables used in the regression.

Empirical Results

Table 3 provides our empirical results. The dependent variable is the total number of university equity

[17] To operationalize this measure we first categorized obvious outliers as either leading or lagging their cohort and then calculated the mean values and standard deviations.

Table 2   Descriptive Statistics

Variable	Mean	Standard Deviation
Equity Share	0.1443	0.1812
Hypothesis 1: Own Technology Transfer Experience		
Age of technology transfer office	14.6452	10.8493
Cumulative number of licenses	148.6906	218.9944
Cumulative number of licenses—squared	69, 293.94	208, 772.6573
Log of average annual industrial research support	13.7728	3.7624
Hypothesis 2: Technology Transfer Budgetary Incentives		
Expectation that TTO will be self supporting	0.4677	0.5030
Hypothesis 3: Relative Technology Transfer Experience		
Lagging cohort	0.2742	0.4497
Leading cohort	0.2258	0.4215
Control Variables		
Has medical school	0.5484	0.5017
Private university	0.3226	0.4713
Is Carnegie I institution	0.6613	0.4771

Table 3   Empirical Results

Own Technology Transfer Experience	Model 1	Model 2	Model 3
Age of technology transfer office	0.0296	0.0249	
	(0.0107)**	(0.0131)**	
Cumulative number of licenses	−0.6924	−0.0073	
	(0.1198)**	(0.020)**	
Cumulative number of licenses—squared		$4.80e^{-06}$	
		$(1.6e^{-06})$**	
Log of average annual industrial		0.2524	
research support		(0.1478)*	
Technology Transfer Budgetary Incentives			
Expectation that TTO will be self	−0.400	−0.4888	
supporting	(0.2416)*	(0.2862)*	
Relative Technology Transfer Experience			
Lagging cohort			0.5843
			(0.3151)*
Leading cohort			0.1233
			(0.3550)
Control Variables			
Has medical school	0.8725	0.7408	0.1370
	(0.2824)**	(0.3146)**	(0.3010)
Private university	−0.3154	−0.0825	−0.6868
	(0.2473)	(0.3185)	(0.2625)**
Is Carnegie I institution	−0.2859	−0.7382	−0.9145
	(0.3562)	(0.4247)*	(0.4005)**
Constant	3.2896	1.5147	1.5833
	(0.4573)**	(4.096)**	(4152)**
Log likelihood	−75.3535	−84.5945	−87.5124
Prob > chi²	0.0000	0.0028	0.0146
N	62	62	62

interests divided by the number of active university licenses in 1998. The equity share of active university licenses is thus a fraction that is truncated at zero and bounded by one at the upper level. There are ten cases for which the number of equity deals was zero, which is the lower bound for our data. We therefore use the lower-bound TOBIT model and the number of 1998 licensing agreement is used as an analytic weight in the model to pt-wide robust estimation (Maddala 1983, Greene 2000).

Models 1 and 2 estimates the use of equity as a function of the university's own technology-transfer experience. The results indicate that the university's prior experience in technology-transfer matters in the

use of equity. The age of the technology-transfer office is positively related to the university's use of equity as expected. The older the university's office of technology-transfer office the greater the use of equity as a percentage of intellectual property transactions. This result is consistent with Bray and Lee (2000) conclusion, based on interviews at 10 university technology-transfer offices. that offices that have been in existence longer are much more likely to consider taking equity than is a fledgling technology transfer program.

The effect of the cumulative number of licensing agreements on the intensity of equity use is more complex. In Model 1, the cumulative number

FELDMAN, FELLER, BERCOVITZ, AND BURTON
Equity and Technology Transfer Strategies of American Research Universities

of licensing agreements is negatively related to the intensity of use of equity—the greater the experience with licensing the less likely the university is to make use of equity. In Model 2, we add a quadratic licensing term that is positive and statistically significant. This indicates that the cumulative licensing experience has a nonlinear relationship on the use of equity. Specifically, universities appear more likely to use equity as they gain experience with licensing but the relationship resembles an inverted U as the use of equity decreases when the university has executed a large number of licenses.

Our final measure of the university's own technology-transfer experience is industrial research support. We find that the log of the amount of average annual industrial research support is positively related to the use of equity in Model 2. In sum, we find support for Hypothesis 1.

The effect of the TTO self-sufficiency is of the expected direction for both Models 1 and 2. University technology-transfer offices that are expected to be self-sufficient make less use of equity, ceteris paribus, providing support for Hypothesis 2.

Model 3 estimates the university's intensity of use of equity relative to the technology-transfer performance of peer institutions. The experience of the technology-transfer office relative to other institutions is measured as a dummy variable that is equal to one if the university respectively lags or leads other universities in its cohort in terms of average annual licensing. We find that those universities that lag their cohort make greater use of equity after accounting for structural characteristics. The coefficient for universities that lead their cohorts is of the expected sign but is not statistically significant. This finding suggests that universities that are average relative to their cohort make less use of equity, confirming Hypothesis 3. The coefficient for institutions that lead their cohort. Hypothesis 4, was of the expected sign but not statistically significant.

Our specifications also include structural characteristics and the results suggest universities make greater use of equity deals in technology transfer if they have a medical school. In addition, Carnegie II research universities appear to make greater use of equity. Model 3 reveals that public universities appear to make greater use of equity when they compare themselves to their cohorts.

In sum, the results support the expectation that universities both learn from their own experience and from the experiences of others. We also find that structural characteristics of the university affect the degree to which the university is able and willing to experiment with equity. Notably, universities with medical schools made greater use of equity in licensing agreements. Carnegie II research universities also seemed to be more aggressive in adopting the new mechanism. This fact seems to bear on the relative standing of these institutions and their desire to advance their position.

Conclusions

Recent trends towards increased university acceptance of equity as compensation for intellectual property rights represents a new strategic perspective on intellectual property management and technology transfer. The older, established view for universities accepting equity in lieu of licensing fees was that equity was the only compensation being offered by cash-starved start-up firms who were the only party that would be interested in the university's patents. We find that equity is increasingly seen by university technology licensing offices as an attractive mechanism that offers advantages in both increasing the upside revenue potential of university technology and improving the alignment between the institution's interests and those of the firm. The adoption of equity may be seem as part of a trend in which universities are becoming more entrepreneurial in light of new opportunities and changing expectations.

These theoretical considerations point to the importance of institutional learning—the product of a university's own experiences and that of other similar institutions, the characteristics of the technology transfer office, and a set of structural variables—which all affect the degree to which an institution accepts equity as a mechanism in its intellectual property licensing transactions. In this paper, we have developed and tested four hypotheses about the effect of direct experience, organizational incentives, and experience relative to a related cohort on the adoption of a new technology transfer mechanism. Our initial results at testing these relationships, using data from a national survey of Carnegie I and II research universities and other measures of academic licensing, support this interpretation.

Our results, though, are limited by both sample size and the absence of attention to changes over time and in university policy. In particular, the recent sharp decline in high-tech stock prices and in IPO share prices may reduce the allure of the equity option. In effect, our view of future trends in university holdings of equity is agnostic. Experience cuts both ways. In many respects, given the recent attention (and hyperbole) associated with university equity initiatives, we would expect the trend to continue, indeed to accelerate. All of our respondents indicated that they expected their university's use of equity would increase or stay the same in the next year. Universities are constantly adapting and learning and our results, and those of other researchers, may relate primarily to the pre-inflexion stage of adoption and diffusion. On the other hand, any prolonged decline in stock prices may quickly lead many technology-transfer offices back into the safe harbor of traditional licensing arrangements. Asking which route may be followed is akin to asking whether it is more profitable in today's market to buy long or sell short. Only time will tell.

Acknowledgments

We wish to acknowledge funding support from the Andrew W. Mellon Foundation for this paper as part of a larger project on evolving university–industry relationships. This is a collaborative research project and the names of the authors vary between publications although each author makes substantial contributions. We would like to thank Scott Shane, David Mowery, Dan Rodriguez and participants at the Georgia Tech Conference on University Entrepreneurship and Technology Transfer for their comments and suggestions. We are indebted to the technology transfer personnel and research administrators at Johns Hopkins University, The Pennsylvania State University and Duke University for generously sharing their time and expertise in identifying salient issues. We also acknowledge and appreciate the cooperation of the technology transfer officials who participated in our survey. We thank Rolf Lehming and Don Siegel for providing data. The views expressed in this paper are, of course, those of the authors, and do not represent the positions of any of the three universities, the individuals interviewed, or the Andrew W. Mellon Foundation.

References

Association of American Universities. 1986. *Trends in Technology Transfer at Universities.* Association of American Universities, Washington, D.C.

Association of University Technology Managers (AUTM) Licensing Survey. 1991–1995, 1996, 1997, 1998, 1999. AUTM, Northbrook, IL.

Bercovitz, J., M. Feldman, I. Feller, R. Burton. 2001. Strategy and structure as determinants of university technology transfer practices: A comparative study. *J. Tech. Transfer* **26** 21–35.

Blake, D. A. 1993. The university's role in marketing research discoveries. *Chronicle Higher Ed.* (May 12).

Bray, M. J., J. N. Lee. 2000. University revenues from technology transfer: Licensing fees vs. equity positions. *J. Bus. Venturing* **15** 385–392.

Di Gregorio, D., S. Shane. 2000. Why do some universities generate more start-ups than others? Mimeo, University of Maryland, College Park, MD.

Desruisseaux, P. 2000. Universities venture into venture capitalism. *Chronicle Higher Ed.* (May 26).

Feller, I. 1990. University patent and technology-licensing strategies. *Ed. Policy* **4** 327–334.

——. 1997. Technology transfer from universities. John Smart, ed. *Handbook Higher Education*, Volume 12. Agathon Press, New York, 1–42.

——, M. Feldman, J. Bercovitz, R. Burton. 2000. A disaggregated examination of patent and licensing behavior at three research universities. Western Economic Association Meeting, Vancouver, B.C., Canada.

Government–University–Industry Research Roundtable. 1986. *New Alliances and Partnerships in American Science and Engineering.* National Academy of Sciences, Washington, D.C.

Greene, W. H. 2000. *Econometric Analysis.* 4th ed. Prentice Hall, Upper Saddle River, NJ.

Henderson, R., A. Jaffe, M. Trajtenberg. 1998. Universities as a source of commercial technology: A detailed analysis of university patenting 1965–1988. *Rev. Econom. Statist.* **81** 119–127.

Jensen, R., M. Thursby. 2001. Proofs and prototypes for sale: The tale of university licensing. *Amer. Econom. Rev.* **91**(1) 240–259.

Kahneman, D., A. Tversky. 1979. Prospect theory: An analysis of decision under risk. *Econometrica* **47** 263–291.

Lerner, J. 1999. The government as venture capitalist: The long run impact of the SBIR program. *J. Bus.* **72** 285–318.

Lerner, J., R. P. Merges. 1998. The control of technology alliances: An empirical analysis of the biotechnology industry. *J. Indust. Econom.* **46**(2) 125–156.

Maddala, G. S. 1983. *Limited-Dependent and Qualitative Variables in Econometric.* Cambridge University Press, Cambridge, U.K.

March, James G. 1988. Variable risk preferences and adaptive aspirations. *J. Behavior Organ.* **9**(1) 5–24.

——, Zur Shapira. 1987. Managerial perspectives on risk and risk taking. *Management Sci.* **33**(11) 1404–1418.

Mowery, D., A. Ziedonis. 1999. The effects of the Bayh–Dole Act on U.S. university research and technology transfer: Analyzing data from entrants and incumbents. Paper presented at the Science and Technology Group, NBER Summer Institute, National Bureau of Economic Research, Cambridge, MA.

——, R. Nelson, B. Sampat, A. Ziedonis. 1999. The effects of the Bayh–Dole Act on U.S. university research and technology transfer. L. Branscomb, F. Kodama, R. Florida, eds. *Industrializing Knowledge.* MIT Press, Cambridge, MA, 269–306.

National Research Council. 1995. *Research-Doctorate Programs in the United States: Continuity and Change.* National Academy Press, Washington, D.C.

National Science Board. 2000. National Science Board, 2000 (NSB-00-1), Arlington, VA.

Rogers, Everett, J. Yin, J. Hoffman. 2000. Assessing the effectiveness of technology transfer offices at U.S. research universities. *J. Assoc. Univ. Tech.* Managers **12** 47–80.

Shane, Scott. 2000. Selling university technology: Patterns from MIT. Paper presented to the Georgia Tech Conference on University Entrepreneurship and Technology Transfer (November).

Siegel, D., D. Waldman, A. Link. 1999. Assessing the impact of organizational practices on the productivity of university technology transfer offices: An exploratory study. Working paper 7256, National Bureau of Economic Research, Cambridge, MA.

Thursby, M., R. Jensen, J. Thursby. 2001. Objectives, characteristics, and outcomes of university licensing: A survey of major U.S. universities. *J. Tech. Transfer* **12** 59–72.

Thursby, J., S. Kemp. 1999. Growth and productive efficiency of university intellectual property licensing. Working paper, Purdue University, West Lafayette, IN.

——, M. Thursby. 2000a. Industry perspectives on licensing university technologies: Sources and problems. *J. Assoc. Univ. Tech. Managers* **12** 9–23.

——, ——. 2000b. Who is selling the ivory tower? Sources of growth in university licensing. NBER working paper no. W7718, Cambridge, MA.

Trajtenberg, M., R. Henderson, A. Jaffe. 1997. University versus corporate patents: A window on the basicness of invention. *Econom. Innovation New Tech.* **5** 19–50.

Tversky, A., D. Kahneman. 1992. Advances in prospect theory: Cumulative representation of uncertainty. *J. Risk Uncertainty* **5** 291–323.

U.S. Patent and Trademark Office. 1992–1999. *Technology Assessment and Forecast Report, U.S. Universities and Colleges, 1992–1999.* Information Products Division, Technology Assessment and Forecast Branch, U.S. Patent and Trademark Office, Washington, D.C.

Vonortas, N., H. Hertzfeld. 1998. Research and development project selection in the public sector. *J. Policy Anal. Management* **17** 621–638.

Williamson, O. 1975. *Markets and Hierarchies: Analysis and Antitrust Implications.* The Free Press, New York.

——. 1985. *The Economic Institutions of Capitalism.* The Free Press, New York.

——. 1991. Comparative economic organization: The analysis of discrete structural alternatives. *Admin. Sci. Quart.* **36**(2) 269–296.

——. 1996. Economic organization: The case for candor. *Acad. Management Rev.* **21**(1) 48–57.

Zacks, R. 2000. The TR university research scorecard. *Tech. Rev.* **103** (July/August) <http://www.techreview.com/articles/july00/ zacks.htm>.

Zucker, L., M. Darby, M. Brewer. 1998. Intellectual human capital and the birth of U.S. biotechnology enterprises. *Amer. Econom. Rev.* **88**(1) 290–305.

Accepted by David C. Mowery and Scott Shane; received December 2000. This paper was with the authors 9 months for 1 revision.

[22]

ELSEVIER

Research Policy 32 (2003) 209–227

research
policy

www.elsevier.com/locate/econbase

Why do some universities generate more start-ups than others?[*]

Dante Di Gregorio [a,b,*], Scott Shane [a,1]

[a] *Robert H. Smith School of Business, University of Maryland, 3321 Van Munching Hall, College Park, MD 20742, USA*
[b] *Anderson School of Management, University of New Mexico, Albuquerque, NM 87131, USA*

Abstract

The results of this study provide insight into why some universities generate more new companies to exploit their intellectual property than do others. We compare four different explanations for cross-institutional variation in new firm formation rates from university technology licensing offices (TLOs) over the 1994–1998 period—the availability of venture capital in the university area; the commercial orientation of university research and development; intellectual eminence; and university policies. The results show that intellectual eminence, and the policies of making equity investments in TLO start-ups and maintaining a low inventor's share of royalties increase new firm formation. The paper discusses the implications of these results for university and public policy.
© 2002 Elsevier Science B.V. All rights reserved.

Keywords: Entrepreneurship; Technology transfer; University intellectual property

1. Introduction

New firms founded to exploit university-assigned intellectual property (TLO start-ups) have become an important economic phenomenon. Roughly 12% of university-assigned inventions are transferred to the private sector through the founding of new organizations (Association of University Technology Managers, 1998). TLO start-ups are also disproportionately successful start-up firms. Of the 2578 technology licensing office (TLO) start-ups that have been founded since 1980, 70% are still in operation (Association of University Technology Managers, 1998). Moreover,

research on the TLO start-ups from the Massachusetts Institute of Technology (MIT) indicates that roughly 20% of these companies experience an initial public offering (Shane and Stuart, 2002). In fact, several major corporations had their origins as TLO start-ups, including Genentech in biotechnology, Cirrus Logic in semiconductors, and Lycos in Internet search engines. Thus, across universities, TLO start-ups are both an important vehicle of technology transfer, and an important mechanism for economic activity.

However, the frequency of TLO start-up activity varies significantly across universities. Some universities, like MIT, routinely transfer their technology through the formation of new firms, while other universities, like Columbia University, rarely generate start-ups. Moreover, rates of start-up activity are not a simple function of the magnitude of sponsored research funding or the quantity of inventions created. For example, Stanford University, with sponsored research expenditures of US$ 391 million generated 25 TLO start-ups in 1997; whereas Duke University, with

[*] An earlier version of this paper was presented at the Microeconomics Workshop at Purdue University and at the 2001 Global Entrepreneurship Research Conference.
* Corresponding author. Tel.: +1-505-246-2060; fax: +1-909-752-5511.
E-mail addresses: digregorio@mgt.unm.edu (D. Di Gregorio), sshane@rhsmith.umd.edu (S. Shane).
[1] Tel.: +1-505-277-3751; fax: +1-505-277-6898.

210 *D. Di Gregorio, S. Shane/Research Policy 32 (2003) 209–227*

sponsored research expenditures of US$ 361 million, generated none. To date we have no systematic explanation for why some universities generate more new companies to exploit their intellectual property than do others.

Explaining cross-school variation in start-up activity is important for at least four reasons. First, university inventions are an important source of knowledge spillovers (Jaffe, 1989), and understanding the different mechanisms by which knowledge from different universities spills over is important to understanding technology creation and economic growth. Second, TLO start-ups tend to locate geographically close to the institutions that spawn them,[2] making them valuable entities for local economic development and agglomeration economies (Zucker et al., 1998). Third, successful TLO start-ups generate significant wealth through initial public offerings, and university inventors and provosts are interested in capturing this wealth. Fourth, university entrepreneurs make different decisions from non-entrepreneurs, leading the creation of TLO start-ups to generate important questions about university norms and policies toward research, teaching, and knowledge disclosure (Cohen et al., 1998; Brooks and Randazzese, 1998).

In this paper, we explore empirically why some universities generate more TLO start-ups than do others. In specific, we examine the number of companies founded to exploit university-assigned intellectual property across 101 US universities over the 1994–1998 period. We investigate four different arguments for cross-institution variation in start-up rates: university policies, local venture capital activity, the commercial orientation of university research, and intellectual eminence. We find that two university policies—making equity investments in lieu of patent and licensing costs, and the inventor share of royalties—and the university's intellectual eminence influence TLO start-up rates. We find no effect of local venture capital activity and only limited support for an effect of the commercial orientation of university research on TLO start-up rates.

This article proceeds as follows: Section 2 presents the four explanations for why some universities

generate more TLO start-ups than others do. Section 3 describes the methodology for the study. Section 4 presents the results. Section 5 presents a discussion and conclusions.

2. The different explanations

TLO start-ups are created when the licensee of a university-assigned invention creates a new company to exploit it. Both micro and macro-level factors influence the decision to create a new company to exploit a university invention. At the micro-level, research has shown that the attributes of technological inventions themselves (Shane, 2001a), inventors' career experience (Levin and Stephan, 1991; Shane and Khurana, 2000), their psychological make-up (Roberts, 1991), and their research skills (Zucker et al., 1998) influence this decision. At the macro-level, research has shown that technology regimes (Shane, 2001b), the strength of patent protection in a line of business (Shane, 2002), and universities' intellectual property (Goldfarb et al., 2001) and human resource policies (Kenney, 1986) influence this decision. Although both micro- and macro-level factors influence the tendency of people to start new firms to exploit university inventions, we do not discuss micro-level factors in this study. The goal of the paper is to examine the effect macro-level factors that vary across universities over time on the rate at which new firms are created to exploit university inventions rather than to develop an overall behavioral model of the decision to found a firm to exploit university inventions.

Prior research suggests four macro-level explanations for cross-university variation in TLO start-up activity. First, universities located in geographic areas rich in venture capital could be more likely generate TLO start-ups because the abundance of venture capital makes resource acquisition easier for entrepreneurs. Second, universities that conduct industry-funded research could be more likely to generate TLO start-ups because they are more likely than other universities to make commercially-oriented discoveries. Third, universities that are more intellectually eminent could be more likely to generate TLO start-ups because intellectual eminence allows schools to produce new technologies of actual or perceived higher quality. Fourth, universities that adopt

---

[2] The Association of University Technology Managers (1999) reports that 79% of the 364 TLO start-ups in 1998 were founded in the state in which the licensing institution is located.

D. Di Gregorio, S. Shane/Research Policy 32 (2003) 209–227 211

certain policies could generate more TLO start-ups because those policies provide greater incentives for entrepreneurial activity. In Sections 2.1–2.4, we develop each of these explanations.

2.1. Venture capital

The first argument for cross-university variation in TLO start-up activity is the availability of venture capital in the area. Venture capitalists play an important role in the innovation process by providing risk capital and operating assistance to new high technology firms (Florida and Kenney, 1988). In fact, venture capital plays a particularly important role in financing university start-ups because it is a major source of funds for new firms in fields in which universities are a major source of new technology, like biotechnology (Zucker et al., 1998).

Because formal venture capital is a major source of equity financing for new technology companies, its availability is important to overcoming capital market barriers to the financing of new technology firms. In addition, venture capitalists serve as "market makers" in a "spot market" for business development resources by connecting new technology companies with potential suppliers, customers, lawyers, manufacturers, and employees (Florida and Kenney, 1988). Finally, venture capitalists provide valuable operating assistance to new technology companies that help those companies to grow and compete.

Venture capital investments tend to be made locally. Moral hazard problems pervade the financing of new technology companies (Sahlman, 1990). Uncertainty and information asymmetry make entrepreneurs privy to information that investors do not have, so it is important for venture capitalists to closely monitor their investments in new ventures. Because interpersonal interaction provides a central mechanism for disseminating information, and this interaction is enhanced by physical interaction and inspection (Sorenson and Stuart, 2001), geographical proximity lowers the cost of monitoring new ventures (Gompers and Lerner, 1999; Gupta and Sapienza, 1992; Lerner, 1995; Sorenson and Stuart, 2001).

Second, to link new technology companies with potential suppliers and customers, venture capitalists rely on networks of contacts. These networks are more easily developed and maintained in a localized geographic area (Sorenson and Stuart, 2001). As a result, efforts to provide new ventures with ties to important stakeholders are facilitated by geographically localized investing.

Third, the provision of operational assistance to new technology companies is enhanced by physical proximity to investment targets (Gupta and Sapienza, 1992). Venture capitalists spend between 4 and 5 h per month on the site of the companies in which they invest, and activities with portfolio companies account for half of a venture capitalist's time (Gorman and Sahlman, 1989). Because travel time reduces the number of ventures with which an investor can interact, geographically localized investing increases the amount of operational assistance that a venture capital firm can make. Moreover, the quality of assistance that venture capitalists can offer start-ups decreases with geographical distance (Sorenson and Stuart, 2001).

Several studies have provided empirical support for the geographical localization of venture capital investments (Gompers and Lerner, 1999; Gupta and Sapienza, 1992; Lerner, 1995; Sorenson and Stuart, 2001). In particular, Sorenson and Stuart (2001) find that the probability that a venture capital firm will invest in a start-up decreases with the geographical distance between the headquarters of the venture capital firm and the start-up firm—the rate of investment in companies 10 miles from a venture capitalist's headquarters is double that in companies located 100 miles away. Similarly, Lerner (1995) finds that geographic proximity influences the composition of the boards of directors of venture capital-backed start-ups—venture capital firms headquartered within 5 miles of a start-up's location are twice as likely to be on the company's board of directors as venture capital firms headquartered 500 miles away.

Evolutionary patterns of regional development, combined with resource endowments, have created different distributions of venture capital in different geographical locations (Lerner, 1995). The vast majority of venture capital in the US is located in a small number of locations like Silicon Valley and Route 128 (Florida and Kenney, 1988). If entrepreneurs use venture capital to found new high technology companies to exploit university inventions, and venture capitalists make geographically constrained investments, then the availability of venture capital in a locality should influence the rate of TLO start-up activity. This

212   *D. Di Gregorio, S. Shane / Research Policy 32 (2003) 209–227*

argument suggests that, ceteris paribus, the greater the availability of venture capital in the university area, the greater the rate of TLO start-up activity.

2.2. Commercially-oriented research

The second argument for cross-university variation in TLO start-up activity is the commercial orientation of university research. Universities differ on the degree to which their researchers focus on industrial problems. Some universities (perhaps because of their state affiliations or their historical involvement with agricultural or industry extension services) focus their research more closely on the needs of industry than do other universities. The commercial orientation of university research is reflected in the source of funding for that research. Commercially-oriented universities receive more of their research budget from industry than do other universities (Rosenberg and Nelson, 1994).

The tendency of a university to conduct industry-funded research and development should increase its TLO start-up rate for three reasons. First, industry tends to fund more commercially-oriented research than the government, and a commercial orientation should increase the likelihood of discovering technologies that have sufficient commercial value for people to found companies.

Second, industry tends to fund less risky research than the government funds (Arrow, 1962). More risky research is more problematic for firm formation because single technology new companies cannot exploit the economies of scope in technology development that allow large firms to diversify these risks (Nelson, 1959).

Third, being more basic, government-funded research tends to suffer from greater information asymmetry problems than does industry-funded research. Because entrepreneurs obtain money through market-mediated transactions,[3] information asymmetry problems result in failures in venture finance markets. Thus, information asymmetry problems make it less likely that entrepreneurs will be able to finance companies to commercialize government-funded research than industry funded research. The above arguments suggest that, ceteris paribus, the greater the amount of commercially-oriented research activity at

the university, the greater the rate of TLO start-up activity.[4,5]

2.3. Intellectual eminence

The third argument for cross-university variation in TLO start-up activity is university eminence. Two different variants of the eminence explanation have been suggested in the literature. The first argument is that better quality researchers are more likely to start firms to exploit their inventions than lesser quality researchers; and, on average, higher quality researchers are found in more eminent universities. In some fields, university entrepreneurs found companies to capture the rents to their intellectual capital (Zucker et al., 1998). Because this intellectual capital is tacit, and belongs to a small set of leading researchers, inventors must become entrepreneurs to exploit it. More eminent schools are more likely to employ leading-edge researchers than are less eminent schools. Therefore, the founding of companies to capture rents to intellectual capital will be more common at more eminent schools than at less eminent institutions.

The second argument is that the university's prestige or reputation makes it easier for researchers from more eminent universities to start companies to exploit their inventions than researchers from less eminent universities. Obtaining the resources necessary to establish a technology company requires entrepreneurs to persuade resource providers to give them money under conditions of information asymmetry and

---

[3] They lack positive cash flow from existing operations.

[4] Readers should note that an alternative argument could be made—the rate of TLO start-ups is inversely proportional to the commercial orientation of university research funding. When a company contributes research funds, it sometimes obtains the right of first refusal to license any discoveries that come from that research. As a result, more industry funding could lead to fewer start-ups because it leads the university to license a greater proportion of its inventions back to the firms that fund the research.

[5] In our regressions to predict the effect of the commercial orientation of university research on the rate of TLO start-up activity, we control for the number of inventions produced in the university-year. This control is important because new firm formation might depend on the attributes of technological inventions themselves (Shane, 2001), rather than on university orientation. As a result, the number of commercially-oriented inventions, rather than the university's commercial orientation might drive the TLO start-up rate. By partialling out the effect of the number of inventions in regression analysis, we can examine the effect of commercial orientation net of the effect of the number of inventions.

uncertainty. Because information problems preclude investors from completely evaluating the technology under question, investors often make their evaluation of entrepreneurs and their ideas on the basis of perceived signals of quality. One signal that investors use is the intellectual eminence of the researchers and the institution spawning the venture (Podolny and Stuart, 1995). Investors believe, rightly or wrongly, that more eminent universities produce technology that is more worthy of funding than less eminent universities, and therefore encourage greater firm formation from more eminent institutions. Both variants of the intellectual eminence argument suggest that, ceteris paribus, the greater the intellectual eminence of the university, the greater the rate of TLO start-up activity.

2.4. University policies

The fourth argument for cross-university variation in TLO start-up activity is that universities differ in their policies toward technology transfer and that those policies shift activities at the margin toward or away from start-up activity. In particular, previous researchers have suggested the importance of four different policies.

First, the distribution of royalty rates between inventors and the university could influence the propensity of entrepreneurs to found firms to exploit university inventions. Universities typically earn profits from their inventions through royalties on the gross sales from licensing that technology. Universities have policies that divide these profits between inventors and the university. This arrangement means that inventors can earn profits from their inventions either from royalties paid by licensees, or from the profits (net of royalties) made from commercializing the technology themselves.[6]

The dual nature of potential inventor compensation from invention creates an inverse relationship between royalties and incentives for inventors to found firms. Assuming constant licensing rates across

---

[6] This argument assumes that the inventor's royalty is not differentially affected by licensing negotiations between the university and the licensing firm, and that that the inventor's income is not differentially affected by the size of after-license consulting contracts, when the licensee is an inventor start-up and when the licensee is an independent entity. Because the current research project cannot examine this assumption, future research should consider its veracity.

different licensees for particular types of technology, the inventor's earnings will increase with his or her share of the royalties if the technology is licensed to an existing firm. In contrast, if the inventor starts a company, his or her earnings will not increase with his or her share of the royalties. Therefore, the greater the inventor's share of the royalties, the greater the opportunity cost of starting a firm to exploit the technology, and the lower the incentive to seek profits from an invention by founding a firm. Therefore, ceteris paribus, the size of the inventor's share of royalties should be inversely related to the TLO start-up rate.

Second, the use of incubators could influence the cost of start-up activity. Most university technologies are embryonic and development on them is necessary before they can be sold in the market place (Jensen and Thursby, 2002). Incubators allow entrepreneurs to "ripen" technologies in close proximity to inventors whose inputs are useful for further development. In addition, incubators reduce the cost of development through subsidies and sharing of general administrative costs. Therefore, ceteris paribus, the use of incubators should increase the TLO start-up rate.

Third, the use of internal venture capital funds could make the acquisition of capital easier for TLO start-ups. Venture capitalists are more likely to invest in companies that are referred to them by colleagues or that are founded by people that they know because these ties provide investors with information that mitigates the information asymmetry problems inherent in financing new technology companies (Sorenson and Stuart, 2001).

However, most university personnel are not members of the information networks of venture capitalists. Their focus on research and teaching does not require interaction with venture capitalists, but instead requires interaction with other economic actors. Because university administrators with whom university personnel interact administer university venture capital funds, potential university entrepreneurs are more likely to have direct or indirect connections to the administrators of university venture capital funds than to general venture capitalists. These connections facilitate the flow of information about the potential entrepreneurs and mitigate the information asymmetry problems in venture finance. Therefore, ceteris paribus, the presence of internal venture capital funds should increase the TLO start-up rate.

Fourth, a university's willingness to take an equity stake in TLO start-ups in exchange for paying patenting, marketing, or other up-front costs could facilitate the formation of start-up companies. Unlike established firms, new firms lack cash flow from existing operations, making them cash constrained. University equity investments made in lieu of paying patent costs or up-front license fees reduce the cash expenditures of new firms, facilitating firm formation (Hsu and Bernstein, 1997). Therefore, ceteris paribus, the willingness of a university to make equity investments in TLO start-ups should increase the TLO start-up rate.

3. Methodology

In this section, we describe the sample and variables included in the analysis, and provide an overview of the analytical methods we employed.

3.1. Sample

Universities regularly retain the right to intellectual property generated by faculty and staff, leading university technology licensing offices to track the life histories of the intellectual property that they create. Because of the interest of universities in tracking their intellectual property, university technology licensing offices are aware of virtually all start-up firms that are created to exploit university intellectual property.

The Association of University Technology Managers (AUTM), a professional association governed by and for TLO officers, annually surveys university technology licensing offices to obtain information pertaining to patenting, licensing, and start-up firm activity, as well as information on funding, staffing, and certain policies. AUTM has collected data pertaining to start-up activity since 1994. Because we use panel data analysis techniques, we gathered data on start-up activity from 1994 to 1998 for the 116 universities for which 2 or more years of TLO start-up data are available from AUTM.

We seek to examine the effect of university policies on the start-up rates. We define a university in our analysis as an entity that operates under a single set of policy rules. Therefore, we aggregated data from multi-campus universities into a single annual observation for the university,[7] except when the different campuses employed distinct policies and procedures and maintained independent TLOs.[8]

Although the dependent variable of interest, TLO start-up activity, was obtained from the AUTM survey, the data for predictor and control variables were obtained from a variety of sources, including venture capital databases, the United States Patent and Trademark Office (USPTO) database, and a survey administered to TLO directors. To obtain information regarding university policies from 1994 to 1998, we surveyed the 116 universities in our sample by both e-mail and telephone. We asked the TLO directors to indicate their policies for each year from 1994 to 1998.

Of the universities surveyed, 101 responded, providing a response rate exceeding 87%. We compared respondents to non-respondents in terms of patenting and start-up activity and found no statistically significant differences at the $P < 0.10$ level. The non-respondents provided a variety of idiosyncratic reasons for not participating (e.g. some do not participate in surveys as a matter of policy, while others had experienced turnover and were unable to provide historical information regarding policies). Therefore, we are confident that non-response to our policy questions does not hinder our analysis.

The sample for our analysis is restricted to the 101 universities that are both in the AUTM database and responded to our survey. Because some universities report start-up data for only some years, our sample consists of 457 university-year observations. However, the sample includes 89 of the 100 top US universities in R&D volume, and accounts for approximately 85% of all US patents issued to universities, based on statistics maintained by the USPTO. Although the exact number of TLO start-ups is unknown, the sample appears to account for the vast majority of the population of such firms, and selection bias does not hinder our analysis of the data.[9]

---

[7] The AUTM licensing data is most often reported at the level of the university system. It is not possible to examine campuses of the same system separately.

[8] Although most state medical schools share a single TLO with the state university, we consider three state medical schools separate institutions due to their distinct policies and administration.

[9] It is important to note that the sample represents the population of universities that generate inventions. It does not represent the population of US educational institutions.

D. Di Gregorio, S. Shane / Research Policy 32 (2003) 209–227 215

To gather data on venture capital activities in different locations, we examined the Venture Economics database, administered by Thomson Financial Services. The Venture Economics database is the leading source of data on venture capital activity in the US (Gompers and Lerner, 1999).

To gather data on intellectual eminence, we utilized the assessment score for overall graduate school quality reported in the Gourman Reports (Gourman, 1994, 1997), a widely used assessment of graduate and professional degree programs. The Gourman Report assessment incorporates the perceived and actual quality of a university's graduate programs in medicine, engineering, business, physical sciences, social sciences, humanities, and other fields into a single measure of graduate school quality.[10] The measure is derived from an assessment of several factors that are believed to influence graduate school quality, including the caliber of faculty, adequacy of facilities, breadth of curriculum, funding levels, and research productivity.

Lastly, we obtained patent data by searching the on-line database of US patents maintained by United States Patent and Trademark Office. For each university-year, we performed a search of the name of the university and/or foundation designated by the university as the assignee for its intellectual property. We then tabulated the total number of patents in each university-year. The results of our search correlated at 0.95 with the self-reported patent data provided by the universities to AUTM.

3.2. Dependent variable

The dependent variable is a count of the number of TLO start-ups from a given university in a given year.

3.3. Predictor variables

3.3.1. Venture capital availability

To measure the effects of venture capital availability on the TLO start-up rate, we examined four measures

of local venture capital: the number of local companies receiving funding from venture capitalists in a given year; the amount of venture capital funding received by local firms in a given year; the number of local venture capital funds in a given year; and the amount of funding provided by local venture capital funds in a given year.[11,12,13] We defined local venture capital as the amount of activity occurring in all telephone area code zones within 60 miles of the each university.[14] Area codes were used to delineate geographic areas in order to avoid errors of inclusion or omission that would be likely to occur by defining regions by state.

3.3.2. Commercially-oriented research

To measure if the commercial orientation of university research increased the TLO start-up rate, we examined the proportion of each university's sponsored research budget in a given year that was industry funded.[15] Because overall magnitude may be more important than percentage allocation, in an alternative specification, we measured commercial orientation as the dollar value of industry funding, while controlling for government funding. We gathered these data from the AUTM licensing survey.

3.3.3. Intellectual eminence

To measure if university eminence increased the TLO start-up rate, we examined the overall academic rating score of graduate schools published in the Gourman Reports (Gourman, 1994, 1997). Because this survey is produced every 3 years, we update the scores in 1994 and 1997. Three medical schools in the

---

[10] We also examined regressions that substituted the engineering school ranking for the overall ranking. The results are substantively the same as those with the overall rankings. We do not report the analysis with the engineering school rankings because the sample size is reduced by 21 universities that do not offer graduate degrees in engineering.

[11] We do not lag the independent variables because we expect that the current year independent variables, rather than past year independent variables, influence the start-up decision.

[12] In our regression analysis, we use the number of local companies receiving venture capital funding in a given year as our primary measure and treat the other measures as tests of robustness in other regressions.

[13] Because the venture capital measures are non-normally distributed, we also examined natural log and square root transformations. The results for the transformed variables are qualitatively the same as those for the untransformed variables. We report the untransformed variables for ease of interpretation.

[14] The area code was available for approximately 85% of the data in the database.

[15] Prior research shows that this proportion captures the university tendency to conduct applied research (Henderson et al., 1998).

216   *D. Di Gregorio, S. Shane / Research Policy 32 (2003) 209–227*

sample do not offer graduate degrees in fields outside of health sciences, and therefore did not receive overall graduate school scores in the Gourman Report. For these universities, we used the scores for their medical schools in our regression analysis. In unreported regressions, we examined the data excluding the three problematic institutions. We find that their inclusion or exclusion does not qualitatively alter the results.

3.3.4. University licensing policies: the inventor share of royalties

To measure if royalty policies influenced the TLO start-up rate, we examined the inventor's share of royalties from technology licensing. The inventors of technologies licensed by universities receive royalties based on a rate that is virtually always explicitly stated in published university policies. The percent of royalties distributed to inventors may be constant, as is the case in the majority of universities included in our sample, or may be established on a sliding scale that typically decreases according to the amount of royalties received by the university. We contend the distribution rate affects start-up activity by altering the perceived opportunity cost of an inventor. Because the inventor's share of royalty rates sometimes forms a range that is affected by the outcome of the license (i.e. declining or increasing percentages as sales increase), inventors cannot know ex ante the exact share of royalties that they will receive. Therefore, in our primary analysis, we use the minimum percent of total royalties distributed to inventors as an indicator of the perceived opportunity cost. In alternative regressions, we measured the distribution of royalties by the amount of royalties an inventor would receive on a patent that yields US$ 1 million in royalties for the university. While this amount clearly exceeds the average amount of royalties received for university patents, inventors are most likely to start a firm to exploit their technology when they believe their invention has better-than-average prospects.

3.3.5. University licensing policies: incubators

To measure if the presence of incubators influenced the TLO start-up rate, we examined whether or not TLO start-ups had access to technology incubators. University officials often argue that they can enhance the start-up rate out of their TLOs by using incubator

facilities to foster new companies. In some instances, university incubators may be independently operated, but work jointly with the university. In other cases, the incubators may be units of the university.[16] In our survey, we asked the TLO directors whether or not the university provided access to either type of incubator for TLO start-up firms during each year from 1994 to 1998. We included a dummy variable of one for the university-year in our regression analysis if the response was affirmative.

3.3.6. University licensing policies: equity policies and practices

To measure if equity policies influenced the TLO start-up rate, we examined whether or not the TLO could make an equity investment in TLO start-ups. Anecdotal evidence suggests that a university policy of making an equity investment in lieu of requiring reimbursement of patenting and licensing expenses will enhance the university start-up rate by reducing capital constraints on firm formation. We measured this practice through the use of a dummy variable of one in the university-year if the information provided by each university to AUTM indicated that the university took an equity stake in at least one licensee in any prior year.

We also tested an alternative measure of equity policies derived from the surveys we sent to TLO directors. We asked the TLO directors whether or not their university was permitted to take an equity stake in licensees of university intellectual property for each of the years covered in the study. This indicator variable took a value of one if the university's policies did not explicitly prohibit the university from taking an equity stake in a licensee in a given year.

3.3.7. University licensing policies: venture capital investment by universities

To measure if university venture capital funds influenced the TLO start-up rate, we asked TLO directors to indicate whether or not their universities were permitted to make venture capital investments in licensees of university technologies. We include a dummy variable

---

[16] As an indicator variable, this measure does not account for variation in size, funding, and quality of assistance among incubators.

D. Di Gregorio, S. Shane/Research Policy 32 (2003) 209–227   217

of one if the university is permitted to make venture capital investments in licensees in a given year.[17]

3.4. Control variables

3.4.1. Number of inventions

Because we expect that the number of TLO start-ups would be related to the number of inventions produced by the university, we control for the production of technology in three different ways. First, we examine the number of patents issued to the university in the year under investigation. Second, we examine the number of invention disclosures in the university-year. Third, we examine the number of licenses and option agreements signed in the university-year.[18] We examine each of these measures of inventive output (in different regressions) because each measure has advantages and disadvantages. Invention disclosures capture the overall inventive activity at a university, whether or not those inventions are of interest to firms. Invention disclosures are also less biased by the patentability of inventions in different types of technology (e.g. software should generate fewer patents per invention than will drugs), than patents. However, universities have different rules about invention disclosures, making them more subject to institutional variation in their measurement than patents, which must meet the same federal requirements. In addition, some universities pre-screen potential inventions and encourage inventors to disclose only if they believe that the inventions are patentable.[19]

Unlike invention disclosures and patents, licenses and option agreements capture the production of tech-

nology that is of interest to the private sector. By controlling for licensing agreements, rather than invention disclosures or patents, we can measure the frequency of start-up activity, ruling out the possibility that we are simply capturing the commercial value of different schools' inventive output. As a result, using this control for inventive output, we capture the idea that there are many inventions that are not of interest to the private sector, and that there are routes to commercialization other than start-ups.

The invention disclosure and licensing data were derived from the AUTM surveys, while patent data were obtained from the United States Patent and Trademark Office database.

3.4.2. Number of technology licensing office staff

The assistance in technology transfer that entrepreneurs require may exceed that required by established companies. In addition, licensing contracts with start-ups often involve exclusive licensing (Jensen and Thursby, 2002), and the negotiations for such contracts may be more time intensive. Therefore, we control for the number of technology licensing office staff, measured in full-time equivalencies (FTEs).

3.4.3. Sponsored research expenditures

Because the intellectual property exploited by TLO start-ups is created through investment in research, the amount of research inputs is likely related to start-up rates. Therefore, we control for the amount of sponsored research expenditures in the university-year. We control for total sponsored research funding, except in a model that includes industry funding (rather than industry funding as a percent of total funding) as a predictor variable. In the latter case, we control for the total amount of government funding.[20] We gather these data from information reported by the universities to AUTM.

3.4.4. Year dummy variables

Patenting and start-up activity is significantly higher in 1997 and 1998 than in other years. To account for annual variations in patenting and start-up activity, we

---

[17] The venture capital investment variable reflects the explicit policies of universities. It is also correlated with the previous variable, equity investment, because a university must first be able to take an equity stake in a licensee (i.e. a passive form of investment) in order to make a direct venture capital investment in the licensee.

[18] We also examined the number of patent applications in place of the number of patents issued. The results are substantively the same with patent applications as with patents issued.

[19] We also explored whether lagging patent applications and invention disclosures changes the effects of these variables. The results are substantively the same when we lag each of these variables by 2 years. Because we do not know the actual lag between invention disclosure or patent application and start-up, the length of the time lag we selected was arbitrary. Therefore, we report the regression analyses with the unlagged variables.

[20] Because this variable is non-normally distributed, we also examined the square root of this variable. The results are qualitatively the same with the transformed and non-transformed variables. For ease of interpretation, we report the results with the non-transformed variables.

218   *D. Di Gregorio, S. Shane / Research Policy 32 (2003) 209–227*

include indicator variables for all but the first year of the sample period.

3.5. Estimation and model specification

We analyzed the 5-year panel compiled for this study utilizing negative binomial models in generalized estimating equations (GEE), which are an extension of generalized linear models applied to longitudinal data (Liang and Zeger, 1986). Our choice of analytic technique depended on five factors: (1) our dependent variable took the form of count data; (2) the standard errors are likely to be auto correlated over time; (3) the covariance structure itself was not of central interest to us; (4) a significant portion of our sample involved schools that generate no start-ups during our observation period; and (5) unobserved school-level heterogeneity likely influences start-up activity.

We employed a negative binomial estimator because our data takes the form of count data with large numbers of zeros. Consequently, ordinary least squares regression is inappropriate. When we examined the distribution of the dependent variable as a Poisson, a goodness-of-fit test rejected the Poisson distribution assumption because of over-dispersion, suggesting that negative binomial models are more appropriate than Poisson models to analyze the data. Therefore, we ran negative binomial models to predict the number of start-ups for each school in each year.

The use of a generalized linear model for time series data corrects for the problem of auto correlation that results from unobserved factors influencing patterns in particular schools over time (Greene, 1990). In particular, the generalized linear model we used corrects for autocorrelation of residuals (Liang and Zeger, 1986).

GEE is also the most appropriate technique for the analysis of non-Gaussian longitudinal data for which the dependence of the outcome on the covariates requires estimation but the covariance structure across time is not of central interest (Liang and Zeger, 1986). Because we had multiple observations for each university and we wanted to account for the covariance relationships over time, we specified the correlation between the error terms to be exchangeable—correlated similarly across time for each school to account for expected correlations between the errors for each school over time. Alternatively, we could

have also justified assuming either an auto-regressive (AR) or an unstructured correlation structure. Therefore, we also estimated AR1 and unstructured models in order to assess the robustness of our results. In both cases, assuming an alternative correlation structure had no meaningful impact on the significance or magnitude of the results.

Of the 101 schools in the sample, 17 had no start-up activity in any year. Typical fixed effects models for estimating panel data cannot estimate effects for samples that include respondents for which there is no variation in the dependent variable over time. However, we expect that universities for which we observe no TLO start-up activity over the observation period are systematically different from those in which there was some start-up activity. Therefore, dropping those observations would likely bias the estimates in the regression analysis. Estimating our regressions using GEE allowed for the inclusion of universities for which no start-up activity was observed during the sample period.

Initially, we also employed random-effects estimators clustered on schools to deal with the potential for unobserved heterogeneity in explaining the start-up rates across schools. However, a Hausman test indicated the assumptions upon which the random-effects model is dependent were untenable. For purposes of comparison, we also report a model without robust clustering on university as well as a random-effects negative binomial model. As is shown below, the results of these models are not markedly different from the core GEE model, lending confidence in the robustness of our results to the choice of analytic technique.[21]

4. Results

Table 1 presents summary statistics for all variables included in the sample. Table 2 presents the results of the regression analysis. In Table 2, model 1 provides the main model. Models 2–9 provide a series of robustness checks using alternative measures for

---

[21] The random-effects model allows us to rule out the possibility that the results we present are artifacts of unobserved heterogeneity in such things as the relative emphases of different schools on different scientific fields and the presence or absence of engineering and medical programs.

D. Di Gregorio, S. Shane/Research Policy 32 (2003) 209–227

219

Table 1
Descriptive statistics

Variable	Observations	Mean	S.D.	S.D. between schools	S.D. within schools	Minimum	Maximum
Number of TLO start-ups in year	457	2.083	3.116	2.523	1.733	0.000	25.000
Number of VC-funded local firms	457	72.591	128.461	115.944	49.631	0.000	1194.000
Number of local VC funds	457	44.842	80.856	76.248	23.218	0.000	421.000
US$ (in millions) provided to local firms	457	591.670	1020.137	841.047	552.975	0.000	9202.840
US$ (in millions) provided by local funds	457	795.501	1803.332	1597.979	771.139	0.000	9604.690
Industry/total sponsored research funds	457	0.104	0.082	0.074	0.036	0.005	0.560
Industry sponsored funding (US$ in millions)	457	15.952	18.666	17.287	5.863	0.303	162.432
Gourman graduate school score	457	3.837	0.762	0.772	0.001	2.080	4.940
Minimum inventor share of royalties (%)	457	35.463	10.272	10.077	2.127	10.000	50.000
Inventor share of royalties from a patent yielding US$ 1 million (%)	457	36.890	9.611	9.567	1.563	15.000	65.000
Has university-affiliated incubator (1 = yes)	457	0.344	0.475	0.460	0.111	0.000	1.000
Has previously taken an equity stake (1 = yes)	457	0.740	0.439	0.420	0.185	0.000	1.000
Permitted to take equity (1 = yes)	457	0.796	0.403	0.386	0.135	0.000	1.000
Permitted to make VC investments (1 = yes)	457	0.435	0.496	0.493	0.066	0.000	1.000
Patents	457	21.260	34.757	31.876	11.141	0.000	415.000
Invention disclosures	457	79.440	89.614	85.227	19.871	0.000	742.000
TLO staff members (FTEs)	457	6.765	11.339	10.826	1.461	0.000	103.500
Total sponsored research funding (US$ in millions)	457	184.182	207.478	199.067	31.486	7.966	1709.929
Government-sponsored funding (US$ in millions)	457	119.217	138.101	128.519	39.156	2.975	933.210
Licenses to all firms in year	452	23.861	29.818	27.617	9.864	0.000	191.000
Licenses to established firms in year	452	21.774	27.948	25.767	9.648	0.000	186.000

220   D. Di Gregorio, S. Shane / Research Policy 32 (2003) 209–227

Table 2
Model estimation

	Model						
	1	2	3	4	5	6	7
Venture capital availability							
Number of VC-funded local firms (in thousands)	1.142 (1.018)	1.064 (0.986)	0.887 (0.655)	1.034 (0.470)	1.110 (0.896)		
Number of local VC funds (in thousands)						0.967 (0.957)	
US$ (in billions) provided to local firms							
US$ (in billions) provided by local funds							0.949 (0.090)
Commercially-oriented research							
Industry/total sponsored research funds	2.035 (2.198)	2.044 (2.260)	1.476 (1.528)	2.625 (2.849)		1.991 (2.169)	1.850 (1.959)
Industry sponsored funding (US$ in millions)					1.013** (0.006)		
Intellectual eminence							
Gourman graduate school score	1.676*** (0.262)	1.812*** (0.271)	1.490** (0.214)	1.533** (0.225)	1.633*** (0.214)	1.679*** (0.258)	1.684*** (0.262)
University licensing policies							
Minimum inventor share of royalties	0.980** (0.006)	0.974*** (0.006)	0.985** (0.006)	0.983** (0.006)	0.980*** (0.006)	0.980** (0.006)	0.981** (0.006)
Inventor share of royalties from a patent yielding US$ 1 million							
Has university-affiliated incubator	1.129 (0.180)	1.294 (0.214)	1.130 (0.165)	1.147 (0.169)	1.111 (0.184)	1.123 (0.181)	1.112 (0.177)
Has previously taken an equity stake	1.886** (0.389)	1.886** (0.389)	1.902** (0.397)	1.836* (0.391)	1.837** (0.378)	1.882** (0.388)	1.869† (0.383)
Permitted to take equity		1.687* (0.372)					
Permitted to make VC investments	0.881 (0.144)	0.825 (0.147)	0.966 (0.148)	0.832 (0.128)	0.933 (0.156)	0.890 (0.151)	0.912 (0.150)
Control variables							
Patents	1.004 (0.004)	1.003 (0.004)	1.004 (0.004)		1.002 (0.003)	1.004 (0.003)	1.005 (0.003)
Invention disclosures			1.005*** (0.001)				
License agreements				1.012*** (0.002)			
TLO staff members (FTEs)	0.990 (0.010)	0.995 (0.010)	0.982** (0.009)	0.982† (0.010)	0.995 (0.007)	0.990 (0.010)	0.991 (0.010)
Total sponsored research funding (US$ in millions)	1.002† (0.001)	1.002 (0.001)	1.001 (0.001)	1.002* (0.001)		1.002† (0.001)	1.002† (0.001)
Government-sponsored funding (US$ in millions)					1.001 (0.001)		
Fiscal year 1995	0.976 (0.126)	1.045 (0.142)	0.949 (0.120)	1.000 (0.130)	1.008 (0.132)	0.977 (0.127)	0.984 (0.128)
Fiscal year 1996	0.987 (0.153)	1.077 (0.169)	0.948 (0.149)	0.977 (0.159)	1.030 (0.156)	0.994 (0.156)	1.020 (0.155)
Fiscal year 1997	1.236 (0.189)	1.355* (0.200)	1.133 (0.163)	1.193 (0.179)	1.258 (0.185)	1.247 (0.179)	1.289† (0.183)
Fiscal year 1998	1.256 (0.189)	1.397 (0.214)	1.190 (0.184)	1.227 (0.178)	1.289† (0.189)	1.267 (0.189)	1.318† (0.200)
Wald X^2 (degrees of freedom)	167.96*** (14)	186.78*** (14)	211.88*** (14)	314.29*** (14)	200.98*** (14)	163.37*** (14)	170.93*** (14)

D. Di Gregorio, S. Shane / Research Policy 32 (2003) 209–227

	8	9	10	11	12	13
Venture capital availability						
Number of VC-funded local firms (in thousands)		1.128 (0.985)	1.142 (0.913)	0.873 (0.490)	1.217 (1.189)	1.147 (0.994)
Number of local VC funds (in thousands)						
US$ (in billions) provided to local firms						
US$ (in billions) provided by local funds	0.990 (0.035)					
Commercially-oriented research						
Industry/total sponsored research funds	1.958 (2.109)	2.276 (2.427)	2.035 (2.272)	2.937 (2.811)	2.745 (2.957)	1.934 (2.021)
Industry sponsored funding (US$ in millions)						
Intellectual eminence						
Gourman graduate school score	1.685*** (0.261)	1.670*** (0.251)	1.676** (0.275)	1.792*** (0.248)	1.818*** (0.300)	1.636*** (0.249)
University licensing policies						
Minimum inventor share of royalties	0.980** (0.006)		0.980* (0.009)	0.985* (0.008)	0.980** (0.007)	0.979** (0.006)
Inventor share of royalties from a patent yielding US$ 1 million		0.974*** (0.007)				
Has university-affiliated incubator	1.124 (0.181)	1.136 (0.181)	1.129 (0.237)	1.146 (0.197)	1.264 (0.218)	1.168 (0.183)
Has previously taken an equity stake	1.876** (0.385)	1.887* (0.392)	1.886** (0.410)	2.087*** (0.407)	1.828* (0.458)	1.924** (0.398)
Permitted to take equity						
Permitted to make VC investments	0.896 (0.154)	0.871 (0.140)	0.881 (0.174)	0.862 (0.142)	0.840 (0.148)	0.895 (0.147)
Control variables						
Patents	1.004 (0.003)	1.003 (0.003)	1.004 (0.004)	1.001 (0.002)	1.003 (0.004)	1.004 (0.003)
Invention disclosures						
License agreements						
TLO staff members (FTEs)	0.991 (0.010)	0.991 (0.010)	0.990 (0.014)	0.998 (0.010)	0.987 (0.010)	0.986 (0.010)
Total sponsored research funding (US$ in millions)	1.002† (0.001)	1.002† (0.001)	1.002* (0.001)	1.001* (0.001)	1.002* (0.001)	1.002* (0.001)
Government-sponsored funding (US$ in millions)						
Fiscal year 1995	0.978 (0.126)	0.970 (0.126)	0.976 (0.156)	1.037 (0.138)	0.959 (0.133)	0.971 (0.126)
Fiscal year 1996	1.001 (0.157)	0.990 (0.155)	0.987 (0.162)	1.008 (0.138)	0.946 (0.149)	0.981 (0.152)
Fiscal year 1997	1.256 (0.178)	1.226 (0.182)	1.236 (0.203)	1.336* (0.177)	1.284 (0.201)	1.232 (0.179)
Fiscal year 1998	1.279† (0.187)	1.257 (0.191)	1.256 (0.214)	1.325* (0.183)	1.256 (0.203)	1.249 (0.190)
Wald X^2 (degrees of freedom)	161.55*** (14)	173.47*** (14)	95.97*** (14)	141.38*** (14)	154.99*** (14)	171.92*** (14)

Dependent variable: start-ups (models 1–13). Number of observations/groups: 457/101 (models 1–3, 5–11 and 13); 452/100 (model 4); 405/86 (model 12). Model specification: GEE, semi-robust (models 1–9); GEE (model 10); NBREG, semi-robust (model 11); GEE, semi-robust, AR1 (model 12); GEE, semi-robust, unstructured (model 13). The coefficients are exponentiated betas. Standard errors are in parentheses.

† $P \leq 0.10$.
* $P \leq 0.05$.
** $P \leq 0.01$.
*** $P \leq 0.001$.

222   *D. Di Gregorio, S. Shane / Research Policy 32 (2003) 209–227*

predictor and control variables. Models 10–13 provide robustness checks by examining alternative estimation techniques. Overall, the results provide substantial evidence that universities' intellectual eminence and licensing policies have a significant impact on TLO start-up activity, while providing little evidence that venture capital availability and the commercial orientation of research influence TLO start-up activity.

The university's intellectual eminence significantly predicts TLO start-up activity. The estimated coefficient for this variable,[22] shown in model 1, implies, ceteris paribus, that an improvement in graduate school quality by one point is associated with a start-up rate of 1.68 times the base rate. Put differently, an increase in intellectual eminence by one standard deviation is associated with approximately one additional start-up firm per year. Thus, more eminent universities appear not only to generate a greater amount of patentable intellectual property, but also—since licenses, patents, and invention disclosures are controlled for in the models we have estimated—create more start-ups to exploit that intellectual property.

Although the precise mechanism through which this effect operates is not entirely clear, we have offered two explanations. First, researchers from more prestigious universities are better researchers and thus are more likely to create firms to capture the rents to their rare and valuable intellectual property (Zucker et al., 1998). Second, since investors use signals, such as institutional reputation or prestige, to help assess the commercial potential of university technologies, inventors from more prestigious universities may be better able to obtain the necessary capital to start their own firms.

Our findings also indicate that two sets of university licensing policies—policies regarding the distribution of royalties to inventors and whether or not the university is permitted to take an equity stake in licensees—appear to influence start-up activity. As in the case of intellectual eminence, these results are robust to different estimation techniques, and are also robust to different operationalizations of the predictor variables. Ceteris paribus, the minimum percentage of royalties distributed to inventors is inversely related to start-up activity such that an increase in the

inventor's share of royalties by 10% implies 0.40 *fewer* start-up firms per year, a decrease of 20% from the mean. When royalties are measured by the amount distributed to inventors on a patent yielding US$ 1 million in total royalties, rather than the minimum distribution rate, the effect size is even greater. By increasing the opportunity cost of starting up a new venture, a high inventor share of royalties provides a disincentive to potential inventor-entrepreneurs.

The other licensing policy that appears to influence start-up activity is equity policy. Ceteris paribus, universities that have previously demonstrated a willingness to take an equity stake in licensees in exchange for paying up-front patenting and licensing expenses have a start-up rate that is 1.89 times that of universities that have not demonstrated a willingness to take equity. When equity practices are assessed by the universities' explicit policies rather than their actual practice, the effect size is slightly diminished. Universities that are permitted to take an equity stake in licensees report a start-up rate 1.69 times that of universities that are not permitted to make equity arrangements. Universities that retain the ability to accept an equity stake in licensees instead of direct reimbursement for patenting and licensing costs appear to foster greater start-up activity by providing greater liquidity to entrepreneurs.

The two additional policy variables that we tested—the presence of a university-affiliated incubator and whether or not the university is permitted to actively make venture capital investments in licensees—do not appear to have an impact on start-up activity. The coefficient on the incubator indicator variable is positive as expected, but is not significant. The coefficient on the venture capital investment indicator variable is actually negative, but is also not significant. Therefore, we find no evidence that these practices influence TLO start-up activity.

Our findings provide little support for the contention that universities that conduct more commercially-oriented research will experience greater TLO start-up activity. When commercial orientation is measured by the percentage of total sponsored research funding that is derived from industry sources, the estimated coefficient is positive but is not significant. However, in an alternative specification in which commercial orientation is measured by the dollar amount of industry funding (model 5), the coefficient for industry

---

[22] In all of the models, we report the exponentiated coefficients for ease of interpretation.

D. Di Gregorio, S. Shane / Research Policy 32 (2003) 209–227   223

Table 3
Model estimation: elite and non-elite sub-samples

	Model							
	1-Elite	2-Elite	3-Elite	4-Elite	1-Non-Elite	2-Non-Elite	3-Non-Elite	4-Non-Elite
Venture capital availability								
Number of VC-funded local firms (in thousands)	2.478 (2.072)	2.354 (2.042)	1.632 (1.425)	2.113 (1.813)	0.943 (1.222)	1.502 (1.855)	0.742 (0.942)	0.991 (1.267)
Number of local VC funds (in thousands)								
US$ (in billions) provided to local firms								
US$ (in billions) provided by local funds								
Commercially-oriented research								
Industry/total sponsored research funds	37.425** (53.790)	33.845** (46.978)	18.586** (21.304)		0.630 (0.874)	0.799 (1.220)	0.546 (0.804)	
Industry sponsored funding (US$ in millions)				1.014* (0.007)				1.008 (0.012)
Intellectual eminence								
Gourman graduate school score	1.826* (0.512)	1.861* (0.523)	1.526* (0.318)	1.615† (0.466)	1.347 (0.637)	1.553 (0.624)	1.493 (0.712)	1.626 (0.783)
University licensing policies								
Minimum inventor share of royalties	0.978** (0.005)	0.974*** (0.006)	0.985** (0.005)	0.976*** (0.005)	0.987 (0.018)	0.974 (0.016)	0.990 (0.016)	0.986 (0.016)
Inventor share of royalties from a patent yielding US$ 1 million								
Has university-affiliated incubator	1.264 (0.252)	1.322 (0.272)	1.292† (0.195)	1.239 (0.261)	1.091 (0.364)	1.428 (0.407)	1.069 (0.352)	0.975 (0.303)
Has previously taken an equity stake	1.549 (0.346)	1.492* (0.269)	1.645* (0.401)	1.573* (0.356)	2.497** (0.756)		2.528** (0.757)	2.316** (0.737)
Permitted to take equity						2.587** (0.800)		
Permitted to make VC investments	0.737† (0.134)	0.701* (0.127)	0.898 (0.126)	0.774 (0.138)	1.127 (0.350)	0.929 (0.295)	1.191 (0.379)	1.150 (0.337)
Control variables								
Patents	1.002 (0.003)	1.002 (0.003)	1.006*** (0.001)	1.000 (0.003)	1.018 (0.012)	1.023† (0.012)	1.003 (0.007)	1.028** (0.011)
Invention disclosures	0.991 (0.007)	0.993 (0.006)	0.981** (0.007)	0.991 (0.006)	1.019 (0.040)	1.037 (0.040)	1.020 (0.045)	1.026 (0.037)
TLO staff members (FTEs)	1.002* (0.001)	1.001* (0.001)	1.001 (0.000)	1.001 (0.001)	1.005* (0.002)	1.005* (0.002)	1.005† (0.003)	1.007† (0.004)
Total sponsored research funding (US$ in millions)								
Government-sponsored research funding (US$ in millions)								
Fiscal year 1995	0.922 (0.145)	0.980 (0.160)	0.888 (0.140)	0.938 (0.149)	1.132 (0.268)	1.188 (0.308)	1.112 (0.256)	1.158 (0.273)
Fiscal year 1996	0.963 (0.196)	1.016 (0.214)	0.898 (0.181)	0.982 (0.195)	1.106 (0.293)	1.126 (0.326)	1.115 (0.308)	1.131 (0.310)
Fiscal year 1997	1.202 (0.241)	1.277 (0.252)	1.041 (0.203)	1.182 (0.236)	1.215 (0.314)	1.350 (0.360)	1.256 (0.317)	1.223 (0.324)
Fiscal year 1998	1.116 (0.210)	1.171 (0.219)	1.010 (0.208)	1.147 (0.217)	1.261 (0.381)	1.498 (0.435)	1.351 (0.379)	1.277 (0.391)
Wald X^2 (degrees of freedom)	112.64*** (14)	107.60*** (14)	173.39*** (14)	137.69*** (14)	126.47*** (14)	99.64*** (14)	91.59*** (14)	119.22*** (14)

Dependent variable: start-ups (all models). Number of observations/groups: 236/51 (models 1-Elite, 2-Elite, 3-Elite and 4-Elite); 221/50 (models 1-Non-Elite, 2-Non-Elite, 3-Non-Elite and 4-Non-Elite). Model specification: GEE, semi-robust (all models). The coefficients are exponentiated betas. Standard errors are in parentheses.

† $P \leq 0.10$.
* $P \leq 0.05$.
** $P \leq 0.01$.
*** $P \leq 0.001$.

224   *D. Di Gregorio, S. Shane/Research Policy 32 (2003) 209–227*

funding is positive and significant. A US$ 10 million increase in industry sponsored research funding is associated with an increase in start-up activity of 0.13 firms (6.7%) per year, ceteris paribus.

Finally, our results provide no evidence that TLO start-up activity is influenced by the local availability of venture capital funding. We operationalized local venture capital availability in four different ways (i.e. models 1 and 6–8), and the coefficients are not significant in any of the models we estimated.

As a robustness check, we examined the predictive validity of our main model on sub-samples of more eminent and less eminent schools by dividing our sample in half at the median on the eminence score. We show these results in Table 3. For the more eminent schools, we find that our results are even stronger than for the entire sample. Intellectual eminence and equity policies have a positive effect and the inventor's share of royalties has a negative effect on the start-up rate. Moreover, the magnitude of the coefficients is greater than that for the overall sample. For this sub-sample, we still find no effect for local venture capital. However, for more eminent universities, the industry share of sponsored research has a positive effect on start-up rates.

In contrast, our model holds less well for less eminent universities. For this sub-sample, we find that only the policy of taking equity appears to influence start-up rates. Overall, the examination of the sub-samples supports our overall findings, but suggests that start-up rates at less eminent universities are driven by more idiosyncratic factors than start-up rates at more eminent institutions.

5. Discussion

In this study, we compared four different explanations for cross-institutional variation in new firm formation rates from TLO offices over the 1994–1998 period—the concentration of venture capital in the area; the reliance of university research and development on industry funding; intellectual eminence; and university policies. The results show that the intellectual eminence of the university, and the policies of making equity investments in TLO start-ups and maintaining a low inventor share of royalties increase new firm formation activity.

We believe that one of the major strengths of this study is that the sampled universities jointly account for the vast majority of university patenting activity in the US. By extension, they most likely account for the vast majority of TLO start-ups. Another major strength of the study concerns the mitigation of selection bias. By examining technology licensing office start-ups, we examine a documented source of new companies, thereby minimizing the problems of selection bias in accounting for start-up activity to exploit other types of new technology developed in universities.

However, our research design limits our sample to the most active research universities, and is therefore not a random sample of all higher education institutions. Moreover, our approach limits our analysis to new firm formation to exploit university-assigned technology. Therefore, our ability to generalize to colleges and universities that are not research-oriented, or to generalize to start-up activity that is not designed to exploit university-assigned intellectual property, is limited. For instance, we have found that a commercial orientation, the availability of venture capital funds, and TLO policies and practices such as the presence of an incubator do not predict TLO start-up activity among the sampled universities. We cannot rule out the possibility that these practices may facilitate start-up activity among colleges and universities that are not research-oriented or influence other types of university start-up activity.

Nevertheless, our findings have four important implications for research on and policy towards university technology transfer and start-up activity. First, we find no evidence to support the argument that capital market constraints limit TLO start-up activity in particular locations. Although other forms of private equity (e.g. angel capital) might influence start-up activity in ways that we cannot observe, we find that the amount of formal venture capital available in a particular location has no significant effect on start-up activity out of TLOs once university technology production is measured. This result is consistent with the work of Zucker et al. (1998) who found that venture capital availability did not significantly influence start-up activity in biotechnology once the distribution of intellectual capital across time and space was considered. Our findings, like Zucker et al. (1998), suggest that capital markets distribute venture capital

D. Di Gregorio, S. Shane / Research Policy 32 (2003) 209–227 225

efficiently over geographic space; and the availability of local venture capital is not a constraint on TLO start-up activity.

This result also suggests that venture capitalists may be late stage investors in university technology. Other sources of funds, such as angels, government agencies, and universities themselves (through equity investment in their own start-ups), may be more important in the early stages, and thus may be catalysts for new firm formation and economic development. Our findings direct further research efforts towards investigating the relative importance of both different funding entities and funding constraints on firm formation as a mode of exploitation of university technology.

Second, although the effect of industry funding on start-up activity may be lagged in ways we cannot estimate, or influence start-up activity in a way that we cannot observe, we fail to find adequate support for the argument that industry funding of university research makes TLO start-up activity more likely. In fact, our results are consistent with anecdotal information on TLO start-ups that suggest that many of these companies seek to exploit basic scientific discoveries (Association of University Technology Managers, 1996).

One reason why the commercial orientation of a university does not predict its start-up rate could be countervailing effects of commercial orientation. Although a commercial research orientation might generate a pool of university inventions that are more appropriate for new firm formation than is generated from a governmental research orientation, the funding structure necessary to generate university inventions might mitigate the benefits of this better pool of inventions. Because private firms might be very likely to license commercially valuable inventions that are generated from research that they fund, any increase in the pool of commercially valuable inventions that a commercial orientation creates may be siphoned off by greater invention licensing by the private sector providers of research funds. As a result, there is no net effect on the TLO start-up rate of the university's commercial orientation.

Nevertheless, the observation that TLO start-ups are as likely to occur when government funds university research as when the private sector does so raises several interesting and important policy questions

that future researchers may wish to explore. For example, how should universities manage TLO start-up activities given that taxpayer funds have been used to fund that research? And what role will universities play in technological development if basic research is transferred to the private sector through proprietary start-up ventures?

Third, we find evidence that several university technology transfer policies enhance TLO start-up activity. In particular, a low inventors' share of royalties and a willingness to make equity investments in TLO start-up companies increase start-up activity. These findings suggest that universities can make policy decisions to generate greater numbers of TLO start-ups. These policy tools are important because start-ups and established firm licensees differ in several important ways, including their tendency to contribute to local economic development, their tendency to generate significant income for universities, and their decisions toward knowledge disclosure and research norms. Understanding the implications of these policy tools is also important because they may generate conflicting incentives. In particular, many universities distribute a high percentage of royalties to inventors in order to encourage the reporting and exploitation of inventions; however, our results suggest that high distribution rates also serve as a disincentive to the creation of start-up firms.

The results also show, however, that many policies advocated as mechanisms to increase TLO start-up activity appear to have little effect. In particular, the effects of university-affiliated incubators and university venture capital funds are insignificant. One reason why the presence of incubators has an insignificant effect on start-up rates may be that potential entrepreneurs do not consider the use of incubators when making the start-up decision. Consequently, the existence of incubators merely shifts the location of start-ups (to incubators from outside) rather than increasing the amount of them. Although we can conclude that having access to an incubator does not influence the rate of TLO start-up activity; our analysis cannot determine if university-affiliated incubators influence the success of TLO start-ups.

One reason why university venture capital funds have an insignificant effect on start-up rates may be that university entrepreneurs develop adequate ties to external venture capitalists to provide the

226   *D. Di Gregorio, S. Shane / Research Policy 32 (2003) 209–227*

investors with information about them through technical due diligence or other activity. As a result, TLO entrepreneurs can obtain adequate amounts of external venture capital. Therefore, university venture capital merely substitutes for, rather than adds to, external venture capital in its effect on start-up activity. Although we cannot be sure why these policies have no effect on start-up rates, we believe that university officials, researchers, and policy makers will find the evidence in support of some policies and not in support of others useful in developing explanations for and procedures toward the management of university technology transfer and TLO start-up activity.

Fourth, our results show more eminent universities have greater TLO start-up activity than other universities. This result is consistent with the argument that leading researchers found companies to earn rents on their intellectual capital (Zucker et al., 1998). It is also consistent with the argument that gathering the necessary resources to found a company to exploit uncertain new technology is easier when the university's status enhances the entrepreneur's credibility.

The tendency for TLO start-ups to come disproportionately from eminent universities also generates important implications for researchers seeking to explain the creation of new technology companies, as well as policy makers interested in influencing the mode of technology transfer out of universities. In particular, the results suggest that researchers and policy makers consider the impact on university technology transfer and industry evolution of the tendency for new technology companies to emerge from eminent universities.

In short, significant differences exist across universities in their generation of new firms to exploit university inventions. Both university policies and intellectual eminence influence this variation, generating important implications for research on and policy towards university technology transfer. Although this paper provides a survey of the effects of university equity investment and royalty policies, intellectual eminence, and funding sources on university TLO start-up activity across a broad spectrum of universities, future research should examine each of these factors in a more fine-grained manner. Hopefully, other scholars will view this study as a springboard for more refined research on these specific topics.

Acknowledgements

The authors contributed equally to the writing of this paper. We would like to thank Rebecca Henderson, David Hsu, Riitta Katilla, Wes Sine, Deepak Somaya, Jerry Thursby, and Rama Velamuri for their helpful comments on an earlier draft of this paper.

References

Arrow, K., 1962. Economic welfare and the allocation of resources for invention. In: Nelson, R. (Ed.), The Rate and Direction of Inventive Activity. Princeton University Press, Princeton, NJ.

Association of University Technology Managers, 1996. AUTM Licensing Survey. Association of University Technology Managers, Norwalk, CT.

Association of University Technology Managers, 1998. AUTM Licensing Survey. Association of University Technology Managers, Norwalk, CT.

Association of University Technology Managers, 1999. AUTM Licensing Survey. Association of University Technology Managers, Norwalk, CT.

Brooks, H., Randazzese, L., 1998. University–industry relations: the next 4 years and beyond. In: Branscomb, L., Keller, J. (Eds.), Investing in Innovation: Creating a Research and Innovation Policy that Works. MIT Press, Cambridge, MA.

Cohen, W., Florida, R., Randazzese, L., Walsh, J., 1998. Industry and the academy: uneasy partners in the cause of technological advance. In: Noll, R. (Ed.), Challenges to Research Universities. The Brookings Institution, Washington, DC.

Florida, R., Kenney, M., 1988. Venture capital financed innovation and technological change the United States. Research Policy 17, 119–137.

Goldfarb, B., Henreksson, M., Rosenberg, N., 2001. Demand versus supply-driven innovations: US and Swedish experiences in academic entrepreneurship. Working Paper, Stockholm School of Economics.

Gompers, P., Lerner, J., 1999. The Venture Capital Cycle. MIT Press, Cambridge, MA.

Gorman, M., Sahlman, W., 1989. What do venture capitalists do? Journal of Business Venturing 4, 231–248.

Gourman, J., 1994. The Gourman Report. National Education Standards, Northridge, CA.

Gourman, J., 1997. The Gourman Report. National Education Standards, Northridge, CA.

Greene, W., 1990. Econometric Analysis. MacMillan, New York.

Gupta, A., Sapienza, H., 1992. Determinants of venture capital firms' preferences regarding the industry diversity and geographic scope of their investments. Journal of Business Venturing 7, 342–362.

Henderson, R., Jaffe, A., Trajtenberg, M., 1998. Universities as a source of commercial technology: a detailed analysis of university patenting, 1965–1988. Review of Economics and Statistics 80, 119–127.

Hsu, D., Bernstein, T., 1997. Managing the university technology licensing process: findings from case studies. Journal of the Association of University Technology Managers 9, 1–33.

Jaffe, A., 1989. The real effects of academic research. American Economic Review 79, 957–970.

Jensen, R., Thursby, M., 2002. Proofs and prototypes for sale: the tale of university licensing. American Economic Review 91 (1), 240–260.

Kenney, M., 1986. Biotechnology: The University–Industrial Complex. Yale University Press, New Haven.

Lerner, J., 1995. Venture capitalists and the oversight of private firms. Journal of Finance 50 (1), 301–318.

Levin, S., Stephan, P., 1991. Research productivity over the life cycle: evidence for academic scientists. American Economic Review 81 (4), 114–132.

Liang, K., Zeger, S., 1986. Longitudinal data analysis using generalized linear models. Biometrika 73 (1), 13–22.

Nelson, R., 1959. The simple economics of basic scientific research. Journal of Political Economy 67, 297–306.

Podolny, J., Stuart, T., 1995. A role-based ecology of technical change. American Journal of Sociology 100 (5), 1224–1260.

Roberts, E., 1991. Entrepreneurs in High Technology—Lessons from MIT and Beyond. Oxford University Press, New York.

Rosenberg, N., Nelson, R., 1994. American universities and technical advance in industry. Research Policy 23, 323–348.

Sahlman, W., 1990. The structure and governance of venture capital organizations. Journal of Financial Economics 27, 473–521.

Shane, S., 2001a. Technology opportunity and firm formation. Management Science 47 (2), 205–220.

Shane, S., 2001b. Technology regimes and new firm formation. Management Science 47 (9), 1173–1190.

Shane, S., 2002. Selling university technology: patterns from MIT. Management Science 48 (1), 122–138.

Shane, S., Khurana, R., 2000. Career experience and firm founding. Academy of Management Best Paper Proceedings.

Shane, S., Stuart, T., 2002. Organizational endowments and the performance of university start-ups. Management Science 48 (1), 154–171.

Sorenson, O., Stuart, T., 2001. Syndication networks and the spatial distribution of venture capital. American Journal of Sociology 106 (6), 1546–1590.

Zucker, L., Darby, M., Brewer, M., 1998. Intellectual human capital and the birth of US biotechnology enterprises. American Economic Review 88 (1), 290–305.

Technology Transfer and
Universities' Spin-Out Strategies

Andy Lockett
Mike Wright
Stephen Franklin

ABSTRACT. Universities may seek to transfer technology from the public to the private sector, and therefore capture the benefits of commercialization, through a number of different mechanisms. This paper examines the option of using technology-based spin-out companies. Based on a survey of technology transfer/business development officers at 57 U.K. universities, we examine their strategies to promote the creation of spin-out companies and how they then manage the development of these companies. Our analysis focuses on the difference between those universities that have been most active in the area and those that have been least active. The results indicate that the more successful universities have clearer strategies towards the spinning out of companies and the use of surrogate entrepreneurs in this process. In addition, the more successful universities were found to possess a greater expertise and networks that may be important in fostering spin-out companies. However, the role of the academic inventor was not found to differ between the more and less successful universities. Finally, equity ownership was found to be more widely distributed among the members of the spin-out company in the case of the more successful universities.

Andy Lockett
Center for Management Buy Out Research
Business School
University of Nottingham
Jubilee Campus
Nottingham NG8 1BB, U.K.

Mike Wright
Center for Management Buy Out Research
Business School and Zeton Ltd
University of Nottingham
Jubilee Campus
Nottingham NG8 1BB, U.K.

and

Stephen Franklin
ANGLE Technology Limited
Enterprise House
Manchester Science Park
Manchester, M15 6SE, U.K.

1. Introduction

The commercialization of university-based technology has become a prominent issue in the policy arena in both the U.S. and the U.K. The spinning-out of inventions into separate companies represents a potentially important but as yet under-exploited option. In the U.S., the transfer of technology from the public to the private sector is increasingly regarded as playing a significant role in new business starts, growth of existing businesses, and new job creation (Siegel et al., 1999). In the U.K., the debate over the role of universities as a source of new spin-out companies has intensified since the publication of reports highlighting the financial and managerial issues that may be critical to their success (Bank of England, 1996; CBI, 1997).

It is not the intention of this paper to provide a comparative assessment of the differing approaches that universities may adopt to the commercialization of university research. Rather, the focus is on identifying areas in which universities can be more successful in the development of spin-off companies. We compare the views of those universities that have been more successful in spinning-out companies with those of the less successful universities with respect to the strategies they pursue and the way in which they manage the process. The more successful companies are defined as the ten most successful universities (V10) in terms of the number of companies that have attracted finance from the commercial sector. The research questions that are explicitly addressed are:

(1) Do universities that are more successful in spinning-out companies adopt different policies and strategies compared to the less successful universities?
(2) Does the role of the academic inventor vary

Small Business Economics 20: 185–200, 2003.
© 2003 *Kluwer Academic Publishers. Printed in the Netherlands.*

in those universities that are more or less successful in spinning-out companies?

(3) Do universities that are more successful in spinning-out companies have access to greater expertise and networks than the less successful universities?

(4) Are there differences between universities that are more successful in spinning-out companies and those that are less successful in terms of who identifies the commercial opportunity?

(5) Does the distribution of equity ownership among the parties involved in spin-out companies differ between those universities that are more or less successful in spinning-out companies?

The paper is structured as follows, section 2 discusses the theory relating to the strategies adopted and implemented by universities concerning spin-out companies. The third section outlines the methodology employed in the study. Section 4 presents the findings from a survey of professionals responsible for the academe-university interface in 57 universities. The final section discusses the findings and their implications for the development of university spin-out companies.

2. Universities' spin-out company strategies

This section discusses the strategies adopted and implemented by universities regarding high technology spin-out companies. In particular, issues concerning: strategies towards spin out companies, the role of academic and surrogate (external) entrepreneurs, the resource base of the university, opportunity recognition, and the distribution of equity ownership in the spin-out company.

Strategies towards spin-out companies

Universities are becoming increasingly motivated by the need for success in commerce as well as academia (Powell and Owen-Smith, 1998). However, there is more than one way in which a University may commercialize its new technology. The dominant way in which technology has been traditionally transferred from the university sector to the private sector is through technology licensing (Siegel et al., 1999). In a licensing arrangement the university may charge a company an initial payment, and then may receive subsequent royalty payments, for the right to use a particular piece of intellectual property. This system has the advantage that the academic and the university are able to capitalise on the technology, and the academic is able to pursue his/her research without having to commit large amounts of time to commercial matters. The downsides to this approach are two fold. First, the nature of the new technology may not be easily patented and transacted via a license agreement. The literature on licensing is clear that the licensing arrangement is only applicable when the assets can be protected by intellectual property law and can be easily stipulated in the form of a contract (Arrow, 1962; Hearn, 1981). Second, universities may not be able to capture the full value of their technology through a licensing arrangement and, therefore, may seek a more direct involvement in the commercialization of new technology through spinning-out a company (Franklin et al., 2001; Samson and Gurdon, 1993).

In contrast to licensing, a spin-out company enables equity ownership by a range of interested parties drawn from inside or outside the university. From inside, equity-holders may include the academic inventor and the university itself. From outside, equity ownership may be held by external managers/entrepreneurs (surrogate entrepreneurs), private companies specialising in the commercialization of technology or financiers. The ownership of equity in the spin-out may increase the potential up-side gain and thus appear an attractive option to universities. There is some evidence from a small sample survey that taking equity in a spin-out company produces a greater average return in the long run compared to the average return available from the average license (Bray and Lee, 2000).

The entrepreneurial role

A key dimension of a strategy to develop spin-out companies relates to the role of the entrepreneur. The academic, as technology originator, may assume the role of the entrepreneur (Samson and Gurdon, 1993). They may leave the university to run the company (Radosevich, 1995) or may alternatively run the company in parallel with his/her academic responsibilities. The involvement of

academic inventors may bring a strong commitment and knowledge of the technology. By the
same token, commercially inexperienced academic
inventors may focus too much on the technical
aspects of the innovation to the detriment of
business dimensions (Daniels and Hofer, 1993).
This problem is not unique to universities as it is
well-recognized that the individual who first
identifies an innovative opportunity may not be
the one to champion its development as he/she
may not have the necessary communication
skills, networks or ability to acquire the resources
necessary for commercializing the project
(Venkataraman et al., 1992).

If the academic becomes involved in the
venture but does not leave the university, there
may be important implications for the amount, and
conflicting demands on, the individual's time. The
academic who remains as an employee of the university must balance a number of different functions that are both academic (research, teaching
and administration), and commerce oriented
(developing and spinning-out the company). The
more involved the academic inventor becomes in
the commercialization of new technology through
a spin-out company, the less time he or she (all
other things being equal) may be able to commit
to their academic role. Although universities are
becoming increasingly interested in the commercialization of their technology there remains a
conflict of interest regarding the role of the
academic inventor. Therefore, although universities may be keen to promote the spinning-out of
companies they may be far less keen to encourage
the academic to devote large proportions of their
time to the commercialization and management of
the spin-out at the expense of their core functions
of research, teaching and administration. If this is
the case, there is potential for tensions between
the demands of academia and the commercial
sector. The more demanding the role the academic
investor performs in the new spin-out company the
greater the potential for conflicts of interest
between academic and commercial activities.

A means of resolving the potential conflicts
between the demands on an academic's time and
their potential lack of skills in commercializing
new ventures is to adopt a strategy of introducing
outside or surrogate entrepreneurs to develop
the spin-out company. Surrogate entrepreneurship

involves an individual (or organization) from
outside the university assuming the role of entrepreneur with the technology originator maintaining their position in the university. It is,
however, key that the academic inventor supports,
and has a commercial interest in, the venture. This
is especially so in the early stages when technology development is a pivotal business activity.
In addition, there may be added benefits from
maintaining a link with the capacity to develop
further technology (Radosevich, 1995). Evidence
suggests that ventures created by "outside
entrepreneurs" with "faculty assistance" become
somewhat larger on average than those created by
the academics themselves (Chrisman et al., 1995).
Therefore, the more successful universities may
be the ones that have a clear strategy to use surrogate entrepreneurs in the management and
development of new technology-based spin-out
companies. However, the academic is expected to
remain as a full-time employee of the university
with a role that is expected to involve more
advisory functions, especially technical ones, than
hands-on, day-to-day management.

Expertise and networks in implementing spinning-out strategies

In order to develop and implement a strategy to
transfer technology through spin-out companies,
universities may need access to key expertise and
networks. The human capital embodied in experienced personnel who are dedicated to the spinning
out of new technology companies may be a key
source of expertise. However, the mere existence
of a commercial office within a university is not
a sufficient condition for in-house expertise
regarding the spinning-out of companies. Rather,
as will be developed below, the expertise of the
individuals in the commercial office of a university may fulfil a very important role in recognizing opportunities. Therefore, it is important that
the university has appropriately experienced staff
to perform this function.

The network of universities' working relationships with both external organizations and individuals may also be crucial to the successful
implementation of spin-out strategies. Low and
MacMillan (1988) suggested that networks are an
important aspect of the context and process of

entrepreneurship. Subsequent studies have found that networking allows entrepreneurs to enlarge their knowledge of opportunities, to gain access to critical resources such as finance and to deal with business obstacles (Johannisson et al., 1994; Sapienza et al., 1996; Hills et al., 1997). In the context of university spin-out companies, networks include: other University commercial companies, venture capital companies, Training and Enterprise Council (TEC) and Business Link, local business angels, and finally local private sector companies which specialise in managing spin-out companies.

The university may develop initiatives that promote the use of networks in helping to spin-out companies. This may be achieved through initiatives that highlight "technologies available" for spin-out companies; the provision of a database of individuals or organizations that have an interest in managing spin-out companies; and the development of initiatives that link into Business Schools as a source of potential (surrogate) entrepreneurs. This approach may aid the development of spin-out companies through bringing together different individuals with complementary forms of human capital. The more successful universities may be expected to have a greater degree of internal expertise in their commercial offices, greater networks with outsiders and greater use of initiatives to promote the availability of technologies.

Opportunity recognition

Opportunity recognition is a critical first step in the entrepreneurial process (Kirzner, 1973). The limited existing research (Ucbasaran et al., 2000) suggests that the ability of an individual to exploit an opportunity is jointly influenced by the characteristics of the opportunity and the nature of the individual (Shane and Venkataraman, 2000). Three potential sources of difference between individuals in terms of their ability to recognize an opportunity are: knowledge (and information) differences; cognitive differences; and behavioral differences (Venkatraman, 1997). In the case of university spin-out companies, there are potentially a number of individuals and bodies, both internal and external to the university, who may have an important role in recognizing an oppor-

tunity: the academic inventor, the university commercial company, a potential surrogate entrepreneur or an external private sector organization.

The academic inventor is assumed to be particularly knowledgeable about his/her area of research, which has resulted in the development of the new technology. However, although the academic may be highly knowledgeable about his/her field of research, he/she may not be able to recognize its commercial potential. The inability to recognize such opportunities is not necessarily the result of a lack of information. Rather, the mindset of the academic may mean that they are not necessarily motivated or interested in considering the potential commercial applications of their research.

If the academic inventor is not necessarily the best individual to recognize an opportunity, this role may be best played by another party. Industry Liaison Offices (ILOs) or commercial companies may help address this issue. Suitable individuals may be more "alert" to, and thus more able to "notice", opportunities (Kirzner, 1973). Suitability may derive from both their better knowledge resources as well as their cognitive mindsets.

Surrogate entrepreneurs may also be involved in the identification of opportunities, particularly where expertise is lacking in the commercial offices of universities. A potential barrier, however, is that as outsiders, surrogate entrepreneurs may be faced with an asymmetric information problem that reduces their access to potentially profitable opportunities, especially at an early stage (Robbie and Wright, 1996). Universities that are more successful at promoting spin-out companies may be expected to draw on all three parties as sources of opportunity recognition.

Equity ownership in the spin-out

The distribution of equity within the spin-out company will have important implications for incentives and the ability to make decisions. As outlined above, a number of different individuals and organizations have an interest in the spin-out company. In order to be committed to the success of the venture, all parties (academic investors, university and surrogate entrepreneurs) require some degree of equity ownership. However, this position may create tensions among the different parties involved. For example, the university may perceive that the academic investor's ownership of equity may be create a conflict of interest as they will become more involved in commercial matters to the detriment of their academic responsibilities. The academic investor may perceive that equity ownership by the university and outsiders removes their control of the technology. Similarly, a surrogate entrepreneur entering the business will require a significant equity stake both as an incentive and to confer a necessary degree of control to enable the implementation of decisions to commercialize the venture. This is a familiar problem in the development of entrepreneurial ventures beyond the start-up phase. One of the differences here concerns the presence of the university as employer of the academic. The more successful universities in spinning-out companies are expected to be more likely to recognize the need to provide academic inventors and outside entrepreneurs, as well as the university, with significant equity stakes. Tensions between the parties may lead to a broadly even distribution of equity amongst the three parties, with no one party having a dominant interest. However, more successful universities are expected to be more likely to enable outsiders to obtain dominant equity stakes in order to provide the incentive to fully exploit growth opportunities.

3. Methodology

Our empirical analysis is based on a comprehensive questionnaire survey of spin-out activity at 57 U.K. universities. The questionnaire gathered data relating to the practice of Spinning-out companies from a university. The research instrument examined issues of the universities strategy towards this practice, their specific resource base for spinning-out companies, which party recognizes the opportunity, the nature of the role of the academic inventor after the company is spun-out and the distribution of equity in the new company. The respondents were invited to score statements on a one to five scale, where five meant that they strongly agreed with the statement and one meant that they strongly disagreed with the statement.

The postal questionnaire was aimed at professionals who have senior positions of responsibility at the academe-industry interface in U.K. universities or university-owned commercialization companies. These individuals are sometimes referred to as business development officers, industry and business liaison officers or technology transfer officers. As there is no single complete list of the relevant individuals, we identified contact names from The Association of University Research and Industry Links (AURIL) and the University Company Association (UNICO). The former organization encompasses practitioners who have a broad role in technology transfer and industrial liaison. The latter association is for universities that have gone as far as setting up a new commercial company to undertake its technology transfer activities, this often being a holding company for new spin-out ventures. There is a significant overlap of membership between the two associations as individuals may be involved in both sets of activities. The mailing lists from these organizations were combined to survey a total of 116 different U.K. universities.

After administration of a reminder questionnaire together with telephone calls, 57 completed questionnaires were received from 57 separate U.K. universities, a response rate of 49.1 percent. Thirty-nine questionnaires were returned by representatives from university industrial liaison offices and 18 from university commercial companies.[1] These 57 universities account for 67% of the total income from research grants and contracts received by U.K. universities.[2] Using total income from research grants and contracts as an approximation of R&D activity, the survey captured 8 out of the top 10 U.K. (V10) universities.

Of the 57 universities that completed questionnaires 16 stated that they had, to the best of their knowledge, no experience in "spinning out" new technology-based companies in the last five years. Among the 41 "venturing" universities, 39 contributed information that suggested they had started a total of 217 new companies between March 1994 and March 1998 inclusive (Table I). Of these 217 new ventures, 115 (53 per cent) had received some form of private sector capital investment, for example risk capital from business angels, venture capital or the public financial

190 *Andy Lockett et al.*

TABLE I

Number of technology-based university spin-out companies (founded between March 1994 to 1998 inclusive) that secured private sector investment among 41 venturing universities

Funding range	V10		Non-V10		Total	
	No.	%	No.	%	No.	%
No funding	47	39.2	55	56.7	102	47.0
Up to £0.2m	46	38.3	25	25.8	71	32.7
£0.2m–£2m	20	16.7	15	15.5	35	16.1
Over £2m	7	5.8	2	2.0	9	4.2
Total	120	100.0	97	100.0	217	100.0

Note: a z-test of proportions on the difference in the percentage of V10 and non-V10 companies receiving funding yields $z = 2.34$, indicating a strongly significant difference between the two groups of universities. One significant member of the V10 did not disclose the total and relative breakdown of the private sector investment secured by its spin-out companies.

markets, but only 4 per cent had received more than £2 million.

Of the 41 "venturing universities", 10 established and secured some degree of private sector funding for more than 5 companies over the five year period. These universities, which are one subset of the total venturing population, we term the V10 sample. The V10 sample is intended to represent "high performers" with regard to establishing new spin-out ventures that have secured private sector investment. The criteria used to select these ten are somewhat simplistic and are not necessarily indicative of the most "successful" universities with regard to spin-out companies. The definition of "success" with regard to universities and spin-out companies is somewhat complex. It is highly dependent upon the perception of the key stakeholders and the relative size and quality of the various university research bases. As noted earlier, it might be anticipated that these experienced universities had differing perspectives from their less successful counterparts about the contributions of academic and surrogate entrepreneurs and in particular may view surrogate entrepreneurs in a more positive light.

The V10 universities are responsible for 120 of the 217 companies (55.3 per cent) established in the five year period. The companies established by the V10 universities were significantly more likely than those established by the 31 venturing

non-V10 universities to receive private sector funding (Table I); 60.9 per cent of V10 companies received private sector funding as against 43.3 per cent of the venturing non-V10 universities' companies. Of the total companies established in the last five years, the V10 universities were responsible for 46 out of the 71 companies (64.7 per cent) that secured up to £200,000 private sector investment, 20 of the 35 (57.1 per cent) that secured between £200,000 and £2m, and 7 of the 9 companies (77.7 per cent) that secured over £2m in investment. It should be noted that one significant member of the V10 did not disclose the total and relative breakdown of the private sector investment secured by its spin-out companies.

4. Results

This section presents the findings of the study in terms of the issues identified in Section 2. We present comparisons of the attitudes and strategies with regard to spin-out companies of the V10 universities and the larger group of 47 less successful universities.[3] Of the 57 universities that contributed to this study, 37 were from long established universities and 20 were from the former polytechnics and colleges which formally became universities in 1992.[4] The "new" universities generally have weaker academic research records than the longer established universities. Nine of the V10 universities were older established universities. Prior to formally coming under the same funding body as older established universities, these "new" universities were funded by local authorities and subject to what may be regarded as a more bureaucratic accountability regime. To the extent that these universities maintain such a management regime and are less well-funded for research than the older established universities, they may perceive there to be significantly higher barriers and challenges to developing spin-out companies. We tested for differences between the old and new universities and comment on the differences where appropriate. Differences between the groups of universities were analysed using Mann-Whitney non-parametric tests. These tests were preferred as they have less rigorous assumptions than parametric tests (De Vaus, 1991).

Strategies towards spin-out companies

The University frequently faces a choice as to how to commercialize a particular technology. The results presented in Table II indicate that the non V10 Universities are significantly more likely to prefer licensing than spin-out companies as a means of commercially exploiting a technology (mean = 3.66) than V10 companies (mean = 2.10); this result was significant at the 1% level. In contrast, the V10 firms were significantly more likely to prefer a spin-out strategy (mean = 3.30) than the non V10 firms (mean = 2.53), this result was significant at the 5% level. Not surprisingly, therefore, the most successful universities at spinning-out companies are those that actually prefer this mode of commercialization over other forms such as licensing.

As well as preferring the spin-out option, V10 universities are also more likely to have a clear strategy for the establishment and development of new technology-based spin-out companies (mean = 4.40) than non V10 firms (mean = 2.79), this result was significant at the 1% level. In addition, the V10 firms were found to have much clearer strategies for using surrogate entrepreneurs/commercial management in new technology-based spin-out companies (mean = 4.30) than non V10 firms (mean = 2.89), this result was also significant at the 1% level. When old and new universities were compared, it was apparent that the former had a significantly clearer strategy towards spin-out companies than did the latter.

The entrepreneurial role

Neither V10 nor non-V10 universities have strategies to proactively encourage academics to manage new technology-based spin-outs (means = 2.60 and 2.64 respectively) (Table III). This is an interesting result that suggests that universities, although keen to transfer technology to the private sector in the case of V10 institutions, do not want the academic to pursue a role in the management of the spin-out. In addition, V10 universities are significantly more likely than non-V10 universities to have strategies to use external surrogate entrepreneurs to develop spin-out companies. Older universities were found to be less sensitive to the need for outside entrepreneurs to bring funding with them in order to gain credibility.

With regard to the actual experiences over the year period among those universities which had spun-out companies, there were no significant differences between the V10 and non-V10 universities concerning the role of academic inventors in spin-out companies (Table IV). However, a number of interesting findings emerge from the data in relation to the overall sample means.

First, the results indicate that it is usual for the academic to remain a full-time employee of the university (overall sample mean = 3.97). It is

TABLE II
University policy/strategy towards spin-out companies

To what extent do you agree or disagree with the following statements in relation to your own institution (5 = strongly agree . . . 1 = strongly disagree)	V10 status	N	Mean	Std. deviation	Std. error mean	Mann Whitney U stat
There is a clear strategy for the establishment and development of new technology-based spin-out companies	non v10	47	2.7872	1.3821	0.2016	89.5***
	v10	10	4.4000	1.2649	0.4000	
It would be fair to say that licensing is the preferred route of commercial exploitation	non v10	47	3.6596	1.1282	0.1646	84***
	v10	10	2.1000	1.1972	0.3786	
It would be fair to say that spin-out companies are the preferred route of commercial exploitation	non v10	47	2.5319	0.9747	0.1422	143.5**
	v10	10	3.3000	1.2517	0.3958	

Significance level: $*p < 0.1$; $**p < 0.05$; $***p < 0.01$.

TABLE III
The role of academic and surrogate entrepreneurs: strategy

To what extent do you agree or disagree with the following statements in relation to your own institution (5 = strongly agree . . . 1 = strongly disagree)	V10 status	N	Mean	Std. deviation	Std. error mean	Mann Whitney U stat
Academics are proactively encouraged to manage new-technology spin-out companies	non v10	47	2.6383	1.1117	0.1622	231
	v10	10	2.6000	1.0750	0.3399	
Academics are proactively encouraged to take advisory roles within technology-based spin-out companies	non v10	46	3.2609	1.1242	0.1658	226
	v10	10	3.2000	1.1353	0.3590	
There is a strategy for using external entrepreneurs/ commercial management in new technology-based spin-out companies	non v10	47	2.8936	1.2893	0.1881	92.5***
	v10	10	4.3000	0.8233	0.2603	
There is an opinion that entrepreneurs/commercial management really need to bring money with them to have credibility	non v10	46	2.9783	0.9998	0.1474	174.5
	v10	10	2.5000	1.1785	0.3727	

Significance level: $*p < 0.1$; $**p < 0.05$; $***p < 0.01$.

TABLE IV
The role of the academic-inventor: Actual experience

Based on the new ventures that you have established in the last 5 years how frequently do the following factors occur in the. (5 = frequently . . . 1 = infrequently)	V10 status	N	Mean	Std. deviation	Std. error mean	Mann Whitney U stat
When the company was formed the academic-inventor became the managing director	non v10	31	3.03	1.47	0.26	113
	v10	10	2.30	1.25	0.40	
When the company was formed the academic-investor had no active role	non v10	31	1.58	0.99	0.18	118
	v10	10	1.20	0.63	0.20	
When the company was formed the academic-inventor became a senior manager	non v10	30	2.94	1.46	0.26	115
	v10	10	3.60	0.97	0.31	
When the company was formed the academic-inventor took an advisory role	non v10	30	2.83	1.37	0.25	118.5
	v10	10	3.30	1.25	0.40	
When the company was formed the academic-inventor became a Technical Director	non v10	30	3.13	1.38	0.25	141.5
	v10	10	3.30	1.34	0.42	
When the company was formed the academic-inventor became a full-time employee of the company	non v10	31	1.65	1.05	0.19	124
	v10	10	1.90	1.20	0.38	
When the company was formed the academic-inventor remained a full-time employee of the University	non v10	31	3.94	1.41	0.25	122.5
	v10	9	4.11	0.60	0.20	

Note: Base for percentages is those universities with experience of spin-out companies.
Significance level: $* p < 0.1$; $** p < 0.05$; $*** p < 0.01$.

much less likely that the academic inventor becomes a full-time employee of the company (overall sample mean = 1.71). This situation may arise because the academic wishes to remain within the university as this is their core function and carries with it security of income. Alternatively, the spin-out company may be unable to pay a full time employee, at least initially. Consistent with earlier findings, the academic may also be discouraged by university liaison staff from managing the spin-out company on a full-time basis.

Although the academic is most likely to remain a full-time employee of the university, the individual may still play a role in the management of the new spin-out company. Our findings suggest it is quite uncommon for the academic inventor to play no active role after the formation of the spin-out company (overall sample mean = 1.49). The second least common role is for the academic inventor to become the Managing Director of the spin-out company (overall sample mean = 2.85). However, there are a number of other roles the academic inventor may perform more frequently in the new company such as that of: senior manager (overall sample mean = 3.10), advisor (overall sample mean = 2.95) and technical director (overall sample mean = 3.18). It appears, therefore, that the most common roles are those that are designed to best exploit the human capital of the academic inventor, allowing him/her to have a technical involvement in the company rather than day to day management. This solution is consistent with universities proactively encouraging academics to become advisors, not managers, of the spin-out company so as not to distract them from their core activities.

In older universities, academics were significantly less likely to have no role in the management of spin-out companies than is the case in new universities.

Expertise and networks in implementing spinning-out strategies

The findings from the survey indicate substantial differences between the two groups of universities regarding the presence of personnel who have experience of spinning-out companies, the networks they have with external bodies who may facilitate the process and the initiatives that the university has in place to facilitate the spinning-out of companies (Table V).

The V10 firms are significantly more likely to have personnel with experience of founding a technology-based spin-out company on the intellectual property of more than one university (mean = 3.20) than non V10 universities (mean = 2.13); this result was significant at the 5% level. In addition, the V10 universities are more likely to have in-house specialists who are dedicated to the establishment of technology-based spin-out companies (mean = 4.80) than non V10 universities (mean = 2.91; this result was significant at the 0.05% level. These findings suggest that the V10 universities have greater resources of expertise at their disposal to facilitate the spinning-out of technology-based companies.

In terms of networks, two results were found to be significant. First, the V10 universities were more likely to have a strong working relationship with at least one venture capital company (mean = 4.20) than non-V10 universities (mean = 2.83); this result was significant at the 1% level. Second, V10 universities were also found to be more likely to have strong working relationships with at least one other university commercial company (mean = 3.60) than non-V10 universities (mean = 2.52). However, no significant differences were found in respect of relationships with other external bodies such as the TEC/Business Link, local business angels, etc.

Finally, there are significant differences between the two groups of universities regarding initiatives to promote spin-out companies. In particular, the V10 universities are more likely to have a database of individuals/organizations from outside the university with an interest in managing spin-out companies (mean = 3.20) than non-V10 universities (mean 1.82), this result was significant at the 1% level. In addition, the V10 universities were found to be significantly more likely to have marketing initiatives highlighting "technologies available" for spin-out companies and initiatives that link into Business Schools as a source of potential entrepreneurs than non-V10 universities. Both of these results were weakly significant at the 10% level.

Older universities have significantly more experience in spinning-out companies and networking

194   *Andy Lockett et al.*

TABLE V
Expertise and networks in the implementation of spin-out strategies

To what extent do you agree or disagree with the following statements in relation to your own institution (5 = strongly agree . . . 1 = strongly disagree)	V10 status	N	Mean	Std. deviation	Std. error mean	Mann Whitney U stat
There is experience of founding a technology-based spin-out company on the intellectual property of more than one university	non v10	46	2.1304	1.2222	0.1802	125**
	v10	10	3.2000	1.3166	0.4163	
There is marketing initiative which highlights "technologies available" for spin-out ventures	non v10	46	2.3913	1.1250	0.1659	149.5*
	v10	10	3.2000	1.3166	0.4163	
There are in-house specialists dedicated to the establishment of technology-based spin-out companies	non v10	47	2.9149	1.5298	0.2232	73$^{\#}$
	v10	10	4.8000	0.4216	0.1333	
There is a database of individuals/organizations from outside the university that have an interest in managing spin-out companies	non v10	45	1.8222	0.9118	0.1359	64.5***
	v10	10	3.2000	0.9189	0.2906	
There are initiatives which tap into Business Schools as a source of potential entrepreneurs	non v10	46	1.9130	0.9849	0.1452	128*
	v10	10	3.1000	1.5951	0.5044	
There is a strong working relationship with at least one other university commercial company	non v10	44	2.5227	1.3380	0.2017	123.5**
	v10	10	3.6000	1.2649	0.4000	
There is a strong working relationship with at least one venture capital company	non v10	47	2.8298	1.2738	0.1858	96.5***
	v10	10	4.2000	0.9189	0.2906	
There is a strong relationship with the TEC/Business link	non v10	44	3.5227	1.2102	0.1824	150
	v10	10	2.7000	1.4944	0.4726	
There is a strong relationship with a local business angel network	non v10	46	2.4565	1.0895	0.1606	183.5
	v10	10	3.0000	1.5635	0.4944	
There is a strong working relationship with a private sector company which specialises in managing spin-out companies	non v10	46	2.0870	1.1513	0.1698	210.5
	v10	10	2.4000	1.5055	0.4761	

Significance level: *$p < 0.1$; **$p < 0.05$; ***$p < 0.01$; $^{\#}p < 0.001$.

with venture capital firms and other university commercial companies. In contrast, new universities have significantly stronger relationships with TECs/Business link organizations.

Opportunity recognition

The 41 companies with spin-out company experience over the five years prior to the survey were asked to identify the most important sources of opportunity recognition. As discussed earlier, a number of different parties may be important sources of opportunity recognition. The most important parties in the recognition of the potential for a spin-out company appear to be those located in University commercial companies (total sample mean = 3.85) and the academic inventor (total sample mean = 3.80) (Table VI Panel A). In contrast, the total sample means for both individuals and private organizations that are external to the University were much lower at 2.52 and 2.39 respectively. These results indicate the impor-

TABLE VI
The recognition of the opportunity

Panel A: A comparison of V10 and non-V10

Based on the new ventures that you have established in the last 5 years how frequently do the following factors occur in the. (5 = frequently . . . 1 = infrequently)	V10 status	N	Mean	Std. deviation	Std. error mean	Mann Whitney U stat
Prior to formation, the academic-inventor recognised the potential for the new company	non v10	31	3.81	1.08	0.19	144
	v10	10	3.60	1.35	0.43	
Prior to formation, the university commercial company recognised the potential for the new company	non v10	29	3.62	1.02	0.19	72.5**
	v10	10	4.50	0.53	0.17	
Prior to formation, an individual from outside the University recognised the potential for the new company	non v10	31	2.61	1.31	0.24	151.5
	v10	10	2.50	0.97	0.31	
Prior to formation, an external private sector organization recognised the potential for the new company	non v10	31	2.39	1.12	0.20	152.5
	v10	10	2.40	1.17	0.37	

Note: Base for percentages is those universities with experience of spin-out companies.
Significance level: $*p < 0.1$; $**p < 0.05$; $***p < 0.01$.

Panel B: Pair wise tests for the relative importance of different groups

	Mean	Standard deviation	Wilcoxon matched pairs Z
Academic inventor v	3.72	1.15	−0.39
University commercial company	3.85	0.99	
Academic inventor v	3.76	1.14	−3.83″
Outside individual	2.59	1.22	
Academic inventor v	3.76	1.14	−4.23″
Private sector organization	2.39	1.12	
University commercial company v	3.85	0.99	−4.00″
Outside individual	2.62	1.23	
University commercial company v	3.85	0.99	−4.65″
Private sector organization	2.38	1.09	
Outside individual v	2.59	1.22	−1.61
Private sector organization	2.39	1.12	

Note: Base for percentages is those universities with experience of spin-out companies.
Significance level: $*p < 0.1$; $**p < 0.05$; $***p < 0.01$; $″p < 0.001$.

tance of individuals who are internal to the university in the recognition of opportunities.

There were significant differences between the two groups of universities with regard to the role of the university commercial company. In V10 universities, the commercial office was found to play a much more important role in the recognition of opportunities (mean = 4.50) when compared to the non-V10 universities (mean = 3.62), this result was significant at the 2% level.

In addition to the group analysis, Wilcoxon pairwise analysis was conducted regarding the relative importance of the academic inventor, the Universities' commercial office, individuals from outside the university and external private sector organizations as sources of opportunity recognition. The scores were calculated on the basis of total sample means and the results of which are presented in Table VI Panel B. The results indicate that both the academic inventors and university commercial companies are significantly more likely to recognize an opportunity than individuals from outside the university and private sector organizations; all these results were significant at the 0.1% level and better. In addition, no significant differences were found between the internal parties (academic inventors and university commercial companies) and between external parties (individuals outside the university and private sector organizations). These findings highlight the importance of internal parties (both academic inventors and university commercial companies) in recognizing opportunities, and that both of these internal parties appears to be equally good at fulfilling the function.

Equity ownership in the spin-out

The findings relating to the distribution of equity ownership (Table VII) suggest it is most common for all parties to obtain an equity stake up to 20% in the spin-out company. The results indicate that all three groups, the university, academic inventor and external management, infrequently hold a dominant equity position of over 50% of the new company.

Significant differences in the equity stake likely to be taken in a spin-out company were identified between the V10 and non-V10 universities. In particular, the V10 universities were less likely to spin-out a company in which the university had no equity stake (mean = 1.00) than the non-V10 universities (mean = 2.29), this result was significant at the 1% level; and to spin-out a company in which the academic inventor had no equity stake (V10 mean = 1.10; non V10 mean = 1.87), significant at the 6% level. These results indicate that the most successful universities at spinning-out companies are less likely to establish spin-out companies in which either the university or the academic investor retain no equity involvement.

Differences between the two groups of universities were also identified regarding the proportion of equity held by the academic inventor or the

external management. More specifically, when the company was formed it was more likely that up to 20% of the equity would be held by the academic investor (mean = 4.00) and the external management (mean = 3.22) in V10 universities than in companies spun-out by non-V10 universities (mean = 2.39 and 2.06 respectively); these differences were significant at the 1% and 5% levels, respectively. The relatively high standard deviations around the mean suggest that, even among V10 universities, there is quite a variation in practice. There was weak evidence that older universities are significantly more likely to take larger, even majority, equity stakes in spin-out companies, and that both academics and external management (i.e. surrogate entrepreneurs) were significantly more likely to have equity stakes of up to 20%.

5. Discussion and conclusions

The transfer of technology from universities to the commercial sector has historically been dominated by the practice of licensing (Siegel et al., 1999). However, licensing is not the only option available to universities and academic inventors as they increasingly seek to capture the benefits that may accrue from the commercialization of their activities. This paper focuses on the option of spin-out companies. The research highlights a number of interesting findings regarding university strategies towards spin-out companies and the way in which they seek to manage the process. In particular, the results suggest a number of tensions exist between the different parties involved in the spin-out which result from their underlying, sometimes divergent, interests. The results indicate that the more successful V10 universities have developed more explicit and proactive strategies towards the development of spin-out companies.

The role of the academic inventor was not found to differ between the more and less successful universities. However, it is clear that the academic inventor will continue to perform some role in the spin-out company. The role of the academic inventor may range from one of top management to a role that is more advisory in capacity, but is more likely to involve the latter. An interesting avenue for future research would be to compare the roles of the academic inventor

TABLE VII

The distribution of equity ownership in the spin-out company: Actual experience

Based on the new ventures that you have established in the last 5 years how frequently do the following factors occur in the. (5 = frequently . . . 1 = infrequently)	V10 status	N	Mean	Std. deviation	Std. error mean	Mann Whitney U stat
When the company was formed the University had no equity stake	non v10	31	2.29	1.42	0.26	65***
	v10	10	1.00	0.00	0.00	
When the company was formed the University had up to a 20% equity stake	non v10	31	2.65	1.50	0.27	104
	v10	10	3.50	1.43	0.45	
When the company was formed the University had an equity stake between 21% and 50%	non v10	30	2.50	1.41	0.26	93.5
	v10	9	3.22	1.30	0.43	
When the company was formed the University had an equity stake greater than 50%	non v10	31	1.77	1.26	0.23	119
	v10	9	2.00	1.22	0.41	
When the company was formed the academic-inventor had no equity stake	non v10	31	1.87	1.26	0.23	101.5*
	v10	10	1.10	0.32	0.00	
When the company was formed the academic-inventor had up to a 20% equity stake	non v10	31	2.39	1.48	0.27	56.5***
	v10	9	4.00	1.12	0.37	
When the company was formed the academic-inventor had an equity stake between 21% and 50%	non v10	31	2.26	1.41	0.25	106
	v10	10	3.00	1.33	0.42	
When the company was formed the academic-inventor had an equity stake greater than 50%	non v10	30	1.9355	1.25	0.23	122.5
	v10	9	1.6667	1.12	0.37	
When the company was formed a commercial manager/management (external to the University) had up to a 20% equity stake	non v10	31	2.06	1.41	0.25	83**
	v10	9	3.22	1.79	0.60	
When the company was formed a commercial manager/management (external to the University) had an equity stake between 21% and 50%	non v10	31	1.74	1.29	0.23	122.5
	v10	9	2.00	1.22	0.41	
When the company was formed a commercial manager/management (external to the University) had an equity stake of greater than 50%	non v10	31	1.42	0.77	0.1336	127
	v10	9	1.22	0.44	0.15	

Note: Base for percentages is those universities with experience of spin-out companies.
Significance level: $*p < 0.1$; $**p < 0.05$; $***p < 0.01$; $^{\#}p < 0.001$.

and the surrogate entrepreneur in the management of the spin-out company. If the motive for bringing the surrogate on board is that he or she offers a range of skills that complement those of the academic inventor, we expect that the two parties will perform different roles in the management of the company that best suit their abilities and knowledge.

The V10 universities were found to have better expertise and networks specific to the spinning-out of companies. These results also highlight an important role for the commercial offices of universities as a mechanism through which academic inventors may be able to access specific knowledge, to arrange initiatives and form relationships with external parties. However, it was evident that even among the V10 universities, links with external network organizations did not appear to be particularly strong.

With respect to new ventures actually formed in the previous five years, the commercial offices in the V10 universities were found to be much more important in recognizing new company opportunities than their counterparts in non-V10 universities. This finding emphasises the important role of commercial offices of universities in the spinning-out of technology-based companies.

Finally, the equity in spin-out companies appears to be distributed among the different interested parties, and it is uncommon for one of the parties to have a dominant equity stake. This finding is consistent with expectations that all interested parties will want to capture a return on the spin-out company through holding an equity stake. The V10 universities were more likely to create spin-outs in which all parties had a substantial equity stake than was the case for the V10 universities. In addition, unlike some non-V10 universities, the V10 group did not spin-out companies in which the university or the academic inventor did not have an equity stake. These findings, however, raise issues as to whether there is an appropriate balance of incentives and control.

The findings of the study have a number of implications for practitioners and policy-makers. There would appear to be a general need, even including the more active universities involved in spinning-out companies, to enhance their external networks. The heavy reliance on industry liaison officers and the relatively low use of surrogate entrepreneurs in identifying opportunities suggests that there may be scope for developing closer active links with the individuals and companies who are interested in managing spin-out companies. The development of university-affiliated Science Parks may be one mechanism for addressing this issue, although their effectiveness has been questioned (Westhead and Storey, 1995). An alternative is for universities to develop their own incubators, such as the University of Manchester's (U.K.) biotechnology incubator strategy, in which surrogate entrepreneurs are recruited who become responsible for identifying, appraising and then establishing new ventures in which they become the founding entrepreneurs. Private sector organizations, such as ANGLE Technology Limited (U.K.), also focus on recruiting high calibre, experienced individuals who are then invested as surrogate entrepreneurs into start-up ventures originated by academics and who receive support from the core organization.

The changes in the role of the university, in terms of the need to develop its own external network of contacts, is also being mirrored by the actions of industry players. It appears as though the boundary between the investor of financial capital and an investor of human capital is becoming increasingly blurred. An example of this are the roles now performed by some specialist venture capitals firms (e.g. Merlin Ventures, U.K., in the life sciences) that will invest finance but also put in an interim management structure. Similarly, the new generation of venture management companies (e.g. ANGLE Technology, U.K., in all technology sectors), that have recognized the market opportunity associated with investing human capital into start-up technology ventures, are now beginning to directly invest financial resources as well. Therefore, specialist venture capital firms, and the new generation of venture management firms, are coming to the same conclusion. That is, to add real value and create a viable new start-up company the venture requires both finance and specialist human capital at the earliest possible stage.

There may also be a need to consider carefully the distribution of equity stakes in spin-out companies. Whilst there is clearly a need to accommodate the interests of universities, academics and surrogate entrepreneurs, the apparent frequent lack of a clear controlling stake may mean that new ventures lack the clear direction necessary for them to develop. This is a familiar problem in the development of new ventures beyond the initial start-up phase. In particular, the lack of incentives created by dispersed equity ownership may "put off" potential surrogate entrepreneurs; and this may create barriers to the development of spin-out companies (Franklin et al., 2001). Therefore, while some universities may be reluctant to cede control to outsiders, there may be greater gains to be had from smaller stakes in more successful ventures.

The less successful universities that seek to keep control of ventures in-house may merely reinforce their lack of success.

Finally, the findings in this paper have implications for further research. First, this paper focused on the views of business development officers regarding university strategies towards the development of spin-out companies. While these respondents are best placed to report on these strategies, we have not been able to comment on the attitudes and strategies of academics and surrogate entrepreneurs towards spin-out companies. Further research might usefully study both these groups of players in the technology transfer process to examine the barriers to the development of spin-out companies and to shed light on how these barriers might be overcome. Such research might usefully compare the attitudes of junior and senior staff towards spin-out companies. Second, this paper has focused on the relatively neglected area of spin-out companies. Given the focus on the nature of universities' strategies towards spin-out companies, it was beyond the scope of the paper to provide a comparative assessment of spin-out companies, licensing and privately sponsored research as approaches to the commercialization of university research. While universities may typically engage in a multi-faceted approach to commercialization, further research is required that sheds light on the conditions determining the appropriate mix of different approaches. For example, under what conditions is more appropriate to license a technology rather than developing a spin-out company and vice versa? Third, examination of the performance of spin-out companies was also outside the scope of this paper. Further research might usefully seek to examine the performance of spin-out companies in terms of profitability, cash flow generation and survival. In addition, comparative analysis of the timing and magnitude of cash flow generation from spin-out companies and licensing arrangements would also be useful. Fourth, further analysis is required concerning the process of strategy implementation. For example, there is a need to examine the organizational arrangements for the development of academic entrepreneurs versus the use of surrogate entrepreneurs, the sanctioning of spin-outs and the commitment of university funding, if any, to such arrangements; there is a need to consider

the influences on the sustainability of spin-out programs; there is a need to consider how universities deal with exit from spin-out companies that are failing, which might include consideration of the impact on the behaviour and careers of the academic entrepreneurs and business development officers concerned as well as the implications of failures for the continuation of spin-out programs. Ultimately, such analyses would assist universities in determining the extent and form of academic entrepreneurship that is appropriate in the context of other, possibly conflicting demands on academics, as well as assisting them to take a view on the most appropriate distribution of the rents from spinning-out companies.

Notes

[1] Universities that are more pre-disposed to spinning-out companies may be more likely to establish commercial companies to promote such activities rather than relying on industrial liaison officers. We tested for differences between the responses from industrial liaison officers and commercial companies and found that the differences were closely in line with the differences identified for successful and non-successful universities as explained below. These findings are not reported in detail here but are available from the authors on request.

[2] Resources of Higher Education Institutions 1996/96, Higher Education Statistics Agency.

[3] We also conducted a comparison of perspectives based on a split of the sample into V10, venturing non-V10 and non-venturing universities. As the findings were very similar to those obtained from the analysis using the V10 versus the rest, they are not presented here but are available from the authors on request.

[4] Unlike the U.S., all but one of the universities in the U.K. are government funded.

References

Arrow, K. J., 1962, 'Economics Welfare and the Allocation of Resources for Invention in the Rate of and Direction of Economic Activity', *Economic ad Social Factors* (NBER), Princeton University Press, p. 609.

Bank of England, October 1996, *The Financing of Technology-based Firms*, Bank of England.

Bray, M. J. and J. N. Lee, 2000, 'University Revenues from Technology Transfer: Licensing Fees vs Equity Positions', *Journal of Business Venturing* 15(5/6), 385–392.

CBI, Feb 1997, *Tech Stars: Breaking the Growth Barriers for Technology-based SMEs*, London: Confederation of British Industry.

Chrisman, J. J., T. Hynes and S. Fraser, 1995, 'Faculty Entrepreneurship and Economic Development: The Case of the University of Calgary', *J. Business Venturing* 10, 267–281.

Daniels, G. and C. Hofer, 1993, 'Characteristics of Successful and Unsuccessful Entrepreneurial Faculty and their Innovative Research Teams', in N. Churchill, S. Birley, W. Bygrave, J. Doutriaux, E. Gatewood, F. Hoy and W. Wetzel (eds), *Frontiers of Entrepreneurship Research*, pp. 598–609.

De Vaus D. A., 1991, *Surveys in Social Research*, Third Edition, London: Allen & Unwin.

Franklin, S., M. Wright and A. Lockett, 2001, 'Academic and Surrogate Entrepreneurs in University Spin-out Companies', *Journal of Technology Transfer* 6(1–2), 127–141.

Hearn, P., 1981, *The Business of Industrial Licensing*, Gower Press.

Hills, G. E., G. T. Lumpkin and R. P. Singh, 1997, 'Opportunity Recognition: Perceptions and Behaviors of Entrepreneurs', in P. D. Reynolds, P. W. D. Carter, P. Davidsson, W. B. Gartner and P. McDougall (eds.), *Frontiers in Entrepreneurship Research 1997*, Wellesley, Massachusetts: Babson College, pp. 330–344.

Johannisson, B., O. Alexanderson, K. Nowicki and K. Senneseth, 1994, 'Beyond Anarchy and Organization: Entrepreneurs in Contextual Networks', *Entrepreneurship and Regional Development* 6, 329–356.

Kirzner, I. M., 1973, *Competition and Entrepreneurship*, Chicago: University of Chicago Press.

Low, M. B. and I. C. MacMillan, 1988, 'Entrepreneurship: Past Research and Future Challenges', *Journal of Management* 35, 139–161.

Powell, W. W. and J. Owen-Smith, 1998, 'Universities and the Market for Intellectual Property in the Life Sciences', *Journal of Policy Analysis and Management* 17(2), 253–277.

Radosevich, R., 1995, 'A Model for Entrepreneurial Spin-offs from Public Technology Sources', *Int. J. Technol. Management* 10(7/8), 879–893.

Robbie, K. and M. Wright, 1996, *Management Buy-ins: Entrepreneurs, Active Investors and Corporate Restructuring*, Manchester: MUP.

Samson, K. J. and M. A. Gurdon, 1993, 'University Scientists as Entrepreneurs: A Special Case of Technology Transfer and High Technology Venturing', *Technovation* 13(2), 63–71.

Sapienza, H. J., S. Manigart and W. Vermeir, 1996, 'Venture Capitalists Governance and Value Added in Four Countries', *Journal of Business Venturing* 11, 439–469.

Shane, S. and S. Venkataraman, 2000, 'The Promise of Entrepreneurship as a Field of Research', *Academy of Management Review* 25, 217–226.

Siegel, D., D. Waldman and A. Link., 1999, 'Assessing the Impact of Organizational Practices on the Productivity of University Technology Transfer Offices: An Exploratory Study', NBER Working Paper #7256, July 1999.

Ucbasaran, A. D., P. Westhead and M. Wright, 2000, 'The Focus of Entrepreneurial Research: Contextual and Process Issues", *Entrepreneurship Theory and Practice*, forthcoming.

Venkataraman, S., I. MacMillan and R. McGrath, 1992, 'Progress in Research on Corporate Venturing', in D. L. Sexton and J. Kasarda (eds.), *The State of the Art of Entrepreneurship*, Boston: PWS-Kent, pp. 487–519.

Venkataraman, S., 1997, 'The Distinctive Domain of Entrepreneurship Research', in J. A. Katz (ed.), *Advances in Entrepreneurship, Firm Emergence and Growth*, vol. 3, Connecticut: JAI Press, pp. 139–202.

Westhead, P., and D. J. Storey, 1995, 'Links Between Higher Education Institutions and High Technology Firms', *Omega, International Journal of Management Science* 23(4), 345–360.

Part IV
The Role of Academic Science in Stimulating Entrepreneurial Activity

[24]

Entrepreneurs in
Academe:
An Exploration of
Behaviors among
Life Scientists

Karen Seashore Louis
University of Minnesota
David Blumenthal
*Brigham and Women's
Hospital* and *Harvard Medical
School*
Michael E. Gluck
Johns Hopkins University
Michael A. Stoto
National Academy of Science

This paper explores entrepreneurship in the research university, a setting in which there has been a marked change over the past half century in norms governing relationships between scholars and the commercial sector. A survey of life science faculty members in research universities is used to distinguish five types of academic entrepreneurship: (1) engaging in large-scale science (externally funded research), (2) earning supplemental income, (3) gaining industry support for university research, (4) obtaining patents or generating trade secrets, and (5) commercialization—forming or holding equity in private companies based on a faculty member's own research. The results suggest models for the different types of entrepreneurship. Individual characteristics and attitudes are the most important predictors of large-scale science and supplemental income, which are more traditional, while local group norms play a more important role in predicting active involvement in commercialization. University policies and structures have little effect on entrepreneurship. Implications for organizational theory and the role of the university are discussed.•

INTRODUCTION

There is increasing consensus in the organizational and management literature that entrepreneurship is a significant factor in organizational effectiveness. According to Benveniste (1987), risk taking and accepting responsibility are interdependent and equally important to an effective professional organization. Peters and Waterman (1982) linked entrepreneurship with invention and innovation and argued that it is causally related to productivity, while Kanter (1983) suggested that there is a critical relationship between entrepreneurship and the overall competitiveness of our corporate sector in the world economy. The role of entrepreneurship in revitalizing ossified or traditional organizations is of particular social importance (Peterson, 1981) and is considered to be one form of strategic management (Mintzberg, 1973). Snow and Hrebiniak's (1980) analysis suggested that entrepreneurial organizational strategies, those based on rapid commercialization of new inventions, engender higher performance in industries operating in uncertain environments.

Interest in the relationship of entrepreneurship to organizational performance and vitality is not limited to the private sector but is also being widely discussed in educational contexts (e.g., Etzkowitz, 1983; Mazzoni, 1987). In this paper we report a study that examined academic entrepreneurship, defined as the attempt to increase individual or institutional profit, influence, or prestige through the development and marketing of research ideas or research-based products.

© 1989 by Cornell University.
0001-8392/89/3401-0110/$1.00.
•
This research was supported by the Andrew Mellon Foundation and the Department of Health and Human Services, grant DHHS-100A-83. We thank our colleagues, Thomas A. Louis, Jack Fowler, Stanley E. Seashore, Ronald G. Corwin, James Hearn, and David Wise for their helpful comments on earlier drafts, as well as three anonymous *ASQ* reviewers. The remaining flaws are, of course, our own.

Universities are not usually viewed as leaders in entrepreneurship. In fact, there is often a tendency to distinguish between the search for truth in science, considered a legitimate function of the university, and the search for invention, which is considered an inappropriate focus on ideas that have potential commercial or practical applicability (Ravetz, 1971; Wade, 1984). Nevertheless, there has been a notable increase in the number of scientists and science watchers who champion increased entrepreneurship in universities. Entre-

Entrepreneurs in Academe

preneurship is believed to contribute to the rapid movement
of scientific ideas into the commercial arena (Blumenthal,
Gluck, and Louis, 1985), to provide a critical contribution of
scientists to the national economy and society (Ping, 1980), to
revitalize the scientific endeavor through new sources of research funds, and to contribute to the university's financial
base through royalties on patents (Blumenthal et al., 1986b).

Sources and Distribution of Entrepreneurship

Whether entrepreneurship is considered good or bad, it is
clearly not evenly distributed: some institutions and individuals demonstrate it more than others. Explanations for this
variable distribution fall into patterns that are familiar to organizational theorists. Organizational psychologists tend to emphasize individual characteristics and attitudes (such as
achievement motivation) as the source of entrepreneurship
(McClelland et al., 1976). Although achievement motivation
does not have strong predictive power (Peterson, 1981),
studies of academics indicate that other individual attributes
may play a part. For example, Liebert (1977) indicated that
past success (as measured by research publications) is associated with effective "grantsmanship." Age and gender may
also be related to incentives. More established scientists may
have more to "sell," may be less motivated by traditional academic incentives (tenure, disciplinary awards), which they
have already achieved, and may have greater financial incentives, such as having children in college (Zuckerman and
Merton, 1972; Etzkowitz, 1983). Women, who have tended
to be less scientifically productive, may also be less likely to
be entrepreneurial (Cole and Zuckerman, 1984). Attitudes can
play a part as well. Etzkowitz (1983) and Peters and Fusfeld
(1982) argued that some scientists seek out industry associations because they are predisposed to commercializing their
ideas, in contrast to scientists who stumble across a marketable finding or wait for industry to take the initiative to seek
them out.

Another line of speculation concerns the importance of cultural support for entrepreneurship. Research indicates that
local culture is more important in this respect than broad social values (Peterson, 1981: 70–71), a point strongly supported by Kanter (1983: 129–138) and consistent with classic
organizational investigations such as Seashore's (1954). In the
world of organized science, Pelz and Andrews (1976) noted,
colleagues in the work group have an impact on the behavior
of individual scientists. This local contextual effect is not related to the size of the work group (Cohen, 1981) but to the
tendency for members to conform to local norms of behavior
regarding entrepreneurship (Peters and Fusfeld, 1982). Local
behavioral norms can be reinforced over time through recruiting, socialization, and retention (Van Maanen, 1976). A
recent analysis of relationships between life scientists and industry found dense institutional networks that are interpreted
as an effect of local norms about entrepreneurship (Ennis,
1986).

A final factor that may account for entrepreneurship is the organizational structures and policies that may affect such activities. Previous research suggests that the size, complexity,
and authority structure of the organization will be associated

with innovativeness in educational settings (Baldridge and Burnham, 1975; Daft and Becker, 1978; Rosenblum and Louis, 1981). Along these lines, Kanter (1983) argued that the matrix structure supports entrepreneurship. Other writers have emphasized the importance of policies and practices, such as reward systems, that may stimulate individual or group entrepreneurship (Kerr and Slocum, 1987).

Despite the high levels of interest in entrepreneurship, there is remarkably little systematic data on the nature of entrepreneurship in the university or other nonbusiness settings. Discussions about what stimulates university faculty to be more entrepreneurial are similarly speculative. The research reported below begins to fill that gap, using data obtained from life scientists located in research-intensive universities. This paper has two main purposes: (1) to describe five different types of entrepreneurship and their incidence and patterns of occurrence in the population of research-intensive universities and (2) to examine a variety of questions that are more directly related to organizational theory, including (a) the structure of entrepreneurship as a behavioral construct, (b) the relation between individual entrepreneurship and several classes of possible predictors drawn from the literature, (c) whether there is such a phenomenon as an entrepreneurial elite, either at the individual or institutional level, and (d) whether there is any institutional patterning that suggests that universities, like other organizations, have distinctive entrepreneurial strategies.

METHOD

The analysis presented below is based on two surveys, both conducted in 1985, one of a sample of life scientists located in major research universities and the other of key administrators in the same universities.

First, university administrators were surveyed in the 50 institutions that receive the most federal research funds. Data on university policies and characteristics were collected in a telephone survey of the 40 university administrators who had been identified as having the most responsibility for the life science departments included in the study. The interviews were conducted by trained professional interviewers. When necessary, other university administrators were also contacted to obtain complete information.

For the faculty survey, only institutions where the key administrator had responded were included, which eliminated 10 of the top 50 institutions. For those 40 universities, the 3,180 life science faculty members listed in published catalogs as members of the departments of biochemistry, molecular biology, genetics, microbiology, biology, cellular biology, or botany were identified (Peterson's Guides, 1984). From this list 1,594 individuals were randomly selected.

Faculty members in the sample were mailed an eight-page questionnaire dealing primarily with his or her research activities. If the questionnaire was not returned within three weeks, they received a second mailing and a follow-up telephone call. One hundred fifty-six respondents were ineligible (deceased, retired, no longer associated with the university, or incorrectly reported as a faculty member in the catalog). Of

Entrepreneurs in Academe

the remaining eligible respondents, 69 percent (997) completed questionnaires. Missing data at the item level in the two surveys reduced the number of usable faculty responses to 778 from 40 universities.

Academic Entrepreneurship

In this paper we define five basic forms of academic entrepreneurship: (1) large-scale science (obtaining large, externally funded research projects), (2) earning supplemental income outside the university, mainly through consulting (knowledge transfer for personal gain), (3) soliciting funds from industry (capitalizing on university-industry relationships to provide new sources of funding for research), (4) patenting the results of research, and (5) forming companies based on the results of research. Although all forms of academic entrepreneurship stimulate occasional controversy in the academic community, the types are roughly ordered from the most to the least compatible with a traditional view of the university-based scientist's role (Etzkowitz, 1983; Krimsky, 1984; Wade, 1984).

Large-scale science. Academic science increasingly requires big laboratories and a large staff. This has affected the basis for evaluating individual performance: the size and number of research grants has come to be an indicator of the individual's disciplinary competence and prestige (Liebert, 1977). University budget processes have been shown to reinforce the importance of grantsmanship (Pfeffer and Salancik, 1974; Pfeffer and Moore, 1980). This type of entrepreneurship may be most challenging for younger scholars, who try to establish their reputations by developing laboratories of their own (Merton, 1968).

Individual involvement in large-scale science was measured by the amount of externally funded research for which the respondent was the principal investigator during the 1984–85 academic year. The median for the sample is $195,000 per year, exclusive of overhead. This level of funding is sufficient to fund a modest laboratory, with a small staff of semiprofessional technicians and perhaps a few doctoral students. However, the standard deviation is rather high ($285,000), suggesting that there is considerable variation in this type of entrepreneurship even within a sample of faculty members associated with research-intensive universities. Ten percent of the faculty members get $3,000 or less of external funding per year, while the top 20 percent of faculty get $251,000 or more of external funding, with a few receiving several million dollars per year.

Supplemental income. After World War II, the belief spread rapidly that scientists could maintain the ideal of basic research without sacrificing contact with the world of practice (Etzkowitz, 1983). Most universities explicitly condone limited consulting, and some form of income augmentation is the norm for most academics. The typical amount of money earned from selling personal scientific expertise is not great, however, and the impacts of consulting on scholarly performance are limited (Boyer and Lewis, 1985).

Supplemental income, which explicitly excludes unearned income, was measured by asking what percentage over basic salary the faculty member earned in recent years. A seven-point categorical scale was used, on which 1 = none, 2 = 1–10 percent, 3 = 11–20 percent, 4 = 21–30 percent, 5 = 31–40 percent, 6 = 41–50 percent, and 7 = over 50 percent. The median response was 2.26, with a mode of 2. About a fifth of the scientists had no supplemental income at all, while half earned no more than 10 percent over their base salary. Fewer than 5 percent supplemented their income by 40 percent or more, a figure that is somewhat lower than for a 1975 random sample of full-time university faculty in all disciplines (Marsh and Dillon, 1980).

Not all forms of supplemental income are viewed as entrepreneurial, however, i.e., teaching additional courses in the summer. Respondents were asked to check the top two sources of supplemental income from a list of 10. Most of the life scientists' extra income was derived from activities that might be considered modestly entrepreneurial, involving the sale of the individual's expertise through nonuniversity employment (10 percent), consulting for profit-making (27 percent) and nonprofit (18 percent) firms, and the lecture circuit (19 percent). The least common major sources of income were the most entrepreneurial (compensated directorships and royalties from licenses, with only 1 percent each). The most traditional forms of earning supplemental income— teaching extra courses and royalties from books—provided significant sources of income for only 5 and 7 percent, respectively.

An estimate of actual supplemental income was calculated using the response to this question and that from another question concerning the respondent's salary. Salary categories were as follows: less than $20,000, $20,000–29,999, $30,000–39,999, $40,000–49,999, $50,000–59,999, $60,000–69,999, and $70,000 or more. Consulting income was estimated by multiplying the midpoint value of the respondent's income category by the midpoint value of his or her consulting category. The mean salary for the population was $50,775, with a standard deviation of $14,997. The median estimated supplemental income was a modest $4,843. In 1975, the average for all faculty was approximately $2,700, which in 1984 dollars would be $5,415. The standard deviation is quite high, however ($7,198). For the nearly 17 percent of the respondents who augmented their income by more than 20 percent, the estimated average supplemental earnings were nearly $27,000.

Industrial support for university research. Recently, the organization of industrial research and basic science research in the university has become increasingly similar (Peters and Fusfeld, 1982; Blumenthal et al., 1986a, 1986b). This has led to exchange of personnel, common research projects and, in some cases, large-scale joint ventures. There are a variety of motivations for scientists to seek funding from industry, but scientists who obtain money from this source are more likely to select research problems because of their potential commercial applicability (Blumenthal et al., 1986b). This supports the contention that this form of entrepreneurship is less traditional than the two previously discussed, although it may be more easily available. In addition, more than 50 percent of our respondents indicated that research support from industry "provides resources for research that could not be obtained

Entrepreneurs in Academe

elsewhere" and "involves less red tape than federal funding." Finally, the market for obtaining industry support is less tied to the applicant's past productivity than federally funded research, which may make industry more attractive to younger scholars or others with weak track records (Liebert, 1977).

Industry funding was measured by calculating the proportion of the total of the respondent's externally funded grants and contracts budget that came from private industry. The median research support from industry was 7.7 percent; again, however, the standard deviation is rather high (21 percent), which demonstrates wide variability in this regard. Only 23 percent of life science faculty members receive some funding from industry, suggesting that this behavior is still the exception rather than the norm. Of those who do receive such funding, fewer than half get more than 25 percent of their external research funding from industry; the mean is 34 percent (see also Blumenthal et al., 1986b). However, there is a small proportion of faculty members who might be assumed to be industry dominated: about 7 percent receive more than half of their external research funds from industry.

Patenting. Patenting is a logical extension of the tendency toward increasing interest in commercially applicable results. The incidence of patents awarded to university scientists or universities has been growing, and many universities now have patent offices or have stimulated independent foundations to deal with patents and royalties (Blumenthal et al., 1986b). In addition, many biotechnology companies report that they have made patent applications based on research that they have funded in universities (Blumenthal, Gluck, and Louis, 1985).

Patent involvement was measured by whether the respondent had applied for or been granted patents or had generated trade secrets. Patenting behavior still involves a minority of life science faculty members in major research universities: 19 percent had applied for or been granted a patent or had generated a trade secret based on their research. Approximately one-third of the respondents indicated that research support from industry or consulting to industry contributed significantly to the work on which patents were based.

Direct commercial involvement. Etzkowitz (1983) pointed out that the emerging characteristics of large-scale science provide faculty members with the management skills that permit easier entry into the private sector. The formation of private firms whose products are based on the university scientists' own research is a logical extension of the trends listed above. This form of entrepreneurship is the most nontraditional and controversial in that it involves potential use of university facilities and graduate students to meet the firm's commercial goals (Blumenthal et al., 1986b).

Direct commercial involvement was measured by asking respondents whether they held equity in companies whose products and services were based on their own research. This form of entrepreneurship is the least common: only about 7 percent indicated that they held equity in such companies, and only a handful held equity in more than one.

The Structure of Entrepreneurship

The literature has not addressed the key question of whether there is an emerging group of "entrepreneurial scholars" who engage in multiple forms of entrepreneurship. If the different forms of entrepreneurship identified above cluster empirically, then such an academic type may be emerging. On the other hand, if the associations between different types of entrepreneurship are not high, then we are drawn to conclude that the above characteristics may be a consequence of different motivations, impulses, or opportunities and represent very different styles of adaptation to the changing scientific and scholarly environment.

Table 1 presents a correlation matrix showing the relationships among the variables. Although the associations are statistically significant, they are not particularly large. The Pearson correlation between equity holding and supplementary income is .33, and this is the strongest relationship in the table. Thus, we reach the preliminary conclusion that the "entrepreneurial scholar" is not common among life scientists.

Table 1

Pearson Correlations Between Five Measures of Entrepreneurship

	1	2	3	4	5
1. Size of research budget	–				
2. Supplemental income	$-.19^{**}$	–			
3. Proportion of funding from industry	$.05^{*}$	$.13^{*}$	–		
4. Patents	$.16^{**}$	$.22^{**}$	$.15^{**}$	–	
5. Equity	$.13^{*}$	$.33^{**}$	$.12^{**}$	$.25^{**}$	–

$^{*} p < .05$; $^{**} p < .01$.

This pattern of relationships does not provide a strong justification for creating a summary scale of entrepreneurship, and a principal components analysis (not shown) produced only a weak first factor. Thus, in the remainder of this analysis we treat entrepreneurship as a multidimensional concept.

Characteristics Predicting Entrepreneurship

Individual-level variables. Measures of individual demographic, career, and attitudinal characteristics in our survey included: *type of appointment,* which measured whether the individual was located in a medical school; *professional age,* measured as years since completing the doctoral degree; *gender,* a dummy variable measured as 1 = male; *risks to science,* measured by a battery of questions indicating the degree to which involvement with industry represents a potential risk to traditional scientific values. Faculty members were asked to indicate whether each of the following posed a great risk, some risk, only a little or no risk: creating pressure for faculty members to spend too much time on commercial activities, shifting too much emphasis toward applied research, undermining intellectual exchange and cooperative

Entrepreneurs in Academe

activities within departments, creating conflict between faculty members who support and those who oppose such activities, altering the standards for promotion and tenure, reducing the supply of talented university teachers, and creating unreasonable delays in the publication of new findings. Responses were added to form the summary risk scale. Two other individual-level variables were measured: attitudes about *university-industry relations,* a single item indicating whether respondents would like to see the involvement between their university and industry increase a lot, somewhat, stay about the same, decrease, or decrease a lot; and *professional productivity* (the number of articles published during an average three-year period over the respondent's professional lifetime). Logarithmic transformations were made of the following variables, which were not normally distributed: size of research budget, percent of research budget from industry, supplemental income, and number of publications.

Another set of individual characteristics that may contribute to a prediction of any particular form of entrepreneurship is, of course, the individual's other entrepreneurial behaviors (OEBs), e.g., all entrepreneurial behaviors other than that being predicted. These were shown to be modestly intercorrelated and are therefore likely to predict each other. In this analysis OEBs were initially treated as a separate group of predictors, in order to further investigate the structure of entrepreneurship behaviors.

Group-level variables. Local norms, defined as the way in which most members of the organization behave, are also likely to influence behavior. For example, a faculty member located in a university where many other faculty members engage in heavy consulting with private industry may be more likely to do the same than one located in a university where such consulting is uncommon. Measures of local norms supporting entrepreneurship were developed by calculating the mean of the responses of the life scientists within each university in the sample for each of the five entrepreneurship variables and attaching the mean of the university to the file of the individual. The formula for calculating the local norms variable for the five entrepreneurial behaviors was as follows:

$$X_{.k} = \left(\sum_{i=1}^{n_k} X_{ik}\right)/n_k,$$

where k = the university, X_{ik} = the measure for individual i in university k; and n_k = the number of individuals in university k. The individual i was included in the calculations of $X_{.k}$ for record i,k. Each institution had between 20 and 45 responses, so the use of this simple model may increase the correlation between the X measured at the individual level and at the contextual level by a maximum of 5 percent. This was considered tolerable for the exploratory analysis presented in this paper.

The local norm measures do not reflect work groups that have routine face-to-face interactions, because most major research universities in our sample had several life science departments. Rather, they are contextual peer groups, as defined by location and role. A substantial body of research supports the utility of using contextual effects of this type in studies of individual behavior (see Burstein, 1980, for a methodological review).

The group-level measures and their indicators, along with the correlations between the individual and local norm variables were as follows: *industry funding,* or the mean percentage of research funding from industry within the life science departments in the university ($r = .25$); *consulting patterns,* measured as the mean proportion of income over and above base salary earned from consulting ($r = .29$); *funded research,* the mean amount of external research funding for life scientists at the university ($r = .35$); *patenting,* the percentage of faculty members that have a history of patenting ($r = .26$); *equity holding,* the percentage of life scientists that hold equity in a firm that uses their research ($r = .28$); and *productivity,* the mean number of articles published over the past three years by life scientists at the university.

Organizational level variables. Organizational structures and policies supporting entrepreneurship vary widely. Some universities have large and complex support units (patent offices) and create institutional incentives (seed money grants to support faculty members' search for external funding) (Peters and Fusfeld, 1982). Auspices may also be important: In general, state universities are viewed as less supportive of entrepreneurship than private universities. However, some land grant colleges and schools with a technical focus have strong traditional ties with industry, while others have been encouraging patenting for some time (Peters and Fusfeld, 1982). Universities can also encourage or discourage faculty consulting and involvement in commercialization through the development and enforcement of policies (Wade, 1984).

Administrative support data were obtained from the survey of university administrators. In each case the administrator's response was linked for analysis to the individual faculty member's file. The measures were as follows: *auspices,* whether the institution is a state or private university; *seed money support,* whether or not money is provided to support faculty members in writing grant and contract proposals for external funding; *patent office size,* the number of professional employees in the university patent office; *traditional industry ties,* measured by an administrator's response to a single three-point item indicating how strong the university's relationships with industry have been in the past; and *university entrepreneurship,* a summary scale indicating the number of mechanisms that the university has for commercializing the research of its faculty members. Scale items included holding equity in faculty-owned firms, holding equity in firms employing faculty members, holding equity in firms providing support to faculty members, having a research foundation to invest in faculty firms, having an office or center for stimulating faculty companies, investing venture capital in life-science firms, and donating land or space to science parks and other commercial enterprises. Also measured were the number of *life science patents* held by the university and *reputation* on the National Academy of Science's average quality rating on a 1–5 scale of all of the sampled departments within each university (Jones, Lindzey, and Coggeshall, 1982).

Entrepreneurs in Academe

RESULTS

Relative Importance of Predictor Groups

Our initial approach to answering the questions regarding the effects of different predictor groups involved looking at the relative contribution of each of the four groups of predictors: individual demographic characteristics and attitudes, other entrepreneurial behaviors, group-level variables measuring local norms, and organizational variables measuring institutional characteristics and policies. Several ordinary-least-squares regression models were calculated. In the first, five forms of entrepreneurship were regressed on each of the four groups of predictors separately. The results are shown in Table 2. This analysis examined the relative importance of each group considered by itself; the names of those variables whose *t* statistics were significant at the .10 level or greater are shown for informational purposes only.

Because the other entrepreneurial behaviors and the local norm variables were composed from the same survey items, it seemed prudent to explore their distinctive contributions to entrepreneurship. Burstein (1980) argued that distinct estimates can be made in regressions in which individual and contextual effect measures are included but not where "frog

Table 2

Regressions of Forms of Entrepreneurship on the Four Groups of Predictor Variables Showing Explanatory Power of Groups

			Dependent Variable		
Variable Group	Research budget	Supplemental income	Industry funding	Patenting	Equity holding
Individual					
R^2	.224•••	.130•••	.0400•••	.056•••	.034•••
	Med +	Med +			
	Age −	Age +			
	Risk −	Risk −	Risk −	Risk −	Risk −
	Pubs +	Pubs +		Pubs +	Pubs +
			Appr UIR +		
Organizational					
R^2	.038•••	.035•••	.000	.012••	.010••
	Seed −		Ties +		
	Repu +	Repu +		Repu +	
OEBs					
R^2	.051•••	.148•••	.031•••	.103•••	.141•••
		Bud +		Bud +	
	Sup +		Sup +	Sup +	Sup +
		Ind +		Ind +	
	Pat +	Pat +	Pat +		Pat +
		Equ +		Equ +	
Local norms					
R^2	.118•••	.080•••	.055•••	.063•••	.071•••
	Bud U +	Sup U +	Ind U +	Pat U +	Equ U +

•$p < .05$; ••$p < .01$.

Note: + and − indicate the sign of the regression coefficient. Med = medical school; Risk = risks to science index; Appr UIR = approval of university-industry relationships; Seed = university provided money for proposals; Repu = university reputation; Ties = strong university ties to industry; Bud/Bud U = $ research funding for individual faculty member/mean $ of research funding in the university; Sup/Sup U = supplemental income for individual/mean supplemental income in the university; Ind/Ind U = industry funding for individual/mean industry funding in the university; Pat/Pat U = individual holds a patent/% of all faculty holding a patent; Equ/Equ U = individual holds equity/% of all faculty holding equity; Pub/Pub U = individual number of publications/mean log of number of publications for all faculty.

pond effects" (the difference between the individual *i*'s score on *X* and the contextual score on *X*) are also part of the equation. However, given the existing controversies about the use of contextual effects data based on attitudes in organizational research, we decided to examine them separately. Table 3 shows the results of the four regression models that were computed. The first two entered individual/university variables as a first step and OEBs or local norms as a second; the third entered individual/university/local norms as a first step and OEBs as a second step; the last entered individual/university/ OEBs as a first step and local norms as a second step.

Perhaps the clearest finding from this table is that university administrative support has little effect on entrepreneurship. In Table 2, the largest amount of variance explained by university administrative support variables was 3.8 percent. University reputation (over which university administrators have little short-term control) is the only institutional characteristic that enters more than one equation (not tabled), which reinforces the conclusion that university policies have little direct impact on faculty entrepreneurial behavior. When OEBs (Table 3, Model 1) or local norms (Model 2) and organizational structure and policy variables are included in the same equation, no university variables achieve significance (not shown).

Overall, individual characteristics, other entrepreneurial behaviors, and local norms appear to be about equally effective in terms of R^2 in explaining entrepreneurship, except in the case of size of research budget, where individual predictors dominate (see Table 2).

Models 1 and 3 in Table 3 indicate, however, that the association between OEBs—or the "entrepreneurship profile" presented by the individual respondent—and size of research budget and funding from industry is sharply reduced when other variables are entered into the model as a first step. In contrast, their strong impact on supplemental income and equity holding is maintained. The independent contribution of

Table 3

Results of Stepwise Regressions to Determine the Relative Importance of OEBs and Local Norms

Effect Modeled	Research budget	Supplemental	Dependent Variable Industry funding income	Patenting	Equity holding
1. Effect of OEBs given individual and university variables					
dR^2*	.011**	.078***	.027***	.060***	.103***
2. Effect of local norms given individual and university variables					
dR^2	.039***	.040***	.042***	.044***	.055***
3. Effect of OEBs given individual, university, and local norms					
dR^2	.010**	.069***	.030***	.035***	.090***
4. Effect of local norms given individual, university, and OEBs					
dR^2	.038***	.031***	.045***	.051***	.042***

* $p < .05$; ** $p < .01$; *** p .001.
* dR^2 is the addition to R^2 associated with the variables entered in the second step.

Entrepreneurs in Academe

OEBs to patenting lies in between. Local norms of behavior significantly increase the multiple R^2 for all of the dependent variables between 4 and 5 percent when added as a second step after other variables (Models 2 and 4).

Models 3 and 4 confirm that OEBs and local norms are measuring different effects. For all five forms of entrepreneurship, local norm variables are significant predictors even when controlling for OEBs, and vice versa.

In the case of the less traditional forms of entrepreneurship —industry funding, patenting, and equity holding—individual characteristics are less likely to be significant predictors when local norm and OEB variables are added to the regression models. For these forms of entrepreneurship, OEBs alone account for 27, 40, and 50 percent, respectively, of the total R^2 that is attained by the full model, and local norm variables account for 41, 32, and 23 percent, respectively, of the total R^2 that is attained by the full models.

Evaluation of Specific Predictors

A second approach to answering the questions posed at the beginning of this paper involved looking at the specific predictors that best account for each form of entrepreneurship. Table 4 shows the results of five regression models that were computed using the 16 individual, OEB, and local norm variables. We excluded organizational variables because they were insignificant in previous regressions. Only variables whose regression coefficients are significant at the .10 level or better are reported in the table.

Two individual-level variables were related to several types of entrepreneurship, as shown in Table 4. First, the individual's concern about the risks to science from working closely with industry was negatively associated with three forms: supplemental income, industry funding, and patenting. This suggests that the deeper their concerns about protecting basic science from pressures to commercialize, the less likely scientists are to behave in an entrepreneurial manner. However, the causal relationship is unclear: Scientists may change their attitudes in order to diminish dissonance between their own behavior and their interpretation of the scientific value system. Alternatively, exposure to entrepreneurship may convince the scientists of the robustness of basic science against corruption through such activities. Second, the individual's publication rate in refereed journals was positively associated with three of the five entrepreneurial behaviors, industry funding and equity holding being the exceptions. Thus, it appears that scientists who meet the highest (quantitative) standards of productivity are most likely to be entrepreneurial.

Table 4 consistently indicates that the local norm variable corresponding to the behavior being analyzed matters the most. In other words, the individual's entrepreneurship of a given type is strongly predicted by the local norms for the same form of entrepreneurship. Local university publication rate was also significant in two cases, research budget and supplemental income. This finding is discussed in more detail below.

Each of the OEBs has a significant effect on at least two other forms of entrepreneurship. Two OEBs stand out: Both

Table 4

Full Regression Model

Variable	Research budget	Supplemental income	Dependent Variable Industry funding	Patenting	Equity holding
Med		−.05			
Age	−.21***	.11***			
Risk		−.08**	−.11**	−.07	
Pubs	.33***	.21***		.11*	
Appr UIR			.09*		
Bud	–	.08*		.08*	
Sup	.08*	–	.10**	.07	.25***
Ind		.08*	–	.10**	.07*
Pat	.07*	.06	.11**	–	.16***
Equ		.22***	.06	.16***	–
Bud U	.30***				
Sup U		.24***			
Ind U			.24***		
Pat U				.24***	
Equ U					.24***
Pub U	−.10	−.11*			
Multiple R	.549	.513	.361	.416	.443
R² (adj.)	.288	.249	.113	.157	.180
F statistic	21.93***	18.13***	7.63***	10.64***	12.38***

* $p < .05$; ** $p < .01$.

Note: + and − indicate the sign of the regression coefficient. Med = medical school; Risk = risks to science index; Appr UIR = approval of university-industry relationships; Seed = university provided money for proposals; Repu = university reputation; Ties = strong university ties to industry; Bud/Bud U = $ research funding for individual faculty member/mean $ of research funding in the university; Sup/Sup U = supplemental income for individual/mean supplemental income in the university; Ind/Ind U = industry funding for individual/mean industry funding in the university; Pat/Pat U = individual holds a patent/% of all faculty holding a patent; Equ/Equ U = individual holds equity/% of all faculty holding equity; Pub/Pub U = individual number of publications/mean log of number of publications for all faculty.

patenting and supplemental income are significant predictors of all other forms of entrepreneurship.

Predicting Forms of Entrepreneurship

Table 4 may be used to address another theoretical issue posed above. Rather than asking about the relative impact of different categories of predictors, we can elaborate on the question posed earlier about the structure of academic entrepreneurship. If entrepreneurship actually consists of a variety of distinctive behaviors, the regressions should produce different patterns of significant predictors.

Research budget. The most traditional form of entrepreneurship—size of research budget—is by far the easiest form of entrepreneurship to predict. Table 2 indicates that for every category of predictor variables except OEBs, the R^2 statistics are highest for size of research budget. The overall adjusted R^2 in the full regression (Table 4) is .288, which is substantially larger than in the other equations.

Individual characteristics and attitudes are relatively more important as predictors of size of research budget than for the other forms of entrepreneurship, accounting for .22 of the .29 R^2 (78 percent) that is attained by the full model. Local norm variables are also significant (particularly the size of the research budget of colleagues), but OEBs barely reach significance and are less important predictors of this form of

Entrepreneurs in Academe

entrepreneurial behavior than other forms. The pattern of significant variables suggests that entrepreneurship based on grantsmanship may coexist easily with traditional academic values: It is associated with high levels of scientific productivity, is not associated with any significant contacts with industry (and presumably other sources of money for applied research), and flourishes in contexts in which other scientists are also productive and engaging in large-scale scientific endeavors. In fact, we might relabel the research budget variable as elite entrepreneurship. These elite entrepreneurs are also younger.

Supplemental income. The pattern for supplemental income is somewhat similar but with clear differences, as well. First, the relationship between this form of entrepreneurship and individual characteristics is more limited (individual variables account for 60 percent of the total explained variance). Second, the elite entrepreneur pattern is complicated by the addition of new predictors. In particular, OEBs are more important, accounting for 28 percent of the total variance explained. Among the OEBs, only industry funding is not a significant predictor of supplemental income. A final difference is that those who earn larger amounts of extra income are likely to be older and to be located in arts and sciences departments (as opposed to medical schools).

It is worth speculating about the contrasting associations between age and these two more common forms of entrepreneurship. On the one hand, it seems probable that incentives to become involved in large, externally funded research projects are greatest among those who are on the fast track in major universities but have not yet necessarily reached the peak of their scientific recognition. The motivation to compete for grants may decline as the scientist's position in the prestige hierarchy stabilizes. Because older scientists are more visible, they are more likely to be sought out as consultants. On the other hand, this may be a cohort effect: Younger scientists are more likely to be in two-career families (minimizing the need to supplement income), or they may be contributing to new norms about the appropriate scale of scientific endeavor (Etzkowitz, 1983).

Funding from industry. Funding from industry presents a somewhat more complicated picture, partly because the level of prediction is weaker than for the other models (only 11 percent of the variance is explained by the full regression model in Table 4). No individual demographic characteristics enter the equations. Attitudinal variables (the risks-to-science index and the variable measuring approval of increasing university-industry ties) are associated, but with the causal inference problems noted above. The individual effects of OEBs are modest compared to the effects of belonging to a group of life scientists who get money from industry. It is clear that the model specified here is not a good predictor, and an alternative organizational-level explanation is explored below.

Patenting and equity holding. The models for the most extreme forms of entrepreneurship—patenting and equity holding—are more similar to each other than they are to either of the two most traditional forms in terms of the predictive power of the variables and the relative importance of different predictor groups. Yet, there are still some differences between them that emerge in Table 4.

Equity holding is better predicted (18 percent of the variance explained) with a simpler model. Only the percentage of life scientists in the university who hold equity and the OEBs (other than size of research budget) exhibit standardized regression coefficients that are significant at the .05 level or better. This supports the contention that equity holding is the most extreme form of entrepreneurship: The variables that significantly predict it are other nonscholarly entrepreneurial behaviors and being in a context in which entrepreneurship is the norm, with the former being by far the most important, accounting for 50 percent of the explained variance. Patenting, however, is both more complex and less stable across the different regression analyses. Like equity holding, the relative importance of local behavioral norms is very important, making up nearly a third of the explained variance. All OEBs are significant predictors in Table 4.

Institutional Patterns of Entrepreneurship

The final theoretical question posed at the beginning of this paper concerns the degree to which these data reveal any evidence that there are entrepreneurial universities, rather than just isolated entrepreneurial academics. The above analyses reveal a consistent finding: For each form of entrepreneurship, the aggregated variable measuring local behavior on this dimension is among the most powerful predictors. To what degree does this statistical association actually reflect a concentration of faculty with certain types of behavior in particular institutions? To examine concentration we generated graphs, shown in Figure 1, that display the concentration of a given entrepreneurial behavior within universities and the association between different forms of entrepreneurship at the level of the university as a whole.

In Figure 1, the X axis measures the cumulative proportion of all faculty members from zero to one. To form this variable, faculty members were grouped by their university affiliation. University groups were then ranked in descending order according to the proportion of faculty members in the university who exhibit the behavior. The Y axis measures the cumulative proportion of faculty members with that behavior on a scale from zero to one. The diagonal line represents an equal distribution of the behavior across all universities. Discrepancies between the diagonal and the curve are a visual representation of the extent to which behavior is institutionally concentrated.

These graphs reveal that the statistically significant associations correspond to what might be considered socially significant facts. As might be expected from the discussion above, the highest levels of concentration are found for equity holding: 75 percent of all faculty members holding equity in a company whose products or services are based on their own research are located in universities containing only about 37 percent of the faculty members in the sample. Similar levels of concentration are found in the case of industrial funding: 70 percent of the faculty members who receive 25 percent or more of their research budget from industry sponsors are located in institutions that contain 40 percent of the faculty

Entrepreneurs in Academe

Figure 1. Institutional concentrations of entrepreneurial behaviors.

Note: The diagonal line represents an equal
distribution of the behavior across all universities.
Discrepancies between the diagonal and the curve
are a visual representation of the extent to which the
behavior is institutionally concentrated.

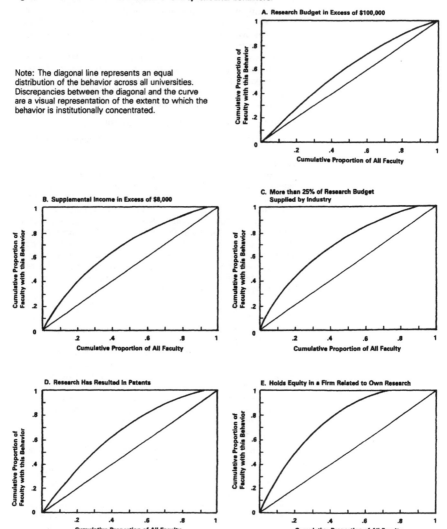

members. Fifty percent of all of the faculty members who have research budgets above $100,000 are located in institutions that contain only 32 percent of the life scientists in the sample; 50 percent of those whose income is supplemented by more than $8,000 a year over their base salary are located in institutions containing only 35 percent of the sample.

We also identified universities that scored in the top quartile on the measures of entrepreneurship. The results are shown in Table 5. We know that the types of entrepreneurship are modestly associated at the individual level. If we look at the most entrepreneurial groups (identified by university affiliation), there are apparent associations at this level as well. For example, among the ten universities that have the highest proportion of faculty members with research budgets larger than the sample median, six are also among the top quartile on two or three other forms of entrepreneurship. Only one institution is characterized solely by high levels of external funding. Similarly, of the ten universities that are in the top quartile on percentage of faculty members holding equity, six are also in the top quartile on supplemental income, while only two are in the top quartile of percentage of research funding from industry. The ranges of faculty behavior among

Table 5

Universities in Top Quartile on Measures of Entrepreneurship

University	Research funds ≥ $195,000*	Measures of Entrepreneurship Supplemental income ≥10%†	Industry funding ≥25%‡	Patenting	Equity holding
Harvard	+	+		+	+
M.I.T.	+	+	+		+
Baylor	+		+	+	+
University of Washington	+			+	+
Yale	+	+			+
University of California, Berkeley	+	+			+
University of Maryland	+				+
Columbia	+	+			
University of Rochester	+		+		
University of Utah	+	+		+	
Stanford	+				+
University of Southern California		+		+	
University of Minnesota		+			+
Purdue			+	+	
Michigan State				+	+
Northwestern	+				
Penn State		+			
Oregon State			+		
Ohio State			+		
Cornell			+		
University of North Carolina, Chapel Hill			+		
University of Florida			+		
Case Western Reserve			+		
Johns Hopkins			+		
University of Pittsburgh				+	
Duke				+	

* This figure is the median for the sample.
† This figure is the median for those who had supplemental income.
‡ This figure is the median for those who received industry funding.

Entrepreneurs in Academe

the top quartile are as follows: mean research budget over $195,000, 80 percent (University of Washington) to 42 percent (Northwestern); mean supplementary income over 10 percent, 59 percent (M.I.T.) to 17 percent (Penn State); mean industry research funding over 25 percent, 38 percent (Oregon State) to 12 percent (Case Western); percent of faculty holding patents, 40 percent (University of Washington) to 12 percent (Baylor); mean percent holding equity, 44 percent (M.I.T.) to 26 percent (Harvard).

There is a significant exception to this generalization: obtaining money from industry. Most of the universities that have close funding ties with industry are not entrepreneurial on any other dimension. Furthermore, several of those that score highest on this form of entrepreneurship, but not on any other, are located in public land-grant institutions. These institutions may be engaged in long-term relationships with state-based industries, and the association may not necessarily be a consequence of a broader local culture of entrepreneurship.

DISCUSSION AND CONCLUSIONS

Entrepreneurship and Science

Many scientists still believe that the search for truth is inconsistent with any interest in profiting from ideas. This view is, however, increasingly controversial as policymakers turn to science as a vehicle for energizing our national economy and society, and administrators and faculty members try to secure more money from both industry and state and national governments to support their research programs.

Irrespective of the position taken, our data suggest that life scientists in research-intensive universities are modestly entrepreneurial. However, despite concerns about weakening the basic science mission of the university (Krimsky, 1984; Wade, 1984; Varrin and Kukich, 1985), there is little evidence in our survey to suggest that most life scientists are more interested in commercial activities than traditional scientific endeavors. Small minorities are involved in more extreme forms of commercial entrepreneurship, and these forms of entrepreneurship are not strongly associated with running a large-scale externally funded research endeavor. In other words, there is no evidence to suggest that a new kind of "entrepreneurial scholar" has taken over most universities.

The data suggest that scientifically productive scholars are more entrepreneurial on several dimensions. Thus, this investigation supports Etzkowitz's (1983) argument that entrepreneurial behavior has evolved naturally within the scientific community and is not incompatible with maintaining the outward manifestations of scholarship. However, scholarly productivity is not an important predictor of the more commercial forms of entrepreneurship, which supports the argument that they may be less compatible with traditional university values.

Our data also suggest that most academic groups do not develop norms that encourage multiple forms of entrepreneurship: only six institutions appear distinctively entrepreneurial. However, the fact that a number of the most prestigious universities are entrepreneurial on multiple dimensions provides support for the concerns of "science watchers." Clark (1983) noted that the evolution of less prestigious higher education institutions is mimetic: Where Harvard, Stanford, and M.I.T. lead in entrepreneurship, will the others be far behind?

Organizational Theory

The analysis supports a tentative conclusion that, at least in academic settings, entrepreneurship is not an either/or condition, nor are the different forms of entrepreneurship minor variations on a similar social phenomenon. The data suggest that the most distinctive patterns occur in the case of obtaining large research grants. The pattern of associations shown throughout the paper suggests that "elite entrepreneurs" are not likely to be drawn toward more extreme forms of entrepreneurship. However, there are also unique patterns associated with each of the other different forms.

Under the assumption that academics are not unique in their motivations and behaviors, we may infer that research on entrepreneurship in private firms might also benefit from efforts to identify different patterns and types. Several of the entrepreneurial forms discussed here may have cognates in other settings. For example, R&D entrepreneurs in industry may be quite distinct from those who are effective in bringing products to market or in organizing new firms.

Our cross-sectional data do not permit drawing definitive conclusions about the causes of academic entrepreneurship. If, however, we look across all of the data a number of hypotheses may be made.

Until recently, research (and popular writing) on entrepreneurship has tended to focus on individual demographic, educational, and employment characteristics rather than on the characteristics of the organizations in which entrepreneurs are located or the groups in which they work. This study suggests that individual characteristics provide weak and unsystematic predictions of the forms of entrepreneurship that are at the center of discussions about the importance of individual action in revitalizing organizations and the economy. This was rather surprising, since several of the individual variables that we examined—gender and age, for example— have been shown to be relatively strong predictors of other faculty members' behaviors such as publication rates (Cole and Zuckerman, 1984), and our analyses suggest that they are very important in predicting the more traditional forms of academic entrepreneurship. To test the robustness of this conclusion, we also conducted additional analyses using alternative individual characteristics (such as rank and actual age) and looked at additional attitudinal batteries in the survey. None of these analyses suggested a powerful effect of individual-level variables.

We therefore hypothesize, based on our data, that for the more nontraditional forms of entrepreneurship, individual characteristics are moderated by institutional location. There are four possible explanations for the relatively strong effect of local norms on individual behavior that would account for the data regarding the concentration of entrepreneurs in particular institutions: (1) self-selection may produce value and

Entrepreneurs in Academe

behavior consensus (individuals are drawn to these settings because they are known to be supportive of or tolerate entrepreneurship); (2) behavioral socialization may operate within a work group (individuals are affected by the behavior of their immediate colleagues and tend to act like them); (3) organizational culture may be a factor (a broader set of institutional policies, procedures, and values reinforces attitudes and behavior regarding entrepreneurship); or (4) strategic management may be a factor (some universities use recruitment to position themselves in the forefront of changing patterns of academic behavior in order to reap the potential benefits in increased prestige and income). We cannot determine which of these is operating, and this issue is worth further exploration. We suspect, however, that it is likely that all of the alternative explanations contribute, in part, to our findings.

Thus, the fact that the university policies and structures identified here have little impact on faculty entrepreneurship should not be taken to rule out an institutional effect, although it suggests that institutions cannot easily engineer entrepreneurship. The measures of university policies were based on actions that university administrators identified as institutional responses to changing patterns of entrepreneurship, but local norms of behavior (as measured here) are also an institutional characteristic and may be a consequence of a variety of other policies and practices that we have not examined. For example, the definition and enforcement of policies relating to consulting or conflict of interest varies quite widely among research institutions (Louis, Anderson, and Swazey, 1988), and this may send significant messages about how faculty members are expected to behave. In addition, departments rarely have complete autonomy in defining personnel needs, and this provides another leverage point for administrators. We hypothesize that these and other policies and procedures reflect underlying values and cultural assumptions about what constitutes appropriate entrepreneurial behavior.

Given the range of controls available to administrators, and the difficulty of managing organizational cultures in large institutions with unclear and conflicting missions, fostering or controlling entrepreneurship from the top may be less effective than working at the departmental or division level. The recruitment of key individuals who may help to alter or set new behavioral norms or the use of task forces to investigate or recommend changes may help to frame new expectations about behavior. Developing specific policies may send a signal, but the organization is basically very dependent on behavioral expectations that are reinforced below. This may, of course, be a finding that is relevant only to organizations, such as universities, that are "loosely coupled" (Weick, 1976). However, the ability of a large organization to maintain a very strong entrepreneurial culture without middle-level support and reinforcement may be questionable even in more tightly structured settings. Overall, since having a productive faculty appears to be so critical, the traditional strategy of continually supporting the recruitment of the best people in the field is a precondition to the effectiveness of other policies that may stimulate (or control) entrepreneurship.

REFERENCES

Baldridge, J. Victor, and Robert A. Burnham
1975 "Organizational innovation: Individual, organizational and environmental impacts." Administrative Science Quarterly, 20: 165–176.

Beneveniste, Guy
1987 Professionalizing the Organization. San Francisco: Jossey-Bass.

Blumenthal, David, Michael Gluck, and Karen Seashore Louis
1985 "Prospecting in academe." Unpublished paper, Kennedy School of Government, Harvard University.

Blumenthal, David, Michael Gluck, Karen Seashore Louis, and David Wise
1986a "Industrial support of university research in biotechnology." Science, 23: 242–246.
1986b "University-industry research relationships in biotechnology: Implications for the university." Science, 23, 1361–1366.

Boyer, Carol, and Darrell Lewis
1985 And on the Seventh Day: Faculty Consulting and Supplemental Income. Washington, DC: Association for the Study of Higher Education.

Burstein, Leigh
1980 "The analysis of multilevel data in educational research and evaluation." In David C. Berliner (ed.), Review of Educational Research, 8: 158–233. Washington, DC: American Educational Research Association.

Clark, Burton R.
1983 The Higher Education System. Berkeley: University of California Press.

Cohen, J. E.
1981 "Publication rate as a function of laboratory size in three biomedical research institutions." Scientometrics, 3: 467–487.

Cole, Jonathan, and Harriet Zuckerman
1984 "The productivity puzzle: Persistance and change in patterns of publication of men and women scientists." In Advances in Motivation and Achievement, 2: 217–258. Beverly Hills, CA: Sage.

Daft, Richard L., and Selwyn W. Becker
1978 The Innovative Organization. New York: Elsevier-North Holland.

Ennis, James G.
1986 "University-corporate links in biotechnology: The network structure of dual affiliations." Unpublished paper, Department of Sociology, Tufts University.

Etzkowitz, Henry
1983 "Entrepreneurial scientists and entrepreneurial universities in American academic science." Minerva, 21: 198–233.

Jones, L., G. Lindzey, and P. Coggeshall (eds.)
1982 An Assessment of Research-Doctorate Programs in the U.S. Washington, DC: National Academy Press.

Kanter, Rosabeth M.
1983 The Change Masters. New York: Simon and Schuster.

Kerr, Jeffrey, and John M. Slocum
1987 "Managing corporate culture through reward systems." Executive, 1: 99–107.

Krimsky, Sheldon
1984 Letter in geneWATCH, 1: 3.

Liebert, Roland J.
1977 "Research-grant getting and productivity among scholars: Recent national patterns of competition and favor." Journal of Higher Education, 48: 164–192.

Louis, Karen S., Melissa Anderson, and Judith P. Swazey
1988 "The university's role in regulating graduate education and research." Paper presented at the annual meeting of the Association for the Study of Higher Education, St. Louis, MO.

Marsh, Herbert, and Katherine Dillon
1980 "Academic productivity and faculty supplemental income." Journal of Higher Education, 51: 546–555.

Mazzoni, Tim L.
1987 "The politics of educational choice in Minnesota." In William Boyd and Charles Kerchner (eds.), The Politics of Excellence and Choice in Education, 1: 109–141. London: Taylor and Francis.

McClelland, David C., John W. Atkinson, Russel A. Clark, and Edgar L. Lowell
1976 The Achievement Motive. New York: Irvington.

Merton, Robert G.
1968 "The Matthew Effect in science." Science, 159 (January): 56–63.

Mintzberg, Henry
1973 "Strategy making in three modes." California Management Review, 16: 44–53.

Pelz, Donald F., and Frank Andrews
1976 Scientists in Organizations. Ann Arbor, MI: Institute for Social Research.

Peters, Lois, and Henry Fusfeld
1982 "Current U.S. university/industry research connections." In National Science Board, University-Industry Research Relationships: Selected Studies. Washington, DC: U.S. Government Printing Office.

Peters, Thomas J., and Robert H. Waterman
1982 In Search of Excellence. New York: Warner.

Peterson, Richard A.
1981 "Entrepreneurship and organization." In Paul C. Nystrom and William H. Starbuck (eds.), Handbook of Organizational Design, 1: 65–83. New York: Oxford University Press.

Peterson's Guides
1984 Peterson's Guides to Graduate Programs in the Biological, Agricultural and Health Sciences. Princeton: Peterson's Guides.

Pfeffer, Jeffrey, and William L. Moore
1980 "Power in university budgeting: A replication and extension." Administrative Science Quarterly, 25: 398–418.

Pfeffer, Jeffrey, and Gerald R. Salancik
1974 "Organizational decision making as a political process: The case of a university budget." Administrative Science Quarterly, 19: 135–151.

Ping Charles
1980 Industry and the Universities: Developing Cooperative Research Relationships in the National Interest. Washington, DC: National Commission on Research.

Ravetz, James
1971 Scientific Knowledge and Its Social Problems. Oxford: Clarendon Press.

Rosenblum, Sheila, and Karen Seashore Louis
1981 Stability and Change: Innovation in an Educational Context. New York: Plenum.

Seashore, Stanley E.
1954 Group Cohesiveness and the Industrial Work Group. Ann Arbor, MI: Institute for Social Research.

Entrepreneurs in Academe

Snow, Charles C., and Lawrence G. Hrebiniak
1980 "Strategy, distinctive competence and organizational performance." Administrative Science Quarterly, 25: 315–334.

Van Maanen, John
1976 "Breaking in: Socialization to work." In R. Dubin (ed.), Handbook of Work, Organization and Society: 67–130. Chicago: Rand McNally.

Varrin, R., and S. Kukich
1985 Letter in Science, 227: 385.

Wade, Nicholas
1984 The Science Business. New York: Priority Press.

Weick, Karl E.
1976 "Educational organizations as loosely coupled systems." Administrative Science Quarterly, 21: 1–19.

Zuckerman, Harriet, and Robert K. Merton
1972 "Age, aging and age structure in science." In M. W. Riley, M. Johnson and A. Foner (eds.), Aging and Society: A Sociology of Age Stratification, 3: 292–356. New York: Russell Sage Foundation.

[25]

Company-Scientist Locational Links:
The Case of Biotechnology

By DAVID B. AUDRETSCH AND PAULA E. STEPHAN *

The emergence of a recent literature (re)-discovering the importance of economic geography[1] might seem paradoxical in a world increasingly dominated by E-mail, faxes, and electronic communications superhighways. Why should geographic proximity matter when technology has advanced in a manner that has drastically reduced the cost of transmitting information across geographic space? This paper explores why geography matters more in certain economic relationships than in others by focusing on the locational incidence of contacts between firms in the biotechnology industry and university-based scientists affiliated with these firms. In particular, we suggest that the specific role played by the scientist shapes the importance of geographic proximity in the firm-scientist link.

* Audretsch: Wissenschaftszentrum Berlin für Sozialforschung and the Centre for Economic Policy Research (CEPR), Reichpietschufer 50, D-10785 Berlin, Germany; Stephan: Department of Economics and Policy Research Center, Georgia State University, Atlanta, GA 30303. This paper was started while Paula Stephan was a visiting professor at the Wissenschaftszentrum Berlin für Sozialforschung. We would like to acknowledge financial support from the North Atlantic Treaty Organization (NATO) under grant number CRG.940792, the College of Business Administration, Georgia State University, and the Policy Research Center of Georgia State University. Richard Hawkins, Meghan Crimmins, Anne Gilbert and Janet Keene coded the data. Steve Everhart provided computer assistance. Earlier versions of this paper were presented at the 1995 meetings of the American Economics Association in Washington, DC; the May 1995 Conference on R&D, Innovation, and Productivity at the Institute for Fiscal Studies in London; the September 1995 annual conference of the European Association for Research in Industrial Economics (EARIE) at Juan-Les-Pins, France; and an October 1995 seminar at INSEAD, Fontainebleau, France. We are also grateful to the suggestions and comments of James Adams, Maryann P. Feldman, Mary Beth Walker and an anonymous referee of this journal. Any remaining errors or omissions are our responsibility.

[1] See for examples Paul Krugman (1991a, b), Robert E. Lucas (1993), Paul Romer (1990), and Audretsch and Maryann P. Feldman (1996).

We shed light on two questions concerning biotechnology companies and the university-based scientists associated with the companies:

1) To what extent are the links between university scientists and biotechnology companies geographically bounded?
2) Is the spatial dimension of geographic links between biotechnology firms and scientists shaped by the role and characteristics of the scientist?

We are able to answer these questions by linking the location of the biotechnology firm with the location of the university-based scientists affiliated with the firm. Thus, while Krugman (1991a) may be correct in pointing out that no "paper trail" exists to facilitate measuring and tracking networks, in this paper we develop a trail of geographic linkages between scientists and firms in biotechnology.

The method used to identify and measure linkages between scientists and biotechnology firms is described in Section I. In particular, we employ a new data base, which includes virtually the entire population of biotechnology firms that prepared an initial public offering (IPO) in the early 1990's, to examine the extent to which the firms and the university-based scientists involved with the firms are located within the same region. In Section II we provide a theory suggesting that the relationship between the locations of a biotechnology firm and a university scientist will be shaped by the potential economic knowledge residing in that scientist and the role that she or he plays in working with the firm. In Section III a probit analysis is undertaken to link the likelihood that a scientist is located in the same region as the biotechnology firm with which she or he is involved to characteristics specific to the scientist and to the role played with the biotechnology firm. Finally, a summary and conclusions are presented.

642   THE AMERICAN ECONOMIC REVIEW   JUNE 1996

I. Measuring Links Between Scientists and Firms

Biotechnology is a new industry that is knowledge based and predominantly composed of new small firms having close ties with university-based scientists. The relative small scale of most biotechnology firms is arguably attributable to the diseconomies of scale inherent in the "bureaucratic process which inhibits both innovative activity and the speed with which new inventions move through the corporate system towards the market" (Albert N. Link and John Rees, 1990 p. 25). Lynne G. Zucker et al. (1994 p. 1) provide considerable evidence suggesting that the timing and location of new biotechnology firms is "primarily explained by the presence at a particular time and place of scientists who are actively contributing to the basic science." More specifically, they find that biotechnology firms are likely to be found in close geographic proximity to where scientists who have published articles on gene sequencing are located. Their work, however, does not explore the geographic linkages among scientists at these institutions and biotech firms. That is, while Zucker et al. show that a region such as the San Francisco Bay Area, which produces a disproportionate amount of research in biotechnology, is home to a disproportionate number of biotech firms, their work sheds virtually no light upon the extent to which biotech firms, once located in the region, establish networks with university-based scientists located in the area. The implicit assumption, of course, is that the networks are overwhelmingly local. Their research design, however, lacks a paper trail linking firms and scientists, and thus can neither affirm nor deny the assumption. Furthermore, they do not explore the variety of roles that university scientists play with biotech firms, but instead focus exclusively on the role of knowledge transfer.[2]

The uniqueness of our approach is that it allows us to determine the actual geographic location of the firm as well as the geographic location of the university-based scientists affiliated with the firm. We are also able to make inferences about the role the scientist plays with the firm since we are able to identify the title they hold with the firm as well as whether the scientist was a founder of the firm. We do this by collecting data from the prospectuses of biotechnology companies that prepared an initial public offering in the United States during the period March 1990 to November 1992. All told, 54 firms affiliated with 445 university-based scientists meet this criterion.[3] By carefully reading these prospectuses, we determine the names of university-based scientists affiliated with each firm, the role they play in the firm, and the name and location of their home institution. Universities and firms are then grouped into regions which are generally larger than a single city but considerably smaller than a state. Certain areas, for example, metropolitan New York, cross several state lines. A straightforward way to examine our data is to determine the percentage of university-based scientists affiliated with the firm that are from universities in the same region as the firm. This is done in the Data Appendix.

Four major conclusions can be drawn from Table A1. First, firms are geographically concentrated in three primary regions (the San Francisco Bay Area, San Diego and Boston), two secondary regions (Philadelphia and New York), and a number of smaller clusters.[4] Second, the degree to which regions rely upon local scientific talent varies substantially. For example, the Boston area firms draw nearly one-half of their scientists from universities located within the region. By contrast, firms located in the San Diego area draw only about one-quarter of their scientists from universities in the region. Third, the degree to which firms rely upon local scientists varies significantly across individual firms. Eighty percent of the scientists employed by Anergen are located in

---

[2] See also Zucker et al. (1995).

[3] The study includes several firms for which the initial public offering was prepared but postponed at the last minute.

[4] Although these data are drawn from a two and one-half year time period, the geographic distribution of the 54 firms in our sample is virtually identical to the entire population of biotechnology firms in the United States. Ernst and Young identify three primary regions, two secondary regions, several other regions with at least 20 companies, and a host of smaller clusters (G. Steven Burrill and Kenneth B. Lee, 1992).

TABLE 1—LOCATION OF SCIENTISTS BY REGION OF UNIVERSITY

	Contacts	Unique firms	Contacts in region	Percentage in region
San Francisco Bay Area	66	28	44	66.7
Stanford University	37	17	24	64.9
University of California, San Francisco	26	14	17	65.4
San Diego, CA	27	13	21	77.8
Scripps College	7	5	5	71.4
University of California, San Diego	16	10	14	87.5
Boston, MA	69	26	41	59.4
Harvard University	43	21	24	55.8
Massachusetts Institute of Technology	15	9	7	46.7
Philadelphia, PA	17	14	8	47.1
University of Pennsylvania	9	8	3	33.3
New York, NY	36	22	9	25.0
Albert Einstein College of Medicine	7	6	1	14.3
Columbia University	11	8	3	27.3
Rockefeller	11	7	4	36.4
Maryland	11	9	1	9.1
Johns Hopkins University	5	4	0	0.0
Seattle, WA	6	5	2	33.3
University of Washington	6	5	2	33.3
Boulder, CO	3	3	1	33.3
Kansas	0	0	0	0.0
Research Triangle, NC	8	8	2	25.0
Los Angeles, CA	13	9	0	0.0
California Institute of Tech	7	5	0	0.0
Dallas, TX	9	5	1	11.1
University of Texas, South Western Medical Center	5	3	0	0.0
Houston, TX	22	9	8	36.4
University of Texas, Anderson Center	11	3	7	63.6
Baylor College of Medicine	7	6	0	0.0
East	37	25	0	0.0
Penn State University	6	5	0	0.0
Pittsburgh University	5	5	0	0.0
Yale University	8	7	0	0.0
Foreign Countries	33	21	0	0.0
Midwest	39	21	0	0.0
Michigan	13	10	0	0.0
South	24	15	0	0.0
Alabama, Birmingham	6	4	0	0.0
West	25	19	0	0.0
University of California, Davis	5	4	0	0.0
Total	445		138	

the San Francisco Bay Area. By contrast, only one of Genta's 19 university-based scientists is located in the same geographic area as the company. The final conclusion to be drawn from Table A1 is that the propensity to draw upon local networks appears unrelated to firm density. For example, the region with the most firms, the San Francisco Bay Area, does not have the greatest propensity to rely upon local-based scientific networks.

Table 1 explores geographic linkages between universities and firms. Eighteen educational regions are defined and within each region institutions with at least five scientific contacts to biotechnology firms are listed. The Table also gives the number of scientist-firm contacts that exist by region and institution as well as the number of firms involved in these contacts. Six important points should be emphasized from Table 1. First, although universities in the San Francisco Bay Area and the Boston-Cambridge Area together supply approximately 30 percent of the scientists, the supply of talent is much less regionally concentrated than are the firms. Second, three institutions are major producers of contacts: Harvard, with 43; Stanford, with 37; and the University of California at San Francisco (UCSF), with 26. Third, universities that are major producers send talent to a large number of firms. Harvard scientists had contact with 40 percent of the firms in our sample; Stanford and UCSF scientists each had contact with over 25 percent of the firms.

Fourth, *commuting patterns* vary by region. For example, two thirds of the university-based scientists in the San Francisco Bay Area work with biotechnology firms located in the Bay Area. By contrast, one fourth of the scientists located in the New York area work with firms in their area. Fifth, commuting patterns also vary considerably according to institutional affiliation. For example, only one in eight of the scientists at the University of California at San Diego (UCSD) commute while six out of seven scientists at the Albert Einstein College of Medicine are affiliated with firms outside the region. Finally, Table 1 indicates the existence of regions in the United States rich in scientific talent but not in biotechnology firms. For example, although 13 of the university-based scientists are located at the University of Michigan, there were no new public offerings filed by biotechnology firms located in the Ann Arbor/ Detroit area during our two and one-half year window of observation.

In Table 2 firms are classified into 13 regions and universities into 18 geographic areas. The final row at the bottom indicates the number of scientists drawn from the 18 distinct university regions and is identical to the summary statistics found in Table 1. The column at the extreme right of the last group indicates the number of university-based sci-

entists affiliated with biotechnology companies from the 13 distinct regions and is identical to the summary entries of Table A1.

The virtue of Table 2 is that it reflects the regional location of biotech talent as well as commuting patterns of university-based scientists. For the 13 regions in which there are both firms and universities, the entries on the diagonal represent the number of university-based scientists involved with firms located within that region. Off-diagonal row entries in Table 2 report the regional source of imported talent.

Table 2 invites two conclusions. First, geographic proximity does not play an important role for most company-scientist location links. Only 138 of the 445 observations lie on the diagonal. Yet, a Chi-square test implies that the null hypothesis of factor independence can be rejected at better than the 0.001 level. Linkages may not be overwhelmingly local but neither are they random. Second, distance does not appear to affect commuting patterns. For example, the hypothesis that scientists are just as likely to make a 2500 mile trip as a 250 mile trip cannot be rejected at the 10-percent level of significance.

II. The Role of University-Based Scientists

The results from the previous section clearly show that in some cases the geographic link between a biotechnology company and a university scientist occurs within the same region, while in other cases geographic proximity does not matter. Here we hypothesize that the locational incidence of contacts between firms and university-scientists is shaped by the particular role played by the scientist with the firm. When university-based scientists are actively involved in knowledge transfer, their knowledge is more easily tapped if the firm is located in the same region as the scientist. But when the scientist plays other roles geographic proximity is considerably less important. Balanced against the benefits of local proximity to the scientist is proximity to other firms and research organizations and also to better inputs. The fewer firms there are in a region, holding all else constant, the less likely the firm would be to locate near scientists in that region with which it has contacts. Also relevant would be unobserved features of the firm,

TABLE 2—GEOGRAPHIC DISTRIBUTION OF FIRM-UNIVERSITY LINKS

	Region of University					
	SF Bay	Los Angeles	San Diego	Boulder	Kansas	Boston
Region of Firm:						
SF Bay	44	9	2	1	0	13
Los Angeles	1	0	0	0	0	0
San Diego	5	1	21	0	0	3
Boulder	1	0	0	1	0	1
Kansas	1	0	0	0	0	0
Boston	4	3	3	1	0	41
Maryland	1	0	0	0	0	1
RTI	0	0	0	0	0	0
New York	5	0	0	0	0	6
Philadelphia	0	0	1	0	0	4
Dallas	0	0	0	0	0	0
Houston	1	0	0	0	0	0
Seattle	3	0	0	0	0	0
Total	66	13	27	3	0	69

	Region of University					
	Maryland	RTI	New York	Philadelphia	Dallas	Houston
Region of Firm:						
SF Bay	2	3	11	2	3	1
Los Angeles	0	0	0	0	0	0
San Diego	2	0	5	4	1	5
Boulder	0	1	0	0	0	0
Kansas	0	0	0	0	0	0
Boston	4	1	6	2	0	0
Maryland	1	0	2	0	0	3
RTI	0	2	0	0	0	0
New York	1	1	9	1	4	1
Philadelphia	1	0	3	8	0	1
Dallas	0	0	0	0	1	3
Houston	0	0	0	0	0	8
Seattle	0	0	0	0	0	0
Total	11	8	36	17	9	22

	Region of University						
	Seattle	East	Foreign	Midwest	South	West	Total
Region of Firm:							
SF Bay	2	9	11	12	10	10	145
Los Angeles	0	2	1	3	1	1	9
San Diego	1	5	9	7	3	5	77
Boulder	0	0	0	0	0	0	4
Kansas	0	0	1	2	1	1	6
Boston	0	3	4	7	3	3	85
Maryland	1	3	0	0	1	0	13
RTI	0	1	0	1	1	1	6
New York	0	3	5	1	1	1	39
Philadelphia	0	8	0	2	1	2	31
Dallas	0	1	1	2	2	0	10
Houston	0	2	1	0	0	1	13
Seattle	2	0	0	2	0	0	7
Total	6	37	33	39	24	25	445

such as where the main participants in the firm that are not university scientists reside.

University-based scientists provide three key functions to biotech firms: they facilitate knowledge transfer from university laboratories to the firm; they signal the quality of the firm's research to both capital and resource markets; and they help chart the scientific direction of the company. The knowledge transfer function of university-based scientists has received the most attention (Gary P. Pisano et al., 1988; Zucker et al., 1994; Zucker et al., 1995; and Henry Etzkowitz, 1983). It occurs, for example, whenever a university-based scientist founds a firm for the explicit purpose of developing knowledge created in the scientist's lab or when a university-based scientist is extensively involved in the research agenda of the firm. It is not the only way that knowledge moves from university labs and companies. Companies can also learn about the research occurring in university labs through social contacts between employees and university scientists and by sending employees to participate in workshops and seminars at the university (Zucker et al., 1995).

In addition to providing knowledge to newly formed biotechnology companies, university-based scientists also signal the quality of the firm to the scientific and financial communities. An effective way to recruit young scientists is to have a scientific advisory board (SAB) composed of the leaders in the field. According to George B. Rathmann, former president and CEO of Amgen, some of the young scientists that Amgen recruited would not have come "without the knowledge that an outstanding scientific advisory board took Amgen seriously" (Burill, 1987 p. 77). University-based scientists can also serve as *bait* to the investment community. In the early stages of development, biotechnology firms miss no opportunity to signal the abilities of their scientists as well as the science they are undertaking. It is not uncommon for prospectuses to read like proposals to the National Institutes of Health, both in terms of the projects they describe and the accomplishments of the scientists. Stephan (1994) has shown that the proceeds raised from an initial public offering as well as the "day one" value of the firm is positively and significantly related to the reputation of the university-based scientist affiliated with the firm.

University-based scientists also help chart the scientific direction of the company. Most biotech companies go public long before they have a flagship product ready for clinical tests. Some go public in the earliest stages of development.[5] Having few employees, and working in what has proved to be an exceptionally risky environment with regard to product effectiveness, firms seek guidance from the scientific community.[6]

The tacit nature of knowledge in biotechnology (Pisano et al., 1988) suggests that knowledge transfer between university-based scientists and biotechnology firms is facilitated by face to face contact and thus geographic proximity. On the other hand, the geographic proximity of all major researchers in a particular subfield is unlikely given the opportunity cost universities face in buying into a single research agenda. The broad-based nature of the knowledge used in biotechnology (Luigi Orsenigo, 1989) also suggests that knowledge links may not be exclusively local.

Scientists whose primary function is to signal the quality of the company are less likely to be local than are scientists who provide essential knowledge to the company. Their quality signal is produced by lending prestige to a venture they have presumably reviewed, a task that can be accomplished with credibility from a distance. The only reason that university-based scientists fulfilling the role of signal bearer might be geographically linked with the company is that the company may find it useful to locate near talent on the assumption that it makes scientific stars that much more willing to be involved. A similar line of reasoning can be made concerning the geographic proximity of scientists whose primary function is to chart the scientific course of the company.

It is, of course, difficult to know the exact functions the university-based scientist fulfills and many scientists undoubtedly fulfill multi-

---

[5] This was particularly true in the early 1990's when companies, sensing an open financial "window," rushed to go public in fear that the window would close and they would find themselves without the resources needed for product development.

[6] Such guidance is also often required by the financial backers and underwriters. Recent examples of product failure in biotechnology underscores the risky nature of the industry (Jim Shrine, 1994).

TABLE 3—ROLE OF SCIENTIST

	Founder	SAB	SAB chair	Majorstock
Nonlocal	16	249	7	20
$n = 307$	(42.1)	(68.2)	(33.3)	(50.0)
Local	22	116	14	20
$n = 138$	(57.9)	(31.8)	(66.7)	(50.0)
Total	38	365	21	40
χ^2	14.04[a]	0.56	13.10[a]	7.41[b]

Note: Percentages of the total are given in parentheses.
[a] Significant at 0.000 or better.
[b] Significant at 0.02 or better.

ple functions. The title the scientists holds at the firm, however, gives some insight into the function performed, and the genesis of the firm also allows for inference. In particular, we expect university-based founders to be a source of knowledge transfer. Presumably scientists start new biotechnology companies because their knowledge is not transferable to other firms for the expected economic value of the knowledge.[7] If this were not the case, there would be no incentive to start a new and independent company. Chairs of scientific advisory boards arguably also play a key role in knowledge transfer. Members of SABs, on the other hand, provide ballast to the masthead and help chart the course of the company. They can also facilitate knowledge transfer by providing the firm, at minimal cost, a full roster of key players doing research in the area.[8]

Table 3 explores the hypothesis that the role played by the scientist in the firm relates to the probability that the linkage is local. Consistent with the above discussion concerning knowledge transfer, we find, using a Chi-square test, that scientific founders are significantly more likely to have a local linkage than are non-

founders. We also find that the university scientists who are chairs of scientific advisory boards are significantly more likely to have a local linkage than are nonchairs.[9] One cannot, however, conclude that chairs and founders who (presumably) provide a source of knowledge do so exclusively for firms in close geographic proximity to where they work. Over 40 percent of the university-based founders establish firms outside of the region of their university; a third of the chairs of SABs are not in the same geographic region as the firm. This is consistent with the idea that while tacit knowledge requires face to face interaction, such interaction does not require that the scientist and the firm be permanently located in the same area.

The table also indicates that the 40 scientists who have sufficient equity holdings in the company (Majorstock) to require disclosure at the time of the initial public offering are more likely to have local ties than those scientists who are not major stockholders. This relates not only to the fact that major stockholders are often founders.[10] It is also consistent with the hypothesis that monitoring is facilitated through geographic proximity. Once again, however, the ties are far from exclusively local. The table also shows that we cannot reject the hypothesis that networks of the 365 SAB members are any more local than networks of other scientists in the data base, as indicated by the Chi-square value of 0.56.

III. Probit Analysis

While suggestive, the results from Table 3 examine geographic linkages only in terms of the role played by the university-based scientist in the firm. No attempt is made to control for personal characteristics of the scientists. Yet, the willingness of a scientist to be involved, as well as the attractiveness of a scientist to a company, undoubtedly influences the extent to which linkages between firms and scientists are geographically bounded. In order

---

[7] Kenneth Arrow (1962), Oliver E. Williamson (1975), and Audretsch (1995) have argued that when new economic knowledge cannot be easily transferred to established firms, perhaps due to organization factors, the holder of such knowledge must start a new firm in order to appropriate the potential economic value of the knowledge.

[8] Members of scientific advisory boards usually receive compensation in the neighborhood of $10,000 per year. In addition, they are often granted options which prove in some cases to be quite valuable (Stephan and Stephen Everhart, 1996).

[9] Twenty-two of the 54 firms designate the chair of the SAB in the prospectus. In all but two instances the chair is employed by a university. In another instance the SAB has co-chairs, both of whom work at a university.

[10] Fifty percent of the major stockholders are founders.

648   THE AMERICAN ECONOMIC REVIEW   JUNE 1996

to examine these relations, we estimate a probit model of the probability that a scientist is located in the same region as the biotechnology firm with which she or he is involved. The probit model permits us to determine how various factors affect the likelihood of being part of a local network as opposed to a nonlocal network. Individual characteristics introduced into the analysis include age, citation history, and Nobel status.[11] Before presenting the results, we discuss the variables and link them to the main hypotheses introduced above. In interpreting the results, it is important to remember that the data do not permit us to examine *who* on university faculties is involved with a biotechnology firm. By definition, *everyone* in our sample is involved. Rather, the analysis focuses upon the geographic dimension of the link between university-based scientists and biotechnology companies—that is, under what circumstances this link occurs within the same geographic space and under which circumstances the scientist and the firm are located in different regions.

A necessary condition for participation is that the firm is aware of the capabilities of the scientist. The dispersion of such information is clearly shaped by the geographic breadth of the scientist's network (contacts). Scientists with limited networks are more likely to be constrained to participate within a local rather than a nonlocal sphere. This suggests that, other things equal, a younger person is more likely to be involved with a local firm than with a nonlocal firm. The expected sign is not only based on factors affecting the size of networks. Life-cycle models of the allocation of time by scientists (David Levy, 1988; and Sharon G. Levin and Stephan, 1991) suggest that in the early stages of their lives scientists invest in human capital in order to build a reputation, while in the later stages of their career scientists trade or *cash in* their reputation for economic return. That is, early in their careers, scientists invest in the creation of knowledge in order to establish a reputation reflecting the scientific value of that new knowledge; with maturity, scientists cash in by seeking ways to

appropriate the economic value of that new knowledge. Thus, we expect older scientists to accept multiple offers of firm involvement. By contrast, younger scientists who have a higher opportunity cost of travel are expected to focus contacts within their own geographic region.

Age is not the only factor shaping the geographic extent of a scientist's network. Scientists who publish are much more likely to be known outside their local network than are nonpublishers. This is especially true if the publications are heavily cited, indicating that the scientific community has a high regard for the work (Robert Merton, 1957; Jonathan R. Cole and Stephen Cole, 1973; and Eugene Garfield, 1979). Thus, just as the involvement of older scientists is likely to be nonlocal in nature, the involvement of scientists with many citations is also likely to be nonlocal. An analogous argument suggests that Nobel laureates are more likely to have nonlocal than local ties.

A major qualification, however, relating to what we call *drawing power,* must be made to the above line of reasoning. Scientists become involved with start-up firms when venture capitalists find the scientist and science she or he is doing sufficiently attractive to warrant financing. Thus, mature scientists with strong reputations have the drawing power to attract firms to locate near them. For example, venture capital and other components of a start-up team for a new biotechnology company will be attracted to locations near scientists with extraordinary reputations to increase the probability that a contact can be established. Whether this drawing power effect outweighs the more general reputation effect is an empirical question.

A different type of qualification is that the higher the density of firms in the region in which any given scientist is located, the greater is the extent of opportunities for her or him within that region. To control for this effect, we include the density of biotechnology firms in the region, measured by the share of the 54 firms located in the scientist's geographic region. The probit model also controls for the role played by the scientist in the biotechnology firm by including a dummy variable defined to be 0 if the scientist founded the firm or chairs the SAB and 0 if she or he did not.

---

[11] Nine of the 445 scientists are Nobel prize recipients and have 10 contacts with biotechnology firms.

The probit regression is estimated for the 312 scientists for whom there is information identifying both their age and citation history. The results are reported in Table 4.[12] The dependent variable is equal to 1 if the link between the scientist and firm is local, and 0 if it is nonlocal. In addition to presenting the probit coefficients and asymptotic standard errors, Table 4 also presents the marginal effect that a one unit change in an independent variable has on the probability of commuting.[13]

The results are striking. The negative and statistically significant coefficient of the age variable suggests that, ceteris paribus, older scientists, are more likely than younger scientists to have contacts with biotechnology firms located outside of the regions of their universities. The marginal effect of an additional year is to increase the probability of a scientist commuting by 0.6 percent; of a decade is 6.0 percent. As expected, the specific role played by the scientist in the biotechnology firm also shapes the geographic dimension of the contact. Those scientists serving as founders of biotechnology firms have a significantly higher propensity to be located in the same region as the firm than those who are not founders. According to the marginal effect, a shift in status from nonfounder to founder increases the likelihood of a contact being local by more than 20 percent. The combined impact (equation (2)) of serving as a founder *or* chair of a SAB is slightly larger.

Having been awarded a Nobel prize significantly increases the propensity for the scientist to engage in local contacts with biotechnology firms.[14] This may reflect the willingness of venture capitalists and other key members of new biotechnology start-ups to locate close to a Nobel prize recipient, and suggests that for scientific stars drawing power overwhelms general reputational effects. On the other hand, there is no evidence that the citation history of a scientist influences the propensity of a scientist to engage in local versus nonlocal contacts.[15] This presumably reflects the offsetting effects of reputation and drawing power discussed in Section II.

One of the concerns in the probit model is that the majority of scientist-firm contacts are concentrated in just two sections of the country: California, which spans the three areas of the San Francisco Bay Area, Los Angeles and San Diego, and the North East, which includes the three areas of Boston, Philadelphia and New York. Because of the proximity of opportunities in neighboring areas, after controlling for density we would expect scientists in the North East and California to have a higher propensity to commute than scientists located in alternative regions of the country. In order to test this hypothesis, we include two dummy variables, the first taking on a value of 1 for scientists located in California, and the other taking on a value of 1 for scientists located in the North East. The results suggest a type of asymmetry between west coast and east coast scientific networks. The positive and statistically significant coefficient on the North East dummy variable implies that despite the large number of opportunities in neighboring areas, scientists located in the North East tend to be insular in their propensity to engage in contacts with firms located in their specific area. By contrast, the coefficient on the California dummy variable, which cannot be considered statistically significant, suggests that proximity of opportunity does not affect commuting patterns for California scientists.

IV. Conclusions

A key finding of this paper is that while a substantial number of university-based scientists participate in networks that are

---

[12] Thirty-one scientists working for three firms are excluded because citation histories were not collected for scientists working for these firms. Of the remaining 414 scientists we found birth dates (and citation histories) for 312, yielding a sample retention rate of 75 percent.

[13] For the continuous variables the marginal effect is evaluated at the mean of the explanatory variable. For the dummy variables the marginal effect reflects the difference between having the characteristic versus not having the characteristic.

[14] The dummy variable for the Nobel prize indicates receipt of the prize since 1970. One scientist received the prize in 1958. The inclusion of this scientist reduces the statistical significance of the coefficient of the Nobel prize dummy variable to being statistically significant at the 10-percent level of significance, for a two-tailed test.

[15] The citation history measure is not statistically significant regardless of the specification by which it is included in the probit equation.

TABLE 4—PROBIT RESULTS FOR PROBABILITY OF SCIENTIST-FIRM CONTACT BEING LOCAL[a]

	(1)	Marginal effect[b]	(2)	Marginal effect[b]	(3)	Marginal effect[b]	(4)	Marginal effect[b]
Constant	−0.45 (0.47)	—	−0.42 (0.47)	—	−0.59 (0.48)	—	−0.56 (0.48)	—
Age	−0.018* (0.008)	−0.006	−0.019* (0.008)	−0.006	−0.022* (0.009)	−0.007	−0.023** (0.009)	−0.008
Citations	0.74×10^{-4} (0.56×10^{-3})	0.25×10^{-4}	0.32×10^{-4} (0.56×10^{-3})	0.10×10^{-4}	0.79×10^{-4} (0.59×10^{-3})	0.25×10^{-4}	0.12×10^{-3} (0.58×10^{-3})	0.40×10^{-4}
Nobel prize	1.13* (0.49)	0.427	1.14* (0.50)	0.430	1.12* (0.50)	0.420	1.12* (0.49)	0.420
Founder	0.62* (0.27)	0.233	—	—	0.67* (0.27)	0.240	—	—
Founder/chair	—	—	0.65** (0.25)	0.242	—	—	0.68** (0.25)	0.250
Firm density[c]	7.39** (0.31)	0.250	7.36** (0.82)	0.248	6.25** (1.37)	0.198	6.15** (1.37)	0.209
California	—	—	—	—	0.38 (0.38)	0.13	0.41 (0.38)	0.14
North East	—	—	—	—	0.87** (0.28)	0.30	0.87** (0.28)	0.30
Log-Likelihood	−142.02		−141.27		−134.72		−134.07	
Sample size	312		312		312		312	

[a] Asymptotic standard errors are listed in parentheses.
[b] See the text for how the marginal effect is computed.
[c] The marginal effect is calculated for a 0.10 change in firm density.
* Statistically significant at the 95-percent level of confidence, two-tailed test.
** Statistically significant at the 99-percent level of confidence, two-tailed test.

geographically bounded, approximately 70 percent of the links between biotechnology companies and the university-based scientists are nonlocal. We conclude that while proximity matters in establishing formal ties between university-based scientists and companies, its influence is anything but overwhelming.

The results clearly suggest that the importance of proximity is shaped by the role played by the scientist. Proximity matters more in the case of founders than for members of scientific advisory boards. It also matters more for chairs of SABs. This presumably reflects the qualitative difference in the services provided by the scientist. In addition, characteristics specific to the scientist shape the geographic dimension of the scientist-firm contact. The status of being a *star*, as reflected by receipt of a Nobel prize, for example, reduces the need to commute outside of the region in which the scientist is located. Apparently, other key components comprising a biotechnology start-up, such as venture capital and managerial competence, may be willing to locate within close proximity to such stars. In addition, we

find that older scientists, other things being equal, are more likely to have links with biotechnology firms that are not geographically bounded. This apparently reflects both the desire of mature scientists to cash in and the geographic breadth of their networks.

Our findings also suggest that the links between scientists and companies involve a multiplicity of dimensions, only one of which is knowledge transfer, and that the importance of local proximity varies considerably across these dimensions. The results also suggest that even in the case of knowledge transfer, scientists and firms are often geographically separated. For example, 40 percent of the university-based founders of biotech firms in the data base are affiliated with firms outside their region. Does this mean that the proponents of the new growth economics may have overemphasized the importance that geography plays? Not necessarily, if one recalls that much of this work stresses the informality of knowledge spillovers while our work focuses on relationships that have been intentionally formed to capitalize on the scientist's knowledge. In both the informal and formal case, the marginal cost of transmitting new economic knowledge, particularly tacit knowledge, across geographic space is nontrivial. This means, as the studies by Audretsch and Feldman (1996) and Adam B. Jaffe et al. (1993) imply, that geographic proximity matters when knowledge spillovers are *informal.* But an important conclusion of this paper is that when knowledge is transmitted through *formal* ties between researchers and firms, geographic proximity is not necessary, since face to face contact does not occur by chance but instead is carefully planned.

Finally, it is important to realize that while geographic proximity between university scientists and firms is valuable, other factors that are related to agglomeration, such as the location of other firms and research organizations, play an important role in mediating the geographic proximity of firms and their affiliated university scientists. These broader types of spillovers have not been examined in this paper. Perhaps future research should shift away from asking *if* geography plays a role to exploring in more depth *how* the role of geography varies by function as well as by characteristics of the region.

APPENDIX TABLE A1—LOCATION OF BIOTECH FIRMS BY REGION

	University-based scientists	Scientists from within region			University-based scientists	Scientists from within region	
		Number	Percent			Number	Percent
San Francisco Bay Area, CA				*Philadelphia, PA*			
Anergen	5	4	80.0	Affinity Biotech	5	1	20.0
Applied Immune Sciences	8	1	12.5	Cephalon	5	1	20.0
Biocircutis	4	2	50.0	DNX	5	2	40.0
Biotime	6	2	33.3	Magainin Pharmaceuticals	6	2	33.3
Cell Genesis	16	2	12.5	Medarex	6	0	0.0
COR Therapeutics	15	5	33.3	Zynaxis	4	2	50.0
Cygnus	5	1	20.0	Total	31	8	25.8
Genelabs Technologies	13	6	46.2				
Genpharm	15	0	0.0	*New York, NY*			
Gilead Sciences	7	1	14.3	Alteon	6	4	66.6
Neurex	22	6	27.3	Biomatrix	6	1	16.7
Oclassen Pharmaceuticals	7	1	14.3	Biospecifics Technologies	5	2	40.0
Protein Design Labs	7	4	57.1	Medicis	9	0	0.0
Sciclone	8	7	87.5	Regeneron Pharmaceuticals	13	2	15.4
Systemix	7	2	28.9	Total	39	9	23.0
Total	145	44	30.3				
				Maryland			
San Diego, CA				Genetic Therapy	7	0	0.0
Amylin	10	3	30.0	Univax Biologics	6	1	16.7
Corvas	9	3	33.3	Total	13	1	7.7
Cytel	9	1	33.3				
Genta	19	1	5.2	*Seattle, WA*			
Idec Pharmaceuticals	2	1	50.0	Cell Pro	7	2	28.6
Immune Response	7	2	28.6				
Ligand Pharmaceuticals	7	4	57.1	*Boulder, CO*			
Protein Polymer Technologie	7	1	14.3	Somatogen	4	1	25.0
Vical	7	3	42.3				
Total	77	21	27.2	*Kansas*			
				Deprenyl	6	0	0.0
Boston, MA							
Alpha-Beta Technology	7	7	100.0	*Research Triangle, NC*			
Cambridge Neuroscience	10	4	40.0	Sphinx Pharmaceuticals	6	2	33.3
Creative Biomolecules	11	4	36.4				
Cytotherapeutics	14	4	28.6	*Los Angeles, CA*			
Epigen	8	2	25.0	Watson Pharmaceuticals	9	0	0.0
Immulogie	11	5	45.5				
Matritech	8	3	37.5	*Dallas, TX*			
Sepracor	7	3	42.8	Carntech	10	1	10.0
Seragen	3	3	100.0				
Vertex Pharmaceuticals	6	6	100.0	*Houston, TX*			
Total	85	41	48.2	Argus Pharmaceuticals	13	8	61.5
				Total	**445**	**138**	**31.0**

REFERENCES

Arrow, Kenneth. "Economic Welfare and the Allocation of Resources for Invention," in Richard R. Nelson, ed., *The rate and direction of inventive activity.* Princeton, NJ: Princeton University Press, 1962, pp. 609–26.

Audretsch, David B. *Innovation and industry evolution.* Cambridge, MA: MIT Press, 1995.

Audretsch, David B. and Feldman, Maryann P. "R&D Spillovers and the Geography of Innovation and Production." *American Economic Review*, June 1996, *86*(3), pp. 630–40.

Burrill, G. Steven. *Biotech 88: Into the marketplace.* San Francisco: Arthur Young High Technology Group, 1987.

Burrill, G. Steven and Lee, Kenneth B., Jr. *Biotech 93: Accelerating commercialization.* San Francisco: Ernst & Young, 1992.

Cole, Jonathan R. and Cole, Stephen. *Social stratification in science.* Chicago: University of Chicago Press, 1973.

Etzkowitz, Henry. "Entrepreneurial Scientists and Entrepreneurial Universities in American Academic Science." *Minerva*, 1983, *21*(2), pp. 198–233.

Garfield, Eugene. *Citation indexing: Its theory and application in science, technology and humanities.* New York: Wiley, 1979.

Jaffe, Adam B.; Trajtenberg, Manuel and Henderson, Rebecca. "Geographic Localization of Knowledge Spillovers as Evidenced by Patent Citations." *Quarterly Journal of Economics*, August 1993, *63*(3), pp. 577–98.

Krugman, Paul. "Increasing Returns and Economic Geography." *Journal of Political Economy*, June 1991a, *99*(3), pp. 483–99.

———. *Geography and trade.* Cambridge, MA: MIT Press, 1991b.

Levin, Sharon G. and Stephan, Paula E. "Research Productivity over the Life Cycle: Evidence for Academic Scientists." *American Economic Review*, March 1991, *81*(4), pp. 114–32.

Levy, David. "The Market for Fame and Fortune." *History of Political Economy*, Winter 1988, *20*(4), pp. 615–25.

Link, Albert N. and Rees, John. "Firm Size, University Based Research, and the Returns to R&D." *Small Business Economics*, 1990, *2*(1), pp. 25–32.

Lucas, Robert E., Jr. "Making a Miracle." *Econometrica*, March 1993, *61*(2), pp. 251–72.

Merton, Robert. "Priorities in Scientific Discovery: A Chapter in the Sociology of Science." *American Sociological Review*, December 1957, *22*(6), pp. 635–59.

Orsenigo, Luigi. *The emergence of biotechnology: Institutions and markets in industrial innovation.* New York: St Martins Press, 1989.

Pisano, Gary P.; Shan, Wiejnian and Teece, David. "Joint Ventures and Collaboration in the Biotechnology Industry," in David Mowery, ed., *International collaborative ventures in U.S. manufacturing.* Cambridge, MA: Ballinger Publishers, 1988, pp. 183–222.

Romer, Paul. "Endogenous Technological Change." *Journal of Political Economy*, October 1990, *98*(5) Part 2, pp. S71–102.

Shrine, Jim. "Telios Offers to Buy Back Shares from Offering." *Bioworld Today*, October 1994, *10*, p. 1.

Stephan, Paula E. "Differences in the Post-Entry Value of Biotech Firms: The Role of Human Capital." Presented at the Conference on the Post-Entry Performance of Firms," hosted by the Bank of Portugal, Lisbon, May 22–28, 1994.

Stephan, Paula E. and Everhart, Stephen. "The Changing Rewards to Science: The Case of Biotechnology." *Small Business Economics*, forthcoming 1996, *8*.

Stephan, Paula E. and Levin, Sharon G. *Striking the mother lode in science.* New York: Oxford University Press, 1992.

Williamson, Oliver E. *Markets and hierarchies: Antitrust analysis and implications.* New York: Free Press, 1975.

Zucker, Lynne G.; Darby, Michael R. and Armstrong, Jeff. "Intellectual Capital and the Firm: The Technology of Geographically Localized Knowledge Spillovers." National Bureau of Economic Research (Cambridge, MA) Working Paper No. 4946, 1995.

Zucker, Lynne G.; Darby, Michael R. and Brewer, Marilynn B. "Intellectual Capital and the Birth of U.S. Biotechnology Enterprises." National Bureau of Economic Research (Cambridge, MA) Working Paper No. 4653, 1994.

[26]

Intellectual Human Capital and the Birth of U.S. Biotechnology Enterprises

By Lynne G. Zucker, Michael R. Darby, and Marilynn B. Brewer *

The number of American firms actively using biotechnology grew rapidly from nonexistent to over 700 in less than two decades, transforming the nature of the pharmaceutical industry and significantly impacting food processing, brewing, and agriculture, as well as other industries. Here we demonstrate empirically that the commercialization of this technology is essentially intertwined with the development of the underlying science in a way which illustrates the significance in practice of the localized spillovers concept in the agglomeration literature and of the tacit knowledge concept in the information literature. Indeed we present here strong evidence that the timing and location of initial usage by both new dedicated biotechnology firms (*"entrants"*) and new biotech subunits of existing firms (*"incumbents"*) are primarily explained by the presence at a particular time and place of scientists who are actively contributing to the basic science as represented by publications reporting genetic-sequence discoveries in academic journals.

By quantifying separable effects of individual scientists, major universities, and federal research support we provide specific structure to the role of universities and their faculties in encouraging local economic development through what are conventionally described in the literature as geographically localized knowledge spillovers.[1] Such localized knowledge spillovers may play fundamental roles in both economic agglomeration and endogenous growth (Paul M. Romer, 1986, 1990; Gene M. Grossman and Elhanan Helpman, 1991). However, our evidence, like the other literature cited here, specifically indicates localized effects without demonstrating that they can be characterized as spillovers (or externalities).

Section I lays out our basic hypothesis. The data are described in Section II. Empirical results are reported and discussed in Section III. A summary and conclusions section (Section IV) and Data Appendix complete the article.

I. The Hypothesis

Innovations are generally treated in the growth literature as a nonrivalrous good—freely useable by an unlimited number of potential

* Zucker: Department of Sociology and Institute for Social Science Research, University of California, Box 951484, Los Angeles, CA 90095, and National Bureau of Economic Research; Darby: John E. Anderson Graduate School of Management, University of California, Box 951481, Los Angeles, CA 90095, UCLA Department of Economics, and National Bureau of Economic Research; Brewer: Department of Psychology, Ohio State University, 1885 Neil Avenue, Columbus, OH 43210. This research has been supported by grants from the National Science Foundation (SES 9012925), the University of California Systemwide Biotechnology Research and Education Program, the University of California's Pacific Rim Research Program, the UCLA Center for American Politics and Public Policy, and the UCLA Institute of Industrial Relations. We acknowledge very useful comments on earlier drafts from two anonymous referees, and from David Butz, Harold Demsetz, Robert Drazin, Martin Feldstein, Zvi Griliches, Keith Head, Adam Jaffe, Benjamin Klein, Josh Lerner, Gary Pisano, Jeff Rosensweig, L. G. Thomas, Ivo Welch, and others. We are indebted to a remarkably talented team of postdoctoral fellows Zhong Deng, Julia Liebeskind, and Yusheng Peng, and research assistants Paul J. Alapat, Jeff Armstrong, Lynda J. Kim, Amalya Oliver, Alan Paul, and Maximo Torero. Armstrong was principally responsible for conducting the analysis and cleaning the firm data set and Torero cleaned the scientist data set; comments from both substantially improved the paper. This paper is a part of the NBER's research program in Productivity. Any opinions expressed are those of the authors and not those of their employers or funders.

[1] Zvi Griliches (1992) has surveyed the importance of R&D spillovers as a major source of endogenous growth in recent "new growth theory" models and the difficult empirical search for their existence. Despite these difficulties, there have been a number of articles reporting evidence of geographic localization of knowledge spillovers, including Adam B. Jaffe (1989), Jaffe et al. (1993), and Edwin Mansfield (1995).

users at a zero marginal cost (Richard R. Nelson and Romer, 1996). A complementary literature recognizes that some information requires an investment of considerable time and effort to master. The human capital developed by this investment is seen as earning a normal return on the cost of the investment, both direct costs and foregone earnings. We believe that some innovations, particularly a breakthrough "invention of a method of inventing" (Griliches, 1957), may be better characterized as creating (rivalrous) human capital—intellectual human capital—characterized by natural excludability as opposed to a set of instructions for combining inputs and outputs which can be protected only by intellectual property rights. This natural excludability arises from the complexity or tacitness of the information required to practice the innovation (see Nelson [1959], Kenneth J. Arrow [1962], Nelson and Sidney G. Winter [1982], and Nathan Rosenberg [1982]).

Based on both extensive interviews and empirical work summarized in Zucker and Darby (1996), we believe that, at least for the first 10 or 15 years, the innovations which underlie biotechnology are properly analyzed in terms of naturally excludable knowledge held by a small initial group of discoverers, their co-workers, and others who learned the knowledge from working at the bench-science level with those possessing the requisite know-how. Ultimately the knowledge spread sufficiently widely to become part of routine science which could be learned at any major research university. After the initial 1973 discovery by Stanley Cohen and Herbert Boyer of the basic technique for recombinant DNA—the foundation of commercial biotechnology as well as of a burst of scientific innovation—the financial returns available to talented recombinant-DNA scientists first rose dramatically as the commercial implications became widely appreciated and then more gradually declined as more and more scientists learned the techniques, until knowledge of the new techniques per se earned only the normal return for the time required for a graduate student to master them. Further, mere knowledge of the techniques of recombinant DNA was not enough to earn these extraordinary returns; the knowledge was far more productive when embodied in a scientist with the genius and vision to con-

tinuously innovate and define the research frontier and apply the new research techniques in the most promising areas.

We hypothesize that entry of firms into biotechnology in a given year thus will be determined by the geographic distribution of stars and perhaps others then actively practicing the new science as well as by the geographic distribution of economic activity. Stars are properly viewed as locationally (semi-)fixed since few star scientists who knew how to do recombinant DNA were willing to abandon their university appointments and laboratory teams to pursue commercial applications of biotechnology. The primary pattern in the development of the industry involved one or more scientist-entrepreneurs who remained on the faculty while establishing a business on the side—businesses which, where successful, resulted in millions or even billions of dollars for the professors who acquired early ownership stakes. Thus, we see the university as bringing about local industrial benefits by permitting its professors to pursue private commercial interests while their faculty appointments tie them to the area. In preliminary work not reported here, we tried to develop measures of local economic activity for industries, like pharmaceuticals, specifically impacted by the new technology, but these attempts never added significantly to the measures of general activity used in the empirical work below. The _local_ availability of venture capital is widely believed to play a significant role in the birth of new biotech entrants (Martin Kenney, 1986; Joshua Lerner, 1994, 1995); so we also include that variable in our regressions.

II. The Data

Data has been collected in panel form for 14 years (1976–1989) and 183 regions (functional economic areas as defined by the U.S. Department of Commerce, Bureau of Economic Analysis [BEA], 1992b). Frequently, the data are aggregates of data at the zip code or county level.[2] Lagged variables

---

[2] The BEA's functional economic areas divide all the counties in the United States into regions including one or more cities, their suburbs, and the rural counties most closely tied to the central city.

include data for 1975 in the unlagged form. See the Data Appendix for more details.

A. *Firms*

Our data set on firms was derived from a base purchased from the North Carolina Biotechnology Center (NCBC) (1992) which was cleaned and supplemented with information in *Bioscan* (1989–1993) and its precursor (Cetus Corp., 1988). We identified 751 distinct U.S. firms for which we could determine a zip code and a date of initial use of biotechnology. Of these 751 firms, 511 were entrants, 150 incumbents, and 90 (including 18 joint ventures) could not be definitively classified. By 1990, 52 of the 751 firms had died or merged into other firms.

We then calculated the number of births in each region by year of initial use of biotechnology for all 751 firms as well as for their identified subcomponents of entrants and incumbents. We also have the stocks of surviving firms, entrants, and incumbents by region and year.

B. *Scientists*

Early in our ongoing project studying the scientific development and diffusion of biotechnology, we identified a set of 327 star scientists based on their outstanding productivity through early 1990. The primary criterion for selections was the discovery of more than 40 genetic sequences as reported in *GenBank* (1990) through April 1990.[3] However, 22 scientists were included based on writing 20 or more articles, each reporting one or more genetic-sequence discoveries.[4] In the 1990's,

sequence discovery has become routinized and is no longer such a useful measure of research success. These 327 stars were only three-quarters of one percent of the authors in *GenBank* (1990) but accounted for 17.3 percent of the published articles, almost 22 times as many articles as the average scientist.

We collected by hand the 4,061 articles authored by stars and listed in *GenBank* and recorded the institutional affiliation of the stars and their coauthors on each of these articles. These coauthors are called *"collaborators"* if they are not themselves a star. Some data on the stars and collaborators who ever published in the United States is given on the left side of Table 1, where the scientists are identified by the organization(s) with which they were affiliated on their first-such publication. The higher citation rate for firm-affiliated scientists is explored at length in Zucker and Darby (1996).

Figure 1 illustrates the time pattern of growth in the numbers of stars and collaborators who have ever published and the total number of firms using biotechnology in the United States. There was a handful of stars who published articles reporting genetic-sequence discoveries before the 1973 breakthrough, but even after 1973 their number increased gradually until taking off in 1980. The numbers of collaborators and firms lagged behind the growth in stars by some years.

To identify those scientists clearly working at the edge of the science in a given year, we term a star or collaborator as *"active"* if he or she has published three or more sequence-discovery articles in the three-year moving window ending with that year. As seen in the right side of Table 1, this stringent second screen provides an even more elite definition of star scientists as well as identifying some very significant collaborators. We count for each year the number of active stars and active collaborators who are affiliated with an organization in each region.

The locations of active stars and firms are both concentrated and highly correlated geographically, particularly early in the period. Figure 2 illustrates this pattern for the whole period by accumulating the number of stars who have ever been active in each region up to 1990 and plotting them together with the

---

[3] See Zucker et al. (1993). As will be obvious, much of the time between 1990 and the initial submission of this paper was spent in developing reasonable measures of intellectual human capital and in collecting and coding data necessary to locate the authors of the discoveries reported in the articles in question and to trace the diffusion process.

[4] Scientists advised that some sequence discoveries are more difficult than others and thus merit an article reporting only one sequence. Therefore we included scientists with 20 or more discovery articles to avoid excluding scientists who specialized in more difficult problems.

TABLE 1—DISTRIBUTION OF STAR SCIENTISTS AND COLLABORATORS
WHO HAVE EVER PUBLISHED IN THE UNITED STATES

Organization type[a]	Full data set		Ever active in U.S.[b]	
	Number of scientists	Citations[c]/ scientist/years	Number of scientists	Citations[c]/ scientist/years
Stars:				
University	158	85.5	108	110.8
Institute	44	63.0	26	98.7
Firm	5	143.7	1	694.3
Dual	0	n/a	0	n/a
Total	207		135	
Collaborators:				
University	2901	10.4	369	30.6
Institute	776	13.7	88	35.8
Firm	324	29.2	43	99.1
Dual	3	7.2	0	n/a
Total	4004		500	

[a] The organization type refers to the affiliation listed on their **first** publication with a U.S. affiliation.

[b] Ever active in the U.S. means that in at least one three-year period beginning 1974 or later and ending 1989 or earlier, the scientist was listed on at least three articles appearing in our data set of 4,061 articles which reported genetic-sequence discoveries and were published in major journals and that the affiliation listed in the last of the three articles was located in the United States.

[c] Citation counts are for 1982, 1987, and 1992 for all articles in our data set (whenever published) for which the individual was listed as an author.

location of biotech-using firms as of early 1990.

C. *Other Measures of Intellectual Human Capital*

Active stars and collaborators may be incomplete measures of location of the scientific base because there are techniques other than recombinant DNA which have played an important role in commercial biotechnology. Some skeptical readers might also think that some simpler measures of regions' relevant academic resources would contain all the information which we have laboriously collected. We found two measures of regional scientific base which entered separately in regressions reported below, but none which were capable of eliminating the effects of the star scientists.

One measure is a count of the number of *"top-quality universities"* in a region where top quality is defined by having one or more *"biotech-relevant"* (biochemistry, cellular/ molecular biology, and microbiology) departments with scholarly quality reputational ratings of 4.0 or higher in the 1982 National Research Council survey (Lyle V. Jones et al., 1982). There are 20 such universities in the United States.[5] Our second measure, *"federal*

[5] The 20 universities were: Brandeis University, California Institute of Technology, Columbia University, Cornell University, Duke University, Harvard University, Johns Hopkins University, Massachusetts Institute of Technology, Rockefeller University, Stanford University, University of California-Berkeley, University of California-Los Angeles, University of California-San Diego, University of California-San Francisco, University of

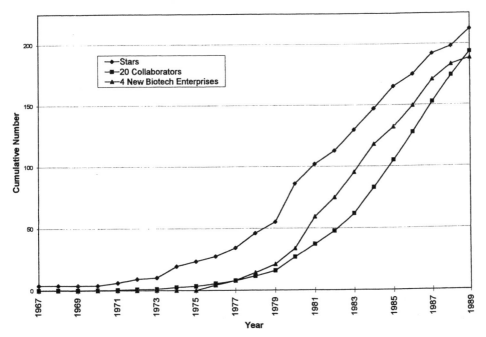

FIGURE 1. CUMULATIVE NUMBER OF U.S. STARS, COLLABORATORS, AND NEW BIOTECH ENTERPRISES, 1967–1989

support,'' is the total number (in hundreds) of faculty supported by 1979–1980 federal grants to all universities in each region for biotech-relevant research.[6] These variables take on the same value for a given region in each year.

D. *Other Variables*

Using listings in Stanley E. Pratt (1982), we measure *"venture capital firms"* as the number of such firms in a region legally eligible to finance start-ups in each year up to 1981. For later years, the number of firms is fixed at the

number in 1981 to avoid possible simultaneity problems once the major wave of biotech founding began.[7] (While great bookstores spring up around great universities, the former should not be counted as causing the latter.)

Since entry of biotech firms would be expected to occur where there is other economic activity, particularly involving a highly skilled labor force, we also include *total employment* in all industries (in millions of persons) and *average wages* (measured by deflated average earnings per job in thousands of 1987 dollars) for each region and year.

Finally, an increase in the (all-equity) cost of capital, as measured by the *earnings-price ratio* on the Standard & Poor's 500 Index would reduce the net present value of entry

---

Chicago, University of Colorado at Denver, University of Pennsylvania, University of Washington (Seattle), University of Wisconsin-Madison, and Yale University.

[6] We also tried a measure of biotech-relevant research expenditures as reported by the universities, but this variable was too collinear with the federal support variable to enter separately and appeared to be less consistently measured across universities.

[7] Instrumental variables would provide a more elegant approach to this problem if suitable instruments had been found.

FIGURE 2. EVER ACTIVE STARS AND NEW BIOTECHNOLOGY ENTERPRISES AS OF 1990

and so should have a negative impact on birth of new firms, entrants or incumbents.

III. Empirical Results

We test our hypothesis using both the full panel data and by regressing the geographical distribution of the data in 1990 on values of the independent variables circa 1980. The former more fully exploit the available information while the latter avoid problems of possible simultaneity which might arise after 1980 when commercial biotechnology became a significant economic factor in some regions. All the regressions reported here, as well as an extensive sensitivity analysis noted below, were estimated in the poisson form appropriate for count variables with numerous zeroes using LIMDEP (William H. Greene, 1992 pp. 539–49), with the Wooldridge regression-based correction for the variance-

covariance matrix estimates.[8] The poisson regressions estimate the logarithm of the expected number of firm births; so the signs and significance of coefficients have the usual interpretation. Although OLS regressions are inappropriate for our count dependent variables with most observations at zero and the rest tailing off through small positive integers, we

---

[8] As discussed in Jerry Hausman et al. (1984), the poisson process is the most appropriate statistical model for count data such as ours. In practice, overdispersion (possibly due to unobserved heterogeneity) frequently occurs. Given the problems with resort to the negative binomial (A. Colin Cameron and Pravin K. Trivedi, 1990), Jeffrey M. Wooldridge (1991) developed a flexible and consistent method for correcting the poisson variance-covariance matrix estimates regardless of the underlying relationship between the mean and variance. We are indebted to Wooldridge and Greene for advice in implementing the procedure in LIMDEP.

reported broadly consistent results using that technique in an earlier version of the paper (Zucker et al., 1994).

In our sensitivity analysis, we ran the same poisson regressions for entrants and incumbents defined both exclusive and inclusive of the arguable case of joint ventures. The results were generally very similar to the subcomponent regressions in Table 4. In other unreported poisson regressions, we found that eliminating those regions with no firms and no stars from the sample did not result in qualitatively different results.

A. The Long-Run Model

Because of concerns about possible simultaneity biases once the industry became a significant economic force, we begin our empirical discussion with models which relate the number of firms in each region at the beginning of 1990 to the distribution of intellectual human capital and other variables as of about 1980. These results provide something of an acid test of our approach.

In Table 2, we present cross-section poisson regressions across the 183 regions explaining the number of firms in each at the beginning of 1990 when our data set ends.[9] Column (a) restrains the analysis to only the numbers of stars and collaborators ever active in each region at any time up through 1980, while columns (b) and (c) add first their squares and then our other intellectual human capital variables. Column (d) considers alternatively other economic variables which might explain entry, and column (e) combines the variables in (c) and (d). Column (f) adds to this model the number of biotech firms existing in 1980.

Column (a) in Table 2 indicates that the number of stars and collaborators active through 1980 is a powerful predictor of the

geographic distribution of biotech enterprises in 1990, since the log-likelihood increases to -871.9 compared to -1401.7 for a constant alone. It is the star scientists that contribute positively, with collaborators having a much smaller negative coefficient in this regression and most of the other long-run models discussed below. We had expected that the coefficient on collaborators would be much smaller than that on stars, but positive. We do obtain a positive coefficient on active collaborators when the squared terms are added in column (b), but that turns negative again upon addition of other variables in the remaining columns of Table 2.[10] (In the annual regressions discussed below, we generally estimate positive effects of active collaborators, but they are often statistically insignificant.)

We can offer two explanations for the generally negative sign on the number of active collaborators in the long-run regressions: (i) This coefficient reflects two partially offsetting influences; collaborators have a positive direct effect on the entry of firms but reduce the effect of stars who are devoting more of their time to training students and relatively less to starting their own firms. Training collaborators is surely a useful and rewarded activity— particularly for the academic stars—but it may take more of the stars' energy than it is worth if firm birth were the only criteria.[11] (ii) The sign and magnitude of the coefficient on collaborators may simply reflect significant multicollinearity among the intellectual human capital variables in the very early years. This is especially likely since when we examine the

---

[9] In an earlier version of this paper we included an alternative form of Table 2 (available from the authors upon request) in order to forestall interpretations that the results in Table 2 may reflect reverse causality. This alternative table reported regressions which explain the number of firms alive at the beginning of 1990 that were born after 1980. Nearly identical results were obtained, reflecting the fact that bulk of new biotechnology enterprises were founded after 1980.

[10] In column (b) of Table 2 (and Table 3), the negative coefficient on the squared term indicates that as the number of stars or collaborators increases, their marginal contribution diminishes eventually passing through zero. For collaborators, in columns (c)–(f) of these tables the sign pattern reverses so that the partial derivative of the log probability of birth with respect to collaborators starts out negative, and increases as their number increases, eventually becoming positive.

[11] In support of this explanation, we note that in our sensitivity analysis we tried regressions which substituted interaction terms multiplying the numbers of active stars and collaborators for the squared terms. In those regressions, we obtain significant positive coefficients on the numbers of stars and collaborators and a significant negative coefficient on their interaction.

TABLE 2—POISSON REGRESSIONS ON THE STOCK OF BIOTECH-USING FIRMS AT THE BEGINNING OF 1990 BY REGION

	(a)	(b)	(c)	(d)	(e)	(f)
Constant	0.911*** (0.014)	0.644*** (0.015)	0.468*** (0.033)	−2.595*** (0.086)	−2.718*** (0.256)	−2.607*** (0.345)
Number stars active at any time during 1976–80	0.567*** (0.029)	0.587*** (0.072)	0.466*** (0.090)	— —	0.877*** (0.076)	0.649*** (0.084)
Number collaborators active at any time during 1976–80	−0.076*** (0.012)	0.175*** (0.033)	−0.183** (0.068)	— —	−0.333*** (0.045)	−0.261*** (0.037)
(Number stars active at any time during 1976–80)^2	— —	−0.028*** (0.007)	−0.019 (0.014)	— —	−0.049*** (0.012)	−0.024* (0.012)
(Number collaborators active at any time during 1976–80)^2	— —	−0.005*** (0.001)	0.002 (0.003)	— —	0.007** (0.003)	0.001 (0.002)
Number top-quality universities in the region	— —	— —	1.388*** (0.150)	— —	1.594*** (0.107)	0.442* (0.195)
Number faculty with federal support in the region	— —	— —	0.263 (0.143)	— —	0.752*** (0.088)	0.711*** (0.051)
Number venture capital firms in the region in 1980	— —	— —	— —	0.017*** (0.002)	−0.045*** (0.003)	−0.013** (0.004)
Total employment (all industries) in the region in 1980	— —	— —	— —	0.222*** (0.019)	−0.009 (0.043)	−0.213*** (0.049)
Average wages per job in the region in 1980	— —	— —	— —	0.166*** (0.004)	0.143*** (0.014)	0.139*** (0.019)
Cumulative births of biotech firms during 1976–80	— —	— —	— —	— —	— —	0.300*** (0.025)
Log-likelihood	−871.9	−707.3	−543.2	−753.9	−416.0	−350.7
Restricted log-likelihood	−1401.7	−1401.7	−1401.7	−1401.7	−1401.7	−1401.7

Notes: N = 183. Standard errors (adjusted by Wooldridge, 1991 Procedure 2.1) are in parentheses below coefficients.
   * Significantly different from 0 at the 5-percent level.
  ** Significantly different from 0 at the 1-percent level.
 *** Significantly different from 0 at the 0.1-percent level.

full cross-section/time-series results just below we obtain (we think more reliable) zero or positive coefficients on collaborators, so the puzzle largely disappears.

The full "fundamentals" model (excepting the decade-lagged dependent variable) is presented in column (e) of Table 2, where all the coefficients are significant except that for total employment. Leaving aside the question of the negative collaborator coefficient, we note the strong, positive, separate effects of stars, top-quality universities, and federal research

grants at universities on birth of firms in a given geographic region. The intellectual human capital variables alone increase the log-likelihood ratio from −1401.7 to −543.2 [see column (c)], with the final three variables bringing this quantity up to −416.0. As to the last three variables, the quality of the labor force, measured by average wages per job, seems much more relevant than its size. Surprisingly, to some observers, the number of venture capital firms in a region enters, but with a significantly negative sign. We interpret the negative sign as evidence that venture capitalists did play an active role in the formation of entrant firms, but they apparently resulted in fewer, larger firms being born in the areas in which they were more active.[12]

This sign of the coefficient of the number of venture capital firms in a region is robust in sensitivity experiments with other forms (not reported here) except for regressions which exclude the intellectual human capital variables such as in column (d). That regression looks good in terms of significance and expected sign pattern although it has a much lower explanatory power than the intellectual human capital variables alone [column (c)]. Just below, we report very similar results in a cross-section/time-series context. Thus, it is certainly easy to see why the evidence for an important positive impact of venture capital firms on the birth of biotech firms may have appeared stronger in previous work than seems warranted based on fuller models: Since venture capital firms have developed around a number of great universities, their presence proxies for intellectual human capital in the absence of more direct measures; if they are the only variable indicating presence of great universities and their faculties, they enter positively even if their packaging activities result in a negative direct effect on births.

The decade-lagged dependent variable is added to the full fundamentals model in column (f) of Table 2. Doing so primarily has the effect of weakening the significance of the top-quality universities variable (but, see the annual model below) due to significant multicollinearity between the variables.[13] One interpretation of this positive coefficient on the lagged dependent variable is that agglomera-

tion effects strengthen the impact of fundamentals on regional development. However, the statistical properties of poisson regressions with lagged dependent variables are somewhat problematic so such regressions and their estimated standard errors should be viewed cautiously.

In conclusion, the intellectual human capital variables play a strong role in determining where the U.S. biotech industry developed during the 1980's. We have been able to identify particular star scientists who appear to play a crucial role in the process of spillover and geographic agglomeration over and above that which would be predicted based on university reputation and scientists supported by federal grants alone. The strong positive role of venture capital variable reported previously is not supported for firm births. Indeed, the data tell us that there were fewer firms founded, other things equal, where there more venture capital firms. It is left to future research to explore whether firms which are associated with particular star scientists or were midwifed by venture capitalists are more successful than other firms.[14]

B. *The Annual Model*

We next report analogous poisson regressions exploiting the panel nature of our data set with observations for the 183 regions for each of the years 1976 through 1989. Tables 3 and 4 report poisson regressions for this entire panel.

Column (a) of Table 3 reports the results using only the counts of stars and their collaborators active each year in each region. As with the long-run models in Table 2, examination of the data suggested that these effects— particularly for stars—were nonlinear so we add squared values in column (b). Again, as the number of stars increases, their marginal contribution diminishes eventually passing through zero.

These nonlinearities might reflect the declining value over time of the intellectual human capital as we have measured it. Basically,

---

[12] This hypothesis was derived from anecdotal evidence, but note that the top nine of Ernst & Young's list of top-ten companies by 1993 market valuation (G. Steven Burrill and Kenneth B. Lee, Jr., 1994 p. 54) were located and founded in regions richly endowed with venture capital firms: Boston (3), San Francisco (3), Los Angeles (1), San Diego (1), and Seattle (1).

[13] In the alternative version of Table 2 (see footnote 9 above), the coefficient on the lagged dependent variable was nearly as large as in Table 2, so the significant positive coefficient does not arise from firms born 1976–1980 appearing in both the current and lagged dependent variables.

[14] See Zucker et al. (1994) for our first effort to assess the determinants of success of firms after birth.

TABLE 3—ANNUAL POISSON REGRESSIONS ON THE BIRTH OF BIOTECH-USING FIRMS BY REGION AND YEAR, 1976–1989

	(a)	(b)	(c)	(d)	(e)	(f)
Constant	−1.591***	−1.918***	−2.148***	−4.447***	−4.491***	−4.687***
	(0.032)	(0.041)	(0.057)	(0.226)	(0.349)	(0.565)
Number stars active in the region and year	0.157***	0.529***	0.270**	—	0.361***	0.282**
	(0.020)	(0.051)	(0.088)	—	(0.080)	(0.103)
Number collaborators active in the region and year	0.043***	0.083*	0.047	—	0.013	0.032
	(0.013)	(0.035)	(0.049)	—	(0.047)	(0.052)
(Number stars active in the region and year)^2	—	−0.022***	−0.014*	—	−0.015**	−0.014
	—	(0.002)	(0.006)	—	(0.005)	(0.008)
(Number collaborators active in the region and year)^2	—	−0.001	0.000	—	0.000	0.001
	—	(0.001)	(0.001)	—	(0.001)	(0.002)
Number stars active in the region and year × DUMMY1986–89	—	—	−0.219	—	−0.298**	−0.245
	—	—	(0.113)	—	(0.102)	(0.128)
Number collaborators active in the region and year × DUMMY1986–89	—	—	0.117	—	0.115	0.027
	—	—	(0.067)	—	(0.064)	(0.081)
(Number stars active in the region and year × DUMMY1986–89)^2	—	—	0.006	—	0.009	0.007
	—	—	(0.007)	—	(0.006)	(0.008)
(Number collaborators active in the region and year × DUMMY1986–89)^2	—	—	−0.001	—	−0.001	0.001
	—	—	(0.002)	—	(0.002)	(0.002)
Number top-quality universities in the region in 1981	—	—	0.444***	—	0.472***	0.462***
	—	—	(0.125)	—	(0.095)	(0.109)
Number faculty with federal support in the region in 1979–80	—	—	0.625***	—	0.982***	0.930***
	—	—	(0.093)	—	(0.094)	(0.093)
Number venture capital firms in the region and year[a]	—	—	—	0.019**	−0.028***	−0.024**
	—	—	—	(0.007)	(0.006)	(0.008)
Total employment (all industries) in the region and year	—	—	—	0.173***	−0.081	−0.117*
	—	—	—	(0.051)	(0.048)	(0.055)
Average wages per job in the region and year	—	—	—	0.153***	0.125***	0.132***
	—	—	—	(0.010)	(0.016)	(0.017)
Earnings-price ratio (Standard & Poors 500) for year	—	—	—	−0.024	−0.026	−0.017
	—	—	—	(0.016)	(0.026)	(0.039)
Number firms active in the region at end of previous year	—	—	—	—	—	0.020
	—	—	—	—	—	(0.013)
Number firms active in all U.S. at end of previous year	—	—	—	—	—	−0.000
	—	—	—	—	—	(0.000)
Births of biotech firms in the region for previous year	—	—	—	—	—	0.054
	—	—	—	—	—	(0.034)
Log-likelihood	−1677.0	−1429.1	−1274.3	−1669.5	−1202.3	−1184.6
Restricted log-likelihood	−2238.5	−2238.5	−2238.5	−2238.5	−2238.5	−2238.5

Notes: N = 2562. Standard errors (adjusted by Wooldridge, 1991 Procedure 2.1) are in parentheses below coefficients.
  [a] For years after 1981, the number of venture capital firms in a region is held constant at the 1981 level to avert simultaneity problems.
    * Significantly different from 0 at the 5-percent level.
   ** Significantly different from 0 at the 1-percent level.
  *** Significantly different from 0 at the 0.1-percent level.

as the knowledge diffuses we expect that more and more stars will result in less and less payoff to any one of them if he or she were to start a firm, and indeed stars are less likely to result

in birth of firms after 1985 than before. This is illustrated in column (c) of Table 3 where we add four interaction terms in which these counts and their squares have been multiplied by a dummy DUMMY1986–89 equal to 1 during 1986–1989 and 0 otherwise, as well as the other intellectual human capital terms. During 1986–1989 the positive effect of stars is sharply reduced while that of collaborators more than triples.[15] Nonetheless, we should view this inference cautiously since the significance values of the interaction terms for stars and collaborators with DUMMY1986–89 fall between 0.10 and 0.05, except for stars in the full fundamentals model in column (e) where the stars interaction term is significant at the 0.01 level.

Thus, we see that (at least during the first decade of this industry) localities with outstanding scientists having the tacit knowledge to practice recombinant DNA were much more likely to see new firms founded and preexisting firms begin to apply biotechnology. There is some evidence that as knowledge about gene splicing diffused and the tacit knowledge lost its scarcity and extraordinary value, the training function of universities became more important relative to the attraction of great scientists to an area. It is interesting that the quadratic term for stars is negative, suggesting diminishing returns (or possibly just proportionately fewer, larger firms) rather than the increasing returns suggested by standard views of knowledge spillovers which posit uninternalized, positive external effects from university scientists.[16] In the same regression in column (c), we see that, beyond the identified stars and collaborators, university quality and federal support are also significant measures of intellectual human capital relevant to firm founding.

Column (d) of Table 3 leads to the same conclusions with panel data as found for the same column in Table 2: The economic variables enter significantly with the expected sign if the intellectual human capital variables are omitted from the regression. However, unlike the previous long-run case, we can now enter the earnings-price ratio.[17] Here this variable enters with the correct sign, but does not even reach the 0.10 level of significance.

Column (e) of Table 3 presents the annual full fundamentals model incorporating the intellectual human capital and other variables. The results for the intellectual human capital measures are robust while the sign of the venture capital variable turns significantly negative as in the long-run model and the employment variable becomes insignificant (and negative).

Column (f) of Table 3, analogously to Table 2, adds a lagged dependent variable to the full fundamentals model. We also included the one-year lagged regional and national counts of firms using biotechnology as dynamic influences reflecting local agglomeration effects and market competition effects, respectively. None of the three dynamic variables enter significantly although their signs are consistent with some geographic agglomeration.

Thus, taken as a whole the results summarized in Table 3 support the strong role of intellectual human capital variables in determining the development of the American biotech industry.

The role of the economic variables, particularly the number of venture capital firms in the region, is explored further in Table 4. This table presents representative results for births in the entrant and incumbent subcomponents of firm entry into biotechnology. We see in columns (a) and (b) that if only the economic variables are introduced we get all the expected signs at appropriate significance [except for employment in (a) and the earnings-price ratio in both], including a result consistent with conventional wisdom that the number of venture capital firms has a signifi-

---

[15] To compute the effects of stars in the 1986–1989 period, we need to add the coefficients of the number of active stars and the coefficient of the same variable interacted with DUMMY1986–89 and then do the same for the two terms involving the squared values of these variables. An analogous approach yields the effect of collaborators during 1986–1989. We examined also interactions with dummy variables for 1976–1980 and with a time trend. Since the coefficients were very small and statistically insignificant for interaction terms involving 1976–1980 dummies, we believe the reported form more accurately reflects the time or diffusion dependence than a negative trend throughout the period.

[16] We are indebted to Jeff Armstrong for this point.

[17] The earnings-price ratio had to be dropped from these analyses because it is available only nationally over time.

TABLE 4—ANNUAL POISSON REGRESSIONS ON THE BIRTH OF BIOTECH-USING ENTRANTS
AND INCUMBENTS BY REGION AND YEAR, 1976–1989

	(a) Entrants	(b) Incumbents	(c) Entrants	(d) Incumbents	(e) Entrants	(f) Incumbents
Constant	−4.726*** (0.284)	−5.798*** (0.563)	−4.843*** (0.409)	−5.673*** (0.902)	−4.928*** (0.669)	−5.228*** (1.285)
Number stars active in the region and year	— —	— —	0.414*** (0.095)	0.323 (0.165)	0.351** (0.124)	0.242 (0.169)
Number collaborators active in the region and year	— —	— —	−0.006 (0.053)	0.000 (0.105)	0.012 (0.059)	0.019 (0.101)
(Number stars active in the region and year)^2	— —	— —	−0.016** (0.006)	−0.016* (0.008)	−0.017 (0.009)	−0.015 (0.011)
(Number collaborators active in the region and year)^2	— —	— —	0.001 (0.002)	0.002 (0.003)	0.000 (0.002)	0.001 (0.003)
Number stars active in the region and year × DUMMY1986–89	—	—	−0.227* (0.113)	−0.519* (0.237)	−0.196 (0.147)	−0.456 (0.251)
Number collaborators active in the region and year × DUMMY1986–89	—	—	0.096 (0.071)	0.233 (0.141)	0.011 (0.090)	0.144 (0.153)
(Number stars active in the region and year × DUMMY1986–89)^2	—	—	0.007 (0.007)	0.018 (0.010)	0.006 (0.010)	0.015 (0.013)
(Number collaborators active in the region and year × DUMMY1986–89)^2	—	—	−0.001 (0.002)	−0.004 (0.003)	0.001 (0.003)	−0.002 (0.004)
Number top-quality universities in the region in 1981	—	—	0.440*** (0.110)	0.479* (0.205)	0.410** (0.126)	0.447 (0.238)
Number faculty with federal support in the region in 1979–80	—	—	0.973*** (0.112)	1.114*** (0.296)	0.932*** (0.107)	1.041*** (0.295)
Number venture capital firms in the region and year[a]	0.023** (0.009)	0.006 (0.013)	−0.029*** (0.007)	−0.027* (0.012)	−0.024** (0.009)	−0.024 (0.013)
Total employment (all industries) in the region and year	0.128 (0.067)	0.296** (0.098)	−0.110 (0.058)	−0.052 (0.098)	−0.149* (0.067)	−0.078 (0.103)
Average wages per job in the region and year	0.156*** (0.012)	0.139*** (0.024)	0.123*** (0.018)	0.113** (0.039)	0.127*** (0.020)	0.114** (0.040)
Earnings-price ratio (Standard & Poors 500) for year	−0.036 (0.021)	−0.033 (0.043)	−0.022 (0.031)	−0.056 (0.070)	−0.016 (0.046)	−0.082 (0.092)
Number firms active in the region at end of previous year	—	—	—	—	0.023 (0.015)	0.024 (0.025)
Number firms active in all U.S. at end of previous year	—	—	—	—	−0.000 (0.000)	−0.001 (0.001)
Births of biotech firms in the region for previous year	—	—	—	—	0.037 (0.041)	0.055 (0.061)
Log-likelihood	−1265.1	−486.3	−945.9	−386.8	−935.8	−382.9
Restricted log-likelihood	−1628.7	−607.9	−1628.7	−607.9	−1628.7	−607.9

Notes: N = 2562. Standard errors (adjusted by Wooldridge, 1991 Procedure 2.1) are in parentheses below coefficients.

[a] For years after 1981, the number of venture capital firms in a region is held constant at the 1981 level to avert simultaneity problems.

* Significantly different from 0 at the 5-percent level.
** Significantly different from 0 at the 1-percent level.
*** Significantly different from 0 at the 0.1-percent level.

cantly positive effect on the birth of new firms but an insignificant effect on the birth of sub-units of existing firms which would not normally be financed by venture capital firms. The full fundamentals model is reported in columns (c) and (d) for births of entrants and incumbents, respectively, which is to be compared to column (e) for all firm births in Table 3. Again, in the presence of intellectual human capital the simple economic story does not hold up: the coefficients of venture capital firms and total employment turn negative, significantly so in the former case. Similar results are obtained in the dynamic versions of the full model reported in columns (e) and (f) of Table 4. The robustness of the negative venture capital coefficient remains a puzzle for future work, particularly in view of Yolanda K. Henderson's (1989) evidence that, despite some significant localization, most investments by venture capitalists cross regional boundaries.

IV. Summary and Conclusions

The American biotechnology industry which was essentially nonexistent in 1975 grew to 700 active firms over the next 15 years. In this paper, we show the tight connection between the intellectual human capital created by frontier research and the founding of firms in the industry. At least for this high-tech industry, the growth and location of intellectual human capital was the principal determinant of the growth and location of the industry itself. This industry is a testament to the value of basic scientific research. The number of local venture capital firms, which appears to be a positive determinant when intellectual human capital variables are excluded from the regressions, is found to depress the rate of firm birth in an area, perhaps due to the role of these venture capital firms in packaging a number of scientists into one larger firm which is likely to go public sooner.

We conclude that the growth and diffusion of intellectual human capital was the main determinant of where and when the American biotechnology industry developed. Intellectual human capital tended to flourish around great universities, but the existence of outstanding scientists measured in terms of research pro-ductivity played a key role over, above, and separate from the presence of those universities and government research funding to them. We believe that our results provide new insight into the role of research universities and their top scientists as central to the formation of new high-tech industries spawned by scientific breakthroughs. By being able to quantitatively identify individuals with the ability both to invent and to commercialize these breakthroughs, we have developed new specificity for the idea of spillovers and in particular raised the issue of whether spillovers are best viewed as resulting from the nonappropriability of scientific knowledge or from the maximizing behavior of scientists who have the ability to appropriate the commercial fruits of their academic discoveries.

DATA APPENDIX

The data used here are generally in panel form for 14 years (1976–1989) and 183 regions (functional economic areas as defined by the BEA). Frequently, the data are aggregates of data at the zip code or county level. Lagged variables include data for 1975 in the unlagged form. These data sets, part of our ongoing project on "Intellectual Capital, Technology Transfer, and the Organization of Leading-Edge Industries: Biotechnology," will be archived upon completion of the project in the Data Archives at the UCLA Institute for Social Science Research. A full description of the data is available from the authors upon request.

Biotechnology Firms

The starting point for our firm data set covered the industry as of April 1990 and was purchased from NCBC (1991), a private firm which tracks the industry. This data set identified 1075 firms, some of which were duplicates or foreign and others of which had died or merged. Further, there were a significant number of firms missing which had exited prior to April 1990. For these reasons, an intensive effort was made to supplement the NCBC data with information from *Bioscan* (1989–1993) and an industry data set provided by a firm in the industry which was also the ancestor of the *Bioscan* data set (Cetus Corp., 1988).

We generally counted entry of firms by adding up for each year and region the number of entrants founded and incumbents first using biotechnology. A few special cases should be noted: Where a firm enters the data set due to the merger of a entrant and another firm, we count it for the purposes of this paper as a continuation of the original entrant and not a new birth (the older entrant if two are involved). If firms already in the data set merge and one continues with the other(s) absorbed, the enterprise is counted as the continuing enterprise and not a new birth.

Scientists

Star scientists and their collaborators were identified as described in the text. Individual scientists are linked to locations through the institutional affiliations reported in their publications in the article data set. The discovery of genetic sequences is recognized by *GenBank*'s assignment to an article of a "primary accession number" to identify each. The 22 additional stars added to the 315 with more than 40 primary accession numbers thus had 20 or more articles with at least one primary accession number and 20–40 primary accession numbers total.

Articles

Our article data set consists of all 4,061 articles in major journals listed in *GenBank* as reporting genetic-sequence discoveries for which one or more of our 327 stars were listed as authors. (A small number of unpublished papers and articles appearing in proceedings volumes and obscure journals were excluded to permit the hand coding detailed below.) All of these articles were assigned unique article ID numbers and collected by hand. For each article, scientist ID numbers are used to identify the order of authorship and the institutional affiliation and location for each author on each article. This hand coding was necessary because, under the authorship traditions for these fields, the head of the laboratory who is often the most prestigious author frequently appears last. Our stars, for example, were first

authors on 18.3 percent of the articles and last authors on 69.1 percent of the 4,031 articles remaining after excluding the 30 sole-authored articles.[18] Unfortunately, only first- and/or corresponding-author affiliations are available in machine-readable sources.[19]

The resulting authorship data file contains 19,346 observations, approximately 4.8 authors for each of the 4,061 published articles. Each authorship observation gives the article ID number, the order of authorship, the scientist ID number of one of our stars and collaborators, and an institutional ID number for the author's affiliation which links him or her to a particular institution with a known zip code as of the publication date of the article.

Citations

We have collected data for 1982, 1987, and 1992 on the total number of citations to each of our 4,061 published articles listed in the Institute for Scientific Information's *Science Citation Index* (1982, 1987, 1992). These citation counts are linked to the article and authorship data set by the article ID number. The citations were collected for articles if and only if they appeared in the article data set; so scientists are credited with citations only insofar as they are to the 4,061 articles reporting genetic-sequence discoveries and published in major journals.

Universities

Our university data set consists of all U.S. institutions listed as granting the Ph.D. degree in any field in the Higher Education General Information Survey (HEGIS), Institutional Characteristics, 1983–1984 (U.S. Department of Education, National Center for Education

---

[18] This positional tradition holds across national boundaries: As a percentage of articles coauthored by their fellow nationals, American stars are 16.4 percent of first authors and 71.2 percent of last authors, compared to 21.2 percent and 63.1 percent, respectively, for Japanese, and 19.7 percent and 69.2 percent for other nationalities.

[19] The *Science Citation Index* lists up to six of the affiliations listed on the paper but only links the corresponding author to a particular affiliation.

Statistics, 1985). Each university is assigned an institutional ID number, a university flag, and located by zip code based on the HEGIS address file. Additional information described in the text was collected from Jones et al. (1982) for those universities granting the Ph.D. degree in biochemistry, cellular/molecular biology, and/or microbiology which we define as *"biotech-relevant"* fields.

Research Institutes and Hospitals

For those U.S. research institutions and hospitals listed as affiliations in the article data set, we assigned an institutional ID number and an institute/hospital flag, and obtained an address including a zip code as required for geocoding. No additional information has been collected on these institutions.

Venture Capital Firms

We created a venture capital firm data set by extracting from the Pratt (1982) directory the name, type, location, year of founding, and interest in funding biotech firms. This information was extracted for all venture capital which were legally permitted to finance startups. This latter requirement eliminated a number of firms which are chartered under government programs targeted at small and minority businesses. This approach accounts includes founding date of firms appearing in the 1982 Pratt directory, excluding those firms that may have either entered thereafter or existed in earlier years but exited before the directory was compiled.

Other Economic Variables

Total employment and average earnings per job by region and year are as reported by the Bureau of Economic Analysis based on county level data in U.S. Department of Commerce (1992b): Total employment is from Table K, line 010 (in millions of persons). Average earnings is from Table V, line 290 (wage & salary disbursements, other labor income, and proprietors income per job in thousands of current dollars), deflated by the implicit price deflator for personal consumption expenditures. The annual

data for the implicit price deflator for personal consumption expenditures were taken from U.S. Department of Commerce (1992a p. 247, line 16) as updated in the July 1992 *Survey of Current Business*, (p. 92, line 16). The S&P 500 earnings-price ratio was taken from *CITIBASE* (1993), series FSEXP.

REFERENCES

Arrow, Kenneth J. "Economic Welfare and the Allocation of Resources for Invention," in Richard R. Nelson, ed., *The rate and direction of inventive activity: Economic and social factors*. National Bureau of Economic Research Special Conference Series, Vol. 13. Princeton, NJ: Princeton University Press, 1962, pp. 609–25.

Bioscan, Vols. 3–7. Phoenix, AZ: Oryx Press, 1989–1993.

Burrill, G. Steven and Lee, Kenneth B., Jr. *Biotech 94: Long-term value, short-term hurdles*. Ernst & Young's Eighth Annual Report on the Biotechnology Industry. San Francisco: Ernst & Young, 1994.

Cameron, A. Colin and Trivedi, Pravin K. "Regression-Based Tests for Overdispersion in the Poisson Model." *Journal of Econometrics*, December 1990, *46*(3), pp. 347–64.

Cetus Corp. "Biotechnology Company Data Base," predecessor source for *Bioscan*. Computer printout, Cetus Corp., 1988.

CITIBASE: Citibank Economic Database. Machine-readable database, 1946–June 1993. New York: Citibank, 1993.

GenBank, Release 65.0. Machine-readable database. Palo Alto, CA: IntelliGentics, Inc., 1990.

Greene, William H. *LIMDEP: User's manual and reference guide, version 6.0*. Bellport, NY: Econometric Software, 1992.

Griliches, Zvi. "Hybrid Corn: An Exploration in the Economics of Technological Change." *Econometrica*, October 1957, *25*(4), pp. 501–22.

_____. "The Search for R&D Spillovers." *Scandinavian Journal of Economics*, 1992 Supplement, *94*, pp. 29–47.

Grossman, Gene M. and Helpman, Elhanan. *Innovation and growth in the global economy*. Cambridge, MA: MIT Press, 1991.

Hausman, Jerry; Hall, Bronwyn H. and Griliches, Zvi. "Econometric Models for Count Data with an Application to the Patents-R&D Relationship." *Econometrica*, July 1984, *52*(4), pp. 909–38.

Henderson, Yolanda K. "Venture Capital and Economic Development." Paper presented to the New England Advisory Council, Federal Reserve Bank of Boston, Boston, MA, July 11, 1989.

Institute for Scientific Information. *Science Citation Index*, ISI compact disc editions, machine-readable database. Philadelphia: Institute for Scientific Information, 1982, 1987, 1992.

Jaffe, Adam B. "Real Effects of Academic Research." *American Economic Review*, December 1989, *79*(5), pp. 957–70.

Jaffe, Adam B.; Trajtenberg, Manuel and Henderson, Rebecca. "Geographic Localization of Knowledge Spillovers as Evidenced by Patent Citations." *Quarterly Journal of Economics*, August 1993, *63*(3), pp. 577–98.

Jones, Lyle V.; Lindzey, Gardner and Coggeshall, Porter E., eds. *An assessment of research-doctorate programs in the United States: Biological sciences*. Washington, DC: National Academy Press, 1982.

Kenney, Martin. *Biotechnology: The university-industrial complex*. New Haven, CT: Yale University Press, 1986.

Lerner, Joshua. "Venture Capitalists and the Decision to Go Public." *Journal of Financial Economics*, June 1994, *35*(3), pp. 293–316.

_____. "Venture Capitalists and the Oversight of Private Firms." *Journal of Finance*, March 1995, *50*(1), pp. 301–18.

Mansfield, Edwin. "Academic Research Underlying Industrial Innovations: Sources, Characteristics, and Financing." *Review of Economics and Statistics*, February 1995, *77*(1), pp. 55–65.

Nelson, Richard R. "The Simple Economics of Basic Scientific Research." *Journal of Political Economy*, June 1959, *67*(3), pp. 297–306.

Nelson, Richard R. and Romer, Paul M. "Science, Economic Growth, and Public Policy," in Bruce L. R. Smith and Claude E. Barfield, eds., *Technology, R&D, and the economy*. Washington, DC: Brookings Institution and American Enterprise Institute, 1996, pp. 49–74.

Nelson, Richard R. and Winter, Sidney G. *An evolutionary theory of economic change*. Cambridge, MA: Harvard University Press, 1982.

North Carolina Biotechnology Center. *North Carolina Biotechnology Center U.S. companies database*, machine-readable database. Research Triangle Park, NC: North Carolina Biotechnology Center, April 16, 1992.

Pratt, Stanley E. *Guide to venture capital sources*, 6th Ed. Englewood Cliffs, NJ: Prentice-Hall, 1982.

Romer, Paul M. "Increasing Returns and Long-Run Growth." *Journal of Political Economy*, October 1986, *94*(5), pp. 1002–37.

_____. "Endogenous Technological Change." *Journal of Political Economy*, October 1990, Part 2, *98*(5), pp. S71–S102.

Rosenberg, Nathan. *Inside the black box: Technology and economics*. Cambridge: Cambridge University Press, 1982.

U.S. Department of Commerce, Bureau of Economic Analysis, Economics and Statistics Administration. *National income and product accounts of the United States, volume 2, 1959–88*. Washington, DC: U.S. Government Printing Office, 1992a.

_____. *Regional economic information system, version 1.3*, CD-ROM, machine-readable database. Washington, DC: Bureau of Economic Analysis, May 5, 1992b.

U.S. Department of Education, National Center for Education Statistics. *Higher education general information survey (HEGIS), institutional characteristics, 1983–84*, machine-readable database, ICPSR 8291. Ann Arbor, MI: Inter-University Consortium for Political and Social Research, circa 1985.

Wooldridge, Jeffrey M. "On the Application of Robust, Regression-Based Diagnostics to Models of Conditional Means and Conditional Variances." *Journal of Econometrics*, January 1991, *47*(1), pp. 5–46.

Zucker, Lynne G.; Brewer, Marilynn B.; Oliver, Amalya and Liebeskind, Julia. "Basic Science as Intellectual Capital in Firms: Information Dilemmas in rDNA Biotechnology

Research.'' Working paper, UCLA Institute for Social Science Research, 1993.

Zucker, Lynne G. and Darby, Michael R. ''Star Scientists and Institutional Transformation: Patterns of Invention and Innovation in the Formation of the Biotechnology Industry.'' *Proceedings of the National Academy of Sciences*, November 12, 1996, *93*(23), pp. 12709–12716.

Zucker, Lynne G.; Darby, Michael R. and Armstrong, Jeff. ''Intellectual Capital and the Firm: The Technology of Geographically Localized Knowledge Spillovers.'' National Bureau of Economic Research (Cambridge, MA) Working Paper No. 4946, December 1994.

Zucker, Lynne G.; Darby, Michael R. and Brewer, Marilynn B. ''Intellectual Capital and the Birth of U.S. Biotechnology Enterprises.'' National Bureau of Economic Research (Cambridge, MA) Working Paper No. 4653, February 1994.

[27]

Capturing Technological Opportunity Via Japan's Star Scientists: Evidence from Japanese Firms' Biotech Patents and Products

Lynne G. Zucker[1]
Michael R. Darby[2]

ABSTRACT. Using detailed data on biotechnology in Japan, we find that identifiable collaborations between particular university star scientists and firms have a large positive impact on firms' research productivity, increasing the average firm's biotech patents by 34 percent, products in development by 27 percent, and products on the market by 8 percent as of 1989–1990. However, there is little evidence of geographically localized knowledge spillovers. In early industry formation, star scientists holding tacit knowledge required to practice recombinant DNA (genetic engineering) were of great economic value, leading to incentives motivating their participation in technology transfer. In Japan, the legal and institutional context implies that firm scientists work in the stars' university laboratories in contrast to America where the stars are more likely to work in the firm's labs. As a result, star collaborations in Japan are less localized around their research universities so that the universities' *local* economic development impact is lessened. Stars' scientific productivity is increased less during collaborations with firms in Japan as compared to the U.S.

JEL Classification: O31

[1] *Professor of Sociology & Director*
Center for International Science,
Technology, and Cultural Policy, SPPSR
UCLA Box 951551
University of California, Los Angeles
Los Angeles, CA 90095-1551
E-mail: zucker@nicco.sscnet.ucla.edu
[2] *Cordner Professor of Money & Financial Markets*
Anderson Graduate School of Management
UCLA Box 951481
University of California, Los Angeles
Los Angeles, CA 90095-1481
E-mail: michael.r.darby@anderson.ucla.edu

> R & D intensity in an industry is largely determined by two key variables – *technological opportunity* and *the ability to appropriate returns from new developments*.
> – Klevorick, Levin, Nelson, and Winter
> (1995, p. 186; their emphasis)

Variations in the degree to which commercially valuable breakthrough knowledge can be captured by persons, firms, industries, and nations provides differential technological opportunities and can translate into sustained competitive advantage in the presence of supporting factors. A stream of recent research on innovation in the U.S. has identified "geographically localized knowledge spillovers" occurring in areas around major universities (Jaffe, 1986, 1989). The underlying assumption is that proximity to a major university itself provides technological opportunity; the localization is assumed to be due to the social ties between university and firm employees or by firm employees attending seminars at the university. In sharp contrast, we find that when we measure the *actual ties* between the university scientists and firms, by using a co-publishing measure that identifies firm scientists who are working at the bench science level with the top university scientists, the effects of other top university scientists working in the same scientific area disappear (Zucker, Darby, and Armstrong, 1998).

We examine whether the same holds true for Japan: When we measure the actual ties between the star university scientists in Japan and firms in Japan, do these ties eliminate the positive, significant effect of untied university scientists? We have already replicated in Japan our U.S. results

Journal of Technology Transfer, 26, 37–58, 2001
© 2001 Kluwer Academic Publishers. Manufactured in The Netherlands.

showing the strong effects of the star scientists making breakthrough bioscience discoveries on the birth of firms adopting biotechnology in Japan, although also documenting the dominance of incumbent firms in Japan compared to the dominance of newly formed firms in the U.S. (Darby and Zucker, 1996; Zucker, Darby, and Brewer, 1998). We now turn to the question of the effects of these scientists on the success of the biotechnology industry in Japan. Here we introduce into our analysis the more commonly used patent measure of innovative output of firms, as well as measures of products in development and on the market that we have used in our earlier U.S. work.

The case of biotechnology is particularly interesting in Japan because Japanese bioscientists are second only to the U.S. in their genetic sequence discoveries, the crucial driving force behind the latest major wave of technology transfer from basic science. The technological opportunity provided by the strong science base meant that Japan's firms had the opportunity to innovate, and our primary question is the role that the top scientists played in this commercialization process. Extensive fieldwork in Japan, and interviews conducted with top bioscientists, top firm officials, and the financial community, provided evidence that there were important ties between the star scientists and firms in Japan. With the many institutional and cultural differences between Japan and the U.S., replicating our earlier results for California would provide strong support for our original conjecture that basic scientific discoveries are commonly appropriated through bench-level scientific collaborations between firm and top university scientists.

Two institutional features of Japan were also explored through our fieldwork. The first is the practice of the top university scientists in Japan of collaborating with firm scientists by bringing these scientists to the university lab, and formally instructing them while informally collaborating with them. The geography of collaboration may well be altered by this practice, since the firm scientists bear the costs of travel or moving. The university and governmental policies underlying this collaboration style will be discussed in more detail below; we use this institutional feature to clarify the differences between the impact of

bench level collaboration between star scientists and firms in Japan and the U.S. The second institutional feature is keiretsu membership. Specifically, we focus on members of each keiretsu's president's club which often gives firms special entre into funding for new projects. Given the high "burn rate" of capital in biotechnology before products can be marketed, substantial funds must be raised early in the process. Access to funding may provide an initial competitive advantage, but our respondents indicated that the advantage might well be lost through the low risk strategies likely to be adopted within the conservative keiretsu structure. We thus enter president's club membership as a variable in our analysis.

Before turning to the empirical analysis, we briefly discuss how the star scientists are identified in Japan, and then discuss the general conditions under which discoveries can be privatized and thus become "appropriable" by discovering scientists, who can then choose to transfer them to a firm. Some basic comparisons of regional bio-industry variations in Japan and the U.S. are presented in Section 2 to clarify the common perception that Japan lags significantly behind the U.S. in its commercialization. We then turn in Section 3 to our main analyses of the market or spillover effects of star scientists on firm success in terms of patents and products in development and on the market. We next examine the effect of commercial ties on the scientific productivity of stars, as measured by number of articles published and their average number of citations. Section 5 presents our conclusions on embodied technology transfer and localized spillovers and on how Japanese institutions have attenuated the local economic development impact of Japan's major research universities.

1. Star scientists and natural excludability of breakthrough knowledge

In a series of papers with our associates (see especially, Zucker and Darby, 1996, 1997a, 1997b; Zucker, Darby, and Brewer, 1998; Darby and Zucker, 1996; and Zucker, Darby, and Armstrong, 1998), we have shown that star scientists play a central role in determining where and when firms enter biotechnology and which of them are most successful. We briefly review here how we identify the star scientists and why they play a crucial role in the commercialization of the breakthrough scientific discoveries.

Identifying star scientists

The breakthrough discovery by Stanley Cohen and Herbert Boyer of the basic technique for recombinant DNA is the foundation both of a burst of related scientific innovation in the biosciences and of commercial biotechnology (reported in Cohen, Chang, Boyer, and Helling, 1973). While other discoveries and techniques have become important in biotechnology, the core technology is the application of genetic engineering based upon the Cohen-Boyer breakthrough of taking a gene from one organism and implanting it in another.[1]

A very important measure of research success is the discovery of nucleotide sequences that determine the characteristics of proteins and other molecules; these sequences and the articles that report them are cataloged in an international scientific data base, GenBank (1990; 1994). In this paper, we analyze gene sequence articles up to 1990 by at least one Japanese scientist (except for our data on tacit knowledge, presented in the next section, that includes international articles through 1992). GenBank assigns to each article one or more "primary accession numbers" to identify each genetic sequence.

Based on these accession numbers, we identified a set of 327 star scientists, 305 with more than 40 genetic sequences through April 1990 and 22 with 20 or more articles (with at least 20 primary accession numbers) to include difficult discoveries that may report fewer sequences per article on average.[2] Of these stars, 52 published with an affiliation to an institution in Japan at least once (for comparison analyses, we also rely on the 207 stars who published with an affiliation to an institution in the U.S. at least once). Affiliation, including both institution and address (country), are not included in GenBank but were hand coded from 4,061 articles authored by stars.[3] When we examine the full GenBank just below, we do not have information on the location/affiliation of most authors, only the top performing scientists and their co-authors.

Tacit knowledge held by the star scientists

Technology transfer by discovering scientists becomes important in determining the success of firms utilizing that technology when a new discovery has both high commercial value and a combination of scarcity and tacitness that defines *natural excludability*, the degree to which there is a barrier to the flow of the valuable knowledge from the discoverers to other scientists. Those with the most information about breakthrough discoveries are the scientists actually making them, so there is initial scarcity. To the extent that the knowledge is both scarce and tacit, it constitutes intellectual human capital retained by the discovering scientists (Zucker, Darby, and Brewer, 1998 and 1994; Data Appendix).

Knowledge provides competitive advantage to the degree that privatization is possible; if none is, then the knowledge is available for all to exploit (and thus there may be few incentives to exploit it). Most, but not all, breakthrough discoveries have a high degree of privatization compared to knowledge produced via "normal science." In the recombinant DNA breakthroughs in bioscience, the discovering scientists initially dominated publication; new scientists entered the area of research, but predominantly by working with at least one other scientist who had previously published in the area.

Scarcity of the new knowledge is reflected in classic diffusion, beginning with just a handful of discoverers and growing at a pace that reflects both the value of the knowledge, where high value discoveries will diffuse more widely and rapidly than those with low value, and its tacitness.[4] When the value is high, as in biotechnology, other scientists are motivated to learn the new knowledge; however when tacitness is high, these other scientists are limited in their ability to learn it depending on the relative scarcity of those who already know it. Scientists desiring to enter the new area of research may need to have hands-on experience at the bench before they are able to enter.[5] Coauthoring, which implies bench level collaboration, provides our measure of tacitness: Degree of tacitness is high when most new authors are publishing with at least one old author defined as those who have published before in GenBank, and low if most new entrants to

GenBank can do the research either by him/herself or with all new authors.

Tacitness appears to be very high in biotechnology: New scientists enter throughout the 1969 through 1992 period predominantly by publishing with old, experienced scientists who have previously published in GenBank, and thus demonstrably know the relevant techniques, with this mode accounting for 81 percent of entry from 1969 through 1992. In our final partial year of data for 1993, new authors entered with old authors 83 percent of the time. Excluding sole-authored articles, which may be dissertations for new authors and review articles by established authors, new authors write exclusively with other new authors 36 percent less frequently than old authors write exclusively with other old authors.[6]

To estimate the significance of these differences, in Table I we examine the choice by each author to write with all old or new authors or not. We find that being a new author significantly decreases the probability of publishing with all the same type of (here, new) author; old authors are more likely to select working with all old authors as the number of articles they have published previously in GenBank increases. The number of authors per article and the year, both entered as control variables, significantly decrease the probability of publishing with all old or all new authors, compared to publishing with mixed old and new authors.

2. Regional variation in Japan and the U.S.

Because we are interested in exploring geographically localized knowledge spillovers, it was important to define for Japan regions similar to the U.S. Bureau of Economic Analysis's functional economic areas within which commuting is sufficiently feasible to think of knowledge as more easily transmitted locally than to other regions of Japan. Our regional definitions are contained in Table II. Since most of the action is within such core prefectures as Tokyo, Chiba, and Kanagawa or Kyoto and Osaka or Aichi, we do not believe that other reasonable classifications would lead to materially different results.

In Table III we report the distribution of firms located in these regions (by principal research location where this differs from headquarters) and their average performance on five different measures of research productivity used in the empirical analysis: numbers of U.S. biotechnology patents granted, numbers of biotech products in development, numbers of human therapeutics and vaccines biotech products in development, numbers of biotech products on the market, and numbers of numbers of human therapeutics and vaccines biotech products on the market. We use data on U.S. patents because of later use of this variable in comparisons with U.S. firms; U.S. patents and Japanese patents have been shown to produce comparable results (Branstetter and Sakakibara, 1998). Of the 368 firms entering biotechnology in Japan 1975–1989, we have product counts (including zeroes but not missing) for 331. In the U.S., where there are many small, privately-held dedicated new biotech firms, we have comparable data for a much smaller percentage: 342 out of 699 firms as of 1990. The greater density of the Japanese population leads us to compare U.S. states to Japanese regions, but even California (with 8 BEA-defined functional economic areas) has only a little over half the share

Table I
Determinants of whether an article's authors will be all old or new (y = 1) or will be mixed old and new (y = 0)
logit analysis

Variables	Coefficients	Standard errors
Constant	60.714***	2.826
Categorical variable = 1 if author i's is a new author; else 0	−0.595***	0.012
Number of articles published by author i this year and before	0.007***	0.001
Number of authors on the article	−0.435***	0.003
Year of publication for the article	−0.030***	0.001

$P^2(4) = 31,755.6^{***}$, Pseudo-$R^2 = 0.124$

N = 238,926

Notes: Probability z > x: * < .05, ** < .01, *** < .001
1. An author is classified as new during the first year the author appears in GenBank (1994) and thereafter is old.
2. There is one observation i, j for each article j authored by each author i (so an article with 5 authors appears 5 times, once for each author). Only articles with more than 1 author are included in the estimation.
3. The coefficients are estimates of the elasticity with respect to the variable of the odds ratio that all authors will be of the same type rather than mixed old and new.

Table II
Definitions of functional economic areas for Japan

Region name	Included prefectures
Hokkaido	Hokkaido
Northern Honshu	Akita, Aomori, Fukushima, Iwate, Miyagi, Niigata, Yamagata
Tokyo area	Chiba, Kanagawa, Saitama, Tokyo
Tokyo ring	Gunma, Ibaraki, Shizuoka, Tochigi, Yamanashi
West-Central Honshu	Aichi, Fukui, Gifu, Ishikawa, Mie
Kansai area	Hyogo, Kyoto, Nara, Osaka, Shiga, Wakayama
Western Honshu	Hiroshima, Okayama, Shimane, Tottori, Yamaguchi
Shikoku	Ehime, Kagawa, Kochi, Tokushima
Kyushu & Nansei Shoto Islands	Fukuoka, Kagoshima, Kumamoto, Miyazaki, Nagasaki, Oita, Okinawa, Saga

of biotech-engaged firms commanded by Japan's Tokyo area.

Consistent with the industry consensus, American firms are far ahead of their Japanese counterparts, reporting more than twice as many patents and also products on the market, both overall and in the highest-tech/highest-value area

of human therapeutics and vaccines. Possibly reflecting differences in our national industry directory sources, the average Japanese firm reports two thirds more products in development than the average U.S. firm overall. However, Japanese firms report human therapeutic and vaccine biotech products in development at a rate one quarter less than in the U.S. While many of our respondents in Japan have expressed concern that their performance persistently lags behind America, we note that Japan has probably done more with its science base than any major European country.

3. Empirical analysis

We report here poisson regressions for three principal measures of success by Japanese firms in using biotechnology: numbers of U.S. biotechnology patents granted, numbers of products in development, and numbers of products on the market. The last two measures are also examined where the products in question are restricted to human therapeutics and vaccines to focus on the highest-value/highest-technology applica-

Table III
Regional variation in firm success in biotechnology Japan and the U.S. as of 1990–1991

			Per-firm averages				
	Firms	Patent	Prod. in dev.	Prod. on mkt.			
Region or state	Number	% total	Totals[a]	All	Human[b]	All	Human[b]
Tokyo area	158	48	0.71	3.51	0.99	1.53	0.13
Kansai area	66	20	0.55	3.59	1.21	1.89	0.45
Tokyo ring	34	10	0.53	3.44	1.24	1.97	0.26
West-central Honshu	29	9	0.00	2.14	0.48	1.59	0.45
Western Honshu	13	4	0.85	2.92	0.92	2.15	0.23
Other Japan	31	9	0.26	1.58	0.68	0.81	0.10
Total Japan	331	100	0.56	3.20	0.98	1.61	0.24
California	96	28	1.72	1.82	1.54	3.97	0.77
Massachusetts	39	11	1.72	2.59	0.86	3.79	0.87
New Jersey	27	8	1.33	2.70	2.15	2.22	0.52
New York	24	7	0.58	1.92	1.29	4.33	0.67
Maryland	16	5	1.63	1.13	0.56	3.50	0.38
Other U.S.	140	41	0.67	1.68	1.09	3.91	0.31
Total U.S.	342	100	1.18	1.89	1.26	3.79	0.55

[a] U.S. biotechnology patents granted through 1991.
[b] Human therapeutics and vaccines.

tions. Poisson regressions are appropriate as here when dealing with count variables with numerous zero values (Hausman, Hall, and Griliches, 1984). All the regressions reported here were estimated using LIMDEP (William Greene, 1992, pp. 539–549), with the Wooldridge regression-based correction for the variance-covariance matrix estimates.[7] The poisson regressions estimate the logarithm of the expected dependent variable; so the signs and significance of coefficients have the usual interpretation.

Sample statistics for these and the other variables used in the empirical analysis are presented in Table IV. The first group of variables are the measures of research productivity to be explained, including both U.S. biotech patent grants with application dates through 1989 and those with grant dates through 1991 (to allow for an average two year lag).[8] We apply the methods developed in the earlier work focusing on the U.S. to the Japanese case in the following poisson regression models taken from Zucker, Darby, and Armstrong (1998) with the addition of two variables to examine differences between the U.S. and Japanese contexts.

The approach is applied to data for individual firms and based on dividing the articles published by academic (university and independent research

Table IV
Descriptive statistics for variables used in analysis of Japanese firms using biotechnology

Variables	Mean	S.E.	Min.	Max.
Measures of research success:				
US biotech patent grants to Japanese firms – applic. dates up to 1989	0.522	2.507	0	34
US biotech patent grants to Japanese firms – grant dates up to 1991	0.539	2.553	0	35
US biotech patent grants to firms – application dates 1986–1989[a]	0.220	0.914	0	12
US biotech patent grants to firms – grant dates 1988–1991[a]	0.285	1.109	0	12
Biotech products in development	3.196	4.107	0	29
Products in Development in human therapeutics & vaccines	0.985	2.375	0	17
Products on the market	1.607	2.134	0	15
Products on the market in human therapeutics & vaccines	0.239	0.846	0	9
Cumulative articles as of 1989 by:				
Stars affiliated to the firm	0.006	0.110	0	2
Stars locally linked to the firm	0.036	0.346	0	5
Stars externally linked to the firm	0.057	0.356	0	3
Stars linked to the firm	0.094	0.545	0	5
Unaffiliated stars in the same region untied to the firm	148.571	93.463	0	297
Other firm characteristics:				
Keiretsu President's Club Membership	0.154	0.362	0	1
Categorical variable = 1 if new biotech firm; else 0	0.082	0.274	0	1
Years of firm experience in biotechnology as of 1989	7.508	3.215	1	15
Categorical variable = 1 if the firm uses rDNA; else 0	0.341	0.475	0	1

N = 331 (37 out of original 368 firms had missing data on products on market)
[a] In these cases, N = 309. 39 firms from the original 368 firms in the full firm data set were born after 1986, and an additional 20 firms had a missing value for the rDNA categorical variable.

institutes) stars in the firm's region into those published with firm coauthors (linked local articles) and all others (untied articles). Proponents of geographically localized knowledge spillovers expect strong positive coefficients on these untied articles while we have concluded in our prior work that localized knowledge effects in this industry have resulted from the tendency of (U.S.) academic stars to work with local firms (of which they are often founders) and the strong effect of star ties on firm's research productivity. As in the U.S. studies, we also include a variable for affiliated stars but in the Japanese case such ties are very rare so that variable serves to dummy out the only firm which has affiliated stars.

As noted above, in Japan it is illegal for national university professors (nearly 90 percent of star university scientists) to also work for or receive compensation from firms. Collaborations with firms and technology transfer are legally part of the professors' official duties, but the university does not provide any rewards for moving these items from the bottom of his or her "to-do list." However, many side arrangements provide incentives for faculty-firm collaborations.[9] Also unlike the U.S., the star scientist does not have to physically do his or her research at the firm's facilities in order for the collaborators to avoid the university's full or co-ownership of any resulting patents. As a result, the collaborations generally involve one of the firm's scientists working in the academic star's university laboratory and serving as liaison to the firm (for example, the star may refer samples to the firm's laboratories for sequencing). Since any firm in Japan can reasonably although not costlessly move one of their scientists to the star's laboratory, it is not surprising that (external) linkages between firms and stars in other regions are relatively much more common in Japan than in the U.S. We alternatively add a count of external linked articles as a separate variable in the regression or combine local and external linked articles in a single variable. In Table IV we report sample statistics for cumulative values up to 1989 of the five different measures of stars' research output in relation to the firm.

The one other alteration to the Zucker, Darby, and Armstrong (1998) set-up is addition of a categorical variable indicating whether or not the firm is represented in a keiretsu presidents' club. Advocates of keiretsus would expect such membership to confer deep pockets and long horizons leading to greater research productivity. Some scientists in Japan have indicated that keiretsus are characterized by older, more conservative chief executives who are less likely to adequately commit company resources to modern biotechnology. This is the first item listed as other firm characteristics in Table IV.

There are only three other variables appearing in the regressions: (a) a categorical variable indicating whether the company is a new biotechnology firm (only 8.3% of the Japanese firms compared to three quarters of American firms using biotechnology) or a prior incumbent firm, (b) experience measured as years elapsed since entry in biotechnology, and (c) a categorical variable indicating whether or not the firm actually applies the recombinant DNA technology.

Patents granted

Table V reports estimates of the process determining U.S. biotechnology patents granted to Japanese firms by application dates 1975–1989 (roughly corresponding to grant dates of 1977–1991). For these regressions only the firms active in biotechnology in any given year are entered and the data on star articles are cumulated to that year. We ran corresponding regressions for patents dated by grant dates with essentially identical results.[10]

Consider first model a in Table V. Collaborations with external stars appear to be very productive in generating patents for the firm. Affiliated stars have a significantly negative coefficient, but for Japan this reflects the comparatively less successful experience of a single firm with affiliated stars compared to what would otherwise be predicted. (Comparison with model b suggests that keiretsu presidents' club membership has a negative impact on predicted patenting success and its inclusion reduces the estimated coefficient of affiliated stars;[11] since only one firm is involved we generally will not further dwell on the affiliated variable.) Not surprisingly, years of experience and the use of the recombinant DNA technology are significant positive factors in generating patents. Interestingly, incumbent firms in

Table V
Poisson regressions for number of U.S. biotechnology patents granted to Japanese firms by firm and year
application dates 1975–1989

	Coefficients (standard errors)			
Variables	model a	model b	model c	model d
Constant	−5.0110***	−4.9910***	−4.9860***	−4.9730***
	(0.1545)	(0.1559)	(0.1575)	(0.1605)
Cumulative star articles:				
Linked local	0.1108	0.0573	–	–
	(0.0616)	(0.0637)		
Linked external	0.4828***	0.4717***	–	–
	(0.0590)	(0.0613)		
Linked local & external	–	–	0.2805***	0.2421***
			(0.0469)	(0.0513)
Affiliated	−1.1100***	−0.8276***	−1.1980***	−0.9343***
	(0.2422)	(0.2457)	(0.2588)	(0.2649)
Untied local stars	−0.0012	−0.0017*	−0.0009	−0.0013
	(0.0007)	(0.0008)	(0.0007)	(0.0007)
Other firm characteristics:				
Keiretsu Presidents' Club	–	−0.5735***	–	−0.5290***
membership		(0.1343)		(0.1404)
Categorical variable = 1 if	−1.3100**	−1.3390**	−1.3230**	−1.3500**
new biotech firm; else 0	(0.4790)	(0.4843)	(0.4906)	(0.4985)
Years of firm experience	0.1750***	0.1868***	0.1658***	0.1769***
in biotechnology in 1986	(0.0136)	(0.0146)	(0.0136)	(0.0152)
Categorical variable = 1 if	2.1380***	2.2360***	2.1630***	2.2580***
firm uses rDNA; else 0	(0.1380)	(0.1432)	(0.1410)	(0.1475)
Log-likelihood	−577.98	−573.44	−581.54	−577.73
Log-likelihood (coefs. = 0)	−723.55	−723.55	−723.55	−723.55
$\chi^2(1)$ for pooling local and	–	–	7.11**	8.58**
external linked articles				

N = 2567
Notes: Probability z > x: * < .05, ** < .01, *** < .001
Standard errors (adjusted by Wooldridge 1991, Procedure 2.1) are in parentheses below coefficients.

Japan appear to have a significant advantage over entrants in Japan in generating patents. Untied local stars have a tiny negative coefficient in all the models in Table V (which is statistically significant in one case), contrary to the predictions of advocates of geographically localized knowledge spillovers. More surprising, given our U.S. results, is the insignificant coefficient on local linked articles.[12]

The weak effect of local star links may simply reflect the fact that in the Japanese context it is not important where the star is located relative to the firm, so we have relatively few local star links which were less productive than average. Models c and d replicate models a and b on the assumption that both types of links should be pooled in Japan. The $\chi^2(1)$ statistics reported at the bottom of the c and d columns indicate that we can reject that hypothesis for these regressions at the 1 percent confidence level. There is a socio-economic explanation for why external links would be more productive than local links in the Japanese context where greater distance does not entail lesser involvement of the star in the collaboration: Since the firm's costs in sending its scientist to work in the star's laboratory will generally be higher when the star is external to the region, the expected payoff to the firm should be higher for external than local collaborations with stars. (See Zucker, Darby, Brewer, and Peng 1996 for more general evidence of this proposition for scientific collaborations.) Thus greater impact of external than local links can be viewed as strongly confirming the importance of embodied technology transfer from particular top academic scientists to particular firms in response to incentives to collaborate and disconfirming the hypothesis of localized knowledge spillovers.

We suspect that such a strong conclusion is over-reaching and prefer an alternative, statistical explanation for the weaker local-linked effects estimated here: The counts of local and external links are highly correlated across firms, so it is difficult to obtain reliable estimates of the two coefficients separately. The case for this explanation is buttressed by the fact that for one of the six dependent variables in Tables V–X local links have a significant positive effect while external links do not and for nearly all the other dependent variables we cannot reject the hypothesis of equal coefficients on the two types of links.

Instead of treating each year for each firm as a different observation, in the cross-section analysis reported in Table VI we treat each firm as a single observation. For the 309 firms which had entered biotechnology by 1986, we cumulate the various star articles up to 1986 to predict the number of U.S. biotechnology patents granted with application dates from 1986 through 1991. The results are rather similar to those obtained by the panel method except: (a) articles by untied stars have a tiny and insignificant positive effect, (b) the negative coefficient on new biotech firms (versus incumbents) are not significant, and (c) whether we can reject pooling the local and external links depends on whether or not the keiretsu presidents' club membership is included in the regression.

Taken together, the robust findings from Tables V and VI are that linked stars (perhaps especially those from other regions), years of experience in biotechnology, use of recombinant DNA technology, and not belonging to a keiretsu presidents' club all increase research productivity measured by patents granted while there is no indication of any geographically localized knowledge spillovers. Since patents may have some problems as an indicator of research productivity (Griliches, 1990), we turn to other indicators more directly related to using biotechnology to create new products.

Products in development

In Zucker, Darby, and Armstrong (1998) we argued that products in development were a good indicator of research productivity, since reaching the stage of clinical trials meant that the product had already passed substantial milestones. In Japan, however, biotechnology is not used so overwhelmingly in the pharmaceutical industry: in Table III we saw that human therapeutics and vaccines account for less than one third of the products in development in Japan compared to two thirds in the U.S. This means that some reported products in development may both be at a somewhat earlier stage of development, of lesser technical difficulty, and of rather different magnitudes in terms of value to the firm than those we considered earlier. Accordingly we also consider an alternative measure counting only human therapeutic and vaccine biotech products in development. Both counts were based on listings in Nikkei Biotechnology's *Biotechnology Guide Japan, 1990–1991* (see Data Appendix for details).

Table VII reports the results for counts of all biotech products in development as of 1990. Both linked local and external stars have large, significant impacts on the numbers of products in development. Again the impact of an article with an external star is larger than one with a local star in terms of the point estimates, but here both are statistically significant and we cannot reject the hypothesis that the impacts are equal. As with patents, the firm with the affiliated stars underperforms. Here there are significant but very small coefficients on articles by local stars not tied to the firm, consistent with geographically localized

Table VI
Poisson regressions for cumulative number of U.S. biotechnology patents granted to Japanese firms with
application dates 1986–1989 by firm

Variables	Coefficients (standard errors)			
	model a	model b	model c	model d
Constant	−4.5830***	−4.6130***	−4.4580***	−4.4700***
	(0.3418)	(0.3338)	(0.3380)	(0.3425)
Star articles up to 1986:				
Linked local	0.0390	−0.0654	–	–
	(0.1743)	(0.1779)		
Linked external	0.5153***	0.5110***	–	–
	(0.0817)	(0.0838)		
Linked local & external	–	–	0.3301***	0.2857***
			(0.0637)	(0.0713)
Affiliated	−0.3351*	−0.0582	−0.5777***	−0.3902***
	(0.1554)	(0.1717)	(0.1239)	(0.1101)
United local stars	0.0012	0.0008	0.0014	0.0012
	(0.0009)	(0.0009)	(0.0009)	(0.0009)
Other firm characteristics:				
Keiretsu Presidents' Club membership	–	−0.5985**	–	−0.4819*
		(0.1924)		(0.2079)
Categorical variable = 1 if new biotech firm; else 0	−0.4312	−0.4892	−0.4225	−0.4662
	(0.4337)	(0.4344)	(0.4610)	(0.4701)
Years of firm experience in biotechnology in 1986	0.2656***	0.2830***	0.2451***	0.2565***
	(0.0356)	(0.0363)	(0.0336)	(0.0361)
Categorical variable = 1 if firm uses rDNA; else 0	1.8750***	1.9870***	1.8770***	1.9680***
	(0.1879)	(0.1928)	(0.1994)	(0.2089)
Log-likelihood	−148.59	−146.84	−150.16	−149.03
Log-likelihood (coefs. = 0)	−210.51	−210.51	−210.51	−210.51
$\chi^2(1)$ for pooling local and external linked articles	–	–	3.14	4.38*

N = 309
Notes: Probability $z > x$: * < .05, ** < .01, *** < .001
Standard errors (adjusted by Wooldridge 1991, Procedure 2.1) are in parentheses below coefficients.

knowledge spillovers, some unmeasured linkages, or both. Experience and use of recombinant DNA technology are again significantly positive, and the effect of being an entrant is significantly negative (as in Table V but not VI). Unlike the case for patents, membership in a keiretsu presidents' club is significantly positive, suggesting that these firms may be more successful at developing products despite relatively fewer patents.

Table VIII reports the results for counts of only human therapeutic and vaccine biotech products in development as of 1990. For these higher value, higher tech products the results are very similar to those for all products except that the impact of linked stars is even stronger, there is no evidence of geographically localized knowledge spillovers or unmeasured linkages, and whether an entrant or incumbent and years of

Table VII
Poisson regressions for number of biotech products in development by Japanese firms as of 1990

Variables	Coefficients (standard errors)			
	model a	model b	model c	model d
Constant	0.1468* (0.0650)	0.1498* (0.0681)	0.1542* (0.0647)	0.1571* (0.0677)
Star articles up to 1989: Linked local	0.1640*** (0.0400)	0.1910*** (0.0418)	–	–
Linked external	0.2705*** (0.0341)	0.2802*** (0.0372)	–	–
Linked local & external	–	–	0.2145*** (0.0268)	0.2345*** (0.0272)
Affiliated	−0.4717*** (0.0643)	−0.5944*** (0.0691)	−0.4888*** (0.0697)	−0.6136*** (0.0716)
Untied local stars	0.0008*** (0.0002)	0.0008*** (0.0002)	0.0008*** (0.0002)	0.0008*** (0.0002)
Other firm characteristics: Keiretsu Presidents' Club membership	–	0.2550*** (0.0498)	–	0.2631*** (0.0486)
Categorical variable = 1 if new biotech firm; else 0	−0.2401*** (0.0681)	−0.2358*** (0.0687)	−0.2405*** (0.0679)	−0.2360*** (0.0686)
Years of firm experience in biotechnology in 1989	0.0428*** (0.0070)	0.0381*** (0.0076)	0.0411*** (0.0070)	0.0365*** (0.0074)
Categorical variable = 1 if firm uses rDNA; else 0	1.0850*** (0.0394)	1.0380*** (0.0401)	1.0920*** (0.0392)	1.0420*** (0.0400)
Log-likelihood Log-likelihood (coefs. = 0)	−833.95 −1072.37	−828.39 −1072.37	−835.21 −1072.37	−829.28 −1072.37
$\chi^2(1)$ for pooling local and external linked articles	–	–	2.51	1.78

N = 331
Notes: Probability z > x: * < .05, ** < .01, *** < .001
Standard errors (adjusted by Wooldridge 1991, Procedure 2.1) are in parentheses below coefficients.

experience are not significant. Taken together, the robust findings from Tables VII and VIII are that linked stars, use of recombinant DNA technology, and membership a keiretsu presidents' club increase research productivity measured by products in development while there is only little or no indication of any geographically localized knowledge spillovers.

Products on the market

Our final measures of research productivity are counts of biotech products on the market (both overall and limited only to human therapeutic and vaccine biotech products) as of 1990. This has both the advantage of not including products that may never make it to market and the disadvan-

Zucker and Darby

Table VIII
Poisson regressions for number of human therapeutic & vaccine biotech products in development by Japanese firms as of 1990

Variables	Coefficients (standard errors)			
	model a	model b	model c	model d
Constant	−1.4990***	−1.4980***	−1.4770***	−1.4760***
	(0.1204)	(0.1244)	(0.1201)	(0.1243)
Star articles up to 1989:				
Linked local	0.2917***	0.3098***	–	–
	(0.0262)	(0.0279)		
Linked external	0.4544***	0.4591***	–	–
	(0.0295)	(0.0322)		
Linked local & external	–	–	0.3692***	0.3834***
			(0.0239)	(0.0247)
Affiliated	−0.5883***	−0.6722***	−0.6072***	−0.7021***
	(0.0373)	(0.0554)	(0.0518)	(0.0640)
United local stars	0.0004	−0.0004	−0.0005	−0.0005
	(0.0003)	(0.0003)	(0.0003)	(0.0003)
Other firm characteristics:				
Keiretsu Presidents' Club membership	–	0.1798*	–	0.2040*
		(0.0844)		(0.0827)
Categorical variable = 1 if new biotech firm; else 0	−0.1148	−0.1156	−0.1176	−0.1183
	(0.1730)	(0.1799)	(0.1734)	(0.1810)
Years of firm experience in biotechnology in 1989	0.0109	0.0076	0.0056	0.0021
	(0.0100)	(0.0106)	(0.0099)	(0.0103)
Categorical variable = 1 if firm uses rDNA; else 0	2.0600***	2.0290***	2.0770***	2.0400***
	(0.0783)	(0.0803)	(0.0779)	(0.0802)
Log-likelihood	−475.31	−474.41	−476.93	−475.77
Log-likelihood (coefs. = 0)	−672.06	−672.06	−672.06	−672.06
$\chi^2(1)$ for pooling local and external linked articles	–	–	3.24	2.72

N = 331
Notes: Probabiliy z > x: * < .05, ** < .01, *** < .001
Standard errors (adjusted by Wooldridge 1991, Procedure 2.1) are in parentheses below coefficients.

tage of being more heavily weighted by lower value products which are faster to the market than pharmaceutical and other products involving more complex development and testing.

Table IX reports the results for all products on the market. Again, linked external star articles, years of experience, and use of recombinant DNA technology are significant and positive. In models a and b, local star links appear to have a significant negative effect, and affiliated stars (for the first time) a significant positive effect, but we see in models c and d that we cannot reject pooling local and external links in which case the overall effect of links is significantly positive and the effect of affiliated stars is insignificant. Thus it appears that results in models a and b reflect the

Table IX
Poisson regressions for number of biotech products on the market by Japanese firms as of 1990

Variables	Coefficients (standard errors)			
	model a	model b	model c	model d
Constant	−0.2727**	−0.2738**	−0.2622**	−0.2632**
	(0.0980)	(0.0979)	(0.0981)	(0.0981)
Star articles up to 1989:				
Linked local	−0.0982*	−0.1043*	–	–
	(0.0445)	(0.0451)		
Linked external	0.1746***	0.1727***	–	–
	(0.0349)	(0.0347)		
Linked local & external	–	–	0.0588*	0.0558*
			(0.0278)	(0.0280)
Affiliated	0.1807**	0.2079**	0.0624	0.0824
	(0.0649)	(0.0693)	(0.0677)	(0.0708)
United local stars	0.0004	0.0004	0.0004	0.0004
	(0.0003)	(0.0003)	(0.0003)	(0.0003)
Other firm characteristics:				
Keiretsu Presidents' Club membership	–	−0.0535	–	−0.0411
		(0.0583)		(0.0583)
Categorical variable = 1 if new biotech firm; else 0	−0.1474	−0.1484	−0.1477	−0.1485
	(0.1034)	(0.1035)	(0.1033)	(0.1035)
Years of firm experience in biotechnology in 1989	0.0583***	0.0592***	0.0566***	0.0573***
	(0.0080)	(0.0080)	(0.0081)	(0.0081)
Categorical variable = 1 if firm uses rDNA; else 0	0.5273***	0.5369***	0.5358***	0.5433***
	(0.0565)	(0.0590)	(0.0562)	(0.0589)
Log-likelihood	−644.15	−644.04	−645.91	−645.85
Log-likelihood (coefs. = 0)	−684.13	−684.13	−684.13	−684.13
$\chi^2(1)$ for pooling local and external linked articles	–	–	3.53	3.61

N = 331
Notes: Probability z > x: * < .05, ** < .01, *** < .001
Standard errors (adjusted by Wooldridge 1991, Procedure 2.1) are in parentheses below coefficients.

fact that the firm with affiliated stars reports relatively more (low value?) products on the market in comparison to other firms with local links. Note that neither membership in a keiretsu presidents' club nor entrant/incumbent status has a significant effect. So – as in Zucker, Darby, and Armstrong (1998) – the results are similar to the other measures of research success, but with generally less precise estimates and less explanatory power (as judged by the increase in the log-likelihood).

There were very few human therapeutics and vaccines on the market in Japan by 1990 and some of those represented licensing of products developed abroad, so the poisson regressions in Table X have comparatively little explanatory power and inferences may be fragile.[13] As usual, the use of recombinant DNA technology and years of experience generally had a significant effect on the number of these products on the market. Like the patent regressions, membership in a keiretsu presidents' club had a significant negative effect on the number of human drugs on the market. This was the only one of our six success measures for which entrant status has a

significantly positive effect. The influence of star scientists on this success measure is difficult to interpret.

The regressions in models a and b indicate that articles by local linked stars and untied local stars had a significant positive effect while external links were insignificantly negative. In models c

Table X

Poisson regressions for number of human therapeutic & vaccine biotech products on the market by Japanese firms as of 1990

Variables	Coefficients (standard errors)			
	model a	model b	model c	model d
Constant	−3.1100***	−3.1100***	−3.1180***	−3.1160***
	(0.2308)	(0.2314)	(0.2303	(0.2310)
Star articles up to 1989:				
Linked local	0.1359***	0.1113**	–	–
	(0.0332)	(0.0340)		
Linked external	−0.0381	−0.0534	–	–
	(0.0689)	(0.0702)		
Linked local & external	–	–	0.0554	0.0355
			(0.0373)	(0.0382)
Untied local stars	0.0033***	0.0032***	0.0032***	0.0032***
	(0.0005)	(0.0005)	(0.0005)	(0.0005)
Other firm characteristics:				
Keiretsu Presidents' Club membership	–	−0.2724**	–	−0.2783**
		(0.0897)		(0.0895)
Categorical variable = 1 if new biotech firm; else 0	0.4362*	0.4281*	0.4371*	0.4289*
	(0.2071)	(0.2038)	(0.2067)	(0.2034)
Years of firm experience in biotechnology in 1989	0.0323*	0.0366**	0.0340**	0.0382**
	(0.0129)	(0.0132)	(0.0128)	(0.0131)
Categorical variable = 1 if firm uses rDNA; else 0	1.5980***	1.6410***	1.5920***	1.6360***
	(0.1242)	(0.1262)	(0.1239)	(0.1260)
Log-likelihood	−204.79	−204.36	−204.96	−204.52
Log-likelihood (coefs. = 0)	−233.81	−233.81	−233.81	−233.81
$\chi^2(1)$ for pooling local and external linked articles	–	–	0.35	0.31

N = 330

Notes: Probability z > x: * < .05, ** < .01, *** < .001

Standard errors (adjusted by Wooldridge 1991, Procedure 2.1) are in parentheses below coefficients.

Affiliated scientists and the observation for the corresponding firm has been dropped from this analysis. The one observation that has affiliate scientists did not have any human therapeutic or human vaccine products on the market as of 1990. As a result, this coefficient on this variable would approach negative infinity to fit the poisson model.

and d, we cannot reject pooling local and external links but end up with a point value for total links which is no longer statistically significant (although an order of magnitude larger than the significant coefficient on untied articles). We suspect that, as with the other five measures of success, star links have a large positive effect on bringing human therapeutics and vaccines to market, but that we observed the process too early in this case to detect it reliably.

Taken together, the products on the market variables give ambiguous results. The overall definition is consistent with significant effects from linked stars and no geographically localized effects while the subset for human therapeutics and vaccines finds evidence of geographically localized effects and little or no statistically significant effects of linked stars.

Quantifying the effects of linked articles by star scientists

It is useful to calculate the predicted effects on firm success due to links to star scientists. Table XI does this for the regressions (model d) in Tables VI, VII, and IX which combine the local and external links and include the keiretsu presidents' club membership variable. The first column in the table gives the number of biotech

patents, products in development, and products on the market predicted by these regression for a firm with no links but otherwise average values of the other variables. The second and third columns give the corresponding predictions if the firm had 2 or 5 linked articles, respectively. (The predicted effect is nonlinear, increasing in the number of links.) The differences are substantial: An otherwise average firm with 2 linked articles could expect to have 77 percent more patents during 1986–1989, and, as of 1990, 60 percent more products in development, and 18 percent more products on the market. For 5 linked articles, the corresponding percentage increases are 317, 223, and 50. The estimated increase for products in development are on the same order of magnitude as Zucker, Darby, and Armstrong (1998) report for California biotech firms while those for products on the market are considerably less than estimated for California. This latter difference may well reflect the long period of product development prior to marketing and the substantial lead of California over Japan (and the rest of the world).

The fourth column of Table XI calculates the effect of linked stars another way. The actual number of biotech patents over 1986–1989 is estimated to be 34 percent higher than would have been the case with no linkages of star scien-

Table XI
Estimated effect of linked articles on measures of success in biotechnology

Measure of success	Number of linked articles[a]			Actual average ÷[b] 0-links value
	0	2	5	
Cumulative U.S. biotech patents granted to Japanese firms – 1986–1989 applications	0.16	0.29	0.68	1.34
Number of biotech products in development as of 1990	2.52	4.02	8.13	1.27
Number of biotech products on the market as of 1990	1.48	1.75	2.24	1.08

Notes: a. The values in the table are the predicted values from model d in Tables VI, VII, and IX assuming that the number of linked articles takes the indicated value and the other independent variables in the regression equal their sample average values.
b. These values are the ratio of the actual average value of the dependent variable in model d in Tables VI, VII, and IX to the predicted value if there were 0 links. They estimate the average increase in success over all Japanese firms due to the links to star scientists.

tists to firms. Similarly, these linkages are estimated to have increased Japan's products in development by 27 percent and on the market by 8
percent.

These numbers illustrate the central role of
linkages to star scientists in determining success
in commercial applications of biotechnology, both
from the point of view of the individual firm and
the country as a whole. They illustrate the very
real importance of reforms under consideration
and underway in Japan to try to increase funding
for academic basic research, focus it on the more
successful investigators, and break down the legal
and institutional barriers to scientists becoming
directly involved in commercialization of their
discoveries.

4. Firm ties and the scientific productivity of star scientists

One of the most surprising results of our examination of commercial ties of U.S. star scientists is
the strong positive correlation between the research productivity of the scientists and the extent of their involvement with firms. In Table XII,
we report comparable measures of Japanese and
American stars' average annual citations to ge-
netic-sequence-discovery articles according to the
nature of their commercial ties. In the U.S., there
is a clear progression in which the average rate of
citation goes up with the extent of commercial
involvement, based on field work which suggests
that stars linked to local firms in the U.S. are
more involved (often as owners) than are stars
linked to firm outside the local region. In Japan,
the two affiliated stars have below average scientific productivity (as measured by citations) just as
their firm has less research success, but otherwise
a moderated version of the same pattern occurs
in Japan as in America.

The smaller differences between linked and
untied citation rates in Japan may be because
some Japanese stars who would be tied to firms in
the U.S. do not find it worth their while with an
incumbent firm and there are many fewer new
biotechnology firms or opportunities to start one's
own firm on the side. However, we also find that
there is a much weaker direct effect of working
with a firm on the scientists' productivity in Japan
than in the U.S. where much greater support for

Table XII
Japanese and American stars' average annual citations by commercial ties

Type of linkage to firm	Average lifetime citations[a]	
	Japanese stars	American stars
Affiliated[a]	77.2	323.0
Local[c]	149.2	159.3
External[d]	131.2	109.4
Untied[e]	105.8	72.2
All stars	118.0	104.4

Notes: A few stars who published in both countries are
counted as both Japanese and American stars.
a. The values are the total number of citations in the *Science
Citation Index* for the 3 years 1982, 1987, 1992 for all genetic-
sequence discovery articles (up to April 1990) in *GenBank* (7)
authored or coauthored by each of the stars in the cell divided
by 3 (years) times the number of stars in the cell.
b. All stars ever publishing a genetic-sequence discovery article and listing an affiliation with a Japanese or American
biotechnology firm, respectively.
c. Any other star ever coauthoring with scientists from a
biotechnology firm in the same region (defined in Table II for
Japan, functional economic areas as defined by the Bureau of
Economic Analysis for the U.S.)
d. Any other star ever coauthoring with scientists from a
biotechnology firm not located in the same region (including
foreign firms).
e. All remaining stars who ever published in Japan or the U.S.,
respectively.

the scientist's work can be extracted from firms
(or from outside investors in one's own firm): In
Japan, the number of articles per year published
by both locally and externally linked stars is significantly higher than untied stars during their
period of linkage (but not before or after). However, unlike the U.S. (see Zucker and Darby,
1997b), we were unable to find any significant
effect on the rate of citations per article to articles written by Japanese stars before, during, or
after firm linkage.

Overall, our examination of the effects of firm
ties on Japanese stars' scientific productivity indicates that it is in the same direction but considerably weaker than in the United States. This is
consistent with the more restricted bargaining
power of Japanese star scientists who cannot
readily access capital markets to start a firm or
even obtain large personal payments or research

grants from incumbent firms with which they collaborate. As a result, the firms obtain a larger share of the perhaps smaller total payoff to star scientist-firm collaborations.

5. Conclusions

Differences in institutional arrangements, laws, and regulations lead to differences in the physical location where academic scientists typically collaborate with firm scientists in Japan and the United States. In Japan, the collaboration typically involves the firm sending one of their best scientists to work in the academic scientist's university laboratory, both learning his or her techniques and serving as liaison to other firm scientists. In the United States, it is more usual for the academic scientist to work at the bench level with firm scientists in the firm's own facilities. This means that there is little difference in the productivity of the process of embodied technology transfer in Japan according to whether the firm is located locally or elsewhere; in the U.S. where the star academic scientists physically travel to the firm, there is a productivity advantage to local collaborations.

These differences are reflected in our analysis of Japanese data. Not only are star scientists' collaborations much less likely to occur locally (compared to the U.S.), links with nonlocal firms are as productive if not more so than local links. External links will appear more productive *ex post* if they are more costly to the firm (travel and relocation costs for employees) and so require a higher *ex ante* or expected productivity to justify their initiation. For the most part there is no positive impact on research productivity of firms of local academic stars who are not linked to the firm, but statistically significant (although very small) impacts are found in some regressions suggesting the possibility of geographically localized knowledge spillovers and/or academic-star collaborations which are not detected by our co-publishing measures.

Our results do not show that there are no spillovers from academic – or indeed firm – research to research in industry. What they do indicate is that such spillovers as do occur appear to be general in nature, equally effecting all firms in Japan (and possibly elsewhere), and not the

geographically localized knowledge spillovers emphasized by Jaffe (1989).

In considering the U.S. case, we find strong local economic development effects of great research universities not because the impact of local links is so much stronger than the effect of external links but because a disproportionate amount of academic star-firm links occur locally. In the Japanese case, these local development effects are virtually absent. Consider Table XIII which details the pattern of collaborations which we have detected between academic star scientists and firms. Tokyo, Nagoya (West-Central Honshu), and the Kansai (mostly Kyoto) contribute nearly equally 94 percent of all the linked articles. Tokyo firms account for some 76 percent of the collaborations, keeping all their local stars and attracting 65 percent of the remaining collaborations. Thus, the ability of large Tokyo firms to send scientists to university laboratories throughout the country has sharply reduced the local benefits that we would have anticipated (based on the U.S. results) from the very strong bio-science base in Nagoya and the Kansai. In Darby and Zucker (1996) we did show for Japan that more firms entered biotechnology near where and when star scientists were actively publishing, but that this effect on entry was significantly smaller than in the U.S. Combining a smaller impact on entry with a small to non-existent localized effect on firm success, there is less role for supporting externalities (not examined here) such as agglomeration effects and cross-industry spillovers for the regions around the science base.

We also found weaker positive effects in Japan on star scientists' scientific productivity during their period of involvement with firms: The large positive effects for affiliated scientists seen in the U.S. were nonexistent for the two affiliated Japanese scientists. For linked scientists there was a significant increase in the number of articles produced per year during their linkage to firms, but no increase in the number of citations per article. We attribute this to the fact that both scientific and pecuniary payoffs to collaboration are lower for Japanese stars who have much more restricted opportunities for exploiting their knowledge commercially than do American academic stars.

Our prior work has shown that for the biotechnology revolution – and, we believe, other scien-

54   *Zucker and Darby*

Table XIII
Regional pattern of articles authored by academic stars and firm scientists Japan, 1975–1989

Region of firm	Percentage of linked articles by regional location of star								
	Northern Honshu	Tokyo area	West-Cen. Honshu	Kansai area	Western Honshu	Shikoku	Kyushu & Nansei S.I.	Other[a]	Total
Northern Honshu	<u>0</u>	0	0	0	0	0	0	0	0
Tokyo area	3	<u>32</u>	21	18	0	0	3	0	76
West-Cent. Honshu	0	<u>0</u>	<u>0</u>	0	0	0	0	0	0
Kansai area	0	0	6	<u>12</u>	0	0	0	0	18
Western Honshu	0	0	3	0	<u>0</u>	0	0	0	3
Shikoku	0	0	0	3	0	<u>0</u>	0	0	3
Kyushu & N.S.I.	0	0	0	0	0	0	<u>0</u>	0	0
Other[a]	0	0	0	0	0	0	0	<u>0</u>	0
Total	3	32	29	32	0	0	3	0	100

Local links are in the underlined cells on the diagonal; external links are off the diagonal.
[a] Other regions (Hokkaido and Tokyo Ring) neither had academic stars or firms involved in star-firm articles.

tific-breakthrough-driven technological discontinuities characterized by natural excludability –
there is initially great value to bench-science involvement in commercialization by the leading
scientists who embody the new discoveries. In the
U.S. context, this resulted in a distinct pattern of
localized effects in which the biotechnology industry arose and succeeded in large part based on
proximity to the star scientists. Japan's academic
structure leads to a distinctly different pattern, in
which access to top academic scientists is no less
important to predicting the research productivity
of firms entering biotechnology, but in which
geographically localized impacts are largely absent. The fact that the institutional differences
lead to such different patterns of economic impact is strong evidence in support of the view that
technology transfer in the case of major breakthroughs involves movement of extraordinarily
talented people responding to economic and scientific incentives.

Acknowledgement

This research has been supported by grants from
the University of California Systemwide Biotech-
nology Research and Education Program, the Al-
fred P. Sloan Foundation through the NBER
Research Program on Industrial Technology and
Productivity, the National Science Foundation
(SES 9012925), and the University of California's
Pacific Rim Research Program.

We are grateful to Mr. Shozo Hashimoto,
Dr. Yoshio Suzuki, Mr. Masayoshi Suzuki, Mr.
Takuma Takahashi, and their colleagues at the
Nomura Research Institute, Ltd., who arranged
most of the interviews for the Japanese fieldwork
and provided valuable comments and insights on
Japanese policies, institutions, and culture. We
also appreciate the very useful comments from
Jeff Armstrong, Akio Tagawa, Maximo Torero,
and Dr. Kazuo Ueda. Akio Tagawa conducted the
initial analysis, co-developed the Japanese firm
data set with Yui Suzuki and Benedikt Stefans-
son, and co-developed the patent data base with
Maximo Torero and Richard Powell. Richard
Mortimer conducted an extensive sensitivity analysis and calculated the Wooldridge corrections.
Gihong Yi was responsible for the analysis of
effects on firm ties on scientists' productivity. We
are also indebted to a remarkably talented team
of post-doctoral fellows Jeff Armstrong, Zhong
Deng, Julia Liebeskind, and Yusheng Peng and to
Alan Wang, who used his computer science
knowledge to make the basic science data base
useable. This paper is a part of the NBER's
research program in Productivity. Any opinions
expressed are those of the authors and not those
of the National Bureau of Economic Research.

Notes

1. The other basic technology is cell fusion (also termed
monoclonal antibodies, MABs, or hybridomas) in which lym-

phocytes are fused with myeloma cells to create rapidly prolif-erating antibody-producing cells (see Sindelar 1992 and 1993 for more detail).

2. These 327 stars were only 3/4 of one percent of the authors in GenBank but accounted for 17.3 percent of the published articles, almost 22 times as many articles as the average scientist. The Genbank data set, methods of identify-ing stars, and productivity of the stars are discussed in more detail in the Data Appendix included in Zucker, Darby, and Brewer (1994) and in Zucker and Darby (1996).

3. The Science Citation Index lists up to six of the affilia-tions listed on the paper but only links the corresponding author to a particular affiliation. Thus, only first- and/or corresponding-author affiliations are available in machine-readable sources and bioscience papers frequently list the head of the lab last. As might be expected, our stars, excluding sole authored articles, were last authors on over 69 percent of the articles, where GenBank articles have on average about 4.8 authors per article.

4. Comparing different scientific breakthroughs to deter-mine the initial starting size of the discoverers, the degree to which learning by doing is involved (coauthoring with "old" scientists as the predominant mode of entry), and the relative rates of "diffusion" is an important next step. For example, a much less tacit process appears to operate in the case of high-temperature superconductors where the know-how was widespread prior to the breakthrough experiment that demon-strated that ceramics incorporating rare earths can work as superconductors at economically interesting temperatures.

5. Exceptions typically include the handful of scientists working in the same very narrow specialized area as the discovering scientists. At the extreme, when initial scarcity and tacitness are very high, transmission of the new knowledge will only be to the graduate students and postdocs working in the same lab as the discovering scientists.

6. Sole-authored articles account for only 6.5 percent of the authorships of new authors and 7.8 percent of the authorships of old authors over this period. Interestingly, new sole authors become more frequent later in the period as the value of the tacit knowledge declined as it became more widespread (see also, Zucker, Darby, Brewer, and Peng, 1996). To illustrate the declining scarcity of the tacit knowledge, note that there were only 11 new authors in GenBank for 1970, compared to 79 in 1975, 868 in 1980, 3,827 in 1985, 9,008 in 1990, and 12,624 in 1992.

7. In practice, overdispersion (possibly due to unobserved heterogeneity) is frequently observed in poisson regressions. Given the problems with resort to the negative binomial (A. Colin Cameron and Pravin K. Trivedi, 1990), Jeffrey M. Wooldridge (1991) developed a flexible and consistent method for correcting the poisson variance-covariance matrix esti-mates regardless of the underlying relationship between the mean and variance. We are indebted to Wooldridge and Greene for advice in implementing the procedure in LIMDEP.

8. We believe that the application dating approach is preferable although the results are very similar.

9. As we will see below, the incentives to get around these restrictions are very large. The key loopholes are that patent rights have *de facto* been given to the inventing professors,

and firms are permitted to supply substantial research re-sources to the professors by sending outstanding researchers employed by the firm as students in the professor's laboratory. Thus, the university does not acquire property rights when the collaboration takes place in university rather than firm labora-tories as is common with U.S. professors. Large cash payments (on the order of $200,000 per year) are also reported to be common and prosecution is rare. For details, see footnote 11 in the earlier version of this article (Zucker and Darby, 1998).

10. The comparisons are made for regressions which allow for an average two year lag between application and grant date: So, grant dates 1977–1991 were substituted for applica-tion dates 1975–1989 in Table V and grant dates 1988–1991 were substituted for application dates 1986–1989 in Table VI.

11. However, note below that membership in the Presidents' club significantly increases the number of products in develop-ment.

12. However, this coefficient is significantly positive and not significantly different from that for external linked star arti-cles in the regressions for products in development discussed below.

13. As noted in the table, a peculiarity of the poisson estima-tor is that a dummy variable for an observation with a 0 value for the dependent variable is not appropriate because log 0 is undefined (or negative infinity). Since affiliated star articles is essentially a dummy variable for a single firm that had none of these products in 1990, that variable was dropped from Table X.

References

Branstetter, L. and M. Sakakibara, 1998, 'Japanese Research Consortia: A Microeconomic Analysis of Industrial Policy', *Journal of Industrial Economics* **46** (2), 207–233.

Cameron, A.C., and P.K. Trivedi, 1990, 'Regression-Based Tests for Overdispersion in the Poisson Model', *Journal of Econometrics* **46**, 347–364.

Cohen, S., A. Chang, H. Boyer, and R. Helling, 1973, 'Con-struction of Biologically Functional Bacterial Plasmids *in vitro*', *Proceedings of the National Academy of Sciences* **70** (11), 3240–3244.

Darby, M.R. and L.G. Zucker, 1996, 'Star Scientists, Institu-tions, and the Entry of Japanese Biotechnology Enter-prises', National Bureau of Economic Research Working Paper No. 5795.

GenBank, 1990, Release 65.0, machine readable data base, Palo Alto, CA: IntelliGentics, Inc.

GenBank, 1994, Release 81.0, machine readable data base, Bethesda, MD: National Center for Biotechnology Infor-mation.

Griliches, Z., 1990, 'Patent Statistics as Economic Indicators: A Survey', *Journal of Economic Literature* **28**, 1661–1707.

Hausman, J., B.H. Hall, and Z. Griliches, 1984, 'Econometric Models for Count Data with an Application to the Patents-R&D Relationship', *Econometrica* 909–938.

Jaffe, A.B., 1986, 'Technological Opportunity and Spillovers of R&D; Evidence from Firms' Patents, Profits, and Market Value', *The American Economic Review* **76** (5), 984–1001.

Jaffe, A.B., 1989, 'Real Effects of Academic Research', *American Economic Review* **79** (5), 957–970.

Klevorick, A.K., R.C. Levin, R.R. Nelson, and S.G. Winter, 1995, 'On the Sources and Significance of Interindustry Differences in Technological Opportunities', *Research Policy* **24** (2), 185–205.

Nikkei Biotechnology, 1990, *Biotechnology Guide Japan, 1990–1991*, Japan-America Management, Ltd., trans., New York, NY: Stockton Press. [Translated from the Section on Japanese Companies in *'89 Sekai no Baio Kigyo 800sha* (The World's 800 Bioindustry Companies.)]

Nikkei Biotechnology, 1994, *94/95 sekai no baio kigyo 2000-sha* ['94/'95 World's 2000 Bioindustry Corporations], Tokyo, Japan: Nikkei Business Publications.

North Carolina Biotechnology Center, 1992, *North Carolina Biotechnology Center Japanese Companies Database*, machine readable data base, Research Triangle Park, NC: North Carolina Biotechnology Center.

Sindelar, R.D., 1992, 'Overview/Preview of Current and Future Recombinant DNA-Produced Pharmaceuticals', *Drug Topics*, Supplement, pp. 3–16.

Sindelar, R.D., 1993, 'The Pharmacy of the Future', *Drug Topics* **137** (9), 66–84.

U.S. Department of Commerce, Patent and Trademark Office, 1993, *Patent Technology Set: Genetic Engineering*, CD-ROM, machine readable data base, Washington, DC: U.S. Department of Commerce, Office of Information Systems.

Weinstein, D.E. and Y. Yafeh, 1995, 'Japan's Corporate Groups: Collusive or Competitive? An Empirical Investigation of *Keiretsu* Behavior', *Journal of Industrial Economics* **43** (4), 359–376.

Wooldridge, J.M., 1991, 'On the Application of Robust, Regression-Based Diagnostics to Models of Conditional Means and Conditional Variances', *Journal of Econometrics* **47**, 5–46.

Zucker, L.G. and M.R. Darby, 1996, 'Star Scientists and Institutional Transformation: Patterns of Invention and Innovation in the Formation of the Biotechnology Industry', *Proceedings of the National Academy of Sciences* **93** (23), 12709–12716.

Zucker, L.G. and M.R. Darby, 1997 (1997b), 'Present at the Revolution: Transformation of Technical Identity for a Large Incumbent Pharmaceutical Firm after the Biotechnological Breakthrough', *Research Policy* **26** (4 & 5), 429–446.

Zucker, L.G. and M.R. Darby, 1997 (1997b), 'The Economists' Case for Biomedical Research', in C. Barfield and B. Smith (eds.), *The Future of Biomedical Research*, Washington, DC: American Enterprise Institute for Public Policy Research and The Brookings Institution (copublishers).

Zucker, L.G. and M. R. Darby, 1998, 'Capturing Technological Opportunity Via Japan's Star Scientists: Evidence from Japanese Firms' Biotech Patents and Products', National Bureau of Economic Research Working Paper No. 6360.

Zucker, L.G., M.R. Darby, and J. Armstrong, 1994, 'Intellectual Capital and the Firm: The Technology of Geographically Localized Knowledge Spillovers', National Bureau of Economic Research Working Paper No. 4946.

Zucker, L.G., M.R. Darby, and J. Armstrong, 1998, 'Geographically Localized Knowledge: Spillovers or Markets?', *Economic Inquiry* **36** (1), 65–86.

Zucker, L.G., M.R. Darby, and M.B. Brewer, 1994, 'Intellectual Capital and the Birth of U.S. Biotechnology Enterprises', National Bureau of Economic Research Working Paper No. 4653.

Zucker, L.G., M.R. Darby, and M.B. Brewer, 1998, 'Intellectual Human Capital and the Birth of U.S. Biotechnology Enterprises', *American Economic Review* **88** (1), 290–306.

Zucker, L.G., M.R. Darby, M.B. Brewer, and Y. Peng, 1996, 'Collaboration Structure and Information Dilemmas in Biotechnology: Organizational Boundaries as Trust Production', in R.M. Kramer and T.R. Tyler (eds.), *Trust in Organizations*, Thousand Oaks, CA: Sage, pp. 90–113.

Data appendix

The data set used here is either drawn directly from or designed to be comparable to that documented in Zucker, Darby, and Brewer (1994, 1998) and Zucker, Darby, and Armstrong (1994, 1998). For additional details, refer to those sources.

New biotechnology enterprises

The data set for Japanese firms began with a data set we had developed for the U.S. We started by licensing a machine-readable database (North Carolina Biotechnology Center, 1992). In line with the U.S. firm data set, we added firms based on listings found in *Bioscan*. Additional firms from *Biotechnology Guide Japan, 1990–91* were included based on a lengthy discussion with Mr. Mitsuru Miyata (Editor-in-Chief) and Ms. Ikuko Uchiyama (Staff Editor) of Nikkei Biotechnology. The discussion enabled us to distinguish those firms actually using the new technologies from those that were listed as a courtesy to subscribers hoping to improve their stock prices. The Nikkei Biotechnology (1994) directory was used to fill in missing data.

The vast majority of the Japanese firms had founding dates prior to their entry into biotechnology, and therefore were classified as incumbents. The remaining 8.2 percent of firms were classified as new biotechnology firms (also termed simply entrants). Apparent response bias led early adopters of biotechnology to report 1975 as the date of entry. We accepted 1975 as the earliest date of entry even though it is doubtful that entry occurred before 1976, given the lag observed in applying the key Cohen-Boyer discovery (Cohen, Chang, Boyer, and Helling, 1973) even in the U.S. In four cases, very early entrants gave dates of entry before 1975, apparently referring to earlier technologies; these were constrained to 1975. This gave us dates of entry for 239 firms. For another 92 firms, no entry dates were available in any of our data sources. Since there was valuable product and patent data associated with these firms, we estimated the entry date of these firms by randomly drawing entry dates from the same distribution as recorded for firms in their prefecture with known entry dates.

Measures of firm performance

Our attempt to categorize firm performance began with products in development and products on the market. To be consistent with the categories we used for the United States, *Bioscan* was used as a starting point. However, consistent data for Japanese firms were not available from this source, so the same categories were carefully applied by Yui Suzuki to the *Nikkei Biotechnology* (1990) directory. From these categories we have shown results from four important areas: Total products in development, products in development in human therapeutics and vaccines, total products on the market, and products on the market in human therapeutics and vaccines.

In the analyses we use a control variable that specifies whether or not the firm reported using the recombinant-DNA technology that is most closely related to the star scientist measure. This portion of the control variable comes from self-reporting as found in our database from the North Carolina Biotechnology Center (1992). However, Yui Suzuki found upon searching the Nikkei Biotechnology directory that many of the firms which did not report to be using the recombinant DNA technology clearly were doing so, and this information was used to supplement the variable.

Information on the number of patents the Japanese firms in our data set had received in the United States were obtained from a CD-ROM data base purchased from the U.S. Department of Commerce Patent and Trademark Office (1993). The patents all came from the Patent Technology Set for Genetic Engineering, Class 935 and Class 435 (subclass 172.3 only). The data contained the dates the patents were granted and the dates for which these successful patents had been applied. In our analyses reported here we use the application date for these patents eventually granted, as this date is much more closely related to the star scientist measures. We use the patent application dates from 1975–1989 for these patents.

Defining stars and their firm affiliation or linkage

Previously, Zucker, Darby, and Brewer (1994) have demonstrated the key role in determining where and when firms are found by intellectual capital, namely by observing where and when "star" scientists are actively publishing. Through *Genbank* (1990), 337 leading "star" researchers were found worldwide on the basis of the number of genetic sequence discoveries and articles up to 1990 for which they were authors. These 337 stars were listed as authors on 4,061 distinct articles in major journals, and these were hand collected and used to identify and locate institutional affiliations for these scientists at the time of these publications. Hand collecting and coding was necessary because databases with this information often failed to identify the specific location for each of the authors. Convention in the field is that the senior author appears as the final author, and databases often specify only the location of the first or corresponding author. There were 6,082 non-star coauthors (or "collaborators") worldwide.

Following Zucker, Darby, and Amstrong (1994, 1998), we have analyzed Japanese firm performance using article level variables; that is, we counted the number of articles written by star scientists and divided them into two distinct categories for our analyses. We call an article "affiliated" to a particular Japanese firm if that firm is listed as the primary affiliation of a star author. Otherwise, they are termed "unaffiliated." Unaffiliated articles are then analyzed with respect to each Japanese firm as either linked to the firm if the star lists his or her primary affiliation as a university or research institute and one or more of the coauthors list their primary affiliations as the firm. Otherwise, we call the unaffiliated article "untied" to this firm (although it may be tied to another firm). Thus, linked stars are those at universities or research institutes who have specific ties to particular firms as identified by their publishing activities with the firm. For the analyses, each firm is geocoded as being located in one of the nine Japanese functional economic areas. In our analyses, we use the expression "local" to mean "in the same region as the firm."

We have five firm-specific article-weighted star variables: a count of the number of articles written by stars working for the specific firm (which we call "affiliated"), the number of star-articles in the region not counted as affiliated but which are linked to the firm (which we call "linked local"), the number of star-articles outside of the region also not affiliated but nevertheless linked to the firm (which we call "linked external"), the total number of star-articles either locally linked or externally linked ("linked local & external"), and finally the number of regional star-articles which are neither affiliated with any firm nor linked to the particular firm (which we call "untied local").

Keiretsu president's club affiliation of Japanese firms

Japanese keiretsu are large corporate groupings of related firms. They are typified by cross-shareholding and financial relations with a central bank. Such industrial groupings are thought to be of central importance in understanding Japanese industrial organization. There are competing definitions for keiretsu; that is, there is no generally agreed definition or listing of which firms are members of which keiretsu. David Weinstein has generously provided us with the data set constructed for Weinstein and Yishay Yafeh (1995) which contains a member listing for four different definitions of keiretsu. For our analyses, we have chosen the narrowest definition, which is called the Big 6 President's Club, which only includes those Japanese firms in the inner circle of the Big 6 keiretsu firms whose CEOs belong to their group's President's Club. Fifty one of the 331 firms in our data set fall into this category.

[28]

To Patent or Not: Faculty Decisions and Institutional Success at Technology Transfer

Jason Owen-Smith[1]
Walter W. Powell[2]

ABSTRACT. We draw on qualitative data derived from field work on two university campuses to develop an explanation for widely disparate rates of new invention disclosure. We argue that faculty decisions to disclose are shaped by their perceptions of the benefits of patent protection. These incentives to disclose are magnified or minimized by the perceived costs of interacting with technology transfer offices and licensing professionals. Finally, faculty considerations of the costs and benefits of disclosure are colored by institutional environments that are supportive or oppositional to the simultaneous pursuit of academic and commercial endeavors.

JEL Classification: L33, M13, M14, O31, O32, and O34

1. Introduction

The last two decades have witnessed a sea-change in relationships between universities, industry, and the federal government. Beginning in the early 1980s, key federal policy changes enabled small businesses, public and nonprofit organizations, including universities, to hold title to intellectual property (IP) developed during the pursuit of federally sponsored research and development (R & D). Since then, research universities have developed increasingly close ties to the world of commerce. Through licensing and other forms of technology transfer, strategic alliances, and spin-off firms, universities have become a driving force in the development of high technology industries (Saxenian, 1994; Rosengrant and Lampe, 1992;

Powell, 1998) and regional economic development (Feldman and Florida, 1994).

Against this backdrop of broad change, institutional prestige for research universities is increasingly defined in terms of both academic and commercial science (Owen-Smith, forthcoming; Powell and Owen-Smith, 1998). Nevertheless, both the process and the success rate for transferring high quality basic science into commercial development varies greatly across U.S. research universities. At some institutions, high profile basic science moves into the commercial realm with few missteps and delays, resulting in healthy revenue streams, close and productive relationships with industry, and broad intellectual property portfolios. In contrast, other campuses with strong basic research programs have floundered in their efforts to commercialize scientific discoveries.

We argue that these differential outcomes are steeped in distinctive institutional contexts that shape the transfer of knowledge from public sources to private firms. On most university campuses, technology transfer offices (TTOs) mediate the interface between university and industry, through procedures and work practices designed to enact university IP and technology transfer policies. In university environments a crucial first step for technology transfer is to convince faculty to disclose their potentially valuable innovations to TTOs.

Most TTOs lack the resources and competencies necessary to search a wide range of laboratories and research groups for commercially viable technologies. Thus, institutional success at patenting depends in part on faculty perceptions of the benefits of patenting, the quality of the TTO, and the institution as a collective enterprise. Faculty

[1] *Stanford University*
509 CERAS Bldg.
Stanford, CA 94305-3084
E-mail: jdos@stanford.edu
[2] *Stanford University*
509 CERAS Bldg.
Stanford, CA 94305-3084

Journal of Technology Transfer, 26, 99–114, 2001
© *2001 Kluwer Academic Publishers. Manufactured in The Netherlands.*

decisions to disclose, then, are shaped by the mixture of individual incentives, local organizational procedures, and institutional milieus. The meanings academic researchers attach to IP and their perceptions of the local patent process color decisions to disclose potentially valuable innovations within the context of a university's history, environment, capacity, and reputation. We draw on 68 semi-structured interviews on two campuses to begin unraveling the effects of distinctive institutional environments on university technology transfer success, focusing empirically on faculty accounts of their decisions to patent.

We begin by introducing the two university cases, pausing briefly to discuss the logic supporting their selection, sampling, and interview methods. We then focus on the institutions' distinct capacities for conducting science and engineering research. This comparison highlights the differential rates of commercial success on the two campuses and examines several possible explanations for the divergence. We suggest that, regardless of important organizational and capacity differences, institutional environments that catalyze or inhibit academic patenting play a large role in explaining the varied outcomes. We then turn to a discussion of faculty perceptions of the positive outcomes of patenting, demonstrating that on both campuses accounts vary significantly by research area. While the perceived benefits of patenting are very similar at both campuses, disclosure rates vary widely at the two schools. Faculty decisions to pursue patents on new technologies are based on perceived benefits of IP protection, but those perceptions appear to be shaped by (a) concerns about the local patenting process and TTO, (b) conceptions of the larger institutional environment in which academic patenting occurs, and (c) perceptions of the potential pecuniary returns to patenting which are themselves forged by institutional histories and environments.

2. Introducing the cases, EPU & BSU

Elite Private University (EPU) and Big State University (BSU) represent two extremes in the pursuit of patents and patent revenue. EPU combines first rank academic science with a highly

successful technology transfer and licensing operation. In contrast, BSU has been less able to transform its high quality basic science portfolio, which excels in the areas of optics, atmospheric science, and cancer research, into commercial success. Table I presents a detailed comparison of EPU and BSU in terms of institutional characteristics, technology transfer infrastructure, R&D capacity, scientific reputation, and commercial success.[1]

Note first the wide disparities between EPU and BSU on all measures of technology transfer activity. EPU faculty disclosed nearly 3 times more than BSU faculty in 1998, and filed more than 8 times the new patent applications. In terms of success, EPU inventors were issued five times the number of patents issued to BSU inventors and EPU received a whopping 128 times more (gross) royalty income. The picture is clearly one of widely disparate commercial outcomes. The first step in empirically examining the sources of these disparities is to explain the gap in faculty propensity to disclose new technologies.

Table I also indicates that EPU and BSU differ in terms of technology transfer capacity. EPU's Technology Licensing Office (TLO) is nearly 20 years older and more than nine times larger than BSU's Technology Transfer Office (TTO). The institutions also differ on measures of academic prestige. EPU ranks higher than BSU on three measures of scientific reputation: National Research Council faculty quality ranking (maximum = 5), a standardized measure of publication impact, and the percentage of faculty holding prestigious (and peer reviewed) NIH or NSF grants.

But despite the wide gulf between the institutions on these measures of reputation, technology transfer capacity and accomplishment, the campuses are rather similar in terms of aggregate research capacity. EPU and BSU are within one standard deviation[2] in terms of number of active researchers, total R&D expenditures, and publication volume. Put differently, relative to Research One universities, these two schools have very similar numbers of science and engineering researchers,[3] spend approximately the same amount of money on R&D, and publish a similar number of science and engineering journal articles. While the institutions differ on several dimensions, both are conducting approximately the same volume of science and engineering research.

The aggregate comparisons highlighted in Table I suggest two explanations for the campuses' differential rates of commercial accomplishment. EPU has both more experience and capacity to pursue patents and license technologies and 'better' science on which to base that pursuit than does BSU. Consider the disaggre-

gated measures of research capacity presented in Table I. These numbers indicate important differences in capacity concentration across the campuses. There are significant differences in the location of EPU and BSU's respective research competencies. While both institutions are accomplished in terms of overall capacity and quality, EPU's capabilities in the key areas of life sciences and engineering are noticeably more developed

Table I
Case comparisons: EPU v. BSU

	EPU	BSU
Institutional characteristics		
Institutional control	Private	Public
Land grant?	No	Yes
Medical school?	Yes	Yes
Agricultural school?	No	Yes
Total enrollment (1998)	15,000	35,000
S & E grad enrollment (1998)	4,600	3,200
S & E post-docs (1998)	1,100	500
Faculty size (1996)	850	1,350
Endowment assets (1996)	> $3 Billion	< $100 Million
# Research doctorate programs (1993)	> 40	< 30
Research capacity		
Total researchers (1998)	6,540	5,040
Total R & D expenditures in thousands (1998)	410,309	302,328
Total articles published (1998)	3,795	2,426
Life science researchers (1998)	1,545	1,523
Life science R & D expenditures (1998)	155,050	75,275
Life science articles published (1998)	807	475
Physical science researchers (1998)	429	587
Physical science R & D expenditures (1998)	58,555	71,248
Physical science articles published (1998)	629	576
Engineering researchers (1998)	2,629	732
Engineering R & D expenditures (1998)	116,364	42,394
Engineering articles published (1998)	741	431
Tech transfer capacity		
Formal TTO?	Yes	Yes
Patent management firm?	No	Yes
Foundation/corporation?	No	No
Licensing FTEs (1998)	18	2.5
Support FTEs (1998)	5.5	4.5
Program founded	1970	1988
Tech transfer measures		
# Disclosures (1998)	247	90
# New applications (1998)	130	16
Issued patents (1998)	86	17
Issued patents (1976–1998)	889	72
New licenses/options executed (1998)	118	32
Licenses yeilding income (1998)	299	45
Gross licensing income (1998)	61,245	477
# Start-ups formed (1998)	9	3
# Licenses with equity (1998)	6	0

than BSU's. Across the academic universe, engineering and biomedical research are the two main drivers of patenting (Owen-Smith, 2000).

Consider, for instance, the disparities apparent across engineering faculty on the two campuses. EPU has three times more active engineering researchers, spends nearly 3 times more on engineering R&D, and produces nearly double the engineering publications that BSU does. A similar pattern obtains across most of the key research areas highlighted in Table I. The same holds true for academic prestige as measured by NRC quality rankings, publication impact, and rates of success in federal grant competitions. Table I tells us that EPU's particular constellation of disciplinary strengths in science and engineering is highly suited to a program of aggressive commercialization. In contrast, at BSU the most prestigious researchers cluster primarily in such areas as astronomy, atmospheric science, archaeology, and management information systems,[4] which are less likely to develop patentable innovations. Thus, even aggressive approaches to patenting by the university may meet with more limited success.

Table I suggests a set of institutional explanations for the divergence in disclosure rates. The TLO at EPU has both the experience and resources to devote more thoughtful effort to searching for new inventors and they are likely to be more successful than BSU has. EPU has more researchers and more resources dedicated to research in areas likely to produce inventions than does BSU and a greater volume of research results in more patentable discoveries. In addition to dedicating more resources to research in key areas, the quality of research conducted at EPU is considered higher than that conducted at BSU, and 'better' science is more likely to result in patentable discoveries. We consider each of these explanations (which we dub the patent capacity, research capacity, and research quality explanations respectively) in turn, arguing that while these differences *are* important, they do not entirely account for the huge gap in disclosure rates across the campuses.

Patent capacity

The TLO at EPU is better funded and staffed than BSU's TTO, but interviews in both offices

suggest that neither dedicates much time and resources to pursuing new disclosures. In both offices, licensing professionals primarily evaluate unsolicited submissions. In rare cases, licensing professionals (LPs) on each campus report that 'word of mouth' referrals led to the discovery of a new faculty inventor, as in these comments by two staff members in the TLO.

> We do not actively seek out disclosures because we do not really need to. Now, having said that, you form certain networks. For instance, I got a call about a year ago from one of my established inventors who I have good rapport with. He said, you should go out and talk to this person, he is a new faculty person from Harvard and he is doing some interesting things. So I went over and talked to him. I introduced myself and learned about some of his research results and then I suggested to him that he might wish to fill out an invention disclosure on them. I am not sure, had I not gone over and chatted with him, whether he would have thought to do that. *Physical Sciences LP, EPU*

> We really have not had to do that [actively solicit] because most of the people know that we are here. The active inventors know that we are here and if they do not know we are here then one of their colleagues does. A lot of times their colleagues will say hey you need to contact the TLO or they will call us with a referral. *Life Sciences LP, EPU*

Notice that neither comment suggests returns to direct searches for new disclosures. Rather, the comments highlight the importance of internal network contacts, office visibility, and campus-wide reputation in determining disclosure rates.

Licensing staff do not actively search for new disclosures for several reasons. Both the TLO and TTO's resources are already strained by managing active IP licenses and evaluating unsolicited invention disclosures. The death of a physical sciences staff member in the TTO at BSU left a single full time professional responsible for evaluating *all* new disclosures. These circumstances kept most physical sciences disclosures from being considered for nearly a year. While the TLO's workload is not as overwhelming, staff there report caseloads ranging from 60 to about 400 active "dockets." No one in either office spends their scarce time searching for extra disclosures under these conditions.

In addition to resource constraints, most licensing professionals lack the expertise necessary to identify potentially patentable technologies across the wide range of disciplines represented by university inventors. Only one staff member in the TLO is Ph.D. trained in science or engineering. While every licensing professional at BSU is Ph.D. trained in a science or engineering field the small staff mitigates against active solicitation of disclosures. Even though individual licensing professionals at BSU have more technical and professional expertise than the average staff member in the TLO, scarce time and resources mitigate against turning this expertise to active solicitation of disclosures.

The TTO's acting director at BSU holds a Ph.D. in chemistry and comes to the office from a background in industrial research and university licensing. He notes that while it might be possible to 'solicit' new inventions, time and staffing constraints at the university mitigate against such searches.

> With all the time in the world I could walk up to the chemistry building and walk up and down the halls and say hey what are you doing. You know, if we had all the time in the world that would be worth doing. I do stimulate a large number of inventions because I sit down and work with people regularly in one area and you are chatting and you hear something and say oh gee, that sounds like it's really a new invention, have you disclosed? So I have solicited in that sense, in the sense of discussion with people. But the people that I discuss with are typically those that have already disclosed, and these may be new inventions by the same people rather than going around knocking on doors and talking to new people. Although I have occasionally done that, it is lower on the priority list so I have not done it often.

These comments explicitly emphasize time and staffing constraints while implicitly suggesting the difficulties inherent in searching for technologies outside of the discipline in which one is trained. This LP would feel confident walking up and down the halls of the chemistry building because of his training and research background but, in addition to his duties as acting director, he is responsible for evaluating and marketing all life sciences disclosures on campus. So he must work in many fields outside his own expertise, which further mitigates against active search efforts.

Increased technology transfer capacity in the form of experience and staff would certainly assist in the evaluation and marketing of new technologies. Even though there is some evidence of re-

turns to scale in licensing revenue (Siegel, Waldman and Link, 1999), a similar relationship does not appear to hold for faculty disclosures. At EPU and BSU more staff do not result directly in more disclosures because neither the TLO nor the TTO devotes time and effort to active solicitation of disclosures. Instead of seeing direct returns to scale in terms of disclosures, we expect that increased staff and experience will yield indirect returns by coordinating the patent process and raising the positive visibility of patenting on campus. Increased technology transfer capacity at EPU, then, does not provide a complete explanation of the disclosure gap, absent a consideration of faculty's reasons for disclosing.

Research capacity

EPU's research capacity is concentrated in areas likely to yield patentable findings. Consequently EPU faculty should discover more potentially valuable technologies than do their colleagues at BSU. Nevertheless, at issue is not the number of potentially valuable discoveries but the number of *disclosures* of such discoveries to university offices responsible for patenting and licensing. We contend that the step from invention to disclosure is a problematic one for faculty and that decisions about whether to pursue patent protection are colored by the incentives and costs associated with patenting in specific university contexts. Under this conception, research capacity is a necessary but not sufficient condition for disclosures. While EPU's higher disclosure rate may result from its greater capability, the relationship should, as with the link between patent capacity and disclosures, be mediated by faculty perceptions of the costs and benefits of patenting.

Research quality

A final explanation suggested by Table I – that the higher profile research conducted at EPU will pay off in more potentially patentable technologies and thus more disclosures than the lower profile research conducted at BSU – elides the distinction between discovery and disclosure in the same manner as the research capacity explanation. Nevertheless, differences in scientific prestige do account for some disparities in disclosure rates (Owen-Smith, 2000).

In the life sciences, high prestige research and patent productivity increasingly go hand in hand (Powell and Owen-Smith, 1998; Blumenthal *et al.*, 1996). Indeed, investigations of the role that 'star' scientists play in biotechnology innovation (Zucker, Darby and Brewer, 1998; Zucker and Darby, 1996; Audretsch and Stephan, 1996) suggest that formal and informal linkages between academic scientists and local firms promote such innovation. The configuration of EPU's high prestige scientists and engineers and their location in a thriving high technology region foster entrepreneurial activity. Moreover, local firms may seek out highly visible scientists and engineers.

By virtue of their physical location and higher prestige, EPU scientists are more likely to be contacted by firms and engaged in commercial research than their colleagues at BSU. Clearly this commercial involvement raises inventor awareness of the value of intellectual property. But does greater awareness lead EPU scientists to disclose inventions to their university? Recent examinations of university technology transfer (Siegel *et al.*, 2000) and our own findings suggest that dissatisfaction with university patent processes may lead faculty inventors to circumvent technology transfer offices by engaging in 'informal' technology transfer through consulting activities or by leaving the academy. The key step in successful tech transfer is creating an entrepreneurial culture among the faculty. Without it, enterprising faculty might well take their IP outside the university. The important step is getting faculty to disclose their inventions to the university and sharing the revenues with the campus at large.

If commercial involvement accompanies higher prestige science, then, in the absence of an institutional environment supportive of both commercial and basic science activities, high quality science may lead to fewer invention disclosures as scientists capitalize on greater contacts with firms to transfer technologies without the knowledge or involvement of their institutions. There are many such efforts to circumvent the university process on both campuses. Physical scientists and engineers at EPU commonly assign title to patents developed during consulting agreements to the firms who hired them. Software and new media projects often rely on copyright rather than patent

protection to escape revenue sharing with the university. Some computer programs are released with open source code, allowing faculty to spin-off service companies without assigning title to the university. Finally, graduate students interested in starting up firms occasionally file incomplete dissertations to maintain their sole ownership of IP developed during graduate school.

At BSU, informants among faculty and in the TTO report shirking on the part of faculty inventors who write incomplete or early stage disclosures in order to have inventions released by the university so they can be pursued independently. In order to facilitate independent pursuit of patent protection, a group of BSU life scientists has founded a small company whose primary purpose is to commercialize inventions released by the TTO. Here again, we contend that the relationship between scientific prestige and invention disclosures is mediated by the effects of local processes and campus environments on faculty decisions to disclose.

Despite the fact that BSU's scientific reputation does not rise to the level of EPU's, it is consistently one of the most prestigious and well funded public research universities and appears in the top quartile of *all* Research One (R1) institutions. Thus, we think it is accurate to argue that while EPU does "better" science than BSU, *both* institutions rank among the most prestigious and productive American universities. While we might expect BSU to trail EPU in commercializing research findings, we suspect that BSU should be accomplishing more than it has been. BSU lags far behind its public peer institutions in terms of patenting and licensing success, ranking in the bottom quartile of R1 institutions in terms of disclosures, patent volume, licenses, and royalty income.

Across R1 institutions commercial success and academic accomplishment are not consistently related (Owen-Smith, 2000). Consider three public universities; Iowa State, Michigan State, and the University of Florida. The former two rank among the top ten patenting universities in 1998, the latter ranks in the top fifteen (Owen-Smith, 2000). Two of these institutions (Florida and Michigan State) ranked among the top ten revenue earners in 1998 (Association of University Technology Managers, 1998). But all three institutions rank in the bottom quartile in terms of academic visibility as measured by citation impact (Owen-Smith, 2000).

The wide disparity in disclosure rates across the campuses is, in our view, not simply the direct result of capacity or prestige differences. Rather, the institutions' differential success at inducing faculty to disclose potentially valuable inventions depends upon the creation of an institutional environment that supports faculty perceptions of the benefits of patenting while minimizing conflicts between commercial and basic science activities. Thus, faculty propensity to disclose is shaped at three analytic levels. One, individual scientists' perceptions of the professional and personal benefits of IP protection generate incentives to disclose. Two, such incentives are magnified or weakened by the ease of the local patent process and inventors' perceptions of the competence and facility of technology transfer offices. Three, the technology transfer process and capacity on each campus is shaped by the unique histories and environments that characterize each institution.

The last two factors depend, in large part, on the work done in technology transfer offices. In our view, one reason that EPU has been able to capitalize on its elite endowment of capacity and talent while BSU has been less successful at transforming its high quality basic research portfolio has to do with the creation and maintenance of an institutional environment supportive of both commercial and academic science and enabling of multiple uses of IP.

We support our claims with data drawn from 68 semi-structured interviews with faculty, licensing professionals, and research administrators on the two campuses. Field work was conducted in Fall, 1999 and Spring, 2000. Twelve physical scientists, twelve life scientists and eleven licensing professionals were interviewed during this time period at EPU. At BSU, 33 interviews with fifteen life scientists, eleven physical scientists and seven LPs or attorneys were conducted. Interviews ranged from 45 minutes to nearly three hours in length and were guided by a protocol of 25 questions. Subject sampling was guided by compiling lists of the most prolific patentors on each campus from patent archives. We then turned to snowball sampling techniques to identify other

inventors and notable scientists who chose not to patent at each institution.

3. Why do faculty patent?

We turn to an extended discussion of academic inventors' reasons for patenting to establish two important findings relevant to the explanation of different disclosure rates at EPU and BSU. First, we demonstrate that the incentives that lead faculty to patent vary significantly across general research areas. We argue that this variance helps explain disclosure rates by suggesting that universities that create processes and environments conducive to multiple uses of IP will maximize disclosures by engaging a broad range of faculty. Second, we determine that faculty perceptions of patent benefits (incentives) do not vary across our cases. EPU and BSU, then, do not have different disclosure rates because faculty are responding to different incentives to disclose. Instead, we argue, similar perceptions of patent benefits are colored by widely disparate local processes and institutional environments resulting in different disclosure rates.

Inventors' responses to two interview questions ("Why do you patent your findings?" and "How do you decide which findings to patent?") reveal that faculty account for their decisions in terms of (1) perceptions of the personal and professional benefits of patenting, (2) perceptions of the time and resource costs of interacting with TTOs, and (3) their general opinions about the campus environment for technology transfer. Scientists' accounts of their decisions to disclose innovations and pursue patents varied across research areas. The director of EPU's TLO captured these differences succinctly when she said, "Physical scientists patent for freedom of action, life scientists patent for strategic advantage." Put differently, life science inventions have a larger potential to open new markets where gaining value from intellectual property will not be constrained by existing products or patents. In contrast, physical sciences inventions, for instance new techniques for magnetic resonance imaging, often enter crowded markets where established products and intellectual property hamper organizations' abilities to gain revenue from IP.

The upshot of this claim is that physical scientists, whose inventions are typically improvements on established processes or products, will use patents to develop relationships with firms and as chips to exchange for the use of other proprietary technology, access to equipment, or other opportunities. In keeping with this more relational approach, physical scientists should (1) expect less direct personal gain from patent royalties, (2) favor non-exclusive licensing arrangements, and (3) be less concerned with finding the "right" licensee, opting instead to open relationships with multiple corporate partners.

The inventions of life scientists commonly involve therapeutic compounds or medical devices. If they are seeking strategic advantage for these novel entities, then these faculty should view patents more as tangible properties to be protected and sold. Rather than using patents to establish relationships with multiple partners, then, these scientists will be concerned with finding the best partner to develop and market a drug or device. In keeping with this more proprietary approach to IP, life scientists should (1) expect personal gains from patent royalties, (2) favor exclusive licensing arrangements, and (3) be concerned with defending IP.

These general patterns hold true in faculty responses to our interview questions. Comments made by physical and life scientists highlight these general differences.

> Our goal is to transfer the technology to industry, it is to build relationships with companies, it is to educate students. That is what we are about. We are not about making money. The money is the tool with which you conduct relationships with the outside world. You need some value that you place on your negotiations so that you arrive at an optimum point. *Senior Physical Scientist, EPU*[5]

> I have to disclose when we think [an invention] might have value. We happen to work on a lot of things that have to do with behaviors and diseases. We do not want to take any chances that we might miss something. So, we just put a disclosure in. Most of them will not make any difference to tell you the truth, but if you miss the golden egg – you might only get a few in your life. Fortunately, we have a few golden eggs. The university could get multi-million dollars from [X technology] and it could get multi-million dollars from [Y technology] at some point in the future. *Senior Life Scientist, BSU.*

These comments underscore general differences between relational and proprietary approaches to

patenting. Note that both these inventors are concerned with outcomes of patent protection – leverage and relationship building in the former case, protection and income in the latter. Conceptions of the benefits of patent protection vary with research areas. These variations result in different motivations to disclose innovations and pursue patents.

Patenting outcomes vary by research area

Table II summarizes beliefs about patent outcomes highlighted by physical and life scientists' accounts of their decisions to disclose. The first column presents general types of outcomes mentioned by EPU and BSU faculty. Both life and physical scientists talked about the value patents have as protection, leverage, and sources of income. Both groups also discussed the intangible benefits of patenting. Interestingly, their accounts of what these outcomes meant varied significantly.

Consider, for instance, the first row of Table II that highlights physical and life scientists' understandings of patent protection in terms of limiting constraints on action and protecting academic freedom. Despite the apparent similarity of these concerns, researchers seem to mean very different things when using protection as a reason to disclose.

> You can go out and tell people things and sign an agreement, what's called a non-disclosure agreement, to try and protect yourself. In recent years, one of the stratagems has been to get ... what is called a provisional patent that gives you a year to try it out on the market.... Suppose I am doing some research and I want to go to your conference and talk about it. One doesn't want to be restricted by this darn patent business. It [a provisional patent] is not too expensive. *Senior Physical Scientist, EPU*

> It is complicated because one of the issues is that if EPU holds a patent that governs the use of a gene they are not going to enforce it in a way that interferes with academic research, whereas a private company might. So there is some incentive to disclose to EPU just to protect academic freedom ... It is certainly an issue in my mind that an incentive to patent is because if someone else were to file a patent on [a gene] that conflicts that could really impair your research or impair academic freedom ... I think that I would do just about everything possible to undermine the commercial companies who want to patent just about everything. *Senior Life Scientist, EPU*

Both of these comments imply that patent protection enables freedom of action but for the first

Table II
Physical and life scientist's perceptions of patent outcomes

Outcome	Physical	Life
Protection	limits restraints on communication	protects academic freedom from commercially held patents
	enables commercialization	enables commercialization/required for drug development
	limits actions of foreign competitors	keeps findings from being 'robbed'
		keeps faculty from being 'skinned' by firms
		keeps faculty from missing 'the golden egg' of a very valuable property
Leverage	enables requests for funds from deans, department chairs	helps convince firms to pay for development research 'beyond the NIH track'
	leads to consulting, sponsored research, and student jobs industry	enables faculty to locate venture capital funding
	aids in obtaining federal grants by leveraging 'cutting edge' equipment from firms	
Money	getting rich	getting rich
Intangibles	curiosity	serving the public good
	validation of research	fighting disease
	increased prestige	increased prestige
	helps forward 'basic science' thinking	helps forward 'basic science' thinking
Education	helps students get jobs	
	reading/writing patents and negotiating relationships is essential training	

scientist that freedom is public, involving the ability to go to conferences and present findings without being restricted by fear of losing potentially valuable property rights. Autonomy also extends to the freedom to market a finding to figure out if it is worth pursuing. In this case, patenting increases freedom by establishing IP protection for the faculty member.

Compare this with the second view. To this life scientist the protections afforded by patenting are not enabling of public presentations of work. Instead, his reasons for pursuing IP protection represent a form of constraint. By undermining the expansive agenda of a potentially aggressive commercial firm he removes their ability to control a key resource, information, and ensures his freedom to conduct research without external restraints. While both scientists express concerns with commercial constraints, the first wishes to maintain the potential value of his technology while trying it out on the market and advertising it at professional meetings. The second scientist

expresses no concern about the value of his technology; instead, he is interested in shielding the private environment of his lab from encroachment by commercial interests. In the end, two very different types of protection are achieved by the same mechanism.

Similar differences are apparent in faculty discussions of the leverage afforded by patents. Note that physical scientists believe patents provide leverage at multiple levels, within the university, in relationships with firms, and in federal grant competitions. Life scientists are more concerned with patents as a means to attract investments in their research from firms and venture capitalists. The life-scientists' image is less one of building a relationship than of capital infusion.

The acting director of the TTO at BSU summarizes incentives for physical scientists to patent in terms of the long run benefits of licensing relationships.

The main [incentive to disclose] is the one I mentioned, we share income with the faculty. That is the upside. The downside is that it is required. Faculty are state employees. Their inventions are state property and they are required as state employees to disclose. So that is the carrot and the stick. Plus the fact that licensing, in addition to personal income, can lead to grant and contract funding, and to sponsored research. Most licenses require further information for corporate development and I encourage the company to support faculty research and to continue working with faculty research teams. That is another reason to disclose.

Contrast this view of the benefits of patent based relationships with the more proprietary approach of a senior life scientist at EPU.

> One of the best ways to get leverage on industry is to have some property. Then you have something to sell, you have something to negotiate. I'm really a firm believer in that ... Because if you want to turn around and start a company or if we want to go to a company and say hey we need a million bucks to take our research to the next phase because it looks too applied to fly through a study section, or if we need a lot more money than an NIH study section would realistically look at for a grant, we would have very little to go on without a patent application or an issued patent. But if you go to the same pharmaceutical company or venture capitalist and say I have an issued patent, then things would look a lot different.

Just as was the case with protection, faculty accounts of the leverage afforded by IP vary widely depending on research area. Similar incentives to disclose patentable technologies are framed very differently by life and physical scientists, but these differences are common across at least two university campuses.

Where protection, leverage, and personal income represent tangible incentives to patent in the form of freedom, negotiating power, and money, a fourth category of patenting outcomes discussed by faculty is much more elusive. Both physical and life scientists highlight intangible personal benefits of patenting. Across research areas many faculty agree that there are status benefits to patenting. Both groups also note that the intellectual exercise of patenting a finding opens new realms of basic science investigation.

Positive relationships between typical academic activities and patenting also result from the view that patenting aids in the development of basic science research programs. A junior physical scientist at BSU emphasizes the scientific benefits of patenting:

> If I try to go into a new research area and try to make a broader scientific impact, I will ask myself some of the

questions I would ask when I evaluate an invention. It also helps in the process of analyzing some types of data. When you start thinking in terms of claims for patents you say I got that result, how can I broaden that claim's impact? So if you ask yourself these questions in terms of your research it gives you immediate new experiments that you need to perform because now you can say I have learned this in that context and that impacts other fields. Then you ask is this new and unexpected? If the answer is yes, we try to initiate experiments looking for principles, for new concepts. So that thinking actually has helped me be more creative in my research.

This comment suggests that the exercise of patenting can actually forward academic research agendas. While there is some disagreement about the relationship between patenting and academic prestige, many inventors reveal that they patent, in part, because they feel it increases their academic visibility and status by reaffirming the novelty and usefulness of their work. In so doing, patenting and commercial activities can reinforce traditional, status based, academic reward structures.

By connecting commercial and academic reward structures, patenting and its varied benefits can have a positive effect on the pursuit of traditional academic rewards. In other words, through protection, leverage, and intangible intellectual and status benefits, commercial activities can help scientists forward their academic accomplishments. Scientists are loathe to relinquish academic benefits for pecuniary returns (Stern, 1999), so mutually supportive linkages between commercial and academic activities should increase disclosure rates.

Faculty decisions to disclose are driven by their perceptions of the potential outcomes and benefits of patenting. In accounts of why they patent, life and physical science faculty highlight the same general types of benefits, but with respect to two important consequences – protection and leverage – their comments suggest divergent understandings and uses of patenting.

4. Perceptions of local policies color patent benefits

There is interesting variation in physical and life scientists' accounts of why they patent. But faculty perception of potential gains do not vary widely between EPU and BSU. Clearly, something other than perceptions of the benefits of IP protection is effecting faculty decisions to disclose on the two campuses. We argue that similar benefits of patent protection are differently colored by faculty beliefs about the costs of pursuing IP through their respective universities.

At EPU, where perceptions of the TLO and its staff are generally high and where a history of spectacular success contributes to an air of optimism, the benefits of patenting discussed above lead more faculty to disclose inventions. In contrast, at BSU, where perceptions of the TTO are generally low and there is no track record of success, faculty who are not already committed to pursuing IP may weigh the potential benefits of inventorship against the potential frustrations of the process and opt out by refusing to disclose new inventions.

A senior EPU life scientist who has patented a technology that is potentially very valuable captures this tradeoff in his discussion of the TLO:

> The people in my group and I, number one, do not want to get bogged down too much in the mechanics of filing the patent. Also, I would say that most of us, certainly including me, are uneasy about the idea of patenting ... Basically, I would just say that when I have the time on my hands and I feel that I can actually deal with the mechanics of it, and I feel like there is something that really has significant commercial potential, then I generally disclose it to the TLO.... If I thought that disclosing something would result in a month's work drafting a patent application, helping them with licensing or anything like that, I don't think they would ever hear a word from me.

Levels of faculty involvement with the patent process run the gamut on both campuses. Several inventors draft entire applications (two EPU faculty are themselves patent agents) while others prefer to avoid the process and cannot even identify the number of patents issued to them. But the comments of scientists who feel uneasy about the entire endeavor are key to understanding differential disclosure rates. On both campuses, the most commercially inclined faculty will pursue intellectual property regardless of perceptions of the process. As an EPU licensing associate noted, "If they [faculty] really want to be involved [in commercialization] they will disclose whatever the office does." With faculty who are aware of their findings' commercial potential but ambivalent about patenting, a less obtrusive and burdensome

process is essential to making the benefits of disclosure worth the perceived costs.

Differences in faculty perceptions of patent processes and infrastructures across the campuses provide one explanation for disparate disclosure rates. Cross-campus process differences cross-cut the physical/life sciences distinction that drives accounts of patent value. Note the striking differences in comments about the patenting process by EPU and BSU inventors.

> I have to say that the TLO does a pretty credible job of making it fairly easy, and they are very considerate. They will come out whenever you have a slot open to get the relevant information. They will do much of the paperwork and so forth for you. So I'm not sure it could get a whole lot easier. *Junior Life Scientist, EPU*

> In our group it is kind of a healthy atmosphere, you patent things and you never know up front how valuable they are going to be. You just don't know, but the process is pretty painless. *Junior Physical Scientist, EPU*

> I do not know whether it is cultural. I do know that when you submit something it is going to die. It will not leave here. So, how can you generate a revenue stream if it never leaves the campus? *Senior Physical Scientist, BSU*

> So the problems that I have had just involve getting that patent through the university... In fact, what happened is that the company [a start-up licensee] has to use its own law firm who then instructs the university's law firm about what to do. Quite honestly, it has been so bad that I probably would make an effort not to disclose things to the university unless I thought it was absolutely essential because I have little confidence in their ability to push it through. *Senior Life Scientist, BSU*

Widely disparate perceptions of the technology transfer process at BSU and EPU shape faculty understandings of the potential benefits of patenting. In cases like that of the scientist whose technology was licensed to his own successful start-up company, frustrations with BSU's patent process deter later disclosures even by commercially involved and successful faculty.

The universities' differential capacities and infrastructures for technology transfer play an important role in explaining disclosure rates. A large and experienced office at EPU enables flexible responses to faculty schedules, relatively quick turn-around, the development of long term relationships with inventors, and the creation of specialty teams who work to address the divergent concerns of life and physical scientists. In contrast, BSU's underfunded and understaffed office is blamed for long delays, inconvenient schedules, lax reporting, and minimal responsiveness to the concerns of academic inventors.

While process failures are partially responsible for BSU's relative lack of invention disclosures, it is important to note that both the difficulties and faculty responses to them do not arise in a vacuum. BSU is a public institution, it is responsible to a broader range of stakeholders than EPU, and is hampered by less flexible policies on intellectual property ownership and technology transfer (Siegel *et al.*, 1999). The problematic relationship between the TTO and faculty inventors at BSU points to larger challenges faced by public research universities. As was suggested by the TTO's acting director, faculty are regarded as State employees first, and entrepreneurs to be assisted by the TTO second. By the same token, faculty inventions are unequivocally regarded as State property.

A smaller staff of licensing professionals has less time to cultivate relationships with faculty. And their lack of success has meant increasing pressure from the State legislature and university governing body to justify their existence. As a result of the need to develop revenue earning properties, the attention of the staff is directed toward landing a blockbuster revenue generating patent.

At nearly all campuses, a small number of patents generate the bulk of the revenue stream (Association of University Technology Managers, 1998). For instance, at Florida State, which falls in the bottom quartile of R1 institutions in terms of patent volume, a blockbuster patent on the use of Taxol as a cancer therapeutic accounts for the lion's share of the revenues which place FSU among the top five royalty earning universities. Hence, BSU's focus on a big hit success is not unreasonable. Indeed, BSU's ex Vice President for Research opines that

> With a couple of exceptions, Columbia being one and MIT being another among the privates, among the publics, most people that make a lot money make it predominantly on one patent. They get lucky. OK, we have not gotten lucky yet... Now I mean in principle we could come up with some blockbuster thing in electronics or optics, but we have not. The pharmaceuticals are where the greatest opportunities and markets are and we have a lot of strength in that area.

This administrator's comments emphasize the importance of big hit patents for developing royalty streams, while explaining BSU's focus on developing a blockbuster in the life sciences.

By virtue of differences between life and physical science approaches to patenting, searching for a blockbuster means emphasizing life sciences innovations at the expense of physical sciences properties and their long term relationship generating benefits. This focus on landing a blockbuster and negotiating the most lucrative licensing deal minimizes the leverage benefits of patenting, alienates physical scientists who feel that their disclosures receive short shrift, and slows the daily operations of the patent process. Our point is that a sole focus on a big success hinders efforts at cultivating high quality researchers who have been hesitant to disclose and patent.

As a consequence of this focus, routine and timely processing of patent applications are delayed, deadlines are missed, and negotiations drag on. In short, a cycle is created where chasing a "bit-hit," under considerable legislative and administrative pressure, creates less productive relationships between faculty and LPs. In turn, the failure to pursue smaller scale "bread and butter" disclosures limits future chances for commercial success by encouraging faculty to bypass the TTO or avoid commercial activities altogether.

5. The environment for entrepreneurial science

We have shown that EPU and BSU faculty account for their decisions to patent by appeal to the outcomes and benefits of IP protection. Perceptions of patent outcomes vary across life and physical scientists. Moreover, variations in the ease and effectiveness of patent processes and technology transfer offices influence faculty thinking about the personal and professional benefits of patenting. The interaction of perceived benefits and potential frustrations, we contend, helps account for some of the differences in disclosure rates across the campuses. But both faculty perceptions and institutional capabilities combine to have broader consequences. Patenting and its outcomes are framed by faculty in terms of a larger institutional environment encompassing peer support of patenting, the effects of prior success, campus wide awareness of commercial activity, and the degree of overlap between commercial and academic science.

We draw on responses to the question: 'Why has (hasn't) EPU/BSU been (more) successful at commercialization?' to highlight the core features of an institutional environment which can be either supportive or oppositional to academic patenting. Against this broader background, faculty conceptions of the patent process and patent outcomes interact to create and maintain distinctive contexts for commercial science.

The catch-all phrase "entrepreneurial culture" is central in informants' explanations of EPU's commercial success. Discussions of a broad campus culture supportive of patenting are almost entirely lacking in interviews conducted at BSU. Entrepreneurial culture has been used to explain the success of high-technology regional economies and has been adopted by faculty and administrators to explain the success of highly commercial universities. A strong culture of patenting attracts faculty interested in pursuing commercial endeavors and socializes new university members into that pursuit. In this kind of environment, status becomes attached to commercial outcomes and technology transfer endeavors come to reinforce traditional academic status hierarchies, linking tangible and intangible patent benefits together with ongoing academic pursuits by blurring the boundaries between commercial and academic science.

The director of EPU's successful TLO describes the effects of an entrepreneurial culture on the university:

> I think there is an entrepreneurial culture out here. I guess my feeling is that since the eighties, since I have been at EPU, you can just see that culture among the faculty. Now it has moved down to the students. They say well I am smarter than so and so and so and so has made millions. I think we all know people who have done really well with equity. So I think that it is now inbred, the competition that is going on.... I think that in the region there is some kind of competition where if you have started a company or if something came of your invention there would be prestige associated with that... It is definitely a risk taking culture.

These comments capture all of the themes present in faculty discussions of a supportive entrepreneurial culture: (1) the effects of success; (2) publicity and widespread awareness of success;

(3) a supportive peer environment; and (4) status benefits ascribed to commercial accomplishments. In contrast, a senior physical scientist at BSU suggests that the very things that characterize EPU's entrepreneurial culture are missing at his institution.

> Commercial success would change the culture, making that part of our research plan. I suppose that to do that we would really have to change our way of thinking about the relative value of patenting to us. I think it would take something really dramatic in that area to change our thinking about the value of patenting...

In short, success begets success and a lack of achievement can be difficult to overcome even when high quality science is present. Indeed, evidence drawn from the BSU case suggests that pursuing some types of commercial success may actually hinder attempts at commercial development on other parts of the campus and may even slow the progress of more academic investigations. A history of success, on the other hand, leads to continued accomplishment by raising awareness, changing the way faculty think about patenting, and reinforcing the tangible and intangible benefits of IP protection. In our view, two key environmental factors will contribute to decisions to disclose despite frustrations with local processes: (1) widespread awareness of patenting procedures and benefits, and (2) publicity about success. EPU and BSU are separated on both these dimensions.

In order for faculty inventors to evaluate the benefits of patent protection or the costs of filing an application they must be aware of the activity. When faculty whose research is potentially valuable are unaware of procedures for or outcomes of IP protection, disclosures will naturally be lower than on campuses where a supportive institutional environment ensures a high level of commercial awareness among potential inventors. Consider the implications of two quotes from interviews with senior life scientists. The first comes from a BSU faculty member who has never disclosed an invention, even though his neurobiological work on a model species of moth that is a notorious crop pest has many potential applications.

> For people like me awareness of patenting is essentially zero. I probably know less about that than I do about Medieval European social history. Really, that happens to

be something that I am interested in. There is no information provided here, no advice urged upon us. If we wanted to do anything about this we would have to be very highly motivated to go out and seek the information, get the advice. We would have to, I think, be more sophisticated than most of us are – than I certainly am – to know when to do that or what sort of thing should trigger it.

Contrast these comments with the thoughts of an EPU faculty member whose patented technologies form the core of a new start-up firm. The BSU faculty member describes an environment where low commercial awareness require "sophistication" and "motivation" on the part of commercially interested faculty members. In contrast, this EPU life scientist paints a picture of an environment buzzing with commercial activity where choosing not to patent would be "rare indeed."

> I think this is an extraordinary place because you have so many people in the peer group or reference group who are running around inventing things, often with NIH money, and going to the technology licensing office asking them to put the capital up to file an invention disclosure and getting first rate patent lawyer to write the patent. Then, after it is done, the university owns the property but they take the strong and, I think, logical position that disembodied technology is relatively worthless. So they usually accede to the wishes of the inventor… I think that faculty members deciding not to patent would be rare indeed here at EPU. Even if you were so inclined it would be hard to ignore how fabulously successful some of your peers are. You know, from the kind of cars they park in the parking lot and your children might be interacting with their children and say hey dad, why does Joe have all of this while we're living in a thatched roof hut? It would just be astonishing not to notice.

These comments describe an institutional environment, shaped by EPU's history and location, supportive of commercial activity that extends beyond the campus into parking lots, local schools, and Little League fields. In such an environment the benefits of patenting will be magnified as commercial successes yield prestige among academic peers and enable inventors to leverage resources for their ongoing academic projects. Under these conditions, tangible and intangible incentives to disclose are magnified by low costs to patenting and an environment which links commercial endeavors with academic success. In contrast, on a campus like BSU where a high level of motivation and sophistication is required even to enter the commercial arena, and the costs

of patenting are high and unconnected to academic success, patent benefits will be minimized, resulting in fewer decisions to disclose.

6. Conclusions and implications

Our aim has been to use the differences in disclosure rates at BSU and EPU as a first step toward unraveling the effects of policy and context on universities' commercial accomplishments. Because technology transfer offices generally lack the resources and expertise necessary to search for potentially valuable innovations, the first step toward success for an institution interested in commercializing science is to convince often ambivalent faculty to disclose new technologies to the university.

Drawing on qualitative data from interviews with 68 faculty and licensing professionals on two Research One campuses, we suggest that faculty decide to patent because of their beliefs about the positive personal and professional outcomes of establishing IP protection. While all faculty mention similar incentives to patent, their understanding of two key benefits, protection and leverage, vary between life and physical sciences research areas. Where life scientists on these campuses focus more on the proprietary benefits of patents as commodities, physical scientists tend to emphasize the relational benefits of patents as markers for exchange.

Faculty beliefs about patent benefits vary by research area, but they do not vary across our university cases. Divergent perceptions of patent benefits cannot explain the different disclosure rates at EPU and BSU. Instead, we argue that the decision to disclose a new finding on these campuses depends upon conceptions of the patent benefits, framed by the costs of interacting with licensing professionals and technology transfer offices.

On each campus, the most commercially oriented faculty are likely to transfer technologies regardless of the costs involved. But inconvenient or frustrating interactions with TTOs may be enough to convince ambivalent inventors that the benefits of IP protection do not outweigh the costs. Process and infrastructure difficulties may recalibrate incentives to disclose. Thus, similarly perceived patenting outcomes are enacted in faculty decisions differently on the two campuses because of widely disparate beliefs about the efficacy of each university's technology transfer office.

Ambivalence about patenting may lead to failure to disclose when the costs of commercial engagement are high. Nevertheless, the distinctive institutional environment in which commercial activities are embedded will color faculty perceptions of both patent benefits and costs. We identify several themes in faculty descriptions of their campus environments: (1) widespread awareness of success and patent benefits, (2) supportive (or perhaps competitive) peer environments, and (3) the ascription of academic status to commercial success. These are three of the factors that contribute to an institutional environment conducive to the simultaneous pursuit of basic and commercial science at EPU. All three factors are absent at BSU where commercial and academic activities remain in opposition. As was the case with beliefs about patent costs, faculty perceptions of their institutional context color decisions about whether to disclose.

Where faculty are highly aware of other's successes, prestige is associated with commercial success. When academic and commercial rewards are linked, incentives to patent are enhanced. In this kind of setting, frustrations with the patent process may be overcome by the general positive reputation of the multiple benefits of IP protection and even ambivalent inventors may begin to disclose. In environments where commercial and academic success remain separate, faculty who wish to patent may be discouraged by their surrounding environment and high costs of pursuing protection through a technology transfer office that is hampered by the need to chase one type of commercial success. On campuses like these, we contend, only the most commercially oriented faculty will seek to disclose new findings and frustrations with the costs of disclosure may drive even those inventors to seek other means of transferring technology.

Acknowledgements

The authors wish to thank the researchers and licensing professionals who took the time to share

their experiences and opinions on university technology transfer. We also thank Janet Bercovitz, Don Siegel and the participants at the Purdue University conference on Organizational Issues in University Technology Transfer for their careful and helpful comments on early versions of this paper. This research was supported by a grant from the Association for Institutional Research (AIR # 99-129-0, Jason Owen-Smith P.I.), and by NSF grant # 9710729 (W.W. Powell and K.W. Koput, Co-PIs).

Notes

1. Some figures in Table I have been rounded to preserve the institutions' anonymity and protect informant confidentiality. In addition pseudonyms have been assigned to institutions and individuals are identified only by general research area and rank.
2. For Research One universities.
3. Faculty, research staff, post-docs, and graduate students.
4. BSU's exceptional optics program is a notable exception.
5. In the interests of maintaining informant confidentiality we classify individuals in terms of seniority (associate professor and above = senior) and general research area.

References

Association of University Technology Managers, Inc., 1998, *AUTM Licensing Survey, Fiscal Year*.

Audretsch, D.B. and P.E. Stephan, 1996, 'Company-Scientist Locational Links: The Case of Biotechnology', *American Economic Review* **86** (2), 641–652.

Blumenthal, D., E.G. Campbell, N. Causino, and K.S. Louis, 1996, 'Participation of life-science faculty in research relationships with industry', *New England Journal of Medicine* **335** (23), 1734–1739.

Feldman, M. and F. Richard, 1994, 'The Geographic Sources of Innovation: Technological Infrastructure and Product Innovation in the United States', *Annals of the Association of American Geographers* **84** (2), 210–229.

Nelson, R., 1993, *National innovation systems: a comparative analysis*, New York: Oxford University Press.

Owen-Smith, J., forthcoming, 'New Arenas for University Competition: Stratification in Academic Patenting', in Jennifer Croissant (ed.), *University Industry Research Relations*, New York: SUNY Press.

Owen-Smith, J., 2000, *Public Science, Private Science: The Causes and Consequences of Patenting by Research One Universities*. Ph.D. Dissertation, University of Arizona.

Powell, W.W. and J. Owen-Smith, 1998, 'Universities and the market for intellectual property in the life sciences', *Journal of Policy Analysis and Management* **17** (2), 253–277.

Powell, W.W., 1998, 'Learning from collaboration: Knowledge and networks in the biotechnology and pharmaceutical industries', *California Management Review* **40** (3), 228–263.

Saxenian, A., 1994, *Regional advantage: culture and competition in Silicon Valley and Route 128*, Cambridge, Mass.: Harvard University Press.

Siegel, D., D. Waldman, and A. Link, 1999, 'Assessing the Impact of Organizational Practices on the Productivity of University Technology Transfer Offices: an Exploratory Study', NBER Working paper W7256.

Siegel, D., D. Waldman, L. Atwater, and A. Link, 2000, 'Transferring Scientific Knowledge from Academicians to Practitioners: Qualitative Evidence from the Commercial-ization of University Technology Transfer Offices', unpublished manuscript.

Stern, S., 1999, 'Do Scientists Pay to be Scientists?' NBER Working paper #7410.

Zucker, L.G. and M.R. Darby, 1996, 'Star Scientists and Institutional Transformation: Patterns of Invention and Innovation in the Formation of the U.S. Biotechnology Industry', *Proceedings of the National Academy of Science* **93** (23), 709–716.

Zucker, L.G., M.R. Darby, and M.B. Brewer, 1998, 'Intellectual Human Capital and the Birth of U.S. Biotechnology Enterprises', *American Economic Review* **88** (1), 290–306.

[29]

Designing Efficient Institutions for
Science-Based Entrepreneurship:
Lesson from the US and Sweden

Magnus Henrekson[1]
Nathan Rosenberg[2]

ABSTRACT. The recent 'scientification' of commercial technology has brought the interface between universities and industry into sharp focus. In particular, academic entrepreneurship, i.e., the variety of ways in which academics take direct part in the commercialization of research, is widely discussed. The purpose of this paper is to suggest a framework for identifying the strategic individual decisions involved when educational choice is translated into science-based entrepreneurship. Identifying these decisions also allows us to hypothesize what incentive structures should be crucial. Our suggested framework is informally tested by an in-depth examination of the experiences of Sweden and the US. Despite large levels of R&D spending and comprehensive government support schemes, science-based entrepreneurship has been far less important in Sweden compared to the US. Our analysis points to weaknesses in the Swedish incentive structure in key respects: the rate of return to human capital investment, incentives to become an entrepreneur and to expand existing businesses, and insufficient incentives within the university system to adjust curricula and research budgets to outside demand. Several policy measures during the 1990s have reduced the weaknesses in the Swedish incentive structure. The current emergence of a more vibrant entrepreneurial culture in Sweden in some areas is consistent with these changes. Our analysis suggests that a policy aimed at encouraging science-based entrepreneurship should focus on strengthening individual incentives for human capital investment and entrepreneurial behavior both within universities and in business.

JEL Classification: J24, O31, O32, O57

[1] *Department of Economics*
Stockholm School of Economics
P. O. Box 6501
SE-113 83 Stockholm
Sweden
E-mail: Magnus.Henrekson@hhs.se
[2] *Department of Economics*
Stanford University
Stanford, CA 94305-6072
U.S.A.
E-mail: nate@leland.stanford.edu

1. Introduction

Nowadays, science-based entrepreneurship looms large in the public policy arena. This is quite natural given the recent 'scientification' of technology; in particular, the most rapidly growing and wealth-creating industries such as biotechnology, computers and telecommunications are progressively more science based. But why does such entrepreneurship flourish in some countries, especially the United States, while there seems to be so much less of it in other countries? The purpose of this paper is to attempt to identify some key institutional factors that are crucial determinants of science-based entrepreneurship. Particular attention will be paid to one important subset of science-based entrepreneurship, namely, academic entrepreneurship. This involves the variety of ways in which academics go beyond the production of potentially useful knowledge and take some sort of leadership role in ensuring successful commercialization.[1]

In the following section we outline a simple informal model of the strategic individual decisions involved when educational choice is translated into science-based entrepreneurship. Identifying these decisions also allows us to examine which incentive structures are likely to be crucial in promoting science-based entrepreneurship.

The rest of this paper constitutes an informal test of our proposed theory. This test consists of an in-depth comparison of science-based entrepreneurship and the relevant incentive structures in the US and Sweden. Section 3 presents a brief comparison of the performance of the Swedish and US economies with particular emphasis on the high-tech sector and new technology-based firms. As shown in Section 4, the two countries

Journal of Technology Transfer, 26, 207–231, 2001
© *2001 Kluwer Academic Publishers. Manufactured in The Netherlands.*

share a common organizational feature: the bulk of frontier research is done in teaching universities. In Section 5, we examine the government support schemes and other bridging arrangements between universities and industry in Sweden and the US. From this examination, it is clear that the relatively low level of science-based entrepreneurship in Sweden cannot be explained by the absence of government support. Sections 6–9 contain in-depth examinations of the relevant incentive structures in Sweden and the US. We identify four key areas in this respect: (1) human capital formation, incentives to (2) become an entrepreneur, (3) expand existing entrepreneurial ventures and (4) the incentives within the university system to adjust the lines of study and the allocation of research budgets to the demand in the private sector and to facilitate for faculty to bridge the gap between academia and the industrial sector. Section 10 contains a brief analysis of the recent entrepreneurial revival in some sectors of the Swedish economy, and whether this revival is consistent with our hypothesis. Section 11 concludes.

2. From educational choice to science-based entrepreneurship

In order to create a large scientific base that in turn gets translated into a great deal of science-based commercial activity a number of crucial steps are involved. The ones likely to be most important are outlined in Figure 1.

The first strategic choice facing an individual takes place in high school when the young individual decides whether to enter the labor market or

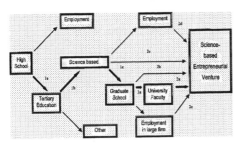

Figure 1. From educational choice to science-based entrepreneurship.

to proceed to the university.[2] Given that the individual enrolls at the university, there is a choice between science and technology-based disciplines and other areas, notably the social sciences. At the point of graduation the natural science graduate can again choose between employment and graduate studies with the aim of getting a Ph.D. After having received a Ph.D. there is yet another choice, this time between a university career and employment.

Keeping in mind that we focus on the emergence of science-based entrepreneurial ventures such ventures are highly dependent on academically trained and motivated individuals. When considering academic entrepreneurship, we think primarily about university faculty assuming an active entrepreneurial and ownership role in these ventures. However, focusing exclusively on this connection is not justified. In addition to university faculty, there are several other important sources for recruiting people to science-based entrepreneurship: From the pool of individuals with either a graduate or an undergraduate exam, and from individuals with that educational background working in other firms.

From Figure 1 it is evident that there are a number of important links that have to function efficiently in order to create an environment where science-based entrepreneurship flourishes. First, the incentives to invest in human capital at the university level (1a, 1b, 1c). Second, the incentives to become involved in science-based entrepreneurial ventures both for university faculty and for nonfaculty with a natural-science training (2a, 2b, 2c, 2d, 2e). Third, the incentives within the university system; to adjust the lines of study to demand in the private sector, to facilitate the transfer from academia to the entrepreneurial sector. This third factor can be expected to have complex repercussions throughout the entire decision tree depicted in Figure 1. Most directly, it will influence the propensity of faculty to get involved in entrepreneurial ventures (2a), but it will also affect students' educational choice (1b, 1c, 3a).

Below we will examine whether the incentives hypothesized to be important for science-based entrepreneurship can indeed be claimed to be of importance. We test our informal model by an in-depth examination of the impact of science-based entrepreneurship in Sweden and the US, but before we assess the pertinent incentive structures we briefly compare economic performance, as well as the input side, i.e., resources going into R&D and government resources spent on arrangements with the purpose of bridging the gap between academia and the commercial sector.

3. Economic performance

Both Sweden and the US emerged from World War II with strong economies, relative to almost all other industrialized countries. No doubt, the US was, in many respects, the technological leader, but by the late 1960s Sweden was not far behind. Given the relatively high income levels of the two countries at the time, both the catching-up effect and the tendency towards income convergence among countries[3] would lead us to expect a low Swedish growth rate relative to the OECD average in subsequent periods. Table I indeed shows that Sweden grew slowly relative to the OECD from 1970 to 1998. However, this is not so for the US. From 1970 up to 1998 the US growth rate was comparable to the OECD average, and if the comparison is limited to the period 1990–98, US performance was markedly superior to the OECD average.

Employment adjusted for population growth rose by approximately 27% in the US between 1970 and 1998, while it decreased by 8% in Sweden during the same period.[4] The share of high-tech output and employment is considerably higher in the US than in Sweden, averaging approximately 3 percentage points higher over the period 1970–1996. Although the high-tech share in Sweden did increase from 11% to 19% between 1990 and 1996, virtually all of this increase can be

attributed to one telecomms firm (Ericsson) and one pharmaceutical firm (Astra).[5]

The view that the increased high-tech production in Sweden is driven by a strong development in a few large firms is supported by complementary evidence showing a low growth rate among new technology-based firms (Utterback and Reitberger, 1982; Rickne and Jacobsson, 1996). Rickne and Jacobsson (1999) study all new technology-based firms founded between 1975 and 1993 (and still in existence in 1993) in Sweden. The employees of the new technology-based firms represented 0.9% of manufacturing employment in the selected industries and 6.2% of employment in manufacturing-related services in 1993. In total they accounted for 2.2% of employment in the industries they belonged to (either manufacturing or manufacturing-related services). Thus, their share of total employment is very small and, perhaps even more importantly, not a single one of the firms had more than 500 employees.

There are also a few Swedish studies that focus exclusively on technology-based firms founded by university faculty. The most extensive of these studies is Olofsson and Wahlbin (1993). The study consists of 569 firms started between 1974 and 1989. It is clear that the direct employment and production effects of the activities of these firms are small: Total sales were approximately SEK 3 billion and the firms employed only 3,500 persons.

Lindholm Dahlstrand (1997a, b) specifically address the issue how new technology-based firms with their roots in universities perform relative to firms with a different origin. This is done by identifying all spin-off firms in the Utterback and Reit-

Table I
The growth rate of GDP and GDP per capita in Sweden, the US and the OECD excluding the US for different periods, 1970–98 (%)

	1970–98		1980–98		1990–98	
	GDP	GDP per capita	GDP	GDP per capita	GDP	GDP per capita
Sweden	1.7	1.3	1.6	1.2	1.0	0.6
The US	2.8	1.8	2.8	1.8	3.0	2.0
OECD excl. the US	2.7	1.9	2.3	1.6	1.8	1.0

Source: OECD, National Accounts 1960–97, Vol. 1, 1999; OECD, Main Economic Indicators, February 2000.

berger (1982) sample (among the 60 firms there are 30 spin-off firms) and by including all spin-offs from the Chalmers Institute of Technology in Göteborg. The author reported that university spin-offs consistently grow much more slowly than other spin-off firms.

In summary, Swedish relative income dropped sharply from 1970 to 1998. The US per capita income relative to the OECD average also dropped at a similar rate until the late 1980s, although the drop took place from a much higher initial level. The US also remained the 2nd richest country throughout this period of relative decline. During the 1990s, however, the US economy grew faster than the OECD average. Regarding employment there was a great difference between the rapid rate of job creation in the US compared to Sweden and Europe, where employment has been stagnant since the 1970s. This has resulted in an hours-adjusted employment level in the US on the order of 35% higher than in Sweden and other European countries. The US high-tech production share has consistently been higher than in Sweden, but the Swedish share has increased sharply during the 1990s. However, there is ample evidence pointing towards a weak performance of new technology based firms.

4. Investment in R&D and output from the university sector

As shown in Table II both Sweden and the US devote a large share of GDP to R&D relative to the OECD norm. Both countries have consistently held the top position together with Japan. Since the mid 1980s, Sweden has in most years had the highest R&D/GDP ratio of all countries.

Perhaps even more important for our purposes is the fact that R&D conducted in the university sector as a share of GDP is consistently the highest in Sweden.[6] The importance of the university sector for total R&D in Sweden is even higher when looking at labor input rather than expenditure.[7] As a matter of fact, an extremely large share of R&D conducted by persons holding a Ph.D. is carried out in the university sector in Sweden—in 1993 the total volume of R&D conducted by Ph.D.'s in Sweden amounted to 9,650 man years, and 52% (5,000 man years) of this volume was carried out at universities (SOU, 1996:70, p. 32).[8]

Finally, the question naturally arises whether an important contributing factor to the Swedish decline in terms of relative income is due to some failure in its university system to make the kinds of research contributions upon which advanced industrial economies have become increasingly dependent. One way of exploring this question is to apply the usual measures of academic research

Table II
Total R&D expenditures and in the university sector as a percentage of GDP in Sweden, the US and the OECD, 1981–97

	Sweden		The US		OECD weighted		OECD unweighted	
	Total	Univ.	Total	Univ.	Total	Univ.	Total	Univ.
1981	2.29	0.69	2.42	0.35	2.09	0.36	1.52	0.32
1983	2.55	0.77	2.66	0.35	2.25	0.37	1.63	0.34
1985	2.89	0.79	2.87	0.37	2.43	0.37	1.77	0.35
1987	2.99	0.86	2.82	0.41	2.44	0.40	1.84	0.37
1989	2.94	0.90	2.73	0.42	2.43	0.40	1.87	0.38
1991	2.89	0.79	2.81	0.40	2.49	0.41	1.93	0.41
1993	3.39	0.87	2.61	0.40	2.38	0.43	1.98	0.43
1995	3.59	0.79	2.54	0.39	2.34	0.42	2.01	0.43
1997	3.85	0.83	2.71	0.39	2.40	0.39	2.07	0.41

Note: Due to data limitations OECD is defined as the following 15 countries: Canada, Denmark, Finland, France, Germany, Iceland, Ireland, Italy, Japan, Netherlands, Norway, Spain, Sweden, the UK, and the US.
Source: OECD, Basic Science and Technology Statistics on diskette, 1997; OECD, Main Science and Technology Indicators, No 1, 1999; OECD, Main Economic Indicators, January 1999.

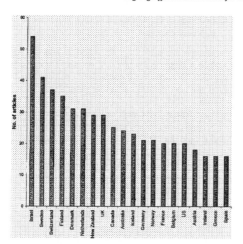

Figure 2. Scientific and technical article output in 20 rich countries, per billion USD of National GDP in 1995.
Source: Science & Engineering Indicators—1998.

productivity to the Swedish university community. When productivity is measured in terms of publications (in recognized professional journals) per billion US dollars of GDP, Sweden fares very well. As shown in Figure 2, Sweden was second to Israel in 1995 in terms of publications relative to the size of the economy, while the US is ranked 20th at less than half the Swedish level. Sweden has also consistently ranked very high in the biology-based disciplines, including especially clinical medicine and biomedical research (*European Science and Technology Scoreboard*, 1999, pp. 34–35).

The conclusion of this section is that, in terms of sheer volume, the Swedish R&D effort is impressive by international standards. The publication rate in international scientific journals is likewise high. At the same time, as documented in Section 3 Sweden does not seem to get full mileage out of its R&D effort in terms of production and job creation in high-tech, high value-added industries. It seems fair to hypothesize that the commercialization of the R&D efforts is a weak link. Most basic research is carried out in the university sector, and there is evidence that spillovers in the form of new viable business ventures tied to the universities are fairly modest in the aggregate. Regarding applied research (development), this is dominated—directly and

indirectly—by a handful of extremely large multinational corporations. Much of the commercialization of this R&D takes place abroad and the spillovers to new businesses are limited (Braunerhjelm, 1998).

5. Government support schemes and other bridging arrangements between universities and industry

As we observed in the previous section, R&D spending as a share of GDP is very high in Sweden compared to most countries, including the US. In addition, it is quite clear that a very large share of (academic) research, in particular research carried out by individuals holding a Ph.D., is carried out at universities. In a country where a large share of research is carried out at universities it becomes even more important that the interface between university research and commercialization is well developed, in order to reap large commercial benefits from research. In this section, we briefly examine the bridging arrangements between universities and industry in Sweden and the US.

The Swedish government has been keenly aware of the importance of an efficient university/industry interface for some time, and the point is emphasized in several recent government commissioned reports (e.g., SOU 1996:70 and SOU 1996:89). This changed view of the role of universities in society at large has been codified in legislation. Before the 1975 university reform, universities were stipulated to "teach and do research based on a scientific foundation". In 1975 a third objective was added to the agenda of universities, namely, to communicate to the surrounding society results emanating from university research and how they can be applied. Gradually this third objective came to be interpreted more broadly as collaboration between the universities, on the one hand, and private industry and the public sector, on the other. In the new regulation of the universities effective from 1998 (SOU 1998:128, pp. 153–154) this is spelled out explicitly. The universities are exhorted to be open to influences from the outside world, disseminate information about their teaching and research activities outside academia, and to facilitate for the surrounding society to gain access to relevant information about research results.

Swedish universities have recently focused on developing university–industry collaboration. These collaborations have assumed at least six forms: (i) research projects commissioned and paid for by an outside agent for commercial reasons; (ii) industry consulting by university personnel, university staff whose salaries are subsidized by an outside firm and adjunct professorships, as well as doctoral studies hosted inside industrial labs; (iii) university employed contact secretaries who act as mediators between university and small and medium size firms; (iv) research institutes and other organizations jointly run by universities and private industry; (v) the creation of firms for commercial exploitation of research; and (vi) financial and advisory aid to research-based firms and to individual researchers in order to facilitate the patenting, licensing or direct commercialization of knowledge and research results originating from universities.

In Sweden, university personnel receive full patent rights for their inventions. The government has been developing a legal and financial infrastructure aimed at facilitating exploitation of these patents and other university ideas. For example, between 1983 and 1997, 17 science parks which host small startups and R&D departments of large multinationals were established. These parks employ more than 10,000 people. However, it is unclear how many of these startups are university spinoffs. In a more direct approach, universities have since 1993 been allowed to set up their own wholly-owned companies for the commercialization of research. It is yet unclear to what extent universities have utilized this new privilege. In addition, all major universities run patent corporations which are intended to facilitate exploitation of patentable innovations emanating from the university.

The government has been active in providing seed financing to technology-based firms through NUTEK, the Swedish National Board for Industrial and Technical Development. In addition, since 1994 seven broker institutions called Technology Bridging Foundations have been established in major university regions. Their task has been to mediate commercialization of R&D from universities, SMEs and individual inventors by facilitating the patenting process, matching up VC funding et cetera. In addition, four foundations, such as the Foundation for Knowledge

and Competence Development, have been established which, among other things, are intended to improve the university/industry interface.

In the US, extensive networks of interaction between universities and the private sector were established in the course of the twentieth century. Consulting arrangements on the part of faculty proliferated, as did other forms of cooperation, involving joint research projects, student fellowships in particular fields, et cetera. The postwar era also marked a drastic departure from earlier years by providing huge budgets to support university research, including basic research. An essential feature of this support is that it was, overwhelmingly, dispensed by mission-oriented agencies of the federal government.

Another distinctive feature of federal government policy in the postwar years was an increasingly solicitous concern for the interests of small business. This was reflected, not only in a continuing exercise of anti-trust activity (with some variation among different administrations), but in various other forms, such as government procurement policies and, especially, new legislation to advance the interests of small business. The thrust of this legislation was strengthened in 1958 by a requirement that government agencies should conduct a "representative" share of their business with small firms. In addition, in the same year Congress passed the Small Business Investment Act, which encouraged the creation of Small Business Investment Companies (SBICs) that could provide small businesses with risk capital. In 1976 a new Office of Advocacy was created at the SBA, with the responsibility of measuring the direct costs and other effects of government regulation on small businesses and make legislative and nonlegislative proposals for eliminating excessive or unnecessary regulations of small businesses (Brock and Evans, 1986, pp. 22–23).

The SBICs became part of a significant experiment in government efforts to provide finance for new, high-risk enterprises. It was the ultimate *failure* of this experiment that created the conditions that led to the eventual rapid growth of the venture capital industry as it now exists in the US. Although the SBICs did, in fact, provide substantial amounts of equity financing to small, fast-growing companies, their further growth came to suffer from serious defects. Since they were heavily dependent upon the leverage provided by low-interest SBA loans, they had to concentrate their activities on debt financing to small companies that were already generating cash flows. Thus, they were seriously restricted in the effort to accommodate the early-stage financial needs of new, start-up firms. Moreover, the availability of government guarantees created familiar moral hazard problems as some SBICs chose to make very high risk investments. The SBICs also suffered from adverse selection. Finally, the program did not prove attractive to the most talented investment managers. The private equity professionals could be paid only salaries, since the provisions of the Investment Company Act of 1940 did not allow them to receive performance-based compensation.

During the economic shocks of the 1970s, many companies failed to meet their obligation to make interest payments on SBIC loans. Numerous highly leveraged SBICs, in turn, could not meet their own repayment schedules, and had to liquidate. Their role as providers of financial support for early-stage entrepreneurs went into a steady decline. The crisis was reinforced by the depressed state of the IPO market.[9]

Our description of the efforts to bridge the gap between universities and industry in Sweden clearly revealed an extensive engagement by the State in this area. Underlying this engagement is the explicitly spelled out premise that government involvement can enhance efficiency and economic growth; left to themselves the scientific research community and the market are likely to achieve less in terms of economic value and new jobs (Gibbons *et al.*, 1994, pp. 162–163).

So if Sweden largely adopted a "top–down" model, which included extensive direct involvement by the government in the transfer of knowledge with commercial potential from universities to industry, the US adopted much more of a "bottom–up" model. Central elements of this model included the institution of a legal framework that promoted the transfer of knowledge to small and new firms. Eventually, as we will see in Section 8, a broad set of rules were introduced, which paved the way for the evolution of the VC industry. This has turned out to be a highly effective institution to bridge the gap between academia and industry. This industry works very

differently from the SBICs, which are more comparable to many of the government-financed support schemes in Sweden.[10]

So what are the missing links? What factors could account for the apparent superiority of the American system in creating economic value from R&D activities at the universities? Our hypothesis is that the answer has to be sought through an in-depth examination of the relevant incentive structures in the respective countries. The next four sections will now be devoted to each one of these issues. Throughout the exposition particular emphasis will be put on how the incentive systems in Sweden and the US are likely to influence the supply of academic entrepreneurship.

6. Incentives to invest in human capital

According to our informal model incentives to invest in human capital, in particular with a natural science orientation, should be important for science-based entrepreneurship. The literature on economic growth also lends strong support to this view—see, e.g., Mankiw, Romer and Weil (1992), Lucas (1988), and Morrison and Siegel (1997).

Given our purpose, we focus almost exclusively on human capital investment at the university level. The US has the highest share of its active population with a university degree of all OECD nations. In 1996, 26% of the population aged 25–64 had a university level education. Sweden, on the other hand, is in an intermediate position at exactly half the US level. Moreover, in the OECD as a whole the share with a university degree tends to decrease with age. In Sweden this pattern does not show up. The propensity to acquire a university degree has dropped precipitously in the most recent generation, from a ratio of 16% among the 45–54 year olds to a ratio of 11% in the youngest group (OECD, 2000). Likewise the share of an age group holding a Ph.D. degree peaked among cohorts born in the 1940s.

As regards the line of study some internationally comparable data are available. In particular, there are data showing the number of science graduates per 100,000 inhabitants aged 25–34. In this regard there is tremendous variation across countries. The number of science graduates per 100,000 inhabitants is roughly five times higher in the UK at the top compared to Italy at the bottom. Sweden is also close to the bottom and the US figure is roughly 50% above the Swedish level (OECD, 1995).

As regards the allocation of academically trained people it is not just that there was a low inclination among Swedish students to specialize in the natural sciences, there was also a very strong tendency to pursue a career in the public sector. During the 1970s two thirds of all academically trained people worked in the public sector. Although this share has decreased somewhat since then, it is still roughly 55%.[11]

But it is well-known that international comparisons of educational levels are imperfect measures of human capital, and therefore a more direct test of the rate of human capital accumulation in Sweden relative to other OECD countries may be obtained by studying changes in the pattern of specialization. Hansson and Lundberg (1995, Ch. 3) show that during the 1980s the structure of industrial production was shifted towards industries with a low level of human and physical capital per person employed. They also examine how the use of human capital per unit of output has changed in Swedish imports and exports during the period 1969–92. The exports/imports ratio remained virtually unchanged during the 1970s, but at the end of the 1970s imports started becoming relatively more human capital intensive. Lundberg (1999) finds that this tendency was further reinforced during the 1990s. These studies show that Sweden appears to have successively lost its comparative advantage in human capital-intensive production.

According to human capital theory (Becker, 1964; Schultz, 1960), the decision to acquire human capital should be analyzed as an individual investment decision. In other words, the individual decision to acquire and use human capital is governed by the rate of return on human capital. Thus, one hypothesis is that the incentives to accumulate human capital have fallen since the 1960s.

A number of such studies have estimated the rate of return on education in Sweden for selected years during the period 1968–91.[12] The Swedish studies are summarized in Henrekson, Jonung, and Stymne (1996) and in Edin and Topel (1997). Comparable estimates are also available for the US covering the same period (Goldin and Katz,

1999). First, it is obvious that the educational premium fell dramatically from the end of the 1960s to the early part of the 1980s in Sweden.

Second, the sharp increase in the college/high school premium experienced in the US between 1979 and 1989 cannot be detected in Sweden.[13] Third, since the 1970s the rate of return on education has consistently been much higher in the US than in Sweden. We conclude that the rate of return on education fell to very low levels in Sweden in the early 1980s, and as Fornwall (1991) shows, the fall was larger for young people.

Accounting for the effect of taxes, Edin and Holmlund (1995) and Björklund and Kjellström (1994) found an even steeper drop in the rate of return in Sweden (compared to educational premia) between 1968 and 1981. The rate of return on higher education was approximately zero in both studies in 1981. The effect of subsidized loans and scholarships on human capital investment is much more difficult to assess. It is of course trivially true that, *ceteris paribus*, the rate of return to attending university is increased (Björklund and Kjellström, 1994; Edin and Holmlund, 1995). On the other hand, loan subsidies and scholarships boost the rate of return by giving rise to income during studies, as opposed to educational premia which give rise to (higher) income after completion of the studies. Thus, loan subsidies and scholarships that are not correlated with the rate of return to the training are likely to lower the incentives to choose the type of education that provides the most human capital investment as measured by the rate of return in terms of relative wages. This effect is reinforced by the fact that no tuition is paid at Swedish universities.

As shown by Fredriksson (1997) and Edin and Topel (1997) the propensity to enroll at universities has been highly correlated to the educational premium. This provides further evidence that the willingness to invest in human capital is greatly affected by the rate of return.

Why did the rate of return to schooling decrease so much in Sweden? Since the Swedish labor force cannot be said to have considerably more schooling than in other countries, it can probably not be explained by a lower scarcity value. Another possibility is that the successful implementation of the solidaristic wage policy resulted in lower educational premiums. Support for this thesis is given by Hibbs (1990) and Edin and Topel (1997).

A third potential explanation for the decline in the rates of return is that the quality of education has deteriorated, despite the fact that Sweden has one of the highest ratios of educational expenditure to GDP of all OECD countries (Fägerlind, 1991; OECD, 2000). This may very well be the case, particularly considering that the incentives to acquire human capital have become weaker. If the rate of return on schooling is low, the individual can adjust to this situation to some extent by consuming education rather than investing in human capital. Hence, human capital investment may be endogenous, in the sense that the individuals have adjusted their actual investment in human capital (as opposed to the number of years of schooling) to the institutionally given rate of return. A further factor that may lead to lower quality in the educational system is the sharp drop in relative wages of educators. As shown by OECD (1995) Sweden has the lowest wage for experienced teachers (high school) relative to PPP-adjusted GDP per capita of all countries compared.

Investment in human capital is crucial for science-based entrepreneurship. In an international comparison the level and rate of human capital investment at the university level is fairly low in Sweden. In particular, it is noteworthy that the propensity to study natural sciences has been low, the share of a cohort acquiring a university degree declined substantially in the 1970s and 1980s, and a disproportionately large share of people holding a university degree work in the public sector.

The analysis in this section has shown that the incentives for individuals to invest in human capital declined in Sweden over time and became very low during the 1970s and 1980s. These incentives were further weakened by the high marginal tax rates on wage income. Furthermore, when the solidaristic wage policy was gradually reformulated into a desire for a general leveling of wages across professions (rather than equal pay for equal work),[14] this had the unanticipated side-effect of a decline in the rate of return on investment in human capital.

7. Incentives to become an entrepreneur

A second important factor likely to determine the contribution of science graduates and university faculty to economic performance by means of science-based entrepreneurship is the relative payoff to becoming an entrepreneur rather than becoming and/or remaining a salaried employee, notably the relative payoff for academically trained people. And once an individual has embarked on an entrepreneurial venture, the contribution of this venture is dependent on whether the institutional environment is beneficial for entrepreneurial ventures.

Self-employment in Sweden declined from 19% of employment in 1950 to 7% in 1991. A slight rise has been registered since then. In an international context as well, self employment in Sweden appears low. A 1992 OECD study (OECD, *Employment Outlook*, July 1992) found that since the beginning of the 1970s throughout the 1980s, Sweden had the lowest rate of self-employment outside agriculture of all the OECD countries. The European Observatory for SMEs (1995) found that in 1992, Sweden had a lower share of self-employed than any of the other 12 countries that comprised the EU at that time. Self-employment as a share of total employment in Sweden was less than half of the average for the 12 EU countries. But does the propensity to be self-employed change with the level of education? Utterback and Reitberger (1982, p. 92), for instance, found that the level of education among entrepreneurs in new technology-based firms was extremely high in Massachusetts compared to Sweden around 1980. From the *Level of Living Surveys* it is possible to obtain more consistent evidence on this point between 1968 and 1991. The share of self-employed with a university degree is about half as large as the share among employees, and again the earlier tendency towards a much higher share of university trained people in the public sector is confirmed. Hence, the educational level of the self-employed is considerably below the level of employees. In the US the rate of self-employment declined in a similar fashion from 19% in 1950 to 9% in 1968. However, it has stayed at that level ever since. Thus the US economy has not since then demonstrated the typical pattern of a declining rate of self-employment as the economy progresses (Fölster, 2001).

To identify the crucial incentives that will induce a university-trained individual to become an entrepreneur is of course a formidable task.

First, it should be noted that these incentives are very much linked to the incentives for extant entrepreneurs to expand their business, since the expected return associated with a transition from being a salaried employee to becoming an entrepreneur is greatly affected by the possibilities for expansion. This will be considered in Section 8.

Second, a highly regulated labor market gives increased power to insiders, thus raising the opportunity cost of transferring to self-employment. Most importantly, the Swedish Employment Security Act (*Lagen om anställningsskydd* or LAS) stipulates the "last in—first out"-principle in case of dismissals caused by redundancy. This implies that tenure at the present employer becomes relatively more important for labor security than individual skill and productivity. This fact increases the individual's opportunity cost of changing employers or of leaving a secure salaried job to become self-employed. This is likely to reduce the spillover of knowledge between industries and firms. Such spillovers contribute to a high social rate of return on R&D and training.

Third, the costs of the unemployment insurance are almost wholly paid by the government, and this is only available for employees, and a host of other social security related benefits are more favorable for employees than for the self-employed. Among these one could mention the unconditional right to leave of absence for studies, the right to demand to work part-time as long as the employee has children below age 10, and generous rules for trade union work at the employer's expense.

A number of arguments have been advanced in favor of the view that it is often beneficial that the academic increasingly adopts the role of the entrepreneur. Stankiewicz (1986, p. 85) mentions three reasons. First, in many cases it is likely that small business units are more innovative than large established companies—see Acs and Audretsch (1990) for evidence. Second, small newly-created companies have certain market advantages as regards new technologies, notably that at early stages they tend to develop in low volume/high price niches that are less attractive for large firms. Olofsson and Stymne (1995) find that independent firms perform better than subsidiaries to large firms in Sweden, *ceteris paribus*. Moreover, there is a great risk that innovative

technological ideas atrophy when they are severed from the original innovator/researcher prematurely. The worst performers were those that were acquired by large firms. For an overview of more recent studies providing corroborating evidence, see Wennekers and Thurik (1999) and Carlsson (1999).

8. Incentives for entrepreneurs to expand

In the previous section we argued that the incentives for a salaried employee to become an entrepreneur may be weak in Sweden. Of equal importance is the fact that, given that somebody chooses to become an entrepreneur, he or she has sufficient incentives to develop the business to its full potential. In fact, the incentives to become an entrepreneur are largely determined by the incentives for extant entrepreneurs to expand. Hence, the factors dealt with in this section in large part apply to the previous section as well.

A number of studies have documented a weak inclination to grow among small firms in Sweden—see Henrekson and Johansson (1999) for an overview. Thus, it is easy to point out a number of studies indicating a lack of motivation to expand among small firms. According to Birch, Haggerty, and Parsons (1995) a few very fast-growing firms, what they call *gazelles* create the majority of jobs in the US. Storey (1994) argues that the small group of high growth SMEs, what he names *flyers*, are the main job creators. In contrast, Swedish researchers (Davidsson *et al.*, 1996; Davidsson and Henrekson, 2001) find little support for the gazelle/flyer hypothesis. Instead they find that the SME contribution to net job creation is largely the result of many small start-ups.

This is likely to show up as a weak evolution of intermediate-sized firms. The pool of firms in the intermediate size classes is tapped through mergers, take-overs and, at least in some cases, expansion into the group of large firms. At the same time, a low willingness to grow should lead to few firms growing out of the very smallest size classes. Thus a gradual depletion of the pool of intermediate-sized firms is likely. Henrekson and Johansson (1999) find this indeed to be the case in Sweden.

Hence, the findings of a number of studies provide direct evidence of constraints on the growth of Swedish firms. In the remainder of this section we will attempt to identify the likely factors contributing to this situation, and make comparisons with the US situation.

Taxation of entrepreneurial income

Several features of the pre-1990 Swedish tax system penalized younger, smaller and less capital-intensive firms and discouraged entrepreneurship and family ownership in favor of institutional forms of ownership. During an extended period of time, for three decades beginning in the early 1960s, there were extreme differences in taxation for different sources of finance and owner categories: (i) debt was the most favored and new share issues the most disfavored; (ii) households/individuals were taxed substantially more heavily than other owner categories. For example, an investment yielding a pre-tax real rate of return of 10% financed by a debt instrument meant that the tax-exempt institution received a real rate of return of 18.3% after tax. In contrast, for a household investing in a newly issued share with the same real rate of return the situation was very different: 10% before tax became −3.7% after tax. See calculations in Södersten (1984, 1993) and Davis and Henrekson (1997). Naturally, tax rules benefiting debt financing relative to equity financing and institutional relative to individual ownership systematically favored large, real capital intensive, publicly traded and well-established firms.

Studies such as King and Fullerton (1984) and Fukao and Hanazaki (1987) also show that Swedish tax policy was extreme in these respects. Furthermore, the Swedish tax system generally subsidized housing investment and has historically had very high marginal tax rates (above 90% in the highest income bracket in the late 1970s) on individual income.

The 1991 tax reform entailed a substantial "leveling of the playing field" for different types of owners and sources of finance, although the leveling was in no way complete. In 1994 the tax code was further reformed and the playing field became for all practical purposes leveled. However, the respite was short-lived as a 1995 act reinstated a higher tax burden on equity financing. Although the tax reform act of 1991 reduced the distortion

between debt and equity financing, there remains a substantial differential today. Furthermore, the tax code still implies a much higher tax burden for investments financed with equity owned by households rather than by institutions.[15] Finally, marginal tax rates have been and remain above 50% for employee income, which to a considerable extent limits owners' ability to extract wealth from their firms.

In order to analyze how the tax system impacts on entrepreneurial behavior it is not sufficient to focus on the taxation of individual owners of firms. To a large extent the return on entrepreneurial effort is taxed as wage income. First, large part of income accruing from closely held companies has to be paid out as wage income. Second, a great deal of the entrepreneurial function is carried out by employees without an ownership stake in the firm or possibly with stock options giving them a potential future ownership stake in the firm should the stock options be exercised.

Finally, it should be noted that the use of stock options to encourage entrepreneurial behavior among employees is highly penalized by the tax system, since gains on options are taxed as wage income when the stock options are tied to employment in the firm. Thus they are subjected both to mandatory social security (33%) and the marginal tax rate. Since the marginal tax rate is roughly 57% this entails a total tax rate of roughly 68% in 1999. The firm that issues the stock options does not pay the social security tax until the stock options are exercised, and hence the firm cannot calculate the cost of its stock option plan.

No doubt, taxation of entrepreneurial income was very high in the US as well before 1980, although it was in no way comparable to the Swedish level. King and Fullerton (1984) report that Sweden was the only country where more than 100% of the real return was taxed away in 1980 for households making corporate investments. Following the comprehensive tax reforms in the early 1980s, the playing field for different types of owners and sources of financing was largely leveled in the US (Jorgenson and Landau, 1993).

Perhaps even more important are the differences between Sweden and the US in the taxation of wage income, capital gains and stock options. The highest marginal tax rate (federal tax) in the US was extremely high until the mid 1960s (91%) and remained at around 70% until 1981. Since then it has been lowered precipitously, reaching a bottom of 28% in 1988–89. The upper threshold for the highest marginal tax rate was set very low—to annual incomes of approximately USD 30,000. Mandatory social security contributions of 15% are also low compared to Sweden. Thus, high wage incomes, which often result from entrepreneurial efforts are taxed at marginal rates that are approximately half the Swedish level.

As a result of the 1978 Revenue Act, the capital gains tax was reduced from 49.5% to 28%. In 1981 it was reduced again, to 20%. In Sweden the capital gains tax is normally 30% since 1991, but for small closely held firms it is in effect 43% since half of the capital gain is taxed as wage income (no social security payments are levied).

The Incentive Stock Option Law of 1981 in the US allowed the use of stock options as compensation by deferring the tax liability to the time when the stocks were sold rather than when the options were exercised. In general, there are (i) no tax consequences to the employee upon the grant or the exercise of the option; (ii) the employee is taxed at capital gains rates when the stock acquired (upon the exercise of the option) is sold after a specified holding period; and (iii) there is no deduction available to the employer.[16] This change in the law shifted the tax risk in the options back to the government, and thus accomplished two things: it increased the potential profit from the stock options and it allowed budget-constrained individuals to sell stocks whenever they chose to do so.

In summary, we have noted in this section that the taxation of entrepreneurial income has been far more beneficial in the US during the last two decades. This emanates from several sources: more favorable taxation of individuals as equity owners, lower rates of capital gains taxes and a more favorable tax treatment of stock options.

Savings incentives

The availability of equity financing is a critical factor for both start-ups and the expansion of existing firms. In general, the riskier the business, the greater the reliance on equity relative to

debt financing. The existence of collateral notwithstanding, a sizeable infusion of equity is often a prerequisite for obtaining comprehensive credits.

The smaller and newer the firm, the more difficult for outside financiers to assess the viability and profitability of the proposed investment project. Thus, *ceteris paribus*, small and newly established firms are more dependent on equity financing than large, well-established firms. Low private savings also exacerbate the inherent problem caused by asymmetric information.

There is substantial scientific evidence supporting the idea that the individual wealth position has important effects for the probability of becoming an entrepreneur and for the propensity to expand. For example, Lindh and Ohlsson (1996, 1998) find that the likelihood of starting a business in Sweden increases significantly among those who receive an inheritance or a lottery gain.[17] They also find that a more unequal wealth distribution covaries positively with the share of self-employed. Similar evidence is found for the US by Holtz-Eakin, Joulfaian, and Rosen (1994). In summary, there is overwhelmingly strong empirical evidence pointing to the importance of personal assets for the degree to which entrepreneurial talent is exploited.

We subscribe to the classical view on entrepreneurship (Knight, 1921, Schumpeter, 1934; Kirzner, 1973; Baumol, 1990) that entrepreneurial talent is unevenly distributed. In this case policies that increase the likelihood that the entrepreneurially talented are not equity constrained are likely to be beneficial. The only really efficient means of increasing this likelihood is to pursue economic policies that promote private wealth accumulation across the board, and in forms that do not preclude that the wealth may be used as equity in entrepreneurial ventures.

Welfare state provisions are likely to remove a number of savings motives as long as the state's commitments are considered credible by the general public. Compensation paid by the social insurance often discourages saving above and beyond the mechanisms discussed above. For instance, Hubbard, Skinner, and Zeldes (1995) find that social assistance discourages saving because it is usually conditional on the individual not having any assets. Other studies find negative effects on precautionary saving of more generous unemployment insurance—see, for example, Engen and

Gruber (1996). Countries like Sweden with large transfer programs tend to have pay-as-you-go pension systems. These tend to lower national savings and investment compared to funded systems (Feldstein, 1996). Thus, in the Swedish welfare state system, total savings motives are much reduced. This has the side effect of decreasing the supply of entrepreneurial capital.

Furthermore, the real rate of taxation on financial savings was extremely high in Sweden for individuals before the 1990/91 tax reform. On interest income it typically exceeded 100% during the 1970s and 1980s. The rate of taxation on saving and wealth accumulation is still high. First, the very high tax rates on wage income makes it hard to save a substantial portion of income that can subsequently be used for equity financing. Second, total taxation on accumulated wealth is high (1999): 30% on the nominal current return, 30% nominal capital gains tax and 1.5% wealth tax on real estate, interest-bearing instruments and prime stock listed on the Stockholm Stock Exchange.

Also, given the level of wealth or national savings, the composition of national savings is not neutral in its impact on entrepreneurship and small business development. The manner in which savings are channeled to various investment activities influences the type of business organization that can obtain credit. Pension funds, for example, are less likely to channel funds to entrepreneurs than business angels or venture capital firms. Hence, if the government forces individuals to carry out most of their savings through a national pension fund system, small business credit availability will suffer relative to an alternative policy and institutional arrangements that allow for greater choice by individuals regarding their savings and investments. In the Swedish case, institutionalized saving in the form of life insurance policies, where the funds are by definition withdrawn from the non-institutional venture capital market, has been and still is highly favored.

As a result of weak savings incentives due to a high rate of taxation and extensive welfare state, the savings rate of Swedish households fell to a very low level in comparison to other OECD countries. Household savings as a share of disposable income has typically been in the 2–3% range since 1970 as compared to typical rates in the range of 10–20% in most other OECD countries. As a result of the consistently low household savings rates in Sweden for several decades, individual financial wealth became low by international comparisons (Pålsson, 1998).

The combination of low private savings and an extremely even distribution (Lindh and Ohlsson, 1998) of these low savings implies that few people either themselves or from their associates, friends or relatives are able to raise the requisite equity to realize their business projects. This deficiency may to quite an extent be substituted for by a well functioning venture capital (VC) market.

The role of the venture capital industry

Before the 1980s, the development of a VC industry in the US was severely hampered by two pieces of legislation passed in 1969.[18] The capital gains tax was sharply increased to 49.5% and tax liabilities on employee stock options were imposed when the options were exercised rather than when the stock was sold. The transformation to a new regime dominated by the limited partnership, a central feature of the US venture capital industry today, took place in the late 1970s and early 1980s. The main elements of this transformation were as follows:

1. The reduction of the capital gains tax in two steps to 28% in 1978 and to 20% in 1981.
2. In 1979 pension fund were allowed to invest in high risk securities issued by small or new companies and venture capital funds. This led to an immediate response in the market for small-company stocks and the new issues market. Public pension funds eventually became the largest investor group in the private equity market.
3. The stock option legislation of 1981 that made it possible to defer the tax liability to the time when the stocks were sold rather than when the options were exercised.

Venture capital firms converted high risk opportunities to a more acceptable risk level through portfolio diversification. This was achieved by means of aligning the incentives of the three agents—investors, VC firms and new high tech startups. The US venture capital industry experienced vastly accelerated growth in the 1980s. The growth in the venture capital stock was also accompanied by a rapid growth in the proportion of the stock that was managed by partnerships. By the late 1980s, the proportion of capital managed by partnerships grew to more than 80%, largely at the expense of independent SBICs, which saw their share of capital fall to virtually nothing.

The role of venture capital in successfully bringing companies to maturity cannot be overstated. This is particularly true in the computer-related and medical and health sectors, where 65% of all IPOs are backed by VC firms.

Within the limited partnership institutional investors enter into an agreement with a venture capital firm in which they are the limited partners, and the senior managers of the venture capital firm act as general partners. The lifetime of such partnerships is generally ten years, during which time the limited partners, as a condition of their limited liability status, are expected to refrain from any active role in the management of their investments. The usual arrangement is one in which the limited partners supply 99% of the capital whereas the general partners supply 1%. In the division of the capital gains, the general partners receive 20% and the limited partners 80%. The general partners, moreover, receive an annual management fee of between 2 and 3% of the total committed capital.

The first responsibility of the venture capital firm, after a partnership has been established, is to screen project proposals. This sorting process is critical, since an outsider can hardly be—or become—as well informed about the true situation as the managers of the firm seeking financial support. Due diligence on the part of the venture capitalist at this point, and careful monitoring of the firms receiving equity commitments, are obviously vital preconditions for success, especially since little information is ordinarily available for firms that are not yet publicly traded. For firms that are supported after the screening process, the venture capital firm will typically play an active role in the day-to-day decision making process as well as in shaping longer-term strategy. Venture capitalists sit on boards of directors, play a prominent role in recruiting key players, and in replacing them when, in their judgment, they are not performing satisfactorily. The leading figures in the startup firm are paid relatively modest salaries and their commitment to the financial success of the firm is established by the receipt of stock options.

An extremely important feature of control in the hands of the venture capitalist is that financial support is doled out in stages, with no more money made available than is necessary for the firm to reach the next stage. Thus, there are multiple opportunities to evaluate performance at each stage and to terminate support if performance is deemed to be unsatisfactory. This discourages opportunistic behavior and strengthens commitment to the firm's long-term prospects for success.

At the same time, there are interesting parallels between the ways in which the VC firm discourages opportunistic behavior on the part of entrepreneurial firms in which they are investing, and the ways in which the limited partnerships constrain the behavior of the VC firms in which they have invested. The VC management receives 20% of the profits from the portfolio, despite their initial investment, which is usually 1%. Hence, a strong direct incentive is in place to encourage the VC firm to ensure the success of the funded firms. Second, limited partnerships are typically undertaken for a ten-year period, at which time the partnership is dissolved and the venture capital firm must seek new sources of investment funds. At this point its most critical asset is its recent track record. Since, moreover, a mature VC firm may have 20 or more limited partnerships, each of eight to 10 years duration, it must have recourse to establishing new partnerships, or renewal of old partnerships, every few years. Hence, the venture capitalist's performance is being continually subjected to market tests. This serves as a powerful force to limit opportunistic misbehavior.

Venture capitalists would have far fewer companies to finance if it were not for *business angels*. VC firms hardly ever participate in the earliest stages of the development of new high tech concepts that eventually make it to the stage of successful commercialization. The earliest financial support is likely to come from affluent friends or relatives or, increasingly, wealthy individuals who have already become rich from similar earlier ventures. If the original funds come from family or friends, kinship ties play a large role in preventing the firm founder/manager from squandering the money. If the original funds come from business people, moral hazard is reduced by screening and by close monitoring of the firm's progress.

Knowledgeable insiders insist that the scale of angel activity is huge, and there is extensive anecdotal evidence to support that assertion—see Zider (1998). A key ingredient is that, in return for undertaking large financial risks, there should be some prospect of earning high rewards—*after* taxes. As a result of the informal nature of these markets, there are no systematic or reliable data on these activities.

The development of a VC industry in Sweden is of more recent vintage, and as we will see it differs from its US counterparts in many respects. Around 1980 Utterback and Reitberger (1982) found that ample supplies of equity capital from private sources outside the firm gave the US firms much lower debt equity ratios, which allowed them to grow faster. They also point out that in those days the large—highly tax favored—Swedish firms played the role filled by venture capitalists and private sources of equity in the US. To the extent that there is reason to believe that large firms are less suitable for assuming this role than venture capitalists, the performance of the new firms suffered.

During the 1980s a VC industry began to develop in Sweden as well, but at least until the mid 1990s these enterprises supplied little capital for the establishment of new firms or in the first critical phase of expansion in the firm's development (NUTEK, 1994). The public sector has tried to offset the lack of private venture capital by introducing numerous support schemes. In 1998 there were more than 140 such schemes. There is no coordination of the different schemes, and the net effect is far from clear (Landell *et al.*, 1998). Moreover, the major portion goes to firms undergoing expansion. Only a tiny portion goes to the start up of new companies as seed financing. More systematic evidence on this point is provided by Isaksson (1998) and Braunerhjelm (1999). No more than 8% of the VC in Sweden in the late 1990s went to the seed and early expansionary phases. Over 50% of the VC was channeled to firms considered to be in the mature phase. Landström (1993) specifically looked at the behavior of business angels. He found that only 25% of the business angels' investments were seed capital in the early 1990s compared to more than 50% in the US in the same period. At the same time, Lindström and Olofsson (1998) show that,

in new technology-based firms that actually succeeded, business angels were instrumental.

According to two new studies—Isaksson (1999) and Karaömerlioglu and Jacobsson (2000)—there has been strong growth in the Swedish VC industry during the latter half of the 1990s. With more complete data Karaömerlioglu and Jacobsson (2000) find that the amount of VC capital in Sweden relative to GDP is the third highest in Europe after the UK and Ireland, and cumulative VC funds relative to GDP had reached 50% of the US level in 1998, up from 25% of the US level in 1983.[19] The amount invested in early phases is also found to be larger than in previous studies (11.6% in 1998). However, compared to their American counterparts Swedish VC firms lack in competence. Isaksson (1999) reports that at most one fifth of the firms that have received VC investment perceive that the VC firm has offered significant inputs in terms of strategic advice, networks and recruitment of key personnel. Similar results are reported for biotech by Rickne (1999) and for the IT industry by E-chron (1998).

In the long run it is also likely that a serious impediment to the growth of the VC market will come from the demand side, i.e., that there may be a lack of potential projects with a development potential due to the factors discussed throughout this study. In this context it is important to note that Gompers and Lerner (1999) find that a crucial factor behind the VC industry growth in the US is that the decrease of capital gains tax rates boosted demand for venture capital as more workers now had an incentive to become entrepreneurs.

In terms of taxation, VC firms in Sweden are at a disadvantage relative to other firms. Dividends are taxed threefold: at a rate of 28% in both the firm itself and the venture capital firm and at 30% at the owners' level. This high tax burden on VC firms is likely to endanger the future supply of VC capital from firms residing in Sweden. Yet another problem is that, according to Swedish tax law, business angels that take active part in the management of the firms in which they invest are taxed at a higher rate. Active owners of unlisted firms are taxed at higher rates than passive owners. This implies that dividends above a fairly moderate threshold (some 9%) will be taxed as wage income, and half of the capital gains tax will also be taxed as wage income and not as capital income. Likewise the income of the general partners in VC firms will be taxed as wage income. Thus, the high rates of taxation of high-tech entrepreneurs, general partners of VC firms and the owners of the VC firms or the business angels result in a substantial reduction in the after-tax return on activities typical for VC firms in the US.

By contrast, in the US investments by venture capital firms are taxed at low rates. If the holding period exceeds five years, the total tax rate is 14%, and since 1997 the capital gains tax from sales of shares in unlisted companies may be deferred indefinitely, if the profits are reinvested within 60 days. Similar systems were introduced in the UK in the early 1990s.

In summary, we note that around 1980 the legal framework in the US became highly conducive to the development of a sophisticated VC industry. The industry itself has then designed a number of efficient incentive schemes that helps to overcome many inherent conflicts of interest between innovators, entrepreneurs, fund managers and investors. In Sweden, on the other hand, the legal framework facilitating the emergence of a highly competent VC industry has not been in place. As a result, the Swedish VC industry has not been able to play the same crucial role in bridging the gap between universities and industry as its US equivalent, although there are signs that the situation has begun to improve.

The functioning of the labor market

Swedish labor organizations successfully pursued egalitarian wage policies from the mid 1960s until the breakdown of centralized wage bargaining in 1983 (Hibbs, 1990; Edin and Holmlund, 1995). The strength of Swedish labor organizations and the centralized nature of the wage-setting institutions appear to have facilitated a remarkable compression of the wage structure during this period, judging by cross-country comparisons of wage inequality trends (Davis, 1992). To the extent that Swedish wage-setting developments drove up wages in the lower tiers of the distribution, relative to outcomes under other institutional arrangements, they reinforced the concentration of economic activity in larger, older and more capital-intensive firms and sectors. This inference follows from the ample evidence that, ordinarily, wages rise with the age, capital intensity and—especially—the size of employers (e.g., Brown and Medoff, 1989; Davis and Haltiwanger, 1999).

Centralized wage-setting institutions may also disadvantage smaller businesses and businesses aiming at promoting an entrepreneurial culture within the firm by implementing standard rate compensation policies that closely tie wages to easily observed job and worker characteristics such as occupation, education, experience and seniority.[20] Efficiency losses associated with the imposition of standard rate compensation policies are likely to be greater for smaller employers. Since smaller and more entrepreneurial employers show greater preference for flexibility and idiosyncrasy in wage determination, standard rate compensation policies are more costly to adopt. This suggests that centralized wage-setting institutions affected the industrial structure and the organization of business activity in Sweden most likely to the detriment of small firms, flexible organizations and firms wanting to remunerate entrepreneurial behavior within the firm (Davis and Henrekson, 2000).

Another feature of the labor market that is important in our context is the existence of job security mandates. Strict employment security provisions are likely to be more harmful for smaller and potentially fast-growing employers. One reason involves the gains from efficiently matching heterogeneous workers to a variety of tasks and positions. As an employer learns about a worker's abilities over time, or as those abilities evolve with the accumulation of experience, the optimal assignment of the worker to various tasks is likely to change. The scope for task reassignment within the firm is likely to rise with firm size. In an unfettered labor market, optimal task reassignment often involves mobility between firms, and such mobility is more likely when the initial employment relationship involves a small business. Thus, any inefficiencies induced by the Swedish Employment Security Act in the assignment of workers to tasks are likely to be more severe and more costly for smaller firms. Furthermore, and for obvious reasons, one bad recruitment is proportionately more costly to bear for a small firm.

There are also theoretical models finding a likely negative effect of employment protection on entrepreneurial firms based on new technology. Hopenhayn and Rogerson (1993) emphasize that the reallocation of labor from old and declining to new and dynamic industries is slowed down. Saint-Paul (1997) finds that countries with a rigid labor market will tend to produce goods at a late stage of their product cycle with a relatively stable demand, while it is more advantageous to produce new goods for which demand is more volatile in countries with a more flexible labor market.

Recent research, sometimes called "the new view of the labor market"[21] suggests that in order to understand in what ways labor market regulations impede growth and employment, one has to analyze the effects on the individual firm. For many firms—and in particular for firms with a good growth potential in terms of productivity and employment—there is a great need for flexibility both to increase the number of employees in response to rising demand and likewise to be able to rapidly contract when demand falls short of expectations. The road from small to large for a gazelle is far from straight, since the activities of new firms in particular are subject to genuine uncertainty. If, under such circumstances, rules are imposed that reduce the firms' leeway to rapid adjustment one should expect both a lower willingness to expand in general and that fewer firms, despite a good product or a viable idea, grow from small to large in a short period of time.

In addition, a strictly applied "last in—first out" principle in case of redundancies implies that tenure at the present employer becomes relatively more important for labor security than individual skill and productivity. This fact increases the individual's opportunity cost of changing employers or of leaving a secure salaried job to become an entrepreneur. This is likely to reduce the spillover of knowledge between industries and firms. Such spillovers contribute to a high social rate of return on R&D and training.

Finally, we note that labor market inflexibility is an element inherently inconsistent with the flexibility, nonhierarchical structures, networking and labor mobility across firms distinguishing an entrepreneurial business culture (Saxenian, 1996).

Summary and conclusions

In this section we have documented a weak willingness to grow among small firms in Sweden. A number of likely factors contributing to this state of affairs have been identified: historically and currently a high tax burden on entrepreneurial income, weak incentives for private wealth accumulation, particularly in forms that promote the supply of venture capital, an unfavorable tax and regulatory system for the VC industry, inflexible wage-setting arrangements rendering the encouragement of entrepreneurial behavior more difficult and strict job security, which is likely to be most detrimental for small, entrepreneurial firms with a high growth potential.

9. Incentives within the university system

Even if all other elements favoring science-based entrepreneurship are at hand—such as conditions encouraging human capital investment, entrepreneurship and firm growth—results in terms of economic performance are likely to be meager, unless the right incentive structure is in place within the university system itself. This structure is of course highly multidimensional. A number of factors are likely to be crucial: (i) the degree to which up to date research results and methods are communicated to students as part of the regular instruction and whether the internal reward systems, be they monetary or nonmonetary, encourage excellence in both teaching and research; (ii) to what extent and how quickly curricula are adjusted to changing demand; (iii) the efficiency with which research budgets can be reallocated across disciplines in response to changes in commercial potential; and (iv) the incentives in a broad sense for faculty to interact with industry in economically beneficial ways.

We begin by examining the incentives for research and teaching in the American system. American universities are highly decentralized and intensely competitive. The decentralization implies that American universities retain a high degree of autonomy, thus pursuing opportunities for solving their own problems and for building upon their own unique strengths and aspirations. Competition takes place along several dimensions: (1) competition for students among universities (including competition between private and state institutions), and at the graduate level among professors for the best students; (2) competition among universities for the best professors in a cultural and economic context where the mobility of professors is very high; (3) competition among professors for research support, which provides released time from teaching and access to research assistants, equipment and other requisite materials. A university that can offer high quality teaching in fields for which there is a strong demand in labor markets can also charge higher tuition fees, which also leads to higher revenues.

As a result of the decentralization and the competition that takes place at so many levels, the US university system has become more responsive to the economic needs of society. In order to justify high tuition fees, students expect a high degree of relevance of the offered curricula. Likewise, professors who are dependent upon research grants in order to be able to pursue a successful research career, are more likely to adjust their research interests to fields that have a high current or expected future economic value.

Because of the decentralization and the competition among universities for professors who are visibly productive, the system tends to result in greater salary dispersion, where salary differences are likely to reflect the economic relevance of the professor's field of specialization as well as his/her higher achievements as a researcher and teacher. Generally, professors active in research prefer to teach at the graduate level, where course content is closer to research at the frontier of the discipline and where graduate students may come to play crucial roles in advancing those frontiers. Rosenberg (1999, 2000) presents evidence showing how rapidly entirely new fields as well as major breakthroughs in established fields have been introduced into the curricula at leading US universities over the years. In the US, therefore, universities can, to a considerable degree, be regarded as endogenous institutions which tend to be characterized by an impressive capability, as well as a strong incentive, to adjust to changes in the outside environment.

In these respects the Swedish and, for that matter, the corresponding systems in most other European countries, differ substantially from the American university system. Traditionally, European professors have, by and large, been civil servants working within the public sector, which implies that a high degree of national uniformity

has been imposed on pay schedules, rules for promotion and recruitment and other working conditions. Essentially, this is still the case also in Sweden, although it should be noted that greater flexibility in terms of pay schedules has been introduced during the 1990s. Nevertheless, the Swedish system differs from the American system in a number of important respects that are likely to impact unfavorably on the inclination to introduce changes in curricula and research orientation in order to accommodate the changing needs of the economy.

First, there is a greater separation of teaching and research. The bulk of undergraduate teaching at Swedish universities is carried out by lecturers who do not do research. This is likely to slow down the pace at which important new research findings are integrated into the curricula. If there are strong complementarities between teaching and research, teaching is likely to benefit when it is delivered by research-oriented faculty. Also, research is probably better when it is carried out in association with advanced students in an intellectual environment that encourages and rewards informed criticism.

Second, in contrast to the US, the Swedish university system is highly centralized. The central government is the body that grants charters to universities, and in practice it also decides on the rules of admittance and the size of a university (through budgetary allocations). Due to this strong influence from the central government there is also much less leeway for individual institutions to allow remuneration to track an individual professor's research and teaching performances more closely and to vary the level of remuneration according to the economic value of the professor's field of specialization. Moreover, greater centralization also makes it more difficult for individual universities to adjust the allocation of its research budget across fields in response to changing demand outside the university.

One way of illustrating this lesser ability to adjust to changing needs is given by the comparison by Jacobsson, Sjöberg and Wahlström (2000) of the number of degrees awarded at the B.Sc. and M.Sc. levels in electrical/electronic engineering and computer science in Sweden and the US, relative to active-age population in the 1977–95 period. For a very long time there was an excess demand for engineers within this specialization in Sweden. Still, the university system was slow to respond to this increased demand through an expansion in teaching. In the US, on the other hand, the number of degrees awarded tripled from 1977 to 1986, while the Swedish expansion did not take off until the number of degrees awarded had already peaked and begun to decrease in the US "market driven" system. When the number of B.Sc. degrees began to decrease, the US experienced a dramatic upgrading, with a large increase in the number of M.Sc. and Ph.D. degrees awarded (National Science Board, 1997).

The point, then, is not that the Swedish higher education system simply failed to respond to a huge increase in the demand for trained personnel in the burgeoning fields of microelectronics and computer science. Rather, the point is that the response did occur, but it occurred, from a purely economic point of view, much too slowly. In considering universities in their specific role as suppliers of trained personnel in appropriate fields of study, timing is a crucial consideration. In competitive world markets, large economic rents are commonly available to those firms (and those countries) that can respond most quickly to economic opportunities opened up by new technologies or new disciplines. But late arrivals are most likely to find that the large financial rewards have already been captured as competitive forces have driven prices down to much lower levels.

Third, in Sweden and other European countries, university degree requirements are typically formulated as a fixed program rather than a flexible accumulation of requirements and credits as in the US. In such a system it is therefore more difficult to make changes than in the American case. Etzkowitz, Asplund, and Nordman (2000) present evidence from their interviews that it is very difficult to change courses quickly and introduce new fields in the old Swedish universities.

The American university system is powerfully driven by competitive forces, especially by competition for financial support to push out the envelope of research frontiers in disciplines that have come to produce useful knowledge. In recent years this has most notably been the case in microelectronics, computer science and molecular biology. An important dimension of American academic competition is reflected in a high degree of mobility on the part of faculty as universities compete

for talent and prestige. Such competition has been taking place in an entrepreneurial culture that has encouraged, or has not constrained, high levels of faculty involvement in business activities. These activities include high tech startups in which there are a variety of potentially high financial payoffs to university faculty whose research produces knowledge that may lead to new products and processes and their accelerated commercialization.

The possibilities for commercial exploitation of university research were strengthened by the passage of the Bayh-Dole Act of 1980, which allowed universities to appropriate the property rights to an invention resulting from university research that was financed by federal grants. As a result of the Bayh-Dole Act, universities can now, in effect, develop contractual arrangements for "profit-sharing" between individual faculty researchers, their departments, and the university. Moreover, universities now have strong incentives to set up their own Office of Technology Transfer. These offices, operating on a fully commercial basis with staffs of lawyers, technology specialists, marketing specialists and accountants, facilitate the commercial exploitation of potentially valuable research findings.

Thus, the broad picture that we have sketched here strongly suggests that the incentives within the US university system encourage active participation by faculty (and also university administrators) in commercial exploitation of research by faculty. What can be said of the corresponding situation in Sweden? At first sight incentives for faculty appear very strong: the 1949 law guaranteeing academic freedom also placed property rights emanating from their research in the hands of faculty members (*lärarundantaget*). However, the outcome has been more complex. A consequence of full faculty ownership of property rights has been that the universities themselves have had little incentive to become involved in technology transfer to the commercial sector. In fact, as emphasized by Etzkowitz *et al.* (2000) it has often been in the interest of universities to discourage contacts between faculty members and industry, since rigid civil servant pay schedules and other constraints have made it very difficult for them to retain highly valued personnel who have established personal ties with industry. Procedures for academic leave have not been adjusted to make it easier for professors to take temporary leave to organize firms in the manner that has become widespread in the US (see also Stankiewicz, 1986, p. 90).

Under these circumstances, Swedish academics are more likely to confine their external involvement to consulting activities, since to proceed further may force them to take a binary decision to leave the university, and few are prepared to do that (Etzkowitz *et al.*, 2000). In a system that discourages faculty involvement with industry beyond consulting and where the property rights rest with the researcher, there is a lower likelihood that the potential commercial benefits of academic research will be reaped. And, as emphasized by Vedin (1993), if the owner of the property rights shows little interest in exploitation, very little is likely to happen. This is also found by Etzkowitz *et al.* who conclude that "[s]ince most professors have little interest in commercializing their rights, or naively presume that discovery should somehow automatically produce rewards, relatively little use was made of these rights."

When property rights rest solely with the individual researcher, there is no "profit sharing" with his/her department. This has probably given rise to anti-entrepreneurial peer pressure at Swedish universities. Informal interviews as well as a recent government report on the collaboration between university and industry (SOU 1996:70, pp. 158–159) point to the existence of such pressure. Anti-entrepreneurial peer pressure also results in tendencies among faculty to be less open about their contacts with industry and, in particular, about the private returns from these contacts. Such surreptitious behavior further reduces the much-needed presence of entrepreneurial role models.

Several scholars studying the Swedish university/industry interface emphasize that, analogous to what Zucker, Darby and Brewer (1998), Audretsch and Stephan (1996) and Siegel Waldman and Link (1999) have found for the US, personal contacts are essential (e.g., Uhlin *et al.*, 1992; Etzkowitz *et al.*, 2000). It is clear, however, that these contacts have been mainly with large firms, and it has turned out that the large firms have preferred that these contacts remain informal in nature. In particular, the large firms have been very unwilling to offer high-powered incentives to academics with whom they cooperate and, as a result, these academics tend to remain consultants. This is, of course, yet another reflection of the Swedish large-firm model of high-tech innovation (Granstrand and Alänge, 1995; Lindholm Dahlstrand, 1997a).

We may conclude that there is much greater flexibility in the US system (a bottom up model) compared to a Swedish or European system. In particular, it should be emphasized that, whatever mode of cooperation between university and industry turns out to be the most suitable for a certain technology, it is more likely to prove feasible in a more flexible and decentralized system.

10. The recent entrepreneurial upturn in Sweden

The analysis in this paper has been wholly long term, i.e., we have focused on the bleak performance of the Swedish economy in a thirty-year perspective and the substantially greater degree of academic entrepreneurship in the US compared to Sweden since the 1970s. At the same time, one should note the highly visible current upturn in entrepreneurial activity in Sweden at the time of finalizing this manuscript (September 2000). The GDP growth rate was 3.0 and 3.8% p.a. in 1998 and 1999, respectively, and aggregate employment grew at an average annual rate of 1.8% during 1998–99.[22] According to Nyhetsbyrån Ticker, the number of IPOs was as high as 105 in 1999, compared to 26 in 1996. New entrepreneurial firms, in particular in the IT sector, were still formed at a rapid rate.

Should this favorable development be seen as a rejection of the thesis in this paper? We do not think so. First, the development is still of recent vintage, and hence it is too early to tell to what extent we are dealing with a cyclical phenomenon. Second, and much more importantly, a number of measures were taken during the 1990s that can be expected to encourage the emergence of a stronger entrepreneurial culture:

- The corporate tax rate has been cut in half and is now 28%, which strongly favors equity relative to debt financing.
- The highest marginal tax rate has been lowered from close to 90% around 1980 to roughly

56%, which has increased the after-tax rate of return on human capital investment.

- The capital and foreign exchange markets have been wholly deregulated.
- The wage bargaining system is now less centralized than before, and in particular wages in the upper decile have increased rapidly in the latter half of the 1990s (Davis and Henrekson, 2000).
- Certain deregulatory measures on the labor market have already been taken, which in practice gives more room for flexibility than before, and more measures can be expected in the near future.
- The deregulation of several previously regulated markets, in particular the deregulation of the market for telecommunications, opened new arenas for entrepreneurial expansion.

Other factors are more fortuitous, but still in line with our thesis. The Stockholm stock exchange had the strongest development of all stock exchanges in the industrialized world during the 1980s and 1990s,[23] and given that 60% of the population own listed shares, this strong wealth creation has made a large number of people wealthy. This should spur entrepreneurial activity. For the first time since the interwar period, new family fortunes were formed, and in many cases that wealth appears to have been instrumental as angel capital in the new IT firms.

Thus, the current boom suggests that favorable changes in the conditions facilitating the emergence of science-based entrepreneurship will ultimately lead to more activity in this arena in Sweden. However, compared to the US the rules of the game are still unfavorable: the taxation of entrepreneurial income (including stock options and the overall taxation of VC firms) continues to be high, the steep rate of labor taxation reduces the rate of return on human capital investment and the labor market remains highly regulated. More specifically, academic entrepreneurship is still hampered by unfavorable incentives within the university system.

11. Conclusions

We outlined a framework for identifying strategic choices made by individuals, and policymakers relating to science-based entrepreneurship.

We examined the implications of this framework, based on an in-depth analysis of experiences in the US and Sweden.

Sweden devoting substantial resources to R&D; R&D spending relative to GDP has been the highest in the world for more than a decade. The country also hosts several world-leading firms with a high R&D intensity, it holds a world class position in terms of publication rates in leading academic journals, and its government invests massively in the building of organizations to bridge the gap between university research and industry. At the same time, the performance record in recent decades has been dismal in many respects. In particular, few new jobs have been created in new technology-based firms and there are few examples of science-based success stories.

To explain why the large volume of research has given rise to comparatively little commercial activity compared to the US, we systematically studied the pertinent incentive structures in the two countries: for human capital investment, for becoming an entrepreneur, for expanding existing entrepreneurial ventures and for universities themselves. We have shown that the relevant incentive structures provide far less encouragement to science-based entrepreneurship and entrepreneurial behavior in Sweden than in the US.

We conclude that a general lack of favorable institutions and pertinent incentive structures that promote the emergence of an entrepreneurial culture is the major explanation for the modest role of academic entrepreneurship in Sweden. Several policy changes have been made in the last decade that strengthen the incentives for science-based entrepreneurship in Sweden. As our analysis would predict, this has been accompanied by a burst of entrepreneurial activity, particularly in the IT sector.

More generally, our analysis suggests that a policy aimed at encouraging science-based entrepreneurship should focus on strengthening individual incentives for human capital investment and entrepreneurial behavior both within universities and in business. Key policy areas include attractive tax rates on entrepreneurial income, a tax structure that is not overly progressive, reasonably deregulated labor markets, and a university system characterized by decentralization and competition.

228 *Henrekson and Rosenberg*

Acknowledgments

Financial support from Jan Wallanders och Tom Hedelius Stiftelse is gratefully acknowledged. We are grateful for excellent research assistance from Per Thulin and Brent Goldfarb.

Notes

1. See Slaughter and Leslie (1997) for a comprehensive examination of the phenomenon in question.
2. One may argue that crucial decisions have been taken even before that, when the student decides whether to focus on natural sciences and technology in high school.
3. Convergence implies a reduction in the variance of income across countries. Convergence does not necessarily imply catching up, since a decreased variance may occur even if the other countries do not approach the income level of the technologically leading country (Barro and Sala-i-Martin, 1995).
4. Source: OECD, *Economic Outlook*, December 1998 (data on disk), OECD, *National Accounts 1960–97*, 1999.
5. The pattern is similar if we look at high-tech exports. Since the mid 1980s the US high-tech export share has been approximately 37%. Sweden's share was at about half the US level until the late 1980s. During the 1990s the Swedish high-tech export share has increased to 27% in 1996, which is roughly the average level in the OECD excluding the US.
6. As used here the term universities also includes colleges.
7. It is approximately 6 percentage points higher when measured as a share of labor input rather than as a share of expenditure—see OECD, *Basic Science and Technology Statistics on diskette, 1997*.
8. According to the same source 76% of total R&D at universities was in technology, natural sciences, biomedicine and agricultural sciences.
9. This and the preceding paragraph are mainly based on Fenn, Liang, and Prowse (1995).
10. One can also point to other countries in addition to the US, where there is substantially more academic entrepreneurship despite very little of bridging institutions and other government support—see, for example, Klofsten and Jones-Evans (2000) for a comparison between Sweden and Ireland. One may also note that Etzkowitz *et al.* (2000) conclude from their interviews: "One opinion is that centralized organizations for external contacts are highly overrated."
11. Zetterberg (1994) and Statistics Sweden, *Labour Force Surveys*.
12. No reliable data set has been collected in Sweden for a date later than 1991. The next *Level of Living Survey* (LNU) will not be available until 2001.
13. According to some studies there was a modest increase in the educational premium in the late 1980s.
14. See Lindbeck (1997).
15. Details are given in Davidsson and Henrekson (2001).
16. See Misher (1984, p. 357).
17. Blanchflower and Oswald (1998) arrive at the same conclusion in an empirical analysis based on British data.
18. Much of the discussion in the subsection regarding the US is based on Fenn, Liang, and Prowse (1995) and Zider (1998).
19. It should be noted, however, that Braunerhjelm (2000) is very skeptical of the Karaömerlioglu and Jacobsson study. He claims that they both exaggerate the size of the Swedish VC market and the degree to which funds are channeled to early investment phases.
20. Blanchflower and Freeman (1992) and Blau and Kahn (1996) provide evidence that unions and other centralized wage-setting institutions compress wages among observationally similar workers by promoting standard rate compensation policies.
21. See Davis, Haltiwanger, and Schuh (1996) for an overview of this research.
22. Statistics Sweden, *National Accounts* and *Labour Force Surveys*.
23. *The Economist* (1999).

References

Acs, Z. and D. Audretsch, 1990, *Innovation and Small Firms*, Cambridge, MA: MIT Press.
Audretsch, D. and P. Stephan, 1996, 'Company-Scientist Locational Links: The Case of Biotechnology', *American Economic Review* **86** (3), 641–652.
Barro, R.J. and X. Sala-i-Martin, 1995, *Economic Growth*, New York: McGraw-Hill.
Baumol, W.J., 1990, 'Entrepreneurship: Productive, Unproductive, and Destructive', *Journal of Political Economy* **98** (5), 893–921.
Becker, G.S., 1964, *Human Capital*, New York: Columbia University Press.
Birch, D., A. Haggerty, and W. Parsons, 1995, *Who's Creating Jobs?* Boston: Cognetics Inc.
Björklund, A. and C., Kjellström, 1994, 'Avkastningen på utbildning i Sverige 1968 till 1991', in R. Eriksson, and J.O. Jönsson (eds.), *Sorteringen i skolan*, Stockholm: Carlssons.
Blanchflower, D.G. and A.J. Oswald, 1998, 'What Makes an Entrepreneur?', *Journal of Labor Economics* **16** (1), 26–60.
Blanchflower, D.G. and R.B. Freeman, 1992, 'Unionism in the United States and Other Advanced OECD Countries', *Industrial Relations* **31** (1), 56–79.
Blau, F.D. and L.M. Kahn, 1996, 'International Differences in Male Wage Inequality: Institutions versus Market Forces', *Journal of Political Economy* **104** (4), 791–837.
Braunerhjelm, P., 1998, 'Varför leder inte ökade FoU-satsningar till mer högteknologisk export?', *Ekonomiska samfundets tidskrift* **51** (2), 113–122.
Braunerhjelm, P., 1999, 'Venture capital, mångfald och tillväxt', *Ekonomisk Debatt* **27** (4), 213–222.
Braunerhjelm, P., 2000, 'Replik till Karaömerlioglu och Jacobsson: Starka slutsatser om venture kapital saknar grund', *Ekonomisk Debatt* **28** (4), 368–373.
Brock, W.A. and D.S. Evans, 1986, *The Economics of Small Businesses: Their Role and Regulation in the US Economy*, New York and London: Holmes and Meier.
Brown, C. and J. Medoff, 1989, 'The Employer Size Wage Effect', *Journal of Political Economy* **97** (5), 1027–1059.

Carlsson, B., 1999, 'Small Business, Entrepreneurship, and Industrial Dynamics', in Z. Acs (ed.), *Are Small Firms Important?*, Dordrecht: Kluwer.

Davidsson, P. and M. Henrekson, 2001, 'Institutional Determinants of the Prevalence of Start-ups and High-Growth Firms: Evidence from Sweden', *Small Business Economics*, forthcoming.

Davidsson, P., L. Lindmark, and C. Olofsson, 1996, *Näringslivsdynamik under 90-talet*, Stockholm: NUTEK.

Davis, S.J., 1992, 'Cross-Country Patterns of Change in Relative Wages', *NBER Macroeconomics Annual Vol. 7*, 239–292.

Davis, S.J. and J. Haltiwanger, 1999, 'Gross Job Flows', in O. Ashenfelter, and D. Card (eds.), *Handbook of Labor Economics*, Vol. 3, Amsterdam: North-Holland.

Davis, S.J., J. Haltiwanger, and S. Schuh, 1996, *Job Creation and Destruction*, Cambridge, MA: MIT Press.

Davis, S.J. and M. Henrekson, 1997, 'Industrial Policy, Employer Size and Economic Performance in Sweden', in R.B. Freeman, R. Topel, and B. Swedenborg (eds.), *The Welfare State in Transition*, Chicago: University of Chicago Press.

Davis, S.J. and M. Henrekson, 2000, 'Wage-Setting Institutions as Industrial Policy', NBER Working Paper No. 7502.

E-chron, 1998, *The Swedish IT/Internet Venture Capital Survey 1998*, Stockholm.

Edin, P.-A. and B. Holmlund, 1995, 'The Swedish Wage Structure: The Rise and Fall of Solidarity Policy?', in R.B. Freeman, and L.F. Katz (eds.), *Differences and Changes in Wage Structures*, Chicago: University of Chicago Press.

Edin, P.-A. and R. Topel, 1997, 'Wage Policy and Restructuring—The Swedish Labor Market Since 1960', in R.B. Freeman, R. Topel, and B. Swedenborg (eds.), *The Welfare State in Transition*, Chicago: University of Chicago Press.

Engen, E. and J. Gruber, 1996, 'Unemployment Insurance and Precautionary Savings', NBER Working Paper No. 5252.

Etzkowitz, H., P. Asplund, and N. Nordman, 2000, 'The University and Regional Renewal: Emergence of an Entrepreneurial Paradigm in the US and Sweden', in G. Törnqvist, and S. Sörlin (eds.), *The Wealth of Knowledge. Universities in the New Economy*, forthcoming.

European Observatory for SMEs, 1995, *Third Annual Report 1995*, Zoetermeer, the Netherlands: EIM Small Business Research and Consultancy.

Fägerlind, I., 1991, 'Utbildningsstandarden i Sverige 1970–1990 och produktivitetsutvecklingen', in E. Wadensjö (ed.), *Arbetskraft, arbetsmarknad och produktivitet*, Expert report No. 4 to Produktivitetsdelegationen, Stockholm: Allmänna Förlaget.

Feldstein, M., 1996, 'The Missing Piece in Policy Analysis: Social Security Reform', *American Economic Review* **86** (2), 1–14.

Fenn, G., N. Liang, and S. Prowse, 1995, 'The Economics of the Private Equity Market', Board of Governors of the Federal Reserve System, Washington, D.C.

Fölster, S., 2001, 'Do Lower Taxes Stimulate Self-Employment?' *Small Business Economics*, forthcoming.

Fornwall, M., 1991, 'Sjunkande avkastning på utbildning', Mimeo. Department of Economics, Uppsala University.

Fredriksson, P., 1997, 'Economic Incentives and the Demand for Higher Education', *Scandinavian Journal of Economics* **99** (1), 129–142.

Fukao, M. and M. Hanazaki, 1987, 'Internationalization of Financial Markets and the Allocation of Capital', *OECD Economic Studies*, **8**, 35–92.

Gibbons, M. *et al.*, 1994, *The New Production of Knowledge*, London: Sage.

Goldin, C. and L.F. Katz, 1999, 'The Returns to Skill in the United States across the the Twentieth Century', NBER Working Paper No. 7126.

Gompers, P.A. and J. Lerner, 1999, 'What Drives Venture Capital Funding?' NBER Working Paper No. 6906.

Granstrand, O. and S. Alänge, 1995, 'The Evolution of Corporate Entrepreneurship in Swedish Industry—Was Schumpeter Wrong?' *Journal of Evolutionary Economics* **5** (2), 133–156.

Hansson, P. and L. Lundberg, 1995, *Från basindustri till högteknologi? Svensk näringsstruktur och strukturpolitik*. Stockholm: SNS Förlag.

Henrekson, M. and D. Johansson, 1999, 'Institutional Effects on the Evolution of the Size Distribution of Firms', *Small Business Economics* **12** (1), 11–23.

Henrekson, M., L. Jonung, and J. Stymne, 1996, 'Economic Growth and the Swedish Model', in N.F.R. Crafts, and G. Tonniolo (eds.), *Economic Growth in Europe since 1945*, Cambridge: Cambridge University Press.

Hibbs, D.A. Jr., 1990, 'Wage Compression under Solidarity Bargaining in Sweden', in I. Persson-Tanimura (ed.), *Generating Equality in the Welfare State: The Swedish Experience*, Oslo: Norwegian University Press.

Holtz-Eakin, D., D. Joulfaian, and H.S. Rosen, 1994, 'Sticking It out: Entrepreneurial Survival and Liquidity Constraints', *Journal of Political Economy* **102** (1), 53–75.

Hopenhayn, H.A. and R. Rogerson, 1993, 'Job Turnover and Policy Evaluation: A General Equilibrium Analysis', *Journal of Political Economy* **101** (5), 915–938.

Hubbard, R.G., J. Skinner, and S.P. Zeldes, 1995, 'Precautionary Savings and Social Insurance', *Journal of Political Economy* **103** (2), 360–399.

Isaksson, A., 1998, 'Den svenska venture capital-marknaden', in E. Landell *et al.*, *Entreprenörsfonder. Riskkapital till växande småföretag*, Stockholm: The Federation of Swedish Industries and NUTEK.

Isaksson, A., 1999, *Effekter av venture capital i Sverige*. B 1999:3, Stockholm: NUTEK Förlag.

Jacobsson, S., C. Sjöberg, and M. Wahlström, 2000, 'Alternative Specifications of the Institutional Constraint to Economic Growth—Or Why Is There a Shortage of Computer and Electronic Engineers and Scientists in Sweden?' *Technology Analysis and Strategic Management*, forthcoming.

Jorgenson, D.W. and R. Landau (eds.), 1993, *Tax Reform and the Cost of Capital. An International Comparison*, Washington, DC: Brookings.

Karaömerlioglu, D. and S. Jacobsson, 2000, 'The Swedish Venture Capital Industry—An Infant, Adolescent or Grown-Up?' *Venture Capital* **2** (1), 61–88.

King, M.A. and D. Fullerton (eds.), 1984, *The Taxation of Income from Capital. A Comparative Study of the United States, the United Kingdom, Sweden and West Germany*, Chicago: University of Chicago Press.

Kirzner, I.M., 1973, *Competition and Entrepreneurship*, Chicago: University of Chicago Press.

Klofsten, M. and D. Jones-Evans, 2000, 'Academic Entrepreneurship in the European Context: A Comparative Study', *Small Business Economics* 14 (4), 299–309.

Knight, F.H., 1921, *Risk, Uncertainty and Profit*, New York: Houghton Mifflin.

Landell, E. *et al.*, 1998, *Entreprenörsfonder. Riskkapital till växande småföretag*, Stockholm: The Federation of Swedish Industries and NUTEK.

Landström, H., 1993, 'Informal Risk Capital in Sweden and Some International Comparisons', *Journal of Business Venturing* 8 (4), 525–540.

Lindbeck, A., 1997, 'The Swedish Experiment', *Journal of Economic Literature* 35 (3), 1273–1319.

Lindh, T. and H. Ohlsson, 1996, 'Self-Employment and Windfall Gains: Evidence from the Swedish Lottery', *Economic Journal* 106 (439), 1515–1526.

Lindh, T. and H. Ohlsson, 1998, 'Self-Employment and Wealth Inequality', *Review of Income and Wealth* 44 (1), 25–42.

Lindholm Dahlstrand, Å., 1997a, 'Growth and Inventiveness in Technology-Based Spin-off Firms', *Research Policy* 26 (3), 331–344.

Lindholm Dahlstrand, Å., 1997b, 'Entrepreneurial Spin-off Enterprises in Göteborg, Sweden', *European Planning Studies* 5 (5), 659–673.

Lindström, G. and C. Olofsson, 1998, 'Teknikbaserade företag i tidig utvecklingsfas', Stockholm: Institute for Management of Innovation and Technology.

Lucas, R.E., 1988, 'On the Mechanics of Economic Development', *Journal of Monetary Economics* 22 (1), 3–42.

Lundberg, L., 1999, *Sveriges internationella konkurrenskraft*, Expert Report to the *Medium-Term Survey* (LU), Stockholm: Fritzes.

Mankiw, N.G., D. Romer, and D.N. Weil, 1992, 'A Contribution to the Empirics of Economic Growth', *Quarterly Journal of Economics* 107 (2), 407–437.

Misher, N., 1984, 'Tax Consequences of Exercising An Incentive Stock Option with Stock of the Granting Corporation', *The Tax Executive*, July, 357–363.

Morrison, C.J. and D. Siegel, 1997, 'External Capital Factors and Increasing Returns in U.S. Manufacturing', *Review of Economics and Statistics* 79 (4), 647–654.

National Science Board, 1997, *Science and Engineering Indicators*, Washington, DC: USGPO.

NUTEK, 1994, *Småföretagen—Sveriges framtid?* B 1994:4, Stockholm: NUTEK Företag.

OECD, 1995, *Education at a Glance*, Paris.

OECD, 2000, *Education at a Glance*, Paris.

Olofsson, C. and B. Stymne, 1995, 'The Contribution of New Technology-Based Firms to the Swedish Economy I: A Literature Survey', Stockholm and Göteborg: IMIT Report 97:88.

Olofsson, C. and C. Wahlbin, 1993, *Teknikbaserade företag från högskolan*, Stockholm: Institute for Management of Innovation and Technology.

Pålsson, A., 1998, 'De svenska hushållens sparande och förmögenheter 1986–1996', Mimeographed. Department of Economics, Lund University.

Rickne, A., 1999, 'New Technology-Based Firms in the Evolution of a Technological Field—The Case of Biomaterials', Mimeographed. Department of Industrial Dynamics, Chalmers University of Technology.

Rickne, A. and S. Jacobsson, 1996, 'New Technology-Based Firms—An Exploratory Study of Technology Exploitation and Industrial Renewal', *International Journal of Technology Management* 11 (3/4), 238–257.

Rickne, A. and S. Jacobsson, 1999, 'New Technology-based Firms in Sweden—A Study of their Direct Impact on Industrial Renewal', *Economics of Innovation and New Technology* 8 (2), 197–223.

Rosenberg, N., 1999, 'American Universities as Endogenous Institutions', Mimeographed. Department of Economics, Stanford University.

Rosenberg, N., 2000, *Schumpeter and the Endogeneity of Technology: Some American Perspectives*, London: Routledge.

Saint-Paul, G., 1997, 'Is Labor Rigidity Harming Europe's Competitiveness? The Effect of Job Protection on the Patterns of Trade and Welfare', *European Economic Review* 41 (3–5), 499–506.

Saxenian, A., 1996, *Regional Advantage. Culture and Competition in Silicon Valley and Route, 128*, Cambridge, MA: Harvard University Press.

Schultz, T.W., 1960, 'Capital Formation in Education', *Journal of Political Economy* 68 (4), 571–583.

Schumpeter, J.A., 1934, *The Theory of Economic Development*, Cambridge, MA: Harvard University Press.

Siegel, D., D. Waldman, and A.N. Link, 1999, 'Assessing the Impact of Organizational Practices on the Productivity of University Technology Transfer Offices: An Exploratory Study', NBER Working Paper No. 7256.

Slaughter, S. and L.L. Leslie, 1997, *Academic Capitalism. Politics, Policies, and the Entrepreneurial University*, Baltimore: John Hopkins University Press.

Södersten, J., 1984, 'Sweden', in M.A. King and D. Fullerton (eds.), *The Taxation of Income from Capital. A Comparative Study of the United States, the United Kingdom, Sweden and West Germany*, Chicago: University of Chicago Press.

Södersten, J., 1993, 'Sweden', in D.W. Jorgenson, and R. Landau (eds.), *Tax Reform and the Cost of Capital. An International Comparison*, Washington, DC: Brookings.

SOU 1996:70, *Samverkan mellan högskolan och näringslivet*, Huvudbetänkande av NYFOR, Stockholm: Fritzes.

SOU 1996:89, *Samverkan mellan högskolan och de små och medelstora företagen*, Slutbetänkande av NYFOR, Stockholm: Fritzes.

SOU 1998:128, *Forskningspolitik*. Slutbetänkande av Kommittén för översyn av den svenska forskningspolitiken (Forskning 2000), Stockholm: Fritzes.

Stankiewicz, R., 1986, *Academics and Entrepreneurs. Developing University—Industry Relations*, London: Frances Pinter.

Statistics Sweden, 1996, *Vetenskaps- och teknologiindikatorer för Sverige 1996*, Stockholm: Statistics Sweden.

Storey, D.J., 1994, *Understanding the Small Business Sector*, London: Routledge.

The Economist, 1999, 'The Foresight Saga.', **353** (8150), December 18th, 65–67.

Uhlin, Å., Å. Philips, and L. Sundberg, 1992, *Forskning och företagande*, ERU-rapport No. 76. Stockholm: Regeringskansliets offsetcentral.

Utterback, J.M. and G. Reitberger, 1982, 'Technology and Industrial Innovation in Sweden: A Study of New-Technology Based Firms', Center for Policy Alternatives, MIT and STU, Stockholm.

Vedin, B.-A., 1993, *Innovationer för Sverige*, SOU 1993:84. Stockholm: Näringsdepartementet.

Wennekers, S. and R. Thurik, 1999, 'Linking Entrepreneurship and Economic Growth', *Small Business Economics* **13** (1), 27–55.

Zetterberg, J., 1994, 'Avkastning på utbildning i privat och offentlig sektor', FIEF Working Paper No. 125, Stockholm.

Zider, B., 1998, 'How Venture Capital Works', *Harvard Business Review*, November–December, 131–139.

Zucker, L., M. Darby, and M. Brewer, 1998, 'Intellectual Human Capital and the Birth of US Biotechnology Enterprises', *American Economic Review* **88** (3), 290–306.

[30]

Available online at www.sciencedirect.com

JOURNAL
of BUSINESS
VENTURING

ELSEVIER

Journal of Business Venturing 20 (2005) 241–263

Entrepreneurship and university-based technology transfer

Gideon D. Markman[a,*], Phillip H. Phan[b,1], David B. Balkin[c,2], Peter T. Gianiodis[a,3]

[a]*Terry College of Business, University of Georgia, Athens, GA 30602-6256, USA*
[b]*Lally School of Management and Technology, Rensselaer Polytechnic Institute, 110 8th Street, Troy, NY 12180-3590, USA*
[c]*Leeds School of Business, University of Colorado at Boulder, Boulder, CO 80309, USA*

Abstract

The success of business incubators and technology parks in university settings is often determined by how well technology is transferred from the labs to their startup firms. University technology transfer offices (UTTOs) function as "technology intermediaries" in fulfilling this role. Yet, entrepreneurship theory and research on the role of the UTTO in business incubation and new venture formation is sparse. To move the research along, we use grounded theory to build a framework to address two questions: (a) Which UTTOs' structures and licensing strategies are most conducive to new venture formation; and (b) how are the various UTTOs' structures and licensing strategies correlated with each other. Our findings reveal a complex set of relationships between UTTO structure and strategies, new venture formation, and business incubation.

Based on interviews with 128 UTTO directors, we show that whereas for-profit UTTO structures are positively related to new venture formation, traditional university and nonprofit UTTO structures are more likely to correlate with the presence of university-based business incubators. Licensing-for-equity strategy is positively related to new venture formation while sponsored research licensing strategy is negatively related. Interestingly, the licensing-for-cash strategy, the most prevalent transfer strategy, is least correlated to new venture formation. A content analysis of UTTO mission statements also revealed an overemphasis on royalty income and an underemphasis on entrepreneurship. The

* Corresponding author. Tel.: +1-706-542-3751; fax: +1-706-542-3743.
  E-mail addresses: gmarkman@terry.uga.edu (G.D. Markman), pphan@rpi.edu (P.H. Phan), david.balkin@colorado.edu (D.B. Balkin), gianiodi@arches.uga.edu (P.T. Gianiodis).
  [1] Tel.: +1-518-276-2319; fax: +1-518-276-8661.
  [2] Tel.: +1-303-492-5780; fax: +1-303-492-5962.
  [3] Tel.: +1-706-542-4666; fax: +1-706-542-3743.

0883-9026/$ – see front matter © 2004 Published by Elsevier Inc.
doi:10.1016/j.jbusvent.2003.12.003

242   *G.D. Markman et al. / Journal of Business Venturing 20 (2005) 241–263*

paper concludes with a discussion that outlines some of the implications and limitations of our model.

Keywords: Entrepreneurship; Technology transfer; Business incubators; UTTO

1. Executive summary

With considerable profits at stake, many research universities are seeking to more effectively manage how their ideas and discoveries are deployed and sold. Perhaps this is the reason why with the exception of such institutions as Harvard, Boston University, Stanford University, and the like, who were already part of new venture "nurseries" or ecologies of emerging organizations, 62% of the universities and their communities in this study are establishing business incubators and building research parks as ways to encourage technology-based new ventures and economic development.

Within this ecology of knowledge creation and business formation, university technology transfer offices (UTTOs) are increasingly functioning as "technology intermediaries" that transmit technological innovations from the lab bench to industry. As we noted in the abstract, the extant entrepreneurship theory and research on the role of UTTO in new business creation and business incubation is sparse and so to advance our understanding of this issue, we use grounded theory to build a framework around the following questions: (a) Which UTTOs' structures and licensing strategies are most conducive of new venture formation? and (b) How are UTTOs' structures and licensing strategies correlated?

Interviews with 128 UTTO directors and a content analysis of university policies revealed that a UTTO is organized into three archetypes: (a) traditional university structure, (b) nonprofit 501(C)1 research foundation, and (c) for-profit private venture extension. These structures grant increasing degrees of autonomy to the UTTO managers in their pursuit of technology commercialization opportunities. A patent-protected technology is commercialized through one of three main licensing strategies: (a) licensing in exchange for sponsored research, (b) licensing for equity in a company, and (c) licensing for cash. While the strategic choice to commercialize proprietary technology depends on many factors, interviewees report that their decisions are strongly influenced by the stage of the technology, which they classify into four overlapping categories including early-stage inventions, proof of concept, reduction to practice, and prototyping.

Results based on qualitative and quantitative data show correlational links between UTTO structures, transfer strategies, the creation of new ventures, and business incubation. For instance, for-profit UTTO structures are positively related to the transfer of new technology via new venture formation. While traditional and nonprofit UTTO structures are uncorrelated with venture creation, they do correlate with the presence of a university business incubator. We found that both licensing in exchange for equity and for sponsored research are related to new venture formation, although the former is negatively so while the latter is positively so. The strategy of licensing for sponsored research is negatively correlated with the existence of a university-based business incubator, which is in part a reflection of the stage of technological maturity. Another important finding is that the licensing-for-cash strategy (the most prevailing transfer strategy in our study) is least related to new venture creation.

The relationships we found between UTTO structures and licensing strategies are also interesting. For example, both traditional and nonprofit structures are related to licensing strategies that favor sponsored research, but the former is positively related while the latter is negatively related. On the other hand, traditional and for-profit structures are positively related to licensing strategies that favor the creation of new ventures. For-profit structures, probably due to UTTOs' competencies in business development, seemed to provide the strongest support for new venture creation.

Taken as a whole, this study advances our understanding in the following ways. With the exception of insightful but narrow case studies there is currently no broad framework for understanding the relationships between UTTO organization, licensing strategies, and the process of technology transfer-inspired new startups. We have done so using a near-census data collection technique that captures the entire phenomenon to develop a model that *simultaneously* explains UTTO strategies, structures, and outcomes.

From a public policy standpoint, taxpayer support for university basic research is traditionally justified by a return-to-society on investment argument. Therefore, universities are pressured to show tangible returns for the research grants they receive. We found that in response universities are increasingly viewing themselves as catalysts of new venture formation and regional development. They view the process of technology transfer as a channel through which this role can be fulfilled. In fact, we found that UTTOs play a key role in economic development by adopting various configurations and enacting different transfer strategies that appear to correlate with varying levels of new venture formation. However, there is an inherent conflict between realizing immediate income through licensing for cash and ensuring long-term cash flows through licensing for equity. Indeed, research shows that in the long run taking equity in startups produces a greater return than the average cash license arrangement. Still, we found that although licensing for equity is more likely to drive new venture emergence, the UTTO motivation to maximize cash flows and minimize financial and legal risks often lead to a strategic choice that undermines new venture creation.

The substantial growth in universities' patenting and licenses activity has prompted policymakers to debate the possible "unintended" effects of the Bayh–Dole Act, such as the apparent shift toward applied research in place of basic research. Our findings that universities employ different UTTO configurations with varying levels of autonomy could raise concerns that expectations of financial returns would, over time, increase the allocation of capital to applied research and reduce the capital to basic research. Although we report that licensing for cash is the predominant licensing strategy, we note that none of the structures are significantly related to the cash strategy. In fact, the for-profit structure was actually negatively related to this licensing strategy. Thus, the "problem" of a shift from basic to applied research may be overstated, at least as it applies to a university's licensing strategy.

244   *G.D. Markman et al. / Journal of Business Venturing 20 (2005) 241–263*

2. Entrepreneurship and university-based technology transfer

At its core, entrepreneurship is about the "why, when, and how opportunities for the creation of goods and services come into existence," (Shane and Venkatramanan, 2000, p. 218) and scientific discoveries are a key precursor to this process (Schumpeter, 1950). Nowhere is scientific discovery more salient to new venture creation than in research-oriented institutions of higher learning, the modern seedbeds for scientific breakthroughs and technological innovation. In fact, research on knowledge spillover and organizational learning suggests that continuous interactions among creators, appropriators, and con-sumers of technology accelerate the richness and reach of knowledge and discoveries (Agrawal and Henderson, 2002; Cockburn and Henderson, 1998; Zucker and Brewer, 1998; Zucker et al., 1998). Thus, the need to organize the process of accelerating technology spillover and innovation in universities is often a principal driver behind the establishment of technology transfer offices, business incubators, and science parks (Link et al., in press; Siegel et al., in press).

The 1980 Bayh–Dole Act, the 1980 Stevenson–Wydler Act, and the 1985 Federal Technology Transfer Act lead to a fundamental change in the way scientific discoveries at universities and Federal laboratories were commercially exploited. Since then, the number of U.S. universities that engage in technology transfer and licensing have increased eightfold, to more than 200, and the volume of university patents has increased fourfold (Mowery and Shane, 2002). The importance of technology commercialization and its impact on new venture creation through business incubation motivates this research. Our objective is to induce a theoretical model that explains the relationship between technology transfer strategies, organization structure, and new firm creation in U.S. research universities.

From 1991 to 1997, university license revenues increased over 315%, from $220 million to $698 million (Association of University Technology Managers [AUTM], 2000, 2002). The number of startup and mature firms that utilize technologies developed by university faculty, staff, and students skyrocketed with the result that venture capitalists are increasingly interested in university-founded technology firms (cf., Small Business Association, 2002). Coupled with Internet-related startups of the late 1990s and the resulting explosion of venture capital financing for technology-based new businesses, universities, sometimes in partnership with regional economic development agencies, intensified their focus on turning their proprietary technology into economic opportunities (Siegel et al., 2003).

Hence, where in the past universities have passively licensed their technologies today many research universities actively search for ways to channel proprietary technology to maximize rents and to spawn new companies (Thursby et al., 2001). Through their office of technology transfer, many U.S. research universities are becoming an integral part of a larger business community that links scientists to a value chain of business startups, incubators, science parks, and industry. For example, at Rensselaer Polytechnic Institute (RPI), a private science and engineering university in Upstate New York, the transfer of university technology into student- and faculty-founded businesses represents a conscious effort to create wealth and increase economic development from scientific discoveries. Budding ventures often relocate from the science labs to the RPI Incubator, which houses more than 35 new ventures

G.D. Markman et al. / Journal of Business Venturing 20 (2005) 241–263 245

at any one time, all of which are student or faculty founded firms. In turn, successful ventures can eventually migrate to the RPI Technology Park. This network of value creation entails many constituencies—inventors, scientists, universities, incubators, and technology parks—and where UTTOs often play a key role. Thus, UTTOs are fundamental to the successful transfer of technology to industry (Link et al., in press; Siegel et al., in press).

In spite of its important role, questions of what UTTO organizational configurations and licensing strategies are most beneficial to new business formation have yet to be fully answered. To this end, we employed a grounded theory approach to build a conceptual model that links the work of UTTOs and the creation of university-spawned businesses. Our primary objective was to address the following two questions: (a) Which UTTOs' structures and licensing strategies are most conducive to new venture formation? and (b) How are UTTOs' structures and licensing strategies related to each other? We next describe the methodology of our research, with special attention paid to the process of data collection for theory building.

3. Theory building methodology

Our paper employs grounded theory, which is an applied methodology of analysis linked with qualitative data to induce a theory (Creswell, 2002; Glaser and Strauss, 1999; Strauss and Corbin, 1998). Grounded theory is prescribed when constructs or phenomena are not well understood (here, the nature of UTTOs as intermediaries of knowledge and opportunities); there is no established theory that explains the links between the phenomena of interest (here, the relationships between UTTO' structure, strategy, and new venture formation); and/or the relationships between constructs that are not well understood in particular contexts (here, at what point transferred technology creates new business opportunities). To answer our questions, we interviewed 128 UTTO directors, who have first-hand experience in the phenomenon being studied and are thus most qualified to provide valuable insights and interpretations of their domain. More importantly, since many UTTOs are recently formed and are still evolving, one cannot rely on an empirical deductive (i.e., hypothesis testing) approach to theory building because we have simply no confidence that existing theoretical frameworks have accounted for the phenomenon in its entirety. In short, theory verification at the emergent stage of a phenomenon is not recommended and so we employ a positivist inductive approach to theory building (Eisenhardt, 1989).

Our primary data collection device is the long interview. We ensured that we always spoke to the Director of the UTTO since this person would be most conversant with university policies and commercialization strategies. We commenced with open-ended interviews with seven UTTO directors, who helped us understand and inventory the organizational config-urations of UTTOs, their transfer strategies, and their missions (cf., Holstein and Gubrium, 1995). Of the initial seven interviewees, three worked for small, medium, and large private universities, while the other four worked for medium and large public universities. To improve response rate and reduce social desirability, we assured the participant's anonymity. The interviews averaged 90 minutes; four were conducted over the telephone while three were conducted in person. Once we understood better the nature of a UTTO's work, we employed structured interviews with an additional 121 UTTO directors using narrower and more focused sets of questions, with each set becoming more focused as we reached theoretical saturation (Eisenhardt, 1989). At this point, an inventory of constructs, the typology of dimensions of the constructs, and the relationships between the constructs became clarified. Specifically, we identified a set of three UTTO structures, three main commercialization strategies, and four technology stages. From the interviews, we then explored the UTTO structures and technology transfer strategies that would most likely lead to new venture creation.

While some might question the external validity of this design, we feel that this is not a serious issue in a positivist approach to grounded theory. First, in building the theoretical model, we deliberately constrained its context to UTTOs in research universities in the United States. Issues of external validity are partially addressed by concentrating on the larger problem of internal validity and reliability and by cross-referencing the qualitative and quantitative data with other sources (e.g., UTTO websites, official university reports, data from various AUTM publications, and internal documents provided by UTTO respondents). We also validated interviewees' accounts with published university policies and internal documents, highlighting those areas for further clarification where our findings may contradict or elaborate on past research. This triangulation approach increased the confidence that the quantitative and qualitative data were accurate and that our interpretations of the data were true to the intentions of the interviewees.

Second, and in contrast to past research on this topic, we used a near-census sample of UTTOs. In total, we interviewed 128 UTTO directors representing over 60% of federal and industry research grants and over 70% of executed licenses, invention disclosures, and new patent applications. Our sample was drawn directly from the universe of 139 U.S. universities in the AUTM for 1999, the most recent list available. Our response rate represented over 92% of the AUTM population. This near-census sample ensured that our model is theoretically saturated and that we have observed the phenomenon in its entirety (Flint et al., 2002).

4. The theoretical model

UTTO personnel administer the commercialization process of a university's intellectual property (IP), defined as patents, copyrights, trademarks, various know-hows, and related assets. At the most general level, UTTO personnel are responsible to (a) evaluate and valuate disclosures of new discoveries; (b) seek legal protection for the technology, primarily through patenting; (c) sell licensing agreements to industry; and (d) collect royalty, oversee, and enforce contractual agreements with licensees. At the same time, because UTTOs are part of a value creation chain, their structures and licensing strategies might have a strong influence on technology transfer outcomes such as new venture creation. Hence, in the following sections we provide aggregated descriptions of UTTOs' structures and licensing strategies as they emerged from the interviews and other data sources provided by the respondents. The data were cross-validated with formal university documents.

G.D. Markman et al. / Journal of Business Venturing 20 (2005) 241–263 247

4.1. Structures: how universities house their UTTOs

Our interviews revealed that UTTOs are organized into three archetypes, which vary by the degree of autonomy granted at the institutional level to pursue technology commercialization opportunities. These structures are (a) traditional university structure, (b) nonprofit 501(C)1 research foundation, and (c) for-profit private venture extension. To establish reliability and convergent validity, we also researched each institution's website to corroborate these organizational structures. As we describe each of these organizational structures, it is important to keep in mind that of the 128 UTTOs studied, over half (52%) conformed to the traditional university structure, 41% were nonprofit research foundation, and 7% operated as for-profit private venture extensions. In the interest of parsimony, Table 1 provides additional descriptions and examples of each configuration.

4.1.1. Traditional university structure

A traditional UTTO is organized as an integral department within a university's administrative structure, usually reporting to the Office of the Provost or Vice President for Research. Such UTTOs are tightly supervised by an assistant or vice president of the university and is generally funded by the research office. Under this structure, which comprised 52% or 67 UTTOs in our sample, personnel are normally untenured university staff with the primary role of pursuing conventional licensing opportunities for royalty income. The direct, and often strong, oversight by a university administration limits the autonomy of UTTO management in matters of decision making, licensing strategies, and incentive systems. As one UTTO director from a public Northwestern school explained:

> Our goal was to have established an incubator by the end of last year to help facilitate entrepreneurial ventures, but we are still [9 months later] waiting for approval from university administration.

As this example illustrates, in addition to seeking patent protection for a discovery or launch a market study to determine the commercial potential of certain technologies, UTTO directors may need to seek formal university administration approval in building the necessary infrastructure to help facilitate their missions, in this example, entrepreneurial activities.

4.1.2. Nonprofit research foundation [501(C)1]

These UTTOs function as independent nonprofit units or part of separately constituted research foundations outside the university's administrative structure. Such research foundations, comprising 41% of 52 UTTOs in our sample, have their own Board of Directors, which is frequently chaired by the university president. Private universities and many large multisystem state universities create nonprofit research foundations to grant greater autonomy to faculty to conduct research and license new technology. In addition, many universities use this structure as it provides stronger legal protection against lawsuits stemming from licensing disputes, IP infringements, and even future product or service liabilities stemming from the university's licensed technology. UTTOs under this structure enjoy a separate budget from

248   *G.D. Markman et al. / Journal of Business Venturing 20 (2005) 241–263*

Table 1
UTTO structures

UTTO structures	Description	Key features	Advantages	(Count/%) Examples
Traditional university structure	UTTO is part of the Office of the Provost for Research, a department within the university structure. It is run primarily by an assistant/vice president of the university and generally is funded by the research office.	UTTO officers are university employees In general, UTTO does more traditional licensing for cash/revenue	UTTO is very simple to manage More direct control to university administration	(67/52%) Ex.: Johns Hopkins, Dartmouth
Nonprofit research foundation (501(C) 3)	UTTO is a separate entity or part of a separate "research" entity outside of the university structure. Research foundation is set by university/state government (for large state universities) specifically to grant greater autonomy to conduct research.	Nonprofit corporation Board of Directors independent of university Separate budget from university In some states, allows university to hold equity President of university is generally chairman of research foundation	Limits liability General autonomy from university Ex.: Provides greater flexibility for employee pay, incentives, etc. (i.e., outside of university grade system) Ex.: Separate budget (i.e., no government entity can "seize" allocated dollars from the foundation to fill budget holes) Allows entity to invest revenues without constraint	(52/41%) Ex.: Land grant universities (University of Minnesota, University of Michigan, etc.); private universities (Cornell, Brown)
For-profit private venture extension	UTTO is either part of university structure or a research foundation, with a private venture extension. The private venture extension generally is focused on economic development and creating startup companies.	Private venture has independent CEO & Board Employees have startup/VC experience Aggressively create startups	Limited liability Greater flexibility/freedom to "incent" employees Greater flexibility to raise outside capital	(9/7%) Ex.: Baylor College of Medicine, Boston University, University of Virginia

G.D. Markman et al. / Journal of Business Venturing 20 (2005) 241–263   249

their affiliated universities, greater autonomy in choosing licensing strategies, and the ability to hold equity in startup companies created to exploit their licensed technologies. As one UTTO director from a public Midwestern University explained:

> ... in addition to giving us better legal protection, this [research foundation] structure offers us greater freedom on hiring and hopefully, one day soon, incenting our officers ...

This example demonstrates that nonprofit research foundations [501(C)1] enjoy more flexibility than the traditionally structured UTTO in terms of granting compensation and incentives to personnel with pay levels that can sometime exceed the university grade system.

4.1.3. For-profit private extension

Only 7% or nine UTTOs in our sample were created as separate private for-profit private venture extensions. Five of these UTTOs were physically housed in a research foundation described above, while four were an integral part of the traditional university campus. The for-profit private extension is focused on economic development and creating startup companies. Private extensions also have an independent CEO and a Board, with personnel who have substantial experience in such areas as IP law, managing companies, and venture capitalism. Our informants told us that private venture extensions were most aggressive at creating startups and raising capital—a fact that was corroborated by our own Web-based searches and analyses. For-profit UTTOs enjoy the greatest autonomy in terms of licensing strategies and compensation systems. As one UTTO director from a private Northeastern university explained:

> ... our scientists are aware of the existing [entrepreneurial] network. Having the freedom to invest capital in these firms, as well as counsel them [on legal issues], provides us with a great opportunity to get in on the ground floor ...

As with a nonprofit research foundation [501(C)1] the benefit to universities is even greater legal insulation against lawsuits. More importantly, such private extensions are freer to raise capital from government or state economic development programs, conduct negotiations with potential licensees and research partners, and act entrepreneurially to fund startup companies.

Although participants from each of the three UTTO structures expressed some interest in new business formation, most of our interviewees suggest that the third archetype would be most conducive to new business formation. This takes us to the first proposition in our model:

Proposition 1: *Of the three UTTO archetypes, the for-profit private venture extension is best positioned to accelerate new business formation.*

4.2. Licensing strategies

Our interviewees suggested that once a technology is patent protected, their office will try to commercialize the discovery through one of three licensing strategies: (a) licensing in exchange for sponsored research; (b) licensing for equity; and (c) licensing for cash.

250

G.D. Markman et al. / Journal of Business Venturing 20 (2005) 241–263

However, since licensing strategies are driven, at least in part, by the technology in question, we begin this section with a short description of how UTTOs characterize the technologies they try to license. Table 2 provides more specific descriptions, culled from the interviews, of each technology stage.

UTTOs classify their technologies into four overlapping types: early-stage inventions, proof of concept, reduced to practice, and prototyping. UTTO directors conceptualized these overlapping categories along two continuums of uncertainty: ambiguity regarding whether a particular technology has market application and ambiguity regarding the robustness of the legal protection over the IP. As one might expect, early-stage inventions refer to discoveries based on basic research with highly uncertain market potential and in many cases unclear IP or prepatent protection status. On the other hand, prototyping refers to a technology with a relatively clearer market application and more robust legal protection (e.g., stronger patents). At the outset, it should be clear that licensing strategies are determined by many factors such as university mission, the budget for such activities, and so forth; so to determine each UTTO's primary licensing strategy we asked interviewees to describe the frequency distribution of their chosen licensing strategies. To be more precise, the question we asked stated, "UTTOs enact different commercialization strategies, including R&D capital; equity; and royalty cash. What is the average distribution of licensing strategies (out of 100%) across these three possibilities at your institution?" For example, the distribution of licensing strategies at a Northwestern U.S. university was 40% for sponsored research, 10% equity, and 50% for cash, whereas the licensing strategy of a prominent Southwestern U.S. university was entirely 100% for cash (0% for sponsored research and 0% for equity). As we describe each of the licensing strategies below, it is important to keep in mind that of the

Table 2
Technology stages

Technology stage	Description
Early stage	An early-stage technology may be an idea that might work should the idea be reduced to practice. This technology could also be a crude extract of some plant or cell that seems to have an in vitro effect. Neither the exact compound in the extract is known, nor has the exact mechanism of the effect been identified.
Proof of concept	An idea or new technology has been developed to the point that it shows signs of having the proposed effect. Similarly, a few target compounds in a crude extract may have been identified, but the mechanism by which they act may not have been discovered yet.
Reduction to practice	At this stage, an experiment on the idea has been replicated several times and the intended results have been reliably and repeatedly reproduced. The mechanism of the compound or compounds may have also been identified and, again, reliable results will have been produced.
Prototyping, formulation, compound	The new technology can now be constructed as a reliable method of producing a given result and/or if it can be predictably manipulated to produce desired results. For instance, a compound from a crude extract would have been either scaled up to industrial scale; based on its identified action, the compound could be used to screen for inhibitors or be used as a diagnostic tool. At this stage, new technologies might be applied in new and different settings.

G.D. Markman et al. / Journal of Business Venturing 20 (2005) 241–263 251

128 UTTOs we studied, 11% sought primarily sponsored research, 17% sought primarily equity licensing, and 72% sought primarily cash royalty as their predominant licensing objectives.

4.2.1. Licensing for sponsored research

Interviewees suggested that this strategy is usually paired with early-stage technologies. Our data show that approximately 11% of the UTTOs we studied used this as their predominant licensing strategy. The interviews revealed several reasons why licensing technology in *exchange for sponsored research* is the least preferred strategy. First, although UTTOs and corporations appreciate the benefits of working together to develop new technologies, both parties are wary of subsequent disputes over research direction and ownership of the future IP. Second, because at this stage the technology is underdeveloped and requires additional R&D capital, firms are reluctant to lock themselves into licensing agreements or incur patenting fees, which can reach $250,000 in the case of an international patent (this cost involves obtaining separate patent protection in foreign countries), without being sure of whether the technology would work, fit their market needs, and provide exclusivity against competing patents. The third and most important reason is best illustrated by legal mêlées between universities, corporations, and inventors.[4] Such uncertainties and legal challenges have left many UTTOs hesitant about and reluctant to enter into licensing in exchange for sponsored research. As one UTTO director from a public Southwestern university explained:

> ... we are well aware of the pending litigation [in California]. The last thing we want to happen is to turn a sponsored research agreement into future litigation ...

While receiving tax-free industry support to fund ongoing research projects enables universities to reallocate their own funds among fewer departments and schools, the legal hazards seem to frequently outweigh the benefits at this stage. Similarly, many universities instruct their UTTOs to focus primarily on developing their royalty stream. As one UTTO director from a private Northeastern engineering school explained,

> Despite the importance of various research undertakings, our job is to generate tangible revenues to the university, not to facilitate research in someone's lab.

Moreover, because licensing for sponsored research involves early-stage or proof of concept technology in which market applications are still unclear, UTTO directors feel that they have to give substantial monetary discounts as incentives to their licensees. Finally, licensing for sponsored research might hinder the UTTOs eventual goals of licensing the technology to any other organizations, including new ventures and corporate partners.

---

[4] Petr Taborsky, an undergraduate student at the University of South Florida, invented a reusable cleanser that can remove ammonia from wastewater (U.S. Patent No. 5,082,813). He was later charged for theft and violation of probation for using his notebooks and for refusing to sign over his patent to the school. This bright student was eventually incarcerated with drug dealers, robbers, and sex offenders.

252   *G.D. Markman et al. / Journal of Business Venturing 20 (2005) 241–263*

4.2.2. Licensing for equity

Our interviewees noted that this strategy is usually paired with proof of concept or reduced to practice technologies. The data show that approximately 17% of the UTTOs we studied used this as their predominant licensing strategy. The financial flexibility afforded by this arrangement allows the technology partner, which is a startup venture in two-thirds of the cases, to bring emerging technologies more quickly to market.

As one UTTO director from a private Mid-Atlantic university explained:

> ... [with] early stage technologies, sometimes taking an equity stake in a company is the only way to get the technology out the door ...

Our informants explained that large or resource-rich firms are less interested in proof of concept or reduced to practice stage technologies because of internal rate-of-return requirements on R&D investments. Additionally, given the inherently low success rate and relatively small commercial impact, a large corporation would view the bureaucratic process of managing a complex relationship with a university economically prohibitive.

Under this licensing strategy the UTTO treats the technology asset as a real option (McGrath, 1997). By investing in what is really a private partnership to further develop the technology, UTTOs bet also on the venture, rather than only on the technology. The objective is to support and harness the energy, aspiration, and motivation of the venture's scientists and founders to create a commercial application from IP. For this reason, UTTOs either leverage their endowed resources (e.g., Boston University, Harvard, and Stanford) with respect to latent incubator capacity (i.e., potential projects for incubators), or create their own incubators in the form of university-affiliated or government-sponsored Research Parks (e.g., RPI, University of Michigan, Cornell University). This explains why some UTTOs may even encourage their licensees to join their local incubator, which provides valuable resources in the form of managerial know-how and skills, business contacts, and social legitimacy (Link et al., 2003). As one UTTO director from a private Northeastern university explained:

> ... taking equity in a firm is a way to legitimize the firm, but sometimes more importantly, to legitimize the technology. Incubators also help in this regard ...

In fact, 62% of the institutions we studied have devoted significant resources into building business incubators that function as complements to and "accelerators" of technology commercialization efforts.

If the bet pays off and the venture successfully launches and makes sales, the university benefits as a claimant to the generated rents. If the venture reaches the stage of an IPO or some other exit pathway, the potential rents would be even higher; the university would enjoy income streams from a public firm while reallocating its resources for investments into other technologies and ventures. In such equity arrangements, the university loosens its control of the technology in exchange for future cash flow rights. In the event that the commercialization attempt is unsuccessful, the licensing agreement is usually terminated, which releases the technology back to the research institution, but hopefully at a more advanced stage, to be relicensed at a future time.

G.D. Markman et al. / Journal of Business Venturing 20 (2005) 241–263 253

There are several advantages to this strategy in the proof of concept or reduced to practice technology stages (cf., Bray and Lee, 2000; Feldman et al., 2002). Informants explained that securing equity positions makes sense when the technology is unresolved, its economic implications are imprecise, and the opportunity costs of foregone licensing and royalty revenues are low. More specifically, real options theory suggests that equity is preferred as it confers licensors the opportunities for future financial gains once licensees develop the technology. Agency theory argues that equity positions in a company provide long-term incentives to align the interests of a university and the firm towards the common goal of commercializing the technology. Such incentive alignment might also mitigate uncertainty regarding IP-related litigations between licensors and licensees (Jensen and Thursby, 2001). Finally, university equity positions in startups send a signal on the university's confidence in the technology and its scientists to potential stakeholders including funding agencies, rivals, suppliers, and customers. Such confidence, so the rationale goes, increases the probability that licensees can secure additional funding, access key distribution channels, and more fully leverage the technology to generate rents.

The benefits of such licensing strategies to new ventures can be substantial. Startups benefit from university-based technologies because in the event of patent infringements, some of the legal burden may shift to the IP owner, which is the university.[5] As one UTTO director from a large Midwestern public research-based university emphasized,

[The] new ventures we spin off often expect us to help them manage promising technologies ... and bear the risks early on in the technology's life cycle.

This point is particularly crucial for startups as infringement trial costs in 1997 reached $3 million for each party (Markman et al., 2004a). New ventures might also negotiate a first rights-of-refusal to cutting-edge proprietary technology with little or no transaction costs. Once an exclusive license is granted, startups enjoy some competitive insulation, while deriving legitimacy from its association with a university-based technology. Another benefit to new ventures is that as licensees they can tap more easily than ever into the knowledge, skills, and expertise of universities' scientists and students.

4.2.3. Licensing for cash

Our informants explained that since licensing choices are driven by the degree of technological resolution and future risk-return scenarios, licensing for cash is almost invariably paired with IP-based technologies at the *prototype* stage, for which a market has been identified. Since the expressed purpose of most UTTOs is to generate rents from scientific discovery, the more predictable the economic value, the more likely a UTTO will choose licensing for cash. Our data show that approximately 72% of the UTTOs in our sample used this as their predominant licensing strategy. A content analysis of UTTOs' mission statements corroborated this finding, as 80% of all mission statements highlight

---

[5] Since infringement cases are exceedingly expensive, universities always try to shift the legal burden to the licensee. For example, universities are less likely to file a lawsuit when the technology is licensed exclusively to a large, resource-rich corporation since the latter will have a natural incentive to protect its own rent streams.

254   *G.D. Markman et al. / Journal of Business Venturing 20 (2005) 241–263*

licensing for cash as a key organizational objective. Interestingly, this is almost fourfold the times mission statements mention entrepreneurship or new-venture creation as their over-arching goal (20.57%). Table 3 outlines the results of our content analysis of the UTTOs' mission statements.

The licensing for cash strategy is also frequently based on a technology that has not only demonstrated a clear path to commercialization but has also shown the potential for diverse applications that may span different industries. As one director from a large Southern public university that licenses primarily in the biotech and agribusiness domains observed,

> ... highly applied discoveries in a single domain, for example, veterinary science, often find applications in other markets and this gives us more licensing opportunities.

Since the path to commercializing applied technology is less uncertain, industry partners are also more willing to license the IP. As licenses for cash are normally exclusive, they reduce some of the risks for the licensee. For instance, exclusive licensing agreements prohibit a UTTO from relicensing the same technology to others, and, naturally, such exclusivity attracts larger industry players. Exclusive licensing agreements for technologies at the prototype stage can generate the most rents and such agreements can be drafted to provide the greatest legal protection to the UTTO as the licensor. In one example, under exclusive licensing agreements companies were more willing to reimburse a UTTO for its IP-related costs, which sometimes exceeded $250,000, and to pay higher up-front fees. Furthermore, although the UTTO cannot relicense the technology, licensees as primary claimants were given the right to relicense to a third party, thus creating additional flow through rents to the UTTO.

Though no exclusionary rights—even those afforded by patents—provide unassailable protection, legal defense under exclusive agreements is simpler because the only parties to the licensing agreement are the UTTO and a single corporation. This strategy is also viewed as a risk-shifting arrangement for the UTTO. The large firm is the main beneficiary of the license and, because of this, also the risk bearer because it has to bear the nontrivial legal costs of protecting the technology.

Table 3
A content analysis of UTTO mission statements

Primary objectives of the UTTO	Percentage of times appeared in mission statement (%)
Licensing for royalties	78.72
IP protection/management	75.18
Facilitate disclosure process	71.63
Sponsored research and assisting inventors	56.74
Public good (disseminate information/technology)	54.61
Industry relationships	42.55
Economic development (region, state)	26.95
Entrepreneurship and new venture creation	20.57

$N = 128$ UTTOs.

G.D. Markman et al. / Journal of Business Venturing 20 (2005) 241–263   255

As the UTTO director of a large West Coast private research university that specializes in IT-based discoveries reports,

> Exclusive licensing generally cuts up-front legal costs and lowers the carrying costs for the UTTO with respect to future legal action.

In addition to reducing legal costs, licensing for cash is also attractive in that the university can direct the resources to complete the technology commercialization cycle even when its technology partner chooses, for commercial reasons, not to bear the costs of final development. When the firm does choose to complete the commercialization process, the frequent engagement with the university's scientists to advance the technology can lead to substantial knowledge spillovers effects. As one UTTO director from a public Midwestern university explained:

> . . . often our scientists are keen to develop strong ties with industry partners in anticipation of future collaboration. When possible, we try to accommodate such requests.

Typically, because exclusive licensing arrangements are tightly defined around specifications of the licensed technology, the knowledge spillovers can result in future discoveries from which the university is free to exploit.

Taken as a whole, our fieldwork shows that while licensing for equity would be most conducive to new business formation, licensing for cash and for sponsored research would mostly likely be negatively related to new business formation. UTTOs in general would always try to license for cash. However, in terms of the other licensing strategies, we surmise from our fieldwork that (a) traditional UTTOs would most likely choose sponsored research and licensing for equity; (b) nonprofit structures would mostly likely avoid sponsored research; and (c) for-profit UTTO structures would mostly likely choose licensing for equity. Thus,

Proposition 2a: *Licensing for equity would be positively related to new business formation.*

Proposition 2b: *Licensing for cash and for sponsored research would be negatively related to new business formation.*

Proposition 3: *Traditional university UTTO structures would be positively related to sponsored research and equity strategies.*

Proposition 4: *Nonprofit UTTO structures would be negatively related to sponsored research strategy.*

Proposition 5: *For-profit UTTO structures would be positively related to equity strategies.*

5. Putting the model together

An important finding from our study is the correlation between UTTO structures, transfer strategy, and the creation of new ventures. The correlation matrix and descriptive statistics

Table 4
Correlation matrix among UTTO structures, licensing strategies, and startups

		1	2	3	4	5	6	7	8
1	Startups 1998–2001								
2	Startups in process	.67***							
3	University incubator	.07	.07						
4	Sponsored research	−.29***	−.13	−.17**					
5	License for cash	−.02	−.16*	−.09	−.53***				
6	License for equity	.30***	.37***	.24**	−.22**	−.56***			
7	Traditional structure	−.06	−.08	.37***	.19**	.10	.25***		
8	503(c) structure	.10	.01	.29***	−.15*	−.03	.11	−.86***	
9	For-profit extension	.19**	.17**	.16*	−.09	−.16*	.31***	−.26***	−.21**

$N = 128$ UTTOs.
 *$P < .10$.
 **$P < .05$.
 ***$P < .001$.

(Tables 4 and 5), culled from interview data and documents, suggest that the for-profit UTTO structure is positively related to the transfer of new technology via new venture formation. Although none of the other structures were correlated with venture creation, they were positively correlated with the presence of a business incubator.

The empirical data confirm that licensing for equity was positively related to new venture formation while licensing for sponsored research was negatively related to new venture formation. Interestingly, the licensing for sponsored research strategy was even negatively correlated with the existence of a university-based business incubator. Another and probably most important finding is that the licensing for cash strategy—the most prevalent UTTO

Table 5
Descriptive statistics

	Mean	Median	S.D.	Range
UTTO structure (1-0)				
Traditional structure	0.52	1.00	0.50	1.00
501(c) foundation	0.41	0.00	0.49	1.00
For-profit extension	0.07	0.00	0.23	1.00
Licensing strategy (%)				
Sponsored research	11	10.00	10.22	40.00
Equity	17	15.00	10.87	50.00
Cash	72	75.00	14.62	100.00
Incubator? (yes/no)	0.62	1.00	0.49	1.00
Average number of startups/university				
In 2001	3	2	4	26
In 2000	3	2	4	31
In 1999	2	1	3	19
In 1998	2	1	3	17

Data sources: AUTM, interviews, UTTO and university websites, UTTO internal documents
$N = 128$ UTTOs.

commercialization strategy—is the least related to new venture emergence. This observation suggests that licensing for cash strategies target mature and resourceful corporations rather than new ventures. This finding is also consistent with UTTO mission statements that emphasize royalties and underemphasize entrepreneurship.

The relationships between UTTO structures and licensing strategies are also interesting. For example, both the traditional and the nonprofit structures are related to licensing strategies that favor sponsored research; however, the former is positively whereas the latter is negatively related. On the other hand, both the traditional university and for-profit structures are positively related to licensing strategies that are more likely to lead to the creation of new ventures. Coincidentally, although one might expect the for-profit UTTOs to seek primarily cash strategies, the correlation matrix does not support this expectation. In fact, as stated above, it appears that the for-profit UTTOs, perhaps due to their focus and personnel's experience in business development, are best positioned to provide strong support for new business creation. As one UTTO director who managed a for-profit UTTO noted:

> ... when I hire personnel, I am looking for them to have worked for a VC or to have other business development experience.

Our interviews also found an important association between technology stage, transfer strategy, and the choice of licensees. Summarized in Fig. 1, the theoretical model illustrates that early-stage inventions are licensed, primarily through sponsored research, to large firms. Large firms are also the primary recipients of technologies at the prototype stage, transferred through cash strategies. In contrast, new ventures are the primary licensing targets of technologies at the proof of concept stage or those that have been reduced to practice.

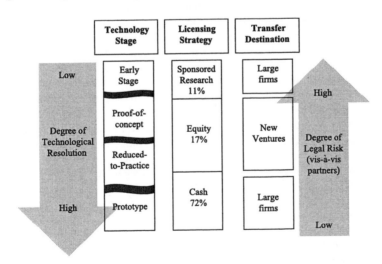

Fig. 1. The relationship between technology stage, licensing strategy, and transfer partner.

6. Discussion and conclusions

Taken together, these findings suggest that universities most interested in generating short-term cash flows from their IP licensing strategies are least positioned to create long-term wealth through venture creation. Although two-thirds of the universities in this study have invested significant resources in incubators and have expressed an interest in new business startups and economic development, most of them have not linked this to their technology transfer strategy choices or to the mission of their UTTOs. This disconnect may be one reason why university incubators tend to remain at the fringe of regional economic development efforts, in spite of the espoused goals of community development in many university mission statements. As one UTTO director from a private Midwestern university remarked:

> ... despite the pressures from the state to focus on local business development, I feel obligated to get the best deal I can for the university [and the administration] ...

To reiterate, this paper was motivated by several gaps in the literature. The various structures by which research institutions house their technology transfer functions, licensing strategies to commercialize proprietary technology, and their links to new venture emergence have thus far been relatively unexplored. Moreover, there has been little theory development vis-à-vis UTTO structures, strategy, and new venture formation. Our paper addressed this gap with the near-census survey of U.S. research universities actively involved in technology transfer activities and, using a grounded theory approach, developed a model to explain the relationships between UTTO structures, licensing strategies, and new venture formation.

Our resulting model argues that for-profit UTTO structures and licensing in exchange for equity are most positively related to new venture formation. More importantly, our model shows that traditional and nonprofit UTTO structures are unrelated to new ventures even though they are correlated with the presence of a university business incubator. Licensing in exchange for sponsored research is negatively related to new venture formation. Interestingly, we also found that licensing for cash—the transfer strategy of choice among 72% of UTTOs we studied—is least related to new venture creation, a disconcerting finding given that the universities in which they operate have overwhelmingly invested in incubators to accelerate new venture creation.

Taken as a whole, this study contributes to theory in several ways. First, with the exception of insightful but narrow case studies there is currently no general framework for understanding the links between UTTO structure, licensing strategies, and new firm creation. Preliminary notions of this process may be found in the technology and knowledge transfer literature (cf., the specialized journals we mentioned earlier), with much of this research providing valuable insight on knowledge flow and spillovers from universities to industry (cf., Agrawal and Henderson, 2002; Jaffe et al., 1993; Link et al., in press) and vice versa (Cohen et al., 1998). However, the adjunct processes of technology transfer to new startups are still poorly understood. Second, our study provides rich insights on the precise structures of UTTOs and proposes a model that *simultaneously* includes UTTO strategies, structures, and technology transfer outcomes. More importantly, based on our near-census data collection technique, we assume that we have described the phenomenon as well as one can reasonably expect with the inherent shortcomings of the long interview.

From a public policy standpoint, taxpayer support for university basic research is traditionally justified by a return-to-society on investment argument (Jensen and Thursby, 2001). Therefore, universities are pressured to show tangible returns for the research grants they receive. Universities that excel at managing proprietary technologies command healthy royalty income streams, which reduce the public burden as taxpayers. For example, in 1999 Columbia University reported over $95 million in gross licensing revenues, with much of it from equity returns. This fact is important as our interviews revealed that U.S. universities' attitudes toward equity can range from policies that are hostile toward equity, to cautious acceptance of equity when cash strategy is ineffective, to aggressively seeking equity whenever possible. For example, as one UTTO director from a private Midwestern university remarked:

> ... the legislature has recently changed the law permitting us to take equity in companies. I am working on my first contract and will aggressively seek equity deals. Some of my colleagues are being more cautious.

Indeed, research has shown that in the long run taking equity in startups produces a greater rate of return than the average cash license arrangement (Bray and Lee, 2000). Others report that UK universities with clearer strategies towards the spinning out of firms and the use of surrogate entrepreneurs in this process are more successful at generating cash flows from their licensing activities (Franklin et al., 2001; Lockett et al., 2003). Our model extends such studies as it helps to define a framework for studying the efficacy of UTTOs' licensing strategies in creating new ventures.

The substantial growth in universities' patenting and licenses activity has prompted policymakers to debate the possible "unintended" effects of the Bayh–Dole Act, such as the apparent shift toward applied research in place of basic research. More specifically, our findings that universities employ different UTTO configurations with varying levels of autonomy could raise concerns that expectations of financial returns would, over time, increase the allocation of capital to applied research and reduce the capital to basic research. Although we report that licensing for cash is the predominant licensing strategy, we note that none of the UTTO structures are statistically significantly related to the cash strategy. In fact, we found that the for-profit structure was even marginally negatively related to this licensing strategy. Also, research has shown that the decrease in average proportion of basic research to total research expenditures between 1977–1980 and 1994–1998 was only 0.005 (Thursby and Thursby, 2002). Thus, the "problem" of a shift from basic to applied research may be overstated, at least in reference to universities' technology licensing strategies.

It has been further suggested elsewhere that the role of the UTTO is "not to develop links between the university and industry, but rather to monitor, facilitate, and regulate the transactions between parties" (Colyvas et al., 2002, p. 65). Our findings challenge this notion as we found that UTTOs play a key role in economic development by adopting various structural configurations and enacting different transfer strategies that appear to correlate with varying levels of new venture formation. Having said this, we have to wonder why licensing for cash was such a predominantly favored strategy. Interviewees explained that since universities are unlikely to thrive unless they recover their R&D and UTTO administration costs, research institutions are increasingly looking at technology commercialization as a source of recurring revenues. Indeed, in an era of budget cutbacks, ensuring healthy operational cash flows has become an important objective for universities. However, the problem of incongruence between incentive systems and goals, which has been noted in previous research (Kerr, 1975) and which we rediscovered in this study, means that universities must remain watchful over the potential trade-offs and conflicts between technology dissemination and revenue generation (Markman et al., 2004b).

Finally, we found that universities are increasingly viewing themselves as catalysts of new venture formation and regional development. As one UTTO director from a public Midwestern university explained:

> ... more and more university administrators have realized that focusing on local economic development can buy a lot of political capital as well as research funding from the state ...

Perhaps this is the reason why 62% of the universities in our sample are establishing business incubators and building research parks in their communities. These are ways to encourage technology-based new ventures and subsequent economic development (Link et al., 2003). With the exception of such institutions as Harvard, Boston University, Stanford University, and the like who were already part of new venture "nurseries" or regional ecologies of emerging organizations, many of our informants told us that those universities without incubators were planning to build one. What we found in this study is that although licensing for equity is more likely to drive new venture emergence, the UTTO motivation to maximize cash flows and minimize financial and legal risks often lead to a strategic choice that does not support new venture creation.

7. Limitations

Most social science research is inherently incomplete, and our study is clearly no exception. For example, although our sample of 128 research universities reflect a 92% response rate, it is restricted to U.S. universities and it does not represent the total population of all research institutions, which may include government research laboratories such the National Institutes of Health (NIH) and the National Institute for Standards and Testing (NIST). However, our sample accounts for over 60% of federal and industry research dollars, and over 70% of licenses executed, inventions disclosures, and new patent applications (cf., Thursby and Thursby, 2002) and so we are confident that our model captures the full phenomenon as far as research-based U.S. universities are concerned. Still, future research on this topic would benefit from studies based on broader sample, including non-U.S. institutions.

Our research design cannot ascertain causality. For example, we cannot tell if licensing strategies or UTTO structures are driven by past UTTO performance, institutional shift towards applied research with strong commercial appeal, or by an increase in demand for university contracts because of cutbacks in industry R&D. This suggests that future studies on this topic, which would involve large sample panel data, should attempt to control for universities' research orientation, industry behavior, and the effect of time.

Nonetheless, the use of interviews and a grounded theory approach has several advantages over previous attempts to document UTTO activities. Attributing meaning to actions and behaviors based on secondary data, mere observation, or without interacting with the UTTO directors can lead to gross misunderstandings (de Vaus, 2001). For example, almost all the universities in our sample have websites explaining the role and work of their technology transfer offices. However, without contextualizing this information with interviews, it would appear that all UTTOs are equally sophisticated in their strategies and successful in what they do. We found differently. With interviews, meanings that resided only in and between the informants are surfaced, giving the researchers a better understanding of the nature of the data. In the context of our study, interviewees gave rich and logical accounts of the decisions and organizational processes within a narrowly defined contextual field. As such, our design and interviews seemed to have achieved a reasonable level of internal, face, and construct validity. Although interview data lack statistical generalizability, we feel the limitations are acceptable because our primary goal was theory building rather than theory testing.

In closing, our paper applies grounded theory to glean insights into the links between UTTO structures, licensing strategies, and new venture creations. Findings indicate how UTTOs are structured, how technological discoveries are categorized, the licensing strategies utilized, and their link to startups. It is our hope that the findings and approach used here will spur other researchers to further elaborate, perhaps longitudinally, which UTTO structure and licensing strategy combinations are more conducive for the creation of new firms.

Acknowledgements

This paper benefited from comments made by the members of the Terry College of Business Brown Bag Seminar (October 2002) and the participants of the RPI conference (April 2003). We also thank Ann Buchholtz, Eileen Fischer, Michael Lubatkin, two anonymous reviewers, and the special issue editors for their insightful comments and suggestions. We acknowledge with gratitude the financial support for this study from the Department of Management at the Terry College of Business and from the John Broadbent Endowment for Research in Entrepreneurship at Rensselaer Polytechnic Institute.

References

Agrawal, A., Henderson, R., 2002. Putting patents in context: exploring knowledge transfer from MIT. Manage. Sci. 48, 44–60.
Association of University Technology Managers, 2000. The AUTM Licensing Survey: Fiscal Year 1999. Association of University Technology Managers, Norwalk, CT.

Association of University Technology Managers, 2002. The AUTM Licensing Survey: Fiscal Year 2000, Survey Summary. Association of University Technology Managers, Norwalk, CT.

Bray, M.J., Lee, J.N., 2000. University revenues from technology transfer: licensing fees vs. equity positions. J. Bus. Venturing 15, 385–392.

Cockburn, I., Henderson, R., 1998. Absorptive capacity, coauthoring behavior, and the organization of research in drug discovery. J. Ind. Econ. 46 (2), 157–182.

Cohen, W., Florida, R., Randazzese, L., Walsh, J., 1998. Industry and the academy: uneasy partners in the cause of technological advance. In: Noll, R. (Ed.), Challenges to the Research University. Brookings Institution, Washington, DC.

Colyvas, J., Crow, M., Gelijns, A., Mazzoleni, R., Nelson, R.R., Rosenberg, N., Sampat, B.N., 2002. How do university inventions get into practice? Manage. Sci. 48, 61–72.

Creswell, J.W., 2002. Research Design: Qualitative, Quantitative, and Mixed Methods Approaches, 2nd ed. Sage, Thousand Oaks, CA.

de Vaus, D.A., 2001. Research Design in Social Research. SAGE, London.

Eisenhardt, K.M., 1989. Building theories from case study research. Acad. Manage. Rev. 14, 532–550.

Feldman, M., Feller, I., Bercovitz, J., Burton, R., 2002. Equity and technology transfer strategies of American research universities. Manage. Sci. 48, 105–121.

Flint, D., Woodruff, R., Gardial, S., 2002. Exploring the phenomenon of customers' desired value change in a business to business context. J. Mark. 66, 102–117.

Franklin, S., Wright, M., Lockett, A., 2001. Academic and surrogate entrepreneurs in university spin-out companies. J. Technol. Transf. 26, 127–141.

Glaser, B.G., Strauss, F., 1999. The Discovery of Grounded Theory: Strategies for Qualitative Research Aldine De Gruyter, New York.

Holstein, J.A., Gubrium, J.F., 1995. The Active Interview Sage, Thousand Oaks, CA.

Jaffe, A., Henderson, R., Trajtenberg, M., 1993. Geographic localization of knowledge spillovers as evidenced by patent citations. Q. J. Econ. 108, 577–598.

Jensen, R., Thursby, M.C., 2001. Proofs and prototypes for sale: the tale of university licensing. Am. Econ. Rev. 91, 240–259.

Kerr, S., 1975. On the folly of rewarding A, while hoping for B. Acad. Manage. J. 18, 769–783.

Link, A.N., Scott, J.T., Siegel, D.S., 2003. The economics of intellectual property at universities: an overview of the special issue. Int. J. Ind. Organ 21, 1301–1322.

Lockett, A., Wright, M., Franklin, S., 2003. Technology transfer and universities' spin-out strategies. Small Bus. Econ. 20 (2), 185–200.

Markman, G.D., Espina, M.I., Phan, P.H., 2004a. Patents as surrogates for inimitable and non-substitutable resources. J. Manage. 30, 529–544.

Markman, G.D., Gianiodis, P.T., Phan, P.H., Balkin, D.B., 2004b. Entrepreneurship from the ivory tower: Do incentive systems matter? J. Technol. Transf. 29, 353–364.

McGrath, R.H., 1997. A real options logic for initiating technology position investments. Acad. Manage. Rev. 22, 974–996.

Mowery, D.C., Shane, S., 2002. Introduction to the special issue on university entrepreneurship and technology transfer. Manage. Sci. 48 (1), v–ix.

Schumpeter, J.A., 1950. Capitalism, Socialism, and Democracy Harper, New York.

Shane, S., Venkatramanan, S., 2000. The promise of entrepreneurship as a field of research. Acad. Manage. Rev. 25, 217–226.

Siegel, D., Waldman, D., Link, A.N., 2003. Assessing the impact of organizational practices on the productivity of university technology transfer offices: an exploratory study. Res. Policy 32 (1), 27–48.

Siegel, D., Waldman, D., Atwater, Link, A.N., 2004. Toward a model of the effective transfer of scientific knowledge from academicians to practitioners: qualitative evidence from the commercialization of university technologies. J. Eng. Technol. Manage. 21, 115–142.

G.D. Markman et al. / Journal of Business Venturing 20 (2005) 241–263 263

Small Business Association, 2002. The Influence of R&D Expenditures on New Firm Formation and Economic Growth. BJK Associates, Maplewood, NJ.

Strauss, A., Corbin, J., 1998. Basics of Qualitative Research: Techniques and Procedures for Developing Grounded Theory, 2nd ed. Sage, Thousand Oaks, CA.

Thursby, J.G., Thursby, M.C., 2002. Who is selling the ivory tower? Sources of growth in university licensing. Manage. Sci. 48, 90–104.

Thursby, J.G., Jensen, R., Thursby, M.C., 2001. Objectives, characteristics, and outcomes of university licensing: A survey of major U.S. universities. J. Technol. Transf. 26, 59–72.

Zucker, L., Brewer, M., 1998. Intellectual capital and the birth of U.S. biotechnology enterprises. Am. Econ. Rev. 88, 290–306.

Zucker, L., Darby, M., Armstrong, J., 1998. Intellectual capital and the firm: the technology of geographically localized knowledge spillovers. Econ. Inq. 36, 65–86.

Name Index